Power AOL: A Survival Guide

KIRK PAUL LAFLER

POWER AOL: A Survival Guide

ISBN (pbk): 1-893115-38-0

Printed and bound in the United States of America 12345678910

Editorial Directors: Dan Appleman, Peter Blackburn, Gary Cornell, Jason Gilmore, Karen Watterson, John Zukowski

Technical Reviewers: Darlynn Lafler, Charles Shipp, Ronald Robinson, Bruce Lafler

Managing Editor: Grace Wong

Project Manager: Sofia Marchant

Compositor: Susan Glinert

Production Editor: Kari Brooks

Indexer: Valerie Haynes Perry

Cover Designer: Tom Debolski

Marketing Manager: Stephanie Rodriguez

Distributed to the book trade in the United States by Springer-Verlag New York, Inc., 175 Fifth Avenue, New York, NY, 10010

and outside the United States by Springer-Verlag GmbH & Co. KG, Tiergartenstr. 17, 69112 Heidelberg, Germany

In the United States, phone 1-800-SPRINGER, email orders@springer-ny.com, or visit http://www.springer-ny.com.

Outside the United States, fax +49 6221 345229, email orders@springer.de, or visit http://www.springer.de.

For information on translations, please contact Apress directly at 2560 Ninth Street, Suite 219, Berkeley, CA 94710. E-mail info@apress.com, or visit http://www.apress.com.

In memory of Herman "Rusty" Morgan-Hobbs,
a great friend and colleague with a great mind,
a curiosity for everything life has to offer,
and someone who always put family and friends first.
You are deeply missed and always remembered.
1956-1994

Contents at a Glance

Contents

Contents

Chapter 5   Searching and Finding Information 107

Chapter 7 AOL Newsgroups *159*

Part Two AOL Services *173*

Chapter 8 AOL Shopping and Services *175*

Chapter 15   Create Your Own Web Page

Chapter 17 Miscellaneous Tips

Index

About the Author

KIRK PAUL LAFLER has worked as a software consultant for the last 25 years. As founder of Software Intelligence Corporation, an IT services provider and trainer, he has helped organizations design and develop application software solutions and comprehensive training. Since 1983, Kirk has provided consulting services and training to Fortune 1000 companies and government installations, lending his expertise in application design and development, training, and custom programming services. As author of two books and more than one hundred articles on technology and software, Kirk is a frequent invited speaker at various user group conferences and events. When he is not consulting, writing, or teaching, he spends much of his time with his wife and son traveling, exploring, and just having fun. He can be reached at: KirkLafler@cs.com or through his Web site at: http://www.software-intelligence.com.

Technical Reviewer Bios

Darlynn Joan Lafler

Darlynn is a Clinical Laboratory Scientist with a leading health care organization in San Diego, CA. She is the author of many articles published in peer-reviewed scientific and medical journals related to her field of work and co-author of the *Year 2000 How To Guide for Medical Laboratories*. From laboratory medicine to researching clinical trial protocols, her career requires that she spend time using the Internet. As an avid user of AOL and CompuServe, Darlynn's favorite time is that spent with her son Ryan who, at almost 3 years old, can't wait for mom to go "on-line." Darlynn enjoys her time off with her son and husband so she can see the many sites in San Diego including Sea World, the Zoo, Seaport Village, La Jolla Shores, and other popular destinations.

Charles Edwin Shipp

Charlie has been an AOL user for many years now. Before that he was an enthusiastic CompuServe user, and still uses that account today. As the father of five children, he and his wife now share the AOL name "MacFamily." Charlie has been active in user group activities around the world and was instrumental in starting the Macintosh and mainframe user groups at Northrop Corporation in California, and was on the initial board of directors for the Los Angeles Macintosh Group. He also served on the second and third Apple Macintosh user group advisory boards, which met personally with Guy Kawasaki and John Sculley. Charlie co-*authored The Year 2000 How To Guide for Medical Laboratories* book and is active in the SAS Institute Books-by-Users Program, having co-authored *Quick Results with SAS/GRAPH Software*. He's also written dozens of computing articles and co-authored numerous award-winning papers.

Ronald Robinson

Ronald is a 10-year-old fourth grade student in the Gifted and Talented Education Program at Descanso Elementary School. He plays soccer, little league and has been in the Boy Scouts for two years. Ronald spends a lot of time on his computer, riding his bike, playing his Gameboy games and is just starting to learn to play the guitar. He also likes to camp, swim and loves fishing. He has lots of friends and likes to hang out with them on the weekends. Ronald lives with his dad, mom and his little sister. He has a great family and loves them all.

Bruce Jeffrey Lafler

Bruce has provided network and software technical support and troubleshooting for companies in Miami, Florida since 1987. Currently, he's a Novell and Microsoft network specialist, working with microcomputer and mainframe network installations, operations support, software security, and Help desk problem solving. Bruce graduated as Valedictorian from the University of Miami, MEED program in 1987. His special interests are computer gaming, amateur astronomy, billiards, electronics, and aquariums.

Preface

AMERICA ONLINE IS THE LARGEST and most widely used Internet Service Provider (ISP) in the world. With well over 30 million users around the world using AOL, and over 100 million using AOL Instant Messaging, America Online has achieved a great deal of success and is driven to become even bigger and better. As a result, this book is intended to be useful for AOL users everywhere. Although AOL is designed to be fairly easy to use, the sheer number of services and features offered in Version 7.0 can become daunting, to say the least.

This book of tips is intended to make it easier for AOL users to take full advantage of the many features and services that AOL offers. I've organized this book to help you learn something about AOL's services and features in 60 seconds or less. The tips are based on years of experience using AOL and other leading ISPs, and are tried and proven for accurate results.

While I assume the reader has some general familiarity with computers, I don't assume any knowledge with AOL to get started with this book. As with any book of this type, examples are an important element to better learning, and this book is filled with step-by-step examples.. By presenting every aspect of AOL's powerful features and content, I am confident that users will have a better and more rewarding online experience.

I hope you'll find my style of informal, conversational writing easy to follow, especially in a world filled with technical jargon on virtually any subject. I'll be happy to receive corrections, new tips, and other suggestions for future editions of this book. Send your ideas to

Kirk Paul Lafler
P.O. Box 1390
Spring Valley, CA 91979-1390
E-mail: KirkLafler@cs.com
http://www.software-intelligence.com

or contact me through the publisher:

Apress
2560 Ninth Street, Suite 219
Berkeley, CA 94710
http://www.apress.com

Acknowledgments

THIS BOOK WAS MADE POSSIBLE because of the support, contributions, and encouragement of many people. I would like to extend my sincerest thanks to each person who encouraged me during the writing and editing process. For as G. B. Stern once said, "Silent gratitude isn't very much use to anyone." So from me to you, thank you to each one of you.

Karen Watterson of Apress for her wonderful support and encouragement in developing each chapter, and during the writing and editing process, Karen acted as a trusted adviser and Technical Reviewer by providing suggestions on ways to improve the content and how each chapter flowed.

Grace Wong of Apress for her leadership, enthusiasm, and assistance with some of the fine points of writing for Apress. Her willingness to support a new imprint and style is greatly appreciated.

Sofia Marchant of Apress for her guidance during the editing process and for allowing me to see the light at the end of the long tunnel. Her encouragement and support during the editing and review process is greatly appreciated.

Kari Brooks of Apress for doing an outstanding job managing the production process and all the production-related issues.

Stephanie Rodriguez of Apress for all the hard work handling the marketing as well as creating a great cover design.

To Susan Glinert at Apress for making this book look wonderful. Her design and formatting expertise made this book come to life on paper.

This book wouldn't have been possible without the hard work of four very important Technical Reviewers. Each spent countless hours working with me, researching topics, reviewing and editing chapter tips, providing expert advice, and much more. Darlynn Joan Lafler provided guidance on the development of each chapter, reviewed content for technical accuracy, and gave encouragement during the long hours of writing and editing the manuscript. Charles Edwin Shipp provided expert advice, reviewed and edited chapter tips, and added Macintosh-specific tips. Ronald Robinson provided enthusiasm, special insights, and expert advice on the chapter on AOL for Kids and Teens. Bruce Lafler provided research expertise in key areas including security, privacy, and other technical areas. Their encouragement and support means more to me than words can say.

To the countless people at America Online who, over the years, have answered so many of my technical questions with a smile and have provided users like myself with great technical support. They do a splendid job providing AOL users around the world with the greatest product support found anywhere.

To all the people that I have worked with and the companies I have worked for. The experiences and memories have been invaluable.

To all the teachers I have had in my life I thank you. Special thanks go to Lawrence Delk (6th grade), Mr. Almeida (12th grade), Professor Carl Kromp (Industrial Engineering), Dr. Joseph J. Moder (Management Science), Dr. Charles Kurucz (Management Science), Dr. John F. Stewart (Computer Information Systems), Dr. Earl Wiener (Management Science), and Dr. Howard S. Gitlow (Management Science).

To my parents and brother for all the wonderful memories. Your love and encouragement through the years has fueled my desire to live life to the fullest.

Finally, to my wife Darlynn and son Ryan for their love and support, and for giving me a sense of balance between family, work, and play. I love you both.

Thank you all!

~ Kirk ~

Introduction

"Seek the wisdom of the children. For the children are my sisters and my brothers ... their laughter and their loveliness would clear a cloudy day. In their innocence and trusting they will teach us to be free. They are a promise of the future and a blessing for today."

By John Denver, Rhymes and Reasons, 1969

POWER AOL: A SURVIVAL GUIDE is designed for AOL users who want to learn all they can about the many features and services provided by America Online. This book is loaded with valuable tips and tricks for getting the most from AOL. Inside, you'll find quick and simple tips written in plain English on how to use AOL more effectively. Both novice and experienced users will learn how to make their online experience more productive and exciting.

My experiences researching other AOL books and talking with other AOL users convinced me that there is a need for a comprehensive and organized collection of AOL tips, much like those written for other software products and tools. But when I looked, I could find no AOL book like it anywhere.

Well, now there is such a book. This is a book for novice, intermediate, and advanced AOL users who want clearly written plain-English tips and techniques organized in a helpful and logical way. It's organized so readers can get faster, easier, and better results without spending inordinate amounts of time reading paragraph after paragraph of text. Power AOL is the perfect companion for the legions of AOL users everywhere. It's the next best thing to having an expert by your side 24 hours a day, 7 days a week.

Organization of the Book

Power AOL is organized so that each chapter will cover a new group of related features and services. It's written so that each chapter can be read sequentially, or you can open the book and access the specific information you need right away. The beauty of this presentation is that users will find the answers they're looking for in 60 seconds or less. Many of the tips are presented with step-by-step instructions and visual aids to enhance the way users learn.

Chapters 1 through 7 introduce the basic but bountiful AOL features and tools. Tips cover topics such as the AOL interface; communicating via e-mail; managing your filing cabinet; tools such as My Calendar; searching and finding information; chat, instant messaging, message boards, and newsgroups.

Chapters 8 through 12 present terrific AOL services including shopping on Shop@AOL; exciting channels for kids and teens including games and homework helpers; content-filled Web channels for young teens and the college bound; resources for 55+ mature online users; and Web channels offering busy families with plenty of good ideas and services to enhance their online enjoyment.

Chapters 13 through 17 provide details on advanced AOL topics including how to ensure computer privacy using security tips and techniques; how to customize AOL services and features; how to use AOL to create your own Web site; how to understand and resolve AOL error messages; and a potpourri of tips covering a variety of exciting new AOL services.

Conventions Used in This Book

The tips presented in this book frequently consist of instructions that you can use to perform some action. You'll be asked to enter one or more AOL Keywords; select from menus, drop-down lists, and radio boxes in order to accomplish what you want to do. Important keywords and button clicks are emphasized using bolding. In many tips throughout the book sample windows, screens, and output pages are displayed to assist in the learning process.

To emphasize specific tip content, the following icons are used throughout this book::

Icon	*Description*
	Identifies useful timesaving tricks or techniques.
	Identifies warnings, errors, and other messages that can cause problems if ignored.

Part One

AOL Features and Tools

CHAPTER 1

Getting Started with AOL

THIS CHAPTER COVERS valuable tips on using AOL. Whether you're an online expert who is comfortable surfing the Internet, sending and receiving e-mail messages and chatting, or whether you're online for the first time—these tips will make your online experience a more rewarding one. By taking the time to learn how the AOL software program communicates with the person using it (this means you), you'll get better results from this powerful and effective tool. You'll learn about each feature step-by-step and in plain English so you can take immediate control of your own destiny.

In this chapter, you'll learn how to:

📖 Start AOL

📖 Choose and manage one or more screen names

📖 Pick passwords

📖 Use the AOL toolbar and navigation buttons

📖 Create and use keyboard shortcuts

📖 Stop and reload graphic image processing

📖 Display channel selections

📖 Obtain online and telephone support

📖 Manage your accounts and billing

📖 Sign off

Setting Up AOL and Connection Tips

1 Installing AOL

Installing AOL is as easy as 1-2-3—just follow these simple steps.

Windows

1. Insert the AOL CD-ROM into your computer's CD-ROM drive.

2. Follow the instructions on your screen and AOL will do the rest. You'll have AOL installed in a few short minutes.

Macintosh

1. Insert the AOL CD-ROM into your computer's CD-ROM drive.

2. Double click the **Install** icon.

3. Follow the on-screen instructions and AOL will do the rest. You'll have AOL installed in a few short minutes.

2 Launching AOL

It's easy to start AOL. Simply locate the AOL icon on the Windows or Macintosh desktop and double-click it. After the program files are activated, the AOL Welcome screen displays a greeting in the title bar (for example, Welcome, KPL Consultant).

3 Using AOL for the first time

Before you can begin using AOL, you need to set up an account, and contrary to what you might think, this doesn't happen automatically when you first install AOL Version 7.0. To set up your account, you will need to start AOL by clicking the AOL V7 icon located on your desktop. Once AOL is active, the Sign On dialog box will appear, shown in Figure 1-1.

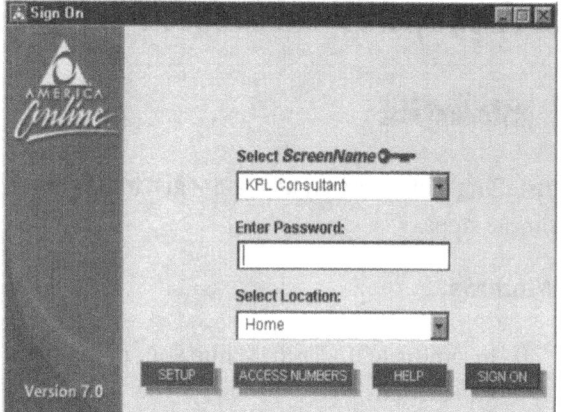

Figure 1-1. Viewing the AOL Sign On screen

Then, click the Expert Setup button to begin the setup process, as you see in Figure 1-2.

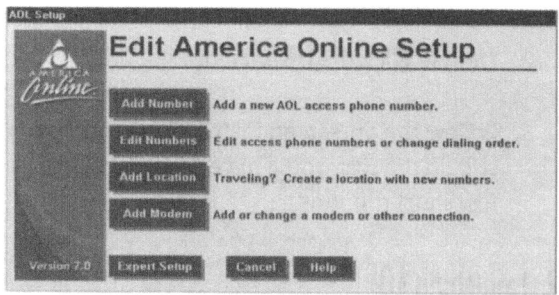

Figure 1-2. Using the Expert Setup button to begin the setup process

4 Choosing local telephone numbers

To avoid unnecessary telephone access charges, try to choose telephone numbers that are local (and are within your area code). You can do this by contacting your local telephone service carrier and verifying that accessing the number will involve no local surcharges. (See tips # 10–13 for information on finding and using different telephone access numbers when you're traveling.)

5 Picking a screen name

Every AOL account can have a maximum of seven screen names (or e-mail addresses) assigned. A screen name is your unique alias to the online world, and will always be the way others find you. Each screen name can have separate passwords, mailboxes, filing cabinets, and favorite places. You'll be asked to enter the screen name and password you chose initially each time you sign on to AOL. This screen name is considered your master screen name and once assigned can't be deleted or changed.

6 Selecting a password

A password is your secret sequence of typed characters and is required to access your AOL account. Anyone who knows your password could sign on to your account and potentially cause a world of havoc, such as deleting mail messages, sending bogus messages that look like they're coming from you, posting messages on public forums that appear to be coming from you, and so on. Because it is so very important, you should really think about the password you select. Don't choose a word that is too obvious or too easy to guess. Also, don't use a word that appears in the dictionary, or is the name of a family member, or a pet's name. These are generally too obvious and make it relatively easy for people or hackers to access your account. You may even consider adding one or more numbers to a screen name to make it unique.

7 Protecting your AOL password

It doesn't matter whether you are the secretive type or not, never give your AOL password to anyone—not even your family members. AOL staff will never ask you for your password for any reason and you should never volunteer your password to others. Giving your password to someone else is the virtual equivalent of handing your car keys to a perfect stranger. If you think your AOL account and password has been compromised, contact AOL immediately by phone or send an e-mail message to screen name TOS Email1.

8 Storing a password

AOL enables you to store your password on your computer. By saving your password, you avoid having to enter it each time you start AOL. Although this feature can be handy and prevent you from typing additional keystrokes, it can be misused if put in the wrong hands. When this feature is used, anyone with access to your computer (such as family members, perhaps even your kids' friends) can sign into AOL with your account. For this reason, you may want to weigh the pros and cons of using this AOL feature.

9 Signing onto AOL as a guest

You can sign onto AOL using any computer as long as the computer has AOL software installed, you have a valid AOL account, and you know your screen name and password. To sign on as a guest, do the following:

1. Select **Guest** from the **Select Screen Name** list on the **Sign On** screen.

2. Click the **Sign On** button.

3. In the **Guest Sign On** window, enter your screen name and password, and click the **OK** button.

4. Any time you spend online as a Guest will be billed to your account.

5. Your address book, filing cabinet, and favorite places cannot be accessed while signed on as a Guest.

10 Connecting tips for the frequent traveler

If you are a frequent traveler and want the benefits associated with an online existence, then there are a few things you should know. The following tips will help improve your online experience as you work from far-off places.

1. Ask the facility you are staying at for a fax line or an analog phone line.

   Analog phone lines are "normal" ones. Digital phone lines have been known to fry modems—so be careful. An increasing number of business hotels also offer high-speed Internet access—generally for a daily surcharge of about $10—and some are also beginning to offer wireless Internet access.

2. If you're trying to connect from an international location, contact your long distance provider—this can prevent costly and unnecessary phone charges.

3. Match your modem speed (see Chapter 17, (Miscellaneous Tips) with the maximum modem speed permitted for connecting to a specific number.

4. Wireless and satellite usage with AOL may cause a poor connection, so attempt to make a connection using a land-based line.

5. Because some International dial tones may not be recognized by your computer's modem, you may need to reconfigure your modem so it will ignore the dial tone and automatically dial the access number. For situations like these, it is recommended that you contact AOL Technical Support for assistance.

6. Line noise is a common problem in some countries. To compensate, try connecting to AOL with a slower modem speed.

7. Shut down any unnecessary programs before using AOL to prevent memory-related problems and ensure top performance.

8. If you have problems and need to contact AOL Technical Support, try to assemble all the information they'll need to resolve the problem (for example, the version of Windows or other operating system you're using, the kind of computer you have, the version of AOL you're running, and the sequence of steps from AOL launch to the occurrence of the actual problem).

11 Accessing AOL's Anywhere Web site

With AOL Anywhere, you can check your mail, portfolio, and calendar from any place and at any time you'd like. AOL Anywhere gives you the ability to access AOL and the World Wide Web, or the Web for short, from your computer, a friend's computer, or while traveling in the U.S. or abroad. The universal AOL Anywhere Web site is: http://www.aol.com.

🖊 *Any combination of lowercase and upper-case characters can be specified.*

12 Changing your local telephone access number online

It is sometimes necessary to change a local tele-phone access number to take advantage of a more reliable connection. AOL lets you make these types of changes during an established online connection using a minimal number of steps. Once you've successfully made the change, AOL will use the new local telephone number you've designated. Here's how it's done.

1. From the **Help** menu option at the top of your AOL screen, select **AOL Access Phone Numbers**.

2. In the **Search** field, enter a state abbreviation (e.g., CA), city (e.g., Spring Valley), or area code (e.g., 619), and click the **Next** button.

3. Select a **country** from the list of countries provided, and click the **Next** button.

4. Select the desired number displayed in the **Select AOL Access Phone Numbers** window, and click the **OK** button.

5. Select one or more **access numbers** from this list and when done click the **Next** button.

6. Select any special circumstances applicable to the selected access number(s) on the **Access Numbers You've Selected** window, and click the **Next** button.

7. Click the **Finish** button on the **Confirm Current Locations** window.

13 Changing your local telephone access number offline

It is sometimes necessary to change a local tele-phone access number to take advantage of a more reliable connection. AOL lets you make the change without first having to sign on. Here's how it's done.

🖊 *You may also make changes to your local telephone access number when you're signed on, see Tip #12.*

1. Sign off AOL.

2. From the **Sign On** screen, select **Setup**.

3. Click **Add a new AOL access phone number** on the AOL Setup window.

4. Enter the area code you are looking numbers for in the **Area Code** field (e.g., 619).

5. Select a **country** from the list of countries provided, and click the **Next** button.

6. Select the desired location in the **Location Name** field from the **Select AOL Access Phone Numbers** window, and click the OK button.

7. Select one or more **access numbers** from this list, and when done click the **Next** button.

8. Select any special circumstances applicable to the selected phone number(s) on the **Access Numbers You've Selected** window, and click the **Next** button.

9. Click the **Finish** button on the **Confirm Current Locations** window.

14 Accessing AOL from anywhere in the U.S. toll free

Having dependable access to AOL from anywhere in the United States and the U.S. Virgin Islands has never been easier. You can access the AOL network by dialing **1-800-716-0023**. There are additional fees for using the 1-800 access number—so consult your specific billing plan before trying GO Billing.

15 Storing alternate access numbers in a new location file

When you're traveling, you may want to dial an alternate number to gain access to AOL. It's easy when you follow these steps:

1. From the **Sign On** screen, select **Setup**.

2. Click the **Add Location** button on the **AOL Setup** screen.

3. Enter a **name** for the new location (e.g., Toll free access number) on the **Add Location** window.

4. Select the **number of times** you want your modem to try connecting to this connection.

5. Click **Select the 800 surcharged access number**, and click the **Next** button.

6. Select any special circumstances applicable to your phone line in the **Get AOL Access Numbers Online** window, and select the **Next** button.

7. The AOL software will dial a toll free phone number to retrieve a **list of 800 surcharged access numbers**, after which it will sign off.

8. Select **one or more** 800 surcharged access numbers from the supplied list, each time clicking the **Add** button.

9. When you're finished adding one or more 800 surcharged access numbers from the list, click the **Next** button.

10. Verify that the correct location is selected, and click **Sign On** from the Sign On screen.

16 Disconnecting from AOL

It is better to disconnect from AOL rather than letting AOL disconnect you because of inactivity. Signing off from an AOL session is a snap. Simply click **Sign Off** from the AOL toolbar located at the top of the screen, and then select **Sign Off** from the drop-down menu items.

Screen Name and Password Management

17 Assigning additional screen names

Every AOL account is allowed a maximum of seven screen names, or e-mail addresses. This comes in handy when you want to assign one or more screen names for family members, such as your spouse, kids, or grandma. Each screen name can have separate passwords, mailboxes, filing cabinets, and favorite places. Remember, the screen name you specified when you first set up your account is considered your master screen name, and can't be deleted or changed. To choose additional screen names for your account follow these steps:

1. Click the **Settings** button on the AOL toolbar and select **Screen Names**.

2. The AOL **Screen Names** window appears, shown in Figure 1-3.

3. Click the **Create a Screen Name** option and the steps for creating a Screen Name will appear.

4. Click **Create Screen Name** button.

5. In the **Choose a Screen Name** window, enter the desired screen name, which will also be your e-mail address, and click the **Continue** button, shown in Figure 1-4.

6. Choose and enter a password once and then again for verification, and click the **Continue** button.

7. Select a **Parental Control Category**, and click the Continue button, shown in Figure 1-5.

8. Confirm your screen name settings, and click the **Accept Settings** button.

9. To begin using your new screen name, sign off AOL and reconnect.

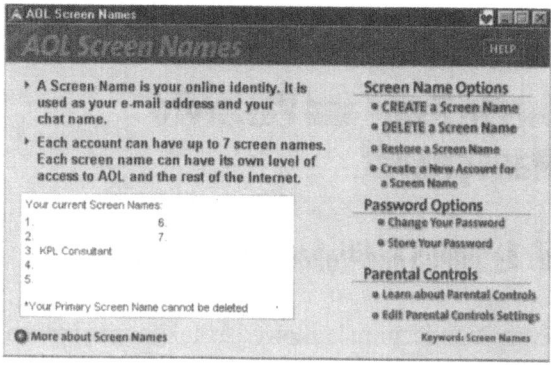

Figure 1-3. Accessing AOL's "Screen Names" window

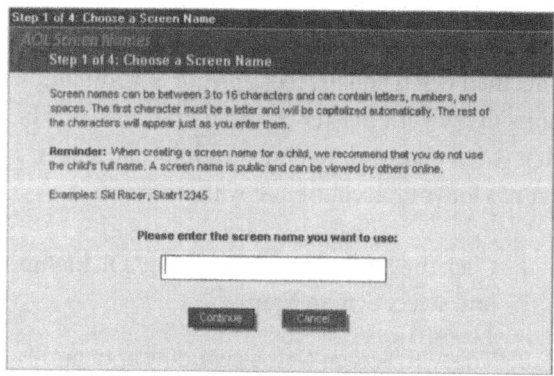

Figure 1-4. Choosing a Screen Name

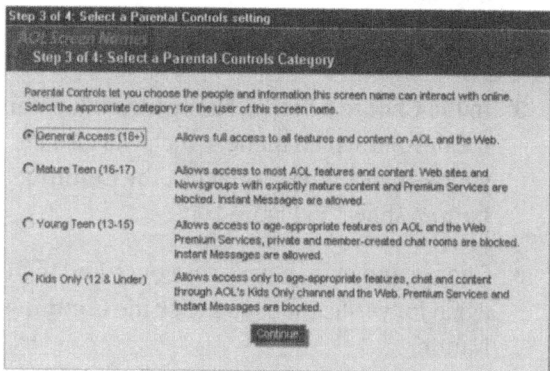

Figure 1-5. Selecting a Parental Controls category

18 Designating an additional master screen name

Each AOL account is allowed a maximum of seven screen names at any one time. There is only one master screen name, which cannot be deleted or changed. Whoever controls the master screen name chooses the additional screen names, and the type of access for each name.

A master screen name has much more power to do certain account-related tasks than non-master screen names. Master screen names can change the account's billing method and price plan, alter parental controls, and create, delete, or restore screen names on the account. For these reasons it is recommended to use extreme care when designating additional master screen names to your account. Having said this, the process of designating additional master screen names is a relatively simple one. The following steps show how it is done.

1. As the primary master screen name owner, sign on to AOL.

2. Click the **Settings** menu on the AOL toolbar located at the top of the screen, and select **Parental Controls** from the drop-down menu list.

3. Click **Set Parental Controls**.

4. From the **Edit Controls** list, select the screen name you want to designate as a master screen name.

5. Click the **General Access** category at the bottom of the window.

6. Click **Additional Master** from the list of custom controls.

7. After reading the information about master screen names, select the check box corresponding to the item **Designate this screen name as a master screen name**.

8. Click the **Save** button.

19 Switching between screen names

If you have assigned multiple screen names to your account, it's nice to know that you can switch between each of the names. The beauty of this feature is that you can make the switch during the same AOL session without having to sign off. Here's how it's done.

1. Click the **Sign Off** drop-down menu located at the top of the AOL screen, and select **Switch Screen Name** from the drop-down list.

2. Select the **Screen Name** you want to switch to.

3. Click the **Switch** button.

4. Enter your **password** and click the **OK** button.

20 Changing your password

To prevent scam artists from getting into your account, it is recommended that you change your password frequently. As a word of caution, never assign the same password to different screen names. This makes it too easy for thieves to compromise, not one, but all of your screen names. To change a password for a screen name, simply follow these steps:

1. Click the **Settings** pull-down menu and select **Passwords**.

2. Select the **Change Password** button on the **Passwords** dialog box.

3. In the **Change Password** window, enter your existing password in the **Old password** box.

4. In the **Enter new password twice** boxes, enter the new password the same way twice.

5. Click the **Change Password** button.

21 Help! I've forgotten my password

If you ever forget or misplace your password, simply call the AOL Customer Service toll-free line 24 hours a day, 7 days a week at the following number. Before calling you should have your account information available (i.e., screen name and credit card number) so account verification can be done.

Screen Name or Password Problems:
1-888-265-8004

22 Removing a stored password

To remove a stored password for any screen name, follow these steps:

1. Using the screen name for which you want the stored password removed, **sign on** to AOL.

2. Open the **Settings** menu on the AOL toolbar and select **Preferences**.

3. Click **Passwords** in the Preferences window.

4. Clear the **Sign On** checkbox.

23 Deleting a screen name

The master screen name (and owner of the account) can create, change, or delete subordinate screen names under that account at any time. To delete a screen name from an account, follow these steps:

1. Using a master screen name, sign on to AOL.

2. Click the **Settings** menu on the AOL toolbar located at the top of the screen, and select **Screen Names** from the drop-down menu.

3. Click **Delete a Screen Name**.

4. Click **Continue** in the **Are You Sure?** Dialog box.

5. Select the screen name you want deleted, and click the **Delete** button.

24 Restoring a screen name

After a screen name has been deleted, it may be possible to restore the deleted screen name for a period of up to six months. A screen name that has not been restored after a period of six months is considered lost and unrecoverable. To restore a screen name, follow these steps:

1. Using a master screen name, sign on to AOL.

2. Click the **Settings** menu on the AOL toolbar located at the top of the screen, and select **Screen Names** from the drop-down menu list.

3. In the AOL Screen Names window, click **Restore a screen name**.

4. Select the screen name you want restored, and click the **Continue** button.

My AOL and Welcome Screen

25 Arranging the windows in My AOL

If several AOL windows are opened at the same time, you can arrange them any way you want by dragging a window from its original location and dropping it into another location. To move a window in My AOL, follow these steps:

1. Using your mouse, point to the gray textured portion of the title bar and click the title bar.

2. Hold the mouse button down while you drag the window to a new desired location (the entire window will be outlined in red).

3. A **Reposition Here** message will display in the area where the window will be moved.

4. To complete the operation, release the mouse button—the window will then appear in its new location.

26 Customizing My AOL

You can customize My AOL by clicking the **Personalize My Page** button located at the top of the My AOL page or click the **Add Content** menu at the bottom of the page.

27 Adding more content to My AOL

Since My AOL is made up of multiple windows, you can customize its content as much, or as little, as you like using either the Personalize or Add Content tools. Add content by clicking the **Personalize My**

Page button located at the top of the My AOL page. Then follow these steps:

1. Click the Personalize My Page button.

2. Click the checkbox corresponding to each window you want to add.

3. Click **Save** and your information will appear.

Content can also be added using the **Add Content** menu as follows:

1. After clicking the **Add Content** menu, click the window(s) you'd like to add.

2. Additional windows will be added to the upper right corner of your my AOL page.

28 Refreshing the contents of My AOL

Since the contents of My AOL changes periodically, you may need to refresh your page (receive updates from AOL) to get the latest news, stock quotes, sports scores, or other information. Click the **Reload** button to have your Web browser recognize the new My AOL settings. You can make this process automatic—setting how often your page should reload in the Refresh My Page area of Preferences.

29 Customizing the Welcome screen with your favorite places

If you've ever wanted to customize the AOL Welcome screen—you're in luck. You can change what appears in the My Places portion of the Welcome screen, shown in Figure 1-6, by entering ten of your favorite destinations, and change them whenever and as often as you'd like. Although AOL selected some of the more popular sites to get you started (e.g., Greetings, Horoscopes, Local News, Maps & Directions, My Portfolios, People Directory, Sports Scores, Stock Quotes, What's New on AOL, and White Pages), it doesn't mean that you can't customize it to satisfy your specific needs.

Figure 1-6. The AOL, Version 7.0 Welcome Screen with My Places

Figure 1-7. AOL's "My Places" window

To customize the My Places portion of the Welcome screen for Version 6.0, follow these steps:

1. Click the **Customize My Places** button located on the upper right side of the Welcome screen.

2. Click **Choose New Place** on any of the buttons you'd like to change—then select an item from the list of categories.

3. When you're done, click the **Save My Changes** button located at the bottom of the screen.

To customize the My Places portion of the Welcome screen for Version 7.0, follow these steps:

1. Click the **More** button located next to the My Places category on the lower right side of the Welcome screen to display the My Places window, shown in Figure 1-7.

2. Click the **Change My Places** button located on the My Places pop-up window.

3. Click **Choose New Place** on any of the buttons you'd like to change—then select an item from the list of categories, shown in Figure 1-8.

4. When you're done, click the **Save My Changes** button located at the bottom of the screen.

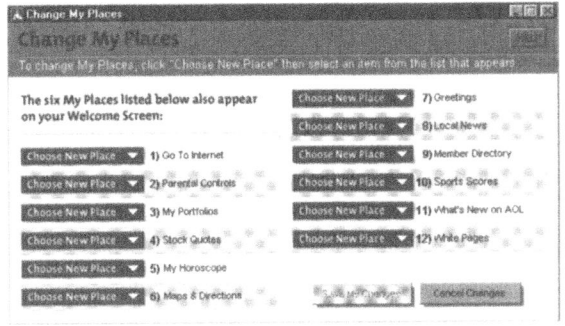

Figure 1-8. Changing My Places of the AOL, Version 7.0 Welcome Screen

30 New Place categories for My Places

New Place categories offer a variety of popular sites and give your Welcome screen a more personal look. The following categories are available:

Computing	People
Entertainment	Personal Finance
Games	Research
Health	Shopping
Interests	Sports
News	Travel

'X' Marks Your Spot

31 Bookmarking your favorite places

As you use AOL to explore what America Online and the Internet have to offer, you're sure to find an area or Web site to which you'd like to return. When this is the case, bookmark it by adding it to your Favorite Places. To add an area or Web page to your Favorite Places follow these steps:

1. Find and display the area or Web site you like.

2. Click the **Favorites** menu on the AOL toolbar located at the top right of your window.

3. Click **Add Top Window to Favorites** in the drop-down menu list.

32 Creating new favorite places folders

After surfing the Web for a while, you may notice that your favorite places list has become a bit long and disorganized. To ease the pain of having to search around for that favorite place, you can create one or more new folders to help group and store your favorite places. It's really pretty easy. Here's how:

1. Click the **My Favorites** button, or choose **Favorite Places** from the **Favorites** toolbar.

2. In the **Favorite Places** window, click the **New** button to open the Add New Folder/Favorite Place window, shown in Figure 1-9.

3. In the **Add New Folder/Favorite Place** window, select the New Folder radio button to create a new folder, shown in Figure 1-10.

4. **Drag** any favorite places, identified with a heart icon, to your new folder in the Favorite Places window, shown in Figure 1-11.

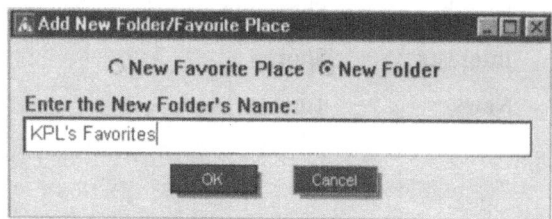

Figure 1-10. Adding a new folder

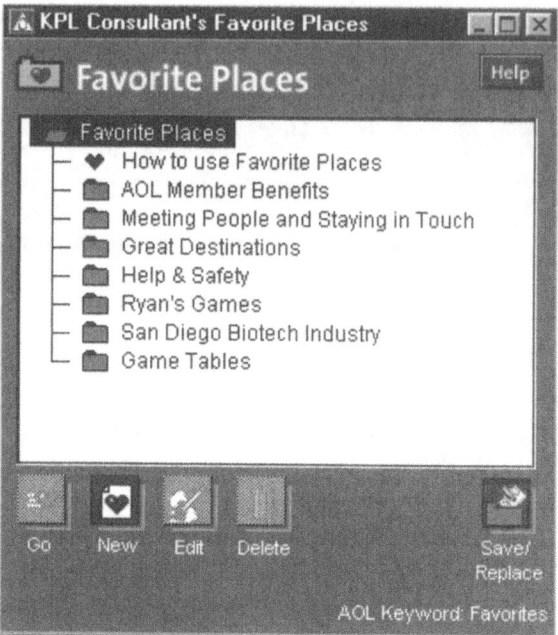

Figure 1-9. Opening the "Add New Folder/Favorite Place" window

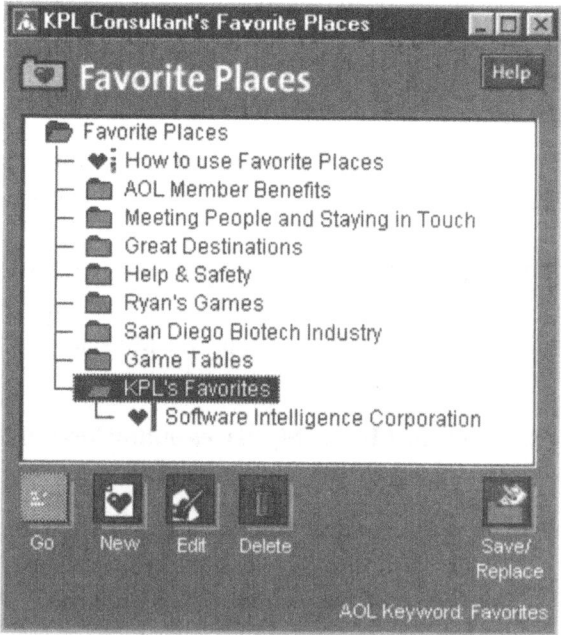

Figure 1-11. Dragging a favorite place to your new folder in the "Favorite Places" window

33 Organizing favorite places

Being able to organize your favorite places is an important feature if you want to locate interesting sites later. The drag-and-drop feature allows you to move items from one folder to another. By holding down the **Shift** key as you click each folder entry, you can select two or more adjacent entries for dragging. When you press the **Ctrl** key while clicking each entry, you can select two or more entries that aren't adjacent to each other for dragging to another folder.

34 Returning to your favorite places

The whole reason for saving your favorites is so you can return to them. Here's how it's done.

1. Click the **Favorites** menu on the AOL toolbar, and select the **Favorite Places** item.

2. In the Favorite Places window, scroll through the list and **double-click** the **favorite place** you want to return to.

35 Renaming your favorite places

Favorite places are automatically given a name when they are saved to a folder. Occasionally, you may want to rename a favorite place to make it stand out from the other favorites in the folder. To rename a favorite, follow these steps:

1. Click the **My Favorites** button from the AOL toolbar, or click the **Favorite Places** item from the **Favorites** menu on the AOL toolbar.

2. In the **Favorite Places** window, open the desired folder by **double-clicking** the folder name.

3. **Select** the favorite you want to rename and click the **Edit** button.

4. Rename the description of your favorite in the **Enter the Place's Description** field, as shown in Figure 1-12.

5. When done, click the **OK** button.

Figure 1-12. Renaming a favorite places folder

36 Saving/replacing your favorite places

Being able to save, transfer, or replace your Favorite Places is a handy feature—especially if you use AOL on multiple computers, want to share them with your family or friends, or just want a backup in the event of a disaster. Whatever the reason, you can easily save and replace your favorite places by following these steps:

1. Click the **My Favorites** button from the AOL toolbar, or click the **Favorite Places** item from the **Favorites** menu on the AOL toolbar.

2. Click the **Save/Replace** button.

3. Select the **Save the Favorite Places for your current screen name** radio box, shown in Figure 1-13.

4. Click the **OK** button.

5. Choose a **location** to save your Favorite Places folder in the **Save Folder** window.

6. Click the **Save** button.

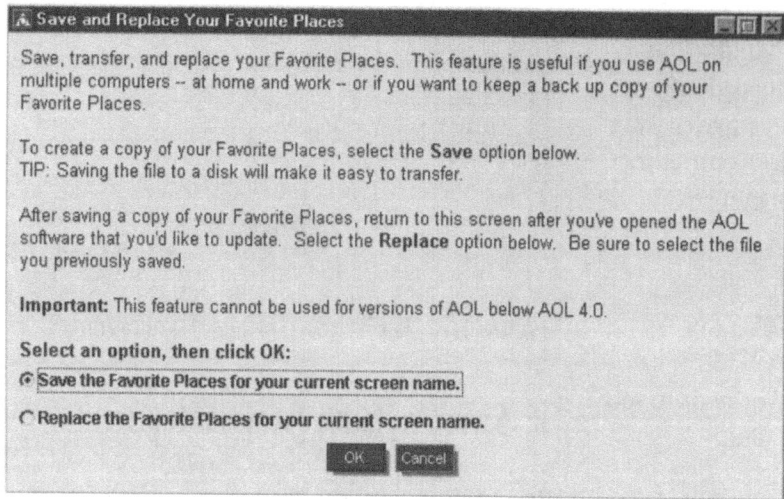

Figure 1-13. Saving and replacing your favorite places

The AOL Interface

37 Understanding the AOL interface

The America Online interface (or the layout of the screen) is one of the easiest and most flexible Internet software packages to use in the world. Its utter simplicity and flexibility make it so easy to use that you may be asking, "What's to learn—I've been using the numerous services from AOL for some time now—what more is there to know?"

Whether you're a seasoned online expert who has been surfing the Internet for some time, sending and receiving e-mail messages, or about to chat online for the first time makes no difference. The AOL Interface is simply the best and easiest screen layout to use anywhere. To get the most from America Online and the numerous services offered, you'll want to become familiar with the AOL Interface. AOL's Version 7.0, as well as 6.0, provides a tried and proven way to communicate online—using a personal Welcome screen, drop-down menus, toolbars, Internet channels (links to Web sites and other interesting areas on the Web), AOL keywords, e-mail, Instant Messaging, buddy lists, and an assortment of other simple and effective tools.

38 Understanding the AOL Menu bar

The AOL Menu bar located at the very top of your screen consists of six drop-down menus—File, Edit, Print, Window, Sign Off, and Help—for performing a variety of functions. When a menu item is clicked, it displays a drop-down list of items beneath it.

39 Understanding File menu options

The **File** menu contains a few selections that you're probably already familiar with such as New, Open, Save, Save as, Print, and Exit from using other software applications. But it also contains a few selections that you may not be fully aware of, including Filing Cabinet, Download Manager, Log Manger, Music Player, Offline Newsgroups, You've Got Pictures, and Voice Recognition.

40 Organizing your Filing Cabinet

Your filing cabinet helps you organize items retrieved online as well as items assembled for the next time you go online. As you begin filing all that e-mail away in your filing cabinet, you will eventually want or need to clean house and organize it.

Organizing it really isn't hard at all. You can begin by creating one or more folders and then drag and drop e-mail items into the folder of choice. Here's how it's done.

1. On the **Mail** menu on the AOL toolbar, click **Filing Cabinet** from the drop-down menu.

2. Click the **Incoming/Saved Mail** folder once to highlight it.

3. Click the **Add Folder** button located at the bottom of the Filing Cabinet window.

4. Enter a **name for the folder** you want to create in the Create Folder dialog box, as you see in Figure 1-14.

5. Click the **OK** button.

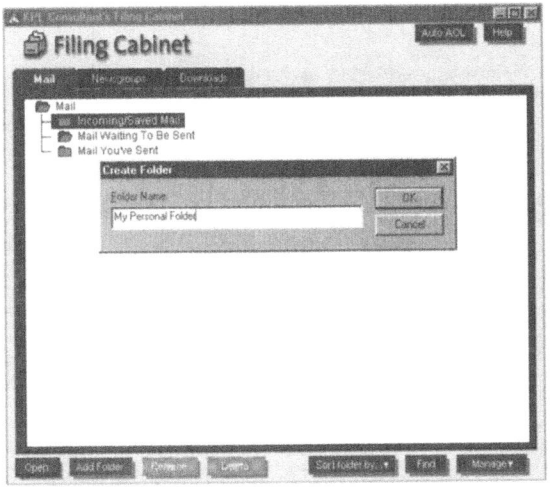

Figure 1-14. Creating a folder in your Filing Cabinet

41 Keeping track of those downloaded files from AOL

The Download Manager helps you keep track of what files have been downloaded from AOL. When opened, it shows the file(s) you have downloaded and allows you to manage the download process through Download Preferences, shown in Figure 1-15.

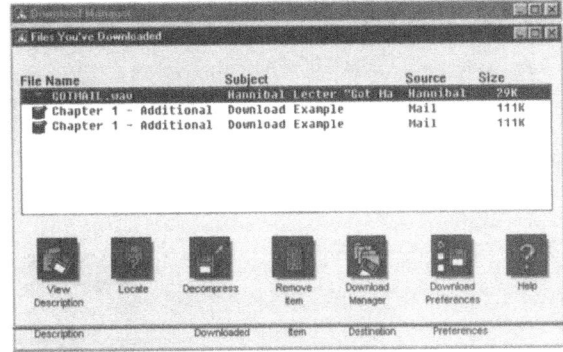

Figure 1-15. Creating a folder in your Filing Cabinet

42 Establishing download preferences

The Download Preferences window allows you to tell the AOL download process how it should work by clicking one or more items displayed in the window. It allows you to decide how AOL is to handle the decompression of ZIP files and whether these ZIP files should be deleted after decompression, whether images should be displayed, and how many downloads information should be retained for.

> *A ZIP file consists of one or more files that has been compressed or compacted to save space. The purpose of a ZIP file is to save space and to keep a group of related files together.*

AOL's Download Preferences window for Version 7.0 is shown in Figure 1-16.

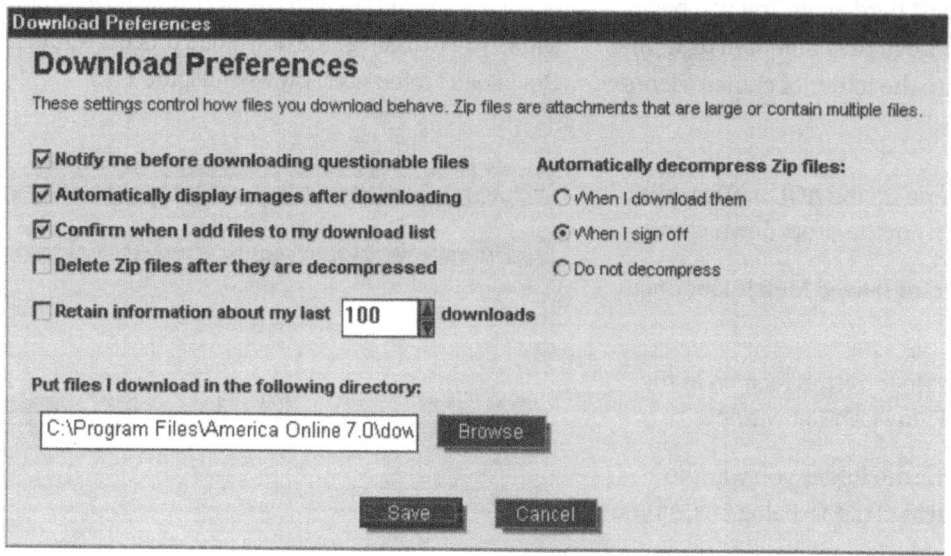

Figure 1-16. Setting AOL's Version 7.0 download preferences

43 Recording and saving a session chat log

There may be times when you want to save text from a chat, an instant message exchange or an article. You can use the Log Manager to transfer online text to a file for viewing or printing later, as you can see in Figure 1-17. Text can be transferred from the following areas:

- Chat rooms and auditoriums

- Instant message conversations

- Message board postings

- News or reference articles

By clicking the **Open Log** button, you inform AOL to store information in a new file. By clicking the **Append Log** button, you attach new information to the end of an existing file.

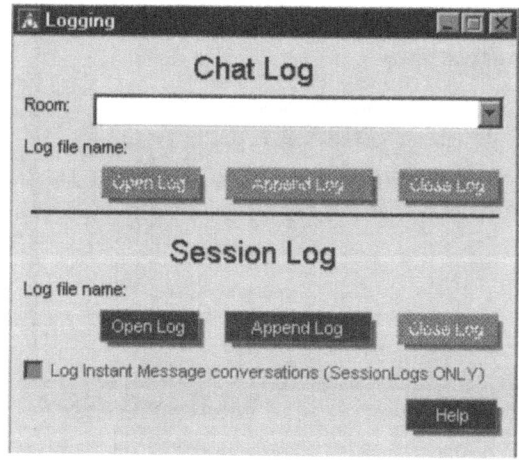

Figure 1-17. Saving a chat log

44 Understanding AOL Web browser controls

The AOL Navigation bar directly beneath the AOL toolbar displays buttons that allow you to go channels, which are links to Web sites and other interesting areas on the Web. The following features displayed from left to right are:

Show/Hide Channels—Show or hide channel selection window.

Back—view previous page.

Forward—return to a viewed Web page.

Stop—turn graphics off and display text only.

Reload—view new graphics and text for pages that change periodically.

Large text box—displays the current Web page address.

Go—launches the Web page displayed in the large text box.

Small text box—enter word or phrase to search AOL and the Internet.

Keyword—open the Keyword window to enter an AOL keyword.

45 Returning to a previously viewed Web site

Anytime during an online session, the AOL Web browser is equipped to quickly return to previously viewed Web pages by clicking the **Back** button located on the AOL Navigation bar. If you back-tracked after viewing one or more Web sites, the **Forward** button will then be highlighted allowing you to move forward with a simple click. (Also see Tip # 47—Using navigation buttons).

46 Understanding the AOL toolbar

The AOL toolbar provides a colorful array of task or menu buttons located at the top of your AOL screen, shown in Figure 1-18. The toolbar is divided into five colored groups:

1. Mail (blue)
2. People (green)
3. AOL Services (violet)
4. Settings (aqua)
5. Favorites (purple)

47 Using navigation buttons

The AOL Navigation bar contains two buttons to control backward and forward movement by the AOL Web browser. The following features displayed from left to right are:

◀ **Back**—view previous page

▶ **Forward**—return to a previously viewed Web page after the Back navigation button has been clicked.

48 Watching the spinning AOL logo

The AOL logo located in the upper right portion of the AOL browser window plays an important role in helping to determine whether a Web page has been completely loaded. When the logo is spinning, this means the current Web page has not been completely downloaded into your computer's memory. The amount of time required to download a Web page generally depends on the number and size of images on the page. A non-spinning logo means the Web page has been retrieved and is ready for viewing.

Figure 1-18. Accessing the AOL toolbar

49 Finding out what AOL version you're using

To figure out the AOL version, the compatible computer operating systems, and revision number you're using, follow these steps:

1. Click the **Help** pull-down menu located at the top of the screen, and select **About America Online** from the menu list.

2. The version of AOL, computer operating system, and revision number are displayed, shown below in Figure 1-19.

50 Understanding the Status Bar

The blue Status Bar located at the bottom of the browser window indicates that the specified Web address has been contacted and is being retrieved. The blue bar shows how much of the Web page has been retrieved or downloaded into your computer's memory. For example, when 25% of the bar is filled in, 75% of the Web page still needs to be downloaded.

51 Stopping the presses

When you don't have time to wait for a Web site containing numerous graphics to download or when a Web site stops responding, it may be necessary to click the **Stop** button located on the Navigation bar. When the Stop button is clicked, the Web page display is halted.

52 Reloading the current Web page

For Web sites containing graphic images that periodically change, you can click the **Reload** button to have the AOL browser recognize these new settings. Otherwise, previous settings may be used in displaying a Web page.

53 Showing/hiding the channel selection window

The AOL Navigation bar permits AOL channels, seen in Figure 1-20, to be shown or hidden by clicking the **Show/Hide Channels** button. Acting as a toggle, the **Show/Hide Channels** window can be displayed or turned off with the click of your mouse.

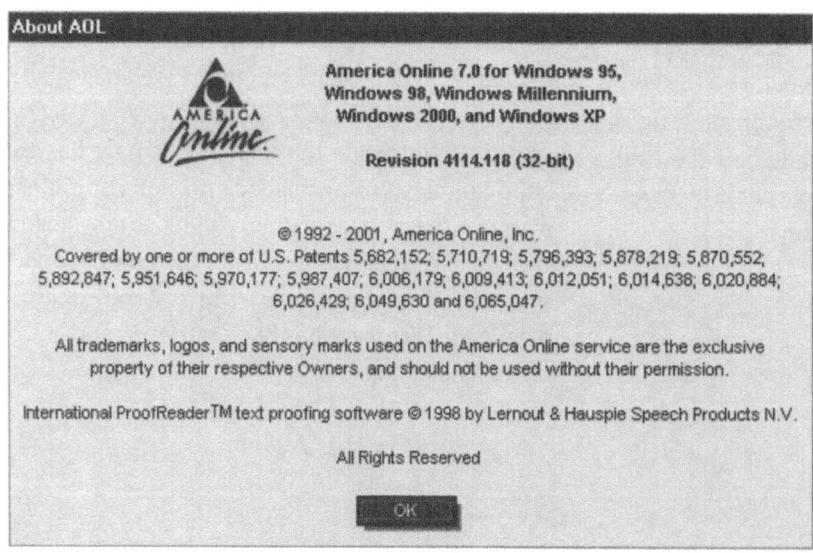

Figure 1-19. Viewing what version of AOL you're using

Figure 1-20. Showing/hiding the channel selection window

54 Understanding the navigation bar history trail

To save keystrokes and time, you can click the arrow located to the right of the large text box on the AOL Navigation bar. This displays the last 25 Web sites you visited in a drop-down list. From this list, commonly referred to as a history trail, you can select a previously displayed site for viewing instead of retyping it again.

55 Is there a spy in my computer?

AOL automatically retains a list of the 25 most recent areas or Web sites you visited. Many see this feature as a great time-saver because it permits the rapid selection of a page that was retrieved earlier. Others see it as intrusive Big Brother looking over their shoulder. To view the list or select a previously viewed area or Web site, you simply have to follow these steps:

1. Click the down-arrow next to the large text box on the AOL Navigation bar located directly beneath the AOL toolbar.

2. Select the area or Web site you'd like to redisplay.

56 Clearing the history trail immediately

As discussed, the history trail is a list of the 25 areas or Web sites you visited most recently. Although many users feel this feature is a great time-saver, others think it's too long and confusing. Also, someone else using your computer could view this list. If you share one computer with others, such as family members, it makes it easy for them to see the Web sites you've been visiting. To maintain your privacy, you can have AOL clear the list at any time during an AOL session by following these simple steps:

1. Click the **Settings** menu on the AOL toolbar and select **Preferences**.

2. In the Preferences window click **Toolbar**.

3. Click **Clear History Now**.

57 Clearing the history trail when signing off

If you feel the history trail containing a stored list of the sites you visited is a bit intrusive, then AOL gives you the option to clear the history trail. In the previous tip you saw how the history trail can be cleared on demand—now you will see how you can clear it each time you sign off. To have AOL automatically clear the contents of the history trail each time you sign off, follow these steps:

1. Click the **Settings** menu on the AOL toolbar and select **Preferences**.

2. In the Preferences window click **Toolbar**.

3. Click Clear history trail after each Sign Off.

Using Netscape with AOL

58 Downloading Netscape for free

You are free to use Netscape as your browser of choice with the AOL network. To use Netscape with AOL, simply sign on to AOL and start Netscape. The Netscape interface, or the layout of the screen, is similar to the America Online interface in that it provides all the navigation tools necessary for Web surfing.

Should you desire to use Netscape as your Web browser, you can download Version 6.01 for free at the following address: http://www.netscape.com. Click the Download button located at the top of the screen to display the Netscape Download & Upgrade page, shown in Figure 1-21, and begin the download process.

59 Understanding Navigation buttons

The Netscape Navigation bar contains two buttons to control backward and forward movement by the Web browser. The following features displayed from left to right are:

◀ **Back**—view previous page.

▶ **Forward**—return to a previously viewed Web page after the Back navigation button has been clicked.

Keyboard Shortcuts

60 Creating keyboard shortcuts

By creating keyboard shortcuts, you can reduce the number of keystrokes you have to type to launch an application or visit the Internet. Once a shortcut is created, you only need to press the CTRL key plus a number from 0–9. By following these steps you can create your own personal shortcuts.

Figure 1-21. Accessing the Netscape Download and Upgrade Web site

1. Click the **Favorites** pull-down menu on the AOL toolbar and point to My Hot Keys.

2. Select **Edit My Hot Keys**.

3. In the Edit My Hot Keys window, type the name of the shortcut in the **Shortcut Title** box.

4. Enter the AOL keyword or Web address in the **Keyword/Internet Address** box.

61 Using AOL keyboard shortcuts

The AOL menu bar provides access to several pull-down menus (File, Edit, Print, Window, Sign Off, and Help) containing common commands such as Open, Save, Help, Copy, and Paste, as well as numerous other commands. These keyboard shortcuts are frequently used to reduce the number of keystrokes. Table 1-1 shows numerous AOL keyboard shortcuts and the tasks they perform.

Table 1-1. AOL Keyboard Shortcuts

WINDOWS	MACINTOSH	TASK
F1 Key <or> ALT-H	⌘-/	Open AOL Help facility
F10 Key	N/A	Direct control to the menu bar located at the top of the screen
ALT-F4 Key	⌘-Q	Exit or Quit AOL
CTRL-C	⌘-C	Copy highlighted text/picture in the active window to paste buffer
CTRL-F	⌘-F	Find one or more occurrences of a word/phrase in an e-mail or file
CTRL-G	⌘-G	Open the **Get a Member's Profile** dialog box
CTRL-I	⌘-I	Open dialog box to send Instant Message
CTRL-Enter	Enter	Send an Instant Message (while in IM session)
CTRL-K	⌘-K	Open the AOL Keywords dialog box
CTRL-L	⌘-L	Open the **Locate Member Online** dialog box
CTRL-M	⌘ M	Open Write Mail form
CTRL-N	⌘-N	Open a simple text editor where text can be entered
CTRL-O	⌘-O	Open the **Open a File** dialog box
CTRL-P	⌘-P	Open the **Print** menu to route file to default printer or printer of choice
CTRL-R	⌘-R	Open your online mailbox
CTRL-S	⌘-S	Open a **Save a File** dialog box to save text/picture to an external file
CTRL-V	⌘-V	Paste text/picture in paste buffer to desired location
N/A	⌘-W	Close the current window
CTRL-X	⌘-X	Cut (or remove) highlighted text/picture in the active window
CTRL-Y	N/A	Open **Add to My Calendar** dialog box
CTRL-Z	⌘-Z	Request the previous action be undone
CTRL-1	N/A	Open the Buddy view
CTRL-2	N/A	Open AOL People Connection to Chat

Table 1-1. AOL Keyboard Shortcuts (Continued)

WINDOWS	MACINTOSH	TASK
CTRL-3	N/A	Open the Calendar
CTRL-4	⌘-/	Open the AOL Help facility
CTRL-5	⌘-7	Open the AOL Internet Connection
CTRL-6	N/A	Open Member Rewards window
CTRL-7	⌘-4	Open the News channel
CTRL-8	⌘-0 (Zero)	Open the Shopping channel
CTRL-9	⌘-5	Open the Stock Quotes window
CTRL-0 (zero)	⌘-1	Open the What's New window
CTRL-=	⌘-=	Launch Spell Check to check for spelling errors in e-mails and files
CTRL-Send Now	N/A	Bypass Spell Check when sending e-mail and this preference is set
CTRL-+ (or ♥)	♥	Add top window to favorite places
SHIFT-F5 Key	N/A	Cascade open window applications like a deck of cards
SHIFT-F4 Key	N/A	Tile open window applications across the AOL interface
TAB Key	TAB Key	In a dialog box, the TAB key moves the cursor to the next field or window
ESC Key	⌘-.	Cancel a running application giving you control back
▬ button	N/A	Minimize active window to an icon
▣ button	N/A	Toggle between regular window size and maximum window size setting
X button	N/A	Close open window (located in the top-right corner of window)
N/A	⌘-2	Open the AOL Store channel
N/A	⌘-3	Sign On a Friend
N/A	⌘-6	AOL Live
N/A	⌘-8	Open the Research and Learn channel
N/A	⌘-9	Entertainment

62 Changing Macintosh keyboard shortcuts

Your Macintosh keyboard shortcuts can be changed to suit your specific needs or preferences. To change your keyboard shortcuts, follow these steps:

1. Click the Window (to the right of the apple in the upper-right of the screen), and select **My Shortcuts.**

2. Select the bottom menu item **Edit Shortcuts.**

3. Change or enter the desired shortcut selections.

Getting Help 24/7

63 Getting the Help you need

The AOL Help Center is your very own personal self-contained, electronic answer guide to a variety of topics and features within AOL. You access the Help Center by pressing the **F1 key** or clicking the **Help** pull-down menu at the top of your screen, and selecting AOL Help. Once the Help Center is launched, you can request assistance by using the Search tool at the top of the Help window or browsing through the various Help topics.

64 Exploring the Help categories

The AOL Help Center has categorized a variety of Help topics for you to browse through. Yes, I know that a lot of the information in this book is also available online, but I've tried to make this even easier to use than AOL's online help—and something you can read when you're not actually online. ? So here are the Help topics:

- Your E-mail
- Instant Messages and Buddy List
- Signing on to the AOL Service
- Parental Controls, Privacy & Security
- Finding Anything Online Quickly
- Personal Finance, Stocks & Quotes
- Exploring the Internet
- Downloading Files & Attachments
- Personalizing Your AOL
- AOL Multimedia Features
- Installing New Version of AOL

65 Searching and finding in Help

The following tips will help you find the information you need, and get the most out of the AOL Help Center.

1. The AOL Help Center screen is organized into different areas. Some areas are updated frequently, such as the new AOL access numbers, billing information, and so one.

2. To search for an answer with the Search tool—enter one or more words in the text box at the top right of the AOL Help Center, and click the **Search** button.

3. You can view any folder or article that matched your requested search by double-clicking on an item displayed in the search window.

4. Verify spelling of key words for accuracy.

5. Use **AND** and **OR** search operators to narrow or expand your search criteria and results. For example, specifying **e-mail AND folders** searches for information containing both words in the search results.

6. Use the **NOT** search operator to negate or ignore a word. For example, specifying **e-mail NOT folders** searches for information containing references to e-mail but not folders.

7. If the search results are not what you were hoping for, try other words that may have the same or similar meaning.

66 Using the Help search tool

The AOL search tool can be the best way to locate needed information. To launch a search, enter one or more words in the text box located at the top right of the Help Center window, and click the **Search** button.

67 Calling AOL for assistance

Depending on the type of problem you are having, you can get help from a live person anytime by calling the AOL Customer Service toll-free line 24 hours a day, 7 days a week. Select from the following list of phone numbers:

AOL Technical Support (Windows version):
1-888-346-3704

AOL Technical Support (Macintosh version):

1-888-265-8007

Screen Name or Password Problems:

1-888-265-8004

Access Numbers:

1-888-265-8005

Billing Inquiries:

1-888-265-8003

Account Cancellation:

1-888-265-8008

68 Checking out Accounts and Billing

You can access your AOL account by clicking the **Accounts and Billing** button located on the right side of the AOL Help Center. When launched, the Billing Center window opens permitting you to update your billing information, view your bill, and display Frequently Asked Questions (FAQs).

CHAPTER 2

Communicating to the World with E-mail

E-MAIL IS ONE OF THE most popular features on AOL. From exchanging messages with family, friends, and associates, to attaching files, documents, and pictures, e-mail is a wonderful way to stay in contact with people without the cost of long-distance phone calls. This chapter supplies e-mail tips that even the savviest online connoisseur will love. You'll learn practical and timesaving tips to help you:

- 📖 Set up e-mail

- 📖 Read, create and send e-mail

- 📖 Send courtesy and blind courtesy copies

- 📖 Jazz up your message text

- 📖 Manage e-mail messages

- 📖 Create and use your address book

- 📖 Format and spell-check message text

- 📖 Add hypertext elements

- 📖 Use signatures, and smileys

- 📖 Manage junk mail

- 📖 Attach and detach files and photos

Setting Up Your E-Mail

1 The AOL e-mail interface

The America Online electronic mail interface is one of the easiest and most flexible Internet e-mail software packages in the world. Its utter simplicity and flexibility make it so easy to use that you may be asking, "What's to learn—I've been using e-mail services from AOL for some time now—what more is there to know?"

Whether you are a seasoned e-mail expert or just clicking your proverbial mouse into the electronic world for the first time makes no difference. To get the most from AOL's e-mail services, as many millions of online users already have, you'll want to at least skim each tip that follows to see if there are any interesting tidbits of information meant just for you. AOL Version 7.0's incredible capabilities and features provide a tried and proven way to communicate online—all through a simple and effective e-mail interface. To help get the most from your e-mail experience, the tips that follow will provide a quick look at each feature one-by-one.

2 Setting up your e-mail account

Before you can begin using e-mail, you must set up an account. When you first install AOL Version 7.0, or an earlier version, it's not automatically set up for you. To set up your e-mail account and other personal information, you'll need to start AOL by clicking the AOL V7 icon located on your desktop. Once AOL is active, the Sign On screen will appear, as displayed in Figure 2-1.

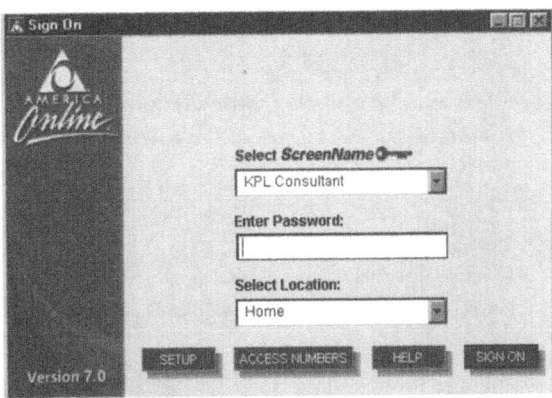

Figure 2-1. AOL's Sign On screen

Then, click the **SETUP** button to begin the online setup process. The Edit America Online Setup screen will appear, as you see in Figure, 2-2.

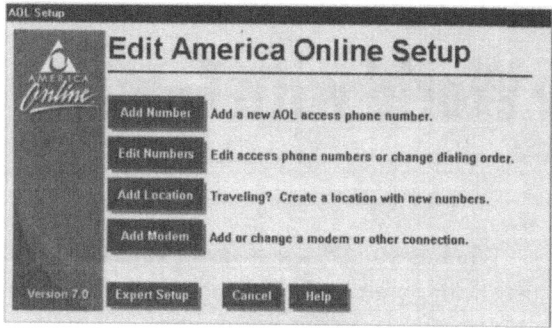

Figure 2-2. Accessing AOL's Online Setup process

3 Securing your AOL password

It doesn't matter whether you are the secretive type or not, never give your AOL password to anyone. AOL staff will never ask you for your password for any reason and you should never volunteer your password to others. Giving your password to someone else is the virtual equivalent of handing your car keys to a perfect stranger. If you receive suspicious-looking e-mail, click the **Forward** button and send it to screen name TOS Email1.

4 Picking mail preferences

You can control how AOL is to behave as you handle your mail. AOL can be made to show e-mail addresses as hyperlinks, automatically display the next message when the current one is deleted, notify you when a message contains a picture (or image) before you actually open it, control how you write your e-mail, and how AOL sends your message. To control the behavior of AOL's mail features, simply set one or more e-mail preferences, and let AOL do the rest.

5 Setting preferences to automatically save e-mail

After e-mail messages have been read, they are automatically sent to your Old Mail box or your Sent Mail box. Mail in your Old Mail box will remain there for 3–7 days, while mail in your Sent Mail box will remain there for 27 days. To alter the way AOL saves your e-mail, follow these steps:

1. From the AOL toolbar, click the **Settings** menu and select **Preferences**.

2. Select **Mail** in the **Communications** section of the **Preferences** window to display the Mail Preferences window, shown in Figure 2-3.

3. Change the number of days in the **Keep my old mail online __ days after I read it** by clicking the increase/decrease button corresponding to the number of days.

4. Click the **Save** button.

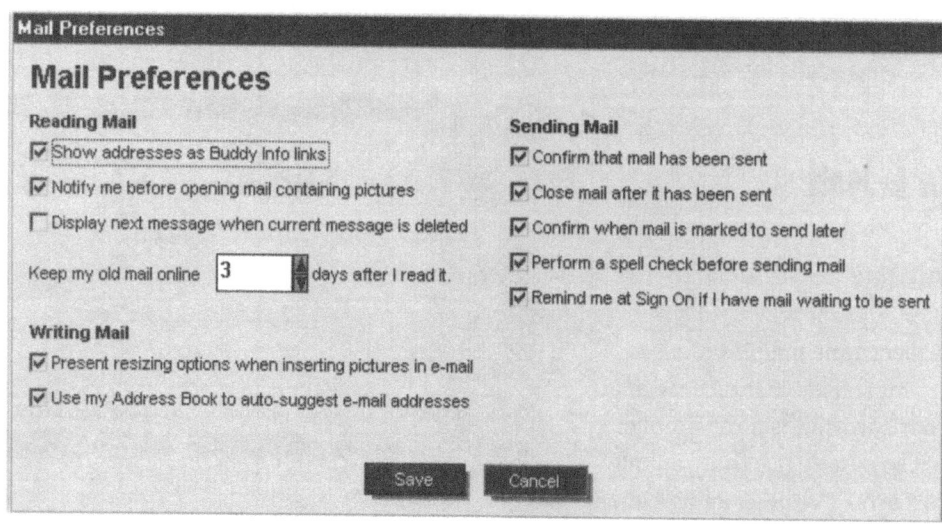

Figure 2-3. Setting preferences to automatically save e-mail

6 Turning on white e-mail headers

To make reading your e-mail easier by having the Subject, Date, From, and To information appear on a white background rather than a gray background, follow these steps:

1. On the **Settings** menu on the AOL toolbar, click **Preferences**.

2. Select **Mail** in the **Communications** section of the **Preferences** window.

3. Click the **Use white mail headers** box.

4. Click the **Save** button.

7 Showing e-mail addresses as hyperlinks

As you read your e-mail, you can send a message back to the sender with a click of the mouse button when you have e-mail addresses listed as hyperlinks. To have addresses displayed as hyperlinks follow these steps:

1. On the **Settings** menu on the AOL toolbar, click **Preferences**.

2. Select **Mail** in the **Communications** section of the **Preferences** window.

3. Click the **Show addresses as hyperlinks** box.

4. Click the **Save** button.

8 Opening e-mail containing pictures

To be notified of e-mail containing images as you read your messages, you can have AOL automatically display a confirmation window. This way, you won't accidentally open an e-mail that could contain a virus without having a confirmation window display first. This is especially useful when you read e-mail from people you don't know. To have AOL notify you of e-mail containing pictures, follow these steps:

1. On the **Settings** menu on the AOL toolbar, click **Preferences**.

2. Select **Mail** in the **Communications** section of the **Preferences** window.

3. Click the **Notify me before opening mail containing pictures** box.

💣 *This may be the default setting—so don't accidentally "unset" this option.*

4. Click the **Save** button.

9 Displaying your next message

To save a few mouse clicks, you can have the next message in your message list automatically open when you delete the current message. Otherwise, if this feature is not turned on, the message list will reappear. To turn this feature on, follow these steps:

1. On the **Settings** menu on the AOL toolbar, click **Preferences**.

2. Select **Mail** in the **Communications** section of the **Preferences** window.

3. Click the **Display next message when current message is deleted** box.

4. Click the **Save** button.

10 Storing old e-mail

To increase or decrease the number of days old mail remains in your online mailbox, follow these steps:

1. On the **Settings** menu on the AOL toolbar, click **Preferences**.

2. Select **Mail** in the **Communications** section of the **Preferences** window.

3. Change the number of days in the **Keep my old mail online __ days after I read it** box by clicking the increase/decrease button associated with the number of days.

4. Click the **Save** button.

11 Confirming when e-mail has been sent

Knowing when an e-mail message has been sent can be a reassuring thing. AOL can be set to display a confirmation window each time you send an e-mail message. To turn this feature on, follow these steps:

1. On the **Settings** menu on the AOL toolbar, click **Preferences**.

2. Select **Mail** in the **Communications** section of the **Preferences** window.

3. Click the **Confirm that mail has been sent** box (located in the **Sending Mail** section of the **Mail Preferences** window).

    🖋 *This may be the default setting—so don't accidentally "unset" this option unless you want to turn it off.*

4. Click the **Save** button.

12 Closing the e-mail window after the message has been sent

To save a little time, you can have the Write Mail message window close immediately after you send your e-mail by following these steps:

1. On the **Settings** menu on the AOL toolbar, click **Preferences**.

2. Select **Mail** in the **Communications** section of the **Preferences** window.

3. Click the **Close mail after it has been sent** box.

4. Click the **Save** button.

13 Confirming when e-mail is marked to send later

A confirmation window can be made to appear each time you click **Send Later**. This handy reminder window alerts you whenever you have mail that is marked to be sent later. To turn this feature on, follow these steps:

1. On the **Settings** menu on the AOL toolbar, click **Preferences**.

2. Select **Mail** in the **Communications** section of the **Preferences** window.

3. Click the **Confirm when mail is marked to send later** box (located in the **Sending Mail** section of the **Mail Preferences** window).

    💣 *This may be the default setting—so don't accidentally "unset" this option unless you want to turn it off.*

4. Click the **Save** button.

14 Spell-checking your message

If your spelling is less than perfect, why not have AOL perform a spell check on your e-mail message before you send it? To perform a spell check before sending your message, follow these steps:

1. On the **Settings** menu on the AOL toolbar, click **Preferences**.

2. Select **Mail** in the **Communications** section of the **Preferences** window.

3. Click the **Perform a spell check before sending mail** box.

4. Click the **Save** button.

15 Setting a reminder when e-mail is waiting to be sent

To have AOL remind you at Sign On with a confirmation window that you have e-mail waiting to be sent, follow these steps:

1. On the **Settings** menu on the AOL toolbar, click **Preferences**.

2. Select **Mail** in the **Communications** section of the **Preferences** window.

3. Click the **Remind me at Sign On if I have mail waiting to be sent** box.

💣 *This may be the default setting—so don't accidentally "unset" this option unless you want to turn it off.*

4. Click the **Save** button.

16 Having AOL resize pictures in e-mail

When writing mail and inserting a picture, you can have AOL automatically display a selection window to help resize the image. To turn this feature on, follow these steps:

1. On the **Settings** menu on the AOL toolbar, click **Preferences**.

2. Select **Mail** in the **Communications** section of the **Preferences** window.

3. Click the **Present resizing options when inserting pictures in e-mail** box.

💣 *This may be the default setting—so don't accidentally "unset" this option unless you want to turn it off.*

4. Click the **Save** button.

17 Using the address book to auto-complete e-mail addresses

Save time by letting AOL auto-complete e-mail addresses you enter in the To and From fields by using addresses in your personal address book. When this feature is turned on, any e-mail address you type in the **Write** window will automatically complete your typing with matches from your address book. To turn this feature on, follow these steps:

1. On the **Settings** menu on the AOL toolbar, click **Preferences**.

2. Select **Mail** in the **Communications** section of the **Preferences** window.

3. Click the **Use my address book to auto-complete e-mail addresses** box (located in the **Writing Mail** section of the **Mail Preferences** window).

💣 *This may be the default setting—so don't accidentally "unset" this option unless you want to turn it off.*

4. Click the **Save** button.

18 Sending e-mail from the "Mail Waiting to be Sent" folder

Any mail that you've identifiedto be sent later by clicking the **Send Later** button on the **Write Mail** window is set-aside in the **Mail Waiting to be Sent** folder. AOL allows you to automatically send it by opening the **Mail Waiting to be Sent** window as follows:

1. Click the **Mail** button on the AOL toolbar.

2. Select the **Mail Waiting to be Sent** menu item from the drop-down menu list.

3. Highlight the mail you want to send and click the **Send** button on the **Mail Waiting to be Sent** window, as you see in Figure 2-4.

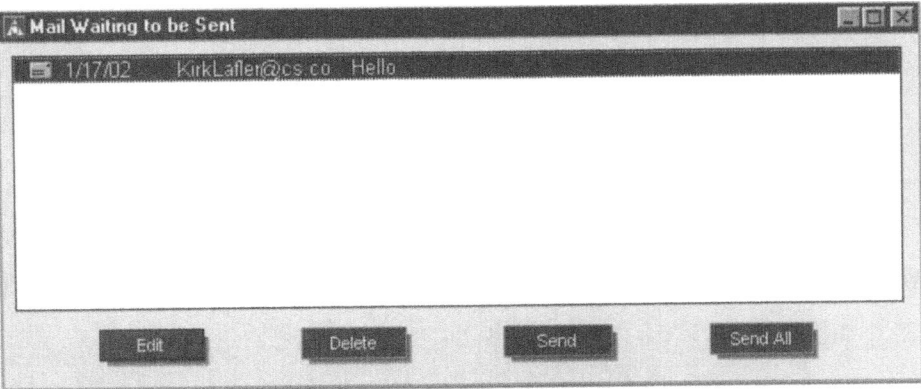

Figure 2-4. Highlighting and sending e-mail in the Mail Waiting to be Sent folder

19 Putting unread e-mail in an "Incoming Mail" folder

Unread mail can be automatically placed in the **Incoming Mail** folder. Follow these steps to have it done.

1. On the **Settings** menu on the AOL toolbar, click **Preferences**.

2. Select **Auto AOL** in the **Communications** section of the **Preferences** window.

3. Click **Get Unread Mail** and put it in **Incoming Mail** folder box, as shown in Figure 2-5.

20 Blocking e-mail attachments

Preventing the download of attached files in e-mail ensures that you won't receive attached files containing viruses and Trojan horse programs, which could steal information from your computer. By following a few simple steps, you can block the downloading of any and all attached files.

1. Click the **Mail** button on the AOL toolbar.

2. Click **Mail Controls** from the **Mail** pull-down menu.

3. From the **AOL Mail Controls** window, select the screen name you want and click the **Customize Mail Controls for this Screen Name** box, as you see in Figure 2-6.

4. Select the **Pictures and Files** button on the AOL Mail Controls window and click the **Block this screen name from sending and receiving mail with pictures and files** box, as shown in Figure 2-7.

5. Click the **Next** button.

6. Click the **Save** button on the AOL **Mail Controls Confirmation** window, as shown in Figure 2-8.

7. Click the **Close** button, as you see in Figure 2-9.

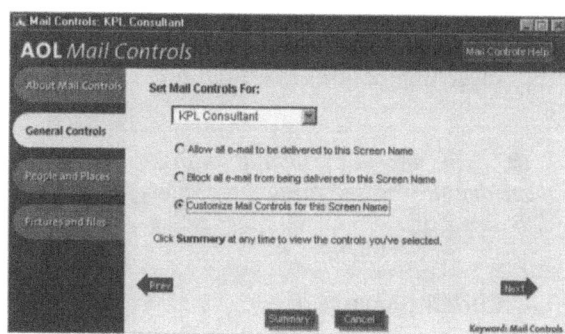

Figure 2-6. Customizing Mail Controls for the selected screen name

Figure 2-5. Setting preferences to have unread mail placed in the Incoming Mail folder

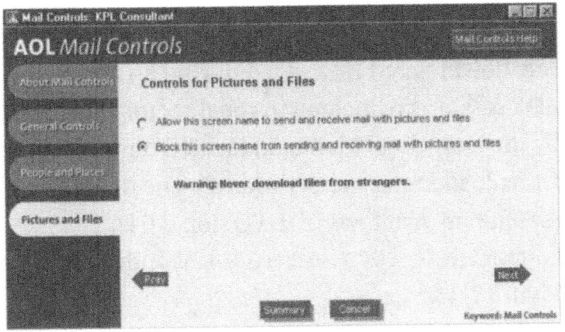

Figure 2-7. Blocking pictures and files for the selected screen name

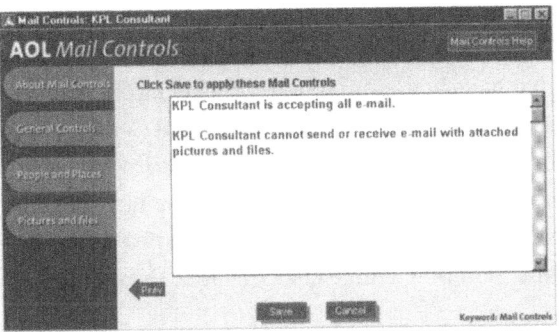

Figure 2-8. Applying mail controls on the Mail Controls Confirmation window

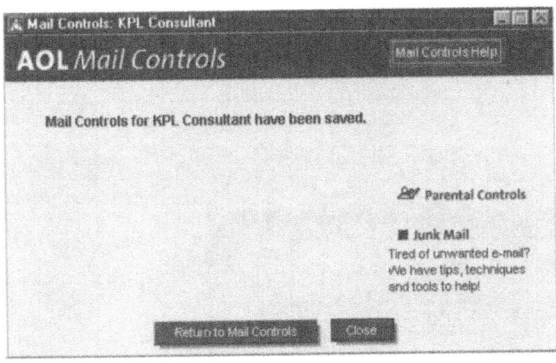

Figure 2-9. Closing AOL's Mail Controls window

21 Scheduling file downloads

You can instruct Automatic AOL to download and save files marked to be downloaded later. Taking advantage of this feature enables you to maximize your time to the fullest by doing time-consuming downloading tasks while you're at the office, after work hours, while on vacation, or while you sleep. When you're ready, sign on and access your personal filing cabinet, and everything will be there waiting for you. This is how it's done:

1. Click the **Settings** icon on the AOL toolbar.

2. Select **Preferences** from the drop-down menu.

3. In the Preferences window, click **Auto AOL** from the **Communications** section.

4. In the Automatic AOL window, click the **Download files market to be downloaded later** box, shown in Figure 2-10.

5. Click the **Schedule Automatic AOL** icon.

6. In the **Schedule Automatic AOL** window, which you see in Figure 2-11, you can specify the days you want it turned on, click **Enable Scheduler**, the starting time, and how often (e.g., every hour, every 2 hours, every 4 hours, every 8 hours, every day).

7. Click the **OK** button.

Figure 2-10. Scheduling file downloads with Automatic AOL

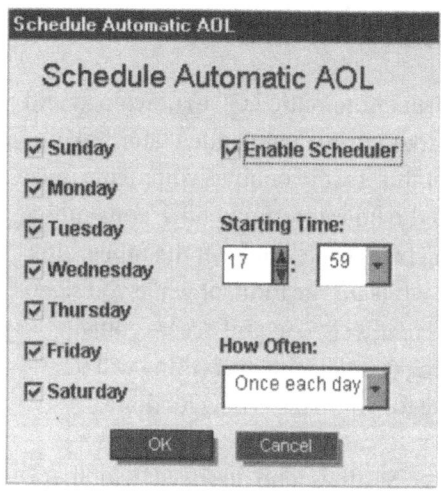

Figure 2-11. Enabling the Automatic AOL Scheduler

22 Selecting the frequency of file downloads

AOL lets you select the frequency of file downloads through a drop-down selection list. Scheduling when and how often an automatic AOL session is to occur is your decision, shown in Figure 2-12.

| Every half hour |
| Every hour |
| Every 2 hours |
| Every 4 hours |
| Every 8 hours |
| Once each day |

Figure 2-12. Selecting the frequency of file downloads from a drop-down list

23 Retrieving downloaded files

Any downloaded files saved during an automatic AOL session are located in the directory specified by the Download Manager, located on the Download Preferences window). The default location in Windows AOL Version 7.0 is: C:\America Online 7.0\download, as shown in Figure 2-13.

Reading E-mail

24 Checking for new e-mail

Your online mailbox contains any e-mail messages that have been sent to you. To check your online mailbox for New Mail, click the **Mail Center** icon on the Welcome Screen. The **Mailbox** window displays any new mail messages you have, as shown in Figure 2-14. You can also view **Old Mail** and **Sent Mail** with a click of your mouse.

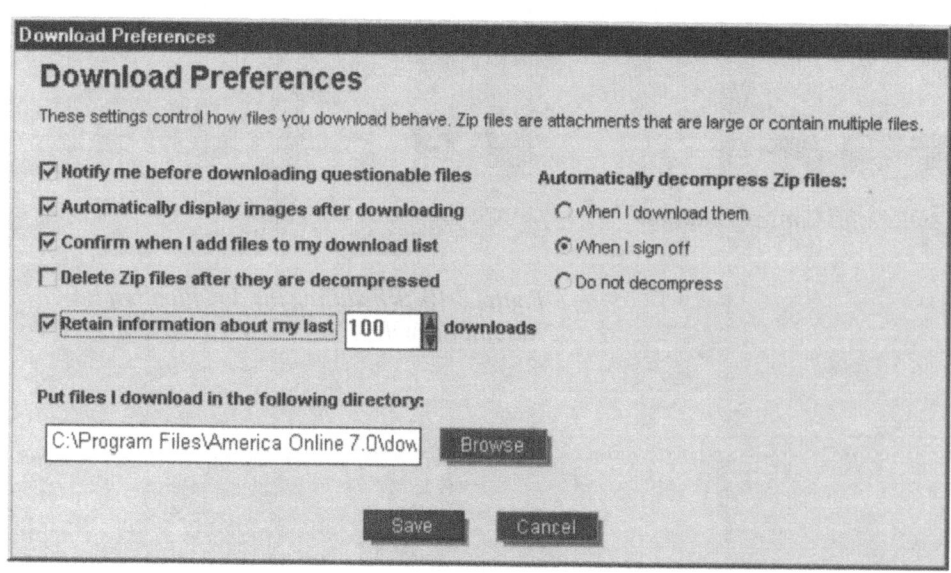

Figure 2-13. Locating downloaded files from an Automatic AOL session

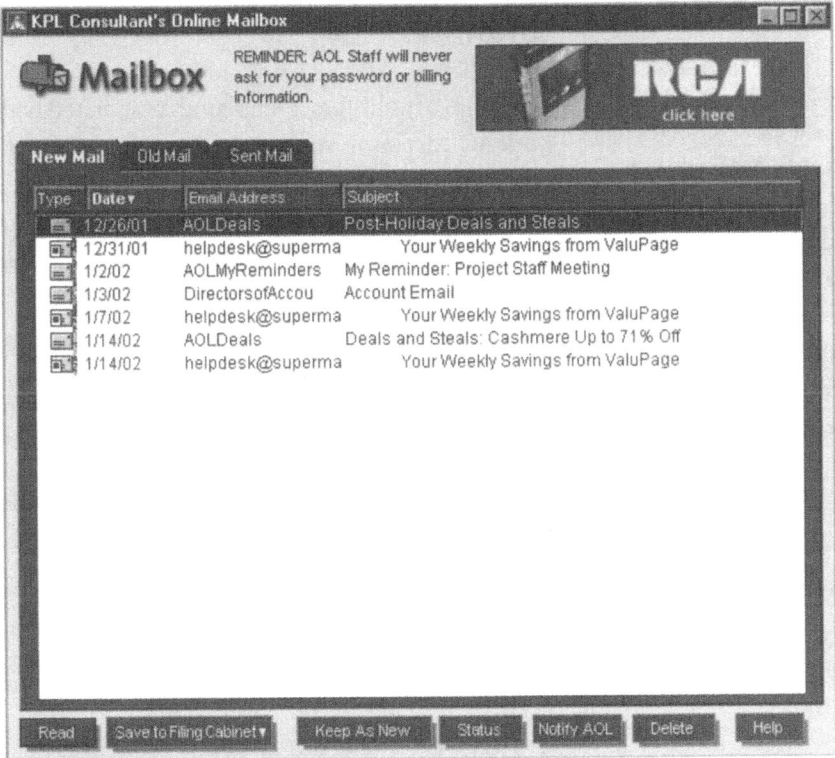

Figure 2-14. Accessing new e-mail in your AOL Online Mailbox

25 Understanding e-mail addresses

Every Internet address (or AOL address) adheres to the form name@organization.domain. For example, my AOL address is KPL Consultant@aol.com. The "KPLConsultant" part of my address is referred to as my AOL or Internet nickname. "AOL" refers to America Online, my Internet provider. The "com" portion refers to the type of domain, designating that "AOL" is a commercial business.

26 Exploring the world of domain designations

There are currently six e-mail address domain designations, with many more to come.

COM	Commercial businesses
EDU	Educational institutions
GOV	Government organizations
MIL	Military establishments
NET	Networks

ORG	Nonprofit organizations
AU	Australia
CA	Canada
UK	Unitcd Kingdom

The International Governing body of domain designations has recently approved seven new e-mail address domain designations. This means that there will be millions of new registrations for these domain names.

BIZ	Businesses
INFO	Information-oriented organizations
NAME	Individuals
PRO	Professional organizations
AERO	Aerospace industry
COOP	Coop organizations
MUSEUM	Museums and galleries

27 Ignoring e-mail messages

While AOL can store as much as 1,000 New Mail messages, 500 Old Mail messages, and 550 Sent Mail messages in your online mailbox per screen name, there are certain time limits. Messages in your New Mail mailbox will be retained for 27 days, in the Old Mail mailbox for 3 days, and Sent Mail mailbox for 27 days—after that it is gone.

Sometimes you may want to simply ignore one or more e-mail messages in your New Mail mailbox. E-mail that you decide to ignore is automatically moved to your Old Mail list. So how do you mark mail that you want to ignore? Follow these steps:

1. Click the **Read** icon on the AOL toolbar.

2. After selecting the **New Mail** tab, right-click the e-mail message you want to ignore and click **Ignore** from the pop-up menu that appears.

28 Sorting messages

Messages in your online mailbox can be sorted by subject, date, or e-mail address to make it easier to find things. Simply click one of the Mailbox tabs located above your messages to arrange and organize them according to your needs. Messages are arranged in ascending alphabetical and/or numerical order (A–Z, 0–9, etc.).

29 Reading e-mail messages online

AOL notifies you of any unread e-mail when you sign on by putting up the flag on the mailbox on the Welcome screen, and if your computer is equipped with a sound card with the words "You've got mail." To read your e-mail messages online, follow these steps:

1. Click the **Read** icon on the AOL toolbar.

2. After selecting the **New Mail** tab, double-click any e-mail message you want to open and read.

30 Reading e-mail messages sent to another screen name

If you have multiple screen names associated with your AOL account, you can read e-mail messages sent to another screen name without signing off. Not only does this save time—it is a handy way to access your other screen names, too. To read e-mail messages sent to another screen name, follow these steps:

1. From the **Sign Off** menu located at the top of your screen, click **Switch Screen Names**.

2. In the **Switch Screen Names** window, double-click the screen name you want to switch to.

3. **Sign on** to your screen name as usual.

31 Reading e-mail messages offline

You don't have to be online to be able to read your e-mail messages. Sometimes it is handy to be able to read all those e-mail messages you downloaded from your online mailbox in an earlier session at a later time. To do this, follow these steps:

1. From the **File** menu located at the top of your screen, click **Filing Cabinet**.

2. Click the **Mail** tab on the Filing Cabinet window, and double-click the desired e-mail message of choice in the **Incoming/Saved Mail** folder.

3. The e-mail message appears so you can read it.

32 Navigating between New Mail, Old mail, and Sent Mail

To view e-mail messages in your online mailbox, as seen in Figure 2-15, follow these steps:

1. **Sign on** to AOL.

2. Click the **Read** icon button on the AOL toolbar.

3. Click one of the tab headings, **New Mail**, **Old Mail**, or **Sent Mail**.

Figure 2-15. Navigating between New, Old, and Sent Mail is easy in AOL.

33 Creating a folder for your e-mail messages

AOL helps you organize your e-mail messages by storing them in your own personal folders. But before a message can be placed in a folder, you must be able to create the folder. So let's see how a folder is created.

1. From the **Mail** menu on the AOL toolbar, click **Filing Cabinet**.

2. Click the **Mail** tab on the **Filing Cabinet** window.

3. Click the **Incoming/Saved Mail** item.

4. Click **New Folder**, and enter the name of the folder you want to create in the Create Folder dialog box.

5. Click the **OK** button.

34 Saving e-mail messages to a folder of your choice

After you've read an e-mail message, you have the choice of leaving it in your online mailbox, deleting it, or saving it to a folder of your choice. Saving it to a folder can be accomplished manually or automatically.

You can save your messages manually by following these steps:

1. From your online mailbox, click the **New Mail**, **Old Mail**, or **Sent Mail** tab.

2. Select the e-mail message you want to save by clicking it once.

3. Click the **Save to Filing Cabinet** menu, and select the location where you want mail saved (e.g., **Incoming/Saved Mail**).

Generally, you'll want to have your messages saved automatically, so follow these steps:

1. Click the **Settings** menu on the AOL toolbar, and select **Preferences** from the drop-down menu.

2. Click **Filing Cabinet** under the **Organization** section of the **Preferences** window.

3. To save all incoming messages, select the **Retain all mail I read in my Filing Cabinet** check box.

35 Printing e-mail messages

If you have a printer and want to print an e-mail message, simply follow these steps:

1. From the **Print** menu located at the top of your screen, click **Print** from the drop-down menu or **Ctrl-P**, and you'll see the window shown in Figure 2-16.

2. Click the **OK** button.

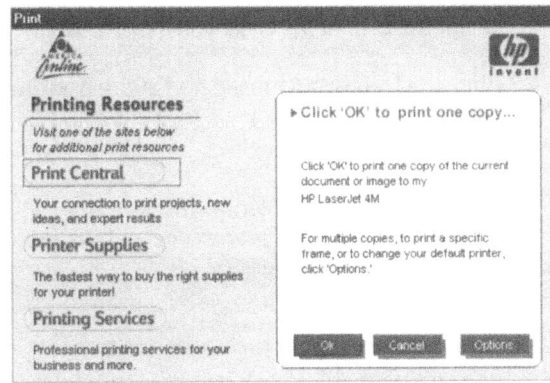

Figure 2-16. Printing an e-mail message from the Print window

36 Marking e-mail messages as unread

To prevent an e-mail message that's been read from being placed in the **Old Mail** folder, you can have AOL treat it as if it were a new message. This gives you a little more time to decide what you want done with it. Here's how it's done.

1. Click the **You've Got Mail** Icon located on the **Welcome** screen.

2. Click the **New Mail** tab, and open the desired message.

3. Close the message when you're done as usual. This will mark the message as being read with a red checkmark in the **Type** field.

4. Click the **Keep as New** button on your online mailbox window.

37 Saying goodbye to those unwanted messages

As a matter of good e-mail management, it may be necessary to delete a message in your mailbox. To accomplish this, follow these steps:

1. Select the e-mail message you'd like to delete.

2. Click the **Delete** button located at the bottom of the Mailbox window.

💣 *Use extreme care when deleting e-mail messages, since the delete process does not verify the action before it is performed.*

You can delete several messages at a time without opening them. Here's how you can delete a group of messages at one time.

1. Hold the **Shift** key down and click on the last message you want to delete. All messages between the first and last selected messages will be included in the selection.

2. Click the **Delete** button.

You can delete two or more messages without selecting all messages in between. Here's how:

1. Hold the **Ctrl** key down and click on each message you want to delete. Each selected message will be included in the deletion.

2. Click the **Delete** button.

38 Undeleting deleted e-mail messages

If you find that you accidentally deleted the wrong e-mail message from your mailbox, don't despair. You may be able to recover recently deleted e-mail messages (if it's been less than 24 hours from the time you deleted it) by following these steps:

1. On the **Mail** menu on the AOL toolbar, click **Recently Deleted Mail**

2. Select the e-mail you want to retrieve in the **Recently Deleted Mail** window.

3. Click **Keep as New** and the e-mail will be restored to your online mailbox.

39 Handling attachments

As a safeguard measure, AOL sends an automatic notification when a message contains a picture. This feature combined with anti-virus software provides some level of security when downloading files from the Internet.

Since viruses usually exist in non-text files they can, if proper precautions are not taken, replicate and spread through your computer system causing havoc if opened. AOL has enabled this feature to alert you when attachments are part of your e-mail.

🖋 *AOL makes it clear that it is not and cannot be held responsible for viruses.*

To disable this feature, follow these steps:

1. Click the **Mail Center** button on the main AOL toolbar and select **Mail Preferences**.

2. Click the **Notify me before opening mail containing pictures** option.

3. Click the **OK** button.

Creating E-mail Messages

40 Writing an e-mail message

AOL makes sending an e-mail message as easy as 1-2-3. You have three ways to display a blank e-mail message window:

- Click the **Write** icon button on the AOL toolbar

- On the **Mail** menu on the AOL toolbar, click **Write Mail**

- Press **CTRL-M**.

Any one of these actions will display the **Write Mail** window, as seen in Figure 2-17.

The **Write Mail** window resembles a text editor and acts as the interface between you and your message. This is where your message will be entered.

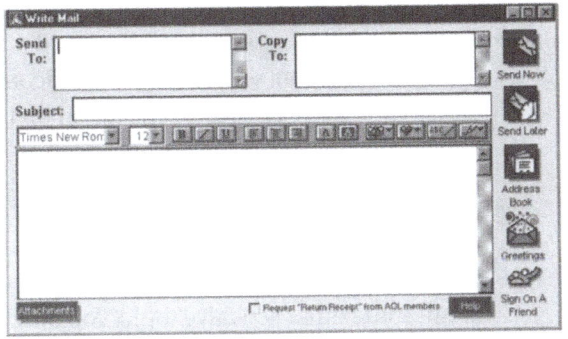

Figure 2-17. Displaying a blank e-mail window

41 Using e-mail message fields

When you create an e-mail message, four principle fields (text boxes) are filled in:

Send To
Copy To
Subject
Message area

The **Send To** text box identifies who the message is to go to, the **Copy To** text box identifies who will receive a courtesy copy of the message, the **Subject** is a brief description of the message, and the

Message text box consists of the message itself. You can move forward between each text box by pressing the **Tab** key (or backward by pressing the **Shift-Tab** key).

42 Getting the address right

Just like regular mail, or snail mail, which requires a name, street address, city, state, and zip code, (and a country for foreign mail), e-mail requires an address too. The **Send To** field in an e-mail message tells AOL who to send the message to. In AOL, your screen name is your e-mail address. You enter the complete e-mail address of the person you want to send the message to, or have your personal address book fill in the field by clicking the person's name. However you decide to do it, an address is always necessary for your e-mail message. To send your e-mail message to more than one recipient separate each address with a comma (,).

43 Using the carbon copy (CC) text box

Sometimes it's useful to have a copy of your e-mail message sent to yourself and/or someone else. Just as you did for the **Send To** text box (see previous tip), you enter the complete e-mail address of the person you want a courtesy copy sent to in the **Copy To** text box. To send your e-mail message to more than one recipient separate each address with a comma (,). For a blind carbon copy (BCC), you can use your address book or type directly in the BCC field.

44 Describing the e-mail subject

You can write anything you like in the subject line of an e-mail message, but it's best if the text corresponds to what is contained in the message itself. Often the subject field is one of the first things, along with the sender's e-mail address, the e-mail recipient will look at to help determine what the message is about and whether the message should be opened. So always try to provide a descriptive heading for your subject line—it can also provide a good way to locate messages at a later time should the need arise.

45 Creating your message text

Your message text can be entered directly in the **Message** text box in the **Write Mail** window. To make your message readable, only use ASCII characters (e.g., 26 upper and lowercase alphabet letters, the numbers 0 through 9, and common punctuation marks).

46 Pasting message text

Sometimes it's easier to compose your message in another text editor (e.g., MS Word). AOL doesn't require you to use the AOL text editor. Instead you can copy-and-paste your text from your favorite text editor right into the AOL message text box. All you need to do is:

1. Compose your message text in the text editor of choice (e.g., MS Word).

2. Highlight the message text in your text editor using your mouse.

3. Press the **CTRL-C** keys simultaneously to copy the highlighted text.

4. In the AOL **Write Mail** window click the message text box, and press the **CTRL-V** keys simultaneously to paste your message text.

5. Your message text will appear in the **Write Mail** window.

🖋 *These control key combinations are the same for Macintosh users.*

47 Composing e-mail messages offline

You can compose one or more e-mail messages even when you're not signed on to AOL. This is a handy feature especially when you're unable to establish a connection with AOL (for instance while waiting at an airport, on the train, or anywhere you can use a computer). To write your e-mail messages offline, follow these steps:

1. Click the **Write** icon on the AOL toolbar.

2. Enter the information in the **Send To, Copy To, Subject**, and **Message** text boxes.

3. Click the **Send Later** icon button.

Minding your E-mail Manners

48 Keeping your tone polite and calm

E-mail has been available for many years now—but many users still know very little about proper e-mail etiquette. Here are some tips for keeping your interchanges cordial:

- Refrain from using ALL CAPITAL letters in your message—not only is it rude, but is frequently interpreted as yelling or screaming.

- Be watchful of the tone of your e-mail messages—message text can easily be misunderstood.

- To prevent being misinterpreted, consider using an emoticon, or smiley. See emoticons and their meanings, presented later in this chapter.

- E-mail is a great way to deal with someone you can't deal with in person, but if you're delivering bad news or communicating about some other sensitive topic, you may be better off getting on the phone.

- Avoid writing e-mail that is hurtful and offensive to others—remember, everyone has feelings.

- Avoid flaming e-mail messages (sending angry messages)—they frequently backfire and make the sender look foolish and immature.

- Never use curse words in your message—this is considered improper etiquette. Rather, use euphemisms and made-up expletives to state a strong opinion.

49 Making your messages look good and read well

The way your e-mail messages appear says a lot about you. Try to be considerate of your readers by presenting your e-mail in the best way possible:

- Make your messages look good—unformatted and sloppy messages are difficult to read.

- Be careful, though, of using too many formatting styles, such as bold, italics, or underline because some e-mail systems may be unable to interpret them correctly and could turn your special formats into gibberish.

- To make your messages readable by all, use only ASCII characters, which are the 26 upper and lower case alphabet letters, the numbers 0 through 9, and common punctuation marks.

- Restrict your message line length to 60 characters because some e-mail systems break text lines in strange places.

- Avoid spelling errors by turning on the AOL Spell Check feature.

- Always include your e-mail address with any message you send.

- Avoid sending e-mail messages without adding a subject line.

- Don't use too many acronyms in your message because not everyone understands them.

- Use short and descriptive subject lines to help others determine what the content of your message is.

50 Being professional in your e-mail messages

When you are using your AOL e-mail account for business purposes, it pays to be polished and polite.

- Don't copy a colleague on an e-mail message unless the message affects them.

- Use blind courtesy copy (BCC) to hide e-mail addresses you don't want others to see.

- Use care when replying to an e-mail message—you could send to a whole list of people accidentally.

- If you're going to use signature files, insert useful information such as your e-mail, web site address, and phone number.

- Avoid using silly signatures for business correspondence—a professional image is everything.

- Reference the original e-mail message when sending a reply.

- When sending attachments—verify that your correspondent has the necessary application software to open it.

51 Saving time for your e-mail recipients

Remember to treat your e-mail message readers, as you would like to be treated—with respect.

- Avoid using the "urgent" flag unless your message really is either time-sensitive or important. Using your best judgment with this feature will show you respect other people's time.

- Don't request a receipt unless the message is extremely important or you've experienced problems with the e-mail system.

- Don't send or follow the instructions specified in chain letters—they are considered unacceptable network behavior.

- Avoid using copyrighted graphics, pictures, and other images in your e-mail, and remember, an inserted graphic, picture, or image will only be seen by other AOL members—and not by non-AOL members.

- Avoid posting messages anonymously since this is unacceptable network behavior.

- Respect another person's time and privacy—don't send junk mail.

Chapter 2

Sending E-mail

52 Sending e-mail messages online

After you've entered an address for the **Send To** and **Copy To** fields, a **Subject** and your message text, you're ready to send your e-mail. Although you don't have to be signed on to AOL to compose your e-mail message, you'll need to be signed on to send it. When your e-mail is ready, click the **Send Now** button located in the upper-right corner of the **Write Mail** window. AOL will immediately send your e-mail, close the **Write Mail** window, and confirm that your e-mail was sent by displaying the message, **Your mail has been sent,** as you can see in Figure 2-18.

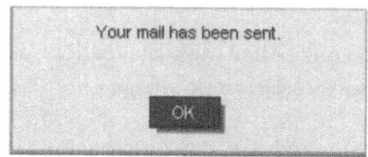

Figure 2-18. AOL's "Your mail has been sent." confirmation window

53 Forwarding e-mail messages

AOL allows you to forward a copy of a message to anyone you wish. So whenever you want to forward an e-mail message, just follow these steps:

1. Open the e-mail message you want to forward, and you'll see the screen shown in Figure 2-19.

2. Click the **Forward** button located on the right side of the **Read** window. AOL opens a new **Write Mail** window, shown in Figure 2-19, complete with the **Subject** line containing the letters **Fwd** for Forward.

3. Enter the address or addresses you wish in the **Send To** and **Copy To** fields, and any message you think is appropriate for forwarding the e-mail.

4. Click the **Send Now** button and your e-mail is forwarded.

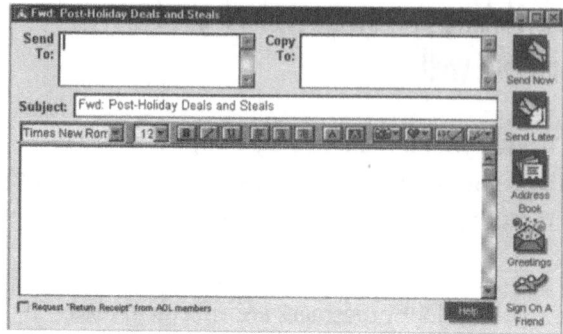

Figure 2-19. Forwarding a copy of an e-mail message to someone else

54 Replying to sender

Anytime you receive an e-mail message, you have the option of replying back with an e-mail of your own. This is typically referred to as **Reply** to sender—and is accomplished by following these steps:

1. Open the e-mail message you want to reply to.

2. Click the **Reply** button located on the right side of the **Read** window. AOL opens a new **Write Mail** window, shown in Figure 2-20, complete with the sender's address in the **Send To** field and a subject in the **Subject** field with the letters Re for Reply.

3. Write any message you'd like to send with your reply, and, if you'd like, enter an address in the **Copy To** field.

4. When finished, click the **Send Now** button.

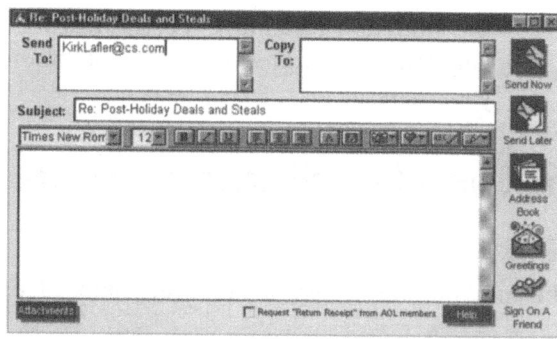

Figure 2-20. Replying to sender with an e-mail of your own

55 Replying to everyone

To have all the recipients in the **Send To** and **Copy To** fields see your reply to an e-mail message, follow these steps:

1. Open the e-mail message you want to reply to.

2. Click the **Reply All** button located on the right side of the **Read** window.

3. Enter any additional e-mail addresses in the **Send To** and **Copy To** fields.

4. Click the **Send Now** button.

56 Quoting from the original message

Sometimes it is useful to quote part of the original message (or the complete message depending on your need) as a reference in your reply. You can quote text by following these steps:

1. Open the e-mail message you want to quote.

2. Highlight the portions of text in the original message that you want to appear in your message.

3. Click the **Reply** button located on the right side of the Read window. A new **Write Mail** window appears with the recipient's e-mail address, subject line, and the portion of text you selected completed. The portion of selected text is bordered with a blue vertical line as well as who wrote it, the date, and time it was sent, as shown in Figure 2-21.

4. Enter any additional text you want included in your e-mail message.

5. Click the **Send Now** button.

57 Requesting a return receipt on sent e-mails

Have you ever sent an important e-mail message and wondered why the recipient doesn't respond, or better yet if your e-mail was even received? If you've found yourself in this position, then you're not alone. AOL provides a handy feature that, when activated, can automatically notify you when another AOL member opens your e-mail. This is how you can request a return receipt on all your important AOL e-mails:

1. Click the **Write Mail** button on the AOL toolbar.

2. Address and compose your e-mail message as usual.

3. Click the **Request "Return Receipt" from AOL members** check box as shown in Figure 2-22

4. Click the **Send Now** button.

🖉 *This feature only works for AOL e-mail addresses.*

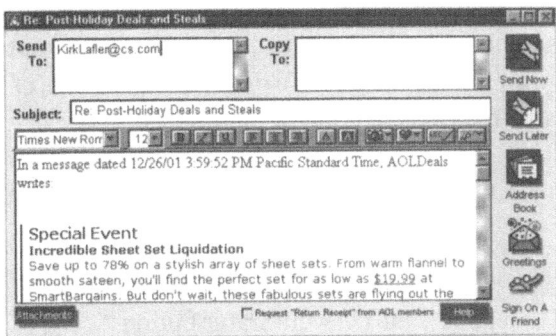

Figure 2-21. Inserting quotes from the original e-mail message is as easy as 1-2-3

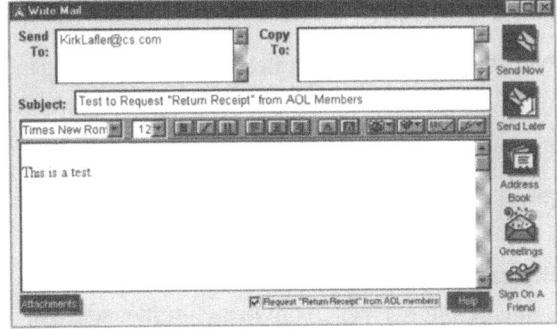

Figure 2-22: Requesting a return receipt on e-mail sent to AOL e-mail addresses

58 Reading date and time stamps

Every e-mail message you send has an automatic date and time stamp applied to it. This information, and much more can be found in the mail header, shown in Figure 2-23, located at the top of every message.

Figure 2-23. Reading date and time stamps in the e-mail header

59 Checking status of sent e-mail

Have you ever wondered if your e-mail message has been opened? AOL can help—at least if you sent the message to an AOL screen name, and not to an Internet address. To determine the status of an e-mail message, follow these steps:

1. On the **Mail** menu on the AOL toolbar, point to **Read Mail** and click **Sent Mail**.

2. Select the e-mail message you want to know about, and click the **Status** button.

Table 2-1 shows the Status Conditions **in the When Read** column:

Table 2-1. E-mail Status Conditions

STATUS CONDITION	DESCRIPTION
Not yet read	Indicates that message has not been opened yet.
Contains date/time	Indicates that message has been opened and cannot be retrieved.
You cannot check status of Internet Mail	Indicates that message was sent to an Internet address, and not to an AOL screen name, and cannot be retrieved.

60 Checking when an e-mail message was read

To see when an e-mail message was read by another AOL screen name, follow these steps:

1. On the **Mail** menu on the AOL toolbar, point to **Read Mail** and click **Sent Mail**.

2. Select the e-mail message you want to know about, and click the **Status** button.

3. The date and time, or other action, will be displayed in the **Status** window.

61 Unsending an e-mail message

Have you ever wished you didn't send an e-mail message? Well you may be in luck—at least if the following conditions are met. If you sent the e-mail message to only America Online screen names, and none of the recipients has yet opened the message, you may be able to "unsend" or retrieve your message. But you must act quickly before your e-mail is opened—once opened you will be unable to retrieve your e-mail.

To retrieve an e-mail message, follow these steps:

1. On the **Mail** menu on the AOL toolbar, point to **Read Mail** and click **Sent Mail**.

2. Select the e-mail message you want to know about, and click the **Unsend** button.

Using Courtesy and Blind Courtesy Copies

62 Sending a courtesy copy

The **Copy To** field allows you to send a courtesy or carbon copy of an e-mail message to one or more designated addresses. You can send courtesy copies to AOL members or to Internet addresses (non-AOL members) around the world.

63 Composing and storing e-mail messages offline

It may be a surprise, but AOL provides a way to compose and store your e-mail messages offline. This is a feature that many users are not aware of. Not only does this free up the telephone lines for greater periods of time while you compose your messages, but it gives you greater freedom in choosing when and where you write your e-mail messages. To take advantage of this features follow these steps:

1. Click the **Write Mail** button on the AOL toolbar.

   🖎 *This can be done even without signing on to AOL.*

2. Address and compose your e-mail message text as usual.

3. When you're done composing your message, click the **Send Later** button.

4. The **Send Later** dialog box will appear informing you that your mail has been placed in the **Mail Waiting to be Sent** folder of your **Personal Filing Cabinet**, as you see in Figure 2-24.

5. Click the **OK** button.

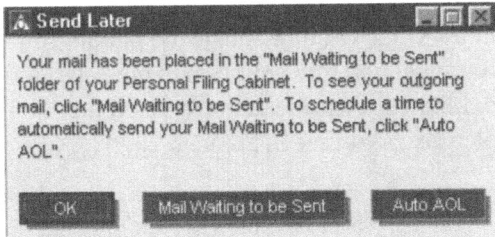

Figure 2-24. Placing mail in the Mail Waiting to be Sent folder

64 Sending e-mail using blind carbon copies (BCC)

Suppose you wanted to send e-mail to someone without everyone knowing you did so (except, of course, you and the person you copied on the e-mail). This process is known as sending e-mail using blind courtesy copies. This protects the privacy of the address or addressee you specify in a blind copy. It also speeds up the process of opening an e-mail message—since fewer addresses are displayed.

To specify a blind courtesy copy for an e-mail address, simply surround each e-mail address in parentheses, for example, (KPLConsultant). To specify a blind courtesy copy for a group of e-mail addresses, separate each address with a comma and then add parentheses around the entire set of addresses, like this: (KPLConsultant, MacFamily). You can also use the Address Book window to send blind copies too—just click the Blind Copy button.

65 Replying to everyone except BCC addresses

To reply to everyone except BCC addresses, just follow these steps:

1. Open the e-mail message you want to reply to.

2. Click the **Reply** button.

3. Enter your message as usual in the **Write Mail** window.

Jazzing Up Your Messages

66 Jazzing up your messages

Sometimes it may be useful to spice up your e-mail messages with special formatting features. You can add color, insert an online greeting, attach a photo, and much more. To take advantage of this feature, follow these steps.

1. Click the **Write** icon on the AOL toolbar.

2. In the **Write Mail** window, click the **Greetings** icon.

3. **Click** the icon associated with the available choices, for example, Greetings, Banners, Mail Art, Photos, Smileys, or Sounds.

67 Justifying your message text

You can change the default alignment of your message text with a click of your mouse. To begin formatting your text, follow these steps:

1. Highlight the portion of text you want to justify.

2. Click the **Align Left** button to left align text, the **Align Center** button to center text, or the **Align Right** button to right align text. These buttons are located above the **Message** field in the **Write Mail** window.

68 Changing text formatting

You can make selected pieces of text appear different from the rest of the e-mail message. To change text formatting, follow these steps:

1. Highlight the text you want a formatting change applied to.

2. Click the formatting features you want to use from the text styling toolbar. The available choices include **Bold**, **Italics**, and **Underline**, **Text Color**, and **Background Color**.

69 Adding some color

You can make selected pieces of text appear different from the rest of the e-mail message. To change your text color, follow these steps:

1. Highlight the text you want a color change applied to.

2. Click the text color you want to use from the text styling toolbar. The available choices include all the colors of the rainbow.

70 Changing your message's background color

You can add background color to liven up your e-mail messages. . To change the background color, follow these steps:

1. Highlight the text you want a background color change applied to.

2. Click the text color you want to use from the text styling toolbar. The available choices include all the colors of the rainbow.

71 Changing the font

If you'd like to change the default Arial typeface in your message, you can choose from the fonts available on your computer. To change your text and font size, follow these steps:

1. Highlight the text you want a font change applied to.

2. Select a font style from the drop-down list.

3. Select a number for the font size, and remember, the smaller the number, the smaller the font.

72 Inserting a picture into a message

Have you ever wanted to insert a picture into your e-mail message text, create a greeting card, or send pictures of family and friends? It's easy to do with AOL. Here's how:

1. Click the **Write** icon on the AOL toolbar.

2. Click the **camera** icon on the **Write Mail** menu style toolbar.

3. Select **Insert a Picture** from the drop-down box.

4. In the **Open** window, locate the picture you want inserted into your e-mail message, and double-click the file name to insert the picture, as you see in Figure 2-25.

✎ *Use the Preview window to verify the picture you want.*

5. If the picture is too small or too large for the page, AOL may ask if you want to resize the picture. It's best to experiment with different sizes to see what is best.

6. Position your cursor before or after the picture and begin typing your message.

7. When you've finished entering your address, subject, and message, just click the **Send Now** button.

🖋 *Only AOL members will be able to view your inserted pictures—not non-AOL members.*

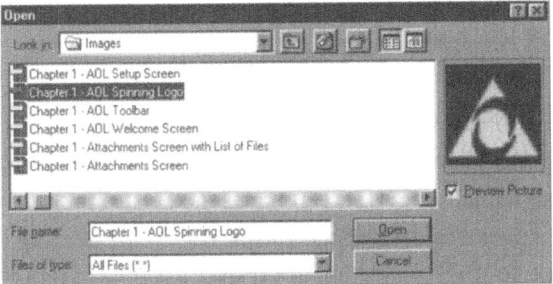

Figure 2-25. Inserting a picture into your e-mail message using the Open dialog window

73 Inserting a graphic background into a message

Inserting a graphic into a message is similar to inserting a picture into a message. The only difference is that you'll be able to type your message on the graphic background. This is how it's done.

1. Click the **Write** icon on the AOL toolbar.

2. Click the camera icon on the **Write Mail** menu style toolbar.

3. Select **Background Picture** from the drop-down box.

4. In the **Open** window, locate the graphic background you want inserted into your e-mail message, and double-click the file name to insert the graphic. Use the **Preview** window to verify the picture you want.

5. Begin typing your message anywhere you'd like—your text will appear on top of the graphic background.

6. When you've finished entering your address, subject, and message, just click the **Send Now** button.

🖋 *Only AOL members will be able to view your inserted graphic backgrounds—not non-AOL members.*

74 Choosing the right type of graphics for your e-mails

AOL allows the following types of pictures and images (identified by the file name's three-character extension) to be inserted into a message: .art, .bmp (bitmap), .gif (Graphics Interchange Format), and .jpg (Joint Photographic Experts Group). To keep the size of your e-mail messages to a minimum, and to reduce the time to send and open messages, inserted pictures and graphic backgrounds should be relatively low-resolution—the higher the resolution or image quality usually results in larger file sizes.

🖋 *To avoid unnecessarily large e-mail transmissions, try to limit the number of graphic insertions or attachments in a message. Also, .gif and .jpg file formats provide good image quality and are usually smaller than .bmp and .tif files.*

Addressing the Address Book

75 Setting up your address book

Your address book contains your very own personal collection of names and e-mail addresses. Not only that, it can be accessed while you're online, offline, or even using a friend's computer. So how do you get started using your own address book? Here's how to do it if you're signed on to AOL.

1. Click the **Write** icon on the AOL toolbar.

2. Click the **Address Book** button located on the right side of the **Write Mail** window.

Here's how to do it if you're not signed on to AOL.

1. Right-click the **AOL** logo on the Windows taskbar located on the bottom right of your screen.

2. Select **Address Book** from the pop-up menu that appears.

76 Adding contact names and addresses

You can add contact names and addresses to your address book any time you feel it's necessary. Here's how:

1. In the **Address Book** window, click the **New Contact** button located at the bottom of the window.

2. Enter the contact's name, e-mail address, and other details in the **Contact Details** window, as you see in Figure 2-26.

3. You can also enter additional information about the contact in the **Home**, **Work**, **Phone**, and **Details** tabs.

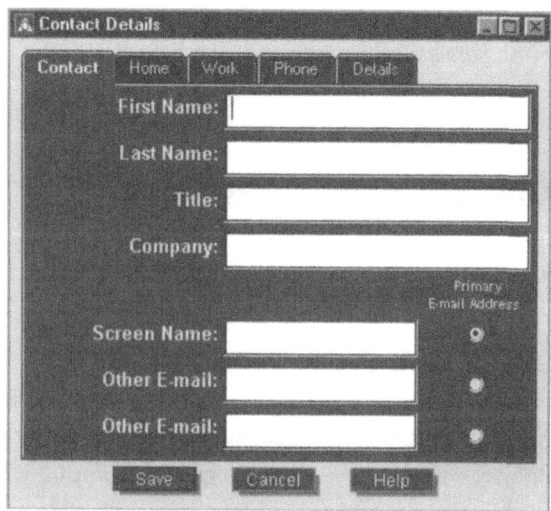

Figure 2-26. Adding a contact name and address information

77 Editing address book contact names

Occasionally you'll need to update one or more address book contacts. You'll find AOL's easy-to-use-screens provide all the help you need to make any adjustments to your address book's information. Here's how:

1. In the **Address Book** window, click the **Edit** button located at the bottom of the window.

2. Update the contact's name, e-mail address, and other details in the **Contact Details** window.

3. Click the **Save** button at the bottom of the **Contact Details** window.

78 Understanding capitalization

Capitalization isn't important when entering e-mail addresses to other AOL members. Neither is spacing. An AOL screen name of 'KPL Consultant' is the same as 'kplconsultant'. But when sending out e-mail to Internet addresses, use care in typing them exactly as they appear. Internet addresses are often case-sensitive.

79 Accessing your address book when sending e-mail

You can easily access your address book to fill in the **Send To** and **Copy To** fields when sending an e-mail message.

1. In the **Write Mail** window, click the **Address Book** button.

2. Select an address from your **Address Book** and click either the **Send To**, **Copy To**, or **Blind Copy** buttons on the left side of the **Address Book** window.

3. The address or addresses will be added as recipients of your e-mail message.

80 Adding an e-mail address to the Address Book from a received e-mail

It's easy to add new addresses to your Address Book from e-mail messages you receive. Just follow these instructions:

1. Open the e-mail message containing the e-mail address you want to add.

2. Highlight the e-mail address you want to add.

✎ *If an address isn't highlighted, the address of the person sending you the e-mail is automatically added.*

3. Click the **Add Address** button located at the bottom-right of your opened window. You can also highlight and add multiple addresses to your Address Book at once.

81 Selecting multiple addresses for copying into your e-mail

You can copy two or more addresses from your address book into your e-mail by clicking the first address you want to select, then holding down the **Ctrl** key, and clicking the remaining addresses you want. If you select one or more addresses you don't want, simply press the **Ctrl** key and click the address again. This action results in the address being deselected. When you're finished selecting the addresses you want, release the **Ctrl** key, and click the **Send To**, **Copy To**, or **Blind Copy** button.

82 Printing your entire address book

If you've ever wanted to print your entire address book as a hard-copy document, you're in luck. With your address book open, click the Print button located at the bottom of your Address Book window. In the Print dialog box that appears, select **Print all contacts**, and click the **OK** button. Your entire address book will be printed.

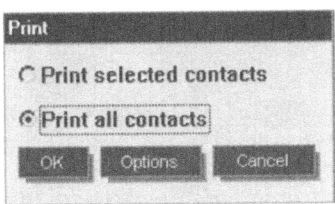

Figure 2-27. Printing the entire address book as a hard-copy document

83 Printing individual entries from your address book

Rather than printing all contacts from your address book, you may want to print only selected contacts. You can do this by selecting one or more addresses and clicking the **Print** button. In the **Print** dialog box that appears select **Print selected contacts** and click the **OK** button. Only your selected contacts will be printed.

84 Finding e-mail addresses in the People Directory or Internet White Pages

Finding an e-mail address of a friend or an acquaintance is possible using the AOL People Directory or Internet White Pages. The People Directory is a searchable database of AOL members who have created a Directory Listing.

To search the **People Directory**, follow these steps:

1. From the AOL toolbar, click the **People** menu and select **People Directory**.

2. You can choose between two search methods: **Quick Search**, shown in Figure 2-28, and **Advanced Search**, shown in Figure 2-29, by clicking the appropriate tab on the **People Directory** window. Enter the search criteria and click the **Search** button.

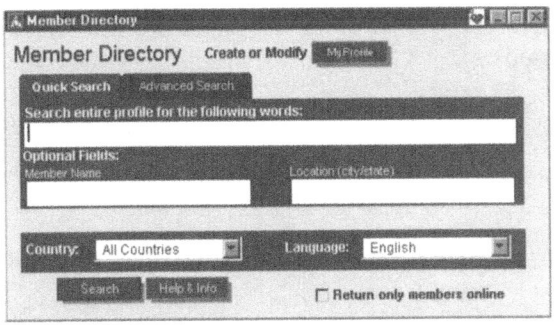

Figure 2-28. Using People Directory Quick Search to find e-mail addresses

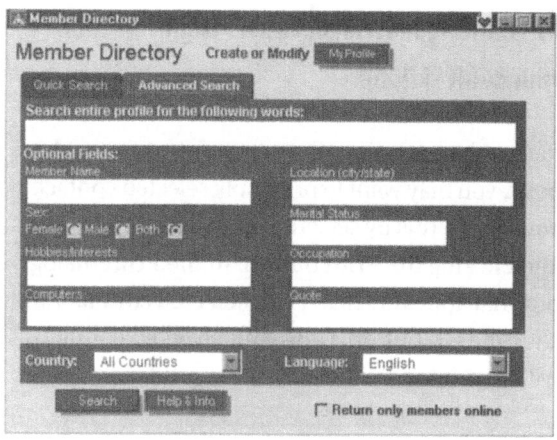

Figure 2-29. Using People Directory Advanced Search to find e-mail addresses

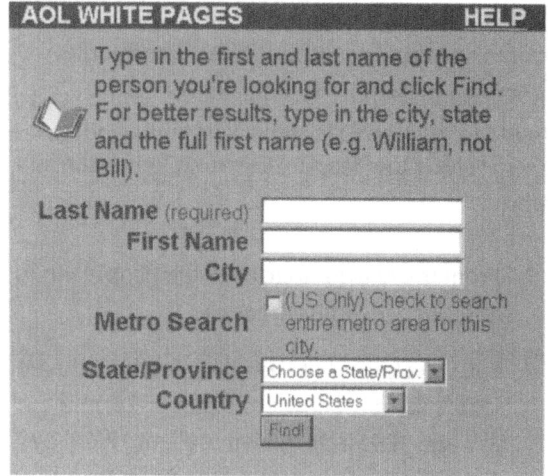

Figure 2-30. Using AOL's White Pages to find e-mail addresses.

To search the **AOL White Pages**, follow these steps:

1. From the AOL toolbar, click the **People** menu and select **White Pages**. The **AOL White Pages** window appears, shown in Figure 2-30.

2. Enter your search criteria and click the **Find** button.

85 Creating group mailing lists

If you find yourself frequently sending e-mail to the same contacts, AOL provides a handy way of treating these contacts as a group in your address book. A group mailing list enables you to handle mass mailing activities to two or more contacts by clicking a single group rather than individually selecting each contact one by one. Everyone in the group is automatically copied into the e-mail with a single click. Here's how to create a group mailing list:

1. Open your address book.

2. In the **Address Book**, click the **New Group** button to create a new group.

3. You'll see the **Manage Group** window, shown in Figure 2-31. Enter a name for the group you're creating.

4. Select the contacts listed on the left side and click the **Add** button to add them to the group.

5. Enter any additional contacts' e-mail address that are not in your address book in the **Additional Contacts in Group** field.

6. Indicate whether you want to be able to share this group at Groups@aol.

7. Click the **Save** button to create your new group.

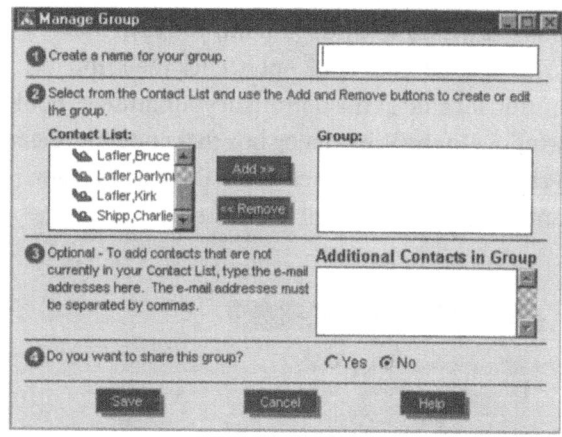

Figure 2-31. Creating a group mailing list with the Manage Group window

86 Adding group mailing list contacts

You can add mailing list contacts to an existing group by selecting the group and clicking the **Edit** button in your **Address Book** window. You can then enter one or more contacts to the group and clicking the **Save** button to save the new contacts.

87 Editing group mailing list contacts

Sometimes you may find yourself needing to edit an existing e-mail address in a group mailing list. When this is the case, you can follow these steps.

1. Open you address book.

2. Select the group you want to edit, and click the **Edit** button.

3. In the **Manage Group** window, select the contact you want added from the left side of item #2 and click the **Add** button to add the contact. Repeat this step for each contact you want added to your group.

4. Enter any additional contact's e-mail address that you'd like in your selected group in item #3 above using commas to separate multiple addresses.

5. When done, click the **Save** button to make your changes permanent.

88 Removing group mailing list contacts

Occasionally you may need to remove one or more contacts in a group mailing list. AOL makes this process a snap.

1. Open your address book.

2. Select the group you want to remove contacts from, and click the **Edit** button.

3. In the **Manage Group** window, select the contact you want removed from the right side of item #2 and click the **Remove** button. Repeat this step for each contact you want removed from your group.

4. When done, click the **Save** button to make your changes permanent.

89 Auto-completing e-mail addresses using your own address book

You can have AOL automatically complete an e-mail address as you are typing by using your personal address book. This feature is automatically enabled when you install AOL. It works by performing a lookup operation as you type an address. If the address you are typing matches one stored in your address book, it automatically displays in the **Send To** or **Copy To** box in the **Write Mail** window.

If you decide to disable this feature, follow these steps:

1. Click the **Mail Center** button on the main AOL toolbar and select **Mail Preferences**.

2. Remove the check mark from **Use my address book to auto-complete e-mail addresses**.

3. Click the **OK** button.

Benefiting from the Spell Checker

90 Spell checking your messages before they are sent

One beauty of e-mail is you can send messages a breakneck pace, but sometimes that means you may overlook grammar and spelling errors. To avoid the obvious but overlooked spelling error, such as words containing switched characters (for example, "the" as "hte"), make sure the **AOL Spell Checker** is enabled. AOL automatically spell checks each message for spelling and grammatical errors before it is sent. To verify or enable the Spell Check feature, follow these steps:

1. Click the **Mail Center** button on the main AOL toolbar and select **Mail Preferences**, shown in Figure 2-32.

2. Click the **Perform a spell check before sending mail** option.

3. Click the **Save** button.

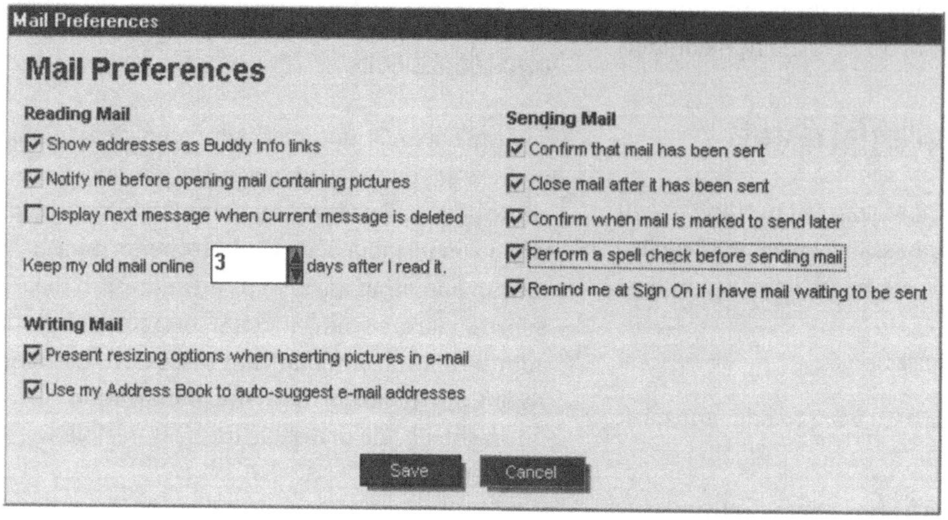

Mail Preferences

Reading Mail

☑ Show addresses as Buddy Info links

☑ Notify me before opening mail containing pictures

☐ Display next message when current message is deleted

Keep my old mail online `3` ▲▼ days after I read it.

Writing Mail

☑ Present resizing options when inserting pictures in e-mail

☑ Use my Address Book to auto-suggest e-mail addresses

Sending Mail

☑ Confirm that mail has been sent

☑ Close mail after it has been sent

☑ Confirm when mail is marked to send later

☑ Perform a spell check before sending mail

☑ Remind me at Sign On if I have mail waiting to be sent

[Save] [Cancel]

Figure 2-32. Enabling AOL's Spell Check feature

91 Replacing a misspelled word

When the spell check process identifies a misspelled word, the spell checking window appears with an explanation of the spelling error and a suggestion to fix the problem. You can click the misspelled word and correct the spelling error or select one of the words in the suggestion list. Once the word has been corrected, click the Replace button.

92 Ensuring good grammar

Because e-mail has a sense of urgency to it, e-mail writers often craft very short, telegraphic messages and leave out important pieces of information in the process. This is not to say that e-mail messages shouldn't be brief, but one-line e-mail messages are often missing important elements, such as a noun or verb, or are not written grammatically. If your message is crafted carelessly, your reader may be left with so many questions about its meaning and context that your message may be overlooked. So take the time to construct your e-mail message. Make sure that you capitalize proper nouns and the first word in every sentence and you use proper punctuation, such as periods at the end of sentences.

93 Knowing what AOL's Spell Checker covers

You can rest a little easier knowing that the **AOL Spell Checker** is designed to catch many of those pesky spelling and punctuations errors, which can make your message difficult to understand or just plain sloppy. So don't forget to turn the **Spell Checker** on so it, rather than you, can do the checking. The **Spell Checker** looks for the following types of errors:

- Words that appear twice in a row
- General punctuation errors and incorrect capitalization
- "A" versus "an"
- Compounding errors such as dead-line instead of deadline
- Hyphenation errors
- Misused words

94 Spell checking a single word

Checking the spelling of a single word in your message is easy. Just highlight the word using your mouse and click the **Spell Check** button in the **Write Mail** window. When you're finished, simply cancel the Spell Check.

95 Customizing advanced Spell Check features

You can apply advanced spelling preferences by following these steps:

1. From the AOL toolbar, click the **Settings** button and select **Preferences.**

2. In the **Preferences** window, select **Spelling** under the **Communications** section.

3. In the **Spelling Preferences** window, click the **Advanced** button to add additional spell-check features.

4. In the **Advanced Spelling Preferences** window, shown in Figure 2-33, you can turn on or off individual spelling rule types by selecting the rule and clicking the **On** or **Off** buttons.

5. When done what rule types you want, click the **OK** button.

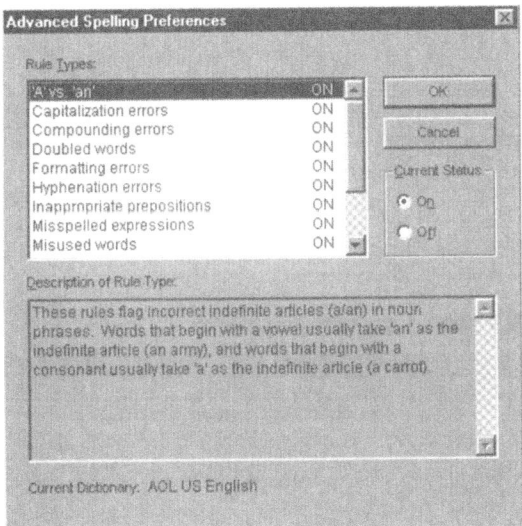

Figure 2-33. Customizing spelling rules in the Advanced Spelling Preferences window

96 Disabling the Spell Checker

To disable the **Spell Checker** follow these simple steps:

1. Click the **Mail Center** button on the main AOL toolbar and select **Mail Preferences**.

2. Deselect by clicking the **Perform a spell check before sending mail** option. In other words, there should not be a check mark in the box.

3. Click the **Save** button.

97 Adding words to your personal dictionary

AOL lets you customize your personal dictionary by adding words to it. Its purpose is to add special words that may be used in your profession or vocabulary to your personal dictionary. This feature makes the spell check feature even more powerful because it checks for standard words as well as special words in your e-mail messages. The steps for adding words to your personal dictionary are easy. Here's how:

1. From the AOL toolbar, click the **Settings** button and select **Preferences**.

2. In the **Preferences** window, select **Spelling** under the **Communications** section.

3. In the **Spelling Preferences** window, click the **Edit** button to add words to your personal dictionary, as you see in Figure 2-34.

4. In the **Personal Dictionary** window, enter one or more words you want added, as you see in Figure 2-35.

5. When done, click the **OK** button.

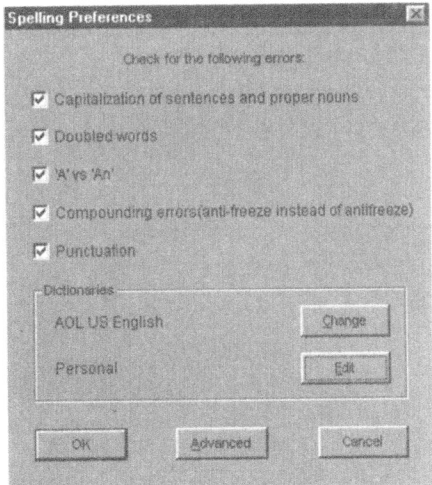

Figure 2-34. Accessing your Personal Dictionary from the Spelling Preferences window

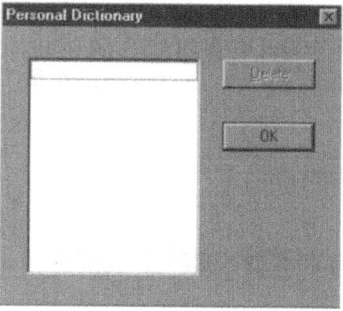

Figure 2-35. Adding words to your Personal Dictionary

Handling Hypertext Elements

98 Turning on Web addresses as hyperlinks

Your e-mail can contain much more than just text: It can include graphics, sounds, and hypertext links. This gives the reader a variety of options with a simple point-and-click of the mouse. All AOL versions after 2.0 provide users with a handy feature—being able to turn on a Web address as a hyperlink. Here's how:

1. Click the **Mail** menu button on the AOL toolbar, and select **Mail Preferences**.

2. In the **Mail Preferences** window, select **Show addresses as hyperlinks** under the **Reading Mail** category, as seen in Figure 2-26.

3. Click the **Save** button to store your preferences.

99 Embedding hypertext address in e-mail

You can share a favorite place with a friend by placing a Web address directly in your e-mail. Available for all versions after 2.0, this handy feature makes it easy for others to view your favorite site by pointing and clicking their mouse on the hypertext address. Here's all you'll need to know to embed a hypertext address and begin using this feature.

1. Click the **Write** icon on the AOL toolbar.

2. Click the **Favorites** icon on the AOL toolbar, and select **Favorite Places**, or click the **My Favorites** button on the AOL toolbar.

3. Drag the heart icon corresponding to your favorite place to the message box in your e-mail message.

4. **Send** your e-mail message as usual.

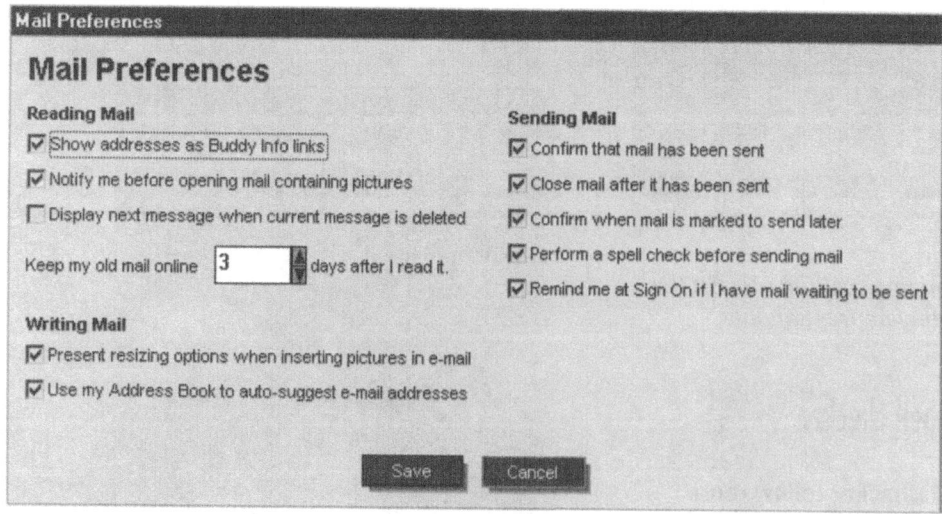

*Figure 2-36. Selecting **Show addresses as hyperlinks** on the Mail Preferences window*

100 Disabling hyperlink addresses

E-mail and Web site addresses are automatically enabled as hyperlinks during set up. To disable this automatic feature, follow these steps:

1. Click the **Mail** menu button on the AOL toolbar and select **Mail Preferences**.

2. Remove the check mark corresponding to the **Show addresses as hyperlinks** option.

3. Click the **Save** button.

101 Testing the mailto hyperlink

It's always a good idea to test the mailto hyperlinks that appear in your e-mail messages before you send your message. This permits you to verify that the hyperlink actually works as intended. Here's how it's done.

1. **Double-click** the mailto hyperlink in the **Write Mail** window.

2. In the **Edit Hyperlink** window, click the **Launch** button, as you see in Figure 2-37.

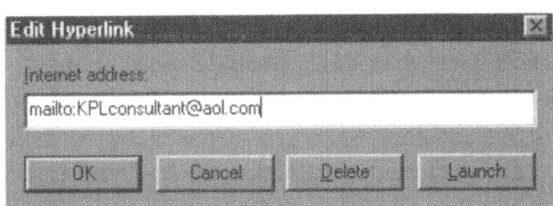

Figure 2-37. Testing the mailto hyperlink in the Edit Hyperlink dialog window

Expressing Yourself with Signatures, Acronyms, and Emoticons

102 Adding a signature to your message

Many AOL users spice up their e-mail messages by adding a signature. Virtually anything you want can be put in a signature, as long as it is character-based text. Some ideas: your full name, title, business, phone or fax numbers, Web site address, or a quotation or motto.

To create a mail signature, follow these steps:

1. Click the **Mail Center** button on the main AOL toolbar and select **Mail Signatures**.

2. Click the **Create** button.

3. In the **Create Signature** window, enter the unique signature name in the **Signature Name** box.

4. **Enter** the desired text to be used as your signature in the **Signature** box.

5. Click the **OK** button, as you see in Figure 2-38.

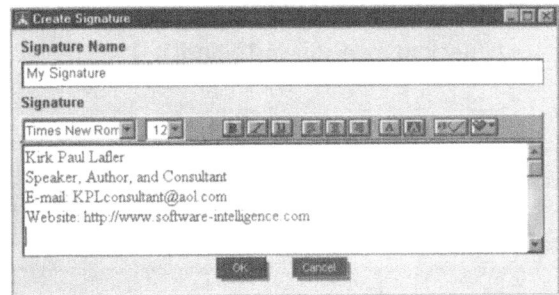

Figure 2-38. Adding a signature is as easy as 1-2-3.

103 Creating up to five different signatures

You can create up to five signatures to be used with your e-mail messages. Just follow these steps to set up your alternate signatures:

1. Click the **Mail Center** button on the main AOL toolbar and select **Mail Signatures**.

2. Click the **Create** button.

3. In the **Create Signature** window, enter the unique signature name in the **Signature Name** box.

4. **Enter** the desired text to be used as your signature in the **Signature** box.

5. Click the **OK** button.

6. Repeat steps 2 through 5 to add additional signatures.

104 Setting up a default signature

With the ability to set up a maximum of five signatures, you'll want to tell AOL which signature to use as your default. After two or more signatures have been created, you will need to designate which signature you want AOL to use as your default in your e-mail messages. Here's how:

1. Click the **Mail Center** button on the main AOL toolbar and select **Mail Signatures**.

2. In the **Set up Signatures** window, select the signature you'd like to use as your default.

3. Click the Default On/Off button, as in Figure 2-39.

4. The default signature will appear with a check mark displayed before it.

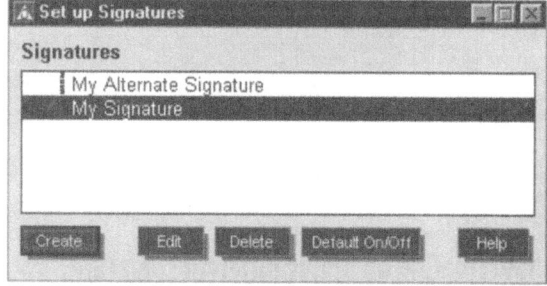

Figure 2-39. Selecting a default signature in the Set up Signatures window

105 Changing your signature

When the information in your signature requires modification, AOL provides a simple way to change or edit an existing signature. Here's how:

1. Click the **Mail Center** button on the main AOL toolbar and select **Mail Signatures**.

2. In the **Set up Signatures** window, select the signature you'd like to change.

3. Click the **Edit** button.

4. Make any necessary changes, and click the **OK** button.

5. **Close** the **Set up Signatures** window by clicking the **X** button in the top right corner.

106 Deleting unwanted signatures

When a signature is no longer wanted or needed, you can remove it by following these steps:

1. Click the **Mail Center** button on the main AOL toolbar and select **Mail Signatures**.

2. In the **Set up Signatures** window, select the signature you'd like to delete.

3. Click the **Delete** button.

4. Close the **Set up Signatures** window by clicking the **X** button in the top right corner.

107 Using acronyms in your messages

Have you ever wished you could speed up the typing process? If you answered a resounding yes to this question—then you're in luck. By using one or more acronyms for commonly used phrases, not only will you speed up the typing process, you'll make your e-mail messages look cool.

Webster defines an acronym as "a word formed from the first (or first few) letters of a series of words." Table 2-2 deciphers all those pesky little words, or acronyms, that many Internet dwellers frequently use in e-mails and in online chat rooms. No longer will you have to remain clueless and wonder what special meaning a particular acronym holds—you'll be able to decipher the message's meaning with the best of them and respond with an acronym of your own. So TTFN.

*Table 2-2. E-mail Acronyms
and Their Meanings*

ACRONYM	MEANING
AAT	And Another Thing
ARTWIT	Are You Thinking What I'm Thinking?
BRB	Be Right Back
BTW	By The Way
BWB	Be Write Back
CMIO	Crying My Eyes Out
CUL	See You Later
CUL8R	See You Later
F2F	Face to Face
FWIW	For What It's Worth
FYA	For Your Amusement
FYI	For Your Information
GD&R	Grin, Duck & Run
GMTA	Great Minds Think Alike
HHOK	Ha Ha Only Kidding
IMHO	In My Humble Opinion
IMO	In My Opinion
IOW	In Other Words
IRC	Internet Relay Chat
L8R	Later
LOL	Laughing Out Loud
OBO	Or Best Offer
OBTW	Oh By The Way
OIC	Oh I See
OTF	On The Floor (laughing)
PC	Politically Correct
PMFBI	Pardon Me For Butting In
PMFJI	Pardon Me For Jumping In
ROFL	Rolling On Floor Laughing
ROTFL	Rolling On The Floor Laughing
RSN	Real Soon Now
RTFM	Read The Freakin' Manual

*Table 2-2. E-mail Acronyms
and Their Meanings (Continued)*

ACRONYM	MEANING
RTM	Read The Manual
SO	Significant Other
SWF	Single White Female
SWM	Single White Male
TANSTAAFL	There Ain't No Such Thing As A Free Lunch
TIA	Thanks In Advance
THNX	Thanks
TNX	Thanks
TTFN	Ta Ta For Now
WB	Welcome Back
WRT	With Respect (Regard) To
WTG	Way To Go
YMMV	Your Mileage May Vary
YW&D	Yakko, Wakko & Dot

108 Expressing yourself with emoticons (or smileys)

Emoticons (or smileys) are text-based smiley faces consisting of various combinations of symbols and letters to add expression to otherwise dull or boring e-mail messages. They are best viewed by looking at the message text and turning your head at a 90-degree angle. Emoticons are a lot of fun to create and insert into text, and can liven up a message or even enhance the meaning of a statement. Emoticons don't have to be just smiling faces either—they can show a range of emotions from happiness to sadness, and surprise to anger. For example, the following statement could be construed as just another outing with your family, or might even be considered an unpleasant chore to some:

> I'M GOING WITH MY FAMILY TO THE
> DEL MAR FAIR NEXT MONTH.

But when the same message contains an emoticon of happiness, the message takes on a happy tone, and the reader is left with little doubt that you are looking forward to this family outing:

I'm going with my family to the Del Mar Fair next month. :-)

Notice the difference an emoticon makes in a message.

109 Picking popular emoticons

Here are the top ten emoticons and their meanings:

:-)	Happy smiley
>:-(	Very angry smiley
B-)	Cool smiley with sunglasses
:-O	Yelling smiley
:-|	Indifferent smiley
;-)	Winking smiley
:-(	Frowning smiley
8-)	Near-sighted smiley
:-D	Laughing smiley
:->	Sarcastic smiley

110 Using (or overusing) emoticons

Many believe that emoticons serve as a universal language. Although this is true for some users, emoticons are hardly universal in their appeal. In fact, many in the Internet community disdain their use and believe that their overuse in e-mail messages shows a lack of maturity or giddiness by the e-mail sender. Whatever your viewpoint, as more Internet-savvy users surf the Web it appears that emoticons are here to stay. So why not just accept the fact that a smile (or smiley) never hurt anyone?

111 Getting to know emoticons

The primary thing to keep in mind when creating and/or using emoticons is that you should have fun with them. Table 2-3, although not comprehensive, illustrates a number of commonly used emoticons to be used as you please in your e-mail messages as well as in online chat rooms. So, have fun!

Table 2-3. Emoticons and Their Meaning

EMOTICON	MEANING	EMOTICON	MEANING
8-O	"Omigod!" smiley	:-*	Kisses smiley
|-{	"Good Grief!" (Charlie Brown) smiley	:-{}	Blowing a kiss smiley
\\-o	Bored smiley	[]	Hugs smiley
][	Feeling separate smiley	(( )):**	Hugs and kisses smiley
}{	Face-to-face smiley	((((name))))	Hug smiley
^5	High five smiley	[ ]	Asking for a hug smiley
^	Thumbs up smiley	}xx	Kisses smiley
_/	"My glass is empty" smiley	[]:*	Hugs and kisses smiley
:-( )	Can't stop talking smiley	@-->-->--	A rose smiley
:-S	Incoherent	:-[	Pouting smiley
:~/	Mixed up smiley	:-P~~	Blowing a raspberry smiley
%-)	Braindead smiley	=)	Variation on a classic smiley
(:|	Egghead smiley	>:-<	Absolutely livid! smiley
=:-)	Hosehead smiley	:-6	Exhausted smiley
:-]	Smiling blockhead smiley	:-[	Un-smiling blockhead smiley
(::()::)	Bandaid; offering help or support smiley		

Avoiding Junk Mail

112 Setting mail controls

Mail controls allow you to block incoming e-mail messages. As the Internet has grown, the problems associated with junk mail have grown as well. To help combat junk mail or spam, as it is sometimes called, AOL lets you set the following mail controls:

- accept e-mail from everyone

- accept e-mail from AOL members only

- accept e-mail only from specified AOL addresses

- accept e-mail from no-one

Here's how to set your mail control preferences:

1. Click the **Mail** menu button on the AOL toolbar, and select **Mail Controls**.

2. Select the screen name you want to set mail controls for in the **Set Mail Controls For** box in the **General Mail Controls** window.

    🖉 *The screen name you use to set mail controls must be a master screen name.*

3. Select the mail controls you want for this screen name.

4. Click the **Save** button.

113 Setting general mail controls for specific screen names

General mail controls allow you to receive all e-mail sent to your selected screen name, or block all e-mail sent to your selected screen name, or customize mail controls for the selected screen name. Here's how it's done:

1. Click the **Mail** menu button on the AOL toolbar, and select **Mail Controls**.

2. Select the screen name for which you want to set mail controls in the **Set Mail Controls For** box in the **General Mail Controls** window.

3. Select one of the three mail control settings by clicking the desired radio button, and click the **Next** button.

4. Review your mail control settings and, if correct, click the **Save** button.

114 Customizing mail controls

There may be times when you'll want to customize your mail controls by allowing or blocking certain e-mail addresses, domain names, pictures, and files. Here's how it's done.

1. Click the **Mail** menu button on the AOL toolbar, and select **Mail Controls**.

2. Select the screen name for which you want to set mail controls in the **Set Mail Controls For** box in the **General Mail Controls** window.

3. Select the **Customize Mail Controls for the Screen Name** radio button, as shown in Figure 2-40.

4. Click the **Next** button.

5. Select the mail controls settings from the five options, as shown in Figure 2-41, and click the **Next** button.

6. Click the **Save** button.

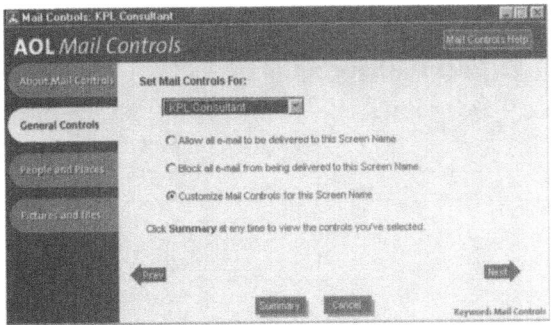

Figure 2-40. Accessing mail controls for a selected screen name

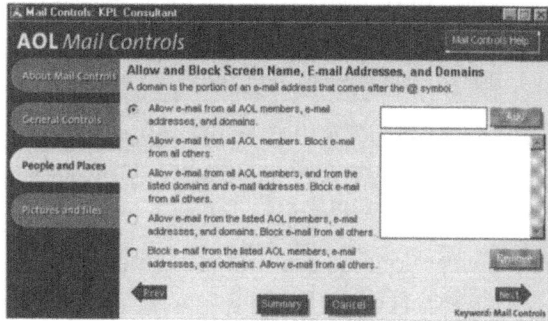

Figure 2-41. Selecting mail controls for a selected screen name

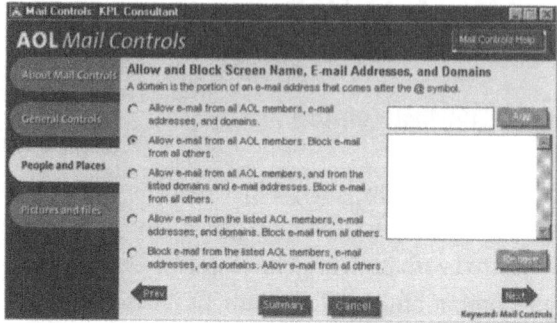

Figure 2-42. Allowing e-mail from AOL members only

115 Allowing e-mail from AOL members only

To allow e-mail from AOL members only while blocking e-mail from non-AOL members, follow these steps:

1. Click the **Mail** menu button on the AOL toolbar, and select **Mail Controls**.

2. Select the screen name for which you want to set mail controls in the **Set Mail Controls For** box in the **General Mail Controls** window.

3. Select the **Customize Mail Controls for the Screen Name** radio button.

4. Click the **Next** button.

5. Select the **Allow e-mail from all AOL members. Block e-mail from all others** radio box, as shown in Figure 2-42, and click the **Next** button.

6. Select the desired mail controls for **pictures and files**, and click the **Next** button.

7. Click the **Save** button.

116 Allowing e-mail from all AOL members and specified e-mail addresses and domains only

You can allow the receipt of e-mail messages from all AOL members and other specified e-mail addresses and domains, but block e-mail from all others. Here's how it's done.

1. Click the **Mail** menu button on the AOL toolbar, and select **Mail Controls**.

2. Select the screen name for which you want to set mail controls in the **Set Mail Controls For** box in the **General Mail Controls** window.

3. Select the **Customize Mail Controls for the Screen Name** radio button.

4. Click the **Next** button.

5. Select the **Allow e-mail from all AOL members, and from the listed domains and e-mail addresses. Block e-mail from all others** radio box, as shown in Figure 2-43, and click the **Next** button.

6. Select the desired mail controls for **pictures and files**, and click the **Next** button.

7. Click the **Save** button.

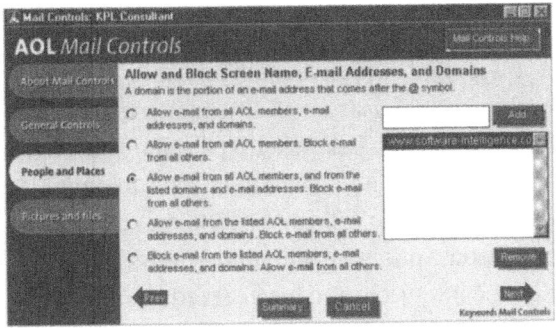

Figure 2-43. Specifying from whom you will receive e-mail

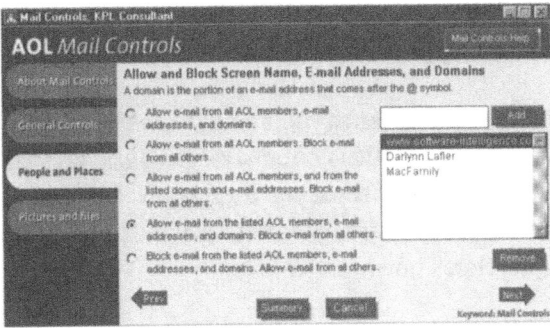

Figure 2-44. Specifying what e-mail addresses you want to receive e-mail from

117 Allowing e-mail from specified AOL members, e-mail addresses, and domains only

To prevent those unwanted messages from appearing in your mailbox, here's how you can allow e-mail only from specified AOL members, e-mail addresses, and domains, and block all others.

1. Click the **Mail** menu button on the AOL toolbar, and select **Mail Controls**.

2. Select the screen name for which you want to set mail controls in the **Set Mail Controls For** box in the **General Mail Controls** window.

3. Select the **Customize Mail Controls for the Screen Name** radio button.

4. Click the **Next** button.

5. Select the **Allow e-mail from the listed AOL members, e-mail addresses and domains. Block e-mail from all others** radio box, as shown in Figure 2-44, and click the **Next** button.

6. Select the desired mail controls for **pictures and files**, and click the **Next** button.

7. Click the **Save** button.

118 Blocking e-mail from specified AOL members, e-mail addresses, and domains, but allowing e-mail from all others

Sometimes it's easier (and a lot less typing) to block the AOL members, e-mail addresses, and domains from which you don't want e-mail, especially if you know the addresses of habitual offenders. In these situations, you simply list the AOL members, e-mail addresses, and domains you want to block. You will be free to accept e-mails from everyone else. Here's how it's done:

1. Click the **Mail** menu button on the AOL toolbar, and select **Mail Controls**.

2. Select the screen name for which you want to set mail controls in the **Set Mail Controls For** box in the **General Mail Controls** window.

3. Select the **Customize Mail Controls for the Screen Name** radio button.

4. Click the **Next** button.

5. Select the **Block e-mail from the listed AOL members, e-mail addresses and domains. Allow e-mail from all others** radio box, and click the **Next** button.

6. Select the desired mail controls for **pictures and files**, and click the **Next** button.

7. Click the **Save** button.

119 Blocking sent and received e-mail containing pictures and files

If security is an issue, you'll want to consider blocking e-mail that contains pictures and files, especially from people you don't know. This will reduce the risk associated with downloading a virus. Here's how:

1. Click the **Mail** menu button on the AOL toolbar, and select **Mail Controls**.

2. Select the screen name you want to set mail controls for in the **Set Mail Controls For** box in the **General Mail Controls** window.

3. Select the **Customize Mail Controls for the Screen Name** radio button.

4. Click the **Next** button.

5. Select the mail control settings you desire, and click the **Next** button.

6. Select **Block this screen name from sending and receiving mail with pictures and files**, as shown in Figure 2-45, and click the **Next** button.

7. Click the **Save** button.

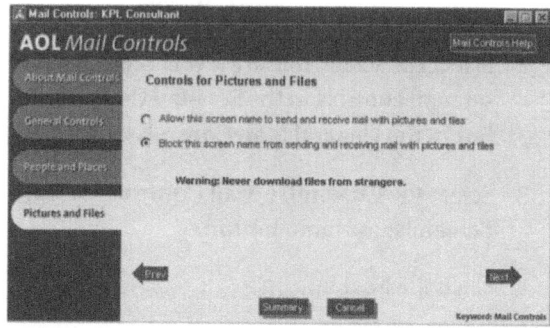

Figure 2-45. Blocking e-mail that contains pictures and files

120 Blocking all junk e-mail

If you're tired of receiving advertisements from businesses, offers from adult-oriented sites, chain letters, and countless other types of unwelcome and unsolicited junk mail, then you can put a stop to it. Never again will you be forced to take time away from your busy schedule deleting mail you have no interest in and never asked for. Take action against this growing menace. AOL makes it easy to eliminate spam while giving greater control over your e-mail situation. Here's how:

1. Click the **Settings** menu button on the AOL toolbar, and select **Parental Controls**.

2. Click **Set Parental Controls** from the AOL **Parental Controls** window.

3. In the **Edit controls for:** field, select the screen name you want to block junk mail for.

4. Click the **E-mail control** button from the **Parental Controls** window, shown in Figure 2-46.

5. Choose the settings you prefer from the **AOL Mail Controls** window, shown in Figure 2-47.

6. Click the **Next** button.

7. Click the **Save** button, shown in Figure 2-48.

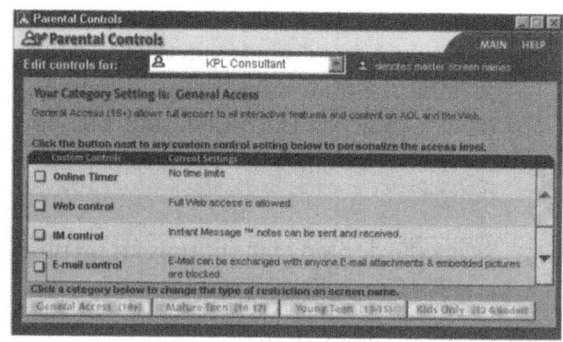

Figure 2-46. Selecting e-mail controls from the Parental Controls window

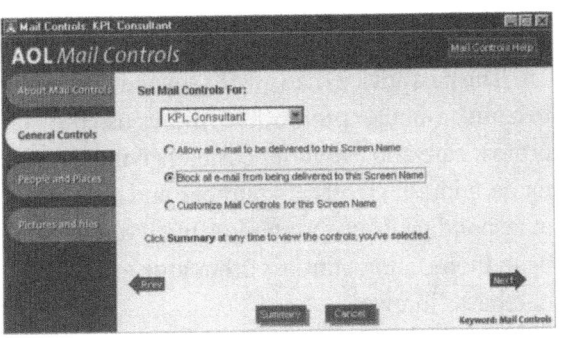

Figure 2-47. Selecting mail control settings on the Mail Controls window

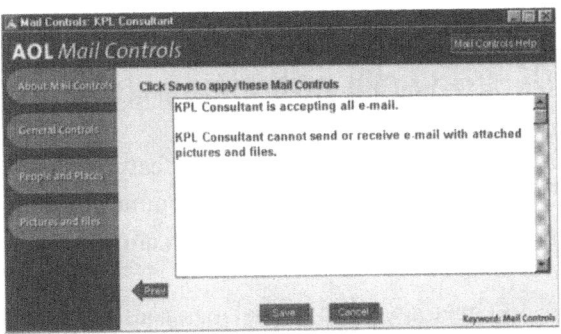

Figure 2-48. Saving mail control settings

121 Obtaining a mail controls summary

You can obtain a quick summary of your mail controls settings for any screen name. Here's how:

1. Click the **Mail** menu button on the AOL toolbar, and select **Mail Controls.**

2. In the **Edit controls for:** field on the AOL Mail Controls window, select the **screen name** you want to obtain summary information for.

3. Click the **Summary** button.

122 Identifying junk e-mail

Junk e-mail is a problem for every Internet user. It is always invasive, annoying, and all too often offensive in nature. AOL members should take extra precautions to be on the outlook for this troubling form of unsolicited mail. You may want to set

up who you can receive e-mail, pictures, and files from using mail controls for any and all of your screen names (discussed earlier in this section). In the absence of mail controls, you can resort to a less than scientific method of identifying junk e-mail. Although there is no perfect technique or methodology for identifying junk e-mail, here are a few ways that I've used over the years. So before you click, keep these tips in mind.

1. **Inspect who sent you the e-mail.** Is it someone you know? If not, then it probably can be classified as unsolicited, and taken a step further, treated as junk e-mail. It's common practice for junk mail senders to use invalid e-mail addresses in the "from" and "reply-to" fields so that if you try to contact them using these addresses the message usually gets sent back to you as being Undeliverable.

2. **Inspect the subject line carefully.** Frequently, junk e-mailers use alluring words such as "Free," "Hot," "Sex," or some other word in its subject line to entice you to open the e-mail and any attachments. Other times a catch phrase is used to attract your curiosity such as "Don't Miss This Opportunity," "Work from Home Part-time," "You've Been Approved," "Want To Be Your Own Boss," and "Make More Money." Another favorite trick is to infer some level of familiarity with you or someone you know such as "Great Meeting You Last Week," "Here Are the Slides You Requested," or "Your Wife Asked For …" The general rule of thumb is that if you don't recognize who the sender is and the subject line infers something too good to be true, it can probably be treated as junk e-mail.

3. **Be skeptical of official sounding addresses.** Junk e-mailers will go to any means to get you to open their message—including using addresses with official sounding names such as TechSupp7, Admin33, or Dept321.

4. **If in doubt, never open an attachment or picture**, and never click on a hyperlink in the e-mail.

123 Reporting junk e-mail violations

Naturally you can delete any and all junk e-mail you receive. But you can step up your campaign a notch and do something about the nuisance created by junk e-mailers. Here's how: You can forward any junk e-mail that violates AOL's Terms of Service to screen name TOSE mail1. If a junk e-mailer sent you an attached files, forward it to screen name TOSFILES. For other types of junk e-mail, whether offensive or not, forward it to screen name TOSSPAM. AOL will review and take the necessary appropriate action against the junk e-mailer.

124 Reducing the amount of junk e-mail you receive

Here are some simple ways to reduce the amount of junk e-mail you get on a day-to-day basis.

1. As mentioned earlier, setting up mail controls is an effective way to reduce junk e-mail. By setting the right controls, you can make yourself virtually junk e-mail free.

2. Create a new screen name blocking e-mail for that screen name. This prevents junk e-mail from being sent to you.

3. Don't create a member profile. Without a member profile, junk e-mailers won't be able to find your name in the **People Directory**.

4. Avoid places like chat rooms that can make you a potential target. Chatting in **People Connection** enables junk e-mailers to find your name all too easily.

125 Finding value in all that junk e-mail

Believe it or not, there may be value in some junk e-mail. But it doesn't come without a price. For example, I've received countless offers to receive free magazine subscriptions, newsletters, and the like—a few worth further investigation but on the whole they always came with a catch. Junk e-mailers always inform you that you can receive several free issues at no risk, and by filling out a simple online

form your subscription will be sent to your door free of charge. Free of charge. Who are they kidding?

The best advice I can give to anyone responding to a junk e-mailer promotion. Always use the utmost care and avoid (if possible) giving out your name, address, credit card number, and other vitals in responding to any promotion. But if you do, you'll be in theirs, and countless other junk e-mailers databases forever.

Sending E-mail Greetings, Postcards, and Banners

126 Accessing AOL greetings and mail extras

AOL gives you value-added e-mail features such as adding greetings, pictures, and sounds to your e-mail. Here's a list of some of the features.

1. **Greetings**—add special messages and electronic cards to your message with greetings from American Greetings Online Greetings store.

2. **Banners**—add decorative images to the top of your message. (Only other AOL members will be able to view your banners.)

3. **Mail Art**—enhance the mood and excitement of your message by inserting clever pictures into your message. (Only other AOL members will be able to view your mail art.)

4. **Photos**—spice up your message by adding one or more high-quality pictures. These pictures will be sure to be noticed. (Only other AOL members will be able to view your photos.)

5. **Smileys**—add a combination of text characters such as a smile, frown, concerned, or more to your message. (Only other AOL members will be able to view your smileys.)

6. **Sounds**—add sound in your message and your greeting will not just be read, but heard. (Only other AOL members will be able to hear sounds.)

127 Sending greetings and mail extras to other AOL members

Only other AOL members will experience the many value-added features found in **Greetings & Mail Extras**. So if you're sending a message containing one or more of these features, non-AOL members won't be able to enjoy the complete experience.

128 Picking e-mail greetings

The top picks for e-mail greetings usually change to reflect the time of the year, season, a current holiday, or some event. For example, during the early summer months you can expect to see Graduation, Bridal Shower, Wedding, Independence Day (4th of July), and all the usual Birthday, Love, and Sorry greetings. So each time you visit, you'll be presented with a recent list of top picks to choose from. Happy picking!

129 Getting to know e-mail greeting categories

E-mail greetings are categorized usually by subject to make the job of finding a particular greeting easier. Here is a sampling of the categories you can choose greetings from.

Baby	Inspirational & Religious
Birthday	Kids
Bridal Showers	Languages & Countries
Business	Love
Collections	Pets
Concern & Support	Seniors
Congratulations	Sports
Engagement	Thank You
Friendship	Top Picks
Holidays	Travel

130 Accessing and sending online greetings

AOL makes accessing and sending an online e-mail greeting as simple as point-and-click.

1. In the **Write Mail** window, click the **Greetings** button located on the right side of your window. The **Greetings & Mail Extras** window will appear, shown in Figure 2-49.

2. Click the **Greetings** button in the **Greetings & Mail Extras** window and make your greeting selection from the available choices.

3. Enter the receiver's e-mail address, a personal message, your e-mail address, and the date you want your greeting sent.

4. Preview your greeting.

5. When your greeting is just the way you want it, click the **Send** button.

Figure 2-49. Accessing and sending greetings in your e-mail messages is easy.

Attaching Files, Photos, and Other Things

131 Attaching multiple files

AOL lets you attach one or more files to your message. You'll be able to attach documents, pictures and images, and other files as easy as 1-2-3. Here's how:

1. In the **Write Mail** window click the **Attachments** button. The **Attachments** window will open, shown in Figure 2-50.

2. Click the **Attach** button and navigate to the directory of choice.

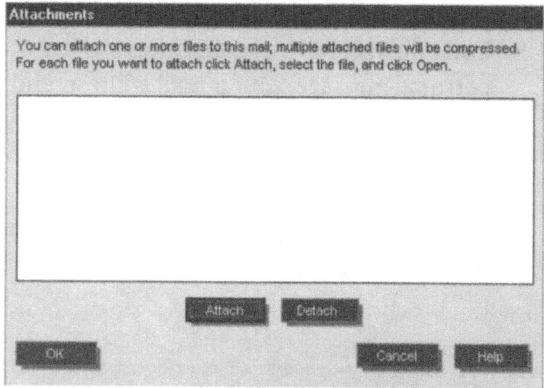

Figure 2-50. Attaching files to your e-mail message

You can select one or more files to any e-mail message you create. Simply double-click the desired file, one at a time, or press the **Ctrl** key as you select multiple files to attach. Files are automatically added to a list in the **Attachments** dialog box, shown in Figure 2-51. When you're done, click the **OK** button to confirm and close the **Attachments** dialog box. You'll be returned to the **Write Mail** window.

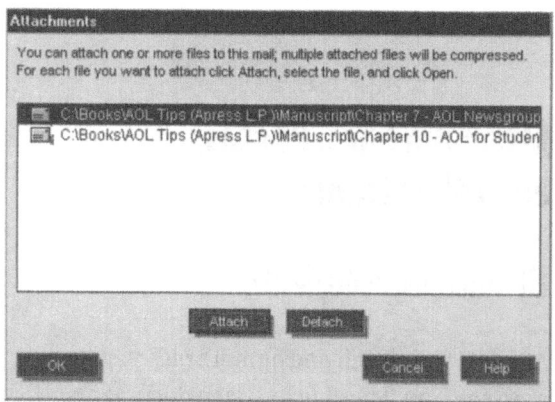

Figure 2-51. Displaying selected files in the Attachments window

132 Understanding the size limit of attached files

AOL attaches and zips, or compresses, any number of file attachments to e-mail; it does restrict the maximum size of all files to 16MB (megabytes). Files are automatically compressed to reduce the allotted storage requirements and to download faster. Windows compressed files usually end with an extension of .ZIP while Macintosh compressed files end with .SIT.

133 Adding mail art to your message

AOL lets you access mail art and include one or more images to your message. You can easily add mail art to any message. Here's how:

1. In the **Greetings & Mail Extras** window, click the **Mail Art** button.

2. Select the mail art you like and click the **Preview** button, or double-click the desired mail art displayed in the list.

3. Click the **Add To Your Mail** button in the **Mail Art Preview** window, shown in Figure 2-52.

🖊 *Only AOL members can see mail art.*

Figure 2-52. Adding mail art to an e-mail message

134 Adding photos to your message

Want to send a special someone a beautiful picture of roses? You can do it by adding a photo of roses to your message. Not only is a picture worth a thousand words, your recipient will treasure your message and the added personal touch enhanced by the picture.

1. In the **Greetings & Mail Extras** window, click the **Photos** button.

2. Select the photo you like and click the **Preview** button, or double-click the desired photo displayed in the list.

3. Click the **Add To Your Mail** button in the **Photo Preview** window, shown in Figure 2-53.

   Only other AOL members will be able to view the picture in your message.

Figure 2-53. Adding photos to your e-mail message in the Photo Preview window

If your message recipient is not an AOL member, you can still send a picture. Instead of using **Greetings & Mail Extras** though, you'll need to send the picture as an attached file.

1. In the **Mail Write** window, click the **Attachments** button at the bottom of the window.

2. Click the **Attach** button in the **Attachments** window, and select the desired photo from your personal library of photos (stored on your computer system).

3. Click the **Open** button in the **Attach** window, shown in Figure 2-54.

4. Send your message as usual.

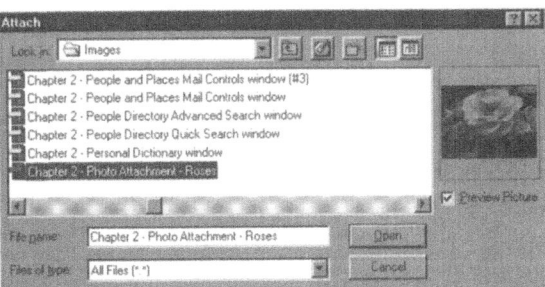

Figure 2-54. Attaching photos to your e-mail message

135 Using AOL's Picture Finder to locate and view pictures and images

Picture Finder makes looking for and viewing your personal library of pictures or images a simple task. You can use **Picture Finder** by following these steps.

1. On the **File** menu, click **Open Picture Finder** from the drop-down list

2. Locate your personal library of pictures or images on your computer system, shown in Figure 2-55.

3. Click the **Open Gallery** button to open the **Picture Gallery** window (contains six images per page), shown in Figure 2-56.

4. Click the right arrow to view the next set of six pictures or images.

5. Select the picture or image you want to use.

6. Click the **Insert in E-mail** button.

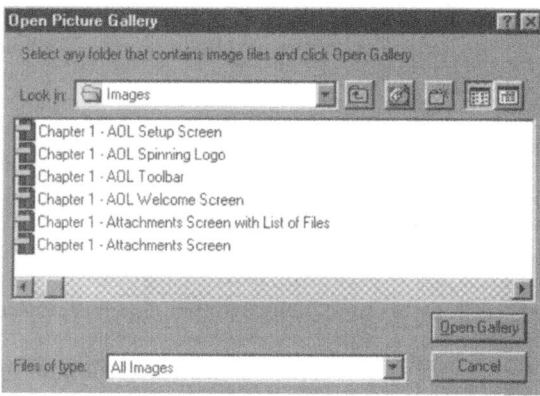

Figure 2-55. Locating a personal library of pictures on your computer

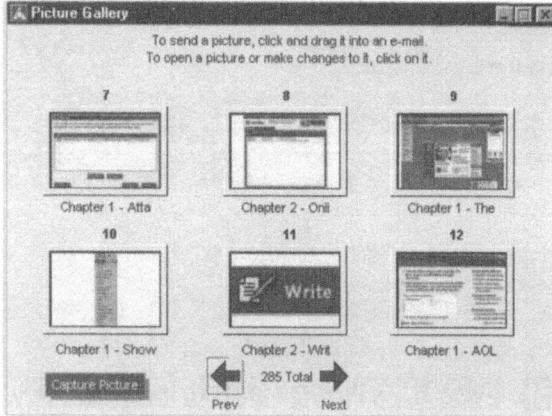

Figure 2-56. Opening your pictures in AOL's Picture Gallery

136 Adding sound effects to your message

Want to send some special sound effects along with your message? If you do, you'll find AOL easy to work with.

1. In the **Greetings & Mail Extras** window, click the **Sounds** button.

2. Select the sound you like to use to complement your message and click the **Preview** button, or double-click the desired sound displayed in the list.

3. For added pleasure and a unique experience, combine sound with pictures.

4. Click the **Add To Your Mail** button.

Only other AOL members will be able to hear the sound in your message.

If your message recipient is not an AOL member, you can still send a sound effect with your message. Instead of using **Greetings & Mail Extras** though, you'll need to send it as an attached file.

1. In the **Mail Write** window, click the **Attachments** button at the bottom of the window.

2. Click the **Attach** button in the **Attachments** window, and select the desired sound effect from your personal library (stored on your computer system).

3. Click the **Open** button in the **Attach** window.

4. Send your message as usual.

137 Understanding AOL supported image types

AOL supports a number of popular image types, usually identified by a filename's extension, and are listed along with their descriptions in Table 2-4.

Table 2-4. Image Types

FILE TYPE	DESCRIPTION
.ART	Represents a compressed graphics file that can be viewed with AOL software.
.AVI	Represents an audio visual file that can be viewed with AOL's Windows software.
.BMP	Represents a graphics bitmap file that can be opened with AOL software.
.EPS	Represents an Encapsulated Postscript File consisting of images designed for drawing programs. These files can't be opened with AOL software.
.GIF	Represents a Graphics Interchange Format type of image that is commonly used everywhere. These files can be displayed with AOL software.
.JPG	Represents a Joint Photographer Expert Group type of image that takes up less space than a .GIF file while maintaining a high-level of quality. These files can be displayed with AOL software.

Table 2-4. Image Types (Continued)

FILE TYPE	DESCRIPTION
.MID	Represents a Musical Instrument Digital Interface type of file containing songs for most sound cards and MIDI boards. These types of files can be played with AOL software.
.MME	Represents a Multipurpose Internet Mail Extension type of file that is used to convert a binary attachment file to text so it can be handled by e-mail. These types of files are handled properly with AOL software.
.MOD	Represents a Musical Module type of file that contains the instruments and score for music. These types of files are heard with a sound card (not MIDI) and a special type of sound program in Windows and on the Macintosh.
.PCX	Represents clip art files and is usually associated with an older types of graphics format. These types of files are opened with AOL software.
.PCT	Represents the original Macintosh graphics format that can be viewed with AOL's Macintosh software.
.SCR	Represents a windows screen saver file. These types of files can't be viewed with AOL software.
.SND	Represents a Macintosh System 7 sound file that can be played with AOL's Macintosh software or converted and played with Windows software.
.TIF	Represents a Tagged Image Format that is popular with desktop publishers. These types of files can't be read with AOL software.
.WAV	Represents a Windows sound file that can be played with AOL's Windows software or converted and played with Macintosh software.

138 Handling MIME files in AOL

MIME (or Multipurpose Internet Mail Extension) establishes guidelines to ensure that attachments (e.g., documents, graphic images, sounds, etc.) sent in e-mails can be opened and read by the recipient. In order for attachments to be handled correctly, both the sender and receiver must use software (e.g., AOL) that is MIME-compliant. AOL, being MIME-compliant, automatically codes any file attachments as long as you click the Attach button on your e-mail form and decodes any attachments. This makes the handling of attachments painless and easy.

139 Encoding and decoding attached files

Swapping files with family, friends, and other e-mail correspondents is a simple process because file encoding and decoding is automatically done for you. AOL and most e-mail software are MIME-compliant making the job of handling attachments a breeze. All you have to do is attach files you want to send with your e-mail and open attached files you've received from others. AOL will do the rest.

140 Using a MIME decoder to read a MIME file

On the rare occasion when an attached file is not automatically decoded by your AOL software, you may need to manually initiate the process. To begin, unless you've already done so, you'll need to download a MIME decoder program from one of the following sources.

Be sure to download the decoder program for the computer system you are running (e.g., PC or Macintosh) and read the instructions for the specific decoder program before use.

For PC users:

WINZIP: V8.0 WinZip for Win95/98/ME/2000/NT
Decodes MIME (.MME) as well as compressed ZIP (.zip) files.

MIMDECODE: V6.0 SR-1 E-mail Decode for Win95/98/2000/NT
Decodes MIME (.MME) with drag and drop.

WINZIP: V6.3 SR-1 for Win31
Decodes MIME (.MME) as well as compressed ZIP (.zip) files.

MIME: V4.3 Decode Shell Extension for Win95/98/NT

Adds a "decode" option to your mouse right-click context menu.

WINCODE: V2.7.3c Encoder/Coder for Win31./3.11

For Macintosh users:

STUFFIT: V5.5 Aladdin Expander for all Macs—OS7.1.1 or later

Uses drag and drop to decode your MIME as well as .SIT, .ZIP, and many other formats.

DECODER: V2.1 Decoder PPC for Power Macs

Uses drag and drop to decode your MIME.

DECODER: V2.1 Decoder 68K for 68K Macs

Uses drag and drop to decode your MIME.

141 Downloading compressed files

More often than not, files that have been uploaded are automatically grouped together and compressed in order to save time during download. You'll be able to tell when your download is in compressed format because the file name will end in .ZIP for PC files and .SIT for Macintosh files.

142 Uncompressing compressed download files

AOL is able to automatically uncompress your downloaded files when specific download preferences are set. Here's how to verify what your preferences are set at and how to customize the settings.

1. Click the **Settings** menu on the AOL toolbar, and select **Preferences** from the drop-down menu items.

2. In the **Preferences** window, click **Download** under the Organization section.

3. In the **Download Preferences** window, shown in Figure 2-57, the available options for decompressing ZIP files are displayed:

    • When I download them

    • When I sign off

    • Do not decompress

4. Select the option which best meets your needs for decompressing downloaded files and click the **Save** button.

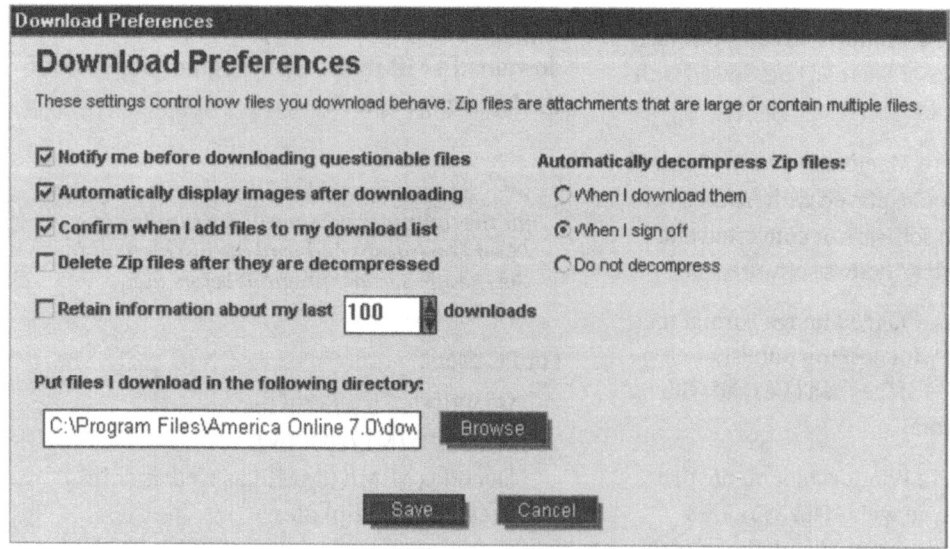

Figure 2-57. Specifying how files are decompressing ZIP files

143 Finding compression/decompression shareware programs

AOL will automatically compress and decompress your file attachments for you—unless you turned this feature off. As an alternative, you can use special software just for the purpose of compressing and decompressing. Many of these shareware programs are available (for a small fee), and can be found by performing a file search using the keyword: **Filesearch**. Then, click **Shareware**, and search on the word "zip."

Managing Your Filing Cabinet

AMERICA ONLINE HELPS YOU store files you've already downloaded and plan to download, organize incoming and outgoing e-mail, manage files and folders, and use search features to locate e-mail quickly. In this chapter, you'll learn how to store all your e-mail on your hard drive, set Filing Cabinet preferences, reclaim unused space in your Filing Cabinet, and manage Filing Cabinet folders, downloaded files, e-mail, unread message board and newsgroup postings.

In this chapter, you'll learn how to:

📖 Use AOL's Mail Center

📖 Organize your Filing Cabinet

📖 Add and rename folders in your Filing Cabinet

📖 Assign and use a password for your Filing Cabinet

📖 Back up information in your Filing Cabinet

📖 Delete items in your Filing Cabinet

📖 Recover unused space in your Filing Cabinet

e-mail. As the brain center or hub for your mail, you'll be able to open and view your e-mail mailbox; create and send e-mails; access powerful mail features such as set mail preferences; access your address book; block junk mail; and much more. Follow these simple steps to access AOL's Mail Center.

From the AOL toolbar:

1. Select **Mail Center** from the **Mail** button located on the AOL toolbar.

2. The Mail Center appears with its various options, shown in Figure 3-1.

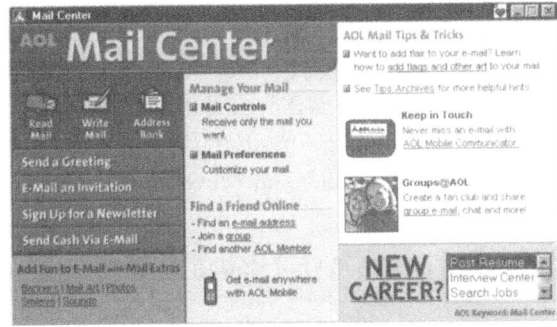

Figure 3-1. AOL's Mail Center lets you manage your mail and send a greeting

Understanding AOL's Mail Center and Your Online Mailbox

1 AOL's Mail Center—using your control and command center

AOL's Mail Center provides a central place to access, create, and manage everything related to

From the Keyword:

1. Click the **Keyword** button.

2. Type **Mail Center** in the **Keyword** dialog box and click the **Go** button.

3. The **Mail Center** appears with its various options.

2 Understanding your Online Mailbox's mail retention features

The first time you access your Online Mailbox you'll find that there's not much there. But as you send and receive e-mails it will begin filling up. Your Online Mailbox will automatically save any incoming and outgoing e-mail, as well as e-mail that you've read. This is a handy feature because it allows you to access each piece of e-mail on AOL's servers until you've decided what to do with it. It's important to note that each piece is handled differently depending on whether your mail is unopened, has been opened and read, or has been sent as outgoing mail. Becoming familiar with these distinctions is important because mail is not automatically retained forever in your Online Mailbox.

Due to the sheer volume of mail America Online handles every day, your Online Mailbox is equipped to store individual pieces of e-mail in your Online Mailbox for only a predetermined number of days. The number of days varies depending on what you did with each piece of e-mail. For each screen name AOL automatically holds in your Online Mailbox up to 1,000 pieces of New Mail for about 27 days, 550 pieces of Old Mail for about 3 days, and 550 pieces of Sent Mail for up to 27 days. This means that mail that has been left unattended beyond the maximum retention periods mentioned above will be unrecoverable and lost.

3 Reading what's in your Online Mailbox

Your Online Mailbox can be accessed anytime you're signed on by clicking the Read button on the AOL toolbar. When your Online Mailbox opens, you'll be able to view New Mail, Old Mail, and Sent Mail by clicking the desired tab. Initially e-mail is listed in chronological order from oldest to newest using the e-mail's date stamp.

To read any e-mail, select the item you want and click the **Read** button or simply double-click the item you want to open.

4 Sorting the contents of your Online Mailbox

As the number of items in your Online Mailbox grows in size, you may find it useful to sort everything in it to allow for better organization. AOL allows you to sort the messages in your Online Mailbox by the type of message (regular mail, mail with attached files, and mail with embedded pictures), the date and time of arrival, the e-mail address of the person who sent the e-mail, or the e-mail subject heading.

1. Sign on to AOL.

2. Click the **Read** icon on the AOL toolbar.

3. Click the **New Mail** tab heading in the **Online Mailbox** window, shown in Figure 3-2.

4. The directional arrow indicates whether the **Online Mailbox** contents are arranged in ascending or descending order.

5. Select a sort option from the following parameter buttons on the **Sort folder by...** menu.

   a. **Mail Type**—arrange e-mail in the following order:

      1. AOL Official mail

      2. Mail containing attached file and embedded image

      3. Mail containing attached file only

      4. Mail containing embedded image only

      5. Mail containing no attached file or embedded image

   b. **Oldest**—arrange e-mail chronologically by oldest to newest using the date stamp.

   c. **Newest**—arrange e-mail chronologically by newest to oldest using the date stamp.

   d. **E-mail Address**—arrange e-mail alphabetically by sender's e-mail address for **Incoming** mail, by recipient's e-mail address for **Outgoing** mail, and by screen name for newsgroup postings.

   e. **Subject**—arrange e-mail alphabetically based on the text in the subject field.

6. **Old Mail** and **Sent Mail** can also be sorted by selecting the corresponding tab.

Figure 3-2. Sorting the contents of your online mailbox is as easy as clicking a tab button.

Managing Your Filing Cabinet

5 Accessing your Filing Cabinet for the first time

As you access your Filing Cabinet for the first time, you'll find that it contains a variety of files and folders in three different categories: Mail, Newsgroups, and Downloads. The Mail category contains Incoming/Saved Mail, Mail Waiting To Be Sent, and Mail You've Sent folders. The Newsgroups category contains Incoming/Saved Postings, Postings Waiting To Be Sent, and Postings You've Sent. The Downloads category contains Files To Download and Files You've Downloaded folders. Following these steps accesses your Filing Cabinet:

1. Select **Filing Cabinet** from the **File** menu located on the AOL toolbar to open your **Filing Cabinet**, shown in Figure 3-3.

2. Select the desired category by clicking the tab located at the top of the window.

3. Double-click the folder name to open it and see what's inside it.

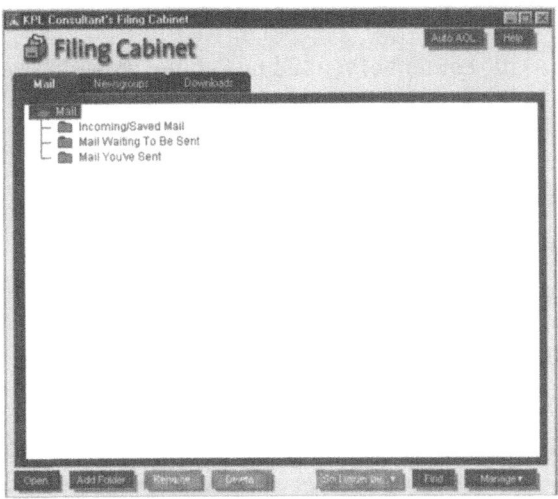

Figure 3-3. Your Filing Cabinet contains three folders the first time you access it.

6 Understanding screen names and individual Filing Cabinets

America Online allows up to seven screen names to be assigned per account. Not only does this give you the ability to create multiple online identities and e-mail addresses, it creates a separate and unique Filing Cabinet for each screen name. Each screen name has its own Filing Cabinet, stored in a single file in the America Online\ORGANIZE folder. To access the folders and information in your Filing Cabinet, you must access it using America Online's software. You can't access your Filing Cabinet by signing on as a Guest from another member's computer.

To access other Filing Cabinet screen names for your account, you'll need to select another screen name by clicking the **Select Screen Name** list from the Sign On screen or click **Switch Screen Name** from the **Sign Off** menu above the AOL toolbar. Once you've successfully connected to the screen name, the **Filing Cabinet** for that screen name will be available.

7 Adding folders to your Filing Cabinet

As the content of your Filing Cabinet grows in size, you may want to consider organizing the e-mail you've saved by creating one or more folders. This can be done at any time. Here's how:

1. Click **Filing Cabinet** from the **Mail** menu located on the AOL toolbar.

2. Select the **Incoming/Saved Mail** folder by clicking it once.

3. Click the **Add Folder** button at the bottom of the Filing Cabinet window to open the **Create Folder** dialog box.

4. Type a name for the folder in the **Create Folder** dialog box and click the **OK** button. The new folder should appear within the **Incoming/Saved Mail** folder.

8 Saving e-mail automatically to your Filing Cabinet

After you've created one or more folders in your Filing Cabinet, you'll be ready to save your e-mail and correspondence to your hard drive. One way of doing this is to let AOL automatically save your e-mail and other correspondence to your hard drive, Zip drive or whatever other storage device you have. By doing this, you'll be able to track, organize, search, and manage all your e-mail much more easily. Here's how it's done:

1. Click **Preferences** from the **Settings** menu located on the AOL toolbar.

2. Click the **Filing Cabinet** link in the **Organization** section of the **Preferences** window to open the **Filing Cabinet Preferences** window, shown in Figure 3-4.

3. Select the **Retain all mail I read in my Personal Filing Cabinet** and **Retain all mail I send in my Personal Filing Cabinet** check boxes.

4. Click the **Save** button to save these settings for the primary and secondary screen names.

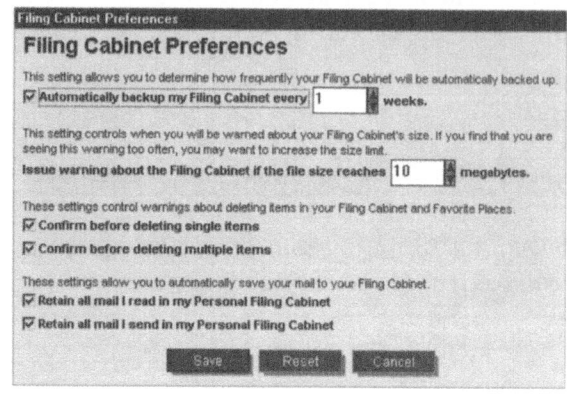

Figure 3-4. Setting preferences to automatically save your mail to your Filing Cabinet

9 Saving e-mail manually to your Filing Cabinet

Saving e-mail to your Filing Cabinet can also be done manually as opposed to automatically (refer to Tip #8 for further details). By manually saving your e-mail, you have greater control over what gets saved and what doesn't. It also prevents e-mail correspondence of little or no importance from being saved and filling up space in your Filing Cabinet.. Here's how it's done:

1. Click the **Read** icon on the AOL toolbar.

2. Click the tab you want to access mail from in your **Online Mailbox**. Your choices are **New Mail, Old Mail**, or **Sent Mail**.

3. Select the piece of e-mail you want to save to your **Filing Cabinet** by clicking it one time.

4. Click the **Save to Filing Cabinet** button located at the bottom of your **Online Mailbox** window.

5. Select the location where you want to save your e-mail from the drop-down menu list, shown in Figure 3-5. The available options are: **Mail, Incoming/Saved Mail, Mail You've Sent**, and **Create Folder**.

6. E-mail will automatically be saved to the location you choose from this menu list.

Figure 3-5. Available options in the Save to Filing Cabinet drop-down option list

10 Renaming a folder in your Filing Cabinet

Renaming a folder in your Filing Cabinet is easy with AOL. Whether you misspelled a folder name or simply want to assign a different name, you can change any folder's name by following these steps.

1. Click **Filing Cabinet** from the **Mail** menu located on the AOL toolbar.

2. Select the folder you want to rename by clicking it once.

3. Click the **Rename** button at the bottom of the **Filing Cabinet** window to rename the selected folder. The folder name will become highlighted allowing you to make changes to the folder name.

4. Make any changes to the folder name as desired and press the **Enter** key.

11 Assigning a password to your Filing Cabinet

You can prevent others from accessing your Filing Cabinet by assigning a password to it. Here's how to be sure unauthorized users won't be able to get into your Filing Cabinet:

1. You'll first have to sign on to the screen name to which you'd like a password assigned.

2. Select **Preferences** from the **Settings** menu on the AOL toolbar.

3. Click **Passwords** under the **Accounts Control** section of the **Preferences** window.

4. Enter the password for your screen name in the **Password** box.

5. Select the **Filing Cabinet** check box, shown in Figure 3-6.

6. Click the **OK** button when done.

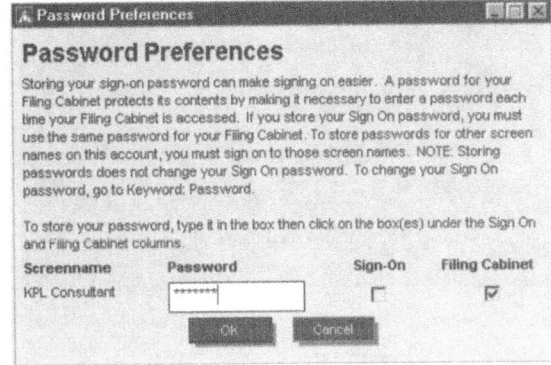

Figure 3-6. Assigning a password to your Filing Cabinet

12 Accessing a Filing Cabinet when a password has been assigned

A password-protected Filing Cabinet guards its contents by requiring the entry of the password before access is granted. If you decide to assign a password to your Filing Cabinet, it is recommended that you carefully select one that is not too obvious, and never write it down or store it so others can find it.

This isn't to say that a password-controlled Filing Cabinet can't be compromised, but if properly done, it just makes it a little harder for an intruder to gain access. Sometimes this is enough to prevent a potential threat or violation from occurring. Accessing a password-protected Filing Cabinet is easy as long as you know the password. Here's how:

1. Click **Filing Cabinet** from the **Mail** menu located on the AOL toolbar.

2. If the **Filing Cabinet** is password protected, the **Please enter your password** dialog box appears, shown in Figure 3-7. You'll need to enter the assigned password in the box.

3. Click the **Continue** button to open the **Filing Cabinet.**

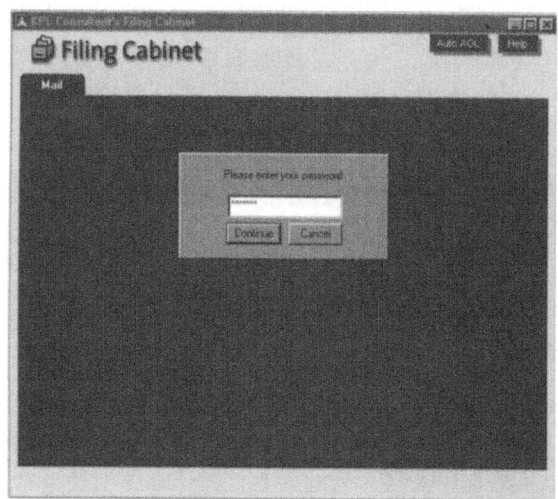

Figure 3-7. *Your Filing Cabinet's password-protected dialog box*

13 Sorting the contents of your Filing Cabinet

As the number of items in your Filing Cabinet folder grows, you may need to organize it by sorting its contents. This can help put some order back into your Filing Cabinet allowing you to find items a bit more easily. Here's how it's done:

1. Select **Filing Cabinet** from the **Mail** menu on the AOL toolbar.

2. If it's not already active, click the **Mail tab** on the **Filing Cabinet** window.

3. Select the folder that you'd like to sort. For example, the **Incoming/Saved Mail** folder could be selected.

4. Click the **Sort folder by...** button and select one of the following sort options from the drop-down list:

   a. **Oldest**—sort items chronologically (oldest to newest) using the arrival date stamp.

   b. **Newest**—sort items in reverse chronological order (newest to oldest) using the arrival date stamp.

   c. **Subject**—items are grouped and sorted alphabetically by what's in the contents of the subject field.

   d. **Mail Type**—sort mail into groups using the following mail types:

      1. AOL Official Mail

      2. Mail containing attached file and embedded image

      3. Mail containing attached file only

      4. Mail containing embedded image only

      5. Mail containing no attached file or embedded image

   5. **E-mail Address**—items are grouped and sorted alphabetically by the sender's e-mail address.

14 Deleting single pieces of e-mail from your Filing Cabinet

There are several ways to delete unwanted or outdated e-mail from your Filing Cabinet. The most common way to delete a single piece of e-mail from your Filing Cabinet is to follow these steps.

1. Select the e-mail you want deleted from your **Filing Cabinet**.

2. Click the **Delete** button located at the bottom of the **Filing Cabinet** window. A confirmation window will appear asking you if you're sure you want to delete the item.

3. Click the **Yes** button to complete the deletion.

15 Deleting multiple pieces of e-mail from your Filing Cabinet

Occasionally you'll have more than a single piece of e-mail to delete. You could take the route of deleting each item separately as explained in Tip #14, but this would be time-consuming and tedious. A more effective way would be to select all the items you want deleted in your Filing Cabinet, and then with a single click of your mouse delete all the items that have been selected. Here's how it's done:

1. Press the **CTRL** key on your keyboard and select each piece of e-mail you want deleted from your **Filing Cabinet**. Using this approach, you're basically building a list of e-mails to be deleted.

2. If multiple pieces of e-mail that are grouped together need to be deleted, you can select all items within the group by holding the **SHIFT** key on your keyboard down on the first item and, while the **SHIFT** key is still being held down, select the last item to select all items in between. This keyboard trick affects how multiple contiguous items are selected and is often referred to as a group selection.

3. If an item is accidentally selected for deletion, simply press the **CTRL** key and select the item to undo the selection. This will not affect any other items that have been selected.

4. Click the **Delete** button located at the bottom of the **Filing Cabinet** window. A confirmation window will appear asking you if you're sure you want to delete the item.

5. Click the **Yes** button to complete the deletion.

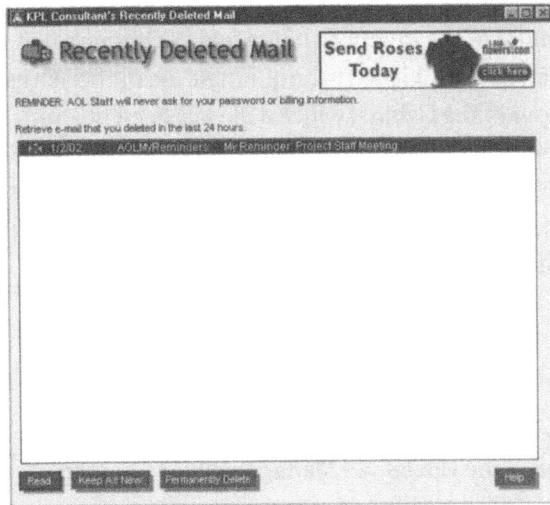

Figure 3-8. A deleted piece of mail is selected for retrieval in the Recently Deleted Mail window

16 Undeleting deleted pieces of e-mail

If you accidentally delete a piece of e-mail from your Online Mailbox, you may be able to "undelete" or retrieve the piece of mail by following a few simple steps. The important thing to remember is that you'll only have 24 hours to perform this operation. After that, the e-mail will be unrecoverable and lost forever. Here's how it's done.

1. Select **Recently Deleted Mail** from the **Mail** menu on the AOL toolbar.

2. From the list of recently deleted mail, select the piece of e-mail you'd like to retrieve by clicking the e-mail in the **Recently Deleted Mail** window, shown in Figure 3-8.

3. Click the **Keep as New** button located on the bottom of the **Recently Deleted Mail** window. The e-mail will automatically be retrieved and placed in the **New Mail** tab in your **Online Mailbox**.

17 Rearranging the contents of your Filing Cabinet

Is it time to perform a little housecleaning in your Filing Cabinet? Rearranging the contents of your Filing Cabinet is easy in America Online. It follows the same drag and drop conventions used in Windows Explorer®. With your Filing Cabinet window opened, just drag a folder or file and drop it onto another folder. The folder or file is moved to the new location, not copied. Here are the step-by-step instructions:

1. Select **Filing Cabinet** from the **Mail** menu on the AOL toolbar.

2. In your **Filing Cabinet**, highlight the folder or file you want to rearrange.

3. Drag a folder or file you want to move to a new location and drop it.

18 Locating files downloaded by the Download Manager

The Download Manager lets you locate files that were downloaded to your computer's hard drive. As you would expect, this operation is performed after at least one file has been downloaded. Downloaded files are automatically saved in the Download folder in the America Online folder, although files can be downloaded to an alternate location such as your Filing Cabinet. Once a file has been downloaded, the Download Manager lets you view the description for any downloaded item. Here are the steps you can follow to locate files downloaded by the Download Manager:

1. Select **Download Manager** from the **File** menu located above the AOL toolbar.

2. Click the **Show Files Downloaded** button in the **Download Manager** window, shown in Figure 3-9.

3. Select the file you want located in the **Files You've Downloaded** window.

4. Click the **Locate** button.

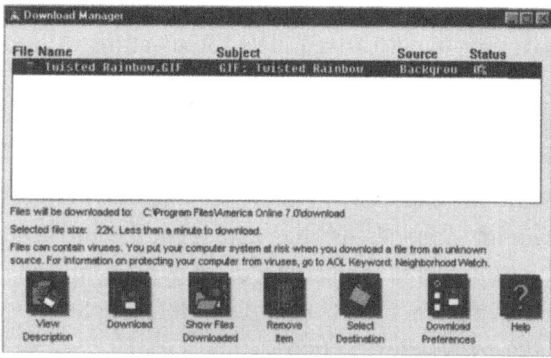

Figure 3-9. The Files You've Downloaded window

19 Downloading stored files to your Filing Cabinet at the end of your AOL session

The download process is the act of transferring a file containing information from someone else's computer to your own computer. The files that are transferred are referred to as downloaded files. You can tell America Online to automatically download and decompress ZIP files at the end of your AOL session. This prevents you from wasting time while you're online to perform the often time-consuming tasks associated with downloading and decompressing ZIP files. All download activities are basically deferred to the time you sign off. Here's how you can

set your download preferences to take advantage of this unique time-management feature:

1. Select **Preferences** from the **Settings** menu on the AOL toolbar.

2. Click **Download** in the **Organization** section of the **Preferences** window.

3. Click the **When I sign off** check box under the **Automatically decompress ZIP files** heading in the **Download Preferences** window, shown in Figure 3-10.

4. Click the **Save** button.

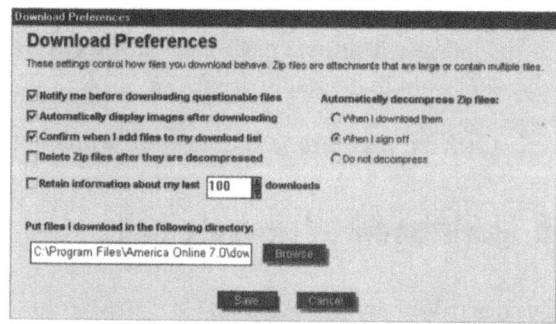

Figure 3-10. Setting the download preference to occur automatically at sign off

20 Resuming an interrupted download

Sometimes a file will be interrupted during the download process. If your connection gets interrupted during a download you may have to try downloading again. If the problem persists, you may want to determine whether your modem or the phone line is the problem. Users are advised to consult the troubleshooting section for modems. Another possible type of download interruption may occur during the download of new AOL software. If this occurs, you may be able to resume where you left off by following these steps.

1. Return to the **Upgrade** area and start the download again.

2. The automatic upgrade process will determine where the download stopped and will resume the download from the point the download was interrupted.

21 Marking stored files to be downloaded by the Download Manager

Mail that is received containing a small disk icon or envelope icon in your New Mail window, means that there's a file attached to the message. Before any attached file can be viewed, you'll have to download it first. Downloading attached files requires additional time and may pose a threat of catching a virus. Although smaller attached files usually take little time to download, this isn't always the case when an attached file is large. To speed up the process of reviewing your New Mail, AOL provides a way to mark attached files for downloading at a later time by the Download Manager. Here's how:

1. Select **Download Manager** from the **File** menu located above the AOL toolbar.

2. Locate and open a file containing a file to be downloaded by double-clicking the file.

3. Click the **Download** button and select **Download Later** from the drop-down list, shown in Figure 3-11.

The Download Manager maintains an internal list of the files that you've downloaded as well as the ones you chose to download at a later time. When a file is marked for downloading later, AOL confirms this decision by displaying a confirmation dialog box. This list provides all the information the Download Manager will need to locate the downloaded files on your hard drive after it's been downloaded. You can access downloaded files by selecting Download Manager from the File menu located above the AOL toolbar.

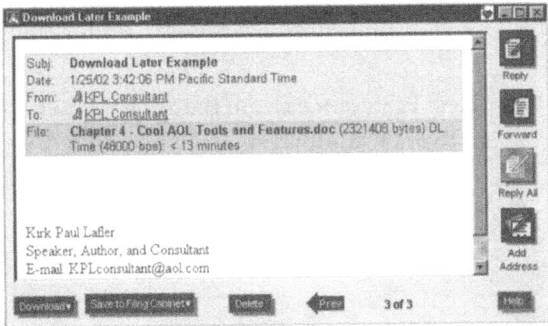

Figure 3-11. Selecting files to be downloaded later from the Download Manager

22 Scheduling Automatic AOL to download your stored files

Automatic AOL acts as your very own robot for a variety of e-mail activities and saves time so you can do other things. From sending and receiving your e-mail, downloading files, and collecting and sending message board and newsgroup postings, automatic AOL can do it all. All you have to do is schedule when the various activities are to take place, activate it, and automatic AOL does the rest. Here's how it's done:

Setting Automatic AOL for the First Time

1. Select **Automatic AOL** from the **Mail** menu on the AOL toolbar.

2. Click the **Continue** button after you've read the **Welcome to Automatic AOL** information window.

3. Answer the series of questions that appears by clicking either the **Yes** or **No** button. You'll be asked whether you want **Automatic AOL** to read e-mail and save it to your personal **Filing Cabinet**; download files that are attached to the e-mail that is being read; send e-mail that you've written offline; download files that you've placed in your **Download Manager**; retrieve unread messages from message board and newsgroup postings; send outgoing message board and newsgroup postings; and what screen name(s) you want **Automatic AOL** activated for.

4. Click the **Continue** button on the **Automatic AOL Walk-Through** window.

5. Click the **Yes** button in the **Schedule Automatic AOL** window.

6. Select the days of the week you'd like to schedule **Automatic AOL** to be activated in the **Which Days of the Week** window and click the **Continue** button.

7. Select how often you'd like to activate **Automatic AOL** each day in the **How Often Each Day** window and click the **Continue** button.

8. Set the starting time to activate **Automatic AOL** each day in the **Starting Time Each Day** window and click the **Continue** button.

9. Click the **OK** button on the **Congratulations** window.

If You've Already Set Up Automatic AOL

1. Select **Automatic AOL** from the **Mail** menu on the AOL toolbar.

2. Select the **Download files marked to be downloaded later** box on the Automatic AOL window.

3. Click the **Schedule Automatic AOL** button on the **Automatic AOL** window to display the **Schedule Automatic AOL** window, shown in Figure 3-12.

4. Select the days of the week, starting time (hour and minutes), and how often.

5. Click the **Enable Scheduler** box.

6. Click the **OK** button.

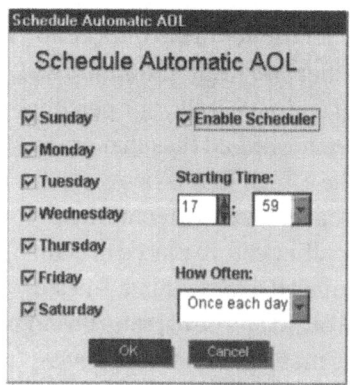

Figure 3-12. Scheduling when and how often Automatic AOL is to run

23 Searching your Filing Cabinet for what you want to find

As the content of your Filing Cabinet grows, you may have more difficulty finding e-mail correspondence that you're looking for. Using the Filing Cabinet Search feature to search for specific folders and e-mail correspondence is much quicker and easier than when manually performed. The Filing Cabinet Search window lets you specify one or more words you want searched in the Find what:

field. You can also click the Match case check box to make AOL perform an exact character-by-character search, or search all folders or only open folders, and scan full text or titles only. To begin searching your Filing Cabinet, follow these step:.

1. Select **Filing Cabinet** from the **Mail** menu on the AOL toolbar.

2. Click the **Find** button to display the **Search** window.

3. Enter your search criteria in the **Filing Cabinet Search** window, shown in Figure 3-13.

4. Select whether you want to match the upper- and lower-case text in your search, the scope of search, and the type of search.

5. Click the **Find Next** button.

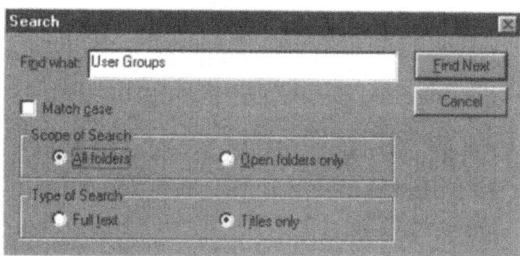

Figure 3-13. Entering search criteria in AOL's Filing Cabinet Search window

24 Controlling the size of your Filing Cabinet

AOL lets you adjust the automatic warnings that correspond to your Filing Cabinet size and the percentage of free space available. This early warning feature lets AOL warn you when your Filing Cabinet approaches the size allocation you've established for it (e.g., 10 megabytes). If you receive this warning too frequently, you can increase the size at any time by following these simple steps.

1. Select **Preferences** from the **Settings** menu on the AOL toolbar.

2. Click **Filing Cabinet** in the **Organization** section of the **Preferences** window.

3. Adjust the warnings associated with the size of your **Filing Cabinet** by clicking the up or down arrow corresponding to **Issue warning about the Filing Cabinet if the size reaches __ megabytes** shown in Figure 3-14.

4. Click the **Save** button to save your new setting when done.

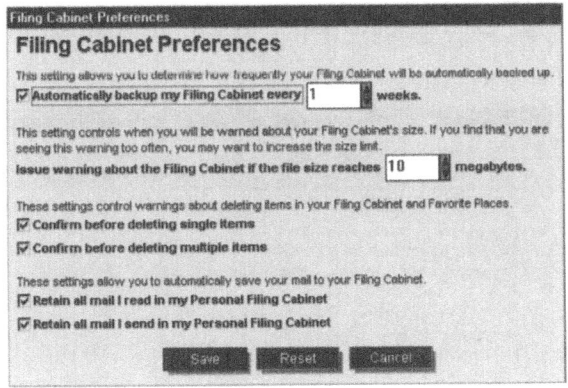

Figure 3-14. Setting Filing Cabinet warning sizes in the Filing Cabinet Preferences window

25 Recovering unused space in your Filing Cabinet

As folders and e-mails are deleted from your Filing Cabinet, the space once occupied by these items is not automatically reclaimed and made available for reuse by your Filing Cabinet. This results in unused space, which is unavailable for storing other things. Not only is this a waste of precious storage resources, it also slows the AOL loading process by requiring AOL to manage something that really isn't there.

In order to recover unused space in your Filing Cabinet and on your hard drive, you'll need to run a utility program to compact the Filing Cabinet database. This will free up any unused space and let you reuse this space for other storage purposes. Here's how it's done.

1. Click the **File** menu located above the AOL toolbar and select **Filing Cabinet** from the drop-down selection list.

2. Click **Manage** and then click **Compact** from the menu that appears in the **Filing Cabinet** window.

3. A performance warning will appear to alert you that your **Filing Cabine**t may have empty space in it. It will confirm whether you'd like to compact your **Filing Cabinet** now. Click the **Compact Now** button, shown in Figure 3-15.

4. When the compacting process is complete, a dialog box appears indicating that your **Filing Cabinet** has been fully compacted. Click the **OK** button to end the process.

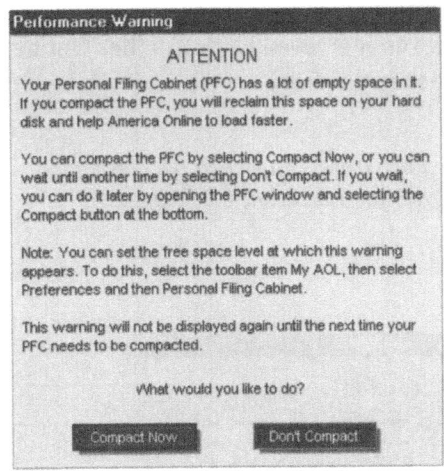

Figure 3-15. A performance warning appears prior to compacting your Filing Cabinet

26 Backing up your Filing Cabinet automatically

Safeguarding the folders and files in your Filing Cabinet should be an important part of any AOL user's data management tasks. It's important because in the event you experience problems with your Filing Cabinet you can restore much or all of the lost information. Rather than putting your important correspondence at risk, you can reduce your stress levels by making sure that important information is backed up. The key to any successful back up plan is to perform regular and timely backups. AOL provides manual and automatic methods of backing up your Filing Cabinet. Here are the steps you can follow to begin backing up your Filing Cabinet and reduce your risk of data loss.

Manually Backing Up Your Filing Cabinet

1. Click the **File** menu located above the AOL toolbar and select **Filing Cabinet** from the drop-down selection list.

2. Click the **Manage** button and then click **Backup** from the menu that appears in the **Filing Cabinet** window. The **Backup Your Filing Cabinet** window appears, shown in Figure 3-16.

3. Click the **Backup Now** button to create a backup copy of your **Filing Cabinet**. Your backup copy is saved to the America Online 7.0 Backup directory.

   🖋 *Version 6.0 users have their backup copy saved to the America Online 6.0 Backup directory.*

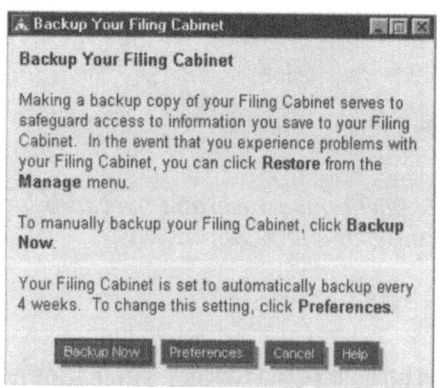

Figure 3-16. The Backup Your Filing Cabinet window and options

Automatically Backing Up Your Filing Cabinet

1. Click the **File** menu located above the AOL toolbar and select **Filing Cabinet** from the drop-down selection list.

2. Click the **Manage** button and then click **Backup** from the menu that appears in the **Filing Cabinet** window. The **Backup Your Filing Cabinet** window appears.

3. Click the **Preferences** button to display the **Filing Cabinet Preferences** window.

4. Click the **Automatically backup my Filing Cabinet every _____ weeks** check box and enter the frequency in weeks you want backups of your **Filing Cabinet** done, shown in Figure 3-17.

   🖋 *Your Filing Cabinet is set to automatically back up every 4 weeks, unless you've changed this default setting.*

5. Click the **Save** button to save the settings.

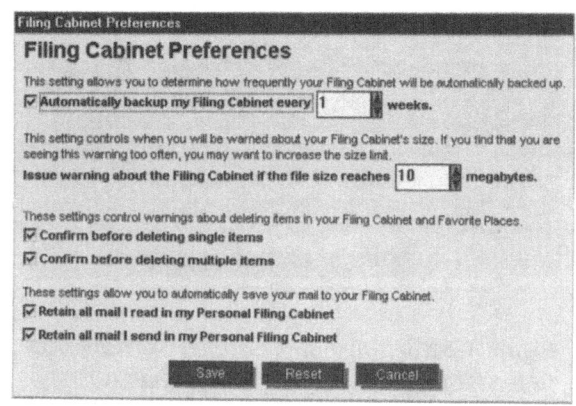

Figure 3-17. Requesting weekly automatic backup of your Filing Cabinet

27 Restoring your Filing Cabinet from your most recent backup copy

Should a loss of information or other problem occur with your Filing Cabinet, you'll be happy to know that everything in your Filing Cabinet from the time of your last back up can be estored (see Tip #26). This provides a degree of security in the event disaster strikes. Here's how it's done.

1. Click the **File** menu located above the AOL toolbar and select **Filing Cabinet** from the drop-down selection list.

2. Click **Manage** and then click **Restore** from the menu that appears in the **Filing Cabinet** window. The **Restore Your Filing Cabinet** window appears confirming that you're about to replace your **Filing Cabinet** with your most recent back up, shown in Figure 3-18.

3. Click the **Yes** button to restore your **Filing Cabinet**. Everything in your **Filing Cabinet** will automatically be restored.

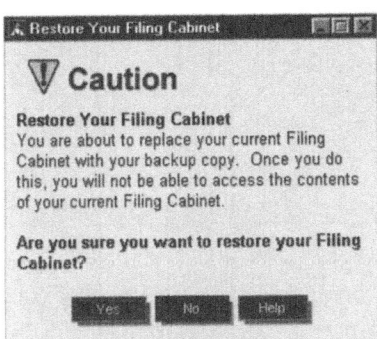

Figure 3-18. Restoring your Filing Cabinet confirmation window

CHAPTER 4

Cool AOL Tools and Features

THIS CHAPTER EXPLORES many of the popular tools and features available with AOL. From accessing AOL anytime and anywhere, and scheduling your personal and business appointments and events, to using multimedia features like playing audio and video files, and capturing and viewing pictures online, you'll find a wealth of extraordinary features that are sure to enhance your life. No matter where you are, you'll be able to receive and manage your e-mail, get stock quotes and oversee your portfolio, get weather reports, see what your horoscope says, and so much more.

In this chapter, you'll learn how to

- Access AOL anytime and anywhere with AOL Anywhere

- Manage My Portfolio

- Use My Calendar

- Enjoy AOL multimedia features

- Capture, save, and view pictures online

Access AOL Anytime and Anywhere

1 Understanding AOL Anywhere and its features

AOL Anywhere provides access to popular AOL member features anywhere, anytime, and at any access speed. The easy-to-use services and features are available beyond the confines of the PC. Members have an array of convenient access options including the familiar AOL 7.0, handheld devices such as Palm® and CE®, mobile services using Internet-ready phones, and a host of other interactive user platforms to accommodate emerging technologies.

Members can easily access AOL Anywhere by clicking the AOL Anywhere button on the AOL toolbar to display a fully customizable Web page, shown in Figure 4-1. Entering the AOL Keyword: **AOL Anywhere** also accesses the AOL Anywhere Web page.

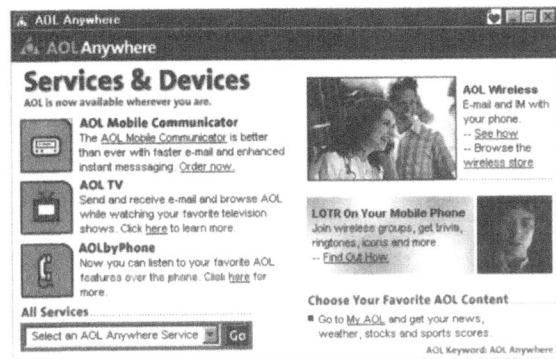

Figure 4-1. The AOL Anywhere Web page permits member access to a variety of services.

Members and non-members alike can also access AOL services and features as long as they're able to connect to the Internet. From any PC or handheld device, simply enter the Web site address: http://www.aol.com to display the AOL Anywhere Web page, shown in Figure 4-2. This handy feature-packed Web site gives you access to your AOL Mail, Portfolio, My AOL, Calendar, news, people and chat, popular channels, AOL shopping, and much more.

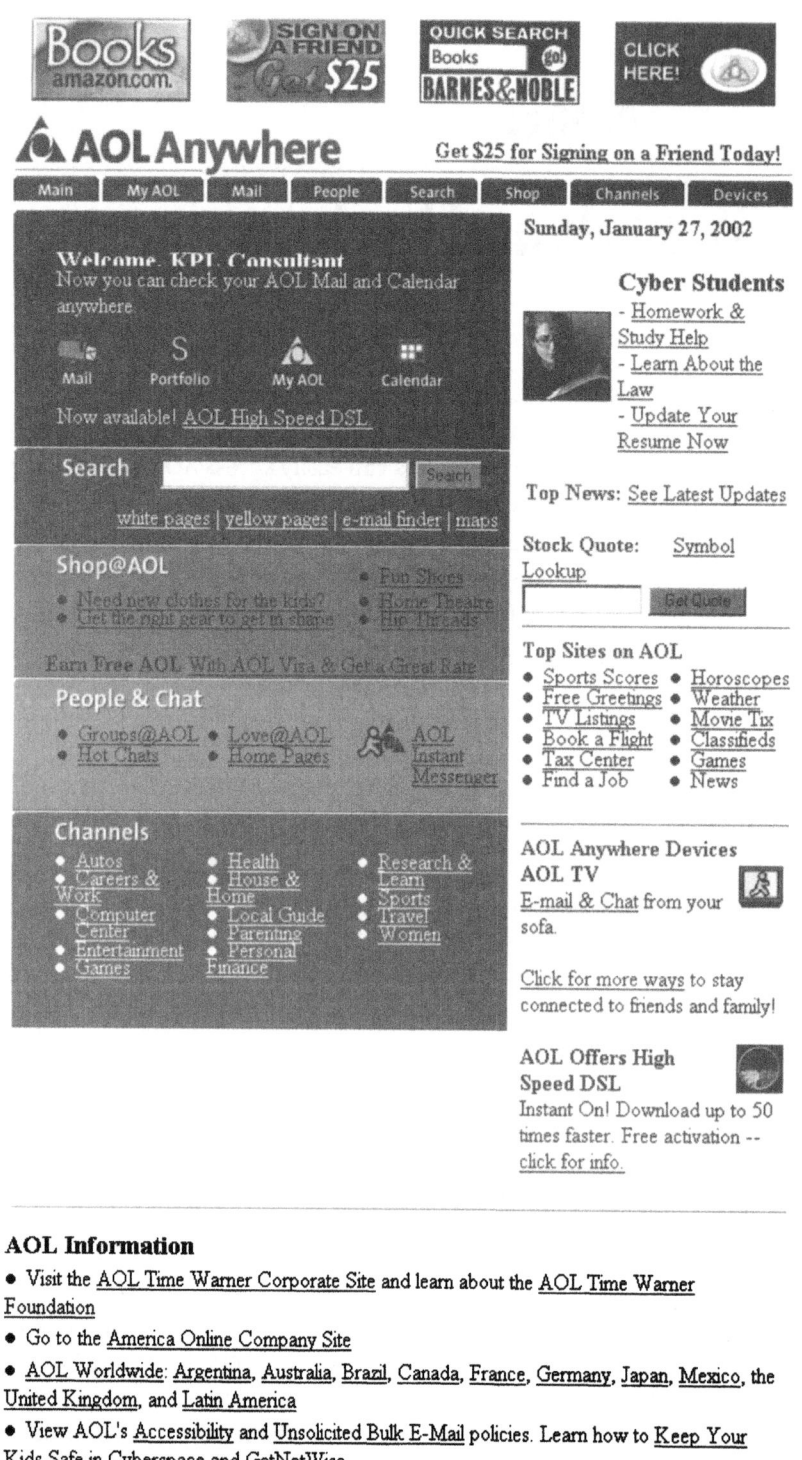

Figure 4-2. The AOL Anywhere Web site for members and non-members alike

2 Accessing your mail from AOL Anywhere

AOL Anywhere provides members with an electronic mail interface to one of the easiest and most flexible Internet e-mail software packages in the world. No matter where you are, on the road traveling, using a friend's computer, using a handheld device, or anyplace else, its utter simplicity and flexibility make it easy and fun to use. AOL Anywhere's Mail interface offers a tried and proven way to communicate online—all through a simple and effective e-mail interface. Here's how it works.

1. After connecting to the Internet, enter the Web site address: http://www.aol.com.

2. Click the **Mail** button on the **AOL Anywhere** Web site.

3. Enter your AOL screen name and password, and click the **Enter AOL Mail** button. You will then be able to view your mail over a secure connection.

4. Click the **Please click here to complete the sign-in process** button from the **Welcome to AOL Mail** Website.

5. Follow the instructions that appear on your screen to gain access to your mail.

3 Managing your mail from AOL Anywhere

AOL Anywhere lets you manage your mail account from anywhere you are. You'll be able to access New Mail, Old Mail, and Sent Mail, reply to messages, compose new messages, access your Address Book, and delete unwanted messages. The AOL Anywhere Mail interface is shown in Figure 4-3. For specific instructions about AOL e-mail capabilities and features, readers are encouraged to review the tips presented in Chapter 2.

Figure 4-3. New Mail appears in the AOL Anywhere Mail Web site

My Portfolio AOL's Financial Manager

4 Accessing My Portfolio

AOL Anywhere provides members with an electronic portfolio. Members can get the latest information on the Dow, Nasdaq, and S&P 500 with the CBS MarketWatch Market Update (quotes are delayed 20 minutes). You'll be able to obtain timely and constantly updated information on the stocks in your portfolio no matter where you are. Here's how you can access your Portfolio:

1. After connecting to the Internet, enter the Web site address: http://www.aol.com.

2. Click the **Portfolio** button on the **AOL Anywhere** Web site.

3. The first time you access your **Portfolio**, you'll see that it's a non-personalized version, shown in Figure 4-4. You'll immediately be able to enter a stock ticker symbol (character symbol used to reference a company—e.g., Merck's ticker symbol is MRK).

4. After entering a ticker symbol and clicking the **Go** button, you'll see the latest numbers including the Stock Exchange the company is on, last price, change in price (percent), high and low price for the day, and a variety of other numbers as shown in Figure 4-5.

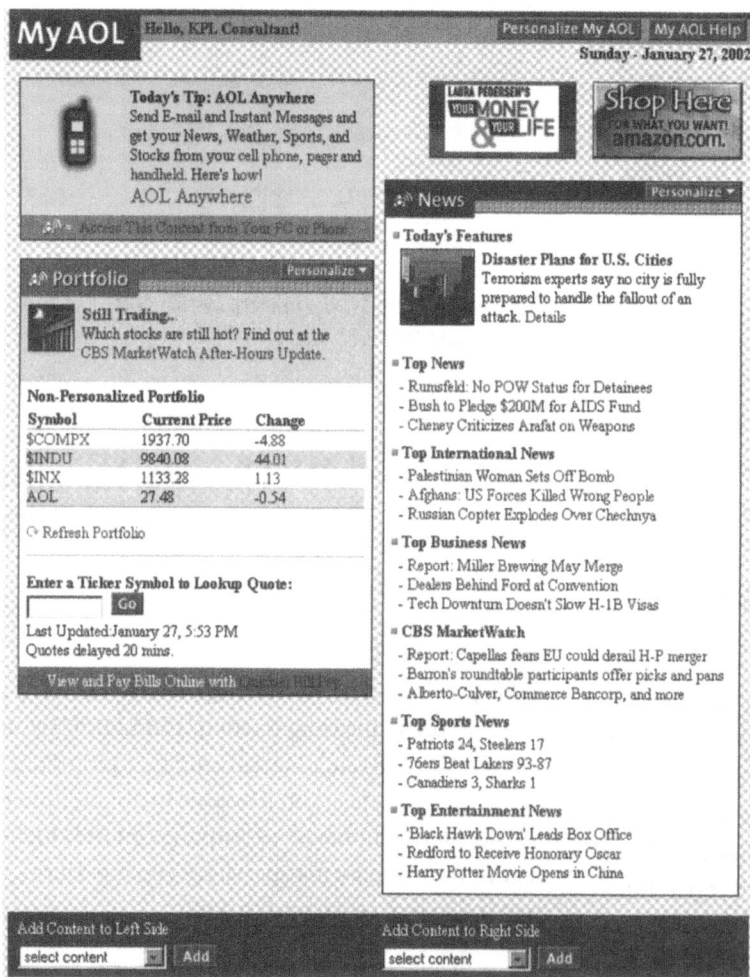

Figure 4-4. Accessing portfolio and stock information from the AOL Anywhere Web site

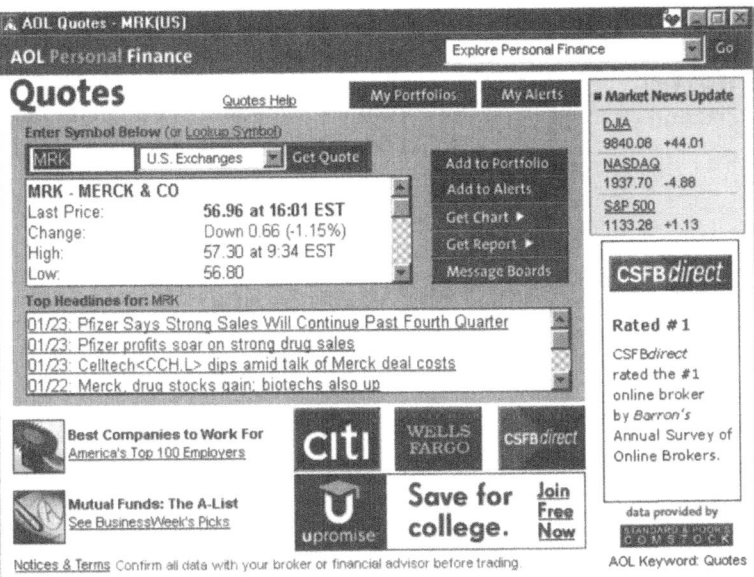

Figure 4-5. The AOL Personal Finance Snapshot window displays the latest quote information

5 Setting up My Portfolio

AOL lets you set up one or more personal portfolios containing the stocks you own. In order to take advantage of this handy feature, you'll need to first add each stock's ticker symbol along with the purchase price and share price to your Portfolio (a maximum of twenty Portfolios can be created per screen name with each Portfolio containing no more than 100 stocks). Once each stock is added, you'll be able to view your Portfolio's constantly updating stock prices. This not only provides a snapshot in time about the health of your investments, but also provides a handy tool to help you manage the stocks in your portfolio. Here are the steps you'll need to follow to set up your portfolio for the first time.

Creating a New Portfolio

1. Click the **Personalize** button in the **Portfolio** window of **My AOL**, and select **Customize** from the drop-down selection list to display AOL's **My Portfolios** window.

2. Click the **Create** button to create a new portfolio.

3. Enter the name you'd like to assign to your new **Portfolio** and click the **Next** button in the **Step 1: New Portfolio Setup** window, shown in Figure 4-7.

4. Enter the stock symbol, number of shares, purchase price, and other optional information about the stock you'd like added to your **Portfolio** in the **Step 2: New Portfolio Setup** window. Click the **Add Item** button to add the stock symbol to your **Portfolio** and click the **Next** button.

5. Enter a cash amount to be tracked in your Portfolio in the **Step 3: New Portfolio Setup** window, select any indices to be tracked by clicking one or more check boxes, and click the **Next** button.

6. You should then see a screen saying **Portfolio _____ has been successfully created** appear. Click the **Next** button.

7. Read the Gramm-Leach-Bliley Act Privacy Notice and if you agree with the terms click the **OK** button.

6 Managing My Portfolio

Over time, you'll want to make changes to your Portfolio. Here's how stocks can be added and deleted in your Portfolio.

Adding and Deleting Stocks in an Existing Portfolio

1. After connecting to the Internet, enter AOL Keyword: **My Portfolios** and click the **Go** button. The **My Portfolios** window appears displaying the name(s) of your personal Portfolio(s).

2. Select (highlight) the desired **Portfolio** and click the **Display** button in the **My Portfolios** window.

3. In the **Portfolio Display** window you'll see the name(s) of your investments and any indices that you selected along with its current activity. You'll be able to add, edit, delete, print, and a variety of other functions in the **Portfolio Display** window, shown in Figure 4-6.

4. To add a new stock to your **Portfolio**, click the **Add** button in the **Portfolio Disp**lay window. Enter the stock symbol you want to add to your **Portfolio** and click the **OK** button in the **Quotes** window in the **Add to Portfolio** window.

5. To delete an existing stock in your **Portfolio**, select the stock and click the **Delete** button in the **Portfolio Display** window. You will be asked to confirm whether you want the stock symbol deleted by clicking the **OK** button.

News and Other Cool Stuff from AOL Anywhere

7 Viewing today's news

You'll be able to view the latest developments in today's news with a touch of your mouse. The news stories include Today's Feature stories, Top News, Top International News, Top Business News, CBS MarketWatch, Top Sports News, and Top Entertainment News. Here's how you can view these news stories and more:

1. After connecting to the Internet, enter the Web site address: http://www.aol.com.

2. Click the **My AOL** button on the **AOL Anywhere** Web site.

3. Click the News headline of interest on the **My AOL** Web site, shown in Figure 4-7.

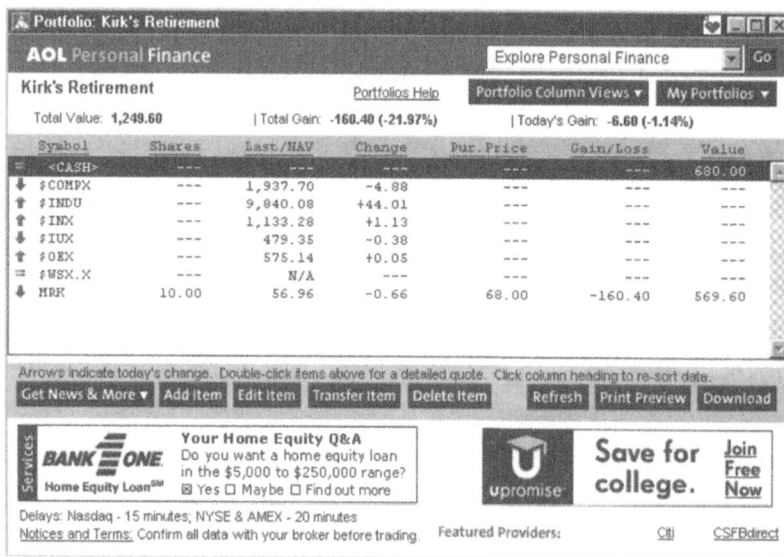

Figure 4-6. Displaying your Portfolio's information in a Portfolio Display window

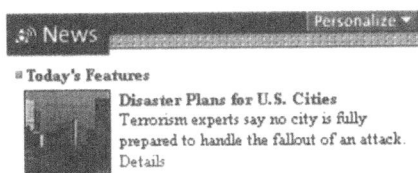

Today's Features

Disaster Plans for U.S. Cities
Terrorism experts say no city is fully
prepared to handle the fallout of an attack.
Details

Top News
- Rumsfeld: No POW Status for Detainees
- Bush to Pledge $200M for AIDS Fund
- Cheney Criticizes Arafat on Weapons

Top International News
- Palestinian Woman Sets Off Bomb
- Afghans: US Forces Killed Wrong People
- Russian Copter Explodes Over Chechnya

Top Business News
- Report: Miller Brewing May Merge
- Dealers Behind Ford at Convention
- Tech Downturn Doesn't Slow H-1B Visas

CBS MarketWatch
- Report: Capellas fears EU could derail H-P merger
- Barron's roundtable participants offer picks and pans
- Alberto-Culver, Commerce Bancorp, and more

Top Sports News
- Patriots Win AFC Championship
- 76ers Beat Lakers 93-87
- Canadiens Score Victory Over Sharks

Top Entertainment News
- 'Black Hawk Down' Leads Box Office
- Redford to Receive Honorary Oscar
- Harry Potter Movie Opens in China

Figure 4-7. Viewing today's News headlines from AOL Anywhere's My AOL Web site

8 Getting weather conditions city-by-city

You'll be able to plan better for that business trip or vacation if you know what to pack. AOL Anywhere's weather conditions and forecasts let you know what the current temperatures and conditions are to make your trip a pleasant one. You'll be able to plan better by using this comprehensive database of over 34,000 cities around the globe. Here's how:

1. After connecting to the Internet, enter the Web site address: http://www.aol.com.

2. Click the **My AOL** button on the **AOL Anywhere** Web site.

3. If you don't see a Weather section on your **My AOL** Web site, click **select content** under either the **Add Content to Left Side** or **Add Content to Right Side** button located at the bottom of your **My AOL** Web site, and select **Weather** from the drop-down selection list. Click the **Add** button to view the **Weather** section of **My AOL**.

4. To get weather conditions for a particular city, enter a city in the **Weather Lookup:** field in the **Weather** section of **My AOL** and click the **Go** button, shown in Figure 4-8.

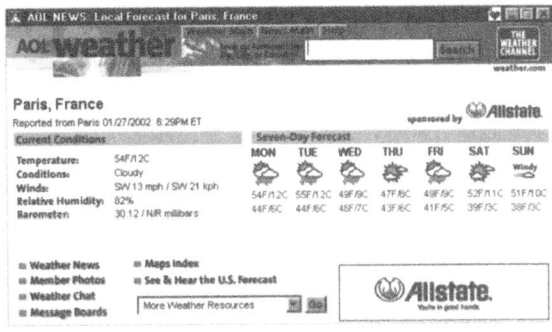

Figure 4-8. Viewing the weather conditions and forecasts for your favorite city

9 Customizing My AOL

My AOL is your main hub when you're on the road, away from home, or beyond the confines of your PC. AOL lets you customize this window with as much or as little information as you want. Consisting of multi-paned windows, My AOL can be personalized with just the information you want for a more rewarding online experience. From up-to-date news, stock quotes, and horoscopes to recipes, travel, and appointment schedules, My AOL is your command and control center while you're away from your PC. Here's how you can control your My AOL settings and content.

Changing My AOL Settings

My AOL is automatically set to never refresh the contents of your page and to display all graphics available on your page. To change either of these default settings, follow these steps:

1. After connecting to the Internet, enter the Web address: http://myaol.aol.com.

2. Click the **Personalize My Page** button located at the top of your **My AOL** page.

3. Change your My AOL settings by checking the desired box in the **Refresh Rate** and **Connection Speed** sections in the **Personalize My AOL** window, shown in Figure 4-9.

4. When you're done customizing, click the **Save** button.

Adding Content to My AOL

You can personalize your My AOL page by adding content or windows. Here's how:

1. After connecting to the Internet, enter the Web address: http://myaol.aol.com.

2. Click the **Personalize My Page** button located at the top of your **My AOL** page.

3. Check each box corresponding to a topic in the **Add or Remove Content** section.

4. When you're done customizing, click the **Save** button.

Removing Content from My AOL

1. After connecting to the Internet, enter the Web address: http://myaol.aol.com.

2. Click the **Personalize My Page** button located at the top of your **My AOL** page.

3. Remove the checked box corresponding to a topic in the **Add or Remove Content** section.

4. When you're done customizing, click the **Save** button.

Customizing a Window's Content in My AOL

1. After connecting to the Internet, enter the Web address: http://myaol.aol.com.

2. Click the **Personalize My Page** button located at the top of your **My AOL** page.

3. Click the **Personalize** button corresponding to the window you'd like to change, and select **Customize** from the list of options: **Customize**, **Remove**, or **Help**.

4. Follow the on-screen instructions in the customization window that appears, and click the **Save** button to make changes permanent.

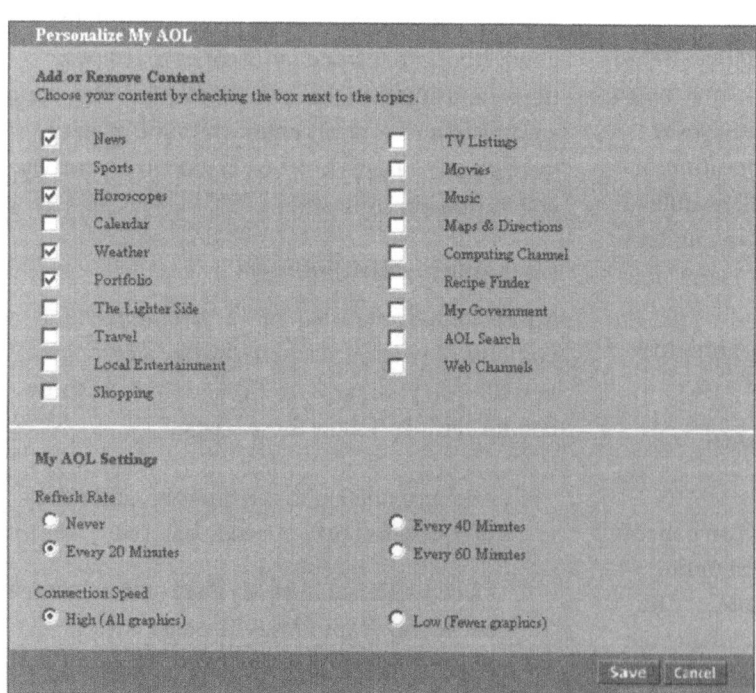

Figure 4-9. Adding/removing content from your my AOL page by checking boxes

Allowing My AOL to Remember Preferences

My AOL uses cookies to remember your specific preferences you've set. My AOL may not work if your Web browser is configured not to accept cookies. Here's how to enable cookies.

1. Click **Preferences** from the **Settings** menu located on the AOL toolbar.

2. Click **Internet Properties (WWW)** on the **Preferences** window.

3. Click the **Security** tab, then the **Custom Level** button on the **Internet Options** window.

4. Click the **Enable** button under the **Cookies** category in the **Security Settings** window, and then click the **OK** button to save new settings.

My Calendar AOL's Electronic Scheduling Tool

10 Registering My Calendar

The first time you use My Calendar, you'll be greeted with a display that asks you to enter your

time zone and zip code. By registering, you'll receive event notifications that occur near you. Here's how:

1. Select the time zone from the drop-down list of choices and then enter your five-digit zip code (U.S. residents only).

2. Click the **Save** button.

11 Checking your calendar from wherever you are

My Calendar is your personalized planner and event service no matter where you are. Its 24/7 accessibility makes it a great tool for viewing current and future appointments while you're home or away. Here's how you can access your Calendar:

1. After connecting to the Internet, enter the Web site address: http://www.aol.com.

2. Click the **Calendar** button on the **AOL Anywhere** Web site. **My Calendar** appears with the current month displayed, shown in Figure 4-10.

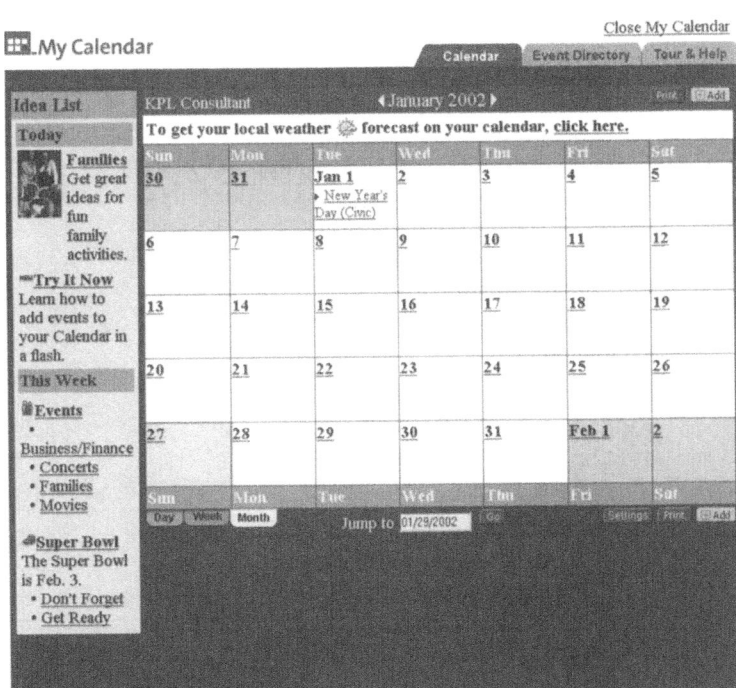

Figure 4-10. Displaying your My Calendar's current month's scheduling information

12 Adding appointments

My Calendar makes it easy to add appointment entries. Adding an appointment requires entering a brief description describing the appointment; the date and time; the length; and optional information such as whether a reminder is needed; any special note; whether this is a recurring or stand-alone appointment; and who should be notified by e-mail (separate multiple e-mail addresses with a comma). My Calendar does the rest. Here's how an appointment is added to My Calendar:

1. After connecting to the Internet, enter the Web site address: http://www.aol.com.

2. Click the **Calendar** button on the **AOL Anywhere** Web site. **My Calendar** appears with the current month displayed.

3. Click the **Calendar** tab and then click the **Add** button located at the top right of the **My Calendar** window.

4. In the **Appointment Details** window, enter the details and optional information about the appointment, shown in Figure 4-11.

5. Click the **Save** button to add the appointment to **My Calendar**.

6. Click the **Calendar** tab and the type of display desired (**Day**, **Week**, or **Month**) from the available tabs at the bottom of the **My Calendar** window. **My Calendar** should display the new appointment as requested, shown in Figure 4-12.

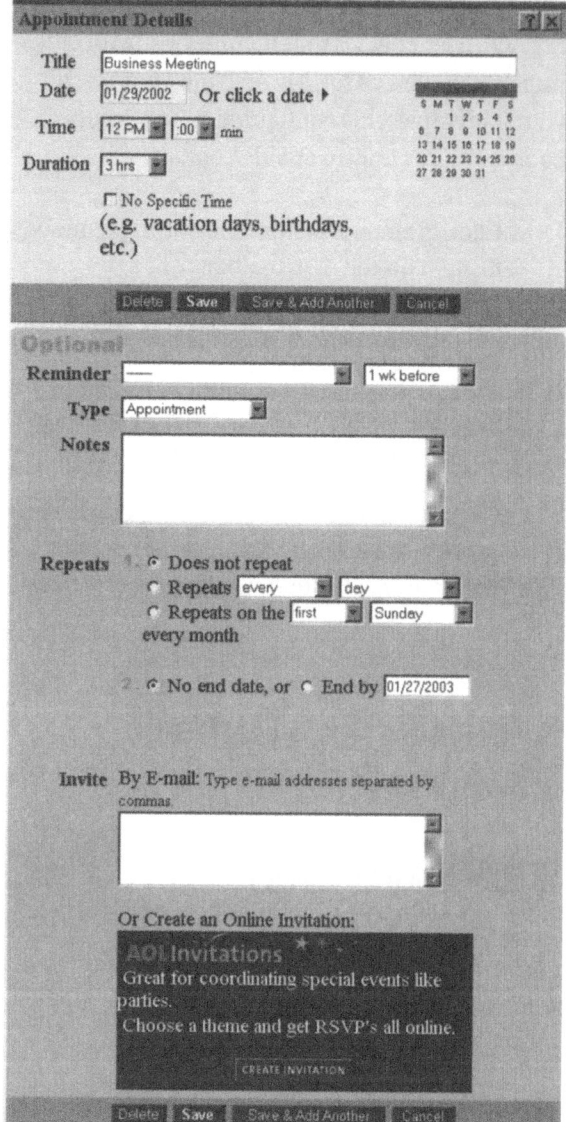

Figure 4-11. Adding an appointment to My Calendar

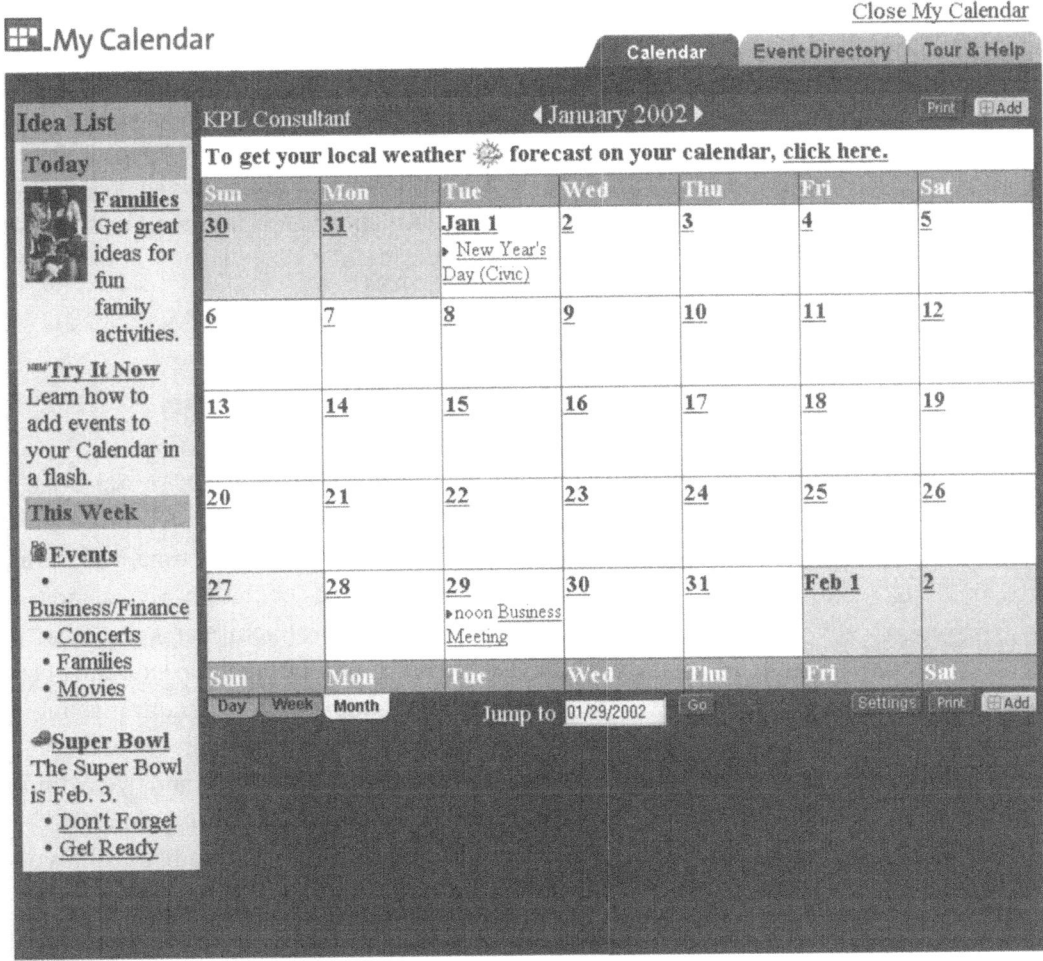

Figure 4-12. Displaying a month view of My Calendar with the scheduled appointment added

13 Adding appointment reminders

My Calendar lets you notify a maximum of three e-mail addresses for an appointment reminder. Here's how:

1. After connecting to the Internet, enter the Web site address: http://www.aol.com.

2. Click the **Calendar** button on the **AOL Anywhere** Web site. **My Calendar** appears with the current month displayed.

3. Click the **Calendar** tab and then click the **Add** button located at the top right of the **My Calendar** window.

4. In the **Add Appointment** window, enter the details and optional information about the appointment as before.

5. Click the **Reminder** drop-down selection box and choose **Alternate Destinations** from the list of choices, select when the reminder should be sent from the drop-down selection box, and click the **Save** button.

6. The **Alternate destinations for reminders** window appears letting you enter a name, type of address, and e-mail address for a maximum of three reminders, shown in Figure 4-13.

7. When you've added the e-mail addresses to have reminders sent, click the **OK** button to save this information along with the appointment entry.

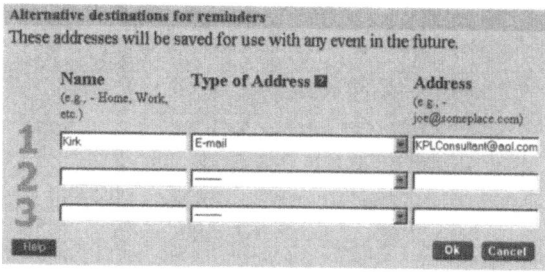

Figure 4-13. Adding an appointment reminder to be sent to an e-mail address

14 Changing appointments

When a meeting or appointment changes, you'll need to make changes to My Calendar to reflect the adjustments. Doing this is easy with AOL. Here's how:

1. After connecting to the Internet, enter the Web site address: http://www.aol.com.

2. Click the **Calendar** button on the **AOL Anywhere** Web site. **My Calendar** appears with the current month displayed.

3. Click the **Calendar** tab and then click the **appointment title** on the calendar itself. By doing this, you'll display the **Appointment Details** window enabling you to change any information that needs adjustment.

4. When you're done making any changes, click the **Save** button to save the changes to the appointment in your My Calendar.

15 Deleting appointments

When an appointment is cancelled, you'll need to update your schedule to reflect the cancellation. Deleting an appointment in My Calendar is easy. Here's how:

1. After connecting to the Internet, enter the Web site address: http://www.aol.com.

2. Click the **Calendar** button on the **AOL Anywhere** Web site. **My Calendar** appears with the current month displayed.

3. Click the **Calendar** tab and then click the **appointment title** on the calendar itself. By doing this, you'll display the **Appointment Details** window enabling you to delete the appointment and any information that associated with it.

4. Click the **Delete** button.

16 Setting recurring appointments

When an appointment is added in My Calendar, it is scheduled as if it were a single occurrence. It occurs on the scheduled day and time, and has a defined start time and conclusion. My Calendar handles these types of appointments with ease. But occasionally, appointments occur more than one time. For example, a project status meeting that is scheduled for the first Thursday of every month occurs one time a month, and twelve times per year. It's easy to schedule an appointment or meeting that occurs a certain number of times per year using My Calendar. Here's how:

1. After connecting to the Internet, enter the Web site address: http://www.aol.com.

2. Click the **Calendar** button on the **AOL Anywhere** Web site. **My Calendar** appears with the current month displayed.

3. Click the **Calendar** tab and then click the **Add** button located at the top right of the **My Calendar** window.

4. In the **Add Appointment** window, enter the details and optional information about the appointment as before.

5. Click the button that represents the type of recurring appointment you're scheduling and select the choices from the drop-down selection boxes for the **Repeats** section of the **Optional** information in the **Add Appointment** window. For example, to add an appointment that occurs on the first Thursday of every month requires you to click the **Repeats on the** radio button, select when the appointment is to occur (first, second, third, last, etc.) from

the drop-down selection box, and select the day of the week from the drop-down selection box.

6. Click the **Save** button.

17 Notifying others about an appointment

Whenever an appointment is added or modified, you can have My Calendar automatically notify others by e-mail. This handy feature makes appointment notification a breeze. Here's how it's used:

1. After connecting to the Internet, enter the Web site address: http://www.aol.com.

2. Click the **Calendar** button on the **AOL Anywhere** Web site. **My Calendar** appears with the current month displayed.

3. If you're adding a new appointment, click the **Calendar** tab and then click the **Add** button located at the top right of the My Calendar window. In the **Add Appointment** window, enter the details and optional information about the appointment as before. Then add the e-mail addresses of the people you'd like to notify in the **Invite** field.

4. If the appointment already exists, click the **Calendar** tab and then click the **appointment title** on the calendar itself. By doing this, you'll display the **Appointment Details** window enabling you to add the e-mail addresses of the people you'd like to notify in the **Invite** field.

5. Click the **Save** button.

6. Add any additional comments in the **Add Comments** field and click the **Send E-mail** button in the **Send E-mail Notification** window, shown in Figure 4-14.

7. **My Calendar** will automatically send an e-mail notification reminding you of your appointment at the time you've requested.

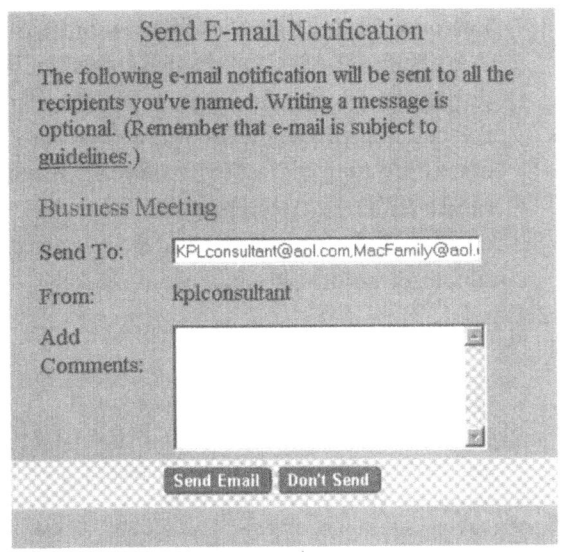

Figure 4-14. Sending e-mail notification to recipients listed in the E-mail Attendees field

18 Sending a calendar reminder via e-mail

Sending an appointment reminder is similar to sending an e-mail notification to recipients listed in the E-mail Attendees field. The only difference is that this feature is typically designed as a handy way to remind you of an upcoming appointment. Follow these simple steps to send yourself a reminder:

1. After connecting to the Internet, enter the Web site address: http://www.aol.com.

2. Click the **Calendar** button on the **AOL Anywhere** Web site. **My Calendar** appears with the current month displayed.

3. If you're adding a new appointment, click the **Calendar** tab and then click the **Add** button located at the top right of the My Calendar window. In the **Add Appointment** window, enter the details and optional information about the appointment as before. Then select a choice from the drop-down selection box and enter the e-mail address to which you'd like to send a reminder in the **Reminder** field, and decide how far in advance you'd like to have it sent (e.g., minutes, hours, days, or weeks).

4. If the appointment already exists, click the **Calendar** tab and then click the **appointment title** on the calendar itself. By doing this, you'll display the **Appointment Details** window. Select a choice from the drop-down box and enter the e-mail address to which you'd like to send a reminder in the **Reminder** field, and decide how far in advance you'd like to have it sent (e.g., minutes, hours, days, or weeks).

5. Click the **Save** button.

6. **My Calendar** will automatically send a reminder of your appointment at the date and time you requested via an e-mail message, shown in Figure 4-15.

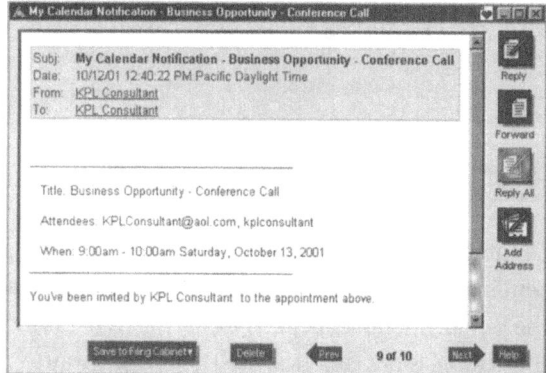

Figure 4-15. An e-mail reminder sent by My Calendar about an upcoming appointment

19 Adding events to your Calendar

Webster's New World Dictionary defines an event as a happening or occurrence, especially one that's important. My Calendar lets you define one or more events of significance from a listing of event categories. Specific events are grouped by category and listed in a directory. Event categories include:

- Cultural Events: Art, Classical Music, Dance, Opera, and Theater

- Family Events: Festivals

- Family Events: Kids and Family Activities

- Finance: Dividends, Earnings, IPOs, and Splits

- Holidays: Civic and Cultural Holidays

- Holidays: Religious Holidays

- Holidays: International Holidays

- Holidays: Celebrate the Day

- Movies: Movies in Theaters

- Music: Concerts

- Special Interest: Wine Events

- Sports: Pro and College Teams

- Television: Favorite Shows

- Trade Shows: Trade Shows and Seminars

- Reference: Horoscope

- Reference: Weather

To find a particular event and add it to your Calendar, follow these instructions.

1. After connecting to the Internet, enter the Web site address: http://www.aol.com.

2. Click the **Calendar** button on the **AOL Anywhere** Web site. **My Calendar** appears with the current month displayed.

3. Click the **Event Directory** tab at the top of the **My Calendar** window to display the Event Directory.

4. Click on a particular event category (e.g., **Kids and Families: Family Events**). The **Family Events – Select a City Web** page appears.

5. Select a city for which you'd like to view **Family Events** (for example, **San Diego**). The **Kids & Family** events Web page for San Diego appears showing the various events that are lined up.

6. Click the desired event to see an overview and event schedule.

7. Click the **Add to My Calendar** button.

8. Click the **Close** button on the **My Calendar** window, shown in Figure 4-16.

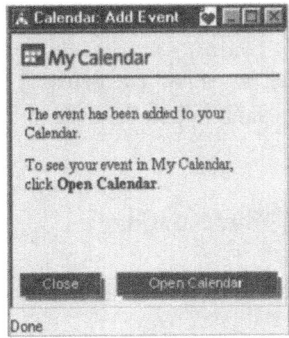

Figure 4-16. Confirming the addition of an event to your My Calendar

20 Adding holidays

You can add an assortment of holidays to your Calendar. From Civic & Cultural, Religious, and International, you have all the holidays to choose from. Just follow these easy steps to add a holiday event schedule to your Calendar:

1. After connecting to the Internet, enter the Web site address: http://www.aol.com.

2. Click the **Calendar** button on the **AOL Anywhere** Web site. **My Calendar** appears with the current month displayed.

3. Click the **Event Directory** tab at the top of the **My Calendar** window to display the **Event Directory**.

4. Click **Holidays** under the **Essentials**: category of the **Event Directory** Web page to display the **Holidays** Web page.

5. To add an entire holiday event schedule directly to your **Calendar**, select a schedule and click the desired holiday sub-category (e.g., U.S.) and select the holidays you want added to your **Calendar** from the list of holidays that is displayed, shown in Figure 4-17.

6. Click the **Add** button to add the checked events to your **Calendar**.

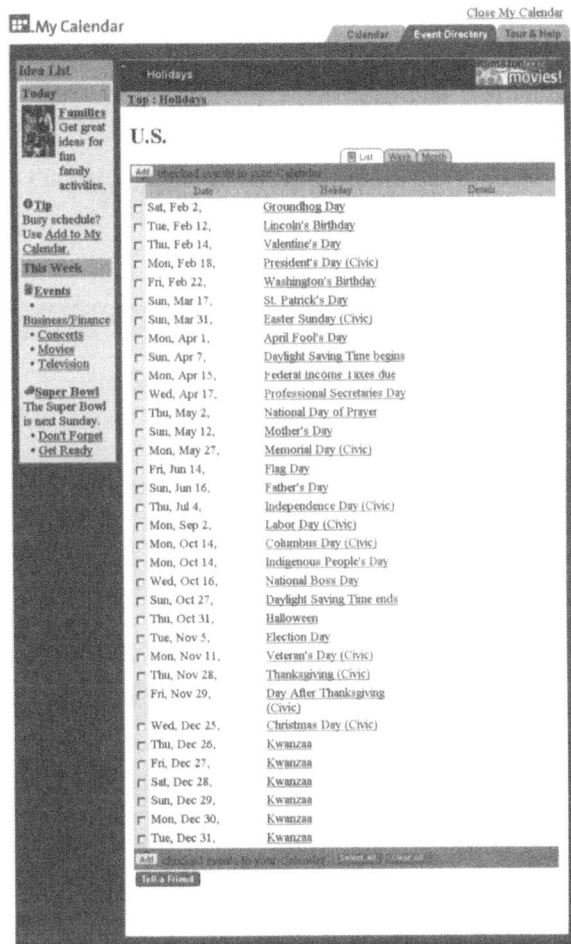

Figure 4-17. Adding checked holidays to your Calendar

21 Removing events from your Calendar

If you need to remove a planned event (e.g., seeing a movie) from your Calendar, you'll find it easy to do. Here's how:

1. After connecting to the Internet, enter the Web site address: http://www.aol.com.

2. Click the **Calendar** button on the **AOL Anywhere** Web site. **My Calendar** appears with the current month's appointments and events.

3. Click the **Calendar** tab and then click the **event title** on the calendar itself. By doing this, you'll display the **Appointment Details** window enabling you to change or delete the actual event from your **Calendar**, shown in Figure 4-18.

4. Click the **Delete** button in the **Appointment** or **Event Details** window.

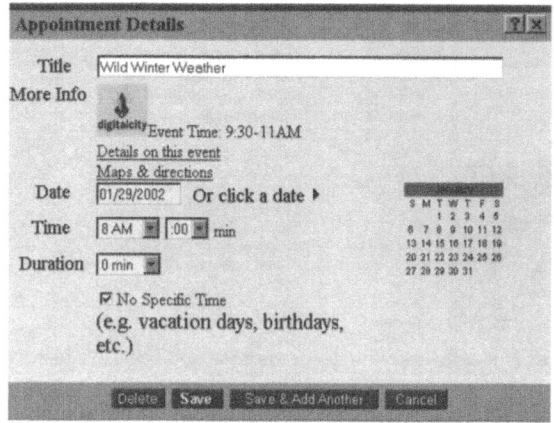

Figure 4-18. Displaying an event in the Appointment Details window before removing it

22 Printing My Calendar

You have three choices as to how you can print your Calendar. My Calendar lets you print your Calendar in Month, Week, or Day view. Individual appointments and appointment notes can also be printed. Here's how to print a month and week view of your calendar.

1. After connecting to the Internet, enter the Web site address: http://www.aol.com.

2. Click the **Calendar** button on the **AOL Anywhere** Web site. **My Calendar** appears with the current month's appointments and events.

Printing a Month View of Your Calendar

1. Click the **Month** tab on your My Calendar window.

2. Click the **Print** button to display the **Printer** dialog box.

3. In the **Printer** dialog box, select the printer and number of copies, and click the **OK** button.

Printing a Week View of Your Calendar

1. Click the **Week** tab located at the top of your **Calendar** window.

2. Click the **Print** button located at the top of your **Calendar** window.

3. In the **Printer** dialog box, select the printer and number of copies, and click the **OK** button.

23 Viewing your calendar with a different date

My Calendar lets you display calendar using the date of your choice quickly and easily. This makes viewing the appointments and events in previous and future months a breeze. Here's how:

1. After connecting to the Internet, enter the Web site address: http://www.aol.com.

2. Click the **Calendar** button on the **AOL Anywhere** Web site. **My Calendar** appears with the current month's appointments and events.

3. Click the back and forward buttons located on either side of the month and year at the top of your **Calendar** to move to the previous month or following month.

4. Click the name of the month and year to display a drop-down menu of choices for month and year. Select the month and year from this list of choices.

5. Your **Calendar** will display the month and year you selected.

24 Notifying others about an event

Whenever an event is added or modified on your Calendar, you can have My Calendar automatically notify others by e-mail. This handy feature makes event notification as easy as 1-2-3. Here's how:

1. After connecting to the Internet, enter the Web site address: `http://www.aol.com`.

2. Click the **Calendar** button on the **AOL Anywhere** Web site. **My Calendar** appears with the current month displayed.

3. Click the desired event on your **Calendar**.

4. Enter the e-mail addresses you want to invite in the **Invite By E-mail:** box on the **Optional** portion of the **Appointment Details.** Click the **Save** button to display the **Send E-mail Notification** window appears, shown in Figure 4-19.

5. Type the e-mail address in the **Send To:** field, add any comments in the **Add Comments:** field, and click the **Send Email** button in the Send E-mail Notification window.

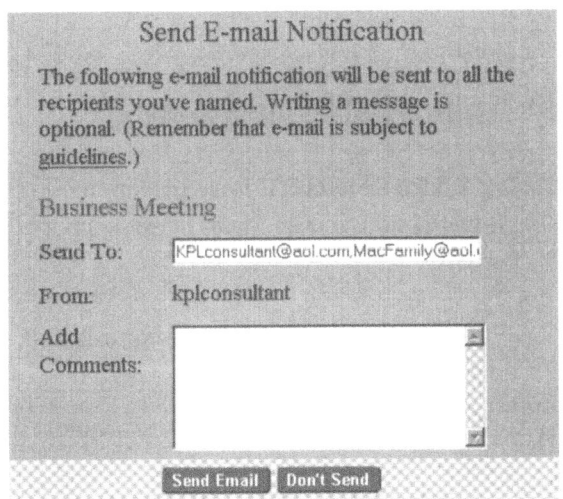

Figure 4-19. Sending an e-mail notification to another e-mail address about an upcoming event

25 Changing the font size on my calendar

You can change the font size your Calendar uses to display text by following these steps:

1. After connecting to the Internet, enter the Web site address: `http://www.aol.com`.

2. Click the **Calendar** button on the **AOL Anywhere** Web site. **My Calendar** appears with the current month displayed.

3. Launch your Internet browser software and select **Text Size** from the drop-down selection list from the **View** menu item. Select the desired text size from the following options: **Largest, Larger, Medium, Smaller,** or **Smallest.**

4. Open My Calendar and make any additional adjustments as necessary by repeating step #3 above.

26 Getting online help with your calendar

Online help is only a few quick mouse clicks away. My Calendar offers many helpful online features, including a My Calendar Help Topics Index with Frequently Asked Questions and My Calendar Guidelines. You can also view an online tour of My Calendar. The Tour describes a few of the features of My Calendar, such as:

- Adding Appointments to your personal calendar

- The Idea List

- The Event Directory

Adding Events from the Event Directory to Your Calendar

Here's how you can access the online help for My Calendar 24/7/365.

1. After connecting to the Internet, enter the Web site address: `http://www.aol.com`.

2. Click the **Calendar** button on the **AOL Anywhere** Web site. **My Calendar** appears with the current month displayed.

3. Click the **Tour & Help** tab on My Calendar. Using the vertical elevator bar, find and select the help topic you're looking for under the **Help Topics** section or begin the tour of **My Calendar** by clicking the **Begin the Tour** button.

AOL Multimedia Features

27 Understanding AOL's Media Player feature

Have you ever wanted to play sound and video files that you found on the Web without first having to download a vast array of additional software? If you answered yes, then AOL's Media Player in the AOL software, Version 7 is for you. AOL provides Media Player as an integrated feature of the AOL software. This means that you don't have to download any other software to play amazing sound and video files.

28 Supported sound and video files

AOL's Media Player supports the following formats:

Sound

WAV
MIDI
MP3*, including MP1, MP2
PLS, M3U playlists
Shoutcast, receipt/playback of streaming MP3
Secure MS Audio & Windows Media (WMA)

Video

AVI
MPEG video

Sound/Video

Real Media* MPEG Layer-3 audio decoding technology is licensed from Fraunhofer IIS and THOMSON multimedia. Supply of this product conveys a license for private, non-commercial use only.

29 Playing sound files stored on your PC

Playing an audio file with AOL is easy. Follow these simple instructions to hear Media Player supported file formats:

1. Turn your computer's volume control to an acceptable level.

2. Select **Open** from the **File** menu located above the AOL toolbar.

3. Locate the desired file stored on your PC using the **Open a File** dialog box.

4. Select the file and click the **Open** button in the **Open a File** dialog box.

5. Click the **Play** button (big round button) on the **AOL Media Player** window to begin playing the sound file, shown in Figure 4-20.

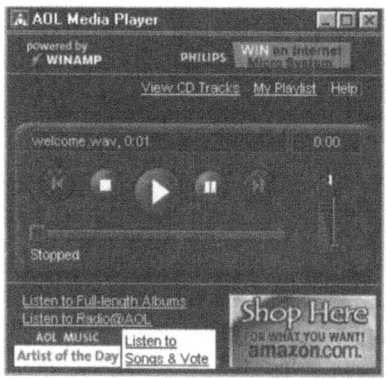

Figure 4-20. Displaying the AOL Media Player(SM) window with various control buttons

30 Playing video files stored on your PC

Playing a video file with AOL is easy. Follow these simple instructions to hear Media Player-supported file formats:

1. Turn your computer's volume control to an acceptable level.

2. Select **Open** from the **File** menu located above the AOL toolbar.

3. Locate the file stored on your PC using the **Open a File** dialog box.

4. Select the file and click the **Open** button in the **Open a File** dialog box.

5. Click the **Play** button (a big round button) on the **AOL Media Player** window

31 Playing audio files in a specific order using My Playlist(SM)

Create and listen to your own personal music library with all your favorite tunes anytime you like. Being able to play your audio files in any specific order requires first creating a My Playlist(SM) and then adding one or more audio files to it. Here's how it's done.

Creating and Adding Files to a Playlist

1. Select **Open** from the **File** menu located above the AOL toolbar.

2. Locate the file stored on your PC using the **Open a File** dialog box.

3. Click **My Playlist** on the AOL Media Player window.

4. Click the **Add Item** button on the AOL Playlist Editor window to add a file to a playlist, shown in Figure 4-21.

5. Locate the files you want to add to your playlist, select each file (multiple files are selected by holding down the **CTRL** key while selecting), and click the **Open** button.

6. Save the playlist consisting of the files you've selected so you can hear them again by clicking the **Save** button on the **AOL Playlist Editor** window.

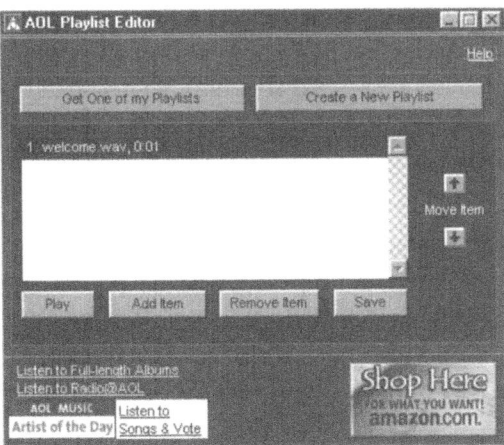

Figure 4-21. Adding a file in the AOL Playlist Editor window

32 Downloading audio and video files from the Web

As you surf the Web you'll frequently discover cool sites that offer an assortment of audio and video files that can be downloaded. This not only is a fun way to build or expand your library of sounds and movie clips, but can be great entertainment for personal use as well. But before you begin downloading, it's worth checking to see if your computer system will properly handle these files after they've been downloaded.

More often than not, files on the Web are compressed in order to save time during download. You'll be able to tell when your download is in compressed format because the file name will end in .ZIP for PC files and .SIT for Macintosh files. America Online software does not automatically uncompress your files for you unless specific download preferences are set. Here's how to verify how your preferences are set and, if necessary, how to customize the settings:

1. Click the **Settings** menu on the AOL toolbar, and select **Preferences** from the drop-down menu items.

2. In the **Preferences** window, click **Download** under the **Organization** section.

3. In the **Download Preferences** window, the available options for decompressing ZIP files are displayed:

   - When I download them

   - When I sign off

   - Do not decompress

4. **Select** the option which best meets your needs for decompressing downloaded files and click the **Save** button.

Once you've verified that your computer system will uncompress downloaded files from the Web, you're ready to proceed with the download process. Here's how:

1. Locate the Web page that contains the link to the **audio** or **video file** you want to download.

2. Click the link to the desired file. A **Save As** dialog box appears allowing you to navigate to the desired folder on your hard drive so you can save the downloaded file.

3. Click the **OK** button to initiate the download process.

33 Managing your audio file playlists

Managing your audio file playlists involves being able to reorder the files in a playlist as well as removing unwanted files from it. Each is important, because it lets you control the selection of sounds based on what your interests are. Here's how it works.

Reordering a Playlist

1. Select **Open** from the **File** menu located above the AOL toolbar.

2. Locate the folder stored on your PC that contains the playlist using the **Open a File** dialog box.

3. Open the playlist by double-clicking it.

4. Select an audio file to move in the **AOL Media Player** window.

5. Click either the **up** or **down arrow** located to the right of the list of files to move the selected file up or down the playlist.

6. Click the **Save** button.

Removing an Audio File from a Playlist

1. Select **Open** from the **File** menu located above the AOL toolbar.

2. Locate the folder stored on your PC that contains the playlist using the **Open a File** dialog box.

3. Open the playlist by double-clicking it.

4. Click **My Playlist** from the **AOL Media Player** window.

5. Select the audio file you want removed from the playlist, and click the **Remove Item** button in the **AOL Media Player** window.

6. Click the **Save** button.

Online Pictures with AOL

34 Accessing Picture Finder

Picture Finder makes looking for and viewing your personal library of pictures or images a simple task. You'll be able to create an electronic photo album for the whole family to enjoy. Follow these steps to access Picture Finder:

1. On the **File** menu, click **Open Picture Finder** from the drop-down list.

2. Locate your personal library (or folder) of images on your computer system by navigating to folders containing images using the **Open Picture Gallery** dialog box.

3. Click the **Open Gallery** button in the **Open Picture Gallery** dialog box to open the **Picture Gallery** window. The gallery automatically displays six images per page, shown in Figure 4-22.

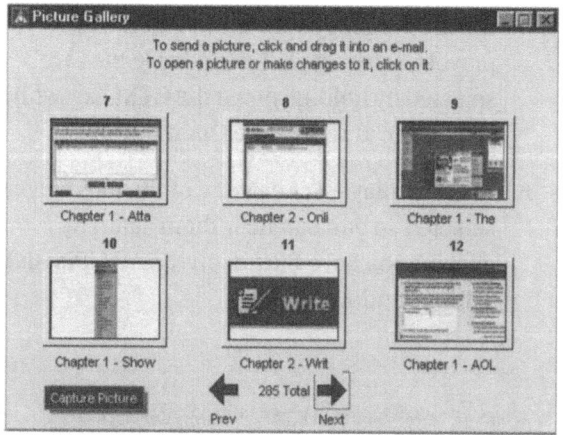

Figure 4-22. Displaying six images at one time with AOL's Picture Gallery window

35 Viewing pictures with Picture Finder

Viewing pictures with Picture Finder is a snap. Not only will it be fun for you and the whole family, you'll be able to view six pictures or images on your screen at one time. Here's how:

1. On the **File** menu, click **Open Picture Finder** from the drop-down list.

2. Locate your personal library (or folder) of images on your computer system.

3. Click the **Open Gallery** button in the **Open Picture Gallery** dialog box to open the **Picture Gallery** window. The gallery automatically displays six images per page.

4. Click the **right arrow** to view the next set of six pictures or images or the **left arrow** button to view the previous set of six pictures or images.

5. To view a single picture separately, select the picture or image you want to use.

36 Editing pictures with Picture Finder

Editing a picture has never been easier than with Picture Finder. You'll be able to rotate the picture, flip the picture horizontally or vertically, zoom in or out, select and crop the picture, increase or decrease the contrast, brighten or dim the picture, invert the picture, or convert the picture to gray scale. Here's how you can edit any picture quickly and easily:

1. On the **File** menu, click **Open Picture Finder** from the drop-down list.

2. Locate your personal library (or folder) of images on your computer system.

3. Click the **Open Gallery** button in the **Open Picture Gallery** dialog box to open the **Picture Gallery** window. The gallery automatically displays six images per page.

4. Click the **right arrow** to view the next set of 6 pictures or images or the **left arrow** button to view the previous set of six pictures or images.

5. Click the picture you want to edit and begin the editing process by clicking one or more of the icons above the picture, shown in Figure 4-23.

6. Click the **Save** button when you've finished editing the picture.

Figure 4-23. Viewing AOL's Picture Finder image editing tools toolbar

37 Understanding Capture Picture

Capture Picture allows you to take pictures directly from your computer's digital camera and save the pictures to your hard drive. This is a handy feature that enables you to easily send saved pictures via e-mail to friends and family members.

38 Saving pictures on your computer

The process of saving pictures to your computer's hard drive is similar to downloading audio and video files. As you surf the Web you'll frequently discover cool sites that offer an assortment of picture files that you'll want to save. But before you begin saving, it's worth checking to see if your computer system will properly handle these files after they've been downloaded.

Often, files on the Web are compressed in order to save time and space during the download process. You'll be able to tell when your download is in compressed format because the file name will end in .ZIP for PC files and .SIT for Macintosh files. America Online software does not automatically uncompress your files for you unless specific download preferences are set. Here's how to verify that your preferences are set properly and how to customize the settings, if necessary.

1. Click the **Settings** menu on the AOL toolbar, and select **Preferences** from the drop-down menu items.

2. In the **Preferences** window, click **Download** under the **Organization** section.

3. In the **Download Preferences** window, the available options for decompressing ZIP files are displayed:

   - When I download them

   - When I sign off

   - Do not decompress

4. Select the option which best meets your needs for decompressing downloaded files and click the **Save** button.

Once you've verified that your computer system will uncompress downloaded files from the

Web, you're ready to proceed with saving pictures to your hard drive. Here's how it's done:

1. Locate the Web page that contains the link to the picture file you want to save.

2. Click the link to the desired file. A **Save As** dialog box appears allowing you to navigate to the desired folder on your hard drive so you can save the downloaded file.

3. Click the **OK** button to initiate the save process.

39 Adjusting picture quality with Capture Picture

If you have a digital camera connected to your computer, you can take advantage of the ability to adjust a picture's quality with Capture Picture. Here's how it works:

1. On the **Edit** menu, click **Capture Picture** from the drop-down list.

2. Click the **Settings** button from the **Capture** window.

3. Select the type of adjustment you want to make from the available options, (e.g., zoom). You'll want to review your camera's specific features by reading the manual that came with your camera before using this feature.

CHAPTER 5

Searching and Finding Information

THIS CHAPTER EXPLORES all the marvelous tools that are available to help you find information on AOL, the Internet, and public and private databases all around the world. You'll be thrilled when you discover those nuggets of information and diamonds in the rough with powerful and easy-to-use search tools. Learn how to use AOL Search to perform simple and advanced searches, access the AOL White and Yellow Pages to locate people and businesses, and delve into the People Directory to find other AOL members with similar interests. Also, you'll find how you can explore popular FTP sites to tap into a wealth of information including art, games, history, images, news, sounds, and so much more right at your fingertips.

In this chapter, you will learn how to

📖 Search databases and folders

📖 Use the AOL White and Yellow Pages

📖 Explore the classifieds

📖 Get to know the People Directory

📖 Understand FTP

Searching Databases and Folders

1 Making AOL your default Internet browser

Here are a few helpful hints to help you decide whether you'll want to make AOL your default Internet browser.

- You'll only be able to assign one default Internet browser under the Microsoft Windows® operating system.

- Selecting AOL as your default Internet browser makes accessing AOL services and features easy to use.

- If you've decided on another default Internet browser, you can always change your mind and go back to AOL—just follow the steps in the next tip.

2 Changing your default Internet software

AOL makes it easy to change your default Internet browser for reading e-mail, viewing Web pages, and reading newsgroups. If you set another Internet browser as your default, you can easily change the settings back to make AOL the default Internet browser. Here's how:

1. Click **Preferences** from the AOL **Settings** menu on the AOL toolbar.

2. Click **Associations** from the **Accounts Control** section of the Preferences window.

3. To make America Online your default Internet browser for your e-mail, Web browsing, and newsgroup needs, click the **OK** button on the **Association Preferences** dialog box.

3 Searching the Filing Cabinet

As the number and size of folders and files in your Filing Cabinet grows, you may need to use a search tool to find the things you've stored in them. AOL provides a simple way of finding whatever it is you want by following these steps:

1. Click **Filing Cabinet** from the **File** menu located above the AOL toolbar.

2. Click the **Find** button at the bottom of the **Filing Cabinet** window to open the Search window.

3. Enter your search criteria (for example, **meeting**) in the **Search** window, choose the Scope Of Search and Type Of Search, and click the **Find Next** button, as shown in Figure 5-1.

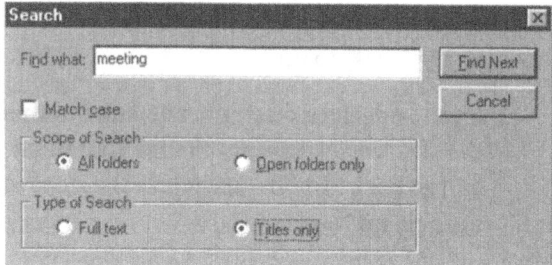

Figure 5-1. Filing Cabinet Search window

4 Searching open Filing Cabinet folders

You can have AOL search only those folders in your Filing Cabinet that are opened by following these easy steps:

1. Click **Filing Cabinet** from the **File** menu located above the AOL toolbar.

2. Click the **Find** button at the bottom of the **Filing Cabinet** window to open the **Search** window.

3. Enter your search criteria (for example, **meeting**) in the **Search** window, and click the **Open folders only** radio button in the **Scope of Search** section.

4. Click the **Find Next** button.

5 Using a title search to search all Filing Cabinet folders

You can instruct AOL to search all your Filing Cabinet folders using a title search by following these easy steps:

1. Click **Filing Cabinet** from the **File** menu located above the AOL toolbar.

2. Click the **Find** button at the bottom of the **Filing Cabinet** window to open the **Search** window.

3. Enter your search criteria (for example, **meeting**) in the **Search** window, click the **All folders** radio button in the **Scope of Search** section, and click the **Titles only** radio button in the **Type of Search** section.

4. Click the **Find Next** button.

6 Locating downloaded files

It's easy to misplace downloaded files, but you can have AOL locate them for you with the AOL Download Manager. It's easy to locate your downloaded files. Here's how:

1. Click **Download Manager** from the **File** menu located above the AOL toolbar.

2. Click the **Show Files Downloaded** button from the **Download Manager** window, which is shown in Figure 5-2.

3. Select the file you want located on your computer.

4. Click the **Locate** button to access the file.

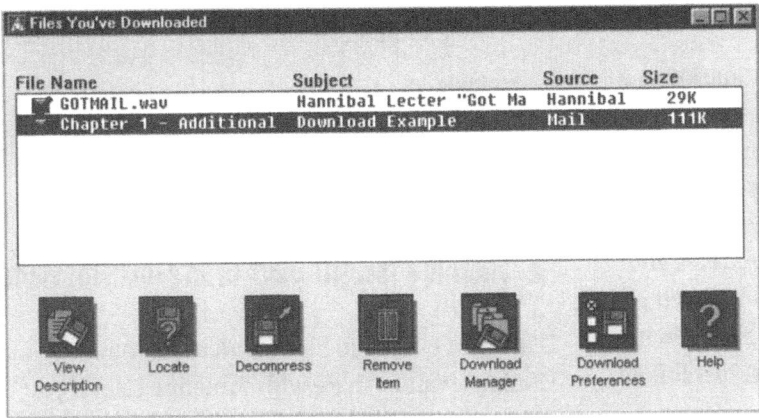

Figure 5-2. Viewing the Files You've Downloaded on the Download Manager

7 Creating a Favorite Places folder

As you search and discover new places with America Online, you're going to want to save some of these discoveries for safekeeping. AOL lets you save your favorite destinations in your own Favorite Places folder on your hard drive. You may even want to create additional folders to help manage your Favorite Places, especially as they grow in number over time. To create one or more additional folders, just follow these simple steps:

1. Click the **heart** icon button located on the AOL toolbar.

2. Click the **New** button in the **Favorite Places** window.

3. Click the **New Folder** radio button and enter the new folder's name in the **Enter the New Folder's Name** text box, shown in Figure 5-3.

4. Click the **OK** button.

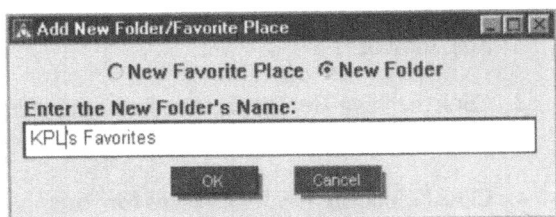

Figure 5-3. Creating a new folder with the Add New Folder/Favorite Place window

8 Bookmarking a favorite place

A bookmark is a convenient way to mark your page in a book to allow easy return at a later time. You can mark or save a Web site address in a similar way by adding a favorite Web destination to a storage area on your hard drive called a favorite place folder. Here's how it's done:

1. Navigate to the Web site you like.

2. Click **Add Top Window to Favorites** from the **Favorites** menu located on the AOL toolbar.

3. Click **Add to Favorites** in the dialog box that appears, shown in Figure 5-4.

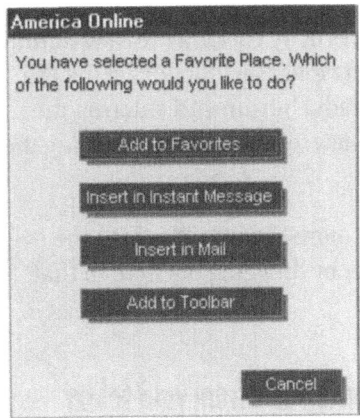

Figure 5-4. Saving a bookmark to a favorite Web destination is as easy as 1-2-3.

9 Returning to your Favorite Places

The ability to return to a favorite destination at a later time is one of the handy features offered by AOL and other Web browsers. With hundreds of millions of Web destinations in cyberspace, you'll want an easy way to bookmark all those cool sites so you can return whenever the urge strikes you. That's the reason your Web browser allows you to save your Favorite Places in the first place. So how do you return to your Favorite Places? Just follow these steps:

1. Click the **heart** icon button located on the AOL toolbar.

2. Double-click your favorite place from the displayed list to return to it.

10 Organizing your Favorite Places

As the number of your Favorite Places increase, you'll need a way to organize all those addresses. This will help prevent bookmark overload. Without the ability to organize your Favorite Places, you'd undoubtedly waste a lot of time searching for the things that matter to you. This is why AOL provides all the tools you'll need to begin organizing all those Web site addresses. Here's how:

1. Click the **heart** icon button located on the AOL toolbar.

2. Create one or more folders to store your Favorite Places in by clicking the **New** button in the **Favorite Places** window, clicking the **New Folder** radio button and entering the name of the new folder, and then clicking the **OK** button.

3. Move one or more Favorite Places to the desired folder by dragging the item to that folder.

11 Deleting a favorite place from your folder

When you no longer want or need a favorite place in your folder, you can delete it with a couple clicks of your mouse. Here's how:

1. Click the **heart** icon button located on the AOL toolbar.

2. Click the favorite place item you want deleted in the **Favorite Places** window.

3. Click the **Delete** button.

12 Sharing a favorite place in an e-mail message

Have you ever found a cool Web site that you couldn't wait to share with someone else? If you have, then you'll appreciate this AOL feature. Instead of typing the address of the Web site by hand into an e-mail message and possibly making a typo or two, just follow these simple steps:

1. Click the **heart** icon located in the top right corner of the Web site you'd like to share.

2. Click the **Insert in Mail** button to display AOL's Write Mail window. The Web address or hyperlink is added directly into the e-mail message.

3. Complete the **Send To:**, **Copy To:**, and send your message as usual.

13 Copying your Favorite Places to another screen name or computer

Have you ever thought about copying your Favorite Places to another screen name? Or wouldn't it be nice to copy your favorites from your home computer to your laptop? AOL lets you transfer all your Favorite Places in just a few steps. Here's how:

1. Select the screen name or computer from which you want to copy your Favorite Places.

2. Click the **heart** icon button located on the AOL toolbar.

3. Click the **Save/Replace** button in the **Favorite Places** window.

4. Click **Select the Favorite Places for your current screen name** radio button, and click the OK button.

5. Enter the desired location and name to save the favorites file in the **Save Folder** window, and click the **Save** button. If you want to copy your Favorites to another computer, then you'll need a blank diskette.

✏ *The file extension for the Favorites file is .pfc.*

14 Replacing your Favorite Places on another screen name or computer

After copying your Favorite Places from one screen name or computer, you're now ready to copy it to another. Here's how it's done:

1. Select the screen name or computer to which you want to copy your Favorite Places.

2. Click the **heart** icon button located on the AOL toolbar.

3. Click the **Save/Replace** button in the **Favorite Places** window.

4. Click **Select the Favorite Places for your current screen name** radio button, and click the **OK** button.

5. Enter the desired location and name to restore the favorites file in the **Select File to Restore** window, and click the **Open** button.

Using Search Engines, Directories, and Hybrids

15 Understanding the difference between search engines and directories

Do you know the difference between a directory and a search engine? And what is a hybrid? If you don't, you're not alone. The fact is that most people are unfamiliar with the available search tools on the Web. You may have used AOL Search, or Yahoo, or even AltaVista. But are there others?

Conservative estimates put the number of search sites on the Web at a staggering 8,000 and with the number expected to grow. You may be wondering why so many are needed, or better yet, which one will best meet your needs. The answer depends on a number of factors including what you're looking for and how much time you have to refine your search. It's been determined that no search site has clear superiority in every way, so it makes sense to bookmark several sites, especially the ones you're most comfortable with. Let's look at the features and differences between search engines, directories, and hybrids.

A search engine uses automated software to collect and index the full text of pages that are found. Search engines rely heavily on crawling, collecting, and indexing text on the Web. In contrast, directories rely more on humans to sift through Web pages by hand to categorize sites by subject while eliminating the inappropriate sites. This human element is central to a directory, because nothing gets into it unless first approved by an editor. Hybrid sites often use features of both a search engine and a directory. For example, a hybrid site may first pass your search to a directory, and then pass the results from the directory to a search engine for processing.

Table 5-1 lists a few search engines, directories, and hybrids that are worth your time trying out:

Table 5.1 Top Search Engines, Directories, and Hybrids

SEARCH SITE	EASE OF USE
AOL Search http://aolsearch.aol.com/	Excellent
AltaVista http://www.altavista.com/	Good
Excite http://www.excite.com	Good
Google http://www.google.com/	Excellent
Lycos http://www.lycos.com/	Good

Table 5.1 Top Search Engines, Directories, and Hybrids (Continued)

SEARCH SITE	EASE OF USE
Northern Light http://northernlight.com/	Good
Yahoo http://www.yahoo.com/	Good

16 Using AOL Search

There is an incredible amount of stuff on the Internet. Some of this stuff is good, but much of it is fluff. That's what makes the Internet so wonderful, and at the same time so overwhelming. To display AOL's Search Web site, simply click the **Search** button located on the right below the AOL toolbar. When you're using America Online, it's crucial to know how to properly use the AOL Search Web site, shown in Figure 5-5. AOL Search provides several useful features to help you find what you're looking for. These features include

- Search box

- Search categories

- Other search tools

- Hot searches

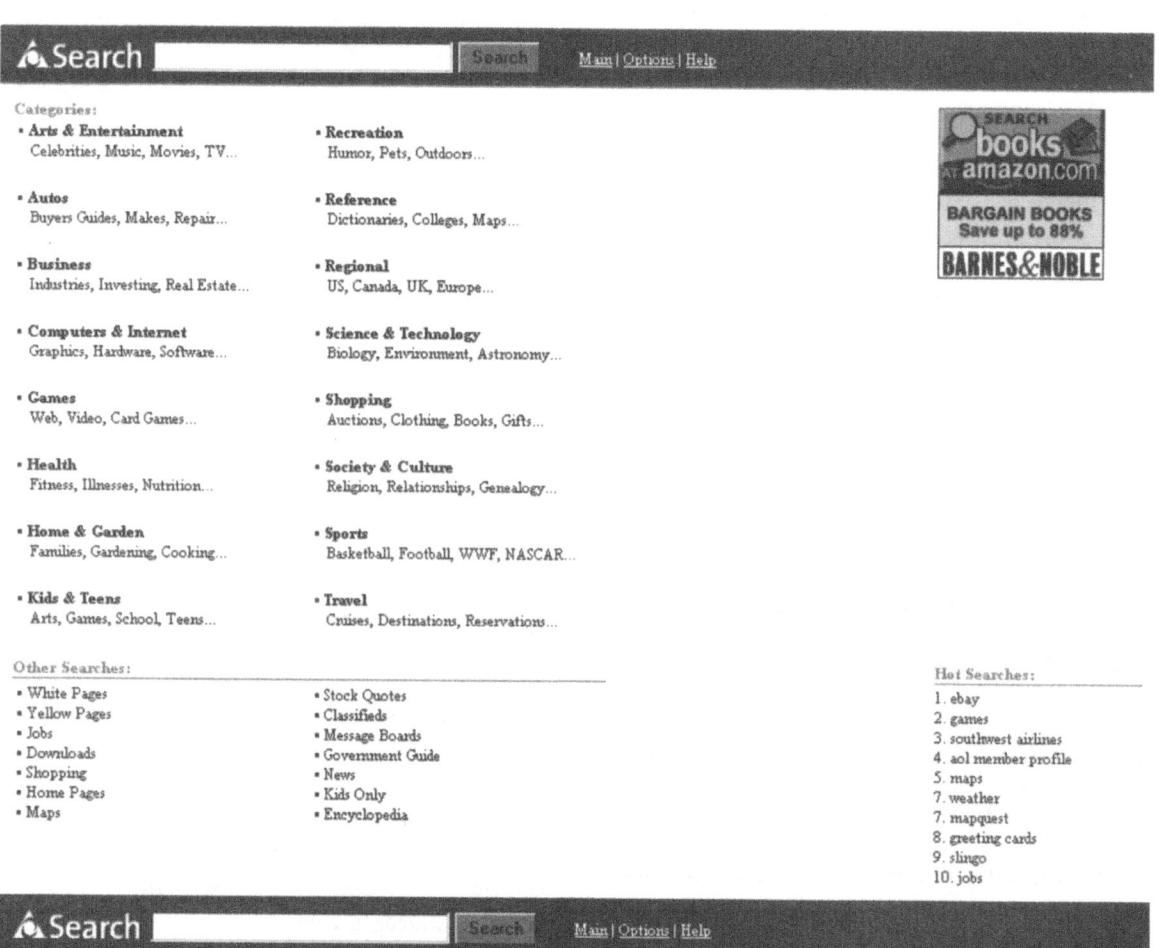

Figure 5-5. Searching is easy with AOL's Search Web site.

17 Finding what you're searching for– useful search tips

Searching on the Internet is not only a necessity—it's a way of life. It's the best way to quickly find the most likely sources of information. But there are a few things you'll want to keep in mind when using with AOL Search.

- Read the instructions included on the site about how to use AOL Search most effectively. Become familiar with the search engine's features and capabilities.

- Be specific—use **multiple keywords** that aren't likely to appear on irrelevant pages.

- Use **quotation marks** (" ") to find an exact match of the keywords used in your search. The words must appear in the exact order that they are specified.

- Save or **bookmark** intermediate pages so you can locate later what you found.

- Click the **Options** button on the AOL Search Web site to further narrow your search criteria.

- On the AOL Search: Search Options page, seen in Figure 5-6, choose What words should be used by clicking one of the following options:

- Any of these words

- All of these words

- Exact phrase

18 Narrowing your search results with Boolean search operators

If you've tried the tips suggested in Tip #17 and are still getting way too many useless or irrelevant results—it's time to try Boolean operators when searching. The term Boolean operator is a fancy way of saying AND, OR, and NOT. Here's how they work:

AND—Searches for all the keywords or search terms. For example, **football AND scores** finds pages on which both words appear. If you leave a space between keywords, AOL Search automatically adds an AND.

OR—Searches any keywords or search terms. For example, **football OR scores** finds pages which have either word, but not necessarily both.

NOT—Excludes keywords or search terms. For example, **football NOT scores** finds pages on which the word football appears but the word scores does not appear.

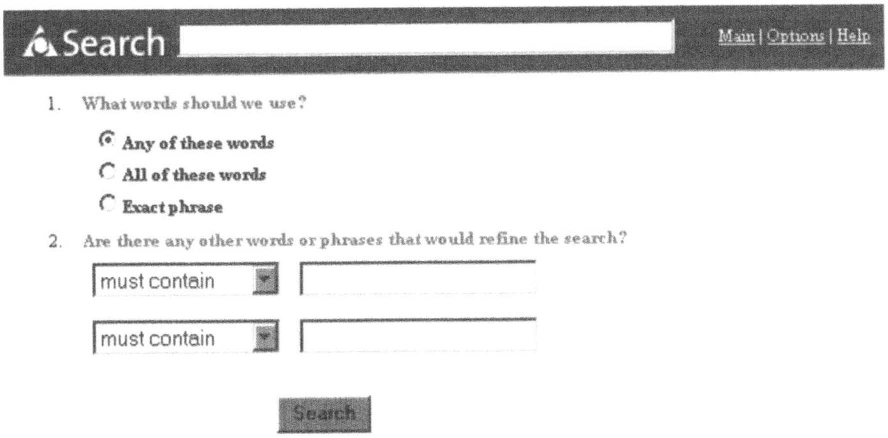

Figure 5-6. Using AOL's Search: Search options for powerful searching

19 Using advanced search operators

Here are a few additional advanced operators that, when correctly used, should improve your search results:

Parentheses ( )—Use parentheses to group search expressions. For example, **(miami dolphins or dolphins)** finds information containing either Miami Dolphins or Dolphins.

W/n—Use the proximity operator to search for information where the right keyword occurs within a specified number of words after the left word. In order to specify the number of words, replace the "n" with the number of words away the keywords can be from each other. For example, **miami W/1 dolphins** finds information where the keyword dolphins occurs within 1 word after Miami.

NEAR—Use the NEAR operator to search for information where the keywords are near each other but the order doesn't matter. For example, **miami near dolphins** finds information containing both words near each other in any order.

?—Searches the keyword using the wildcard operator. For example, **dolphin?** finds information containing the words *dolphin* and *dolphins.*

20 Searching by search categories

AOL's Search Web site provides a variety of search categories. These are best used when you're able to identify the topic area of your search. For example, if you were looking for information on **movies**, you'd probably concentrate your search in the **Arts & Entertainment** category. Here's a list of the different search categories AOL Search provides:

Arts & Entertainment	Recreation
Autos	Reference
Business	Regional
Computers & Internet	Science & Technology
Games	Shopping
Health	Society & Culture
Home & Garden	Sports
Kids & Teens	Travel
News	

21 Other AOL search categories

AOL's Search Web site also provides a variety of other search categories. These are most often used when you want to expand your search using a variety of specific types of tools. For example, if you were looking for information on employment opportunities in the Northwest of the U.S., you might want to begin your search by clicking Jobs in the Other Searches category. Here's a list of the other search categories AOL Search provides:

White Pages	Stock Quotes
Yellow Pages	Classifieds
Jobs	Message Boards
Downloads	Government Guide
Shopping	News
Home Pages	Kids Only
Maps	Encyclopedia

22 Top 10 AOL searches

AOL's Search Web site lists the 10 hottest search topics for your searching pleasure. These change depending on who and what is in vogue at any particular time. So check the AOL Search Web site from time to time to get the updated list. Here's the list the last time I accessed it:

Slingo	Eminem
Britney Spears	Jokes
Maps	Tickets
Greeting Cards	Scooters
Jobs	Weather

23 Using search engines and directories outside of AOL—Do you Yahoo or Google?

You've undoubtedly heard about Yahoo, but how about Google? Both provide the virtues of being a directory as well as a search engine. This melding of features provides a "best-of-both-worlds" scenario. So what are the features that a Yahoo or a Google provide users?

Yahoo and Google Features

Google http://www.google.com/	Very easy to use and returns relevant results. Results are returned from a directory and search engine. There are over 1 billion pages that have been indexed.
Yahoo http://www.yahoo.com/	Very easy to use and returns results from directory and search engine.

24 Searching message boards

Have you ever wanted to find message boards to share your interests with others? There are numerous message boards to choose from all over AOL. With subjects from aardvark to Zulu and everything in between, AOL probably has a message board for you to share your thoughts and ideas with others. The wonderful feature of AOL's message boards is that messages are posted for others to read and respond to and often remain on the boards for months.

So how do you find a particular message board? Click the Keyword button located at the top of your screen and enter AOL Keyword **Message Board**, and click the Go button. AOL provides two handy search tools: Quick Search and Custom Search to help you get the best results from your search. For example, say you're a sailing enthusiast who wants to share your recent sailing experiences with others. You could begin your search for message boards that have something to do with sailing, as you see in Figures 5-7 and 5-8 by entering a search word or phrase, selecting the language option (English, French, and German), and clicking the Search button. The results from the search would display all the different subjects and board names related to your search request, as you see in Figure 5-9. Along with each search result, AOL assigns a score (a percentage from 1 to 100) to indicate how well the message board matches your search criteria and orders them from highest to lowest score.

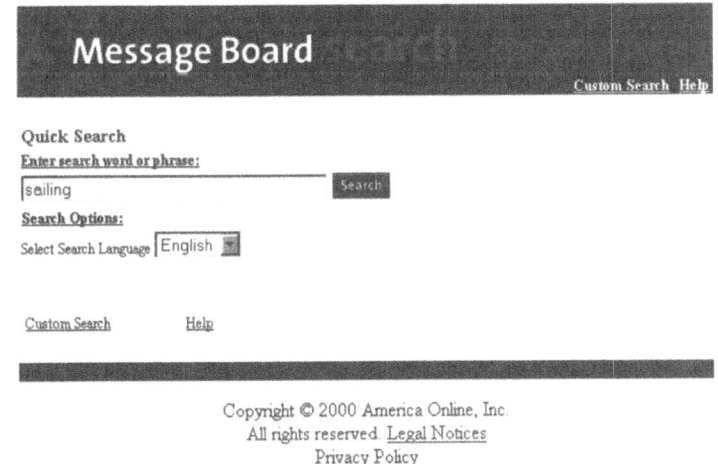

Figure 5-7 Using AOL's Message Board Quick Search is fast and easy.

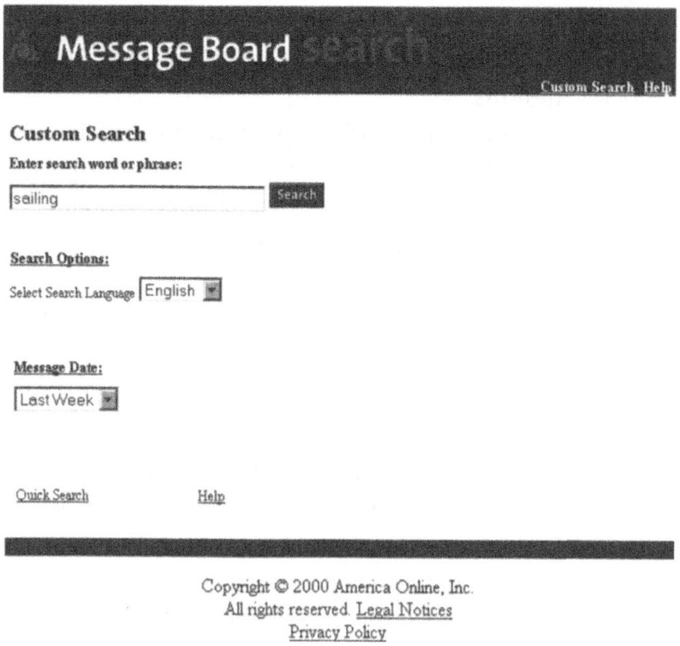

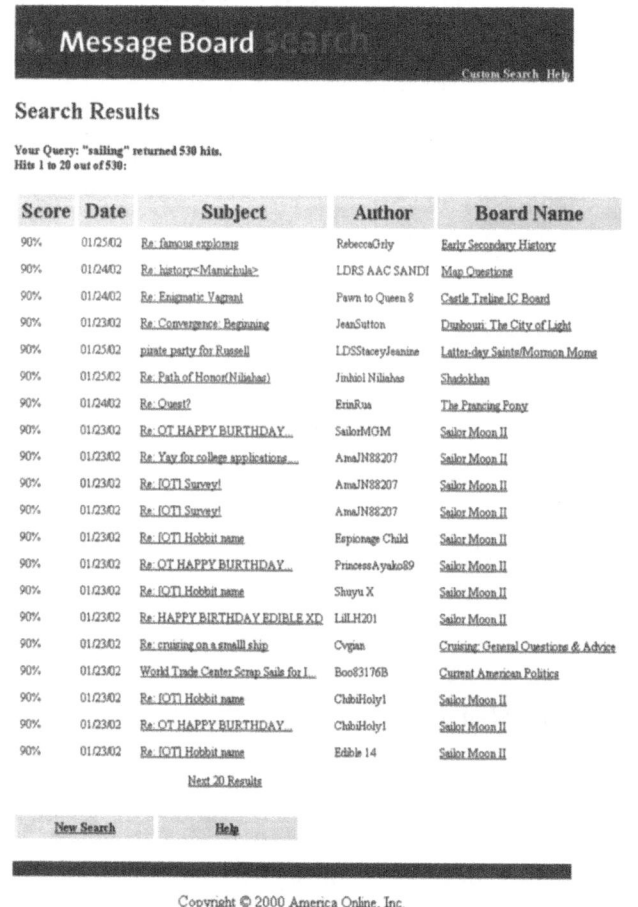

Figure 5-8. Accessing AOL's Message Board Custom Search by message date

Figure 5-9. Viewing search results with AOL's Message Board Search Web site

25 Searching online for software

Are you looking to purchase software for your home or business? Then why not use AOL's online search tools to help? You'll find a nicely organized and categorized list of software products and tools to choose from. Here's how:

1. Click the **Keyword** button.

2. Type **AOL Search** in the **Keyword** dialog box and click the **Go** button.

3. Click **Software** under the **Computers & Internet** category in the AOL Search window.

4. Choose the type of software you'd like to further explore from the list of software sub-categories.

26 Finding shareware files and programs

If you're looking for shareware files and programs, then AOL Search can provide thousands of shareware sub-categories for you to choose from. Here's how:

1. Click the **Keyword** button.

2. Type **AOL Search** in the **Keyword** dialog box and click the **Go** button.

3. Select **Software** under the **Computers & Internet** category in the AOL Search window.

4. Select **Shareware** from the list of software sub-categories.

5. Select the Shareware sub-category that you'd like to further explore, as you see in Figure 5-10.

27 Searching online for books

Are you searching for a few great books to read? Use AOL's online search tools to help. You'll find thousands of books in such categories as art, collecting, business, children, fiction, health, history, home and garden, music, mysteries, poetry, sports, travel, and much more. Here's how:

1. Click the **Keyword** button.

2. Type **AOL Search** in the **Keyword** dialog box and click the **Go** button.

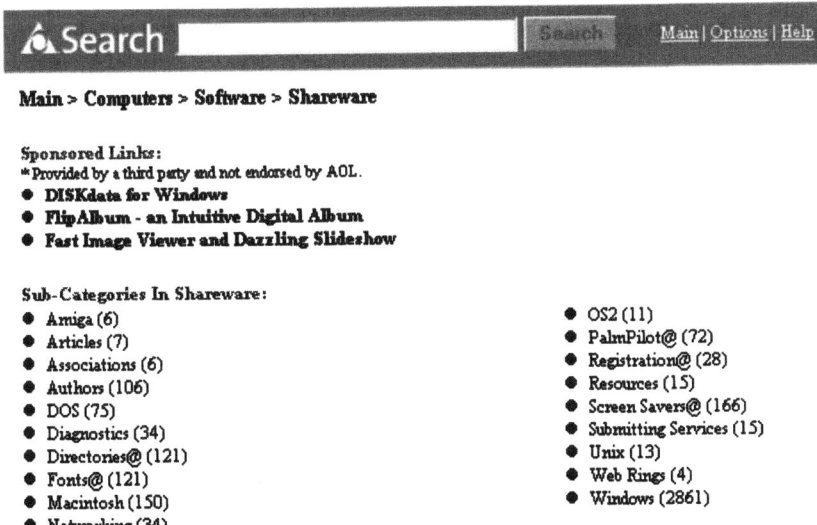

Figure 5-10. Searching for shareware files in AOL's Search: Shareware Sub-Categories

3. Select **Books** under the **Shopping** category in the AOL Search window.

4. Choose the type of software you'd like to further explore from the list of software sub-categories.

28 Finding science journals and magazines

Are you looking for the current issue of your favorite science journal or magazine? Use AOL's online search tools to help find it right from the convenience of your home or office. Here's how:

1. Click the **Keyword** button.

2. Type **AOL Search** in the **Keyword** dialog box and click the **Go** button.

3. Select the **Science & Technology** category in the AOL **Search** window.

4. Select **Publications** from the list of Science sub-categories in the **AOL Search: Science** page.

5. Select **Journals and Magazines** from the list of Publications sub-categories in the **AOL Search: Science>Publications** page.

6. Choose the list of journal and magazine you'd like to explore from the list of sub-categories.

29 Shopping anyone?

AOL's Search Web site provides the ultimate online shopping experience with numerous categories containing everything from antiques to weddings. Here's a list of the different search categories AOL Search provides. If these don't whet your appetite and get you jump-started, nothing will.

Antiques & Collectibles	Jewelry
Auctions	Music
Autos	Niche
Book	Office Products

Children	Pets
Classifieds	Photography
Clothing	Publications
Computers	Recreation &
Consumer Electronics	Religious
Crafts	Retailers
Directories	Sports
Entertainment	Tobacco
Ethnic & Regional	Tools
Flowers	Toys & Games
Food	Travel
Furniture	Vehicles
Gifts	Visual Arts
Hobbies	Weddings
Health & Beauty	Wholesale
Holidays	
Home & Garden	

30 Getting to know the other sites in the shopping category

Here are a few other cool sites in the Shopping category especially designed for the "Shop 'til you drop" shopper to explore. Shop and have fun!

Other Sites in the Shopping Category

KEYWORD	DESCRIPTION
AOL Rewards	Shop and earn points
Message Board	AOL Shopping channel board
Catalog City	Shop at dozens of online stores
Deals Newsletter	Free newsletter for the latest sales
DealTime	Comparison shop online
eLuxury	Shop online for luxury items

Other Sites in the Shopping Category (Continued)

KEYWORD	DESCRIPTION
Respond.com	Interactive shopping service
Shopping	Find merchant by category
Quick Checkout	Shop online—highest security
Shopping List	Create personalized wish list
Shopping Help	Customer service related questions
Shop@ICQ	Shop for special products recommended by ICQ

Using the AOL White and Yellow Pages

31 Searching the AOL White Pages

If you're looking for a phone number, street address, or e-mail address of a long-lost family member or friend, then the AOL White Pages can help. By using the White Pages you can stop those expensive calls to directory assistance. The AOL White Pages is your single source for names, street addresses, phone numbers, e-mail addresses, neighborhood maps, driving directions, and much more. Here's how you search the White Pages:

1. Click **White Pages** from the **People** menu on the AOL toolbar.

2. Enter the last name of the individual you're looking for and, if possible, the first name, city, state/province, and country, as you see in Figure 5-11.

3. Click the **Find** button.

32 Searching the White Pages

Here are a few tips to keep in mind when using the AOL White Pages search tool. Not only will they help you find who you're looking for, it's easy to use, too. Just keep these simple tips in mind:

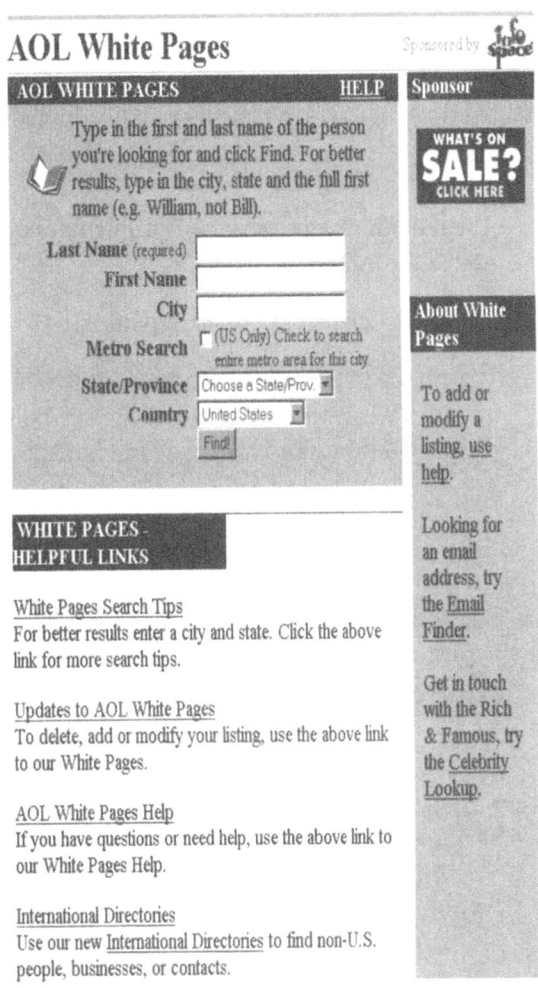

Figure 5-11. The AOL White Pages

1. Verify your spelling accuracy as you enter the person's last name, which is required, and their first name.

2. The City field is optional, but if you enter it make sure you avoid any abbreviations; for example, type **New York City** instead of **NYC**.

3. The State/Province field is optional, but if you enter it make sure you enter the correct spelling or two-letter abbreviation, such as **CA** or **California**.

4. Make sure you select the country where the person currently resides from the list of selections.

33 Finding celebrities

The AOL White Pages is a great way to find the street address, city, state, zip, and e-mail address for many of your favorite celebrities. Here's how:

1. Click **White Pages** from the **People** menu on the AOL toolbar.

2. Click the **Celebrity Lookup** hyperlink.

3. As you see in Figure 5-12, enter the full name of the celebrity you're looking for (for example, Oprah Winfrey), and click the **Find** button.

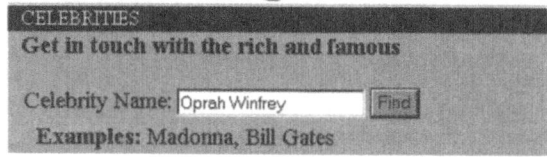

Figure 5-12. Finding the rich and famous with AOL's White Pages—Celebrity Search

You can combine the AOL White Pages search with AOL Search results for even more information on your favorite celebrities. Click the Arts & Entertainment sub-category Celebrities on the AOL Search site. You'll be amazed how much you'll find—all the latest gossip, photos, and news. You can also access fan clubs, memorabilia, message boards, and chat rooms for added fun.

34 Adding your listing to the AOL White Pages

Would you like to be listed in the AOL White Pages? You can be by completing a simple online form at this Web site address: http://www.infospace.com/ aolwp.aols/kmaint/kdbadd.html
Just complete the form, shown in Figure 5-13, and any optional information that you'd like to provide, and click the **Add Listing** button at the bottom of the form. You'll receive an e-mail message reply from InfoSpace (the company that powers the AOL White Pages) verifying the information you provided. Your listing will then be added to the AOL White Pages and E-mail Finder on AOL.com.

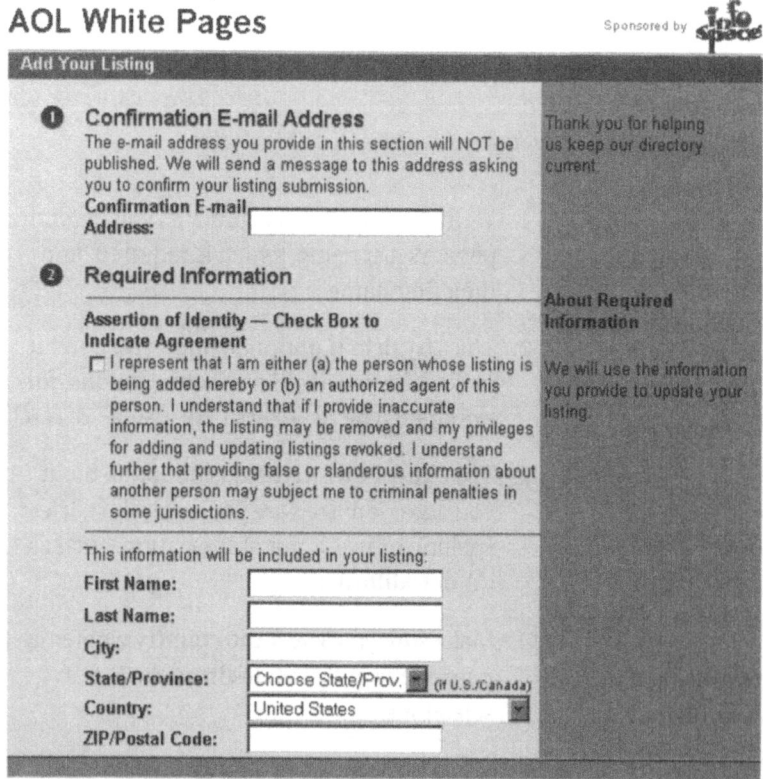

Figure 5-13. Adding your listing to the AOL White Pages

35 Searching international directories

The AOL International Directories can help you find people, businesses, and Web sites from around the world. You'll find country directories for Argentina, Australia, Austria, Belgium, Bermuda, Bulgaria, Canada, Chile, China, Colombia, Costa Rica, Croatia, Czech Republic, Denmark, Estonia, Finland, France, Germany, Greece, Hong Kong, India, Indonesia, Ireland, Italy, Japan, Latvia, Lithuania, Luxembourg, Malaysia, Netherlands, New Zealand, Norway, Pakistan, Paraguay, Peru, Portugal, Puerto Rico, Romania, Russia, Singapore, Slovenia, South Africa, Spain, Sweden, Switzerland, Turkey, United Kingdom, and Venezuela. You should note that some country listings might be in the native language for the country you're searching. Follow these instructions to search international directories:

1. Click **White Pages** from the **People** menu on the AOL toolbar.

2. Click **International Directories** in the **White Pages – Helpful Links** section at the bottom of the AOL White Pages site.

3. Make your country selection from the list provided on the AOL International Directories site by clicking the **Country** hyperlink.

For example, click the White Pages hyperlink for Australia.

4. In the selected country's White Pages, enter the required information. For example, to perform a search in the Australian White Pages, you'll need to enter the following information: Family/Business name, State, Area, and Search Type.

36 Searching the online Yellow Pages

If you're looking for a business and other pertinent information, then the AOL Yellow Pages can help. The AOL Yellow Pages is an excellent source for business users and businesses everywhere. Here's how you search the Yellow Pages:

1. Click the **AOL Keyword** button located beneath the AOL toolbar at the top of your screen, enter **Yellow Pages**, and click the **Go** button.

2. New Yellow Pages users will need to enter a street address (optional), city, state, or zip code to set your location. Click the **Set Location** button, shown in Figure 5-14.

3. Enter the required information such as a business name or business category.

4. Click the **Search** button.

5. View the search results, shown in Figure 5-15.

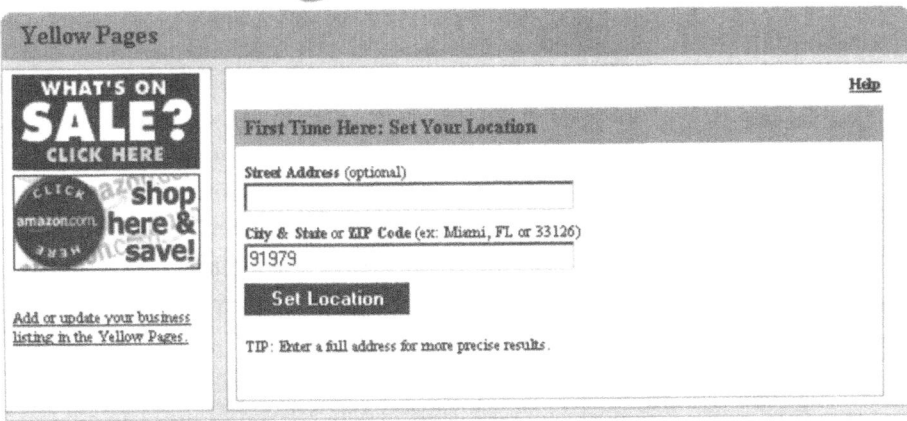

Figure 5-14. Setting your AOL Yellow Pages location

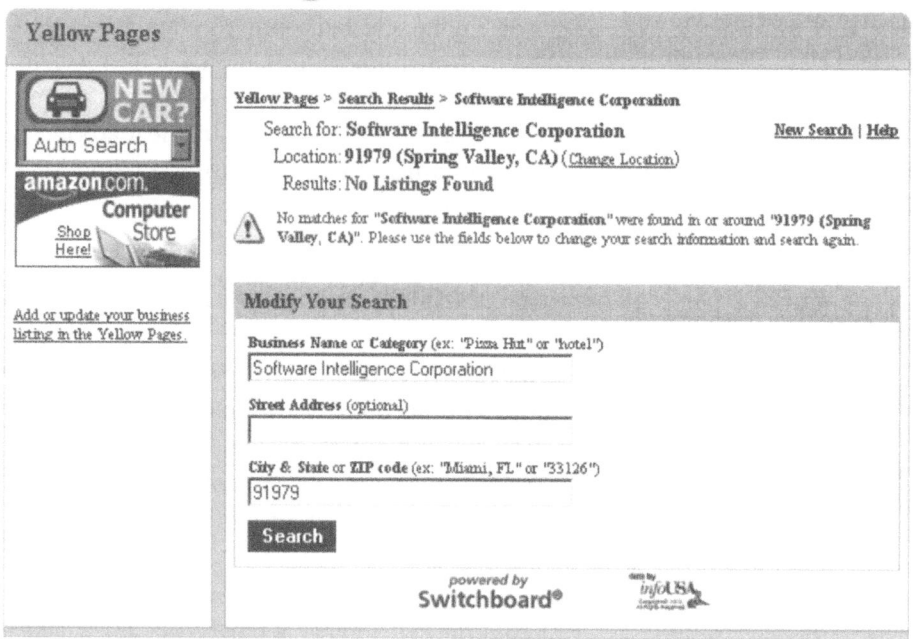

Figure 5-15. Viewing the AOL Yellow Pages search results

37 Searching the Yellow Pages

Here are a few tips that will help you search the
AOL Yellow Pages more effectively:

- You must choose a state from the list of states.

- Select a business category from the list of
  categories or enter a word related to the
  type of business you're searching for. For
  example, if you enter **software**, the Yellow
  Pages will return a list of all categories that
  contain the word.

- Enter an entire business name or a partial
  name.

- When you're not sure of the spelling of a
  business name, you can use the wild card
  character, asterisk (*), to represent one or
  more letters or words. For example, entering
  Soft* will find Soft, Softy, and Software, anywhere in the business name.

- Enter a value for city when you want to
  narrow your search of businesses to a particular city.

38 Performing simple Yellow Pages searches

You don't have to enter a lot of information to do a
simple Yellow Page search. The only required information is the state and either the business name or
business category. However, the more information
you provide about the businesses you're looking
for, the more precise your search results will be.

39 Finding businesses by category in the Yellow Pages

AOL lets you find virtually any business by category.
You'll be able to search from arts and entertainment,
autos and boats, business and professional,
community, computers and electronics, education
and training, family guide, health and medicine,
home guide, money and finance, personal and
fitness, shopping guide, sports and recreation, and
travel. Here's how it's done:

1. Click the **AOL Keyword** button located
   beneath the AOL toolbar at the top of your
   screen, enter **Yellow Pages**, and click the
   Go button.

2. New Yellow Pages users will need to enter a street address (optional), city, state, or zip code to set your location. Click the **Set Location** button.

3. Click the business category your interested in from the AOL Yellow Pages Web site (for example, **Shopping Guide**).

4. Further refine your search by clicking the sub category you're looking for.

40 Performing distance-based Yellow Pages searches

Would you like to limit your search to businesses based on their proximity to your home or business? The AOL Yellow Pages allows you to do just that. You determine whether 15 miles, 10 miles, or even 1 mile is too far to drive. Naturally

the choice you make determines what businesses are displayed in your search results. It's a handy feature that's easy to use. Here's how:

1. Click the **AOL Keyword** button located beneath the AOL toolbar at the top of your screen, enter **Yellow Pages**, and click the **Go** button.

2. New Yellow Pages users will need to enter a street address (optional), city, state, or zip code to set your location. Click the **Set Location** button.

3. Click the business category your interested in from the AOL Yellow Pages Web site (for example, **Shopping Guide**).

4. Further refine your search by clicking the sub-category you're looking for to view the businesses in order of closest to you, as you see in Figure 5-16.

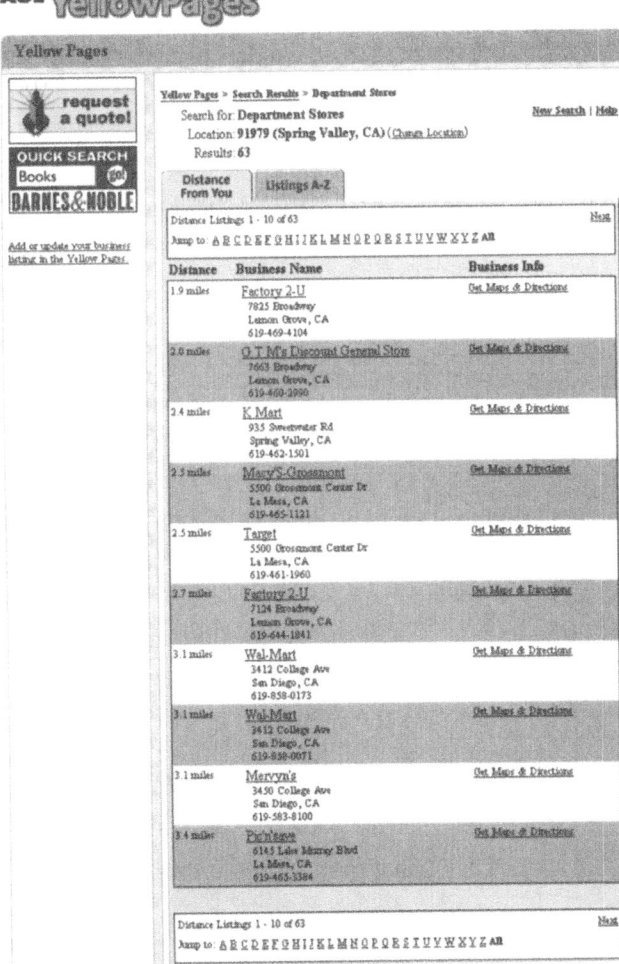

Figure 5-16. Displaying businesses based on distance

Exploring the Classifieds

41 Searching online for Classifieds with ClassifiedPlus

Would you like to browse over 2 million ad listings in 10 major categories? With AOL's ClassifiedPlus you can. With more than 45 million users on America Online, CompuServe, Netscape, and Digital City you'll have a great opportunity to find what you're looking for, and if you're an AOL member, you'll be able to create and display your own ads for people to see all over the world. And AOL members can place a free ad in most categories. Before you place your own ad, you should take the time to familiarize yourself with the various categories and see how others have placed ads with ClassifiedPlus. Here's how you can start searching the Classifieds:

1. Click the **Keyword** button.

2. Type **Classifieds** in the Keyword dialog box and click the **Go** button.

3. Click the **Enter ClassifiedPlus** button in the **ClassifiedPlus** window.

4. Enter the word or words you'd like ClassifiedPlus to search for and click the **Search** button, as you see in Figure 5-17.

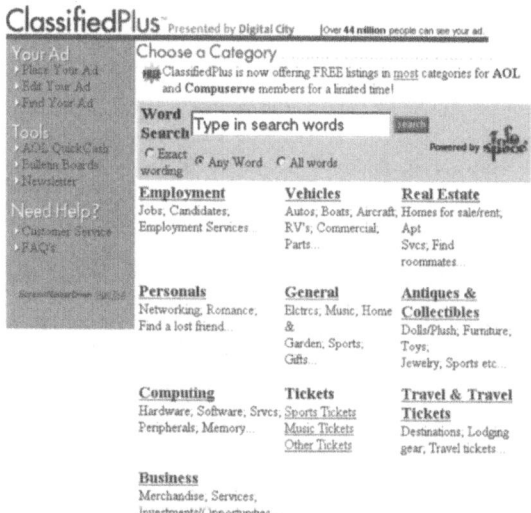

Figure 5-17. Searching AOL's ClassifiedPlus Web site

42 Getting familiar with classified categories

AOL's ClassifiedPlus provides 10 ad categories for you to choose from. Whether you'd like to browse the Personals or place an ad to sell your used car in Vehicles, ClassifiedPlus provides the type of service to get it noticed. Here's a list of the categories you'll have to choose from:

Employment	General
Personals	Tickets
Computing	Real Estate
Business	Antiques & Collectibles
Vehicles	Travel & Travel Tickets

43 Featuring ClassifiedPlus ads

ClassifiedPlus allows you to place, edit, or find ads. You can place an ad for free as long as you're an AOL member. You're limited to a maximum of 20 simultaneous ads per account. Your listing can consist of the following features:

- Standard heading to attract viewers

- Unlimited words to describe your ad

- Insertion of one photo per ad

- Exposure to users on AOL, AOL.COM, CompuServe, Netscape, and Digital City

44 Placing your ad

Using ClassifiedPlus to place an ad is simple. Before you begin going through the following steps, it's recommended that you prepare a brief outline of what you want your ad to say. This preparation will save you lots of time and aggravation as you enter your ad. Let's see how it's done.

1. Click the **Keyword** button.

2. Type **Classifieds** in the Keyword dialog box and click the **Go** button.

3. Click the **Enter ClassifiedPlus** button in the **ClassifiedPlus** window.

4. Click **Place Your Ad** in the **Your Ad** box.

5. Choose the category where you'd like to place your ad (for example, **Computers**).

6. You'll be asked to fill out the ClassifiedPlus Registration online form. Click the Next button when done. This is only required one time for each screen name.

7. To place a computer ad, select the radio button corresponding to what it is you're selling (for example, **hardware**, **software**, or **services**), enter the location of the item or service you're selling, and click the **Continue** button.

8. Select your subcategory, enter a price, click whether your price is **Firm** or **Best Offer**, enter an ad title and description, and click the **Continue** button in the **Place an Ad – Services** window, as shown in Figure 5-18.

9. You'll be asked to preview your ad in the **Preview** window by clicking the **Continue** button.

10. If your ad is the way you want it as displayed in the Preview window, click the **Continue** button.

11. Select the ad start date. Your ad will run for a period of one month or until you delete it. Click the **Continue** button to proceed.

12. ClassifiedPlus will then display a summary of your ad for your files, your ad, the category it's in, and the time frame for the ad.

13. Before your ad is actually placed in the classifieds for others to see, ClassifiedPlus Customer Service will review your request and send an e-mail either accepting or rejecting your request to place an ad.

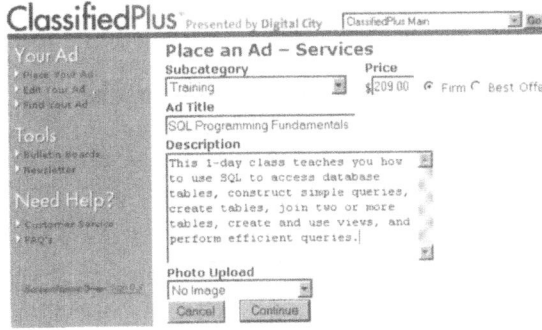

Figure 5-18. Placing your ad with ClassifiedPlus is quick and easy.

45 Changing your ClassifiedPlus ad

If you find the ad you placed with ClassifiedPlus has a typo or requires a change, you can follow these easy steps to edit your ad. You should know that AOL permits you to change your ad a maximum of two times.

1. Click the **Keyword** button.

2. Type **Classifieds** in the Keyword dialog box and click the **Go** button.

3. Click the **Enter ClassifiedPlus** button in the **ClassifiedPlus** window.

4. Click **Edit Your Ad** in the **Your Ad** box.

5. You'll be asked to fill out the ClassifiedPlus Registration online form. Click the **Next** button when done.

This is only required one time for each screen name.

6. Click the **Edit** button at the bottom of your ad.

✎ *If you've already changed your ad two times, you won't be able to edit your ad.*

7. Make the needed change(s) to your ad.

8. If your ad is the way you want it as displayed in the **Preview** window, click the **Continue** button.

9. ClassifiedPlus will then display a summary of your ad with the requested changes for your files.

46 Deleting your ad

When you no longer need or want your ad, you may remove it from ClassifiedPlus. This will prevent having to respond to requests from interested people viewing your ad. Here's how it's done:

1. Click the **Keyword** button.

2. Type **Classifieds** in the **Keyword** dialog box and click the **Go** button.

3. Click the **Enter ClassifiedPlus** button in the **ClassifiedPlus** window.

4. Click **Find Your Ad** in the **Your Ad** box.

5. When your ad displays, click the **Delete** button at the bottom of your ad.

Getting to Know the People Directory

47 Creating your own member profile

You can have your screen name and other personal information such as your name, address, gender, marital status, hobbies, and other information listed in the searchable People Directory. Initially, AOL keeps this information private as an extra security measure for your online safety, but you can add your personal member profile so anyone in the AOL community can view it by following a few simple steps.

Do remember that information posted in your member profile can be viewed by anyone in the AOL community; so use caution when listing information about yourself that you may want to keep

private. Since your AOL member profile can be viewed by anyone in the AOL community, you may want to avoid posting your full name, address, or phone number.

1. Click **My Directory Listing** from the **Settings** menu on the AOL toolbar.

2. Enter the information you want others to see about you in the **Edit Your Online Profile** window (see figure 5-19). You can enter as much or as little information as you want to in your member profile listing.

3. When you're done, click the **Update** button.

4. An America Online dialog window will display confirming that your member profile will be created within 24 hours.

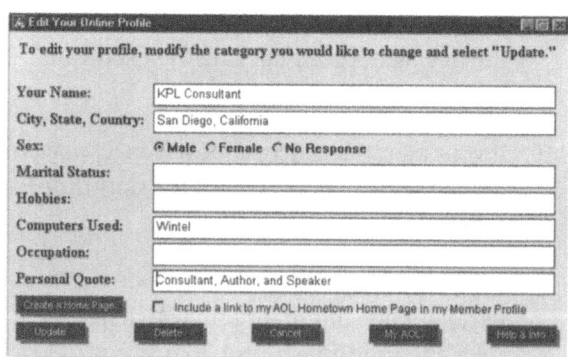

Figure 5-19. Creating your online profile with the Edit Your Online Profile screen is easy.

48 Modifying your existing member profile

If you change your marital status, name, address, or just want to update your member profile information, you can do it by following these simple steps:

1. Click **My Directory Listing** from the **Settings** menu on the AOL toolbar.

2. Modify the information displayed in your member profile in the **Edit Your Online Profile** window. You can modify as much or as little information as necessary to update your member profile listing.

3. When you're done, click the **Update** button.

49 Deleting your member profile

Your personal information is yours alone and you control when it is displayed. AOL realizes this and does everything possible to prevent your privacy from being compromised. This is why they have provided a way to delete your member profile at anytime. Once AOL receives your request to delete your member profile they will remove it from the searchable database, usually within 24 hours. Here's how:

1. Click **My Directory Listing** from the **Settings** menu on the AOL toolbar.

2. Click the **Delete** button in the **Edit Your Online Profile** window.

3. In the **Are you SURE you want to delete all your information?** dialog window, click the **Yes** button.

4. An America Online dialog window will appear confirming that your member profile will be deleted wi.hin 24 hours.

50 Searching the People Directory

Do you want to find other AOL members who share your interests, live nearby, are currently online, or work in the same profession as you? You can find this information and more about AOL members who have created a member profile. A member profile contains information that is shared with others, so always use caution when creating it.

The AOL People Directory also allows you to search for members located anywhere in the world. But if you want to narrow your search to a defined region of the world or a specific country you can do that too. Search locations include Argentina, Australia, Austria, Brazil, Canada, France, Germany, Hong Kong, Japan, Switzerland, Sweden, the United Kingdom, and the United States. AOL makes searching the People Directory easy by following these steps.

1. Click **People Directory** from the **People** menu on the AOL toolbar. The **Member Directory** window appears showing two tabs: **Quick Search** and **Advanced Search**. Click the desired tab.

2. The **Quick Search**, shown in Figure 5-20, allows you to search AOL member profiles for specific words, by member name, city, state or country and language

3. The **Advanced Search**, shown in Figure 5-21, displays additional selection criteria allowing you to narrow your search results to a more manageable size, for example, accessing only members that are currently online.

4. After making one or more selections in either window, click the **Search** button.

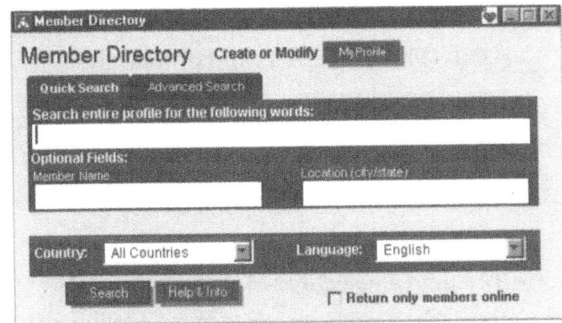

Figure 5-20. Searching AOL's Member Directory with Quick Search

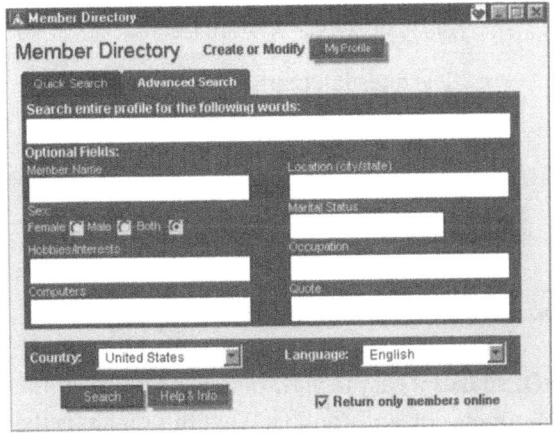

Figure 5-21. Narrowing your search results with advanced searching criteria

51 Searching member names and profiles

Keep these search tips handy as you use the People Directory to search member names and profiles.

- Search words must be at least three characters long. Words that are shorter than three characters long will not be accepted.

- A space between search words (e.g., Miami Dolphin) is treated as if an AND were inserted between the two words, so it's **Miami AND Dolphin.**

- Boolean expressions can be used in your search to limit or expand your search results. The following Boolean expressions can be used:

  - **AND**—Finds members and profiles that contain all search words.

  - **OR**—Finds members and profiles that contain any word.

  - **NOT**—Finds members and profiles that do not contain the word that follows the NOT expression.

- The following wild card characters can be used when you're not sure of the spelling of a person's name:

  - ***** The asterisk is used to represent any number of characters following the specified word. For example, entering **Smit*** will find members and profiles containing Smith, Smithe, and Smits.

  - **?** The question mark is used to replace a single character in a word. For example, entering **Smit?** will find members and profiles containing Smith and Smits, but not Smithe.

52 Searching for members currently online

AOL makes it easy to view member profiles of members currently online. What this means is that the search results will automatically exclude any members not signed on at the time the search is performed. Here's how:

1. Click **People Directory** from the **People** menu on the AOL toolbar.

2. After making one or more selections in either Member Directory window, click the box *Return only members online.*

3. Click the **Search** button.

53 Getting help using the People Directory

AOL provides a comprehensive online Help facility where you can get assistance while using various People Directory features. Here's how you can get help and information whenever you need it:

1. Click **People Directory** from the **People** menu on the AOL toolbar.

2. Click the **Help & Info** button on the Member Directory window.

3. Review the displayed help information for suggestions on using Quick Search on the Member Directory, and when you're done close the window.

54 Performing advanced searches

The Advanced Search feature allows you to construct a more specific search request than with the Quick Search feature. In addition to the search criteria provided with Quick Search, additional fields are provided for you to select from such as gender, hobbies/interests, computers, marital status, occupation, and quote. These additional fields let you narrow your member search results even more than before. Take the time to become familiar with AOL's advanced search features so you can obtain a list of screen names that exactly satisfy your search needs.

Understanding File Transfer Protocol (FTP)

55 Understanding how FTP sites work

An FTP site is a computer that makes files available for downloading and uploading by using special software known as File Transfer Protocol (FTP). FTP provides a standard way of transferring files from one computer to another on the Internet. By using an FTP program you'll be able to share your favorite books, games, images, software, sounds, and much more.

56 Accessing My FTP Space

AOL sets aside an area of free disk space for every AOL member on the members.aol.com Web server. This disk space is called **My FTP Space** and has the sole purpose of allowing you to make files available to anyone using America Online or other Internet services. This mechanism for sharing files is available for each screen name you create under your AOL account (a maximum of seven screen names can be created per account).

Each screen name is given a maximum of 2MB of storage space (maximum of 14MB per account) to use as you wish. Your **My FTP Space** is found at the following Web address:

http://members.aol.com/screenname

For the last part of the URL, replace "screenname" with your own AOL screen name without any spaces.

To access your personal **My FTP Space** to store and share Web pages and any files you create, display the **My FTP Space** window by typing **AOL keyword: My FTP Space**, shown in Figure 5-22.

Figure 5-22. Accessing your My FTP Space

57 Accessing AOL's FTP services

To access the vast collection of books, games, images, software, sounds, and countless other content offered on the Internet, AOL offers users FTP services. FTP services from AOL gives you a standard way of transferring files from one computer to another on the Internet. To find out more about AOL's FTP services, type **AOL keyword: FTP**. To access FTP sites offered by AOL, click the **Go To FTP** button on the **File Transfer Protocol** window.

Many FTP sites require you to have an established account with user name and password before you're given permission to access the FTP site and upload or download files. If you don't have or don't want an account, you can use anonymous FTP to access several FTP sites to retrieve files that are available to the general public. By clicking the **Go To FTP** button, AOL's Anonymous FTP window displays providing you with access to several FTP sites, shown in Figure 5-23.

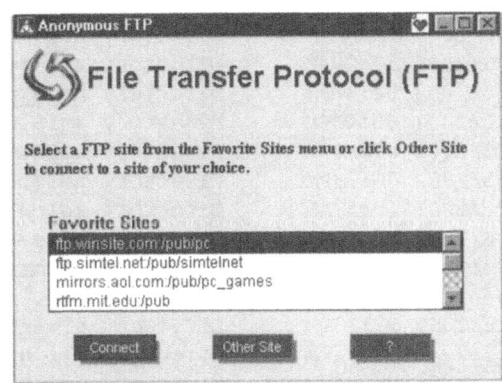

Figure 5-23. Accessing AOL's Anonymous FTP window

To access any of the FTP sites listed in AOL's Anonymous FTP window's selection list, select the site you'd like to visit from the Favorite Sites selection list and click the **Connect** button.

58 Connecting to FTP sites

You can use AOL's Anonymous FTP window to access other FTP sites by clicking the "Other Site" button to display the Other FTP Site window.

You can use AOL's built-in browser to access FTP sites. In the text entry box on the navigation bar at the top of your screen, type **ftp** immediately followed by a colon (:), two forward slashes (//), the site's address, and then click the **Go** button.

For a listing of FTP sites available on the Internet, access the AOL Search Web site: ftp.aol.com. Figure 5-24 illustrates what this FTP listing looks like.

FTP root at ftp.aol.com

```
01/25/2002 04:13PM     Directory .
01/25/2002 04:13PM     Directory ..
05/17/2000 12:00AM          776 .message
08/03/2000 12:00AM     Directory AOL_Select
06/12/2001 12:00AM     Directory MetaStreamComponents
08/21/2001 05:07PM     Directory NASCAR
09/24/1999 12:00AM          351 Welcome
10/10/2000 12:00AM     Directory WinPDA
08/02/2000 12:00AM     Directory addons
06/15/2001 12:00AM     Directory addressbook
08/30/2000 12:00AM     Directory aim
02/13/2001 12:00AM     Directory aim-france
01/08/2001 12:00AM     Directory aim-hk
11/28/2001 03:30PM     Directory aim-japan
12/20/2001 02:23PM     Directory aimgen
08/03/2000 12:00AM     Directory aol
08/03/2000 12:00AM     Directory aol-reg
01/25/2002 04:36PM     Directory aol4.0
01/25/2002 05:46PM     Directory aol5.0
11/26/2001 01:24PM     Directory aol6.0
01/25/2002 06:53PM     Directory aol7.0
11/26/2001 10:57AM     Directory aolca7.0
04/06/2001 12:00AM     Directory aolcanada
08/02/2000 12:00AM     Directory aolmail
08/04/2000 12:00AM            7 bin
01/28/2002 12:13PM     Directory clients
12/18/2001 02:03PM     Directory clientsca
12/18/2001 02:07PM     Directory clientscf
08/04/2000 12:00AM     Directory cscanada
10/08/2001 03:43PM     Directory dev
08/04/2000 12:00AM     Directory etc
01/31/2001 12:00AM     Directory iplanet
08/03/2000 12:00AM     Directory netmail
09/25/2001 04:07PM     Directory newline
04/10/2001 12:00AM     Directory palm
04/10/2001 12:00AM     Directory pub
06/28/2001 12:00AM     Directory radio
08/07/2000 12:00AM     Directory real
01/17/2002 03:10PM     Directory tax_forms
03/26/2001 12:00AM     Directory taxforms
02/08/2001 12:00AM     Directory twnscp
08/03/2000 12:00AM     Directory usr
```

Figure 5-24. Viewing AOL's listing of FTP sites at address: ftp.aol.com

59 Typing FTP addresses

Some FTP addresses are case-sensitive and require their address to be entered using lowercase letters. So if you're unable to connect to a site when capitalizing one or more letters in an address, try typing the entire site address in lowercase letters. As long as the site address isn't misspelled, you should be able to access it.

> 🖋 *Internet and FTP addresses don't contain spaces separating words.*

60 Using FTP to search for files

Have you ever wanted to search for books, games, images, software, sounds, or other content on the Web? If you have, you might be surprised to learn that these and other precious gems are sometimes easier to find on FTP sites than using Web-based tools. Are you interested? Here's how you can use FTP to find all sorts of goodies on public FTP sites:

1. Click the AOL Keyword button and type **AOL Search** and click the **Go** button.

2. Type in **AOL FTP sites** and click the **Search** button.

3. Double-click on the sites that interest you in the **Search Results** window.

61 Downloading files with FTP

Assuming you have permission to use a given FTP site, here's how to download a file to your computer's hard drive or other storage device:

1. Click the AOL Keyword button and type **My FTP Space** and click the **Go** button.

2. Click the **Go To FTP** button.

3. Select a site from the selection list or click **Other Site** and type in an FTP address, and click the **OK** button.

4. Navigate to the directory and folder of the folder you'd like to download.

5. Click the **Download Now** button.

6. Navigate to the directory and folder on your hard drive where you'd like the downloaded file to go.

7. Click the **Save** button.

62 Unlocking zipped files

Files on the Web are frequently zipped (or compressed) to speed up the download process and save storage space. There are two basic reasons for zipping files: 1) to reduce a larger file to a smaller size, and 2) to package a number of files into one bundled space. Whenever a file or set of files can be made smaller you lessen the time needed for transfer from one computer to another. You can usually tell whether you have a zipped file by looking at the extension. Windows compressed files always end in .zip while Macintosh compressed files end in .sit. But there is a catch. Before a zipped file can be read or used, it must first be unzipped (or decompressed). AOL can automatically do this for you, as long as you follow these steps:

1. Click **Preferences** from the **Settings** menu on the AOL toolbar.

2. Click **Download** under the **Organization** section of the **Preferences** window.

3. Select the radio button, **When I download them,** from the **Automatically decompress Zip files: options** section, and click the **Save** button.

63 Uploading files with FTP

To upload pictures, Web pages, and other things from your computer's hard drive to your personal **My FTP Space**, follow these instructions:

1. Click the AOL Keyword button and type **My FTP Space** and click the **Go** button.

2. Click **See My FTP Space** in the **My FTP Space** window.

3. Navigate to the directory and folder where you'd like to place the uploaded file.

4. Click the **Upload** button.

5. Type the name of the file to be used for the uploaded and stored file in you're **My FTP Space** in the **Remote Filename** dialog box.

6. Select **ASCII** for text files or **Binary** for programs and graphics, and then click the **OK** button.

7. Click the **Select File** button in the **Upload File** window.

8. Navigate to the file in the directory and folder where you want to upload, and double-click the desired file.

9. Click the **Send** button to upload the file.

64 Exploring the best FTP sites

Table 5-2 lists some great FTP sites containing terrific content. Here's a list of the best FTP sites for you to visit.

Table 5-2. Best of FTP

FTP NAME	ADDRESS	DESCRIPTION
AOL	ftp://mirrors.aol.com/pub/pc_games	This FTP site covers PC games and programming.
Electronic Frontier Foundation	ftp://ftp.eff.org/	This FTP site provides directories containing information on activism, campaigns, censorship, congress, global, images, jobs, legal, media, net culture, news, privacy, state and local, sounds, statistics, templates, and much more.
Finnish University	ftp://ftp.funet.fi/pub/msdos/games/	The Finnish University and Research Network serves up a wide range of games and game info: adventure, arcade and board games, card games, editors, patches, programming, puzzles, and strategy.
Swedish University	ftp://ftp.sunet.se/pub/pictures	At the Swedish University Network you can download images of all sorts of things: architecture, art, comics, computers, flags, flowers, fractals, fun, history, maps, money, music, paleontology, people, plants, satellite-views, space, sports, and vehicles.
Washington University	ftp://wuarchive.wustl.edu/multimedia/images/	The Washington University Graphics Archive provides many directories containing .gif and .jpeg images on hundreds of topics.

Chat, Instant Messaging, and Message Boards

AMERICA ONLINE LETS YOU stay in touch with loved ones and friends, as well as make new acquaintances anytime you want with a variety of online services and member communities. From chatting in live online group areas to sending instant messages, AOL provides exciting ways to stay in touch with family and friends. You'll also see how you can meet people who share your interests by reading and posting messages to online message boards. These tips will help you discover and explore the exciting world of chat, instant messaging, and message boards—all AOL features that are sure to give the whole family hours of enjoyment.

In this chapter, you'll learn how to

- Enjoy AOL's chat feature
- Use Instant Messenger (AIM)™
- Manage and access Buddy Lists®
- Get the most out of electronic message boards

The World of Chatting

1 Finding a chat room—chat communities

With hundreds of public chat rooms to choose from, you're bound to find lively group interaction where you can share your knowledge and experiences with others, or simply sit back and watch the discussions between other chatters.

AOL provides two types of public chat rooms: those created by People Connection, and those created by AOL members. Some chat rooms are hosted and open around the clock while others have scheduled events such as presentations or classes. Knowing how to find a chat room of particular interest to you is a lot easier than you think. AOL lets you either browse a list of public chat rooms or search the database of People Connection chat rooms to find what you're looking for. Here's how it works.

Browsing the Public Chat Rooms

1. Select **Find a Chat** from the **People** menu on the AOL toolbar.

2. Select either the **created by People Connection** or **created by AOL Members** tab in the **Find a Chat** window.

3. Select a chat category from the list of categories in the left selection window and click the **View Chats** button.

4. Select a chat room from the list of rooms in the right selection window and click the **Go Chats** button.

Searching the Database of People Connection Chat Rooms

1. Select **Find a Chat** from the **People** menu on the AOL toolbar.

2. Click the **Search All People Connection Chats** button in the **Find a Chat** window.

3. Enter a search word in the Search field in the **Search Featured Chats** window and click the **Search** button, shown in Figure 6-1.

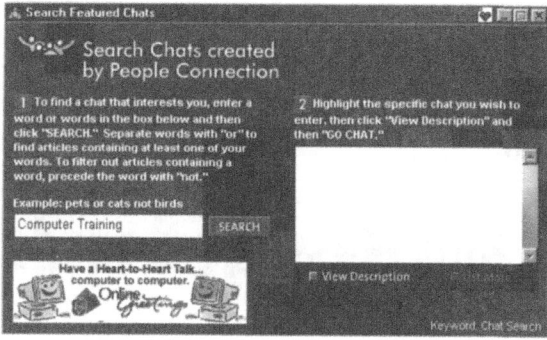

Figure 6-1. Searching the People Connection featured chats database

2 Types of public chat rooms

AOL offers hundreds of public chat rooms to help make your online experience an exciting and rewarding one. Because of the number of chats available, each is organized by topic or category. An alphabetical list of the available categories for chats created by People Connection and those by AOL Members consist of the following categories:

> AOL ArgentinaLife
>
> AOL BrazilNews, Sports & Finance
>
> AOL MexicoPlaces
>
> Arts and EntertainmentRomance
>
> Canada—EnglishSpecial Interests
>
> Canada—FrenchTown Square
>
> FriendsUK
>
> Japan

3 Chat room etiquette

Chat rooms are among the most popular forums on America Online. They're an exciting electronic medium and are meant to be fun for everyone. Chat rooms are not the same as message boards because conversations are immediate. Chat rooms are monitored by hosts who can give you a helping hand if necessary and keep the dialogue running smoothly. Because chat conversations are live, they can be monitored by AOL personnel and must conform to certain rules of conduct as stated in the AOL Online Content Guidelines.

First, messages should not contain vulgar language, explicit sexual content including slang words that discuss a person's anatomy, hate language or speech, and any type of offensive language to any person or group of people. Second, photos revealing frontal nudity should never be posted. Next, depictions of illegal drug use as acceptable forms of behavior are not permitted. Finally, graphic images containing blood and gore, and/or violence are not acceptable behavior and should never be posted. These are meant to serve as guidelines to proper use of AOL and chat rooms, and if you identify offensive behavior, you can naturally ignore it, or you may report it by typing AOL Keyword: Notify AOL.

The following tips offer a few suggestions to help you better understand the proper chat room etiquette. Take the time to learn the correct etiquette so you'll be able to enjoy the excitement offered by this medium. And most importantly, don't forget that manners and politeness go a long way for a more rewarding online experience.

4 Viewing member profiles in chat rooms

A member's online profile, assuming the AOL member took the time to fill one out and save it, is useful information about a member. If properly filled out, it captures a member's name, city, state, country, sex, marital status, hobbies, occupation, personal quote, and computers used. You can even link your profile to your home page, if available. This online record is stored in a searchable database with millions of other profiles. Its purpose is to help others understand who you are so they can determine whether to contact you in a chat room, Instant Message, or message board. Here's how you can view a member's profile while in a chat room:

1. Find and open a chat room of choice.

2. In the **People Here** section of the chat window, double-click the screen name of the person you'd like to view a profile for.

3. Click **Get Profile** in the **Information** window that appears.

5 Viewing a member's profile without entering a chat room

Sometimes getting into a busy chat room is next to impossible, let alone seeing who is on there. In these situations you can still see who's chatting as well as view member profiles by following a few simple steps.

1. If you don't have a chat window open, select **Find a Chat** from the **People** menu on the AOL toolbar.

2. In the **Find a Chat** window, select the chat category and room you'd like to view member profiles for.

3. Click the **Who's Chatting** button in the **Find a Chat** window.

4. Select the screen name you want to view a profile for and click the **Get Member Profile** button, shown in Figure 6-2.

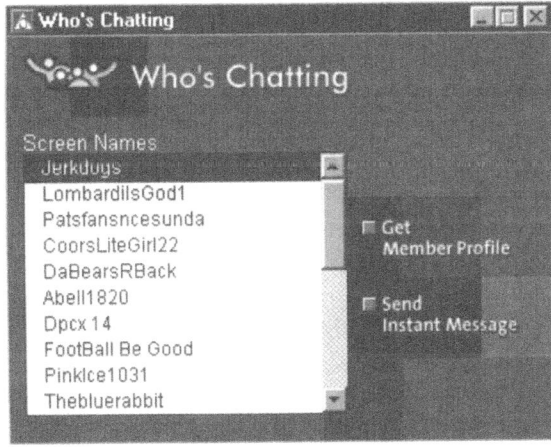

Figure 6-2. Displaying a list of screen names in the Who's Chatting window

6 Creating a screen name for chatting

Screen names created for e-mail correspondence are publicly visible for everyone to see while you're online. Whether you're communicating with others via e-mail, chat, message boards, or any of the other communication mediums, your screen

name is always visible for other to see. Sometimes having a single screen name for all your online activities will trigger unwanted and unsolicited correspondence. For this reason, AOL members often create additional screen names to use for accessing the other online communication features such as chat and message boards. Every AOL account can have a maximum of seven screen names, each with separate passwords, mailboxes, filing cabinets, and favorite places. The screen name you specified when you first set up your account is considered your primary master screen name, and can't be deleted or changed. To assign additional screen names to your account, follow these steps:

1. Click the **Settings** button on the AOL toolbar and select **Screen Names**. The AOL **Screen Names** window appears.

2. Click the **Create a Screen Name** option and the steps for creating a **Screen Name** appears.

3. Click **Create Screen Name** button.

4. In the **Choose a Screen Name** window, enter the desired screen name (e-mail address), and click the **Continue** button.

5. Choose and enter a **password** once and then twice for verification, and click the **Continue** button.

6. Select a **Parental Control Category**, and click the **Continue** button.

7. Confirm your screen name settings, and click the **Accept Settings** button.

8. To begin using your new screen name, sign off AOL and reconnect, or select **Switch Screen Name** from the **Sign Off** menu above the AOL toolbar.

7 Setting chat preferences

You can set and save special chat preferences that enable you to get the most from your online chat experience. For instance, you can have AOL notify you when members enter or leave a chat room, enable chat room sounds, alphabetize the member list in a chat room, even double-spacing incoming messages for enhanced readability. It's easy to let AOL know whether you want these features on or off. Here's how:

1. Select **Preferences** from the **Settings** menu on the AOL toolbar.

2. Click **Chat** under the **Communications** section in the **Preferences** window.

3. Select the specific chat preferences you want by clicking the desired check boxes, and click the **Save** button, shown in Figure 6-3.

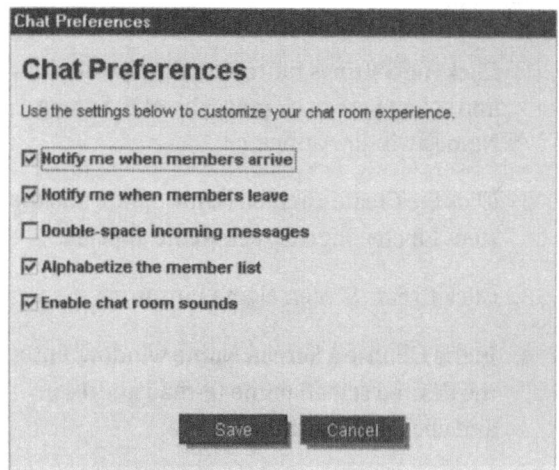

Figure 6-3. Selecting chat preferences from the Chat Preferences window

8 Starting your own chat

Are you a chat fanatic? Do you and your buddies have a special interest in a topic that you'd like to make available to others? Are you having a difficult time finding an existing chat on your topic? Or do you want to create a private chat for just you and your buddies? AOL lets members create their own public or private chat rooms to satisfy all these needs. This is an especially handy feature for members who have an understanding of how chats work, and/or for those who can't seem to find a chat that addresses their particular needs. Here's how you can start your own chat:

1. Select **Start Your Own Chat** from the **People** menu on the AOL toolbar.

2. Determine the type of chat you want to start:

   • Public (member) chat—listed in the Find a Chat directory

   • Private chat—not listed in the Find a Chat directory.

3. Click **Member Chat** to start a public chat or **Private Chat** from the **Start Your Own Chat** window.

4. Select the category where you want your chat to appear in the **Find a Chat** directory, and enter the name of your chat in the field provided on **the Start Your Own Member or Private Chat** window, shown in Figure 6-4.

5. Click the **Go Chat** button to go to your chat room.

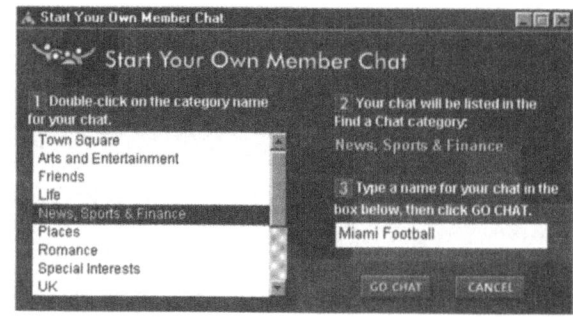

Figure 6-4. Entering a name for your own member chat

9 Blocking hyperlinks in chat rooms

AOL 4.0 users or higher can block the blue underlined text links, commonly referred to as hyperlinks from appearing in your chats. This prevents any links to external sites from appearing as well as the redirection to an external site or Web page caused by accidentally clicking a link. Here's how you can turn hyperlinks off:

1. Verify that you're currently signed on as the primary or master screen name.

2. Select **Parental Controls** from the **Settings** menu on the AOL toolbar.

3. Click **Set Parental Controls** in the **AOL Parental Controls** window.

4. Click **Chat control** under the **Custom Controls** heading in the **Parental Controls** window.

5. Select the check box **Block viewing and using hyperlinks in rooms** in the **Custom Control Settings: Chat** window, and click the **Save** button, shown in Figure 6-5.

6. Click the **OK** button in the **Your changes to Chat Controls have been saved** dialog box.

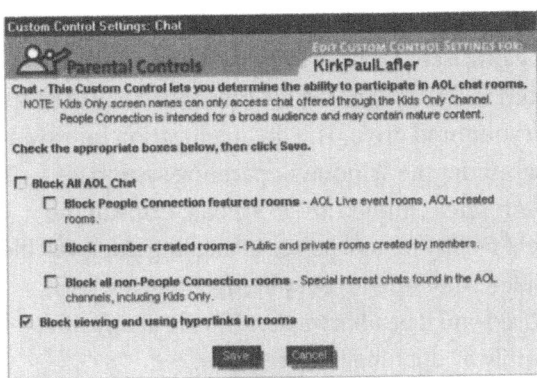

Figure 6-5. Selecting the Block viewing and using hyperlinks in rooms check box

10 Blocking e-mail or selected e-mail

Blocking e-mail or selected e-mail is easy in AOL. Sometimes it's easier (and a lot less typing) to block the AOL members, e-mail addresses, and domains you don't want e-mail from, especially if you know the addresses of habitual offenders. In these situations, you simply list the AOL members, e-mail addresses, and domains you want to block receiving e-mails from. You will be free to accept e-mails from everyone else. Here's how it's done:

1. Click the **Mail** menu button on the AOL toolbar, and select **Mail Controls.**

2. Select the **screen name** you want to set mail controls for in the **Set Mail Controls For** box in the **General Mail Controls** window.

3. Select the **Customize Mail Controls for the Screen Name** radio button, and click the **Next** button.

4. Select the **Block e-mail from the listed AOL members, e-mail addresses, and domains. Allow e-mail from all others** radio box, and click the **Next** button.

5. Select the desired mail controls for **pictures and files**, and click the **Next** button.

6. Click the **Save** button.

11 Setting Parental Controls

You can control what type of access is available for a particular screen name through Parental Controls. The Parental Control assigns a safety net for members to prevent unauthorized contact by other members while online. This feature controls member access while using Instant Message, chat rooms, newsgroups, message boards, and other online communication mediums. AOL lets you set Parental Controls for the following age categories:

- Kids Only (ages 12 and under)

- Young Teens (ages 13–15)

- Mature Teens (ages 16–17)

- General Access (ages 18 and older)

Here's how you can set Parental Controls for any screen name.

1. Verify that you're currently signed on as the primary or master screen name.

2. Select **Parental Controls** from the **Settings** menu on the AOL toolbar.

3. Select the screen name you want to assign parental control settings for from the **Edit controls for:** list.

4. Click **Chat control** under the **Custom Controls** heading in the **Parental Controls** window.

5. Click the check box corresponding to the chat options you want to allow or restrict , and click the **Save** button.

12 Saving chat room conversations to a log file

Chat room conversations can be fast and furious. Some of the more popular rooms have discussion going on around the clock 24 hours a day. With people coming and going from one chat room to the next, hours of chat conversation can roll by quicker than you think. And let's face it, sometimes you're just too busy to sit and watch a chat discussion for any length of time. AOL can help by letting you save any chat room conversation to a log file on your PC's hard drive. The process of saving a chat room's conversations is called *logging*. Here's how it's done:

1. Enter the chat room you'd like to log a conversation from. Only an open chat room can be logged.

2. Select **Log Manager** from the **File** menu above the AOL toolbar.

3. Click the **Open Log** button located in the **Chat Log** section of the **Logging** window, shown in Figure 6-6.

4. AOL automatically assigns a name to the log file it creates. Click the **OK** button to accept this name designation or change the name in the **Windows Open Log** dialog box.

5. Continue to participate in the chat discussions as normal.

6. When you're ready to stop logging the chat conversations, click the **Close Log** button located in the **Chat Log** section of the **Logging** window.

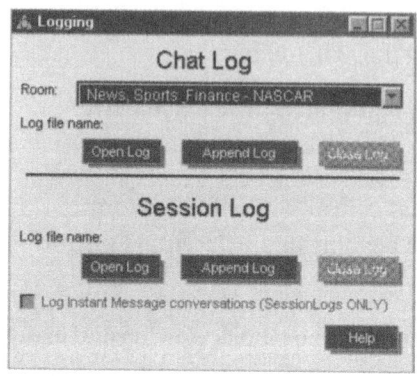

Figure 6-6. Saving the chat discussion in the News, Sports, Finance—NASCAR to a log

13 Reading saved chat room conversations

Logging a chat room's conversations saves every word to the designated file (described in Tip #12) on your hard drive. The default location for saved logs under the Windows operating system is c:\America Online 7.0\Download. Consult the Help facility for assistance in locating the saved file under other operating systems. Once the log is closed you'll be able to view the file at any time simply by opening it. Here's how:

1. Select **Open** from the **File** menu above the AOL toolbar.

2. In the **Open a File** dialog box, navigate to the directory and folder containing your saved log file.

3. Once the saved log file is found, you'll want to open it by double-clicking the file in the **Open a File** dialog box. If the file is too large to open using the AOL software, you may need to open it with your system's word processing software (e.g., MS Word).

Using AOL Speaks

14 Making chatting easier with AOL Speaks— a voice recognition program

Are you tired of typing your messages on your keyboard? Would you rather compose your message by speaking into your computer's microphone? Well now you can with AOL Speaks—the voice recognition program that allows you to dictate your message by speaking into your computer. Before you can begin using AOL Speaks, you'll need to set it up and configure the software to make sure all the necessary files are created, check that your microphone is installed and working properly, and, most importantly, train the software to recognize your vocabulary and speech patterns.

15 AOL Speaks system requirements

To run AOL Speaks, you'll need to make sure your computer meets the following minimum system requirements:

- A 200MHz Pentium processor with MMX technology

- Windows 95/98 or Windows 2000 with at least 48MB RAM or Windows NT 4.0 with at least 64MB RAM

- At least 250MB free hard disk space

- An industry-standard 16-bit sound card or built-in audio system with input quality equal to or greater than the Creative Labs Sound Blaster 16

- A microphone with an earphone or headset, and speakers for the multimedia Help system

- A CD-ROM drive

16 Before installing AOL Speaks

Before you begin installing AOL Speaks, you should do the following:

1. Turn off any virus checking software—the installation process may activate a virus report even when one doesn't exist.

 Refer to the documentation or Help information for activating and deactivating software.

2. Install a sound card if one doesn't exist.

3. Assemble and connect a microphone headset.

17 Installing and launching AOL Speaks on your computer

Installing AOL Speaks is easy if you follow these instructions:

1. **Insert the AOL 6.0 or greater disc** in your CD-ROM drive. During installation of AOL, a "Free AOL Extras" folder is placed in the directory where AOL is installed. Check to see if this folder exists. You may also see the **Free AOL Extras** icon on your computer desktop.

2. Double-click the **Install AOL Speaks** shortcut located in the **Free AOL Extras** directory or double-click the **Install AOL Speaks** icon on your desktop.

3. The installation will start automatically where the **Setup wizard** will appear and guide you through the installation process.

4. At installation completion, indicate whether you want to view the Readme file.

5. Reboot your computer.

6. To start AOL Speaks, click the **Start** menu, choose **Programs**, and select **AOL Speaks**.

18 Configuring AOL Speaks audio settings

Once your AOL speech files are created, you're ready to configure your audio settings. Click the **Run Audio Settings** wizard button and follow the on-screen instructions. Accept the wizard's default settings and, when finished, click the **Next** button.

19 Testing AOL Speaks audio settings

After configuring your audio settings using the Run Audio Setup wizard, you'll want to test the audio settings. The test process should determine whether the sound quality is acceptable, by testing the following elements:

1. Verify that the **headset** produces a strong sound quality without interference or static. Also verify its ease of use and that it is comfortable.

   🖎 *Verify that there are no bare or frayed wires.*

2. Verify that the **microphone** is connected and is capable of recording sound, and that the microphone on /microphone off and mute buttons function properly.

3. Verify that the **sound card** is not an older model and that it provides sufficient levels of power to the microphone so it can operate.

   🖎 *If the sound card is an older model, you may need to upgrade.*

20 Tips on using AOL Speaks

To get the greatest benefit from AOL Speaks, you'll want to follow these simple tips:

- **Read** the "first timers" online Help instructions and the AOL Speaks User's Manual for specific help.

- **Create speech files.** Each person who uses AOL Speaks will need to create his or her own unique speech file.

- **Train AOL Speaks** to recognize your voice, unique speech patterns, and pronunciation of words.

- **Have AOL Speaks back up your speech files.** By default, AOL Speaks backs up each person's speech files every fifth save. This can be changed according to your preferences.

- **Test your sound system** consisting of your microphone, speakers, sound card, or built-in audio system.

21 Using AOL Speaks for the first time— the New User Wizard

The AOL Speaks New User Wizard leads you through the customization process asking you to enter certain information and accept certain recommendations. The first-time user can expect AOL Speaks to conduct the following tasks:

- **Creating user speech files,** including the selection of a speech model and vocabulary.

- **Configuring and testing** your audio hardware and settings.

- **Training AOL Speaks** to recognize your speech patterns and pronunciation of words.

- **Customizing your vocabulary** so AOL Speaks can learn your writing style, including your use of special words and phrases.

22 Creating new AOL Speaks speech files

Before you can begin using AOL Speaks, you'll need to create new speech files. These speech files will contain information about your voice, your pronunciation of words, and your use of words. The wizard will prompt you for the following information or to accept the recommended preference:

1. You'll be asked to provide a unique name for your speech files (e.g., your name with or without blanks).

   🖎 *Special characters such as commas, slashes, equal signs, and quotation marks can't be used as part of your name.*

2. You'll then be asked to accept a speech model containing the sounds of words.

3. Finally, you be asked to accept vocabulary containing words that AOL Speaks recognizes.

23 Training AOL Speaks to recognize your speech patterns and sound of your voice

After you've completed the audio setup, you're ready to begin training AOL Speaks to recognize your speech patterns and the sound of your voice. Training AOL Speaks involves running General

Training consisting of a two-step process: 1) a brief initial stage, and 2) a longer, more complete stage. It is recommended that both steps be done during the same session.

The first stage of General Training requires you to read a few paragraphs out loud. When you are finished, General Training performs an initial calibration.

The second stage of General Training requires you to read out loud from one of several texts. At the completion of the second step, General Training processes the data for approximately five minutes.

24 Personalizing your AOL Speaks vocabulary with Vocabulary Builder

After completing the General Training stages to recognize your speech patterns and sound of your voice, the New User wizard will run Vocabulary Builder. Vocabulary Builder customizes AOL Speaks so that it recognizes your writing style and the words you use, adding words you choose to the active vocabulary, and customizing the language model in accordance with the vocabulary. Here's how you can customize your vocabulary:

1. Spell check a document to be used in the Vocabulary Builder process. Correct any identified errors.

2. Click the **Run Vocabulary Builder** button.

3. Run Vocabulary Builder with at least one document representing the type of text you'll be dictating into AOL Speaks. Note: The document can be one of the following types:

   - Text file (.TXT)

   - MS Word file (.DOC)

   - HTML file (.HTML)

   - Rich Text Format file (.RTF)

   - Corel WordPerfect file (.WPD)

4. New words are listed in the **New Words from Document** dialog box. Select any words you want added, and click the **Build** button.

   A maximum of 250 words can be added during each Vocabulary Builder session.

5. Follow the on-screen instructions.

25 Saving AOL Speaks speech files

It's always a good idea to save your speech files after you use the Vocabulary Builder or Vocabulary Editor, run training, train words, or correct speech recognition mistakes. AOL Speaks recognizes speech files changes and prompts you to save them.

Failing to save changes made during the current session won't impact changes made in previous sessions.

26 Backing up AOL Speaks speech files

Backing up your speech files, as with other important data and files, can help safeguard them against computer hardware and software failures. Yes, things can and do go wrong with computer hardware and software. A computer system isn't immune to serious ailments—in fact when they do occur, they usually happen when least expected and without notice. So don't let a hardware or software failure leave you unprepared and without the ability to access your speech files. Follow these simple instructions to back up your speech files each time you use the Vocabulary Builder or Vocabulary Editor, run training, train words, or correct speech recognition mistakes:

1. Click **Back Up** on the User menu.

2. Save your speech files to a permanent location in your AOL Speaks folder on your hard drive.

   If you have a Zip drive, you might want to save your speech files to a Zip disk.

27 Restoring AOL Speaks speech files

Restoring damaged or lost speech files is a snap, as long as you performed at least one backup during a prior session. Here's how:

1. Click **Restore** on the User menu.

2. The restore process takes the last backup that was made and saves it with a different name.

3. Open the restored speech file to work with it.

28 Dictating your chat message with AOL Speaks

Dictating text and messages with AOL Speaks is a great way to capture or compose your messages, but it will take a little getting used to. As with anything new, you may want to practice a bit so you can become familiar with the technology. Here are a few tips on becoming a pro with AOL Speaks.

- Turn the microphone on.

- Speak clearly and naturally into your microphone—unless you're a seasoned radio announcer or disc jockey, you may want to practice a bit.

- Speak at normal speed.

- Speak in longer phrases rather than short abrupt words.

- Say the e-mail address so it appears in the Send To field. Immediately correct an incorrect address by saying "Correct" and typing in the correct address in the Correction dialog box.

- Pause briefly between voice commands so AOL Speaks recognizes it as a command rather than normal dictation.

- Press and hold down the **Ctrl key** while saying the command—this will force AOL Speaks to recognize the command as a command.

- For normal dictation, press and hold down the **Shift key**. This will force AOL Speaks to recognize these words as dictation.

- Correct speech recognition errors by saying "Correct That" or pressing the minus key immediately after AOL Speaks make a recognition error. The Correction dialog box appears displaying a list of recognized words and a list of different interpretations.

🖉 *Each time you correct speech recognition errors, AOL Speaks improves the way it understands your speech patterns.*

AOL's Instant Messenger (AIM) and Buddy Lists

29 Launching the Instant Message window

Are hectic schedules, budget constraints, time zone differences, and the rising cost of postage preventing you from staying in touch with friends and loved ones? AOL can help by providing a great feature to bridge the communication gap. AOL's widely heralded Instant Message feature provides a totally live and private one-on-one chat environment between two people who are currently online. You'll find chatting with friends or collaborating with coworkers rewarding and fun.

Best of all, AOL's Instant Messenger (AIM) is free and easy to use. Plus you don't have to be an AOL member to take advantage of this feature, as you'll see from the next tip. There are several ways of launching the Instant Message (IM) window right away so you can begin communicating as often as you want. Here's how:

1. Sign on to AOL (or if you're a non-AOL member, see Tip # 30).

2. Click the **IM** button located on the AOL toolbar or select the **Send Instant Message** option from the **People** menu on the AOL toolbar or press **Ctrl+I** keys, or click the **Send IM** button in your **Buddy List** window, or click the **IM** button in your **Address Book** (see Chapter 2 for more information about the Address Book).

3. The **Send Instant Message** window appears.

4. Type your message and click the **Send** button, shown in Figure 6-7.

Figure 6-7. Sending an Instant Message note is just a mouse click away.

30 Chatting with non-AOL members in real time using Instant Messenger (AIM)

You might have wondered how you can stay in contact with friends and loved ones who aren't AOL members. Well stop wondering and start chatting. AOL lets you have free private online chats with non-AOL members just like you do with AOL members. All non-members have to do is sign up for AOL's Instant Messenger Service at Web site: http://www.aol.com or enter AOL keyword: **Instant Messenger** or **AIM**. AIM stands for AOL Instant Messenger and offers the ability to exchange instant messages with non-AOL members everywhere. The sign up process is simple and fast. Here's how it's done:

1. Connect to the Internet using your preferred service provider.

2. Connect to the **AOL Anywhere** Web site at: http://www.aol.com.

3. Click the **AOL Instant Messenger** icon located in the **People and Chat** section of the **AOL Anywhere** Web site.

4. Click the **AOL Instant Messenger** download icon and follow the onscreen instructions.

5. Complete **Step 1** of the AOL Instant Messenger Sign Up process by entering your unique screen name, password, e-mail address, and date of birth information and click the **Next** arrow.

6. Complete **Step 2** by clicking the appropriate icon to download the AOL Instant Messenger software for your computer's operating system. Available choices include: Windows, Macintosh, or Other (includes WinCE, Palm, Linux, Mac68K, and beta versions), shown in Figure 6-8.

7. Complete **Step 3** to install the downloaded software on your computer.

8. Complete **Step 4** to begin using AOL Instant Messenger by clicking the AIM icon located on your desktop. You'll need to enter the screen name along with your password you chose in Step 1.

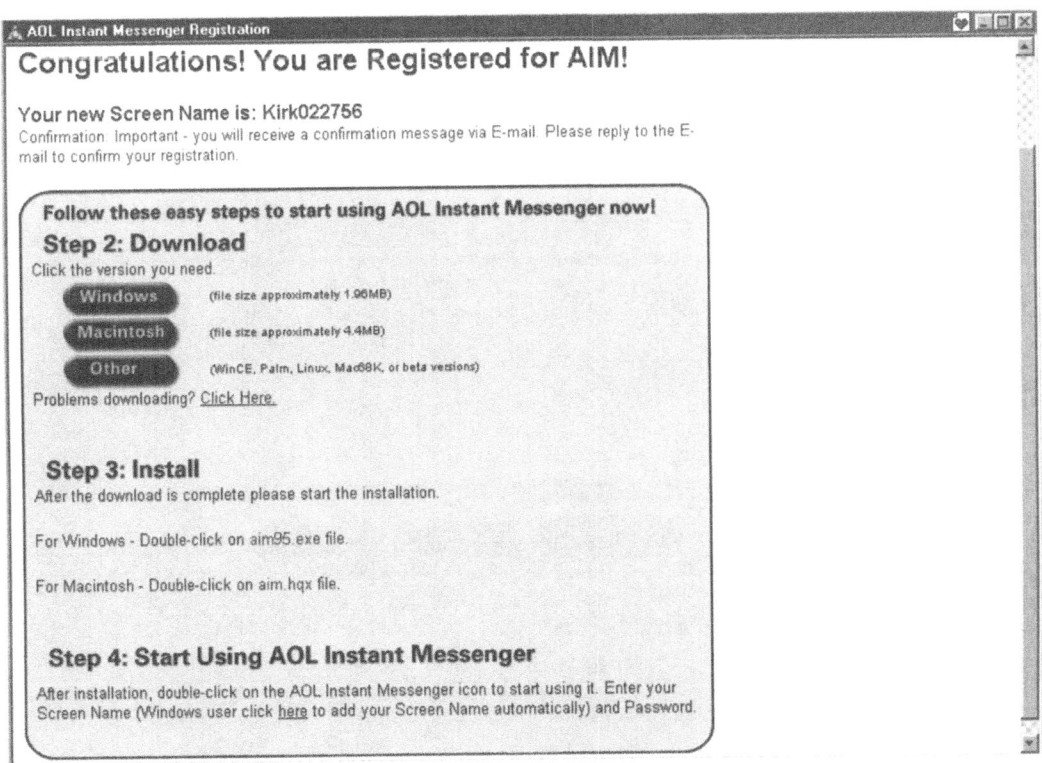

Figure 6-8. Registering for AOL Instant Messenger is fast, free, and easy.

31 Sending and receiving Instant Message notes

Participating in an Instant Message (IM) conversation with another online person is as easy as 1-2-3. After opening the **Instant Message** window, enter the screen name of the person you want to send a message to in the **To:** field, enter your message in the message box, and click the **Send** button to send the message.

If you receive an IM from someone else, you can reply to the IM by clicking the **Respond** button to continue the conversation. If you are unable to reply, AOL lets you cancel the IM by clicking the **Cancel** button.

32 Locating a buddy in your Buddy List

AOL lets you determine the whereabouts of buddies stored in your Buddy List who are currently signed on. From your Buddy List, select the screen name you want to locate and click the **Locate** button in your Buddy List window. Another way of locating a member online is to press the **Ctrl+L** keys, enter the desired screen name in the box, and click the

OK button. The resulting information will let you know whether your buddy is in one of the many chat areas or not.

33 Viewing a buddy's profile

As an AOL member, you can view any other AOL member's profile if they have taken the time to create it. The profile or directory listing is available to the entire AOL community and contains information such as a member's name, city, state, gender, marital status, hobbies, occupation, and a personal quote. AOL members are cautioned that they may prefer not to post information such as street address, telephone numbers, or other sensitive information because the entire AOL community can see it. To view a buddy's profile, follow these simple steps:

1. Press **Ctrl+G** to display the **Get a Member's Profile** window.

2. In the **Get a Member's Profile** window, enter the screen name you want information on.

3. Click the **OK** button to display the member's profile, shown in Figure 6-9.

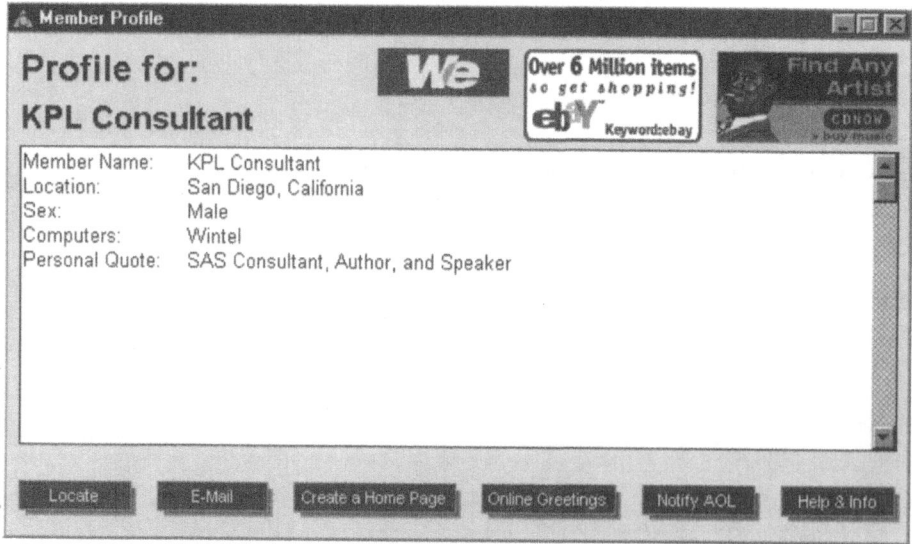

Figure 6-9. Displaying a member profile is easy.

144

34 Using the timestamp for Instant Message notes

To help you determine whether a message that has been sent to you is recent or has been sitting there for a while unnoticed, AOL provides a great feature called time stamping. *Timestamping* is the process of displaying a time to the right of the screen name. It's especially useful when you have several IM windows open at the same time and are unable to monitor the actions in each window as carefully as you'd like. By default, AOL turns this feature off, but you can turn it on or off at anytime. Here's how you can take advantage of this useful feature:

1. Click the **Setup** button on the **Buddy List** window.

2. Click the **Preferences** button on the **Buddy List Setup** window.

3. Click the **IM** tab on the **Buddy List Preferences** window.

4. Click the **Display timestamp on IM** checkbox under the Instant Message Preferences heading, shown in Figure 6-10.

5. Click the **Apply** button to save the requested changes.

6. Click the **Save** button.

35 Formatting your Instant Message notes

Instant Message notes can be formatted to express your individuality. There are two ways to control how your IM notes will look: assigning in your Preferences, or assigning in the Instant Message window itself. Both methods let you control what font and special formatting will be used.

Assigning Font, Size, Style, and Color in Preferences

The default font used in your IM notes is controlled by what has been set in your font, text, and graphics Preferences. These settings control not only what your IM notes look like, but also what the text will look like when you send e-mail and chat. To assign a preferred default font, size, style, and color for all your message text, follow these steps:

1. Select **Preferences** from the **Settings** menu on the AOL toolbar.

2. Click **Font, Text, & Graphics** from the Communications section on the **Preferences** window.

3. Select the desired font, size, style, and color to be used for your IM, e-mail, and chat notes, shown in Figure 6-11.

4. Click the **Save** button.

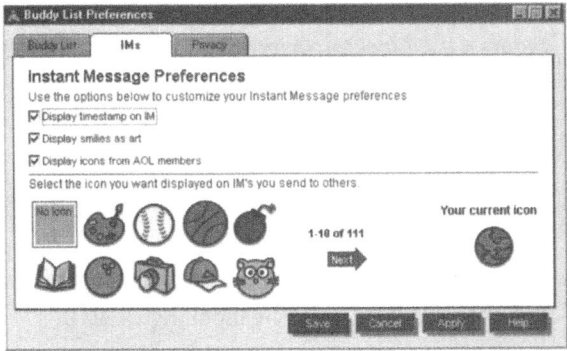

Figure 6-10. Selecting the timestamp to display on IM messages

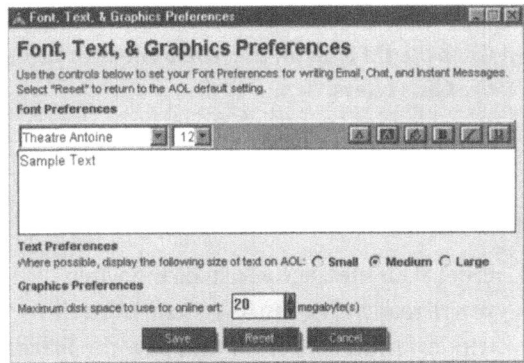

Figure 6-11. Assigning a default font, size, style, and color for IM, e-mail, and chat notes

**Assigning Font Size, Style, and Color
in the IM Window**

The default font used in each IM window is
controlled by what has been set as your font, text,
and graphics Preferences. These font and text
settings can be overridden by assigning unique font
formatting controls in a window. The advantage of
this method is that the font you assign to an individual IM window does not change the font and
text formatting properties assigned in your Preferences—so your e-mail and chat notes are not
affected. To assign a preferred font size, style, and
color in a single IM window, follow these steps:

1. Launch an IM window by pressing the
   Ctrl+I keys.

2. In the open IM window, select the desired
   font size, style, and color to be used in a
   single IM window.

3. Enter your IM notes as usual, and then click
   the **Send** button.

36 Adding hyperlinks in Instant Message notes

Have you ever wanted to share a favorite place on
the Internet with someone else? AOL lets you add
to your IM a hyperlink which, when clicked, takes
the user to another Web page or document. To add
a favorite place hyperlink to an Instant Message
note, just follow these steps:

1. Click the **IM** icon on the AOL toolbar or press
   the **Ctrl+I** keys.

2. Enter the screen name of the person you
   want to chat with in the **To:** box of the **Send
   Instant Message** window.

3. Enter your message as usual, and when
   you're ready, drag the heart icon from the
   window title bar or from your Favorite Places
   window to the open IM window. This automatically adds a hyperlink to the IM note.

4. When you're done typing your message, click
   the **Send** button.

37 Blocking Instant Message notes

You can block the receipt of Instant Message notes
at any time in the same way you block IMs for Kids
Only and Young Teens. This is a handy feature,
especially when you're too busy to deal with receiving
and responding to IM notes. Here's how it's done:

1. Select **Parental Controls** from the **Settings**
   menu on the AOL toolbar.

2. Click the **Set Parental Controls** icon on the
   AOL **Parental Controls** window.

3. Click the **IM control** icon under the **Custom
   Control** heading.

4. Click the **Block Instant Message notes**
   checkbox in the **Custom Control Settings:
   Instant Messages** window, shown in
   Figure 6-12.

5. Click the **Save** button.

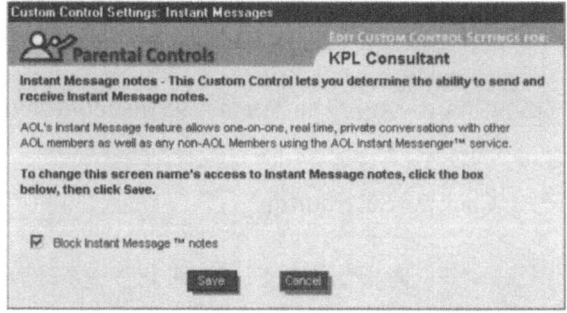

*Figure 6-12. Blocking Instant Message notes on the
Custom Control Settings window*

38 Blocking Buddy List and Instant Message notes

AOL lets you apply privacy preferences to your
Buddy List and IM notes by blocking all AOL
members and non-members. This action prevents
anyone from seeing that you're online and from
contacting you with an IM note. To block Buddy
List and Instant Message notes, follow these steps:

1. Select **Buddy List** from the **People** menu on
   the AOL toolbar.

2. Click the **Setup** button in the **Buddy List** window.

3. Click the **Preferences** button in the **Buddy List Setup** window.

4. Click the **Privacy** tab in the **Buddy List Preferences** window.

5. Click the **Block All** checkbox under the **Choose Your Privacy Preferences** heading and then click the **Buddy List and Instant Message** checkbox under the **Apply Preferences to the Following Features** heading, shown in Figure 6-13.

6. Click the **Apply** button.

7. Click the **Save** button.

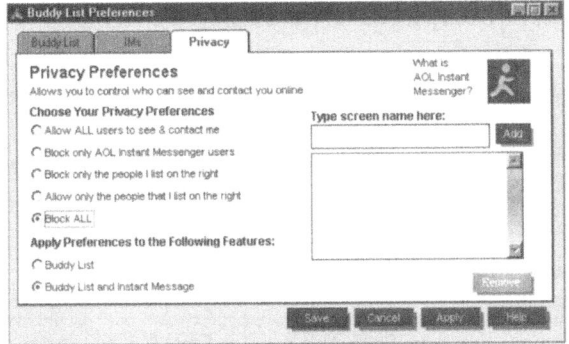

Figure 6-13. Blocking all Buddy List and Instant Message notes

39 Chatting with emotion using emoticons (smileys)

An actual dialogue between two people is always augmented with emotion, whether voluntary or involuntary. We express our emotions in a live conversation with a smile, a frown, an act of surprise, or a wink using our eyes and mouth. An online discussion between two or more people can also benefit from using expressions, sometimes known as emoticons or smileys.

Emoticons are human-face drawings composed of text characters or as artwork, depending on your AOL preference settings. Available artwork emoticons are displayed in a drop-down selection list, shown in Figure 6-14. To activate the selection list,

simply click the smiley-face button on the Instant Message window.

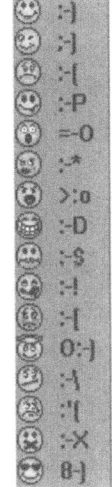

Figure 6-14. Smileys for adding fun to your IMs

40 Inserting emoticons (smileys) in Instant Message notes

AOL lets you use emoticons or smileys in your Instant Message notes to express feelings of emotion. Emoticons can be displayed as art or as text. To insert art-based emoticons, you'll need to verify that your Buddy List Preferences have the **Display smiles as art** checkbox checked. Here's how it's done:

1. Select **Buddy List** from the **People** menu on the AOL toolbar.

2. Click the **Setup** button in the **Buddy List** window.

3. Click the **Preferences** button in the **Buddy List Setup** window.

4. Click the **IMs** tab in the **Buddy List Preferences** window.

5. Click the **Display smiles as art** checkbox in the **Buddy List Preferences** window.

6. Click the **Apply** button.

7. Click the **Save** button.

Once the **Display smiles as art** checkbox is checked, you're then ready to insert art-based smiles into your IM notes. Here's how it's done.

1. Launch an IM window by pressing the **Ctrl+I** keys.

2. In the open IM window, select the desired font size, style, and color to be used in a single IM window.

3. Enter your IM notes as usual.

4. Click the **smiley face** button to display a drop-down list of smiley faces.

5. Click the desired smiley face from the selection, shown in Figure 6-15.

6. When done, click the **Send** button.

Figure 6-15. Inserting a smiley in the Send Instant Message window

41 Selecting an icon to display on Instant Messages you send others

AOL members using version 6 or higher can display an icon, or picture, from a selection of choices for all your buddies to see on your Instant Message (IM) windows. Customize your IM window with your favorite animal, instrument, food, or other icon from an assortment of icons. This feature allows you to personalize your IM window and display an icon in the lower left corner of your buddies IM window. Here's how you can personalize your IM window with your very own icon:

1. Select **Buddy List** from the **People** menu on the AOL toolbar.

2. Click the **Setup** button in the **Buddy List** window.

3. Click the **Preferences** button in the **Buddy List Setup** window.

4. Click the **IMs** tab in the **Buddy List Preferences** window.

5. Scroll through the available icons by clicking the **Next** and **Prev** buttons.

6. When you find one you like, simply click the icon and click the **Apply** button in the **Buddy List Preferences** window.

7. Click the **Save** button.

42 Displaying icons from other AOL members

If you're using version 6 or higher, you can display icons from other AOL members as you chat in their Instant Message (IM) window. By turning this feature on, you'll be able to see your buddy's personalized icon in the lower left of the IM window. It's easy to turn on. Here's how:

1. Select **Buddy List** from the **People** menu on the AOL toolbar.

2. Click the **Setup** button in the **Buddy List** window.

3. Click the **Preferences** button in the **Buddy List Setup** window.

4. Click the **IMs** tab in the **Buddy List Preferences** window.

5. Click the **Display icons from AOL members** checkbox in the **Buddy List Preferences** window.

6. Click the **Apply** button in the **Buddy List Preferences** window.

7. Click the **Save** button.

43 Double-spacing incoming messages

To avoid the normal clutter associated with incoming messages, you can have the Instant Message (IM) window automatically double-space incoming message text. This makes your buddy's incoming message text not only more readable, but helps reduce eye fatigue. Here's how to set this valuable feature in AOL:

1. Select **Preferences** from the **Settings** menu on the AOL toolbar.

2. Click **Chat** from the Communications section on the **Preferences** window.

3. Click the **Double-space incoming messages** checkbox on the **Chat Preferences** window, shown in Figure 6-16.

4. Click the **Save** button.

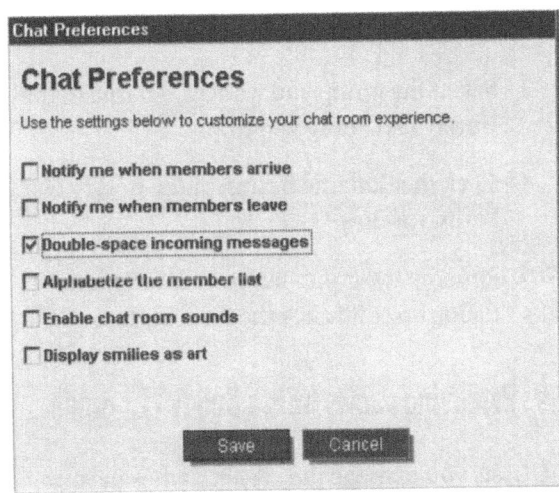

Figure 6-16. Setting Chat preferences to double-space incoming messages

44 Adding a buddy to your Buddy List

AOL offers a great feature for storing screen names or AOL Instant Messenger (AIM) names of your buddies. Your buddies can be almost anyone such as friends, family members, co-workers, and so on. Not only does it store your buddies in a handy list, but it also lets you know automatically when they sign on or off AOL. This makes for easy and spontaneous communication using the Instant Message feature. Here's how you can add one or more buddies to your Buddy List:

1. Select **Buddy List** from the **People** menu on the AOL toolbar. This will open your **Buddy List** window.

2. Click the **Setup** button in the **Buddy List** window.

3. Select the desired **Buddy List group** from the following selections: Buddies, Family, or Co-Workers.

4. Click the **Add Buddy** button in the **Buddy List Setup** window.

5. Enter the screen name or AOL Instant Messenger (AIM) name in the **Add New Buddy** dialog box and click the **Save** button.

45 Creating a Buddy List group

Initially your Buddy List consists of three empty groups: Buddies, Family, and Co-Workers. You can use these existing groups to add one or more screen names or AIM names as desired, or you can customize your Buddy List by creating one or more new groups. When a new group is needed, you can follow these easy steps to create a new Buddy List group:

1. Select **Buddy List** from the **People** menu on the AOL toolbar. This will open your **Buddy List** window.

2. Click the **Setup** button in the **Buddy List** window.

3. Click the **Add Group** button in the **Buddy List Setup** window.

4. Enter a name for the new Group, for example **Conference Contacts**, in the **Add New Group** dialog box and click the **Save** button.

5. The new Group will be added and listed in your **Buddy List** window.

46 Knowing when your buddies are online and other cool things

Your Buddy List displays useful information about whom on your list is signed on, screen names that recently signed on or signed off, and how many screen names in each group are signed on out of the total number of screen names in the group. This information is provided using special symbols. So if you want to better understand what's happening in your Buddy List, get to know the following symbols:

- *** Asterisk**—appears next to the screen name who most recently signed on. The asterisk disappears after a couple of minutes.

- **( ) Parentheses**—appears around the screen name who most recently signed off. Once a person has signed off, you'll be unable to exchange Instant Messages (IM) with that person or locate that person. The parentheses disappear once another person in your Buddy List has signed on or signed off.

- **(i/n)—(i)** displays how many people in your Buddy List group are currently signed on versus the total number of screen names for that group (n). For example, (2/7) means that two of the seven people in your Buddy List group are currently signed on.

47 Displaying your Buddy List when you sign on

AOL lets you control whether your Buddy List is open or closed when you sign on. Many people prefer to have their list open when they sign on, eliminating the need to activate it from the People menu on the AOL toolbar. AOL makes it easy to set it up so your Buddy List is open when you sign on. Here's how:

1. If your Buddy List isn't open, select **Buddy List** from the **People** menu on the AOL toolbar.

2. Click the **Setup** button in the **Buddy List** window.

3. Click the **Preferences** button in the **Buddy List Setup** window.

4. Click the **Buddy List** tab in the **Buddy List Preferences** window.

5. Click the **Show me my buddy list at sign-on** checkbox in the **Buddy List Preferences** window.

6. Click the **Apply** button in the **Buddy List Preferences** window.

7. Click the **Save** button.

48 Changing the name of a Buddy List group

AOL lets you rename a Buddy List group at any time by following a few easy steps. Here's how:

1. If your Buddy List isn't open, select **Buddy List** from the **People** menu on the AOL toolbar.

2. Click the **Setup** button in the **Buddy List** window.

3. Select the group you want to rename in the **Buddy List Setup** window.

4. Click the **Rename** button in the **Buddy List Setup** window.

5. Rename the group name in the **Rename** dialog box and click the **Save** button.

49 Removing names from a Buddy List group

AOL lets you manage the screen names in your Buddy List groups. Just follow these easy instructions and you can remove any screen names that are no longer active.

1. If your Buddy List isn't open, select **Buddy List** from the **People** menu on the AOL toolbar.

2. Click the **Setup** button in the **Buddy List** window.

3. Select the group you want to remove screen names from in the **Buddy List Setup** window.

4. Highlight the screen name you want to remove from your group's list.

5. Click the **Remove** button in the **Buddy List Setup** window.

6. Click the **Yes** button when the **Are you sure you want to delete the selected item?** question appears.

7. Repeat steps 4–6 as many times as necessary to remove unwanted screen names.

50 Setting sounds to indicate when a buddy signs on or off

You can set AOL to play sounds when a buddy in your Buddy List signs on or off. When sound settings are turned on, AOL defaults to a squeaky door opening when a buddy signs on and a door slamming closed when a buddy signs off. Otherwise no sound is played. This notification feature is easy to use and can be set at anytime by following these simple steps:

1. If your Buddy List isn't open, select **Buddy List** from the **People** menu on the AOL toolbar.

2. Click the **Setup** button in the **Buddy List** window.

3. Click the **Preferences** button in the **Buddy List Setup** window.

4. Click the **Buddy List** tab in the **Buddy List Preferences** window.

5. Click the **Play sound when buddies sign on** and **Play sound when buddies sign off** checkboxes in the **Buddy List Preferences** window.

6. Click the **Apply** button in the **Buddy List Preferences** window.

7. Click the **Save** button.

51 Using alternate Buddy List sounds

The default sounds you hear when a buddy signs on or off AOL can be changed to alternate sounds. This is part of the AOL customization process and requires you to download the Buddy Sound Installer from the AOL Sound Library. The Buddy Sound

Installer is available only under the PC operating system. Once the installer is downloaded, you'll be able to select various .WAV (Windows Audio Format) files for the BuddyIn and BuddyOut sound events. Here's how it works.

1. If your Buddy List isn't open, select **Buddy List** from the **People** menu on the AOL toolbar.

2. Click the **Setup** button in the **Buddy List** window.

3. Click the **Preferences** button in the **Buddy List Setup** window.

4. Click the **Buddy List** tab in the **Buddy List Preferences** window.

5. Click the **Go to Sound Library** button in the **Buddy List Preferences** window.

6. Click the **Buddy List Sound Library** button in the **Buddy List Sounds** window.

7. Select the sound you want to download from the **Buddy List Sounds** selection window and click the **Download Now** button, shown in Figure 6-17.

8. Save the selected .wav sound file in the desired location using the **Download Manager** window. The default download location on your hard drive for AOL version 7.0 is C:\America Online V7.0\download.

9. Click **Sounds** from your **Windows Control Panel** and point the BuddyIn and BuddyOut sound events to the desired .wav files.

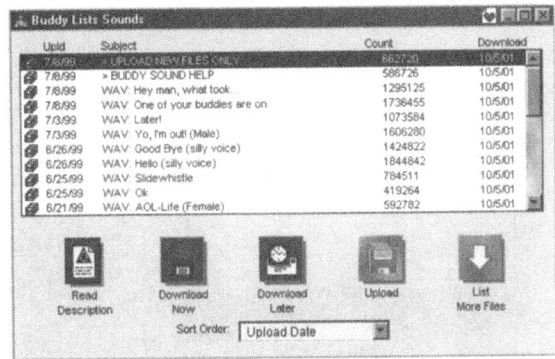

Figure 6-17. Selecting "alternate" sounds from the Buddy List Sound Library

151

52 Displaying a "Gone Fishing" notice when out of the office

If you're planning on leaving your computer for a while or don't want to be disturbed, you can display a brief message to anyone who tries to send you an Instant Message (IM). This handy feature, often referred to as an "Away Notice," lets you notify others that you're not available. Here are the easy steps you can follow to set up an "Away Notice" the next time work or anything else takes you away from your computer.

1. If your Buddy List isn't open, select **Buddy List** from the **People** menu on the AOL toolbar.

2. Click the **Away Notice** button located at the bottom of your **Buddy List** window.

3. Select the type of message you want to display in the **Away Message** selection window. The available categories to choose from are: I am Away, On the Phone, At Lunch, and Be Right Back, shown in Figure 6-18.

4. Click the appropriate button on the **Away Message** selection window to indicate whether you want to enter a new message using **New**, modify an existing message using **Edit**, or delete an existing message using **Delete**. Once the selection is made, click the **OK** button.

5. Enter a title and message in the corresponding **Enter Title** and **Enter New Message** fields, and click the **Save** button, shown in Figure 6-19.

6. The new message will automatically display in the **Away Message** selection window. Click the **OK** button.

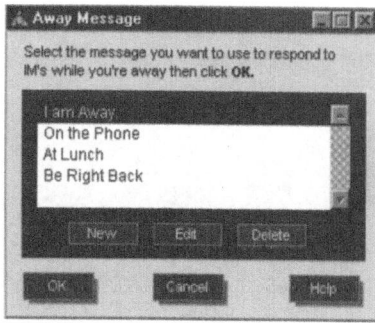

Figure 6-18. Selecting the type of message you want to use to respond to IMs while you're away

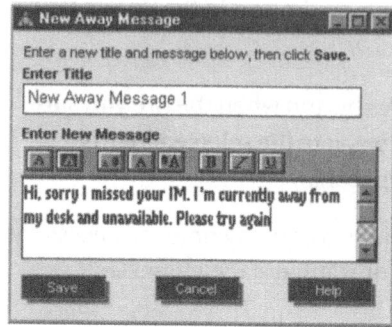

Figure 6-19. Entering a New Away Message

53 Deleting a Buddy List group

When you no longer need a Buddy List group or its contents, you can delete individual buddies or the entire group. Here's how it's done:

1. If your Buddy List isn't open, select **Buddy List** from the **People** menu on the AOL toolbar.

2. Click the **Setup** button in the **Buddy List** window.

3. Select the group you no longer want in the **Buddy List Setup** window and click the **Remove** button.

54 Security concerns with Instant Messages

When you are messaging with your friends, you need have little concern about security, because viruses don't transmit via AOL Instant Messenger (AIM). This is an advantage to using a service like AOL over communicating with e-mail on the Internet.

Still, if you receive a request from someone you don't know for chat on Instant Message and you become suspicious, you can click on the button to notify AOL. Your message window will close and the AOL Security Team will look into it.

🖉 *AOL correspondence always is sent in a blue envelope on your screen. That way you know it's official.*

Using Message Boards

55 Message board etiquette

With the great selection of AOL message boards, you'll have no problem finding others who share your interests. Message boards are not the same as chat rooms because conversations are not immediate. Instead, messages are posted and saved for months so others can read and respond to them. They are also frequently monitored by AOL personnel and must conform to certain rules of conduct as stated in the AOL Online Content Guidelines.

First, messages should not contain vulgar language, explicit sexual content, hate language or speech, and any type of language offensive to any person or group of people. Second, photos revealing frontal nudity should never be posted. Next, depictions of illegal drug use as acceptable forms of behavior are not permitted. Finally, graphic images containing blood and gore, and/or violence are not acceptable and should never be posted. Should you identify offensive behavior, you can naturally ignore it, or you may report it by typing AOL Keyword: **Notify AOL**.

56 Finding message board communities

Message boards are a electronic bulletin boards covering practically any type of topic and community you can think of. So you may be wondering, how can I access them? That's easy. Practically every AOL window you'll access has a message board area. So look for the phrase "message boards" in the windows that display. Chances are you'll find just what you're looking for.

One way to begin your search for AOL message boards is to access the message board Search Web site at AOL Keyword: **message board**. All you need to

do is enter a search word or phrase in the search field and click the **Search** button, shown in Figure 6-20.

Figure 6-20. Entering a word or phrase in the Quick Search Message Board Search Web site

You can customize the specific search options using message board Custom Search, which provides a more flexible searching mechanism. From drop-down boxes you can select the search language to use and the dates for which you want to display messages.

Another way to access AOL's message board communities is to type in AOL Keyword: **Hometown**. The categories of communities make it easy to access a particular interest. They include Business Park, Careers & Money, Cultures & Beliefs, Education & News, Entertainment & Games, Family & Home, Food & Travel, Health & Wellness, Hobbies & Interests, Local, Personal Interests, Sports & Recreation, and Women's Interests.

You can usually access a community of message board forums by clicking the folder button located at the top of each message board window. The list, once displayed, will identify the topics and subjects available in that category of AOL message boards. As an example, a partial list of Professional message board forums is shown in Figure 6-21.

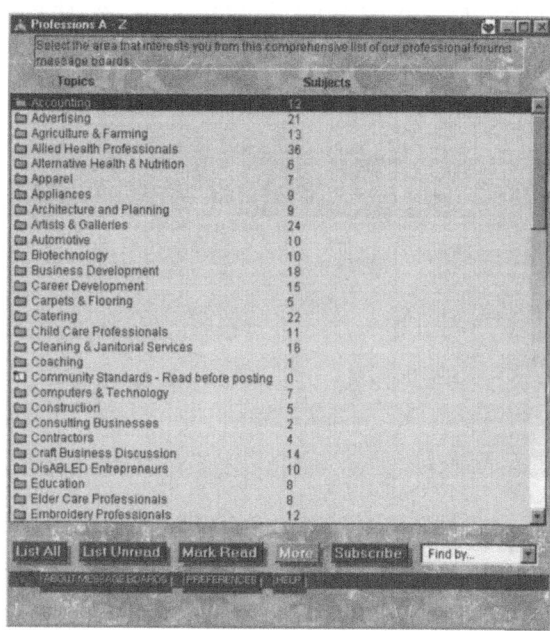

Figure 6-21. Some Professional message board forums

57 Finding messages

To find messages related to your specific interests, enter a search word or phrase in the top field of the Custom Search window. For example, entering **Consulting** in the search box (combined with the search language and dates you choose) results in the search results being displayed in the AOL message board window. The information displayed in the Search Results window consists of a score indicating how closely the results matches your search word or phrase, the date the message was posted, the subject of the message, the author's screen name, and the message board where the message was found, shown in Figure 6-22.

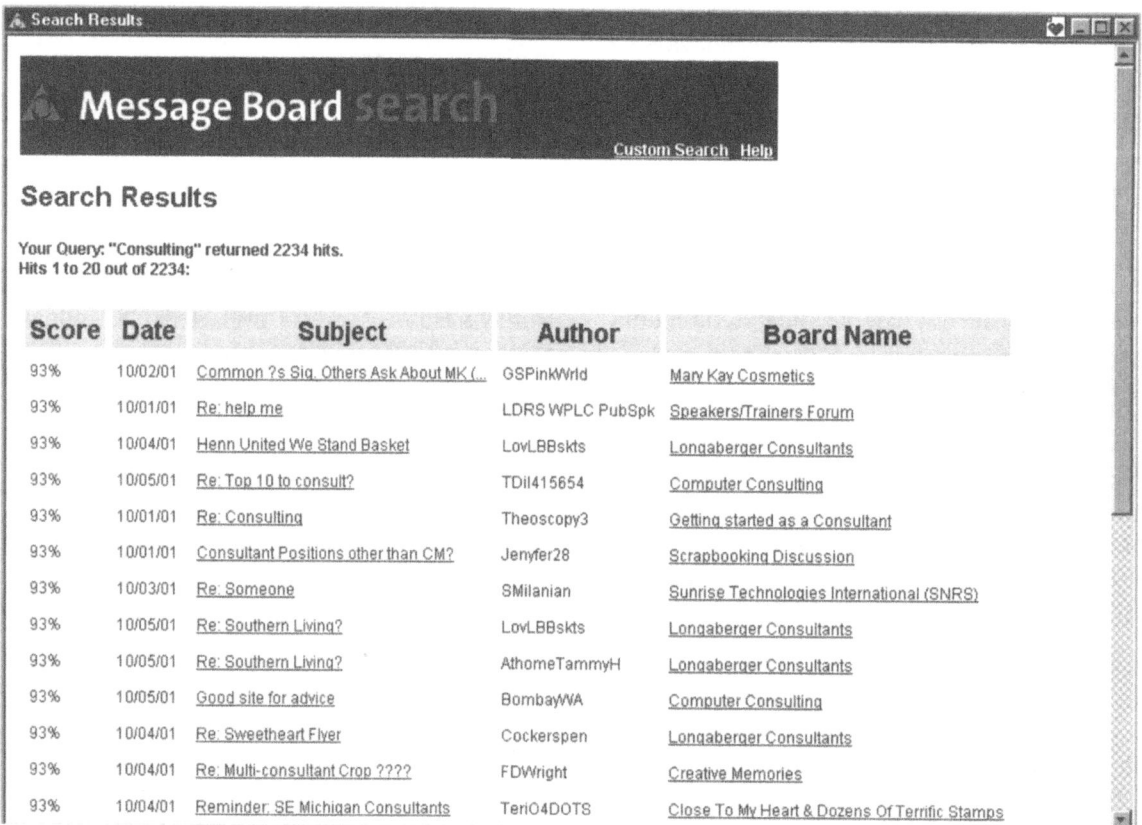

Score	Date	Subject	Author	Board Name
93%	10/02/01	Common ?s Sig. Others Ask About MK (...	GSPinkWrld	Mary Kay Cosmetics
93%	10/01/01	Re: help me	LDRS WPLC PubSpk	Speakers/Trainers Forum
93%	10/04/01	Henn United We Stand Basket	LovLBBskts	Longaberger Consultants
93%	10/05/01	Re: Top 10 to consult?	TDil415654	Computer Consulting
93%	10/01/01	Re: Consulting	Theoscopy3	Getting started as a Consultant
93%	10/01/01	Consultant Positions other than CM?	Jenyfer28	Scrapbooking Discussion
93%	10/03/01	Re: Someone	SMilanian	Sunrise Technologies International (SNRS)
93%	10/05/01	Re: Southern Living?	LovLBBskts	Longaberger Consultants
93%	10/05/01	Re: Southern Living?	AthomeTammyH	Longaberger Consultants
93%	10/05/01	Good site for advice	BombayWA	Computer Consulting
93%	10/04/01	Re: Sweetheart Flyer	Cockerspen	Longaberger Consultants
93%	10/04/01	Re: Multi-consultant Crop ????	FDWright	Creative Memories
93%	10/04/01	Reminder: SE Michigan Consultants	Teri04DOTS	Close To My Heart & Dozens Of Terrific Stamps

Figure 6-22. The message board displays the search results using the requested search criteria.

58 Viewing message board messages

It is not uncommon for the message board search results to return a large number of messages, especially for popular topics. In these circumstances, you may need to scroll through the results by clicking **Next 20 Results** at the bottom of your Search Results window. You'll see the relevancy of the results, when a message was posted, the subject line, by whom it was posted, and to what message board it was posted. This is useful information and frequently helps in determining whether a message should be read.

59 Reading message board messages

Reading a message board message is easy. From the Search Results window, select the message you'd like to read. With the message opened, the first thing you'll notice is its resemblance to an e-mail message. Message board messages consist of a subject line, the date the message was posted to the board, the screen name of the person who posted the message, and then the message itself.

There are a number of buttons located at the bottom of the message window that allow you to do the following: move from message to message within a subject, move from subject to subject, mark a read message as unread, list all subjects in that board, show subjects that haven't been read, or display more message text.

60 Setting message board preferences

To set your personal message board window settings, you'll need to select a board name in the Search Results window, and then click the **Preferences** button located at the bottom of the message board window. For example, selecting **Computer Consulting** from the list displayed in Search Results displays a message board window containing one or more messages, shown in Figure 6-23. This action opens the **Global Message Board Preferences** setting the actions for every board you open, and it consists of three tab categories: **Viewing**, **Posting**, and **Filtering**. Once selections are made

on each tab, click the **Save** button to apply the custom settings you've chosen.

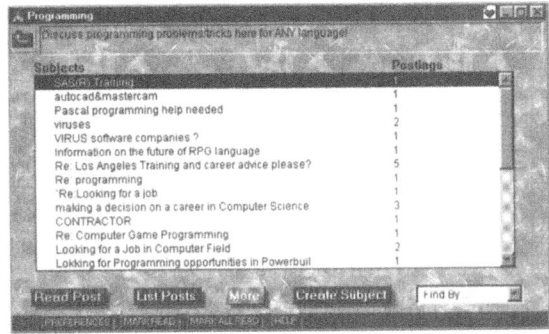

Figure 6-23. Programming message board window

61 Posting a message to a message board

Posting a message to a message board is as easy as creating and sending an e-mail message. You have two basic choices: You can create the message to be posted as the first post of a new subject, or you can reply to an existing post that you're currently reading (see next tip). To create a new subject to be posted, follow these instructions:

1. Open a message board of interest, if it isn't already open.

2. Click the **Create Subject** button located at the bottom of the **message board** window. The **Post New Message** window will appear.

3. Enter a subject line in the **Subject** text box and then enter your message, adding whatever formatting and hyperlinks you want, shown in Figure 6-24.

4. Once you've had time to review your message and are satisfied with what it says, click the **Send** button.

5. Click the **OK** button in the dialog box that displays **Your message has been sent**.

6. Your message will appear in the list of messages within a few minutes.

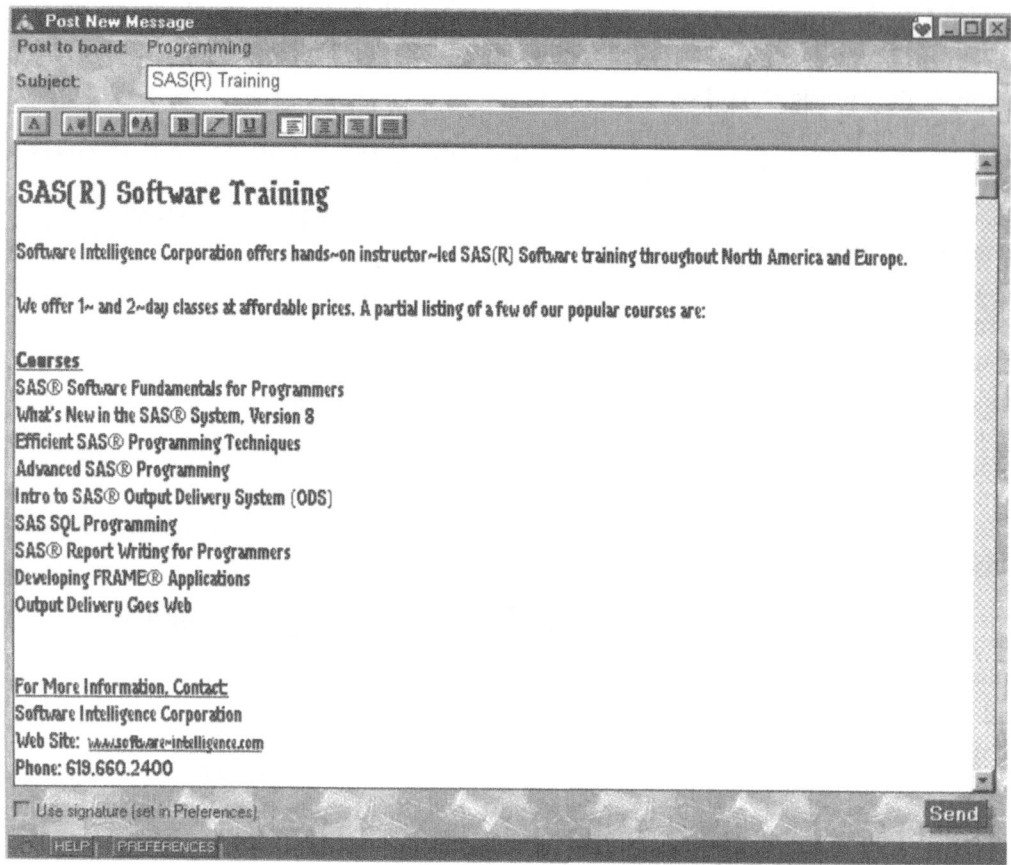

Figure 6-24. Posting a message to a message board

62 Replying to a message board message

AOL makes replying to a message board post easy. You can either reply to the message board itself, making your reply visible by everyone, or you can reply in a more private setting to the person who wrote the post by sending an e-mail. The choice is yours. You can reply by sending a message directly to the message board, sending a message via e-mail, or if in doubt, sending a message to both.

Replying to a Posted Message on the Message Board

1. Open a message board of interest, if it isn't already open.

2. Click the **Reply** button located at the bottom of the **message board** window. The **Reply** window appears.

3. In the **Reply** window, click the **Post to message board** checkbox to send your reply to the message board, shown in Figure 6-25.

4. Enter your reply message and click the **Send** button.

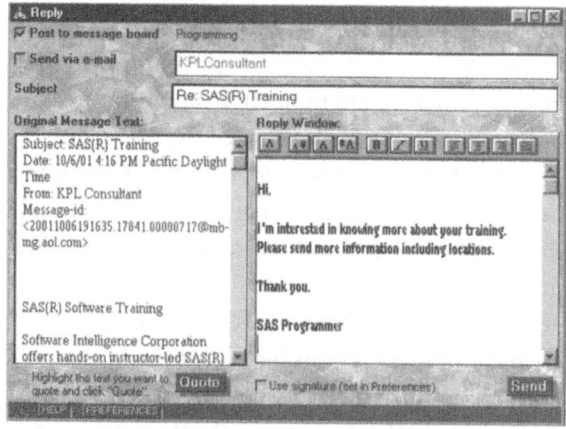

Figure 6-25. Replying to the message board where the message resides

Replying to a Posted Message via E-mail

1. Open a message board of interest, if it isn't already opened.

2. Click the **Reply** button located at the bottom of the **Message Board** window. The **Reply** window appears.

3. In the **Reply** window, click the **Send via e-mail** checkbox to send your reply to the message board.

4. Enter your reply message and click the **Send** button.

63 Removing a post from a message board

If you want to remove a post that you've made to a message board, you'll need to contact the forum leader for the message board. This contact information can usually be found in the area of the message board and is sometimes identified by a label such as "Meet the Staff," "About this Area," or some other identifying label. Review any folders or articles related to suggestions on using the board and you may find instructions on removing a post once it's been made. Follow the instructions, identify the screen name of the forum leader, and request the removal of the posted message.

CHAPTER 7

AOL Newsgroups

THIS CHAPTER EXPLORES a popular AOL communication medium commonly referred to as newsgroups. You'll uncover secrets, shortcuts, and tips about newsgroups that will help you communicate more effectively with people who share the same interests as you. Although similar to message boards (see Chapter 6), newsgroups offer an even wider range of discussion topics, from modern art to biotechnology, business to finance, pizza to religion, and virtually any other topic under the sun, you'll find a discussion group to pique your interest. And best of all, AOL members can participate free of charge. To enhance your online experience, you'll discover ways to filter out the "junk" from the content that matters most to you. Newsgroups contain strong and diverse communities as well as fascinating conversations.

In this chapter, you'll learn how to

- Find and subscribe to newsgroups

- Set personal preferences

- Use proper netiquette behavior

- Read and post messages

- Search and post to newsgroups offline

- Express yourself with emoticons

- Manage newsgroup messages and mail

Getting Started with Newsgroups

1 AOL newsgroups–communicating with like-minded people

Over the years newsgroups have become increasingly popular primarily for their ability to allow communication on a variety of diverse topics. Their appeal has grown so much that virtually any topic now exists on the Internet. Because of this they have become a very popular medium for AOL users in general. Many users prefer newsgroups to other mediums such as message boards because they have greater control over posting and reading message posts. Another reason is that newsgroups have been around for a long time, so they have become an important part of the online culture.

2 Accessing popular newsgroup categories

Newsgroups exist on virtually any topic. Because of their diverse nature, they're organized into categories to aid in their search. Each category is structured in a hierarchy, similar to a Windows or DOS directory structure. Here's a sampling of popular categories:

AOL	Health
Apparel	Home
Art	Hobbies
Automotive	Legal
Beliefs	Life
Biotechnology	Local

Business	Marketing
Careers	Money
Catering	News
Child care	Personal
Computers	Recreation
Construction	Regional
Consulting	Religion
Cultures	Sports
Education	Travel
Elder care	Weather
Entertainment	Wellness
Family	Women's Issues
Food	World
Games	

3 Finding newsgroups of interest

Newsgroups are pretty much concentrated in one area on AOL rather than being scattered all over the Internet, the way message boards are. Finding one or more newsgroups related to your specific interests requires that you enter either a search word or phrase as part of your search. For example, if you enter "Consulting" in the search box, you'll get your results displayed in the AOL Newsgroups window. You'll notice a score indicating how closely the results matches your search word or phrase, the date the message was posted, the subject of the message, the author's screen name, and the message board where the message was found. To help find newsgroups that satisfy a particular interest, just follow these steps.

1. Click the **Keyword** button located on the AOL toolbar and enter AOL Keyword: **Newsgroups** and click the **Go** button, or click the **AOL Services** button located on the AOL toolbar, then select **Internet** from the drop-down menu choices and click **Newsgroups**. Either method displays the **Newsgroups** window, shown in Figure 7-1.

2. Click the **Search All Newsgroups** button on the **Newsgroups** window.

3. In the **Search All Newsgroups** window, enter a word or phrase in the search field and click the **List Articles** button, shown in Figure 7-2. Click the **More** button to see another twenty entries in the result display.

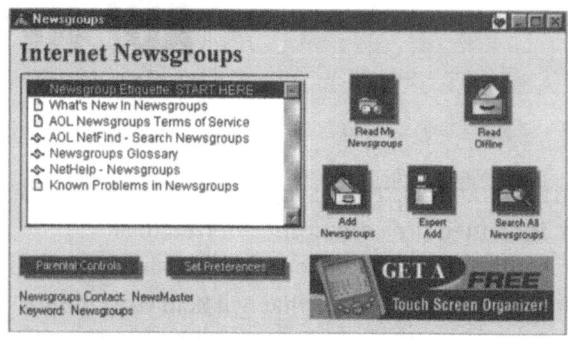

Figure 7-1. Accessing AOL's Newsgroups channel

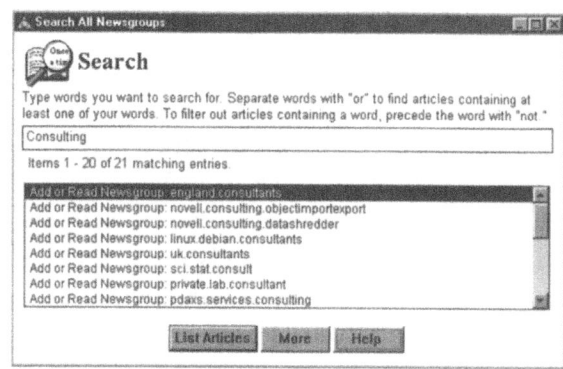

Figure 7-2. Newsgroup search results

4 Getting help with newsgroups

You can get online assistance for many of your newsgroup questions by accessing the online Help facility, called Help, or Frequently Asked Questions (FAQs). Here's how:

1. Click the **Keyword** button located on the AOL toolbar and enter AOL Keyword: **Newsgroups** and click the **Go** button, or click the **AOL Services** button located on the AOL toolbar, then select **Internet** from the drop-down menu choices and click **Newsgroups**. Either method displays the **Newsgroups** window.

2. Click the **Search All Newsgroups** button on the **Newsgroups** window.

3. Double-click the newsgroup to open it.

4. With the newsgroup of choice opened, click the **Help** button, usually located at the bottom of the window or some other convenient location.

5 Searching for additional newsgroup communities with AOL Search

You can use AOL Search to expand your search of newsgroup communities. AOL Search provides a Web site that allows you to enter one or more search words to search for additional newsgroup communities. Here's how it works:

1. Click the **Keyword** button located on the AOL toolbar and enter AOL Keyword: **AOL Search** and click the **Go** button. The **AOL Search** Web site appears.

2. In the **AOL Search** Web site, enter **AOL Neighborhood** in the search field.

3. Click **AOL Neighborhood**. This displays the **AOL Neighborhood Newsgroups** Web site.

6 Acquiring good newsgroup netiquette

With the large selection of AOL message boards, you'll have no problem finding others who share your interests. Newsgroups are similar to message boards in that conversations are not immediate. Newsgroup messages are posted and saved for months so others can read and respond to them. AOL personnel may moderate some newsgroups, but most are not moderated. Regardless of whether a newsgroup is moderated or not, you should make every attempt to conform to the rules of conduct as stated in the AOL Online Content Guidelines. A summary follows:

1. Messages should not contain vulgar language, explicit sexual content, hate language or speech, and any type of language offensive to any person or group of people.

2. Photos revealing frontal nudity should never be posted.

3. Depictions of illegal drug use as acceptable forms of behavior are not permitted.

4. Graphic images containing blood and gore, and/or violence are not acceptable. Content of this nature should be avoided at all times. Should you identify offensive behavior, you can naturally ignore it, or you may report it by typing AOL Keyword: **Notify AOL**.

When posting a message, always remember that it'll only be posted on a single newsgroup. AOL doesn't allow a single message to be posted to several newsgroups. This activity is commonly referred to as cross posting. Not only is it an unacceptable newsgroup behavior, it causes increased traffic across newsgroups.

Posting messages to newsgroups with objectionable content may result in a terms of service action levied by AOL. AOL members must follow the rules of proper newsgroup use and etiquette in order to prevent a suspension or possible termination of your account. The following terms of service guidelines should be adhered to:

1. Avoid commercial content that sells, promotes, or advertises products or services. Newsgroup participants strongly object to these types of posts.

2. Avoid posting chain letters.

3. Avoid posting objectionable material containing crude comments, hate mail, sexual images, and other negative messages.

7 Subscribing to a newsgroup

AOL lets you subscribe to newsgroups free of charge. By subscribing, you're informing AOL that you'd like to access the messages that are posted. As a convenience to you, AOL tracks the messages that its already sent so you'll only receive new messages. This eliminates the possibility of reading the same message twice—a true time saving feature. Here's how you can subscribe to a newsgroup:

1. Click the **Keyword** button located on the AOL toolbar and enter AOL Keyword: **Newsgroups** and click the **Go** button, or click the **AOL Services** button located on the AOL toolbar, then select **Internet** from the drop-down menu choices and click **Newsgroups**. Either method displays the **Newsgroups** window.

2. Click the **Add Newsgroups** button on the **Newsgroups** window to view a list of newsgroups.

3. Double-click a category that interests you from the **Add Newsgroups—Categories** window.

4. Double-click a category that interests you.

5. Highlight the specific newsgroup displayed on the list, and click the **Subscribe** button, shown in Figure 7-3.

6. Click the **OK** button in the **You have been subscribed to** _____ newsgroup dialog box.

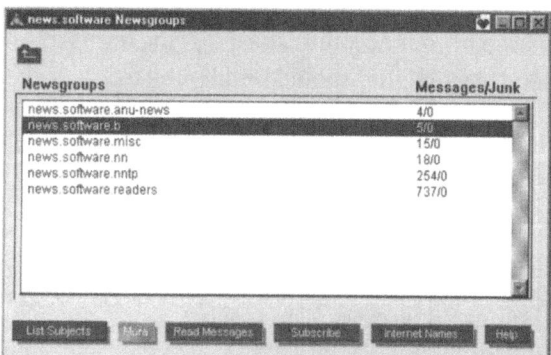

Figure 7-3. Selecting and subscribing to a newsgroup

8 Canceling or unsubscribing from a newsgroup

If the newsgroup you subscribed to is not what you expected or is no longer interesting, you can cancel or unsubscribe at anytime. Just follow these simple steps to cancel your subscription:

1. Click the **Keyword** button located on the AOL toolbar and enter AOL Keyword: **Newsgroups** and click the **Go** button, or click the **AOL Services** button located on the AOL toolbar, then select **Internet** from the drop-down menu choices and click **Newsgroups**. Either method displays the **Newsgroups** window.

2. Click the **Read My Newsgroups** button on the **Newsgroups** window to view a list of newsgroups.

3. Select the newsgroup you want to cancel from the **Read My Newsgroups** window, and click the **Remove** button.

9 Selecting newsgroup messages to read offline

Messages that are posted to newsgroups can be retrieved and stored in your Filing Cabinet using Automatic AOL while you're offline. This is a handy feature because it lets you decide when AOL should be accessed to retrieve the messages in a newsgroup. This means that you don't have to manually sign on and capture the newsgroups message posts, but have AOL automatically do it for you. Only new messages will be downloaded to your Filing Cabinet. Here's how to do it:

1. Click the **Keyword** button located on the AOL toolbar and enter AOL Keyword: **Newsgroups** and click the **Go** button, or click the **AOL Services** button located on the AOL toolbar, then select **Internet** from the drop-down menu choices and click **Newsgroups**. Either method displays the **Newsgroups** window.

2. Click the **Read Offline** button on the **Newsgroups** window to view a list of newsgroups that you've subscribed to.

3. Highlight the newsgroups you'd like to read offline and click the **Add** button in the **Choose Newsgroups** window, shown in Figure 7-4.

4. Click the **OK** button in the **Choose Newsgroups** window.

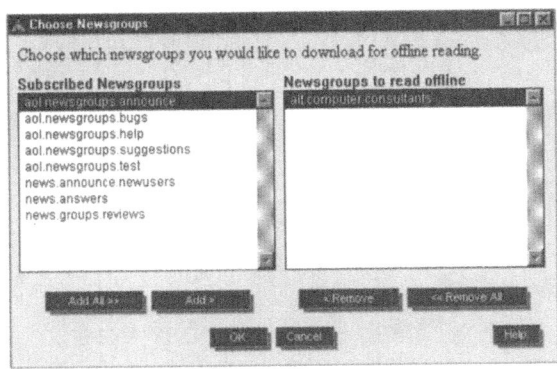

Figure 7-4. Choosing newsgroups to download for offline reading

10 Searching for newsgroup posts

With AOL, you'll be able to search for newsgroup posts quickly and easily. AOL lets you search in the subject lines, newsgroup descriptions, and message text to find what you're looking for. Here's how it works.

Searching Newsgroup Subject Lines

1. Click the **Keyword** button located on the AOL toolbar and enter AOL Keyword: **Newsgroups** and click the **Go** button, or click the **AOL Services** button located on the AOL toolbar, then select **Internet** from the drop-down menu choices and click **Newsgroups**. Either method displays the **Newsgroups** window.

2. Click the **Read My Newsgroups** button on the **Newsgroups** window to view a list of newsgroups.

3. Double-click the newsgroup you subscribe to in the **Read My Newsgroups** window.

4. Click **Find in Top Window** (or press CTRL+F keys) from the **Edit** menu located above the AOL toolbar.

5. Enter the word or phrase you're searching for in the **Find in Top Window** dialog box, shown in Figure 7-5.

6. Click the **Find** button in the **Find in Top Window** dialog box. Click the **Find** button again to locate additional occurrences of the word or phrase. Any subjects that match your search criteria will be highlighted in the **Subjects** window.

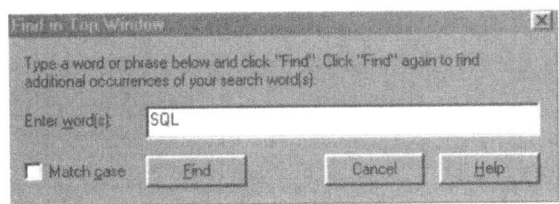

Figure 7-5. Entering a word to search newsgroup subject lines

Searching Newsgroup Posts

1. Click the **Keyword** button located on the AOL toolbar and enter AOL Keyword: **Newsgroups** and click the **Go** button, or click the **AOL Services** button located on the AOL toolbar, then select **Internet** from the drop-down menu choices and click **Newsgroups**. Either method displays the **Newsgroups** window.

2. Click **AOL NetFind—Search Newsgroups** located in the scrollable selection window on the **Newsgroups** window to search for specific articles or entire newsgroups.

3. Click either the **Newsgroup Articles** or **Descriptions** radio button, and enter a keyword to search for.

4. Click the **Find** button.

5. Your results will be displayed in a **Google Search Results** window, shown in Figure 7-6.

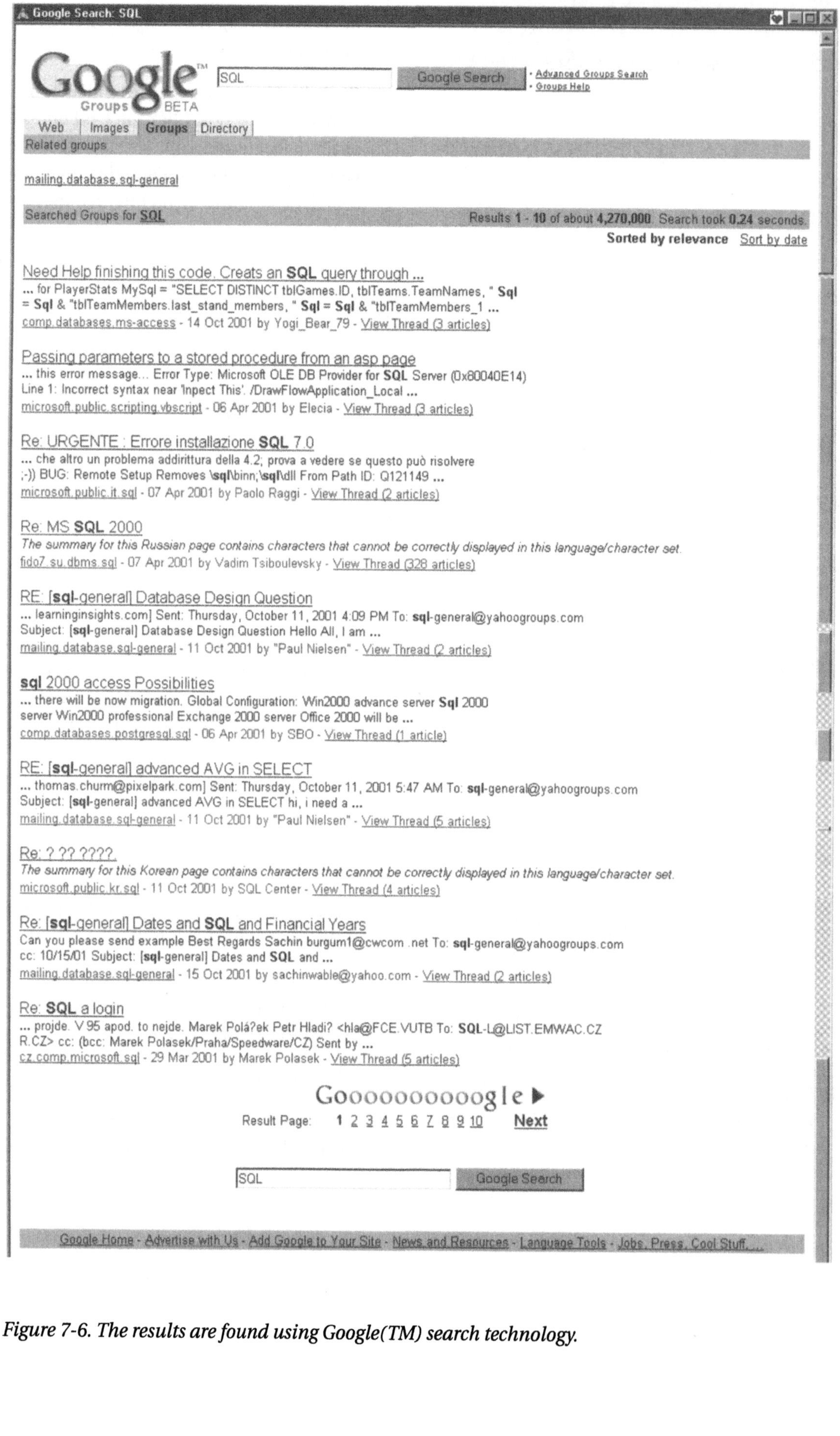

Figure 7-6. The results are found using Google(TM) search technology.

11 Setting personal newsgroup preferences

AOL lets you designate specific preferences for each newsgroup you visit. You'll be able to hide binary files, read newsgroup postings offline, limit the length of displayed messages, restrict how old messages can be, and assign filters to display messages that suit your interests. Here's how it works.

1. Click the **Keyword** button located on the AOL toolbar and enter AOL Keyword: **Newsgroups** and click the **Go** button, or click the **AOL Services** button located on the AOL toolbar, then select **Internet** from the drop-down menu choices and click **Newsgroups**. Either method displays the **Newsgroups** window.

2. Click the **Add Newsgroups** button on the **Newsgroups** window to view a list of newsgroups.

3. Double-click a category that interests you from the **Add Newsgroups – Categories** window.

4. In the opened newsgroup window, click the **Preferences** button.

5. Set the newsgroup preferences in the **Group Preferences** window that appears and click the **Save** button, shown in Figure 7-7.

12 Setting global preferences

AOL also lets you set global preferences to control all newsgroups. By setting your global preferences you'll be able to control whether postings containing encoded sounds, images or software can be downloaded; whether newsgroup postings can be read offline; whether long postings are read; whether old postings are displayed; and whether filtering should be applied to postings to restrict what is displayed. Here's how it's done:

1. Click the **Keyword** button located on the AOL toolbar and enter AOL Keyword: **Newsgroups** and click the **Go** button, or click the **AOL Services** button located on the AOL toolbar, then select **Internet** from the drop-down menu choices and click **Newsgroups**. Either method displays the **Newsgroups** window.

2. Click the **Set Preferences** button in the Newsgroups window.

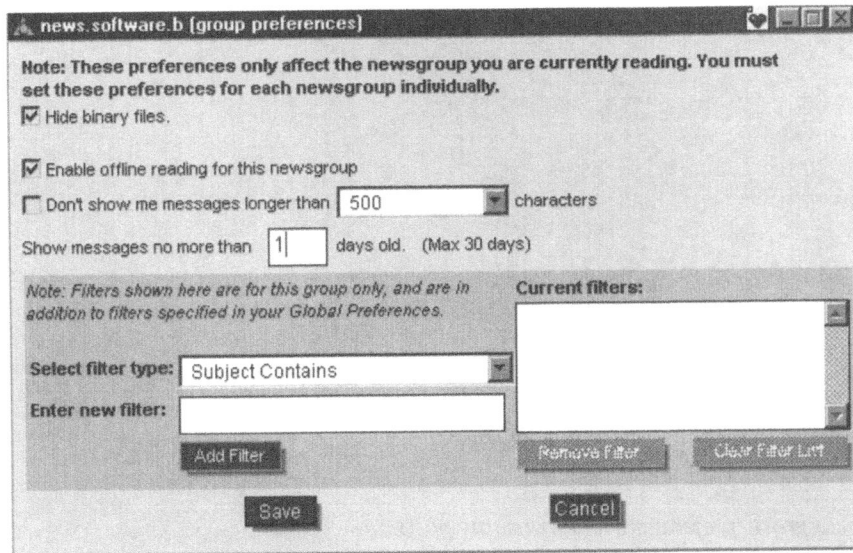

Figure 7-7. Setting newsgroup preferences

3. Click the **Viewing** tab and select the desired preferences for viewing newsgroups in the **Global Newsgroups Preferences** window, shown in Figure 7-8.

4. Click the **Posting** tab and select the desired preferences for posting newsgroup messages in the **Global Newsgroups Preferences** window. Enter a name that you want to appear after your e-mail address in all your posts, and an optional signature consisting of a maximum of 254 characters.

5. Click the **Filtering** tab and select the desired preferences for restricting junk newsgroup messages in the **Global Newsgroups Preferences** window.

6. Click the **Save** button to save your global newsgroup preferences settings.

13 Limiting your child's access to newsgroups

Unlike message boards, newsgroups are open to anyone on the Internet and therefore aren't subject to AOL's terms of service guidelines. Because postings could contain objectionable content such as vulgar language, sexual comments, or files of an unsuitable nature, you may find it necessary to limit your child's access to newsgroups. AOL lets you control how much or how little your child can interact with newsgroup content. Here's how:

1. Click **Parental Controls** from the **Settings** menu on the AOL toolbar.

2. Click **Set Parental Controls** from the AOL **Parental Controls** window.

3. From the **Edit controls for** list, select the screen name you want to block downloads for.

4. Click **Newsgroups** from the **Parental Controls** window.

5. Click the appropriate check box to control what your child can or can't do in newsgroups from the **Custom Control Settings: Newsgroups** window. For example, to block access to all newsgroups click the **Block all newsgroups** check box.

6. Click the **Save** button to save new settings.

7. Click the **OK** button in the **Your changes to Newsgroup Controls have been saved** dialog box.

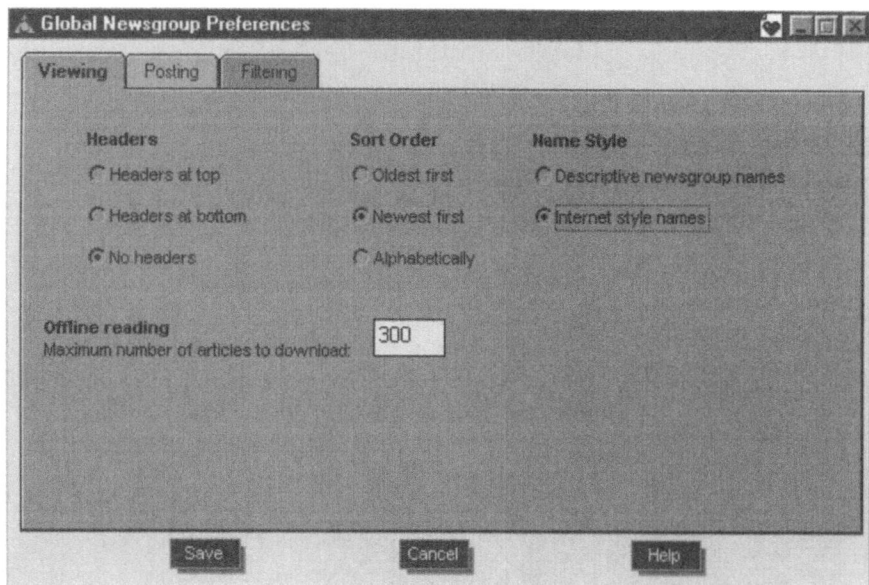

Figure 7-8. Selecting global newsgroup preferences when viewing posts

14 Downloading from newsgroups

Occasionally binary files are posted to newsgroups. Binary files are non-text files that contain bits and bytes of non-printable text such as executable machine code, graphic images, sound, or video. Although all AOL accounts are preset to automatically block binary downloads from newsgroups, this setting can be changed by the master screen name at any time by following a few simple steps. Here's how it's done:

1. Click **Parental Controls** from the **Settings** menu on the AOL toolbar.

2. Click **Set Parental Controls** from the AOL **Parental Controls** window.

3. From the **Edit controls for** list, select the screen name you want to unblock downloads for.

4. Click **Newsgroups** from the **Parental Controls** window.

5. Remove the check mark from the **Block newsgroup file download** check box to permit the downloading of binary files in the **Custom Control Settings: Newsgroups** window.

6. Click the **Save** button to save new settings.

7. Click the **OK** button in the **Your changes to Newsgroup Controls have been saved** dialog box.

Once a binary file is posted to a newsgroup, it is automatically converted to an encoded format. The downloading of a file from a newsgroup causes AOL to automatically convert or decode the file's encoded format using a special software feature known as File Grabber.

✎ *When downloading files from newsgroups, you should always check for viruses and Trojan Horse programs before opening them.*

15 Blocking downloads

Because downloaded files may contain computer viruses or Trojan Horse programs, or objectionable graphic images that may compromise or cause harm to your hardware or software, AOL automatically prevents binary downloads from newsgroups. In the event that this setting has been reset, you can prevent the downloading of binary files for any screen name by following these steps:

1. Click **Parental Controls** from the **Settings** menu on the AOL toolbar.

2. Click **Set Parental Controls** from the AOL **Parental Controls** window.

3. From the **Edit controls for: list**, select the screen name you want to block downloads for.

4. Click **Newsgroups** from the **Parental Controls** window.

5. Click the **Block newsgroup file download** check box from the **Custom Control Settings: Newsgroups** window.

6. Click the Save button to save new settings.

7. Click the **OK** button in the **Your changes to Newsgroup Controls have been saved.** dialog box.

16 Unable to add a newsgroup

If you've received an error that says you can't add a newsgroup to your newsgroup list, one of the following problems may exist:

1. The newsgroup may have an invalid name that is not recognized or is misspelled. Check to make sure the correct spelling of the newsgroup is being specified.

2. Parental control settings may be blocking the newsgroup from being added. To allow access to the newsgroup, reset parental controls using the master screen name.

3. The newsgroup may not be found because it hasn't been added to the AOL servers yet. Wait a few days and try accessing the newsgroup again.

17 Reading postings offline

In order to read newsgroup postings while offline, you'll need to first set up Automatic AOL to sign on to AOL and have AOL automatically read postings for you. Here's how it's done:

1. Click **Preferences** from the **Settings** menu on the AOL toolbar.

2. Click **Auto AOL** from the **Communications** section on the **Preferences** window.

3. Click the **Get unread postings and put in "Incoming Postings" folder** check box and schedule when **Automatic AOL** is to run by clicking the **Schedule Automatic AOL** button.

4. Click the **OK** button in the **Schedule Automatic AOL** window.

5. Select the screen name to use and enter the password for the screen name.

Once you've set up Automatic AOL, you're ready to read newsgroup postings offline that have been stored to your computer's hard drive. Here's how it's done:

1. Select **Offline Newsgroups** from the **File** menu located above the AOL toolbar.

2. Enter your password for the selected screen name.

3. Open the **Incoming/Saved Postings** folder by double-clicking it.

4. To read a posting, double-click it.

18 Viewing and reading newsgroup messages

It is not uncommon for the newsgroup search results to return a large number of matched entries, especially for popular topics. In such circumstances, you may need to scroll through the results by clicking the **More** button at the bottom of your Search Results window. This action lets you view all newsgroup topics that match your original search criteria. A directory of newsgroups appears providing a drill-down interface so you can open each item by double-clicking your mouse button

on the item desired. Here's how you can view newsgroup messages:

1. Click the search result entry of interest from the **Search All Newsgroups** window. Click the **More** button to view additional entries as needed.

2. Click **List articles in newsgroup** in the **Add or Read Newsgroup** window. This will display a newsgroup subject window.

3. In the **Newsgroup Subjects** window, shown in Figure 7-9, scroll through the various subject titles and select one of interest by double-clicking it.

4. The **Message** window will open allowing you to read it. To view and read other messages, if they exist, for the subject you've chosen, click the **Message** button located at the bottom of the **Message** window. This will move you to the next message.

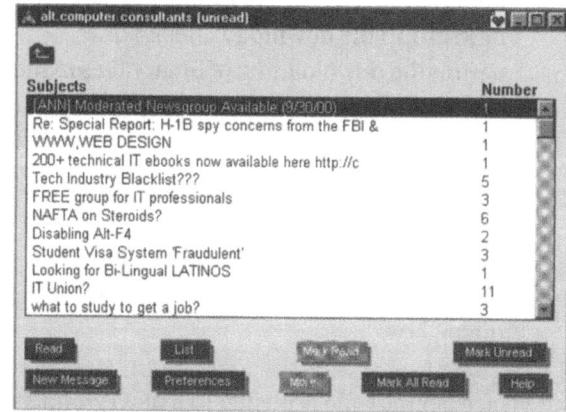

Figure 7-9. Viewing the number of messages in a newsgroup subject list

19 Posting messages

When posting a message, it's useful to keep a few things in mind. First, create an informative subject line for your post. This makes it considerably easier for others to find and open only the messages that interest them. Second, only post messages that provide useful content. Avoid posts that contribute little or nothing to a newsgroup. Finally, when responding to a post, quote portions of the original message to make the conversation easier for everyone to follow. Here's how:

1. Click the **Keyword** button located on the AOL toolbar and enter AOL Keyword: **Newsgroups** and click the **Go** button, or click the **AOL Services** button located on the AOL toolbar, then select **Internet** from the drop-down menu choices and click **Newsgroups**. Either method displays the **Newsgroups** window.

2. Click the **Read My Newsgroups** button on the **Newsgroups** window to view a list of newsgroups.

3. Double-click the newsgroup you want to post to from your list of subscribed newsgroups in the **Read My Newsgroups** window.

4. Click the **New Message** button in the newsgroup you've opened.

5. Enter a subject line and text message in the **Post New Message** window, and click the **Send** button, shown in Figure 7-10.

6. Click the **OK** button in the **Message has been sent** dialog box.

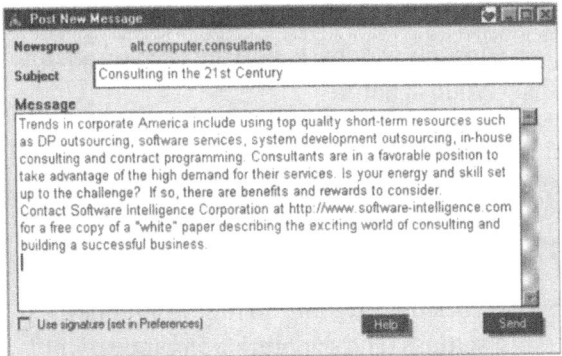

Figure 7-10. Posting a new message to a newsgroup of choice

20 Responding to postings offline

Postings that you've read offline can also be responded to while offline. The important thing to remember is that you'll need to set up Automatic AOL to sign on to AOL and have AOL automatically read postings for you. Once that's done, you're ready to respond to newsgroup postings offline. Here's how it's done.

1. Select **Offline Newsgroups** from the **File** menu located above the AOL toolbar.

2. Enter your password for the selected screen name.

3. Open the **Incoming/Saved Postings** folder by double-clicking it.

4. Double-click a posting to read it.

5. Select a portion of the message you want to quote from, and either click the **Reply to Group** button to post a message to the message board, or click the **Reply to Author** button to send a reply to the author of the post via e-mail.

6. Enter your response and click the **Send Later** button.

Advanced Topics

21 Lurking before contributing

There's nothing worse than restating what's already been posted or being out of step with the conversations in a newsgroup. Before you begin posting or responding to newsgroup messages, it's a good idea to acquaint yourself with the newsgroup first. The process of reading a newsgroup's posts without posting is referred to as lurking. Lurking makes it more likely that you'll come up with thoughtful and useful posts and that you'll get responses to your posts rather than being ignored.

22 Understanding moderated newsgroups

Although most AOL newsgroups don't have anyone keeping track of the postings on a subject, some do. For these newsgroups, a moderator's responsibility is to filter out the posts that have little or nothing to do with the conversation flow, and keep out the junk. The content of a moderated newsgroup is usually better, and consequently the group may be more popular with users who want to share worthwhile information. To determine whether a newsgroup is moderated or not, look for the word "moderated" in the title of the newsgroup.

23 Posting pictures and sound

AOL lets you post pictures and sounds to newsgroups as binary files. Binary files are non-text files that contain bits and bytes of non-printable text such as executable machine code, graphic images, sound, or video. Before you'll be able to post a binary file, you may need to download and install the encoding UUencoder software on your computer's hard drive. To find the necessary software, go to AOL's Download Center at AOL Keyword: **Download Center** and download it, noting the name and location where you store it. After that, you'll be able to post your binary files to a newsgroup.

Once a binary file is posted to a newsgroup, it's automatically converted to an encoded format. When this encoded formatted file is later downloaded, the file is automatically converted or decoded back to binary by AOL using a special software feature known as File Grabber. Here are the steps to posting your pictures and sounds to any newsgroup:

1. Run the **UUencode** program on the file you want to post to a newsgroup. Be sure you know what the name and location of the encoded file before you proceed.

2. Click the **Keyword** button located on the AOL toolbar and enter AOL Keyword: **Newsgroups** and click the **Go** button, or click the **AOL Services** button located on the AOL toolbar, then select **Internet** from the drop-down menu choices and click **Newsgroups**. Either method displays the **Newsgroups** window.

3. Click the **Read My Newsgroups** button on the **Newsgroups** window to view a list of newsgroups.

4. Double-click the newsgroup you want to post to from your list of subscribed newsgroups in the **Read My Newsgroups** window.

5. Click the **Send New Message** button in the newsgroup you've opened.

6. Locate the encoded file and open it. Cut and paste the file's contents into the message field.

7. Click the **Send** button.

24 Adding a signature to your postings

Many AOL users spice up their message posts by adding a signature. A signature is any combination of characters that you choose to use to close an e-mail message. Virtually any character-based text can be put in a signature

To create an automatic signature on your newsgroup posts, follow these steps:

1. Click the **Keyword** button located on the AOL toolbar and enter AOL Keyword: **Newsgroups** and click the **Go** button, or click the **AOL Services** button located on the AOL toolbar, then select **Internet** from the drop-down menu choices and click **Newsgroups**. Either method displays the **Newsgroups** window.

2. Click the **Set Preferences** button in the **Newsgroups** window to add the text you ant for your signature.

3. Click the **Posting** tab, and enter the desired text to be used as your signature in the **Signature** box in the **Global Newsgroups Preferences** window, shown in Figure 7-11.

4. Click the **Save** button to save your new settings. The signature won't appear until your message is posted to the newsgroup.

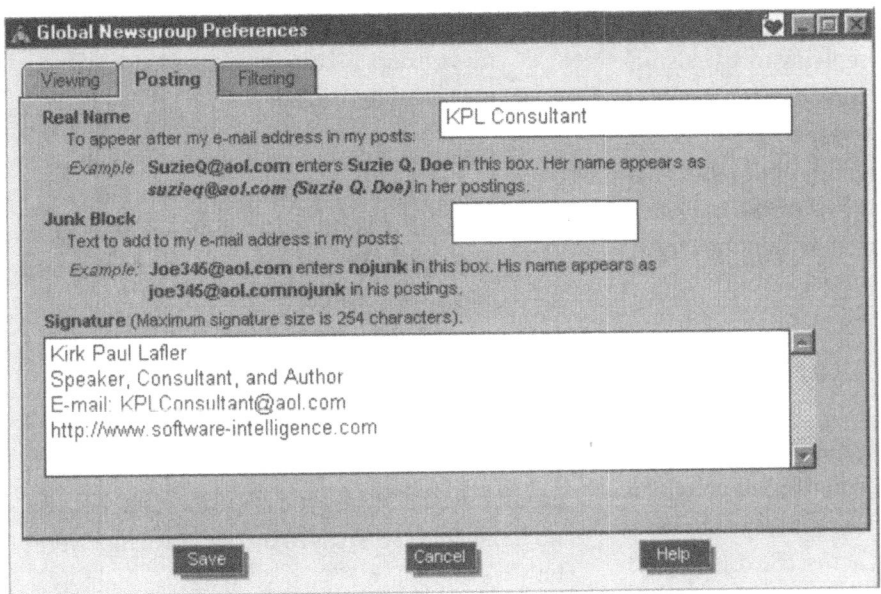

Figure 7-11. Entering a signature that will appear on all your newsgroup postings

25 Managing newsgroup posts

Popular newsgroups can receive many posts over the course of a day, week, or longer. AOL lets you set up Automatic AOL to retrieve messages posted to the newsgroups you've subscribed to. These messages are stored in your filing cabinet so you can read and respond to them at a later time. To prevent being swamped with hundreds, or even thousands, of posts in your filing cabinet, AOL lets you manage the newsgroup posts you receive. The best way to organize the posts in your filing cabinet is to store them in one or more personal folders. Before a message can be placed in a folder however, you must first create the folder or folders. So let's see how a folder is created:

1. From the **Mail** menu on the AOL toolbar, click **Filing Cabinet**.

2. Click the **Mail** tab on the **Filing Cabinet** window.

3. Click the **Incoming/Saved Mail** item.

4. Click **New Folder**, and enter the name of the folder you want to create in the **Create Folder** dialog box.

5. Click the **OK** button.

After you've read a post, you have the choice of leaving it in the folder it's in, deleting it, or saving it to a folder of your choice. Saving a post to another folder can be accomplished manually by dragging the message to another folder.

As a matter of "good" message management, it may be necessary to delete a message in your filing cabinet. To accomplish this, follow these steps:

1. **Select** the message you'd like to delete.

2. Click the **Delete** button.

26 Threading your conversations

AOL boasts countless newsgroup topics on a variety of themes and subjects. Many topics are broad in scope and appeal to a broad audience, such as newsgroups about cars, fashions, foods, pets, etc. To accommodate the needs of a huge diverse audience, AOL allows broadly based newsgroup topics to be splintered into conversations consisting of tightly focused topics covering a specific subject, such as Maseratis, evening gowns, pizza, and gerbils. These narrow conversations are often referred to as threads within the broader topic of a newsgroup.

The most common way to create a thread in AOL is to post a message with a new subject line. This means that instead of replying to an existing post, you're creating a new thread or topic within the broader topic of the newsgroup. New threads are created all the time using this approach. The origins of a thread can always be traced back to a single message that was posted within the larger topic of the newsgroup.

27 Throwing flames

Newsgroups are long on tradition. Ever since their beginning, newsgroups have permitted people to express themselves practically any way they felt necessary to get their point across. So, many people with strongly held opinions and beliefs express themselves without holding back, often at the expense of others. Posts of this type are referred to as flames. The process of posting a flame is called flaming.

Although flaming isn't necessarily bad netiquette, it can quickly get out of hand and become more of a nuisance than anything else. After all, how many people really enjoy being the brunt of rude and offensive posts? So if you must flame, try posting at newsgroups like alt.flame, alt.tasteless, or the popular "Hall of Flame" newsgroup at alt.flame.hall-of-flame. And remember, what seems funny or just a joke to some may be construed as hurtful or in bad taste to others.

28 Trolling at your own risk

Trolling is another form of bad netiquette. A person who initiates this type of behavior in a newsgroup is referred to as a troll. A troll's sole purpose is to incite anger or provoke others within a newsgroup. Trolling often initiates a series of flames in response, but this type of response frequently backfires, because this is what the troll wants. Here are a few tips to beat a troll at their own game:

1. If you're in a moderated newsgroup, you can ask your moderator to stop posting the troll's posts.

2. Send a response to the troll saying, "Your post was inappropriate and unnecessary to this newsgroup. Please do not post similar messages here again."

3. If all else fails, ignore the remarks or posts levied by the troll. This generally works because trolls love attention and when they don't get it, they often leave the newsgroup and go elsewhere.

29 Deleting your newsgroup posts

Have you ever wanted to delete your own newsgroup posts? AOL lets you remove posts that you no longer want displayed on a newsgroup. Here's how it's done:

1. Click the **Keyword** button located on the AOL toolbar and enter AOL Keyword: **Newsgroups** and click the **Go** button, or click the **AOL Services** button located on the AOL toolbar, then select **Internet** from the drop-down menu choices and click **Newsgroups**. Either method displays the **Newsgroups** window.

2. Click the **Read My Newsgroups** button on the **Newsgroups** window to view a list of newsgroups.

3. Double-click the newsgroup you want to open from your list of subscribed newsgroups in the **Read My Newsgroups** window.

4. Find the message that you'd like to remove in the list of messages (it must be your message—not someone else's), and double-click it to open it.

5. Click the **Delete** button located at the bottom of the message window.

Information Superhighway

Part Two

AOL Services

CHAPTER 8

AOL Shopping and Services

EXPLORING AOL's one-stop Shopping channel is simple, fast, and fun. In this chapter you'll be able to locate your favorite stores, products, and brands. You'll also learn where to find and print valuable coupons that will save you big bucks when you shop—all from your PC. Another exciting feature is the AOL Rewards program. It lets you earn points for each item purchased, and when you're ready, lets you redeem the points you've accumulated for fabulous gifts and services. So take a few minutes to explore the variety of merchants, products, and services that are available. It's fast and easy, and most of all fun for the entire family. Happy shopping.

In this chapter, you'll learn how to

📕 Shop the simple and easy way

📕 Find specials, discounts, and all sorts of bargains

📕 Find gifts for anyone

📕 Purchase those big-ticket items

📕 Save big bucks with coupons

📕 Earn and redeem rewards for every dollar you spend

📕 Shop safely anyplace and anytime you'd like

📕 Get help when you need it

Shopping the Simple Way

1 Shopping convenience on AOL's Shop@AOL

The days of fighting traffic, crowds, and finding a parking spot are a thing of the past. AOL offers an exciting one-stop shopping experience for AOL members everywhere. Discover the convenience of online shopping; from home, work, or anywhere else—you'll be amazed by the time you'll save shopping online.

Shop@AOL lets you buy everything you need in one convenient virtual marketplace. Powerful tools help you find all your favorite stores, departments, and products, bringing them to your computer's screen in living color. Find and buy everything you need around the clock, 365 days a year, from the privacy of your computer and at your convenience, not others.

From department stores to home and garden shops; from beauty and fragrance products to books, music, and videos; and from electronics and computer equipment to the latest fashions—everything is available on Shop@AOL. Anything that's at your local brick-and-mortar department store can be bought safely online, and often at wonderful savings too. And best of all, it's brought right to your doorstep. Follow these steps, for a shopping experience like no other:

Click the **Keyword** button located on the AOL toolbar and enter AOL Keyword: **Shop** and click the **Go** button, or click the **AOL Shopping** channel located on the left side of your screen. Either method displays the **Shop@AOL** window, shown in Figure 8-1.

Figure 8-1. Offering an exciting one-stop shopping experience at AOL's Shop@AOL

2 Checking out–AOL's Quick Checkout

Shopping at your favorite stores on America Online isn't only safe and easy—it saves time too. With AOL's Quick Checkout, you'll only have to enter your credit card and shipping information once. AOL will automatically remember it for you after that. Your private information is stored safely and securely for future shopping visits. Once you've found all the products you'd like to purchase, take your shopping cart to the front of the line with Quick Checkout. Quick Checkout only asks for your secret password each time you checkout. Billing and mailing information is processed safely to the credit card you specified. Here's how you can find out more about AOL's Quick Checkout feature:

1. Click the **Keyword** button located on the AOL toolbar and enter AOL Keyword: **AOL Quick Checkout** and click the **Go** button.

2. Click the **Sign Up Now!** button on the **Quick Checkout** Web site.

3. Enter your **Zip Code** and click the **Continue** button.

4. Enter the requested information on the **Quick Checkout Signup** application form and click the **Continue** button, shown in Figure 8-2. The application process consists of five easy steps: Credit Card information, Shipping information, Shopping Password, Security Question and Answer, and Mailing List.

5. Follow the remaining on-screen instructions to set up the **Quick Checkout** process.

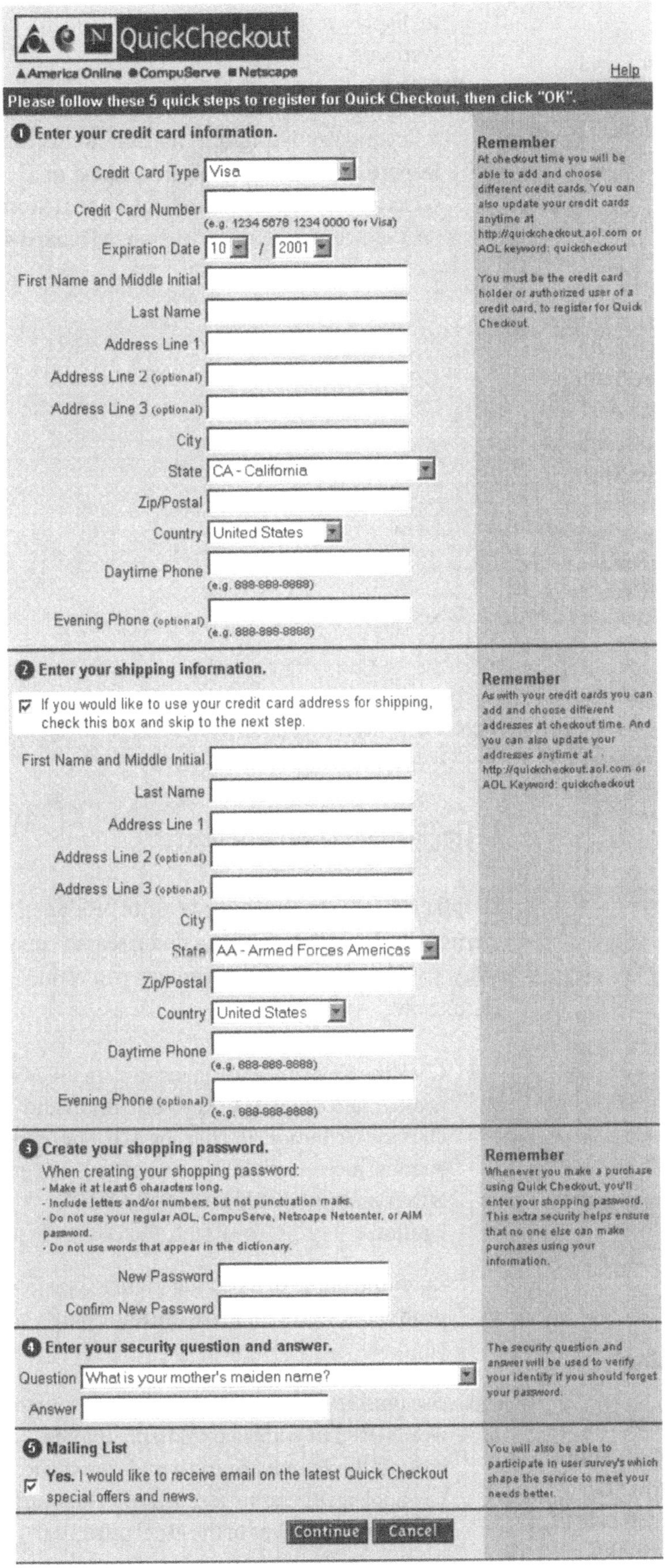

QuickCheckout

▲America Online ●CompuServe ■Netscape

Help

Please follow these 5 quick steps to register for Quick Checkout, then click "OK".

① Enter your credit card information.

Credit Card Type [Visa ▼]

Credit Card Number [ ]
(e.g. 1234 5678 1234 0000 for Visa)

Expiration Date [10 ▼] / [2001 ▼]

First Name and Middle Initial [ ]

Last Name [ ]

Address Line 1 [ ]

Address Line 2 (optional) [ ]

Address Line 3 (optional) [ ]

City [ ]

State [CA - California ▼]

Zip/Postal [ ]

Country [United States ▼]

Daytime Phone [ ]
(e.g. 888-888-8888)

Evening Phone (optional) [ ]
(e.g. 888-888-8888)

Remember
At checkout time you will be able to add and choose different credit cards. You can also update your credit cards anytime at http://quickcheckout.aol.com or AOL keyword: quickcheckout

You must be the credit card holder or authorized user of a credit card, to register for Quick Checkout.

② Enter your shipping information.

☑ If you would like to use your credit card address for shipping, check this box and skip to the next step.

First Name and Middle Initial [ ]

Last Name [ ]

Address Line 1 [ ]

Address Line 2 (optional) [ ]

Address Line 3 (optional) [ ]

City [ ]

State [AA - Armed Forces Americas ▼]

Zip/Postal [ ]

Country [United States ▼]

Daytime Phone [ ]
(e.g. 888-888-8888)

Evening Phone (optional) [ ]
(e.g. 888-888-8888)

Remember
As with your credit cards you can add and choose different addresses at checkout time. And you can also update your addresses anytime at http://quickcheckout.aol.com or AOL Keyword: quickcheckout

③ Create your shopping password.

When creating your shopping password:
- Make it at least 6 characters long.
- Include letters and/or numbers, but not punctuation marks.
- Do not use your regular AOL, CompuServe, Netscape Netcenter, or AIM password.
- Do not use words that appear in the dictionary.

New Password [ ]

Confirm New Password [ ]

Remember
Whenever you make a purchase using Quick Checkout, you'll enter your shopping password. This extra security helps ensure that no one else can make purchases using your information.

④ Enter your security question and answer.

Question [What is your mother's maiden name? ▼]

Answer [ ]

The security question and answer will be used to verify your identity if you should forget your password.

⑤ Mailing List

☑ **Yes.** I would like to receive email on the latest Quick Checkout special offers and news.

You will also be able to participate in user survey's which shape the service to meet your needs better.

[Continue] [Cancel]

Figure 8-2. Registering for AOL Quick Checkout

3 Locating your favorite stores

Your favorite stores are only a mouse-click away with Shop@AOL. With a global A–Z alphabetical directory of online stores, catalogs, and local stores, you won't have a problem finding your favorite vendor. Here's how:

Accessing the AOL's Shop@AOL A –Z Store Directory

1. Click the **Keyword** button located on the AOL toolbar and enter AOL Keyword: **Shop** and click the **Go** button, or click the **AOL Shopping** channel located on the left side of your screen. Either method displays the **Shop@AOL** window.

2. Click **A to Z Directory** on the **Shop@AOL** window to display the **A–Z Store Directory** Web site, shown in Figure 8-3.

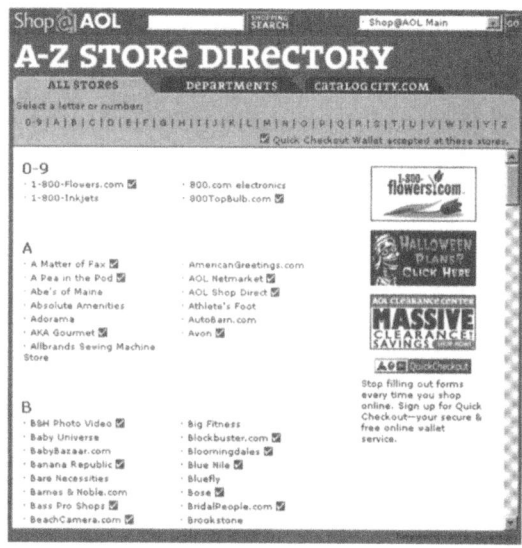

Figure 8-3. Accessing AOL's Shop@AOL Online alphabetical Store Directory

Accessing AOL's Shop@AOL Local Guide

1. Click the **Keyword** button located on the AOL toolbar and enter AOL Keyword: **Shop** and click the **Go** button, or click the **AOL Shopping** channel located on the left side of your screen. Either method displays the **Shop@AOL** window.

2. Click **Local Stores** on the **Shop@AOL** window to display your area's **Local Store Directory** Web site.

3. Click where you want to shop from the following list: **Shopping Districts, Malls, Department Stores,** or **Local Auctions,** or select a category from the **Find a Local Store** drop-down selection box, shown in Figure 8-4.

Figure 8-4. Accessing Shop@AOL Categories of Online Store Departments

4 Finding your favorite products

Shop@AOL lets you find your favorite products anytime and anyplace. Using a quick search capability, you'll always find the products you want. Here's how:

1. Click the **Keyword** button located on the AOL toolbar and enter AOL Keyword: **Shop** and click the **Go** button, or click the **AOL Shopping** channel located on the left side of your screen. Either method displays the **Shop@AOL** window.

2. Enter the name of a product in the **Type in a product or brand** field on the **Shopping** window.

3. Use **double-quotes (" ")** to find a match of the words used in your search. Using quotes around the search criteria avoids having to use Boolean operators (see Tip #6). The words don't need to appear in the exact order that they're specified. For example, **"Operating System"** would find all product references containing the words **Operating System** or **System Operating** in the title or description.

5 Locating a favorite brand

Brand loyalty is an important element to many consumers. People in general are loyal to a particular brand, especially when they've had a positive experience with it. Shop@AOL lets you find your favorite brands anytime and anyplace. Using a quick search capability, you'll always find the brands you want. Here's how:

1. Click the **Keyword** button located on the AOL toolbar and enter AOL Keyword: **Shop** and click the **Go** button, or click the **AOL Shopping** channel located on the left side of your screen. Either method displays the **Shop@AOL** window.

2. Enter the name of a brand in the **Type in a product or brand** field on the **Shopping** window.

3. Use **double-quotes** (" ") to find a match of the words used in your search. Using quotes around the search criteria avoids having to use Boolean operators (see Tip #6). The words don't need to appear in the exact order that they're specified. For example, **"Microsoft Windows XP"** would find all brands containing the words **Microsoft Windows XP, XP Microsoft Windows** or any combination of these words, in the title or description.

6 Narrowing your search results with AND, OR, and NOT

AOL lets you be specific in what you're searching for. If you're still getting way too many useless or irrelevant results (or in some cases too little) from your product or brand searches, it's time to use AND, OR, and NOT in your search requests. You see, AND, OR, and NOT are known as Boolean operators. Used properly, they tell Shop@AOL exactly how to perform a search. Here's how they work:

> **AND**—Searches both words it separates. Both words must exist in order for it to be listed in the search results. For example, **Windows AND XP** finds information having both words in a title or description.

> **OR**—Searches either word it separates. Only one of the words needs to appear for it to be listed in the search results. For example, **Windows OR XP** finds information having either word (not necessarily both) in a title or description.

> **NOT**—Searches the word or expression preceding the operator NOT and omits the keyword or expression following the operator NOT. For example, **Windows NOT XP** finds information containing the word Windows without any references to XP.

You can further qualify your search by combining your search criteria with two or more search operators to control what appears in your search results. For example, **Windows AND XP NOT Books**, finds information having Windows and XP in a title or description, but not anything to do with Books. This is a handy way to restrict what appears in your search results.

7 Shopping local

AOL's Shop@AOL lets you shop at local merchants for all the products and services you buy. You can visit your local Shopping Districts, Malls, Department Stores, and Auctions all at the touch of your mouse. You'll also be able to use powerful search tools to find the stores, products, and brands you've come to love. As an added bonus, you can visit another city's stores without leaving your chair. This feature is handy for business or vacation travelers planning to visit another city. Follow these simple instructions to begin shopping online at all your favorite local stores:

1. Click the **Keyword** button located on the AOL toolbar and enter AOL Keyword: **Shop** and click the **Go** button, or click the **AOL Shopping** channel located on the left side of your screen. Either method displays the **Shop@AOL** window.

2. Click **Local Stores** on the **Shop@AOL** window to display your area's **Local Store Directory** Web site.

3. Click where you want to shop from the following list: **Shopping Districts**, **Malls**, **Department Stores**, or **Local Auctions**, or select a category from the **Find a Local Store** drop-down selection box.

4. Use the built-in search feature to locate your favorite stores from the **Find a Local Store** drop-down selection list. The available categories include

Automotive	House & Home
Books, Music & Movies	Jewelry & Watches
Clothing & Accessories	Kids & Baby
Computers	Lawn & Garden
Crafts & Hobbies	Malls
Department Stores	Office & School Supplies
Electronics & Photo	Outlets, Discount & Thrift
Flowers & Gifts	Pets
Food & Entertaining	Sports & Outdoors
Grocery Stores	Toys & Games
Health & Beauty	Weddings & Parties

8 Comparing prices as you shop

Shop@AOL lets you compare prices as you shop. This handy feature is used to help determine which stores offer the product or service you're looking for as well as who offers it at the best price. Here's how it works:

1. Click the **Keyword** button located on the AOL toolbar and enter AOL Keyword: **Shop** and click the **Go** button, or click the **AOL Shopping** channel located on the left side of your screen. Either method displays the **Shop@AOL** window.

2. Enter the name of the product or service you want to search for in the **Shopping Search** field on the **Shopping** Web site. For example, entering **windows and xp and software** would find all products related to the Windows XP operating system software.

🖊 *Upper- and lowercase characters are treated as the same.*

3. Select the category that best satisfies your needs from the **Shop@AOL Search Results** Web site.

4. Click the **DealTime™** button located at the bottom of the **Shop@AOL Search Results** Web site. You can also access the **DealTime** Web site by entering AOL Keyword: **DealTime**. Select the product category that best corresponds to your search request from the **DealTime** Web site. For example, to view only those products corresponding to Operating System Software, select **Operating Systems Software.**

5. The search results for the product you selected initially displays in alphabetical order by **Store Name**, shown in Figure 8-5.

6. DealTime lets you refine your search results by using the following user-friendly selection boxes: **Type**, **Version**, **Platform**, **Brand**, **Keyword**, **Minimum Price**, and **Maximum Price**. If your budget only allowed you to spend a maximum of $300 for Windows XP software, you could change the amount in the **Max. Price** field to 300.00 and click the **Search** button. Only those products matching your search criteria would be redisplayed.

Specials, Discounts, and Bargains

9 Signing up for AOL newsletters, perks, and benefits

America Online offers members a great way to get free newsletters, earn wonderful perks, and learn about exciting benefits each time you shop. You'll be able to find great deals with AOL's Shop Direct, Weekly Specials, AAdvantage Rewards, Netmarket, Travel Discounts, AutoDirect, AutoAdvantage, and other perks and member benefits, and this also makes you eligible to win exciting prizes each time you shop. You'll first have to sign up. Here are a few cool sites that offer some great perks and other stuff after you sign up:

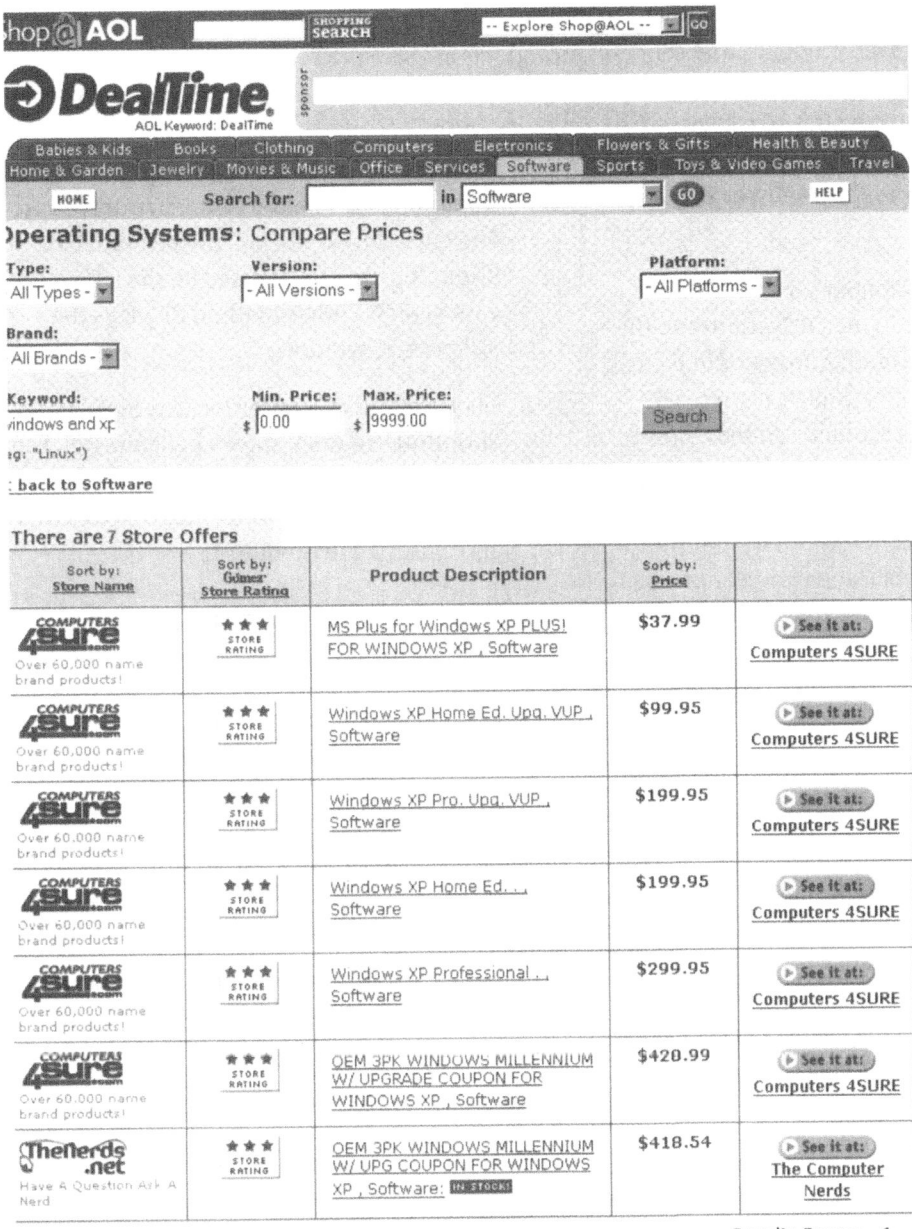

Figure 8-5. Viewing the list of products matching your search

- Save up to 60% on featured products and other selected items by typing AOL keyword: **Shop Direct** from the **AOL Member Perks** window. Enter your e-mail address and click the **Sign Up** button to subscribe to the **AOL Shop Direct Newsletter**. This **Newsletter** alerts you to the latest product news and specials being offered.

- Find exciting weekly specials and business perks by typing AOL keyword: **Member Perks**, and click **Business Perks: Weekly Specials** from the **AOL Member Perks** window. Just follow the instructions to find cost-saving opportunities.

- Earn miles while you shop online, on the ground, or in the air, then spend the miles you earn on the travel, products, and services you want. Sign up for this exciting member program by typing AOL keyword: **Perks**, and click **AOL AAdvantage Rewards: Enroll Free** from the AOL **Member Perks** window.

- If you love online shopping, try a free three-month membership to **AOL Netmarket,** the online superstore containing products in these categories: electronics, cameras & optics, computers & office supplies, home & leisure, sports & fitness, toys & collectables, and jewelry & fragrance. Members receive a 200 percent low price guarantee, **AOL Netmarket** cash, and two-year product warranty coverage on everything they buy. To join, type AOL keyword: **Perks**, and click **AOL Netmarket:** from the **AOL Member Perks** window.

- If you're a frequent traveler or just like to get away once in a while, try a free three-month membership with AOL **Travelers Advantage**, the **24/7 Travel Discount Club**. Save money on airlines, hotels, car rentals, and more, all with low price guarantees, last minute deals, members-only specials, and value vacation packages. To join, type AOL keyword: **Perks**, and click **Travel Discounts:** from the AOL **Member Perks** window.

- If you love cars, you'll love **AOL AutoDirect** or **AOL AutoVantage**. It lets you compare vehicles, read reviews, build your dream car, get an instant price, and even buy your dream car online. Type AOL keyword: **Perks**, and click **AOL AutoDirect:** or **AOL Auto-Vantage:** from the **AOL Member Perks** window.

10 Shopping for clearance and discontinued items

If its great deals and bargains you're looking for, then **Shop@AOL** has everything you'll want for exciting clearance and discontinued items. You'll find bargains and deals on clearance and discontinued items in a variety of departments including women's, men's, and children's clothing; electronics; home

décor, jewelry; music and movies; and sports and outdoors. This great Web site offers well-known products at value prices. Here's how you can get quality products at below-market prices:

1. Click the **Keyword** button located on the AOL toolbar and enter AOL Keyword: **Shop** and click the **Go** button, or click the **AOL Shopping** channel located on the left side of your screen. Either method displays the **Shop@AOL** window.

2. Click **Clearance Center** located on the **Shopping** channel, shown in Figure 8-6. You can also go directly to the **Clearance Center** by entering AOL Keyword: **Clearance Center**, and clicking the **Go** button.

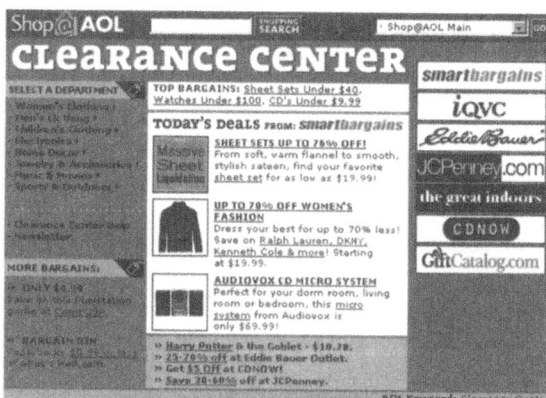

Figure 8-6. Shopping at AOL's Clearance Center can save you big money on popular products.

11 Saving more with closeouts

If saving money on leading products and brands is your goal, then you'll be able to save even more on product closeouts. Product closeouts are a fact of life in product merchandising and become available when a product isn't going to be manufactured or stocked by the store anymore. These products may have been leading sellers at one time too. Stores run closeout specials to clear these items from their inventories, thereby making room for new products. You'll often be able to purchase great products at prices way below discount. Here's how:

1. Click the **Keyword** button located on the AOL toolbar and enter AOL Keyword: **Shop** and click the **Go** button, or click the **AOL Shopping** channel located on the left side of your screen. Either method displays the **Shop@AOL** window.

2. Enter **Closeouts** in the **Type in a product or brand:** field and click the **Shopping Search** button on the **Shopping** window.

3. The product categories containing the word **Closeouts** will appear in the **Shop@AOL Search Results** Web site. Click the category from the **Results** display that appears.

12 Bidding for bargains online

Online auctions are very popular for buying and selling merchandise. You'll be able to find and bid on cool merchandise, and sell your own stuff on eBAY.com® and uBid™. Here's how you can get quality products often at below market prices:

1. Click the **AOL Shopping** channel located on the left side of your screen and then click **Auctions** located on the **Shopping** channel or you can also go directly to the **Auctions Web** site by entering AOL Keyword: **Auctions**, and clicking the **Go** button.

2. Click one or more items listed in the **Top Auctions** section, or view the **Specials** of the day listed on the **Auctions** Web site.

Gift Buying

13 Finding a gift in every size

With Shop@AOL's Gifts & Registries Web site, you'll be able to find the perfect gift for any occasion. Whether you're purchasing a gift for an upcoming holiday, birthday, wedding, anniversary, graduation, or anything else, the Gifts & Registries Web site has whatever you're looking for. Here's how you can find gifts for friends, family, or that special someone.

1. Click the **Keyword** button located on the AOL toolbar and enter AOL Keyword: **Shop** and click the **Go** button, or click the **AOL Shopping** channel located on the left side of your screen. Either method displays the **Shop@AOL** window.

2. Click **Gifts & Registries** located on the **Shopping** channel. You can also go directly to **Gifts & Registries** by entering AOL Keyword: **Gifts & Registries**, and clicking the **Go** button. **Shop@AOL**'s Gifts + Registries Web site appears, shown in Figure 8-7.

14 Purchasing gift certificates

Do you have to buy a gift for someone who is hard to buy for? If so, then you might consider giving a gift certificate. Gift certificates make great gifts and can be purchased for an amazing range of products directly from Shop@AOL. Here's how:

1. Click the **Keyword** button located on the AOL toolbar and enter AOL Keyword: **Shop** and click the **Go** button, or click the **AOL Shopping** channel located on the left side of your screen. Either method displays the **Shop@AOL** window.

2. Click **Gifts & Registries** located on the Shopping channel or enter AOL Keyword: **Gifts & Registries** and click the **Go** button.

3. Type **Gift Certificates** in the **Type in a Product or Brand** field on **Shop@AOL**'s Gifts & Registries Web site to display the products matching the search results.

15 Shopping at the last minute–gifts for every occasion

Do you need to purchase and send a gift to a friend, family member, or loved one, but you just don't have enough time to shop, package, and mail the gift? Shop@AOL may not only be able to help you find a gift, but also deliver it in time. It offers last-minute gift ideas that can be ordered and delivered within 24 to 48 hours. AOL also offers many gifts that can be ordered and delivered the

Figure 8-7. Making your gift giving easy with the Gifts & Registry Web site

same day—talk about quick service! Here's how you can take advantage of this great service when you're strapped for time:

1. Click the **Keyword** button located on the AOL toolbar and enter AOL Keyword: **Shop** and click the **Go** button, or click the **AOL Shopping** channel located on the left side of your screen. Either method displays the **Shop@AOL** window.

2. Click **Gifts & Registries** located on the **Shopping** channel or, enter AOL Keyword: **Gifts & Registries** and click the **Go** button.

3. Click **Last-Minute Gifts** on the **Gifts & Registries** channel to display **Shop@AOL's Last-Minute Gifts** channel.

16 Sending money with AOL's QuickCash (SM)

Now gift buying is made even easier. AOL lets you send and receive money via e-mail using QuickCash. To enroll in this flexible service, you'll first need to register. Approval and terms of service are through Citigroup, FSB, Member FDIC. Once your application for enrollment has been approved, you'll be able to send and receive cash quickly and easily anytime with a simple e-mail. Here's how you can get started with this terrific service.

Navigating to AOL QuickCash

1. Click the **Keyword** button located on the AOL toolbar and enter AOL Keyword: **Shop** and click the **Go** button, or click the **AOL Shopping** channel located on the left side of your screen. Either method displays the **Shop@AOL** window.

2. Click **Gifts & Registries** located on the **Shopping** channel or, enter AOL Keyword: **Gifts & Registries** and click the **Go** button.

3. Click the **Sign up now** button on the **AOL QuickCash** Web site to enroll.

Registering for AOL QuickCash

1. Enter all the requested information on the **QuickCash Enrollment Application** and click the **Next** button.

2. Review the information you entered, and click the **Next** button.

3. Review the **Terms and Conditions**, click the desired **Privacy choices**, and click the **Next** button. You may print this information by clicking the **Print** button.

Big Ticket Purchases

17 Shopping for luxury

If luxury is what you're looking for, Shop@AOL offers extravagant, one-of-a-kind products and services from well-known names around the world. This is your premier online source for luxury and is provided for the enjoyment of AOL members everywhere. Whether you're looking for the finer things that money can buy, or doing a little virtual window-shopping, Shop@AOL is dedicated to your discriminating tastes. Also, members have access to expert commentary and purchase recommendations to help you make an informed decision.

Here's how you can satisfy your yearning for the finer things that life has to offer with Shop@AOL's Luxury channel:

1. Click the **Keyword** button located on the AOL toolbar and enter AOL Keyword: **Shop** and click the **Go** button, or click the **AOL Shopping** channel located on the left side of your screen. Either method displays the **Shop@AOL** window.

2. Click **Luxury + Designer** located on the **Shopping** channel or, enter AOL Keyword: **Luxury** and click the **Go** button. **Shop@AOL's Luxury + Designer channel** appears, shown in Figure 8-8.

Figure 8-8. Shopping for those one-of-a-kind gifts on the Luxury channel

18 Shopping for beauty and fashion

AOL members can purchase all their beauty and fashion products from the Shop@AOL's Luxury channel. Whether you're shopping for Women's, Men's, Body & Fragrance, or Beauty products, Shop@AOL's Luxury channel offers well-known products offered by such manufacturers as Neiman Marcus, Ralph Lauren, Dolce & Gabbana, Kate Spade, Re Vive, La Mer, Creed, Chantecaille, as well as others. Here's how you can access this popular Web site:

1. Click the **Keyword** button located on the AOL toolbar and enter AOL Keyword: **Shop** and click the **Go** button, or click the **AOL Shopping** channel located on the left side of your screen. Either method displays the **Shop@AOL** window.

2. Click **Luxury + Designer** located on the Shopping channel or, enter AOL Keyword: **Luxury** and click the **Go** button to display the **Luxury** channel.

3. Click **Beauty & Fashion** on the **Luxury** channel to display **Shop@AOL's Beauty + Fashion** channel.

19 Shopping for a car, truck, or boat

If you're looking for that special luxury car or SUV you've always wanted, AOL members can drive away in style using Shop@AOL's Luxury Autos channel. Members have two luxury channel choices: Autos showcasing Lexus cars and SUVs, and the Autos channel featuring leading luxury U.S. and foreign auto manufacturers. You'll also find information about buying a car, finance and insurance options, and an assortment of other valuable buyer and seller assistance programs. Here's how you can access these popular Web sites.

Accessing the Autos Channel Featuring Lexus Cars and SUVs

1. Click the **Keyword** button located on the AOL toolbar and enter AOL Keyword: **Shop** and click the **Go** button, or click the **AOL Shopping** channel located on the left side of your screen. Either method displays the **Shop@AOL** window.

2. Click **Luxury + Designer** located on the Shopping channel or, enter AOL Keyword: **Luxury** and click the **Go** button to display the **Luxury** channel.

3. Click **Autos** on the **Luxury** channel to display **Shop@AOL's Autos** channel.

Accessing the Autos Channel Featuring Luxury U.S. and Foreign Cars and SUVs

1. Click the **Keyword** button located on the AOL toolbar and enter AOL Keyword: **Autos** and click the **Go** button to display the **AOL Autos** channel.

2. AOL members have a wonderful resource consisting of **Auto Essentials, New** and **Used Car** purchase options, and **Local Resources** choices.

20 Shopping for your next vacation or business trip

Shop@AOL provides AOL members with one-stop vacation planning services. Business travelers will also be able to make airline, hotel, and car rental reservations quickly and easily with one-stop shopping services. Here's how you can plan and schedule your next vacation from popular travel destinations.

Shop@AOL's Travel + Leisure Vacation Planning Channel

1. Click the **Keyword** button located on the AOL toolbar and enter AOL Keyword: **Shop** and click the **Go** button, or click the **AOL Shopping** channel located on the left side of your screen. Either method displays the **Shop@AOL** window.

2. Click **Luxury + Designer** located on the Shopping channel or, enter AOL Keyword: **Luxury** and click the **Go** button to display the **Luxury** channel.

3. Click **Travel & Leisure** on the **Luxury** channel to display **Shop@AOL's Travel + Leisure** channel, shown in Figure 8-9. You'll be able to book exotic cruise vacations right at your fingertips.

Figure 8-9. Offering one-stop vacation shopping on AOL's Travel + Leisure channel

AOL members can book all their business travel needs including airline, hotel, and car rentals on the AOL Travel channel. Expedia, along with Travelocity are the largest online travel agency in the world. Travelocity provides AOL members with a flexible service, low rates,flexible service, low rates, convenient business tools, restaurant finders, maps and directions, and a variety of other useful resources with an easy-to-use travel channel. Here's how you can access the AOL Travel channel.

AOL Travel Channel for the Business Traveler

1. Click the **Keyword** button located on the AOL toolbar and enter AOL Keyword: **Business Travel Center** and click the **Go** button to display the **AOL Travel** channel for business travelers.

2. AOL member business travelers have a wonderful resource for booking airline, hotel, and car rental reservations for all your business needs.

3. Click the services of interest from the available links that are displayed.

21 Shopping for Real Estate

Are you looking to buy a new home, town home, or rental property? AOL's Real Estate channel and ClassifiedPlus Real Estate Web site provide comprehensive resources for homebuyers and

sellers everywhere. You'll have powerful search engines to help locate over 1.3 million new and existing homes and properties anywhere in the United States or Canada. You'll also have a handy reference center to help you find a mortgage lender as well as a realtor, locate a neighborhood best suited to you or your family's needs, find home repair contractors in your area, as well as a variety of other resources including mortgage calculators, home valuation centers, and message boards. Here's how you can find the home, town home, or rental property of your dreams.

AOL's Real Estate Channel

1. Click the **Keyword** button located on the AOL toolbar and enter AOL Keyword: **Real Estate** and click the **Go** button. The **AOL House & Home: Real Estate** channel appears, shown in Figure 8-10.

2. Click the topics of interest from the **Essentials and More Resources** categories or begin your search for existing or new homes for sale, as well as apartments and rentals anywhere in the United States or Canada.

Figure 8-10. Accessing AOL's Real Estate channel for real estate resouces

For additional real estate resources, AOL provides the ClassifiedPlus Real Estate Web site consisting of homes for sale by realtors, homes for sale by owner, rental properties, new home sales, builders, room mates services, commercial prop-erties, home improvement resources, travel accommodations, and a wealth of other valuable resources.

AOL's ClassifiedPlus Real Estate Web Site

1. Click the **Keyword** button located on the AOL toolbar and enter AOL Keyword: **Home for Rent** and click the **Go** button. The **ClassifiedPlus Real Estate** Web site appears.

2. Use the built-in search engine to find resources applicable to your needs or click the topics of interest from the available links that are displayed.

Coupon Shopping

22 Saving big bucks with coupons

Coupons are a great way to save money on the products you buy. AOL lets you get coupons on deals in your area or brand name products redeemable nationwide. You'll be able to access stores in your area's ValuPages or have manufacturers brand name coupons mailed to you to save big bucks on many of the products you and your family enjoys. Here's how:

1. Click the **Keyword** button located on the AOL toolbar and enter AOL Keyword: **Coupons** and click the **Go** button. The AOL **House & Home Coupons & Savings** channel appears, shown in Figure 8-11.

2. From the **Coupons & Savings** channel, enter your **zip code** and click the **Search** button to print valuable coupons or click the **Get Coupons** button to get exclusive brand-name coupons mailed to you.

Figure 8-11. Getting coupons for deals and products you buy is simple on AOL.

23 Registering and using ValuPage coupons for instant savings

Stores in your area list valuable offers and coupons in the form of ValuPages. You'll be able to get huge savings such as free samples, rebates, and offers specifically designed around your shopping habits. You'll also be able to see recipes for the products listed on the ValuPage. To begin taking advantage of your local stores ValuPages, you'll need to register. After you've registered (a one-time process), you'll be on your way to big savings. Here's how it's done:

Registering for Supermarket ValuPages

1. Click the **Keyword** button located on the AOL toolbar and enter AOL Keyword: **Coupons** and click the **Go** button to display the AOL **House & Home Coupons & Savings** channel.

2. Enter your **zip code** and click the **Search** button on the **Coupons & Savings** channel. The **ValuPage** for the stores in your area appears.

3. Click the **Want to Register?** button on the ValuPage screen.

4. Enter your first and last name, e-mail address, and zip code, and click the **Enter Info** button.

5. Check the supermarkets where you want to use your **ValuPage** list of offers at and click the **Enter Info** button.

6. Enter specific information about you and your family and click the **Enter Info** button.

7. Click **Get my ValuPage** button to view the supermarket you selected **ValuPage** of values. Your **ValuPages** will be mailed to your e-mail address on a weekly basis.

8. You'll be assigned a unique password that you'll use with your e-mail address.

Accessing your ValuPage

After you've successfully registered, you'll be on your way to receiving valuable savings at your local supermarkets. When you receive your supermarket's ValuPage in an e-mail, simply open the e-mail and print it to your printer. Here's how you can access your favorite stores ValuPage listing of offers:

1. Click the **Keyword** button located on the AOL toolbar and enter AOL Keyword: **Coupons** and click the **Go** button to display the AOL **House & Home Coupons & Savings** channel.

2. Enter your **zip code** and click the **Search** button on the **Coupons & Savings** channel. The **ValuPage** for the stores in your area appears.

3. Enter your e-mail address and **ValuPage** password and click the **Go** button.

4. Click the **Get All Offers** button on the **ValuPage**. The **ValuPage** will appear, shown in Figure 8-12.

Using your Supermarkets ValuPages

Using your ValuPage listing of offers is easy. Here's how it's done:

1. Select one or more of the items listed on your **ValuPage** of offers.

2. Give your **ValuPage** to the cashier at the beginning of your checkout process.

3. The cashier will give you **Web Bucks** which can be used to purchase anything on your next trip back to the supermarket. Law must not prohibit items that are purchased with **Web Bucks**.

24 Printing coupons for instant savings

Shopping with coupons has never been easier or more rewarding. SmartSource.com, in partnership with AOL, provides exclusive grocery, health, and household coupons that can be printed, as well as offering free samples. Once you've registered, you'll receive valuable coupons that can be printed on your printer and used at your favorite stores. Here's how it works:

1. Click the **Keyword** button located on the AOL toolbar and enter AOL Keyword: **Coupons** and click the **Go** button to display the AOL **House & Home Coupons & Savings** channel.

2. Click the **Get Coupons** button from the **Coupons & Savings** channel. This will display the AOL **House & Home SmartSource.com** Web site.

3. Click the **printable** button on the **SmartSource.com** Web site.

4. If this is your first time using **SmartSource.com** to print coupons, then you'll need to click the **Register Now!** button. You'll need to create your unique profile by completing the **My Profile—About Me** portion of the registration, and when finished click the **Next** button. Complete the **My Profile—My Household** portion of the registration and click the **Next** button. Finally, complete the **My Profile—My Preferences** portion of the registration and click the **Next** button.

5. After you've completed the registration process, you're then ready to sign in using your username and password that you entered when you created your profile.

6. Click the **Get Print Manager** button and once the print manager is downloaded, click the **Print Coupons** button. The printable coupon page(s) will appear, shown in Figure 8-13.

	Buy These Items	**Web Bucks Earned**
Baking Needs	TWO (2) 3-Strips **Fleischmann's**® Yeast, Active Dry or RapidRise, and earn 50¢ in Web Bucks® - OR - Buy THREE (3) or more 3-Strips **Fleischmann's**® Yeast, Active Dry or RapidRise and earn 99¢ in Web Bucks® [This coupon prints at end of order and may have a slight delay in printing]	up to 99¢
	TWO (2) boxes of **Fleischmann's**® Bread Machine Mixes, any variety, and earn 60¢ in Web Bucks® - OR - Buy THREE (3) or more boxes of **Fleischmann's**® Bread Machine Mixes, any variety, and earn $1.00 in Web Bucks® [This coupon prints at end of order and may have a slight delay in printing]	up to $1.00
	ONE 4 oz. jar of **Fleischmann's**® Yeast, Active Dry or Bread Machine	75¢
Cheese & Deli	TWO (2) **Kaukauna**® OR **WisPride**® Cheese Items (Cups, Balls, or Logs only)	75¢
Spices & Seasonings	ONE **McCormick**® PURE Vanilla Extract (excludes Imitation Vanilla)	35¢
	THREE (3) **McCormick**® Gravy Mixes (any variety, EXCLUDING Country Gravy Mixes)	50¢
Breads & Snacks	ONE box of **Entenmann's**® CEREAL BARS	35¢
Baby Items	ONE Jumbo package or larger of **HUGGIES**® Diapers (EXCLUDING Pull-Ups®)	$1.50
	ONE **HUGGIES**® Baby Wipes (64 ct. or larger) - **Cleans Like a Washcloth**® -	75¢
	THREE (3) tubs of **Beech-Nut**® **Table Time**® Toddler Dinners	50¢
	THREE (3) individual jars of **Beech-Nut Naturals**® Stage 3® Baby Food	50¢
	FIVE (5) individual jars of **Beech-Nut Naturals**® Stage 1® or Stage 2® Baby Food	50¢
	ONE **Beech-Nut Naturals**® 32 oz. Juice	50¢
	ONE box of **Beech-Nut Naturals**® Cereal	50¢
Grocery Items	ONE jar of **Pace**® Sauce or Salsa (16 oz. ONLY) and earn 40¢ in Web Bucks® - OR - Buy TWO (2) jars of **Pace**® Sauce or Salsa (16 oz. or larger) and earn $1.00 in Web Bucks® [This coupon prints at end of order and may have a slight delay in printing]	up to $1.00
	ONE container of **Carapelli**® Olive Oil (any variety, 17 oz. or larger)	$1.00
	ONE **Herb-Ox**® Bouillon (any variety)	75¢
	ONE jar of **Prego**® PASTA BAKE Sauce (Pasta Bake Sauce varieties ONLY)	75¢
Cereal	ONE box of **Brown Sugar & Oats Total**®, **Whole Grain Total**®, **Total**® Corn Flakes, or **Total**® Raisin Bran	40¢

Figure 8-12. Viewing a ValuPage listing of valuable offers

Figure 8-13. Selecting printable coupons for instant savings

25 Having coupons mailed directly to your home

Are you tired of looking for and cutting out coupons from your newspaper? Would you prefer to have savings coupons mailed to your home so all you have to do is redeem them at your local store? SmartSource.com, in partnership with AOL, provides exclusive grocery, health, and household coupons that can be automatically mailed to your home. Once you register for the service, you'll be able to select valuable coupons online and have them mailed directly to your home via first-class mail. These savings coupons can then be redeemed at participating stores nationwide. Not only is it hassle-free, it'll enable you to save money in the process. Here's how it works:

1. Click the **Keyword** button located on the AOL toolbar and enter AOL Keyword: **Coupons** and click the **Go** button to display the AOL **House & Home Coupons & Savings** channel.

2. Click the **Get Coupons** button from the **Coupons & Savings** channel. This will display the AOL **House & Home SmartSource.com** Web site.

3. Click the **by mail** button on the **Smart-Source.com** Web site.

4. If this is your first time using **SmartSource.com** to have coupons mailed to you, then you'll need to register by clicking the **Register Now!** button. This will enable you to create a unique personal profile by completing all the required information. When done, click the **I'm Done** button to begin saving money with coupons mailed to your home.

5. After you've completed the registration process, you're then ready to sign in using your username and password that you entered when you created your personal profile.

6. The **SmartSource.com** Internet coupons will appear asking you to select the coupons that interest you. When done, click the **I'm Done** button.

AOL Reward and Savings Programs

26 Earning points while you shop

Do you want to earn valuable reward points each time you shop? You can by using the AOL Visa card, which lets you earn one AOL Visa Reward point for every $1 purchase you make with your Visa card. Points are automatically accumulated and never expire. Here's how you can apply for an AOL Visa account:

Click the **Keyword** button located on the AOL toolbar and enter AOL Keyword: **AOL Visa** and click the **Go** button to display the AOL **Visa Cardmember Services** channel.

27 Saving a bundle on magazines

Would you like to get two free additional months of your favorite magazines when you subscribe? Now AOL members can at MagazineOutlet.com. You'll be able to enjoy many popular consumer-oriented magazines for an additional two months at no cost to you. This means that you'll be able to read about the latest trends, news, sports, and other information free of charge. Plus as an added bonus, you'll also be able to subscribe to popular magazines at huge discounts over the newsstand prices. Here's how to take advantage of this great offer.

1. Click the **Keyword** button located on the AOL toolbar and enter AOL Keyword:

MagazineOutlet.com and click the **Go** button to display the **Shop@AOL's MagazineOutlet.com** Web site, shown in Figure 8-14.

2. Select the **2 months at no cost to you** image on the **MagazineOutlet.com** Web site. This will display the magazine selection page.

Figure 8-14. Saving on magazines from MagazineOutlet.com

28 Exciting travel program with AOL Travelers Advantage

AOL's Travelers Advantage lets you research, explore, book, and save on travel destinations at your computer. You'll be able to take advantage of vacation offers, cruises, specials, and a vast array of resources all with a low price guarantee. Plus, as an added bonus, new members get a free hotel night just for joining. Here's how to take advantage of this great travel resource:

1. Click the **Keyword** button located on the AOL toolbar and enter AOL Keyword: **Travelers Advantage** and click the **Go** button to display the AOL **Travelers Advantage** channel.

2. Click the **Click Here!** button to access the AOL **Travelers Advantages** resources or to become a new member. Once you're a member, you'll be able to take advantage of all the great offers and discounts for your next vacation or travel destination.

29 Protecting yourself while you drive with AOL AutoVantage

You get 24-hour roadside assistance, car buying resources, travel discounts, free gas coupons, free oil changes, care and truck rental savings, and much more when you join AOL AutoVantage. AOL gives you a 3-month trial membership to experience how AutoVantage will give you peace of mind while you drive. Here's how you can take advantage of this great service:

1. Click the **Keyword** button located on the AOL toolbar and enter AOL Keyword: **AutoVantage** and click the **Go** button to display the AOL **AutoVantage** channel.

2. Click the **Member Sign-in** button to access the AOL **Autovantages Sign-in** channel. If you're not a member, you'll need to click the **Yes, I want it!** button. Click the **Join** button and complete the 3 months for free trial application process.

30 Signing up for newsletter alerts

Whether you're looking for bargains, coupons, or hot new deals, you'll want to sign up for the newsletters available on AOL and its partners. Three of the best newsletters available for shoppers at AOL Shopping are Deals & Steals, Web Flyer, and ShoppersAdvantage. Each provides valuable offers, advice, and savings tips.

AOL Shopping: Deals & Steals is a free newsletter designed for the AOL Shopping Channel Bargain Shopper. It's packed with deals on the things you like to shop for. Once you subscribe, you'll receive the weekly newsletter in your online mailbox every Wednesday. Here's how you can get great deals and steals on the many of the things you buy:

1. Click the **Keyword** button located on the AOL toolbar and enter AOL Keyword: **Deals News** and click the **Go** button to display the AOL **Shopping Deals & Steals** channel.

2. Click the **Subscribe** button.

Web Flyer is the frequent flyer authority and offers great last minute airfare deals, a variety of travel-related services, and a rewards program. To sign up for the Web Flyer newsletter, follow these easy steps:

1. Click the **Keyword** button located on the AOL toolbar and enter AOL Keyword: **InsideFlyer** and click the **Go** button to display the **Web Flyer** Web site.

2. Click **Subscribe Today to our FREE Newsletters** located on the left of the Web site. This will display the **Newsletter Sign-Up** Web site.

3. Enter the requested information on the membership application, click the **Subscribe** button corresponding to the **Newsletter** you want, and click the **Continue** button.

ShoppersAdvantage offers a 3-month trial to their newsletter for $1. Once you become a member, you'll be advised of special bargains, price drops, rewards, and benefits via e-mail updates. ShoppersAdvantage purchases earn a

3.5 percent ShoppersAdvantage cash bonus that can be applied to future purchases. Members receive a two-year product warranty coverage at zero cost to you. To sign up for the ShoppersAdvantage newsletter, follow these simple steps:

1. Click the **Keyword** button located on the AOL toolbar and enter AOL Keyword: **Advantage Store** and click the **Go** button to display the **ShoppersAdvantage** Web site.

2. Click **Newsletter Sign-Up** located at the bottom of the Web site under the **Contact & Info** section. This will display the **Newsletter Sign-Up** Web site.

3. Click the **Become a Member** button.

4. Enter the requested information on the membership application and click the **Become a Member** button.

Services, Security, Privacy, and Shipping

31 Accessing credit alert services

Another free service provided by AOL is Credit Alert by PrivacyGuard. Credit Alert lets you get 3 months free by seeing the data that banks and credit card companies see, as well as who has accessed your credit report. This service lets you get one free credit report plus monthly credit alerts to help you protect your financial security. Once you join, you'll get copies of your credit, driving, and medical records allowing you to check and correct inaccuracies in all your records. Here's how you'll be able to take advantage of this handy free service:

1. Click the **Keyword** button located on the AOL toolbar and enter AOL Keyword: **CA** and click the **Go** button. The **Credit Alert by PrivacyGuard** window appears.

2. Review the offer details by clicking the **Try Now** button. Read the offer carefully before enrolling.

32 Receiving reminders

Never forget that birthday, anniversary, holiday or special occasion again. Just register the dates for which you want reminders in AOL's confidential database. Fourteen days before the holiday or special occasion AOL's free reminder service sends a friendly reminder e-mail message. It can also be made to send a second reminder 4 days prior. Here's how it works:

1. Click the **Keyword** button located on the AOL toolbar and enter AOL Keyword: **Reminder** and click the **Go** button to display the **Free Reminder Service** channel.

2. Click the **Create Your Reminder** button to enter your name, gender, and the date you'd automatically like to be reminded of, shown in Figure 8-15.

3. Click the **Continue** button to display your **Personal Reminder** list. Your **Personal Reminder** list appears.

4. Click the **OK** button in the **Thank You! Your Reminder Team** dialog box.

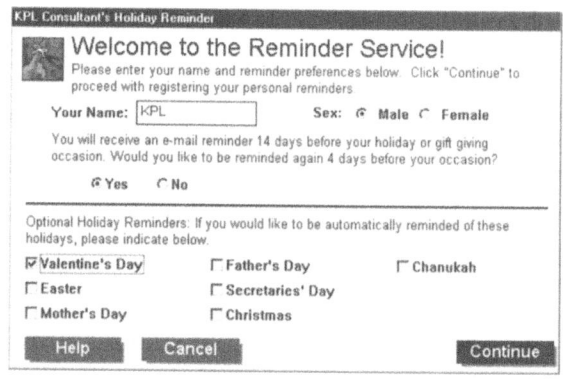

Figure 8-15. Registering your personal reminders to the Reminder Service

33 Protecting your online security and privacy

Maintaining a high level of security and privacy is a high priority for AOL. It's also important that you take responsibility to ensure that your online security and privacy isn't compromised. To accomplish this, always be on the lookout for online security and privacy breeches. The following tips will help you understand the types of problems to look for and better protect the security and privacy of your AOL account:

- Never give out your password or billing information to anyone. AOL personnel will never ask for this information.

- Create a password that is a minimum of six characters in length and uses a combination of characters and numbers, such as jet7run or run4fun7 or 8is4plus4.

- Whenever you think that your account has been compromised, change your password immediately as well as for any other screen names on your account.

- Setting up a member profile serves a useful purpose when accessing online communities, but they are public information that everyone can view. Never list any personal information such as name, address, phone number, or other identifying information.

- Never open a file attachment sent to you from a stranger. The attached file could contain a virus or Trojan horse program that could attack and destroy your computer files. Attached files containing Trojan horse programs often end with the extension .SHS, and sometimes .EXE—beware.

- Use the AOL mail controls to block e-mail messages containing attached files being sent to you.

- Set up download controls for your children so they can't download files from software libraries or FTP transfer sites containing offensive material and/or pictures.

- Avoid electronic greeting card scams where a scam artist sends you what appears to be a greeting card, but in actuality contains a Trojan horse program that compromises your system by accessing your billing information.

- AOL personnel will never send attached files.

- Create a separate screen name for your online and Internet purchases that block others from sending attached files and pictures.

34 Preventing unauthorized online purchases

Do you worry that your kids may buy online without your permission? To prevent screen names on your account from making online purchases, you can follow these simple steps:

1. Sign on to your account using the master screen name or one that has been designated as being an additional master screen name.

2. On your **Settings** menu located on the AOL toolbar, select **Parental Controls**.

3. Click **Set Parental Controls** from the **Parental Controls** window.

4. Select the **screen name** you want to prevent from making online purchases from the **Edit controls for:** list.

5. Select a designation of **Mature Teen (16–17)**, **Young Teen (13–15)**, or **Kids Only (12 and under)** for the screen name selected. Selecting **Mature Teen** or **Young Teen** permits the screen name to view online shopping areas, but not to make purchases. Selecting **Kids Only** prevents the screen name from viewing and purchasing items from online shopping areas.

35 Filling out a shipping form once

Are you tired of filling out payment and shipping forms with every purchase you make online? America Online offers a hassle-free way to check out and save time shopping online. The service is called QuickCheckout. Not only is it fast, easy, and safe, it's also free. The number of online stores participating in this service is growing rapidly, so the checkout process for these stores will only be a point and click away. If you decide to take advantage of QuickCheckout, you'll need to sign up just one time. From that point on, your personal information is privately saved and stored using state-of-the-art technology so you only have to enter it once.

Updates to your personal shopping information can be made at any time as well. Here's how you can take advantage of this time-saving online wallet service:

1. Click the **Keyword** button located on the AOL toolbar and enter AOL Keyword: **Shopping** and click the **Go** button to display the **Shop@AOL Shopping** channel.

2. Click **Quick Checkout** located on the **Shopping** channel to display the **QuickCheckout** Web site.

Registering for QuickCheckout

1. Click the **Sign Up Now!** button on the **QuickCheckout** Web site. Enter your Zip/Postal Code and click the **Continue** button.

2. Complete the five easy steps of the registration process: **Credit Card Information, Shipping Information, Create Your Shopping Password, Enter Your Security Question and Answer**, and **Mailing List**, and click the **Continue** button.

Using QuickCheckout

Whenever you shop online, look for the **Quick-Checkout** button or the **Buy Now** button. By clicking either of these buttons, you'll use the personal information you saved.

Reaching Customer Service for Shopping Help

36 Getting help whenever you need it

AOL provides three convenient ways for you to get shopping assistance anytime you want. Customer representatives are available 24 hours a day, 7 days a week to assist with your every need. Here's how you can contact them:

- Chat Now: Get immediate, live help from one of AOL's shopping consultants. You must be logged onto AOL to use this option.

- By Phone: 1-800-349-1945. AOL's consultants are standing by to answer your questions.

- By E-mail: Please e-mail AOL at AOL Screen Name ShopHelp.

If you need to get in touch with a specific merchant's customer service department or with an AOL representative, follow these easy steps:

1. Click the **Keyword** button located on the AOL toolbar and enter AOL Keyword: **Shopping Customer Service** and click the **Go** button to display the AOL **Customer Service** channel.

2. Click the desired **Shopping Customer Service** department from the selection list of departments.

3. If you're not getting the assistance you feel you deserve, click the **Email Shopping** button and describe your situation and transmit the e-mail message.

37 Chatting with live customer service representatives

Would you like to chat with a live customer service representative about a technical or billing problem you're having? You can get the assistance you need anytime, 24 hours a day, 7 days a week, and it's free. Here's how it works:

1. Click the **Keyword** button located on the AOL toolbar and enter AOL Keyword: **Customer Service** and click the **Go** button to display the AOL **Customer Service** channel.

2. Click **Get Live Online Help** from the customer service options.

3. Click **Technical** to contact a technical representative with questions related to connection problems, error messages, or other technical issues. Click **Billing** to contact a billing representative with questions related to account

information changes, pricing plans, or surcharges.

38 Contacting AOL by phone

America Online is available to answer your AOL questions 24 hours a day, 7 days a week. Before calling on of their toll-free numbers, you should have your account information available (i.e., screen name and credit card number) so account verification can be performed. Select the phone number from the list below.:

AOL Technical Support (Windows version):
1-888-346-3704

AOL Technical Support (Macintosh version):
1-888-265-8007

Screen Name or Password Problems:
1-888-265-8004

Access Numbers:
1-888-265-8005

Billing Inquiries:
1-888-265-8003

Account Cancellation:
1-888-265-8008

39 Contacting customer service by e-mail

America Online makes it easy to contact customer service representative with a technical or billing

problem you're having. You can get the assistance you need anytime, 24 hours a day, 7 days a week by e-mail, and it's free. An AOL staff member will send a reply to your question directly to your online mailbox within 72 hours. Here's how it works:

1. Click the **Keyword** button located on the AOL toolbar and enter AOL Keyword: **Customer Service** and click the **Go** button to display the AOL **Customer Service** channel.

2. Click **Contact Customer Service by E-mail** from the customer service options.

3. Click **Technical** to contact a technical representative with questions related to connection problems, error messages, or other technical issues. Complete the detailed information on the form and select the dropdown selection options that best describe your computer, and click the **Send** button.

4. Click **Billing** to contact a billing representative with questions related to account information changes, pricing plans, or surcharges. Complete the detailed information on the form and select the dropdown selection option that best relates to your question, and click the **Send** button, shown in Figure 8-16.

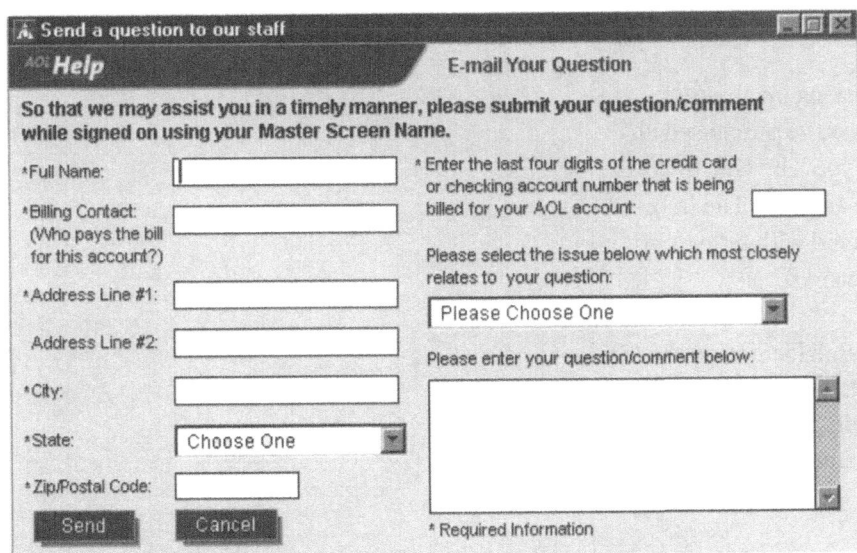

Figure 8-16. Sending a billing question is a snap.

40 Having a problem with a purchase—contact ShopHelp

If you're having a problem with an online purchase and need to get it resolved, you can contact Shopping Help. America Online gives you three ways to get the help you need: by e-mail, by Instant Message Chat, or by phone. Here's how you can get the latest information for the help you need.

1. Click the **Keyword** button located on the AOL toolbar and enter AOL Keyword: **Shopping Help** and click the **Go** button to display **the Shop@AOL's Shopping Help** Web site.

2. For e-mail assistance, open a **Write** window, enter the screen name **ShopHelp** in the **Send To** field, enter your screen name in the **Copy To** field, and describe your problem in the message text field. When you're done, click the **Send Now** button.

3. For immediate online chat assistance, click the **Keyword** button located on the AOL toolbar and enter AOL Keyword: **Customer Service** and click the **Go** button to display the AOL **Customer Service** channel. Click **Billing** to contact a billing representative with questions related to account information changes, pricing plans, or surcharges.

4. For telephone assistance, call tool-free **1-800-349-1945** to talk to an AOL representative right now, 24 hours a day, 7 days a week.

41 Checking on an order online

America Online makes checking on an order online a simple process. If you've purchased an item on AOL's Shop Direct, you'll be able to get the assistance you need online anytime. The information is provided on demand with little or no time waiting. Here's how it works:

1. Click the **Keyword** button located on the AOL toolbar and enter AOL Keyword: **Shop Direct** and click the **Go** button to display the AOL **Customer Service** channel.

2. Click **Order Status** under the **Contact Us** section on the AOL **Shop Direct** Web site.

3. You'll need to enter your **order number** and **zip code**, and then click the **Submit** button.

4. The online system will find your order status information and display it on your screen.

CHAPTER 9
AOL for Kids and Teens

THIS CHAPTER IS DEVOTED to kids and teens everywhere. In fact, parents will also find the kid-friendly content a marvelous way for their young ones to build a life-long desire for learning. This chapter presents fun and amazing tips that will pique your interest in the world around you. Whether your interest is in finding and playing the latest online or multi-user dungeon games, reading books, exploring the many wonders of the world, the planets, or deep space, this chapter will wow and amaze parents, kids, and teens everywhere.

In this chapter, you'll learn how to

- 📖 Surf safely

- 📖 Use the Online Timer

- 📖 Explore the Kids Only channel

- 📖 Find the coolest teen sites

- 📖 Get educational

- 📖 Use acronyms and smileys

- 📖 Research and learn

- 📖 Have fun with hobbies and other stuff

Surfing Safely

1 Playing it safe online

AOL offers extensive information and educational features; however, not everything on AOL or the rest of the Internet is suitable for kids and teens. As a parent, you should use AOL's Parental Controls feature to control your child's online experience and ensure that it is safe, fun, and enriching. The Parental Controls let you determine the people and places your child can access based on your comfort level and your child's maturity level. There's also an Online Timer that allows you to determine the number of hours your child can spend online, and what times and days of the week. For more information, go to AOL Keyword: **AOL Parental Controls** on AOL.

2 Learning top safety tips for kids and teens

Creating a safe online environment is something every parent should ensure for their children's safety and enjoyment. Here are some safety tips for your kids to remember each time they get online:

- Tell your parents about any bad or threatening language you see.

- Never give your AOL password to anyone.

- Never tell anyone your name, address, telephone number, or school name without your parents' permission.

- Never respond to anyone who makes you feel bad, uncomfortable, or unsafe. Instead, contact keyword: **Tell AOL**. Remember that people aren't always who they say they are.

- Get your parents' permission before telling someone you'll meet them in person.

- Never accept e-mails, file attachments, pictures, or Web site addresses from someone you don't know.

- Don't degrade, harass, or discriminate against other people.

- Don't swear or use vulgar language.

3 Getting a Kids Only account

Kids Only (KO) Accounts are special accounts that make playing online a fun and safe experience. A KO account displays a special Welcome screen with your child's screen name on it. Your kid will be able to play at KO and surf the net at KO Netfind. The best feature of all is that you'll know your child is safe online because AOL checks out all the Web sites and makes sure they're safe before kids can explore them. So use Parental Controls to set up a KO account for your kids today. You'll be glad you did.

4 Safe searching for kids and teens

AOL provides search Web sites just for kids and teens. KO Search (AOL keyword: **KO Search**) makes it easy to find the coolest kids-only sites on the Web, shown in Figure 9-1. And teens will be glad to surf the The Kids and Teens Search site at http://aolsearch.aol.com/. The best part is that AOL editors have handpicked all of the sites for a fun and safe Internet experience.

Using the Online Timer

5 Limiting time online with the Timer

As a parent, you are responsible for making your child's online experience pleasant and safe. This may involve setting limits on the number of hours you want him or her to spend online. If your child uses AOL to access the Internet, you can limit the number of hours your child spends online with the use of the AOL Online Timer.

> 🖋 *If your child uses some other software to access the Internet, the online timer will not work.*

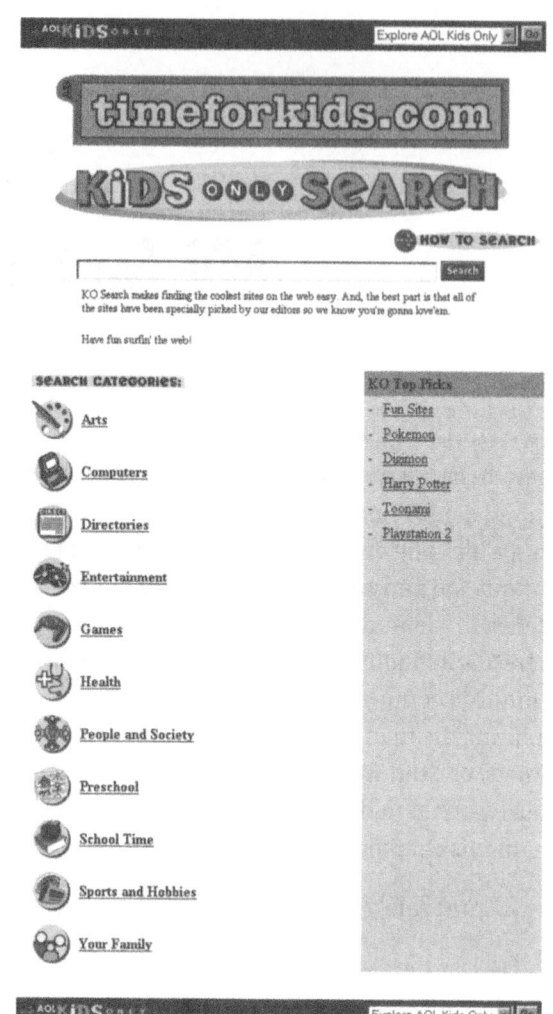

Figure 9-1. Accessing AOL's Kids Only search channel is as easy as 1-2-3.

6 Setting the Online Timer

The AOL Online Timer is pretty easy to set. Just follow these steps:

1. Click the **Settings** menu located on the AOL toolbar, and select the **Parental Controls** option.

2. Click the **Set Parental Controls** option.

3. Select the screen name for which you want the online timer in the **Edit Controls for** box.

4. Click the **Online Timer** control.

5. Follow the four-step process by clicking the **Next** button each time.

7 Modifying the Online Timer

You can modify the Online Timer any time you like by following these steps:

1. Click the **Settings** menu located on the AOL toolbar, and select the **Parental Controls** option.

2. Click the **Set Parental Controls** option.

3. Select the screen name for which you want the online timer in the **Edit Controls for** box.

4. Click the **Online Timer** control.

5. Follow the four-step process by clicking the **Next** button.

8 Setting the Timer for different times on different days

To provide flexibility, the Online Timer permits you to set different time limits for different days of the week. This is a handy feature that recognizes the following settings:

- Restrict daily activities to the same time limit for each day of the week.

- A different time limit for weekday and weekend activities.

- A different time limit for each day of the week.

- Unlimited use.

9 Checking the Timer

When your child first signs on to AOL, he or she will automatically be notified as to how much time is left for the day. Your child can also type the AOL Keyword: **Timer** at any time to see how much time is left for the day.

10 Running out of time

Once the allotted time for any given day has expired, your child's screen name will automatically sign off. They will not be able to sign back on to AOL until their next session of allotted online time begins.

Exploring the Kids Channels

11 Getting to know the AOL Kids Only channel

The Kids Only (KO) channel is geared entirely for kids. An AOL Kids Only account gets a special Welcome screen. It provides basic links to your kid's online mailbox, local weather forecasts, cool tips, online help, and entrance into the Kids Only channel. Accessed by typing AOL Keyword: **Kids Only** or **KO**, it's simple to use and provides hours of fun and enjoyment for the whole family. By moving your mouse over each of the six buttons: TV Movies & Music, Games, Homework Help, Growing Up, Art Studio, and News+Sports, you'll sneak a peek at what each button has in store. KO, shown in Figure 9-2, is packed with great stories, terrific features, and hours of enjoyment.

Figure 9-2. Accessing AOL's Kids Only channel

12 Exploring the top 10 kids channels

Here's a list of great Kids Only channels, shown in Table 9-2, that kids everywhere are sure to enjoy. So explore, learn, and most importantly have fun by visiting these true treasures.

Table 9-2. Top 10 Kids Only Web Sites

KEYWORD	DESCRIPTION
KO Harry Potter	Take a look at movie previews, toys and other goodies. Also download a free screensaver, print bookmarks and scenes, and visit the Official Harry Potter Movie site.

KO Cartoon Dolls	Download a free cartoon doll, customize her, and submit your doll creation to see if it makes the top 100-doll gallery.
Pokemon	Learn about everything that is Pokemon including the official site for games, pictures, downloads, comics, poke-games, books, toys, and movies.

KO Clubhouse	Check out a variety of Kids Only clubs for birthdays, cartoons, collecting, computers, cooking, dinosaurs, games, jokes, movies, pets, space, and stickers.
KO Toy Fair	Sneak a peek at the toys of the week, action toys, movie and TV toys, tech toys, and learn what's in the toy hall of fame. Also talk about the toys you've seen on the Toy Fair message board.

Table 9-2. Top 10 Kids Only Web Sites (Continued)

KEYWORD	DESCRIPTION
KO Games	Download fun games including Arnold vs. Sewer King, Urban Racer, Pillow Fight, Golf, Trivia Dunk-off, and more. Also play online games and get video game codes.

KO Pet of the Week	Pet of the Week allows you to send a picture and story about your pet. It could be the featured pet for the week.
KO Art	The KO Art Studio gives you a variety of cool art tools. Create cartoons, greeting cards, fliers, announcements, or anything your heart desires with these fun art tools.
KO Music	Get the latest information on kids-only music including who sings the lyrics to hit movies and songs. Also learn more about your favorite musical artists.
KO Homework Help	Do you need help with your homework? Are those math problems getting you down? Is that science project due tomorrow? You can get help with English, reading, math, science, and social studies right away. You can even ask a teacher.

13 Getting the KO newsletter

Want to get the coolest newsletter for kids and teens delivered direct to your mailbox twice a month? The Kids Only newsletter contains cool information for kids and teens, and it's free too. To subscribe, simply follow these instructions:

1. Click **Kids Help** on the KO main screen.

2. Click the **Everything List** icon located at the bottom left hand corner of your screen.

3. Click on the **Subscribe** button to get the KO newsletter, which is sent twice a month.

14 Finding other fun and entertaining Web sites

Here's a great list of AOL-sponsored fun and entertaining sites on the Web, shown in Table 9-3. AOL put these together just for kids.

Table 9-3. AOL-sponsored Web Site

Amazing Braino	`http://aol.amazingbraino.com/`
Ant Kids	`aol://1722:antkids/`
Cartoon Network	`http://www.cartoonnetwork.com/`
CBS SportLine	`http://www.sportsline.com/u/kids/`
FunSchool	`http://www.funschool.com/`
HarryPotter Games	`http://aol.kidsreads.com/HarryPotter/games.html`
Kidsreads.com	`http://www.kidsreads.com/`
MaMaMedia	`http://www.mamamedia.com/`
NancyDrew.com	`http://www.nancydrew.com/aol/`
Nickelodeon	`http://www.nick.com/`
PBS Kids	`http://www.pbskids.org/`
Timeforkids.com	`http://www.timeforkids.com/`
White House	`http://www.whitehouse.gov/kids/`

15 Checking out the PBS Kids Web site

The PBS Kids Web site is full of fun games and information about the popular Public TV shows including Arthur, Barney, Dragon Tales, Jay Jay, Mister Rogers, Teletubbies, Tots TV, Zoboomafoo, and much more, shown in Figure 9-7. To access this wonderful kids site type AOL Keyword: **PBS Kids**.

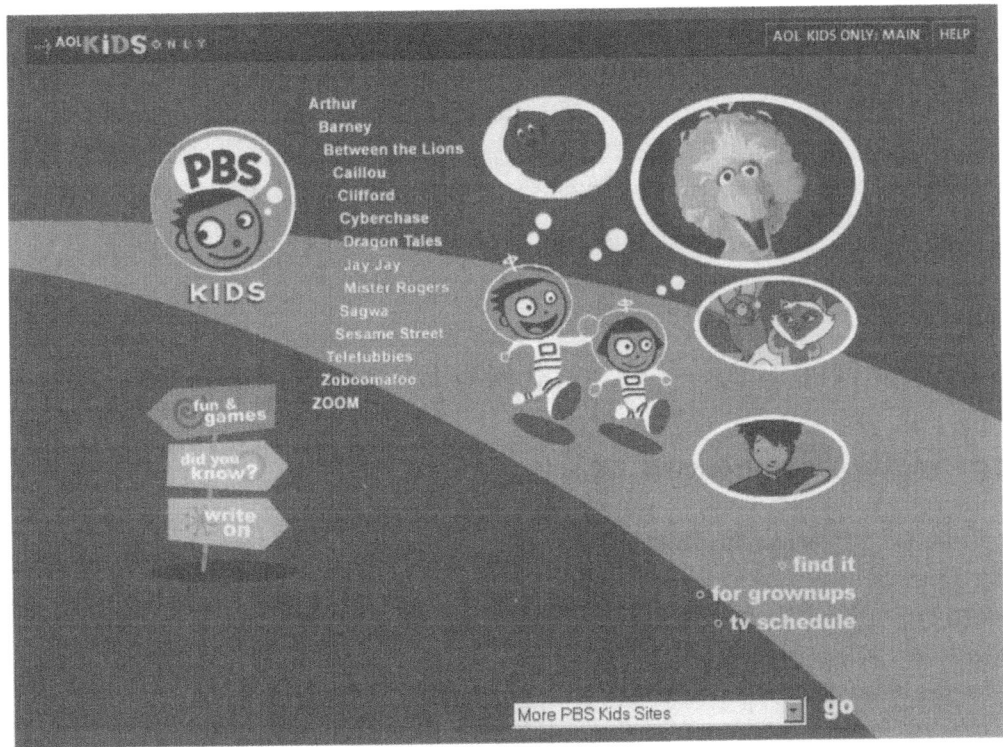

Figure 9-7. Having fun and learning with the PBS Kids Web site

16 Making believe

Have you ever played make-believe where you pretended you were a wizard, astronaut, ballerina, professional baseball player, ship captain, or doctor? Playing make believe is a wonderful past time for kids of all ages. Kids love to play make believe. Table 9-4 shows a list of some creative and wonderful make believe Web sites that kids are sure to enjoy.

Table 9-4. Make-Believe Web Sites

SITE NAME	ADDRESS	DESCRIPTION
Daily Life Ancient Egypt	`http://member.aol.com/donnclass/egyptlife.html`	Learn about Egyptian life
Grandfather Reads	`http://www.grandfatherreads.com/`	Inspire children to read
Inventors Gallery	`http://invention.psychology.msstate.edu/`	Inventors gallery
Land of Make Believe	`http://www.lomb.com/`	New Jersey's Water Amusement Park

Table 9-4. Make-Believe Web Sites (Continued)

SITE NAME	ADDRESS	DESCRIPTION
Life in the Fourth Grade	http://now2000.com/bigkidnetwork/kidschron2.html	Kids chronicle of life in the 4th grade
NASA Apollo Mission 11	http://www.ksc.nasa.gov/history/apollo/apollo-11/apollo-11.html	NASA Apollo Mission Apollo 11
Oz Encyclopedia	http://www.halcyon.com/piglet/	Land of Oz information, movies, books
Planet Mars	http://www.marshome.com/	Planet Mars home page
Tropical Rainforest Animals	http://www.ran.org/ran/kids_action/animals.html	Pretend you're in a tropical rainforest

Finding the Coolest Teen Sites

17 Getting started with the AOL Teens channel

The AOL Teens channel offers teens everywhere chats and message boards, games, celebrity fan clubs, music, sports, movies and TV, style, real life, and much more, shown in Figure 9-8. The AOL Teens channel provides hours of fun and is accessed by typing AOL keyword: **Teens**.

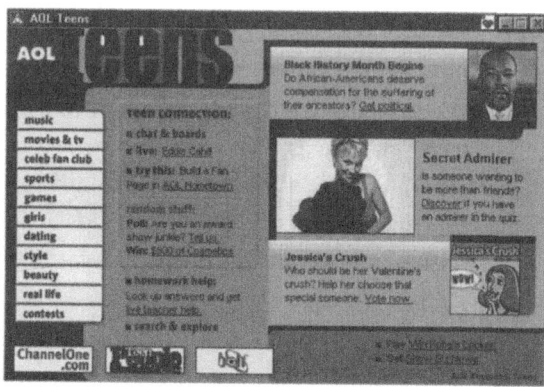

Figure 9-8. Accessing AOL's Teens channel for games, music, sports, and much more

18 Accessing the top 10 Teen channels

Here's a top-ten list of some great teen sites, shown in Table 9-5. Each can be accessed from AOL's Teens channel. Teens everywhere will enjoy exploring, learning, and having fun with these cool destinations. Simply access each category by clicking the hyperlink on AOL's Teens channel.

Table 9-5. Top 10 Teen channels

KEYWORD	DESCRIPTION
Music	Read about your favorite music artists, get music news, and look at concert photos.
Movies & TV	Get the latest on TV shows, top TV picks, and photos. Also, post messages and chat online.
Celeb Fan Club	Want to know more about your favorite celebrities? Then this is the place to for you. You'll also find celebrity trivia, photos, and places to post messages and chat online live with your favorite stars.
Games	Play lots of online games, and learn about the latest downloadables and games.
School	At this site you'll find school news and issues including popularity, pressures and grades, classes, money, and college. Also post your thoughts about these issues.

Table 9-5. Top 10 Teen channels (Continued)

KEYWORD	DESCRIPTION
Sports	Dig into sports news and info on your favorite teams and athletes from high school and college to the pros. Also post messages and chat with other sports fans.
Girls	Get all girly with tips on dating, style, and beauty secrets. Also post messages and chat.
Real Life	Real Life covers all sorts of news and issues confronting teens including school, dating, health and more.
Chat & Boards	Chat online and post your messages with like-minded teens. Choose from a number of chat and message board topics.
Style	Get the latest fashion information including fashion style quizzes, style message boards and chat lines.

19 Learning about chat and message boards

Chat and message boards are popular among teens. Finding the many chat and message board communities is simple with AOL. Type AOL Keyword: **Teen Chat**. A sample chat room lobby is shown in Figure 9-9.

Figure 9-9. Displaying a sample chat room lobby

20 Accessing one of the teen chat rooms

AOL provides a number of teen chat rooms to join in conversations with friends and family. The following chat room communities can be accessed from AOL's Teen Chat channel. Each room's name distinguishes it from the others. How? Only teens know for sure.

gold	brass
platinum	mercury
copper	zinc
silver	bronze
nickel	brick
rust	paper
carbon	plastic
steel	concrete
iron	crystal
tin	aluminum

The following teen message boards are available within AOL.

Music—Artists A to Z	Extreme Sports
Music—Genre	Girls Only
Movies	Style & Fashion
Television Shows	News & Issues
Celebrities	School
Videogames	Dating
High School Sports	Health
Pro & College Sports	Real People

Getting Educational

21 Learning and interacting online

Here are a few fun and educational interactive Web sites that kids as well as the whole family can enjoy.

CyberSurfari	http://www.cybersurfari.org/
DiscoverySchool	http://school.discovery.com/
EducationWorld	http://www.educationworld.com/
Kids Domain	http://www.kidsdomain.com/
LearningNetwork	http://familyeducation.com/k12/

22 Keeping up on the news at Time for Kids

The Time for Kids Web site is an educational site for kids and teens. You access it by typing the Web site address: http://www.timeforkids.com/TFK/. So what's available? You'll find articles, news, games, magazines, and cool things to explore, for all different ages. This is a great site for having fun while you learn.

23 Going to AOL@School

AOL@School, shown in Figure 9-10, provides a wealth of information for kids and students of all ages. You begin by selecting your grade level to get matched to activities and resources just right for you. The grade level groupings are:

- Primary (K–2)

- Elementary (3–5)

- Middle (6–8)

- High School (9–12)

You can get help with homework, research a topic, learn about current events, and find lesson plans on a variety of subjects including Math, Science, Social Studies, Arts, and Language Arts.

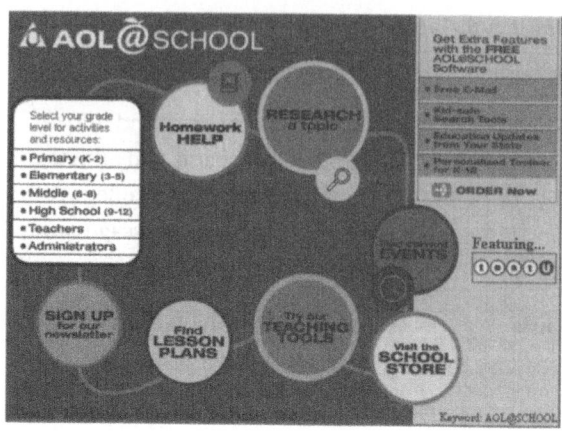

Figure 9-10. Accessing the AOL@School Web site for all your information needs

24 Learning online with homework helper

Have you ever wanted help with your homework? AOL provides a Homework helper by typing AOL keyword: **Homework**. Get the help you need to solve a math problem, research topics for an upcoming science project, post an English or reading question, or get an answer for your social studies class. You can even ask a teacher by posting a question and, yes, you'll get an answer.

Online learning is an increasingly popular way to learn. It is convenient, and Web-based learning can be enjoyed anywhere a Web browser is available. Teens can get help with research papers, by using an encyclopedia, thesaurus, dictionary, and live tutoring from teachers available through the AOL Research & Learn homework helper. Just type AOL Keyword: **Homework Help**.

25 Digging into books and stuff

Find out about cool new children's books and their creators at AOL Keyword: **Kids Reads**. The Kids Reads channel, which you see in Figure 9-20, provides reading lists, book reviews, information on home-schooling, and lots more for kids, teens, and parents.

Figure 9-11. Accessing AOL's Kids Reads channel is fun for the whole family.

A Web site showcasing books for teens, author chats, featured books, and book reviews is found at TeenReads.com and can be reached at:
`ttp://aol.teenreads.com/index.asp`.

26 Discovering and learning

If you need to access reference resources such as a desktop encyclopedia or a dictionary to help with your child's education or homework, you won't want to miss the AOL Research & Learn channel. Accessed by typing AOL Keyword: **Research**, it provides a vast library of research material on subjects such as history, art, science, biographies, mythology, reading & writing, consumer & money matters, law & government, health, geography & maps, and many other topics.

Visit PBS Online, shown in Figure 9-12, for even more research-related material, and to discover the subjects you enjoy most, from news to history, business to finance, science to arts and culture, and technology to current events. PBS Online provides superb content and previews upcoming PBS TV shows and specials. You can access this site by clicking the **PBS Stay Curious** button located at the bottom of the Research & Learn channel window or typing the address: `http://aolsvc.pbs.aol.com/researchandlearn/`.

Figure 9-12. The PBS Online Web site

27 Exploring far away places and things

The AOL Research & Learn channel lets your mind soar to far away places and adventures with special interest topics like ballooning, rafting, skydiving, and more. Explore the world from your computer screen by typing AOL Keyword: **Adventure**.

28 Exploring multimedia—pictures, sounds, and movies

Kids and teens can find multimedia resources including pictures, sounds, and movies from a variety of AOL channels including Science, History, Maps & Geography, Math Forum, and Reading & Writing, among others.

29 Getting scientific

Kids and teens will have great fun exploring the world of science at AOL keyword: **Science**. Learn the latest news from the world of science and explore planet Earth, space, archaeology, and much more.

30 Getting wild in the animal kingdom

Explore the animal kingdom at AOL keyword: **Nature**. Learn all about lions, tigers, and bears, and view the photo gallery, chat online with others, and post messages on the message board.

31 Researching natural history

Have you ever wondered who our ancestors were, what they ate, or how they lived? Find answers to these and other natural history questions at AOL Keyword: **Anthropology**. Learn about prehuman ancestors, mummies, what new fossils have been found, and much more. You can also chat online about your research findings, and post messages on the boards.

32 Exploring our planet

Hurricanes, tornadoes, forest fires, and nature's other deadly forces—have you ever wondered what causes

them? Find these answers and more at AOL Keyword: **Planet Earth**. Access Planet Earth resources, chat online, and post messages on the boards.

33 Blasting into space and beyond

Find out about stellar space facts like, what is the star closest to planet Earth, what are the planets made of, and what is the temperature of Mars? These answers and more await you at AOL Keyword: **Space**. Be the first in your school or neighborhood to join an astronomy club, explore space, the planets, and stars. Chat online with other future astronomers, and post messages on the boards about your latest research findings.

Using Acronyms and Smileys

34 Keeping it short and sweet with kids- and teens-only acronyms

Table 9-6 deciphers all those cool little words known as acronyms that are used so frequently by Internet-savvy kids in e-mails, online interactive games, and kids' chat rooms. You'll be able to understand and respond with an acronym of your own. So sy.

Table 9-6. Kids and Teens-Only Acronyms

ACRONYM	MEANING	ACRONYM	MEANING
2	to/too/two	OIC	Oh, I see!
411?	Tell me more	OMG	Oh My GOSH!
???	What? / Explain	OTF	On The Floor
AFK	Away From Keyboard	p911	parents here
AKA	Also Known As	P911	My parents are coming in the room.
AP	Absolutely Positive	POS	Parent Over Shoulder
BAK	Back At Keyboard	QT	Cutie
BrB	Bathroom Break	ROTF	Rolling On The Floor
BRB	Be Right Back	SA	Sibling Alert!

Table 9-6. Kids and Teens-Only Acronyms (Continued)

ACRONYM	MEANING	ACRONYM	MEANING
BTW	By The Way	SK	Super Kid!
cul8er	see you later	SUL	See You Later
CUL8R	See You Later	sup	What's up?
D/L	Downloading	sy	see ya!
E-M me k?	E-mail me o'k?	TTFN	Ta-Ta For Now!
GB	Good Bye	HH	Hey Host
GTG	Got To Go	TTYL	Talk To You
H5!	High Five	U	you
IAB	I Am BORED!	UGG	You Go Girl!
IGJ	I Gotta Jet	WB	Welcome Back!
ILY	I love you!	WTG	Way To Go
jj	just joking	Y	Why?
L8TR	Later	Yme?	Why me?
LOL	Laughing Out Loud	zzzzz	Boring or tired

35 Getting cute with kids- and teens-only smileys

Show emotion in all your e-mail and chat room discussions with these popular text-based smileys, commonly referred to as emoticons.

Table 9-7. Kids and Teens-Only Smileys

SMILEY	MEANING	SMILEY	MEANING
:-)	Happy smiley	~:o	Baby smiley
:-))	Really happy smiley	~:-)	Baby smiley
:-]	Another happy face! smiley	~(:O	Baby crying smiley
:-D	Laughing smiley	B-}	Have got eyes for you smiley
:-(	A little sad or grumpy smiley	:-X	I promise not to tell smiley
:-((	Really sad smiley	~:|	Don't bother me smiley
:-C	Very sad smiley	L:)	Loser smiley
;-)	Wink, Wink, Know what I mean? smiley	~</:-)	Party hat smiley
;^)	Winking smiley	+<:-)	Nun smiley

Table 9-7. Kids and Teens-Only Smileys   (Continued)

SMILEY	MEANING	SMILEY	MEANING
:-(	Frowning smiley	+:-)	Doctor smiley
:-[	Pouting smiley	<:-)	Dunce smiley
:-|	Ho Hum – A bored smiley	(:o (|)	Homer Simpson smiley
: (_____)	Bored or tired smiley	(:V)	PacMan smiley
:-*	Kissing smiley	(|XO|)	Big Mac smiley
:X	Kissing smiley	~8-)	Harry Potter smiley
O:-)	Like an angel smiley	o->-</:	Skater Dude smiley
(-:	Left-handed smiley	o{-</:	Skater Dude smiley
/:-(	Worried smiley	(o---<)	Sounds fishy smiley
:-/	Confused smiley, Skeptical	X(	Fed up or angry smiley
=:-O	Scared smiley	:-OI	Mouth full smiley
:-@	Screaming smiley	:-p	Smiley with tongue sticking out
:`-)	Happy tear smiley	:-&	Tongue-tied smiley
:-()	Yelling smiley	[:-)	Wearing a walkman smiley
|-I	Asleep smiley	:-~(	Got the flu smiley
:-]	Talk to me smiley	:-(E	Sloppy eater smiley
d:-)	Wearing a baseball cap smiley	%-)	Cross-eyed smiley
:-#/	Wears braces smiley	:-X	"My lips are sealed"
:>)	Can't keep his mouth shut smiley	8(:-)	Mickey Mouse smiley
*<:-{{{	Santa Clause smiley	(:>)( )( )	Snowman smiley
s-]	Silly smiley	:-----------)	Pinocchio smiley
:-s	Don't know what to say smiley	M-),:X,:-M	See no evil, hear no evil, speak no evil smiley

Having Fun with Hobbies and Other Stuff

36 Finding all AOL games

Wouldn't it be nice to find out all the games available on AOL? Here's a Web site that groups and alphabetically lists all the available AOL games that you can play. You can reach the AOL Games Web site at http://aolsvc.aol.com/games/index.adp.

37 Getting active indoors and out

Do you enjoy doing fun and exciting indoor and outdoor activities with family and friends? Do you enjoy working with crafts? Or do you like to spend the day working in the garden? If you like doing any of these activities then AOL has some great hobbies and activities channels for you to look into. For starters, the AOL House & Home: Crafts channel, serves up a wealth of crafty ideas. Accessed by typing AOL Keyword: **Crafts**, you'll have numerous projects to choose from including quilting, jewelry & beading, woodworking, among others as well as receiving a free weekly newsletter with tips and ideas.

38 Tuning into amateur radio

Do you want a high-tech hobby that is fun and exciting and has something for everyone? Do you want to communicate with others around town or around the world? Ham radio operators use two-way radio stations from their homes, cars, boats, and outdoors to connect with people using voice, computers, or Morse code. There's no age, gender, or physical abilities required to become an amateur radio operator. You can find out more about radio communications on the Radio Communications Forum by typing AOL Keyword: **Ham Radio**.

You can also participate in The Ham Radio Club by selecting **The Ham Radio Club** option in the Radio Communications Forum channel. The Ham Radio Club channel offers access to information such as Call Sign updates, digital ham radio, news bulletins, packet radio, space ham radio, solar flare information, weather/disaster operations, message boards, and software libraries.

39 Visiting amusement and theme park sites

Looking for the right amusement or theme park to take your family to? You'll be able to access a list of amusement and theme parks near you including distances and driving directions. You'll also be able to access message boards and chats to make your vacation planning a successful event. Entering AOL Keyword: **Amusement Parks** displays the AOL Theme Parks Web site.

40 Signing on for sports stuff

Get sports news, scores, and statistics on your favorite team anytime. Enter AOL Keyword: **KO News & Sports** or click the **News + Sports** button on the Kids Only channel.

Teens can get sports information at the Teens Sports channel by typing AOL Keyword: **Teens Sports**. Find the latest sports scores on high school, college, and pro events. You'll also be able to find the latest information on extreme sports.

41 Finding more fun stuff for kids and teens

Are you having a hard time finding things to do in your spare time? If so you'll want to visit these AOL ideas channels. For kids, visit the Kids Only Fun channel by typing AOL Keyword: **KO Fun**.

The AOL Kids Only Fun channel offers kids with an assortment of games, cool art tools, and chat rooms. Play with drawing and online art tools to help them create that lasting masterpiece. Also, kids can visit the AOL Kids Only Art Studio (shown in Figure 9-13) by typing AOL Keyword: **KO Art**.

Figure 9-13. Drawing, writing, and creating on AOL's Kids Only Art channel

For teens, AOL offers a hot channel called Boredom Busters by entering AOL Keyword: **Bored**. Here teens can tune into music, fashion, crafts, and other cool stuff. Check it out!

CHAPTER 10
AOL for Students

AOL OFFERS MANY HELPFUL resources to students of all ages, from young teens to the college bound and beyond. You'll learn how to access online encyclopedias, dictionaries and book reviews, find out about history and ancient civilizations, and uncover secrets and mysteries of the past. The possibilities are endless. Students also benefit from using sites that give advice on selecting a college, financial aid, and career choices. Sit back, relax and enjoy a game or two using AOL's access to entertainment sites, or read the latest movie and film reviews. Although this chapter is entitled AOL for Students, anyone can benefit from the myriad resources described on the following pages.

In this chapter, you'll learn how to

- Take advantage of the many learning resources offered by AOL

- Use student tools such as online dictionaries, encyclopedias, and thesauri

- Use student aids and other resources to find colleges, apply for financial aid, and access the computer center

- Discover vocation and career resources that will improve your career possibilities

- Access entertainment resources such as comics, games, puzzles, and sports

Research & Learn Channels

1 Finding adventure

If adventure is what you seek, then look no further than AOL's Adventure channel. Discover far-away places, explore the West as Lewis and Clark did,

trek through the Amazonian rainforest, balloon race around the world, look for treasures in sunken cities, experience Africa's culture and wildlife, and have countless other adventures—all without leaving your desk. Here's how:

Click the **Keyword** button located on the AOL toolbar and enter AOL Keyword: **Adventure** and click the **Go** button. The **Adventure** channel appears.

< or >

Click the **Research & Learn** channel button located on the left side of your screen and click **Adventure** under the **Subjects** heading. The **Adventure** channel appears.

2 Discovering ancient history's peoples, places, and beliefs

Learn how ancient civilizations lived, worked, and played, and even what people ate during ancient times. The Ancient History channel lets you discover empires of two thousand years ago, explore the secrets of the Pharaohs, journey to long-lost cities, understand the timeline of ancient history, research the origin and history of the gods, and much more. You'll be amazed to find that many cultures of today are based on ancient civilizations of long ago. Come discover ancient history as never seen before. Here's how:

Click the **Keyword** button located on the AOL toolbar and enter AOL Keyword: **Ancient History** and click the **Go** button. The **Ancient History** channel appears.

< or >

Click the **Research & Learn** channel button located on the left side of your screen and click the **History & Biography** button under the **Subjects** heading. Then, click **Ancient History** under the

Subjects heading on the **History** channel. The **Ancient History** channel appears.

3 Uncovering the secrets and mysteries of the past

The Archaeology/Anthropology channel lets you explore the secrets of the Pharaohs, uncover long-lost cities, and discover how ancient undertakers used oils, waxes, and fats to embalm the dead. Understand human origins, access the Encyclopedia Smithsonian archives of Natural History, and much more. You'll be spellbound as you explore library after library of Natural History information and databases from around the world. See for yourself what awaits you on the Archaeology/Anthropology channel. Here's how you can access this great resource:

Click the **Keyword** button located on the AOL toolbar and enter AOL Keyword: **Anthropology** and click the **Go** button. The **Anthropology** channel appears.

< or >

Click the **Research & Learn** channel button located on the left side of your screen and click the **Science** button under the **Subjects** heading. Then, click **Archaeology/Anthropology** under the **Subjects** heading on the **Science** channel. The **Archaeology/Anthropology** channel appears.

4 Expanding your understanding of the artistic world

Expand your understanding of the artistic world and learn about art, dance, fashion and costumes, films and movies, museums, music, opera, and theater. The Arts channel lets you discover artistic expression at its best by providing an understanding of the principles behind making or doing things that display form, beauty, and unusual perception. Wander through virtual museums and view masterpieces that have been cherished for generations. Learn about folk songs, sheet music, and all things musical. Check out local and international performing arts and media. Visit the Arts channel and explore your artistic side.

Click the **Keyword** button located on the AOL toolbar and enter AOL Keyword: **Arts** and click the **Go** button. The **Arts** channel appears, shown in Figure 10-1.

< or >

Click the **Research & Learn** channel button located on the left side of your screen and click **Arts** under the **Subjects** heading. The **Arts** channel appears.

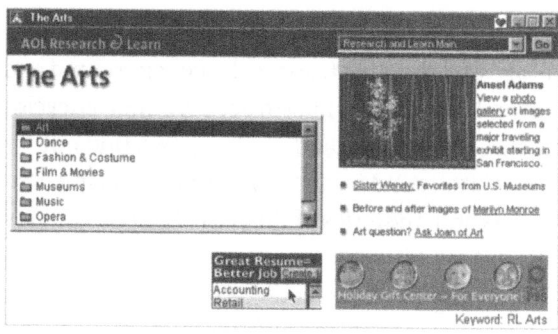

Figure 10-1. Finding artistic expression on AOL's Arts channel

5 Exploring the lives of notable figures through their biographies

Learn about the lives of notable figures in history. The Biographies channel lets you explore the people who made a difference for humankind. You'll find historical biographies, facts about famous mathematicians, scientists, sports figures, inventors, distinguished women of the past and present, the person of the week, as well as a wealth of other resources. Research and learn about people who were dedicated to their professions and became famous for it. Here's how:

Click the **Keyword** button located on the AOL toolbar and enter AOL Keyword: **Biographies** and click the **Go** button. The **Biographies** channel appears.

< or >

Click the **Research & Learn** channel button located on the left side of your screen and click **Biographies** under the **Subjects** heading on the **History & Biography** channel. The **Biographies** channel appears.

6 Accessing leading books and periodicals from around the world

Find out popular fiction and nonfiction books as well as leading periodicals such as The New York Times, Time, The Christian Science Monitor, Business Week, Entertainment Weekly, and Sports Illustrated for Kids. Read the latest book reviews, find out what books have hit the bestseller list, and learn what events your favorite author is planning to participate in. This and much more is yours when you visit the Books & Periodicals channel. Here's how you can access this great channel:

Click the **Keyword** button located on the AOL toolbar and enter AOL Keyword: **Library** or AOL Keyword: **Periodicals** and click the **Go** button. The **Books & Periodicals** channel appears.

< or >

Click the **Research & Learn** channel button located on the left side of your screen and click **Books & Periodicals** under the **References** heading. The **Books & Periodicals** channel appears.

7 Understanding the world through geography

Get a better understanding of the world and its people through geography. Learn about any country, its location, size, population, languages, boundaries, ethnic divisions, religions, history, and other information. The Geography channel contains a wealth of information including maps, photos, and learning games. Here's how you can access this terrific site:

Click the **Keyword** button located on the AOL toolbar and enter AOL Keyword: **Geography** and click the **Go** button. The **Geography** channel appears, shown in Figure 10-2.

< or >

Click the **Research & Learn** channel button located on the left side of your screen and click **Maps & Geography** under the **References** heading. The **Geography** channel appears.

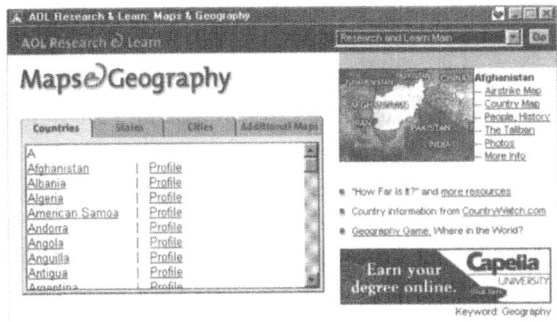

Figure 10-2. Accessing maps on any country in the world on AOL's Geography channel

8 Understanding history and world events for a better tomorrow

Learn about history and world events from the ancient past to the current day. Gain a better perspective on the world and its many peoples by discovering the different countries of the world, their cultures, and what wars were fought. Read essays about American history, the inaugural addresses of U.S. Presidents, and facts about your ancestors. The History channel contains a wealth of information consisting of encyclopedias, photos, and learning games. Here's how you can access the history of the world:

Click the **Keyword** button located on the AOL toolbar and enter AOL Keyword: **History** and click the **Go** button. The **History** channel appears.

< or >

Click the **Research & Learn** channel button located on the left side of your screen and click **History & Biography** under the **Subjects** heading. The **History** channel appears.

9 Getting help with your homework

Are you looking for a tutor who is available to help you with your homework 24 hours a day, 7 days a week? The Homework Help channel is the answer. It provides online assistance for students in elementary school, middle school, high school, college, and beyond. You'll get all the assistance you need with help from real teachers, cool science fair project ideas, research papers, reference materials, and writing tools. Visit the Homework Help channel the next time you or your child needs help with their studies. Here's how:

Click the **Keyword** button located on the AOL toolbar and enter AOL Keyword: **Homework** and click the **Go** button. The **Homework Help** channel appears.

< or >

Click the **Research & Learn** channel button located on the left side of your screen and click **Homework Help** under the **Education** heading. The **Homework Help** channel appears.

10 Exploring the world's peoples, languages, and cultures

Do you want international news, or information about foreign business, travel, or sports? The International channel has information on what's happening around the world. It provides news by region or country, foreign newspapers, international weather forecasts, international meeting places, foreign chats, international business news and opportunities, international music programming, language translators, currency converters, maps, sporting events, and much more. Make the International channel your first choice for world news, business, weather, and sports information. Here's how:

Click the **Keyword** button located on the AOL toolbar and enter AOL Keyword: **International** and click the **Go** button. The **International** channel appears.

< or >

Click the **International** channel button located on the left side of your screen to display the **International** channel.

11 Learning games for the entire family to enjoy

AOL offers many online games that let you play for knowledge or just for the fun of it. The Learning Games channel features quiz-oriented games such as Where in the world?, Who am I?, Mysteries of the wild, and other types of games. Here's how to access this treasure-trove of thinking games fun for the entire family:

Click the **Keyword** button located on the AOL toolbar and enter AOL Keyword: **Learning Games** and click the **Go** button. The **Learning Games** channel appears.

< or >

Click the **Research & Learn** channel button located on the left side of your screen and click **Learning Games** under the **Subjects** heading. The **Learning Games** channel appears.

12 Learning network for parents, teachers, and students

One of the most comprehensive sites for parents, teachers, and students is the Learning Network. With a multitude of tips, guidelines, reference tools, games, and other learning resources, the Learning Network has it all. You'll find resources for parents, teachers, kids, and teens in an integrated and user-friendly site. For parents there are resources to help answer a child's questions, tips, guidelines, and other family education activities. For teachers there are resources such as a lesson planning center, teacher tools, and a professional development center. For students there are resources to help with homework assignments, college planning guides, SAT and ACT test preps, reference tools such as encyclopedias and almanacs, and learning games. Visit the Learning Network Web site—the family education center. Here's how:

Click the **Keyword** button located on the AOL toolbar and enter AOL Keyword: **Learning Network** and click the **Go** button. The Learning Network Web site appears, shown in Figure 10-3.

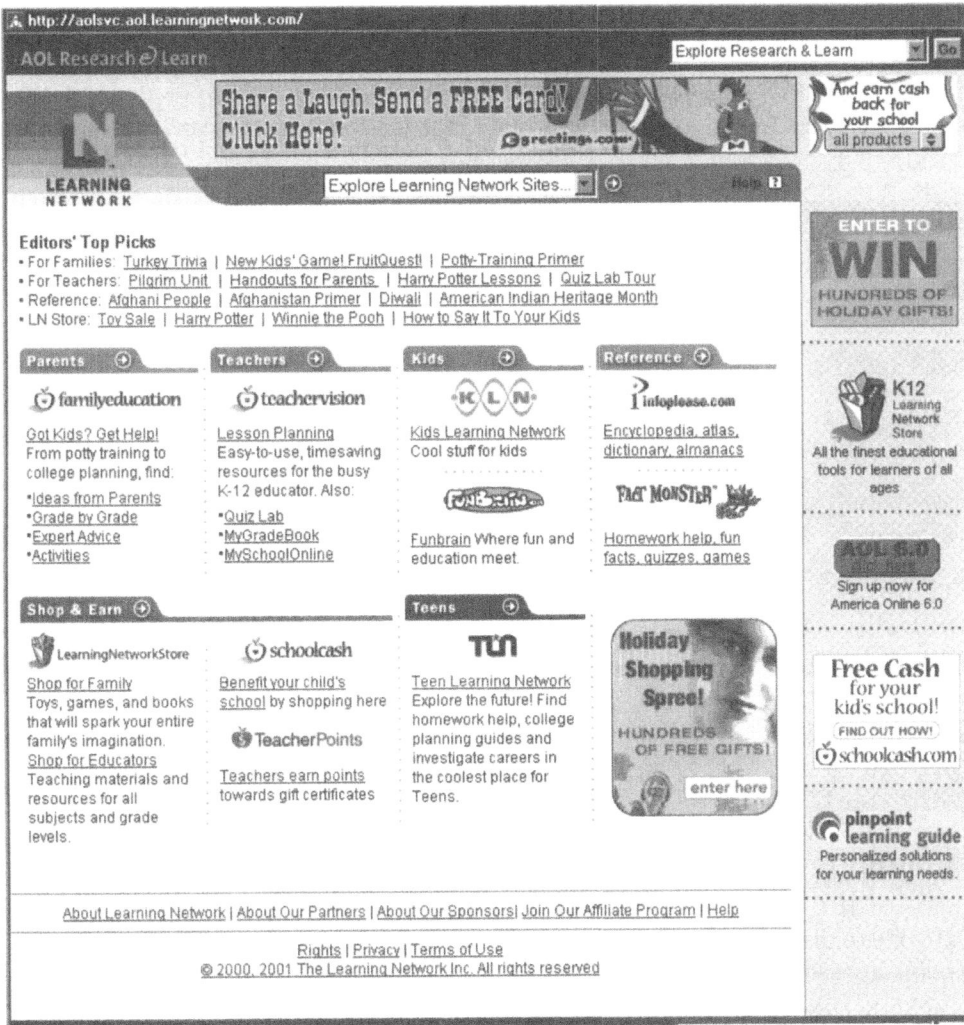

Figure 10-3. Accessing a comprehensive education center on the Learning Network

13 Stepping back in time with living history

Converse about the reenactment of historical events that shaped the world we live in. The Living History channel lets you become part of a history community that offers message boards, chats, home pages, and other items of interest for the history enthusiast. Reenact historical events that took place during the Renaissance, or the 18th, 19th, and 20th centuries. Visit the Living History channel and relive history's greatest events. Here's how:

Click the **Keyword** button located on the AOL toolbar and enter AOL Keyword: **Living History** and click the **Go** button. The **Living History** channel appears.

14 Researching the Library of Congress

The Library of Congress Web site preserves a collection of nearly 121 million items including books, maps, film and television clips, and other resources. You'll find news and events stored in electronic format, congressional committee reports and legislative schedules, digitally reproduced historical collections of papers and photographs, Copyright Office forms and applications, interactive presentations for kids and families, online exhibitions of historical events, and a comprehensive online search catalog to help find what you're looking for. Visit the Library of Congress

Web site for a better understanding of how our government works. Here's how:

Click the **Keyword** button located on the AOL toolbar and enter AOL Keyword: **LOC** and click the **Go** button. The **Library of Congress** Web site appears, shown in Figure 10-4.

Figure 10-4. Accessing the wonderful resources of the Library of Congress

15 Getting help with math

The Math channel provides online assistance to help improve your math skills. From flashcards to homework helpers, worksheets to game rooms, metric conversions to an assortment of math resources, introductory to advanced topics, you'll discover an abundance of tools to help master math. The next time you need assistance with your math homework, visit the Math channel. Here's how:

Click the **Keyword** button located on the AOL toolbar and enter AOL Keyword: **Math** and click the **Go** button. The **Math** channel appears.

16 Accessing references on virtually anything

The More References channel provides a comprehensive online resource on virtually anything. You'll find three major areas: Subjects, References, and Information Sources. A sampling of Subjects includes Ancient History, Biography, Law, Government, Nature, Science, World History, and much more. A sampling of References includes Almanac, Ask-A-Teacher, Barron's Booknotes, Courses Online, Financial Aid, Foreign Languages, Resources

for Parents & Teachers, and more. A sampling of Information Sources includes Books & Periodicals, Knowledge Databases, Maps, Quotations, and more. Visit the More References channel and you'll acquire your very own reference library of resources. Here's how:

Click the **Keyword** button located on the AOL toolbar and enter AOL Keyword: **More References** and click the **Go** button. The **More References** channel appears.

17 Listening to the music of today and yesterday

If you love music, you'll want to tune into the Music channel. You'll be able to find music styles such as classical, country, jazz, and much more. Listen to your favorite music via digital download or on Internet radio. Access free music cards, listen to party or patriotic songs. Visit the Music channel for all your music interests. Here's how:

Click the **Keyword** button located on the AOL toolbar and enter AOL Keyword: **Music** and click the **Go** button. The **Music** channel appears.

< or >

Click the **Music** channel button located on the left side of your screen to display the **Music** channel.

18 Learning nature's secrets

Nature's wildlife can be experience firsthand by browsing through over 1,400 video clips. The Nature & Wildlife channel offers mysteries of the wild, nature conservation, bird watching, ocean habitats, desert oasis, shark encounters, poisonous animals, creatures of the night, and much more. Visit the Nature & Wildlife channel and experience everything nature has to offer. Here's how:

Click the **Keyword** button located on the AOL toolbar and enter AOL Keyword: **Nature** and click the **Go** button. The Nature & Wildlife channel appears.

19 Accessing our nation's news and politics

The Nation channel is your gateway to our nation's news and politics. It provides news and other information about our government, the White House, Congress, Supreme Court, federal agencies, elected officials, election news, crime and courts, states, health and science, news releases, and much more. You'll get up-to-the minute news and politics from around our great nation. Visit The Nation channel anytime you want information about the decisions that help shape our nation.

Click the **Keyword** button located on the AOL toolbar and enter AOL Keyword: **Nation** and click the **Go** button. The Nation channel appears.

20 Getting today's happenings from a variety of publications

Have your own newsstand right at your fingertips. The AOL Publications channel provides popular publications for your viewing pleasure. From American Journalism Review to the Atlantic Monthly, National Review to The Christian Science Monitor, Business Week to Time, CBS.SportsLine.com to The Sporting News!, and much more, you'll be able to view timely and well-written articles from your favorite publications. You can also get news and commentary from the team at National Public Radio (NPR). Visit the AOL Publications channel and relax while you enjoy some of the world's most popular online magazines. Here's how:

Click the **Keyword** button located on the AOL toolbar and enter AOL Keyword: **Publications** and click the **Go** button. The AOL **Publications** channel appears.

21 Reading and writing resources

AOL has assembled comprehensive reading and writing resources and made them available on the Reading & Writing channel. With books and periodicals, grammar and style guides, dictionaries, language and usage references, folk and fairy tales, poetry, quotations, book reviews, and much more. Here's how to access this treasure trove of reading and writing resources:

Click the **Keyword** button located on the AOL toolbar and enter AOL Keyword: **Reading** and click the **Go** button. The **Reading & Writing** channel appears.

< or >

Click the **Research & Learn** channel button located on the left side of your screen and click **Reading & Writing** under the **Subjects** heading. The **Reading & Writing** channel appears.

22 Researching and learning from AOL's top sites

If access to a comprehensive research and learning library of resources is what you want, then you're in luck. The AOL Research & Learn channel has everything a student could want, and then some. You'll have access to the arts, adventure, biographies, history, learning games, reading and writing resources, science, encyclopedias, dictionaries, almanacs, white and yellow pages, and much more. Visit AOL's Research & Learn channel anytime and anywhere for the latest information on a variety of research subjects, references, and educational resources. Here's how:

Click the **Keyword** button located on the AOL toolbar and enter AOL Keyword: **Research** and click the **Go** button. The AOL **Research & Learn** channel appears.

< or >

Click the **Research & Learn** channel button located on the left side of your screen to display the AOL **Research & Learn** channel.

23 Discovering what's happening in the world of science

The Science channel provides timely science news from around the world. AOL updates this fact-filled channel with timely information and knowledge for budding scientists. Visit the Science channel the next time you need help on that science project or just want to find out what's happening in the world of science. Here's how:

Click the **Keyword** button located on the AOL toolbar and enter AOL Keyword: **Science** and click the **Go** button. The **Science** channel appears.

< or >

Click the **Research & Learn** channel button located on the left side of your screen and click **Science** under the **Subjects** heading. The **Science** channel appears.

24 Exploring space and astronomy

AOL offers comprehensive resources for future astronomers and astronauts on the Space channel. You'll find information on the earth and space, space news, scenes from space, famous space flight stories, resources from the national air and space museum, societies and clubs, online homework helpers, chats and message boards, and much more. Here's how you can access this marvelous site:

Click the **Keyword** button located on the AOL toolbar and enter AOL Keyword: **Space** and click the **Go** button. The **Space** channel appears.

< or >

Click the **Research & Learn** channel button located on the left side of your screen and click **Science** under the **Subjects** heading. Click the **Space** channel button on the **Science** channel to display the **Space** channel.

25 Unlocking the events and stories that shaped U.S. History

AOL's U.S. History channel offers historical resources including biographies of the U.S. presidents, historical documents (1400–2000 A.D.), inaugural addresses, wars and battles, historic places, articles, maps, chat groups, and message boards. Find out about strategic battles, military leadership, relations among the States, social issues, and much more. Visit the U.S. History channel for a magnificent collection of American historical resources. Here's how:

Click the **Keyword** button located on the AOL toolbar and enter AOL Keyword: **US History** and click the **Go** button. The U.S. **History** channel appears.

< or >

Click the **Research & Learn** channel button located on the left side of your screen and click **History & Biography** under the **Subjects** heading. Click the **U.S. History** channel button to display the **U.S. History** channel.

26 Understanding world history

AOL's World History channel provides a comprehensive historical reference for ancient history, and world history from the year 1–to 2000 A.D.). The ancient history section covers events from 4.5 billion–600 B.C., and 599–1 B.C. World history resources include PBS, H.G. Wells, and Infoplease. Visit the World History channel for a magnificent collection of resources. Here's how:

Click the **Keyword** button located on the AOL toolbar and enter AOL Keyword: **World History** and click the **Go** button. The World History channel appears.

< or >

Click the **Research & Learn** channel button located on the left side of your screen and click **History & Biography** under the **Subjects** heading. Click the **World History** channel button on the **History** channel to display the **World History** channel.

Student Tools

27 Accessing the Merriam-Webster Dictionary

The Merriam-Webster Dictionary provides a comprehensive reference for students to use when looking up words or phrases. Visit this useful online dictionary for all your writing needs. Here's how:

Click the **Keyword** button located on the AOL toolbar and enter AOL Keyword: **Dictionary** and click the **Go** button. The **Merriam-Webster Dictionary** appears, shown in Figure 10-5.

< or >

Click the **Research & Learn** channel button located on the left side of your screen and click **Dictionary** under the **References** heading to display the **Merriam-Webster Dictionary**.

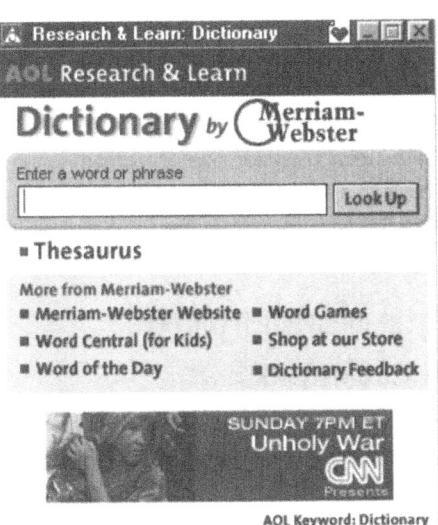

AOL Keyword: Dictionary

Figure 10-5. The Merriam-Webster Dictionary is your online word or phrase source.

28 Using the Merriam-Webster Thesaurus

The Merriam-Webster Thesaurus provides a comprehensive reference of synonyms and antonyms for students to use when looking up words or phrases. Visit this wonderful online thesaurus for all your writing needs. Here's how it's accessed:

Click the **Keyword** button located on the AOL toolbar and enter AOL Keyword: **Thesaurus** and click the **Go** button. The **Thesaurus** by **Merriam-Webster** appears.

< or >

Click the **Research & Learn** channel button located on the left side of your screen and click **Thesaurus** under the references section to display the **Merriam-Webster Thesaurus**.

29 Using correct grammar and style

Do you need help forming and structuring your words? AOL provides a great Grammar & Style tool that helps you use the proper rules for speaking and writing the English language. You'll find these classic language resources: The Elements of Style, Writing Research Papers, Grammar Guide—WEB, Book of English Usage, The King's English, Writing a Book Report, and Books on Grammar. Visit the

Grammar & Style channel for the tools you'll need to make you look like a pro. Here's how it's accessed:

Click the **Keyword** button located on the AOL toolbar and enter AOL Keyword: **Grammar** and click the **Go** button. The **Grammar & Style** channel appears.

< or >

Click the **Research & Learn** channel button located on the left side of your screen and click **Reading & Writing** under the **Subjects** heading. Click the **Grammar & Style Guides** folder on the **Reading** channel to display the **Grammar & Style** channel.

30 Accessing the World Book Encyclopedia

The World Book Encyclopedia serves as a comprehensive, objective, and reliable reference for students and adults. AOL members receive unlimited access to the World Book Online. All you have to do is type in a word in the Search field, and click the Search button. World Book results often reference links to related information consisting of maps, charts, audio and visual clips, animations, Web sites, magazine and newspaper articles, or other World Book articles or reference materials. Visit this wonderful online encyclopedia for all your research needs. Here's how you access it:

Click the **Keyword** button located on the AOL toolbar and enter AOL Keyword: **Research** and click the **Go** button. The AOL **Research & Learn** channel appears with the ability to search the **World Book Encyclopedia**.

< or >

Click the **Research & Learn** channel button located on the left side of your screen to display the **World Book Encyclopedia**.

31 Translating from one language to another

Have you ever wanted to translate a word, sentence, or paragraph from one language to another? AOL's Online translation Web site lets you to do just that. You select the language you'd like to have the one language converted to, type or paste the text or URL you'd like to have converted in the text box, and then click the **Translate** button. You'll be able to select from the following languages: Dutch, English, French, German, Italian, Portuguese, and Spanish. Visit this wonderful online tool for all your language translation needs. Here's how it's accessed:

Click the **Keyword** button located on the AOL toolbar and enter AOL Keyword: **Foreign Dictionary** and click the **Go** button. The AOL **Online Translation** Web site appears with the ability to translate text or URLs, shown in Figure 10-6.

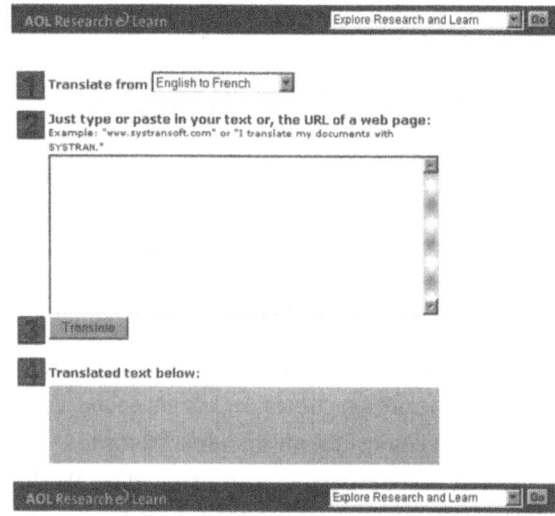

Figure 10-6. Translate text easily with this handy online translation tool.

Student Aids and Other Resources

32 Getting high schoolers ready for the college lifestyle

The AOL@School High School Web site provides a wonderful resource for high school students everywhere. You'll get help finding the college that's right for you, get the inside scoop written from a teen's point of view on hundreds of colleges and universities, take free full-length SAT and ACT practice exams, explore your options for paying for college, and much more. This is a must-see site for high school students who plan to go to college. Visit the AOL@School High School Web site for all

the details you need to make an informed decision. Here's how it's accessed:

Click the **Keyword** button located on the AOL toolbar and enter AOL Keyword: **High School** and click the **Go** button. The **AOL@School High School** Web site appears. Click **College** under the **Get the Facts** heading located on the left side of the Web site.

33 Finding the information you need on colleges and universities

The College channel also lets you search for Colleges and Universities by entering a school name, location, field of study, or sport. You'll learn how to apply to Colleges and Universities online, market yourself to admission counselors, list the top schools and their rankings, prepare for the SAT exam, register for the SAT online, and much more. Visit the College channel and see first hand what it's like to be a college student. Here's how:

Click the **Keyword** button located on the AOL toolbar and enter AOL Keyword: **College** and click the **Go** button. The **College** channel appears.

< or >

Click the **Research & Learn** channel button located on the left side of your screen and click **Reading & Writing** under the **Subjects** heading. Click **College** under the **Education** section to display the **College** channel.

34 Planning resources for college entrance exams

The College Board Web site connects students to colleges and opportunities. You'll find useful tips on how to plan for college, prepare for the SAT with real practice questions, find the best college for you, write a winning application and apply online, and get financial aid information to help make college affordable. This is a great site for any student who wants to make their college experience a more rewarding one. Visit the College Board Web site and get a head start on finding the right college for a brighter future. Here's how:

Click the **Keyword** button located on the AOL toolbar and enter AOL Keyword: **College Board** and click the **Go** button. The **College Board** Web site appears, shown in Figure 10-7.

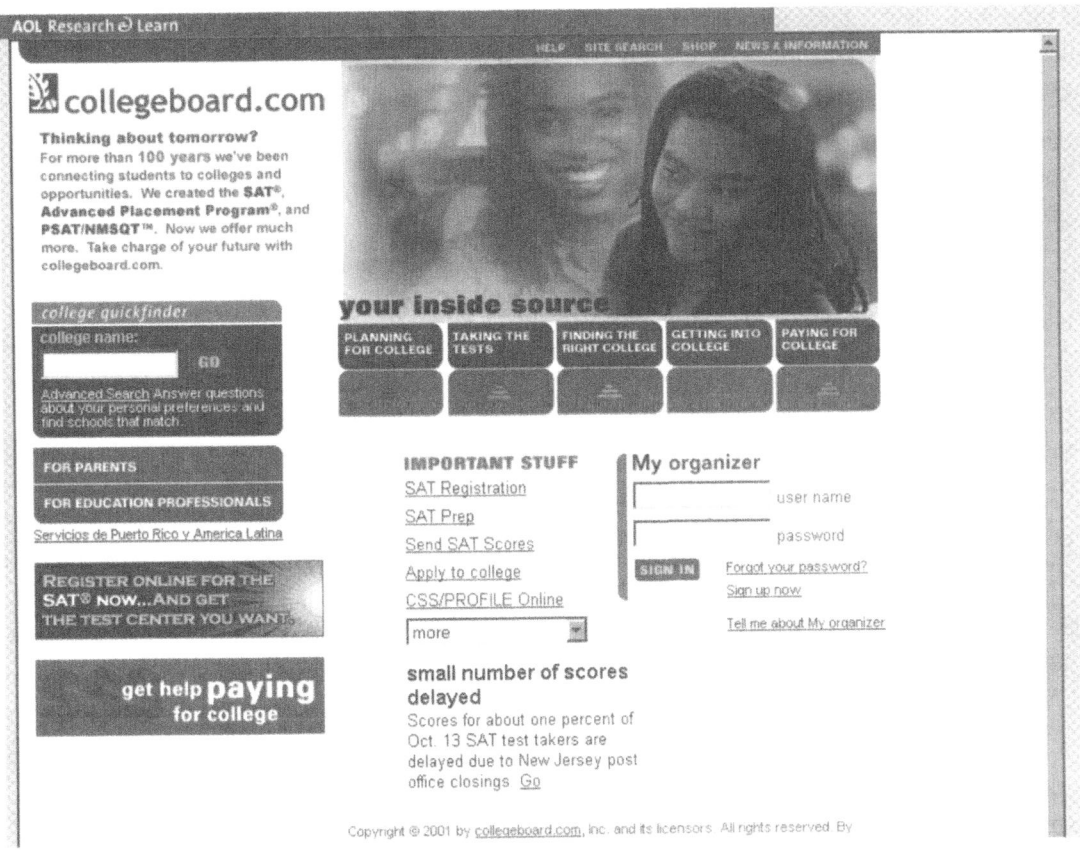

Figure 10-7. The College Board Web site can help you prepare for college with helpful information

35 Getting the most out of college

Want to get the most out of your college experience? The trick is to do the necessary planning before you get there. The College Bound channel provides advice from students on what to do during your junior and senior year in high school, how to apply to your college online, what you should do before making your final decision on which college to attend, and much more. This is a must-see site for high school students who plan to go to college. Visit the College Bound channel and learn from other students' experiences. Here's how:

Click the **Keyword** button located on the AOL toolbar and enter AOL Keyword: **College Bound** and click the **Go** button. The **College Bound** channel appears.

36 Determining what college or university is right for you

Are you uncertain about which college is right for you? Do you need more information about a college to help you make a decision? The College Guide Web site asks a series of simple questions and, based on your answers, provides a comparison guide of the colleges that are right for you. The colleges are listed side-by-side to help you make a better decision. This is a must-see site for high school students who plan to go to college. Visit the College Guide Web site for the details you need to make an informed decision. Here's how it works.

1. Click the **Keyword** button located on the AOL toolbar and enter AOL Keyword: **College Guide** and click the **Go** button. The **College Guide** Web site appears.

2. Click the **Q&A** button to step through a question-and-answer guide for selecting a college. You'll be asked the following questions:

- Select which location of the United States you'd like to go to college in (e.g., New England, Mid-Atlantic, Southeast, North Central, South Central, Northwest, and Southwest). Click one or more boxes representing the locations you'd consider.

- Select the type of campus life you prefer (e.g., student housing, freshmen retention rate, ROTC program).

- Select the type of college (e.g., private or public, gender classes, religious affiliation).

- Select how competitive you want the college admissions to be based on your SAT or ACT scores.

- Select the maximum amount you can spend for tuition each year (e.g., in-state versus out-of-state tuition).

- Select the importance of a low student-faculty ratio, and what major you're interested in.

- Select the importance of men's and women's NCAA sports (e.g., baseball, basketball, football, tennis, etc.).

- Select certain factors that are most important to you (e.g., preferred location, preferred student body size, more selective admissions, and cost).

3. Click the **Compare** button to find a specific college enabling you to compare them side-by-side.

37 Preparing for college life

Perterson's.com College Quest Web site provides a terrific all-in-one resource to help search for the college that's right for you, get help on SAT and ACT practice exams questions, explore your options for paying for college, and much more. Visit Peterson's College Quest Web site for all the details you need to make an informed decision. Here's how it's accessed:

Click the **Keyword** button located on the AOL toolbar and enter AOL Keyword: **Petersons** or **College Quest** and click the **Go** button. **Peterson's.com College Quest** Web site appears.

38 Searching for a college or university

The College Guide Web site lets you search for a college or university anywhere in the United States. This is a must-see site for high school students who plan to go to college and want to know more information about a college or university. Visit the College Guide Web site for the details you need for an informed decision. Here's how it works:

Click the **Keyword** button located on the AOL toolbar and enter AOL Keyword: **College Guide** and click the **Go** button. The College Guide Web site appears. Enter one or more search words and click the **Search** button.

> ✎ *If you're getting too many or too few results from your search, you may want to refine your search.*

Here are a few tips to keep in mind when entering your search criteria:

1. Enter multiple words as your search criteria. You may also want to try entering phrases rather than a single word to increase the chance of finding what you're looking for.

2. A space between search words (e.g., University of Miami) is treated as if an AND were inserted between each word (e.g., "University AND of AND Miami"). Boolean expressions are explained below.

3. Capitalizing words has no affect on the search results.

4. Boolean expressions can be used in your search to limit or expand your search results. The following Boolean expressions can be used:

   AND—Finds results that contain both search words.

   OR—Finds results that contain either word.

   NOT—Omits results that contain the word you insert following NOT.

5. Wild card characters can be used when spelling variations exist (e.g., Smith, Smithe, Smit, etc.). The following wild card characters are available:

—An asterisk is used to represent any number of characters following the specified word. For example, entering "Univ" will search colleges containing Univ., University, and University of.

? —A question mark is used to replace a single character in a word. For example, entering "Univ?" will find colleges containing Univ., not University.

39 Accessing your personal computer center anytime you like

Would you like to access a computer center from your home or office? Now you can with AOL's Computer Center channel. You'll be able to access product reviews on computers and software, download screensavers and wallpaper, get the help you need to deal with computer viruses, access PC games and downloads, find help with the Internet and Web building, review buying guides on desktop computers and printers, use a built-in search engine, and much more. This is a great site for anyone who wants something for his or her computer. Visit the Computer Center channel for all your computing needs. Here's how it's accessed:

Click the **Keyword** button located on the AOL toolbar and enter AOL Keyword: **Computer** and click the **Go** button. AOL's **Computer Center** channel appears.

40 Searching for financial aid and scholarship programs

The Financial Aid channel is a resource for all your financial aid questions. You'll find help with Federal and State loan assistance programs, an online Free Application for Federal Student Aid (FAFSA) that you can complete and submit, valuable information to fund your education and help make college affordable, built-in search tools to find scholarships, college cost calculators, and

much more. Visit the Financial Aid channel so you don't have to worry that you don't have enough money for college. Here's how it's accessed:

Click the **Keyword** button located on the AOL toolbar and enter AOL Keyword: **Financial Aid** and click the **Go** button. The **Financial Aid** channel appears.

41 Understanding personal finance for a brighter tomorrow

The Personal Finance channel is a comprehensive online financial adviser that serves up advice, tips, tools, and other useful information. It's designed to provide business news, stock market reports, mutual fund investing tips, money management techniques, retirement planning information, home equity loan advice, real estate market reports, free personal finance e-mail newsletters, chats, message boards, and helpful advice from leading experts. This is a great site for anyone who wants to attain some level of financial freedom. Visit the Personal Finance channel to find ways to stretch your dollars. Here's how it's accessed:

Click the **Keyword** button located on the AOL toolbar and enter AOL Keyword: **Personal Finance** and click the **Go** button. The **Personal Finance** channel appears.

42 Thinking about going to graduate school

The Graduate School channel lets you find a degree program you'd like to pursue, prepare for the GRE and GMAT with real practice questions, find out what needs to be done about the application process and when, determine whether a Master's or PhD program is right for you, apply online to a graduate school, take classes online with many off-campus degree programs, and much more. This is a great site for anyone contemplating getting an advanced degree. Visit the Graduate School channel and learn how an advanced degree can open up greater opportunities as well as a higher salary. Here's how:

Click the **Keyword** button located on the AOL toolbar and enter AOL Keyword: **Graduate School** and click the **Go** button. The **Graduate School** channel appears.

43 Accessing the White & Yellow Pages

If you're looking for the phone number, street address, or e-mail address of a long-lost family member or friend, then the AOL White Pages can help. For even more online assistance, the AOL Yellow Pages is your single source for finding businesses everywhere. With access to Chamber of Commerce, associations, international, and toll-free directories, you won't need to make any more expensive directory assistance calls. These directories are your source for names, street addresses, phone numbers, e-mail addresses, neighborhood maps, driving directions, and much more. Here's how you can access these great directories:

Click the **Keyword** button located on the AOL toolbar and enter AOL Keyword: **Phonebook** and click the **Go** button. The **White & Yellow Pages** channel appears.

Vocation and Career Resources

44 Finding a career you'll love

The AOL Career Finder Web site lets you find a career that best suits your personality. Find a treasure-trove of resources to help you identify what your calling in life is, self-help resources such as a resume and interview center, learning tools, salary guide, self-assessment analyzers, job Q&As, job search center, book store, chat, message boards, and much more. Here's how you can access these great resources:

Click the **Keyword** button located on the AOL toolbar and enter AOL Keyword: **Career Finder** and click the **Go** button. The **Career Finder** Web site appears.

45 Connecting with career-minded people

As a student, you'll want to connect yourself with career-minded people. The AOL Career Talk Web site lets you connect with people who share your interests about careers and work. Access a collection of resources to help explore options for your future including an assortment of professional communities and forums, a career development center, job search database, small business center, information on online education, writers' columns, artists' galleries, home pages, free newsletters, chat, message boards, and much more. Here's how you can access these great resources:

Click the **Keyword** button located on the AOL toolbar and enter AOL Keyword: **Career Talk** and click the **Go** button. The **Career Talk** Web site appears.

46 Finding a job or career

The Careers & Work channel lets you find over 250,000 job listings by profession and location, get resume help, post your resume online, find jobs by e-mail, compare salary by city, research a company, improve yourself, get professional training, access chat and message boards, and much more. Visit the Careers & Work channel and find a job or career you love. Here's how:

Click the **Keyword** button located on the AOL toolbar and enter AOL Keyword: **Career** and click the **Go** button. The **Careers & Work** channel appears.

< or >

Click the **Careers & Work** channel button located on the left side of your screen to display the **Careers & Work** channel.

47 Improving yourself for greater success

The Improve Yourself channel lets you further your education to enhance your career opportunities, find the perfect career for your personality, search a database containing over 250,000 job listings by profession and location, get resume help, post your resume online, learn effective time management techniques, acquire negotiating skills, avoid common mistakes when changing careers, get professional training, access chat and message boards, and much more. Visit the Improve Yourself channel and get the help you need to improve yourself for greater success. Here's how:

Click the **Keyword** button located on the AOL toolbar and enter AOL Keyword: **Improve Yourself** and click the **Go** button. The **Improve Yourself** channel appears.

< or >

Click the **Careers & Work** channel button located on the left side of your screen and click **Improve Yourself** from the **Careers & Work** channel to display the **Improve Yourself** channel.

48 Interviewing and negotiating tips

Would you like to prevent interview jitters or learn to negotiate a higher salary? The Interview & Negotiate channel provides resources to help achieve greater interviewing and negotiating success. You'll learn why practicing your interviewing techniques is so important, how to exude confidence, how to develop a checklist and other tools to gauge your performance, how to effectively negotiate salary and benefits, and much more. Visit the Interview & Negotiate channel and get the help you need to improve your interviewing and negotiating skills. Here's how it's accessed:

Click the **Keyword** button located on the AOL toolbar and enter AOL Keyword: **Interview** and click the **Go** button. The **Interview & Negotiate** channel appears.

49 Searching for that job of a lifetime

The Job Search channel lets you search over 245,000 job listings by profession and location. You'll also be able to build and send your resume online, develop a cover letter to send with your resume, store up to five versions of your resume, and much more. Visit the Job Search channel and get the results you want by narrowing your search with this handy tool. Here's how it's accessed:

Click the **Keyword** button located on the AOL toolbar and enter AOL Keyword: **Job** and click the **Go** button. The **Job Search** channel appears, shown in Figure 10-8.

< or >

Click the **Careers & Work** channel button located on the left side of your screen and click **Job Listings** under the **Find a Job** section on the **Careers & Work** channel to display the **Job Search** channel.

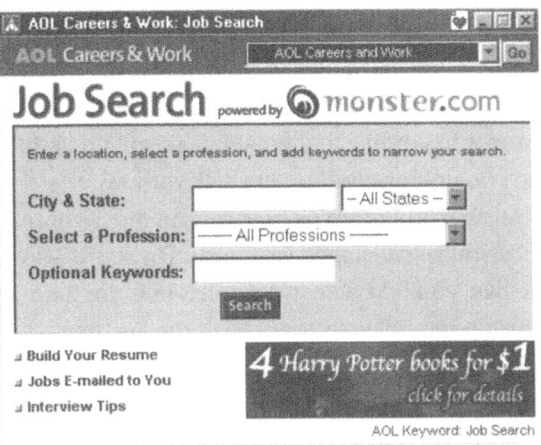

Figure 10-8. Finding the job of a lifetime with the Job Search channel

50 Researching a company

Would you like to get the inside scoop on a company before taking a job? The Research a Company channel lets you research more than 51,000 companies so you can find out what employees and employers say about their company. You'll also be able to see what companies made the Fortune 100 list, research a company by the industry they're in, and much more. Visit the Research a Company channel before you take that job to make sure it's a good fit. Here's how it's accessed:

Click the **Keyword** button located on the AOL toolbar and enter AOL Keyword: **Research a Company** and click the **Go** button. The **Research a Company** channel appears.

< or >

Click the **Careers & Work** channel button located on the left side of your screen and click **Research a Company** on the **Careers & Work** channel to display the **Research a Company** channel.

51 Getting help developing a resume

You only have one chance to make a great first impression to a potential employer. Why not do it in style? The Resume Center channel provides comprehensive resources to model your resume on and get your resume to stand out from the crowd. You'll learn how to build a resume step-by-step, avoid the pitfalls that could hurt your chances in landing that great job, create powerful and convincing cover letters, talk with experts using chat and message boards, and much more. Once you've developed your resume just the way you like, you'll be able to submit it to more than 70,000 potential employers. Visit the Resume Center channel and get all the help you need to make that great first impression. Here's how:

Click the **Keyword** button located on the AOL toolbar and enter AOL Keyword: **Resume** and click the **Go** button. The **Resume Center** channel appears.

< or >

Click the **Careers & Work** channel button located on the left side of your screen and click **Resume Center** under **Find a Job** on the **Careers & Work** channel to display the **Resume Center** channel.

Entertainment and Miscellaneous Resources

52 Satisfying all your entertainment needs

The Entertainment channel is your all-in-one source for movies, movie tickets, television listings, music and celebrity news, fun & games, books & art, photos, rant & rave, chat, message boards, and much more. You'll get the most up-to-date and comprehensive information on entertainment to help you stay current with what's happening. Visit the Entertainment channel for your daily dose of entertainment news and trivia. Here's how:

Click the **Keyword** button located on the AOL toolbar and enter AOL Keyword: **Entertainment** and click the **Go** button. The **Entertainment** channel appears.

< or >

Click the **Entertainment** channel button located on the left side of your screen to display the **Entertainment** channel.

53 Finding fun facts

Every day, the Fun Facts channel brings you a new word, a quote of the day, and a history lesson fact. The objective of this channel is to educate while having a little fun. You'll also be able to e-mail and print each fun fact anytime you like. Visit the Fun Facts channel for your daily dose of trivia and fun. You won't be disappointed. Here's how it's accessed:

Click the **Keyword** button located on the AOL toolbar and enter AOL Keyword: **Fun Facts** or **Fact a Day** and click the **Go** button. The **Fun Facts** channel appears.

54 Having fun with online games

From downloadable games to online games, you'll have a blast with these all-time favorites. The Games channel offers Pogo games, word and puzzle games, card and board games, arcade and trivia games, and much more. You'll also have access to free games, game news, chat, and message boards. Visit the Games channel and compete against yourself, a friend, or anyone on the Internet. Here's how to access it:

Click the **Keyword** button located on the AOL toolbar and enter AOL Keyword: **Games** and click the **Go** button. The **Games** channel appears.

< or >

Click the **Games** channel button located on the left side of your screen to display the **Games** channel.

55 Sending out invitations for that party or other event

Do you want to plan a get-together, throw a party, or celebrate an event? AOL's Invitations Web site lets you create an invitation representing the theme of your event, and then send it to anyone with an e-mail address. When your guests receive the invitation containing a link to the AOL Invitations site, they can view the details of your party and send their RSVP and any comments. You'll be able to see the invitations you sent and the RSVPs you've received. Plus, you'll be able to include driving directions and a map in your invitation, making it easy for your guests to find your party or event. Visit AOL's Invitations Web site and you'll be able to organize and manage the guest list like a pro. Your guests will appreciate it too. Here's how:

Click the **Keyword** button located on the AOL toolbar and enter AOL Keyword: **Invitation** and click the **Go** button. AOL's **Invitations** Web site appears, shown in Figure 10-9.

Figure 10-9. Sending party invitations like a pro with AOL's Invitations Web site

56 Playing puzzles and word games

If you like playing word and puzzle games, then the Word & Puzzle Web site is for you. It offers word games such as Crossword, Sports Crossword, Word Search, Word Whomp, and other games. You'll also have access to puzzles such as Animal Ark, Bump, Overflow, Photons, Poppit!, Sweet Tooth, and other puzzle games. Visit the Word & Puzzle site and you, friends, and family will have a blast. Here's how this popular site is accessed.

Click the **Keyword** button located on the AOL toolbar and enter AOL Keyword: **Puzzle** and click the **Go** button. The Word & Puzzle Web site appears.

< or >

Click the **Games** channel button located on the left side of your screen and click **Word & Puzzle** on the **Games** channel to display the **Word & Puzzle** Web site.

57 Listening to Radio@AOL

If you're using the Windows® 95/98/2000/ME/XP operating system, have a sound card and speakers connected to your computer, a 28.8Kbps or faster modem, AOL version 5.0 or higher, RealPlayer® G2 or higher, and a stable connection to the Internet, you can listen to music and talk radio on the Internet. The Radio@AOL channel provides more than 75 programmed AOL stations for your listening pleasure including classical, country, jazz, inspirational, Latin, lite sounds, news, sports, talk, pop, rock, rap, hip-hop, soundtracks, and more. You'll also be able to listen to exclusive performances and live interviews from popular artists. Visit the Radio@AOL channel 24/7 for your listening pleasure. Here's how:

Click the **Keyword** button located on the AOL toolbar and enter AOL Keyword: **Radio** and click the **Go** button. The **Radio@AOL** channel appears, shown in Figure 10-10.

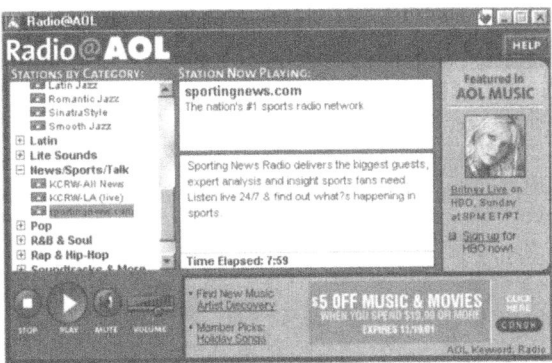

Figure 10-10. Listening to music, news, sports, and talk on the Radio@AOL channel 24/7

231

58 Getting sports scores and other sports information

If you like sports, then the Sports channel is the right ticket. It provides sports scores and details on auto racing, baseball, boxing, golf, basketball, football, hockey, soccer, tennis, and numerous other sports. You'll be able to access categories such as scores, teams, fantasy, sports talk, columnists, locker room, photos, games, chat, and message boards. Visit the Sports channel for all your sporting needs. Here's how:

Click the **Keyword** button located on the AOL toolbar and enter AOL Keyword: **Sports** and click the **Go** button. The **Sports** channel appears.

< or >

Click the **Sports** channel button located on the left side of your screen to display the **Sports** channel.

CHAPTER 11
AOL for Seniors

AOL FOR SENIORS offers a multitude of resources for the over 55, mature online user. Whether your interest is booking an adventure to the Amazon, communicating with other seniors, finding living arrangements, or staying in touch with the grandkids, AOL is there for you. Access AARP and SeniorNet to get the latest information on health and wellness or get assistance on estate planning and retirement. Mature online users will enjoy great content, a variety of features, knowledge resources, and entertainment without having to do a lot of unnecessary searching around.

In this chapter, you'll learn how to

🕮 Access communities for computer-using seniors

🕮 Find housing and health communities

🕮 Discover entertainment resources for seniors

🕮 Access retirement and estate planning resources

center, online learning tools, libraries and archives, a quarterly newsletter, and much more, SeniorNet Online will be your one-stop destination on the Internet. Here's how it's accessed:

Click the **Keyword** button located on the AOL toolbar and enter AOL Keyword: **SeniorNet** and click the **Go** button. The **SeniorNet**™ channel appears, shown in Figure 11-1.

Figure 11-1. Enhancing your life with the wonderful tools on the SeniorNet Online channel

Communities for Computer-Using Seniors

1 Using SeniorNet Online

The SeniorNet Online channel is an international community of computer-using seniors, ages 55 and older. It provides education about computer technology and the Internet to enhance their lives and enable them to use their new knowledge and wisdom. Consisting of forums, an active community

2 Accessing the AARP network

AARP, formerly known as the American Association of Retired Persons, aims to improve the quality of life for all people as they get older. The AARP channel provides member services and discounts, information on computers and technology, articles on health and wellness, and online learning opportunities. It's also a great place to get the latest facts on legislative issues, tips on leisure and fun activities, help with life transitions, advice on money and work, and much more. The AARP channel is your gateway to a wealth of knowledge, publications, and services. Here's how to get there:

Click the **Keyword** button located on the AOL toolbar and enter AOL Keyword: **AARP** and click the **Go** button to display the **AARP** channel, shown in Figure 11-2.

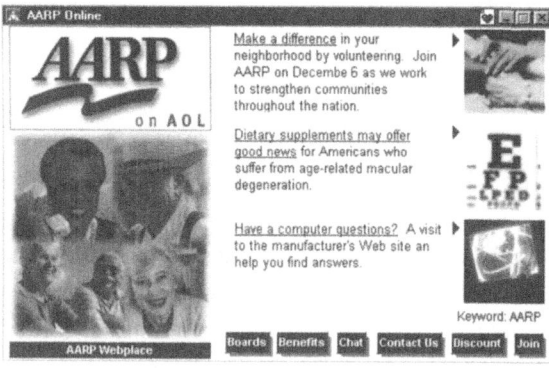

Figure 11-2. Improving the quality of your life by accessing the AARP channel

3 Communicating with other seniors— SeniorNet Forums

It's fun to reach out and touch someone online. Communicating with other seniors is easy using the SeniorNet Message Boards. Message board communities exist for a variety of topics such as arts and leisure, civic and social topics, health and wellness, computer and online topics, generation, World War II memories, and more. Here's how they're accessed:

1. Click the **Keyword** button located on the AOL toolbar and enter AOL Keyword: **SeniorNet** and click the **Go** button to display the **SeniorNet Online** channel.

2. Click the **SeniorNet Forums** button on the **SeniorNet** channel to display the **SeniorNet Message Boards**. Double-click the message board of interest to join any discussion already in progress.

4 Chatting on the online Community Center

The SeniorNet Community Center is a chat room designed for adults 55 and older. The people chatting

in the Community Center are the friendliest people I've ever found on the Internet. They'll make you feel right at home with lively chat and engaging conversations. Here's how it's accessed:

1. Click the **Keyword** button located on the AOL toolbar and enter AOL Keyword: **SeniorNet** and click the **Go** button to display the **SeniorNet Online** channel.

2. Click the **Community Center** button on the **SeniorNet** channel to display the **SeniorNet Community Center** chat room, shown in Figure 11-3. Once in the chat room, you can watch the messages or join in the chat discussion.

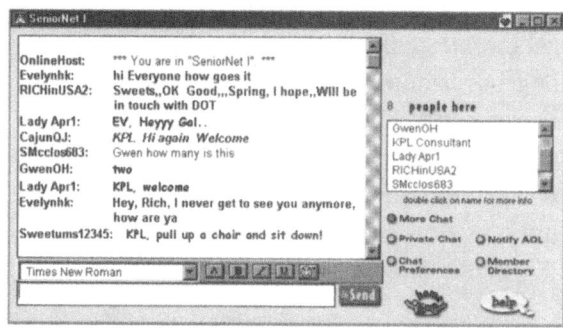

Figure 11-3. Chatting on the SeniorNet Community

5 Learning online with the Online Learning Center

The SeniorNet Online Learning Center provides different ways to learn computer and communication technologies including tips, message boards, a computer tools library, living archives, and more. Here's how it's accessed:

1. Click the **Keyword** button located on the AOL toolbar and enter AOL Keyword: **SeniorNet** and click the **Go** button to display the **SeniorNet Online** channel.

2. Click the **Online Learning Center** button on the **SeniorNet** channel to display the **Online Learning Center** selection window.

6 Accessing SeniorNet on the Web

The nonprofit SeniorNet Web site provides wonderful content and technical education for individuals 50 and older. With over 39,000 members and hundreds of discussion topics in the SeniorNet RoundTables, you can get and give information about finance, travel, gardening, genealogy, health matters, arts & entertainment, computers, and much more. Members and non-members alike are able to share questions and expertise with others. SeniorNet also operates 220 Learning Centers around the United States, provides discounts on major computer products, and publishes a quarterly newsletter. Here's how this useful site accessed:

1. Click the **Keyword** button located on the AOL toolbar and enter AOL Keyword: **SeniorNet** and click the **Go** button to display the **SeniorNet Online** channel.

2. Click the **SeniorNet Showcase on the Web** button on the **SeniorNet** channel to display the **SeniorNet** Web site.
   < or >
3. Enter Web site address: http://www.seniornet.org and press Enter to access **SeniorNet** on the Web.

7 Accessing Libraries & Archives

The SeniorNet Libraries & Archives site contains folders of downloadable files such as graphics, sounds, recipes, computing tools, transcripts, and much more. The description for each file can be viewed, and if desired, can be downloaded to your computer's hard drive. Here's how these folders and files are accessed:

1. Click the **Keyword** button located on the AOL toolbar and enter AOL Keyword: **SeniorNet** and click the **Go** button to display the **SeniorNet Online** channel.

2. Click the **Libraries & Archives** button on the **SeniorNet** channel to display the **SeniorNet Libraries & Archives** selection window.

3. Double-click the desired folder or click the **Open** button to open and view its contents.

4. Select the desired file from the open folder and click the **Download Now** or **Download Later** button to download the file to your computer's hard drive.

8 Increasing or decreasing the text size on SeniorNet on the Web

Do you have a problem reading the small text displayed on the SeniorNet Web site? SeniorNet recognized that this could be a problem for many members and non-members alike, so they made it easier to view the text displayed on the SeniorNet Web site by allowing you to increase the size of the text. Not only does it make it easier to read, you'll see the larger text when you print it, to. Here's how to increase and decrease the text size whenever you want.

Increasing the Text Size

1. Click the **Keyword** button located on the AOL toolbar and enter AOL Keyword: **SeniorNet** and click the **Go** button to display the **SeniorNet Online** channel.

2. Click the **SeniorNet Showcase on the Web** button on the **SeniorNet** channel to display the **SeniorNet** Web site.

3. Click the **Increase Text Size** button located on the top right side of any displayed page. The page will redisplay using larger font sizes when displaying text.

Decreasing the Text Size

1. Click the **Decrease Text Size** button located on the top right side of any displayed page to decrease the text size. The page will redisplay using the original font sizes when displaying text.

9 Staying in contact– long-distance grandparenting

The Grandparents channel offers a wealth of information, advice, chat, message boards, and much more. Whether your grandkids are near or far away, you can get useful information about being a grandparent. Read about your rights, long-distance grandparenting, raising grandchildren, saving for your grandchildren's college education, and more. Visit the Grandparents channel for community chat and message boards, or the next time you want a helping hand about grandparenting from afar. Here's how:

Click the **Keyword** button located on the AOL toolbar and enter AOL Keyword: **Grandparents.** Click the **Go** button to display the **Grandparents** channel, shown in Figure 11-4.

Figure 11-4. Staying in contact with family and friends on the Grandparents channel is easy.

10 Finding answers to your computer questions on the Internet

Have you ever had a problem installing computer hardware or received a computer error message you didn't understand? If you answered yes to either of these questions, then you'll be happy to know that there's help. The How To Find Answers Web site recognizes that many problems are not the result of something you did, but something the manufacturer did. Consequently, many problems and their answers are found on the manufacturers' Web sites. Although finding answers to your technical questions varies from manufacturer site to site, you should be able to navigate through most, if not all, of these sites relatively easily. Here's a list of some major manufacturers and their Web site addresses:

Adaptec Inc.
http://www.adaptec.com

Adobe Systems Incorporated
http://www.adobe.com

American Power Conversion
http://www.apccc.com

Apple Computer, Inc.
http://www.apple.com

Canon Computer Systems Inc.
http://www.canon.com

Compaq Computer Corp.
http://www.compaq.com

Dell Computer Corp.
http://www.dell.com

Diamond Multimedia Systems
http://www.diamondmm.com

Eastman Kodak Co.
http://www.kodak.com

Epson America, Inc.
http://www.epson.com

Gateway, Inc.
http://www.gateway.com

Hewlett-Packard Company
http://www.hp.com

IBM Corp.
http://www.ibm.com

Intuit Inc.
http://www.intuit.com

Iomega Corp.
http://www.iomega.com

Kensington Technology Group
http://www.kensington.com

Lexmark International, Inc. Inc.
http://www.lexmark.com

Logitech
http://www.logitech.com

Matrox Graphics Inc.
http://www.matrox.com

McAfee Associates
http://www.mcafee.com

Micron Electronics Inc.
http://www.micronpc.com

Microsoft Corp.
http://www.microsoft.com

Netscape
http://www.netscape.com

Okidata
http://www.okidata.com

Panasonic
http://www.panasonic.com

Plextor
http://www.plextor.com

Qualcomm Inc.
http://www.eudora.com

Samsung Electronics Co., Ltd.
http://www.samsung.com

Seagate Technology
http://www.seagate.com

Sony Electronics
http://www.sony.com

Symantec Corp.
http://www.symantec.com

Toshiba America
http://www.toshiba.com

Tripp Lite
http://www.tripplite.com

U.S. Robotics
http://www.usr.com

ViewSonic Corp.
http://www.viewsonic.com

Xerox Corporation
http://www.xerox.com

The How To Find Answers Web site is pretty easy to use: It provides links to many of the popular computer manufacturers to help you answer your questions as quickly as possible. Here's how you can access it:

1. Click the **Keyword** button located on the AOL toolbar, enter AOL Keyword: **AARP** and click the **Go** button to display the **AARP** channel.

2. Click **Have a Computer Question?** on the **AARP** channel to display the **How To Find Answers** Web site.

11 Accessing military veterans message boards

Military veterans will be excited to know that SeniorNet on the Web provides message boards designed just for them. You'll be able to join in discussion groups with other veterans or others who want to talk about wars. Discussion group topics include: World War II Memories, Effects of the GI Bill, Korean War Comrades Remembered, Vietnam War, World War I, Veterans Benefits, Widows/Widowers of Military Personnel, and more. The SeniorNet Veterans and Wars Web site provides a way for military veterans who lived through war to discuss their feelings with like-minded individuals. Here's how to find the site:

1. Click the **Keyword** button located on the AOL toolbar and enter AOL Keyword: **SeniorNet** and click the **Go** button to display the **SeniorNet Online** channel.

2. Click the **SeniorNet Showcase on the Web** button on the **SeniorNet** channel to display the **SeniorNet** Web site.

3. Click **Site Index** located at the top of the SeniorNet Web site.

4. Scroll down to **Veterans** under the **Discussion Areas** category and click **Veterans** link to display the **Veterans and Wars** Web site.

12 Getting politically active

Are you politically active? Do you enjoy talking about politics, government, policy, and other topics? If so, the SeniorNet Web site provides message boards designed just for you. You'll be able to join in discussion groups with other individuals who enjoy talking about government policy, the executive, legislative and judicial branches of government, political news, global foreign policy, and much more. Here's how to get there:

1. Click the **Keyword** button located on the AOL toolbar and enter AOL Keyword: **SeniorNet** and click the **Go** button to display the **SeniorNet Online** channel.

2. Click the **SeniorNet Showcase on the Web** button on the **SeniorNet** channel to display the **SeniorNet** Web site.

3. Click **Site Index** located at the top of the **SeniorNet** Web site.

4. Scroll down to **Politics** under the **Discussion Areas** category and click **Political Issues** link to display the **Political Issues** Web site.

13 Subscribing to SeniorNet Newsletters

To keep you informed about computer and technology issues, and to inspire you to contribute your knowledge and wisdom through various activities and programs, SeniorNet offers two types of Newsletters: SeniorNet Newsline and Inside SeniorNet. Both newsletters are for members only and offer a wealth of information. The SeniorNet Newsline newsletter is published quarterly in print format and is mailed to all members. The Inside SeniorNet newsletter consists of monthly updates by SeniorNet President Ann Wrixon. Here's how you can subscribe to either or both of these newsletters:

1. Click the **Keyword** button located on the AOL toolbar and enter AOL Keyword: **SeniorNet** and click the **Go** button to display the **SeniorNet Online** channel.

2. Click the **SeniorNet Showcase on the Web** button on the **SeniorNet** channel to display the **SeniorNet** Web site.

3. Click **Newsletters** located at the top of the **SeniorNet** Web site to display the **SeniorNet Newsletters** Web site.

4. Click the newsletter you'd like to subscribe to and follow the on-screen instructions.

Senior Living—Housing and Health

14 Living independently

AOL's Independent Living Web site provides information you'll need to determine whether independent living is right for you. It takes into

account a number of factors in making this assessment: overall physical and emotional health, the level of physical assistance and personal care needed, the amount of social interaction desired, the availability of health services, and the level of personal freedom wanted. It also lets you order a free senior housing directory simply by answering a few questions, entering your e-mail address and mailing address. This site is a great resource for determining whether you or your loved one is a candidate for an independent living community. Here's how it's accessed:

1. Click the **Keyword** button located on the AOL toolbar and enter AOL Keyword: **Senior Living** and click the **Go** button to display AOL's **Senior Living** Web site.

2. Click **Independent Living** under the **Know Your Options** heading on the **Senior Living** Web site to display the **Independent Living** Web site.

To find independent living communities in your city or another city, just follow these simple steps:

1. Click the **Keyword** button located on the AOL toolbar and enter AOL Keyword: **Senior Living** and click the **Go** button to display AOL's **Senior Living** Web site.

2. Check the **Independent Living** box under the **Select your type(s) of housing or care** heading on the **Senior Living** Web site to display AOL's **Independent Living** Web site, enter your city and state, and click the **Go** button.

15 Housing alternatives—Assisted Living

What types of housing alternatives do you or your loved one qualify for? AOL's Assisted Living Web site provides information to help determine whether assisted living is right for you or your loved one. It takes into account a number of factors in making this assessment: overall physical and emotional health, the level of physical assistance and personal care needed, the amount of social interaction desired, the availability of health services, and the level of personal freedom wanted.

You'll also be able to order a free senior housing directory simply by answering a few questions, entering your e-mail address and mailing address. This site is a great resource for determining whether you or your loved-one is a candidate for an assisted living community. Here's how it's accessed.

1. Click the **Keyword** button located on the AOL toolbar and enter AOL Keyword: **Senior Living** and click the **Go** button to display AOL's Senior Living Web site.

2. Click **Assisted Living** under the **Know Your Options** heading on the Senior Living Web site to display AOL's **Assisted Living** Web site.

To find assisted living communities in your city or another city, just follow these simple steps.

1. Click the **Keyword** button located on the AOL toolbar and enter AOL Keyword: **Senior Living** and click the **Go** button to display AOL's Senior Living Web site.

2. Check the **Assisted Living** box under the **Select your type(s) of housing or care** heading on the Senior Living Web site to display AOL's **Assisted Living** Web site, enter your city and state, and click the **Go** button.

16 Nursing home living

AOL's Nursing Home Web site provides information to help determine whether you or your loved-one needs 24-hour skilled nursing care. It takes into account a number of factors in making this assessment: overall physical and emotional health, the level of physical assistance and personal care needed, the amount of social interaction desired, the availability of health services, and the level of personal freedom wanted. You'll also be able to order a free senior housing directory simply by answering a few questions, entering your e-mail address and mailing address. This site is a great resource for determining whether you or your

loved one is a candidate for a skilled 24-hour nursing care facility or community. Here's how it's accessed:

1. Click the **Keyword** button located on the AOL toolbar and enter AOL Keyword: **Senior Living** and click the **Go** button to display AOL's **Senior Living** Web site.

2. Click **Nursing Home** under the **Know Your Options** heading on the **Senior Living** Web site to display AOL's **Nursing Homes** Web site.

To find skilled nursing care facilities and communities in your city or another city, just follow these simple steps:

1. Click the **Keyword** button located on the AOL toolbar and enter AOL Keyword: **Senior Living** and click the **Go** button to display AOL's **Senior Living** Web site.

2. Check the **Nursing Home** box under the **Select your type(s) of housing or care** heading on the **Senior Living** Web site to display AOL's **Nursing Homes** Web site, enter your city and state, and click the **Go** button.

17 Continuing care retirement communities

AOL's Continuing Care Residential Communities Web site provides information to help determine whether you or your loved one requires living conditions that have continuing care. It takes into account a number of factors in making this assessment: overall physical and emotional health, the level of physical assistance and personal care needed, the amount of social interaction desired, the availability of health services, and the level of personal freedom wanted. You'll also be able to order a free senior housing directory simply by answering a few questions, entering your e-mail address and mailing address. This site is a great resource for determining whether you or your loved one is a candidate for an independent living environment with the availability of services often found in an assisted living environment or even a skilled 24-hour nursing care facility or community. Here's how it's accessed:

1. Click the **Keyword** button located on the AOL toolbar and enter AOL Keyword: **Senior Living** and click the **Go** button to display AOL's **Senior Living** Web site.

2. Click **Continuing Care** under the **Know Your Options** heading on the **Senior Living** Web site to display AOL's **Continuing Care Retirement Communities** Web site.

To find continuing care retirement communities in your city or another city, just follow these simple steps:

1. Click the **Keyword** button located on the AOL toolbar and enter AOL Keyword: **Senior Living** and click the **Go** button to display AOL's **Senior Living** Web site.

2. Check the **Continuing Care (CCRC)** box under the **Select your type(s) of housing or care** heading on the **Senior Living** Web site to display AOL's **Continuing Care Retirement Communities** Web site, enter your city and state, and click the **Go** button.

18 Taking care of special situations like Alzheimer's/Dementia

AOL's Alzheimer's/Dementia Care Web site provides information to help determine whether you or your loved one requires living conditions that can provide specialized and continuing care. It takes into account a number of factors in making this assessment: overall physical and emotional health, the level of physical assistance and personal care needed, the amount of social interaction desired, the availability of health services, and the level of personal freedom wanted. You'll also be able to order a free senior housing directory simply by answering a few questions, entering your e-mail address and mailing address. This site is a great resource for determining whether you or your loved one is a candidate for the specialized living environment required by people with this disease. Often people afflicted with this disease require a

specialized living environment with skilled 24-hour nursing care facilities. Here's how it's accessed:

1. Click the **Keyword** button located on the AOL toolbar and enter AOL Keyword: **Senior Living** and click the **Go** button to display AOL's **Senior Living** Web site.

2. Click **Alzheimer's Care** under the **Know Your Options** heading on the **Senior Living** Web site to display AOL's **Alzheimer's/Dementia Care** Web site.

To find continuing care retirement communities in your city or another city, just follow these simple steps:

1. Click the **Keyword** button located on the AOL toolbar and enter AOL Keyword: **Senior Living** and click the **Go** button to display AOL's **Senior Living** Web site.

2. Check the **Alzheimer's Care** box under the **Select your type(s) of housing or care heading** on the **Senior Living** Web site to display AOL's **Alzheimer's/Dementia Care** Web site, enter your city and state, and click the **Go** button.

19 Accessing senior health communities

The SeniorNet Health Matters Web site provides articles of special interest to adults over 50 as well as roundtable discussions on a variety of health-related topics. Articles and health guides include: Healthy habits, How to Get the Best Cancer Care, Heart Disease, Osteoporosis, Prostate Enlargement, Stroke, and more. RoundTable discussion topics include: Alcoholism, Anger Management, Asthma, Death and End of Life Issues, Health Insurance, Wrist Problems, and hundreds more. This site is a great resource containing up to date articles, health forums, and support groups. Here's how it's accessed:

1. Click the **Keyword** button located on the AOL toolbar and enter AOL Keyword: **SeniorNet** and click the **Go** button to display **SeniorNet's** Web site.

2. Click **Health Matters** on the SeniorNet Web site to display **SeniorNet's Health Matters** Web site.

3. Click the **Roundtable** discussion group of interest by using the vertical scroll bar located at the right of your screen.

20 Accessing AARP Online Bulletins

The AARP Bulletins Online Web site provides news and perspectives for adults 50 and older. Topics include: News, Social Security, Medicare, Consumer Alert, Long-Term Care, Your Health, Your Money, Your Life, Make a Difference, and Faceoff. This site is a great resource containing news, articles, publications, and much more. It's easy to use and you'll be able to enrich your life while having fun every step of the way. Here's how it's accessed:

1. Click the **Keyword** button located on the AOL toolbar and enter AOL Keyword: **AARP** and click the **Go** button to display AOL's **AARP** channel.

2. Click the picture above the words AARP Webplace on the **AARP** channel to display the **AARP** Web site.

3. Click **AARP Bulletin News** under the **Popular Choices** heading to display the **AARP Bulletin Online**.

21 Making a difference by volunteering

The AARP Volunteering Web site asks AARP members to make a difference in society by volunteering in their communities. The site lists several Day of Service Partners that you can contact for ways to get involved in your community. Visit the AARP Volunteering Web site and enrich your own life as well as those of others in your community. Here's how it's accessed:

1. Click the **Keyword** button located on the AOL toolbar and enter AOL Keyword: **AARP** and click the **Go** button to display AOL's **AARP** channel.

2. Click **Make a Difference** on the **AARP** channel to display the **Serve your Community, Strengthen Our Nation** Web site.

Entertainment Resources for Seniors

22 Reading local newspapers

AOL Anywhere's Online Newspaper Directory lets you read local news coverage online. From the Akron Beacon Journal to the Grand Rapids Press, the Hartford Courant to the Norfolk Virginian-Pilot, and the Oklahoma City Daily Oklahoman to the Worcester Telegram & Gazette, you'll find news from virtually anyplace in the United States. Visit the Online Newspaper Directory Web site and read what's happening in local communities around the country. Here's how:

1. Click the **Keyword** button located on the AOL toolbar and enter AOL Keyword: **Newspapers** and click the **Go** button to display AOL's **Online Newspaper Directory** Web site.

2. Double-click the newspaper of interest to view it online.

23 Viewing online magazines and publications

View your favorite magazines and publications online with the Magazines channel. AOL provides access to a variety of online sources including Time, The New York Times, CBS News, Atlantic Monthly, Business Week, Entertainment Weekly, National Review, The Christian Science Monitor, The Sporting News, and others. Plus, as an added bonus, you'll be able to get news and commentary from the team at National Public Radio (NPR). Visit the Online Newspaper Directory Web site and read what's happening in local communities around the country. Here's how:

1. Click the **Keyword** button located on the AOL toolbar and enter AOL Keyword: **Magazines** and click the **Go** button to display AOL's **News and Publications** channel, shown in Figure 11-5.

2. Double-click the publication you'd like to view online from the **News and Publications** window or click one of the images (e.g., Time, The NY Times, or CBS News).

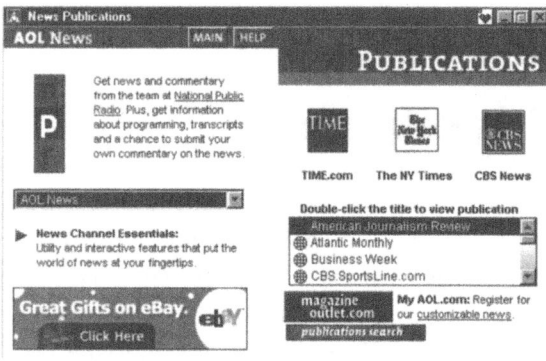

Figure 11-5. Viewing popular magazines and publications on the News & Publications channel

24 Reading your horoscope

The Horoscopes channel lets you discover what's in your future. From predictions using tarot and numerology, you can find out about your love life and compatibility, money and career, and a treasure trove of other resources. You'll also find much more, such as Astrology.com, Astronet, Free Psychic Readings, the Crystal Ball Forum, and Redbook Horoscopes. Visit the Horoscopes channel and see what your future has in store for you. Here's how:

1. Click the **Keyword** button located on the AOL toolbar and enter AOL Keyword: **Horoscope** and click the **Go** button to display AOL's **Horoscopes** channel.

2. Select your sign from the drop-down selection box and click the **Go** button.

25 Accessing AARP's radio and TV

AARP's Radio and Television Web site provides radio and television broadcasting for your listening pleasure 24/7. You'll find one-hour weekly radio interview programs focusing on the wide-ranging interests of listeners 40 and older, daily news and radio programs, and weekly video releases covering

topics such as finance, health, and social issues. Visit the AARP Radio and Television Web site the next time you want prime time news, radio with a mature focus, and broadcast video news. Here's how it's accessed:

1. Click the **Keyword** button located on the AOL toolbar and enter AOL Keyword: **AARP** and click the **Go** button to display AOL's **AARP** channel.

2. Click **Radio and Television from AARP** from the Feature Finder selection box and click the Go button to display the **Radio and Television from AARP** Web site.

26 Playing card and board games online

The Card & Board channel offers popular board games that you can play online. From card games such as Bridge, Cribbage, Euchre, Hearts, Solitaire, and Spades to board games such as Backgammon, Checkers, Chess, and Dominoes, you'll have hours of fun. You'll also find exciting games in other categories such as Word & Puzzle, Free Casino & Lottery, Arcade and Trivia, and more. Visit the Card & Board channel the next time you want to challenge a friend, loved one, or anyone else to a game of hearts. Here's how:

1. Click the **Keyword** button located on the AOL toolbar and enter AOL Keyword: **Card** or **Board** and click the **Go** button to display AOL's **Card & Board** channel.

2. Click the card or board game you'd like to play from the listed games.

27 Getting door-to-door driving directions

Getting door-to-door driving directions has never been so easy. The MapQuest Web site provides maps, driving directions, and much more that you can use for your next trip or just for having fun. Visit MapQuest the next time you need driving directions, traffic reports, city guides, or trip planners. Here's how:

1. Click the **Keyword** button located on the AOL toolbar and enter AOL Keyword: **Directions** and click the **Go** button to display the **MapQuest™** Web site.

2. Click the **Driving Directions** icon button to display the Driving **Directions From and To** Web site, shown in Figure 11-6.

3. Enter as much information as you know in the **From** portion and as much information as you know about the **To** portion, and click the **Get Directions** button.

28 Getting live traffic reports

Get live traffic reports for the city where you live or for countless other cities—it's as easy as 1-2-3 with DigitalCity.com's Traffic Conditions Web site. You'll

see traffic conditions for each main road or highway and the type of incident, such as accident, construction, delays, object on the roadway, or hazardous driving conditions.. Visit the Traffic Conditions Web site the next time you drive for live traffic condition reports—it could save you time. Here's how:

1. Click the **Keyword** button located on the AOL toolbar and enter AOL Keyword: **Traffic** and click the **Go** button to display **DigitalCity.com's Traffic Conditions** Web site.

2. Click the city you'd like to see traffic conditions for or click **See a complete listing of cities by state** to display all major cities.

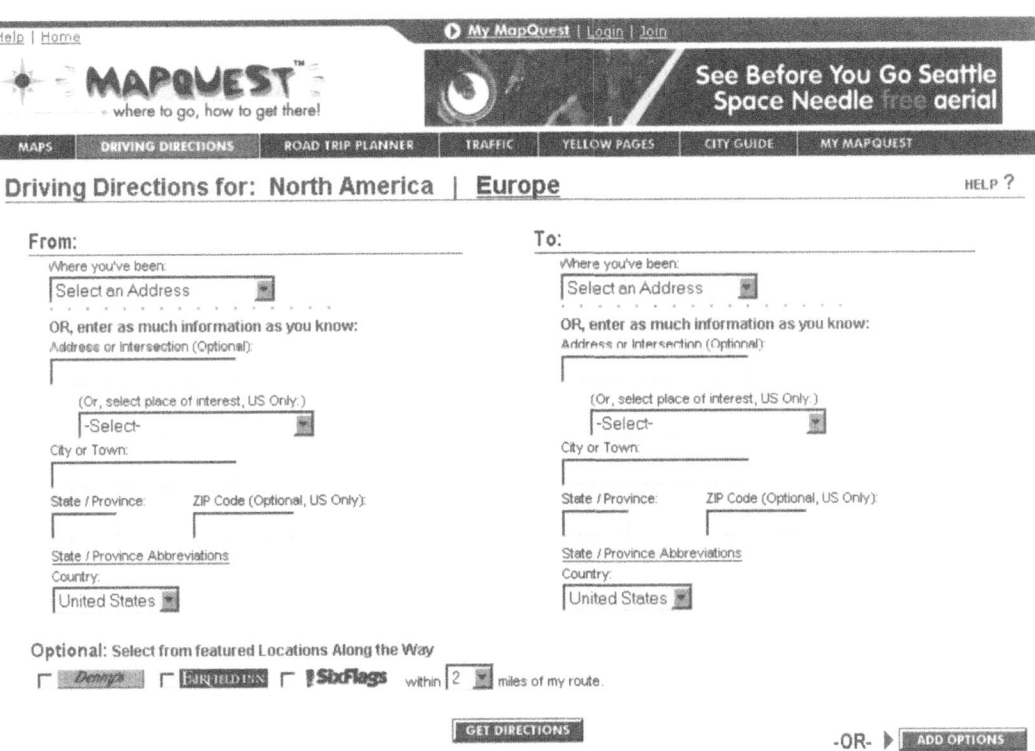

Figure 11-6. Getting detailed driving directions

29 Finding fun and adventure-travel destinations

Find fun and adventure on AOL's Adventure & Outdoors Web site. Whether it's a daytrip, weekend getaway, or a vacation, you'll find great opportunities for adventures that are packed with fun and excitement. You'll have countless activities to choose from such as biking, birding, camping, caving, climbing, driving, fishing, hiking, hunting, paddling, skiing, snorkeling, wildlife viewing, and many others. Visit the Adventure & Outdoors Web site the next time you want an adrenaline rush or just want a little adventure—you'll find packages, gear, and a tremendous amount of information right at your fingertips. Here's how to get there:

1. Click the **Keyword** button located on the AOL toolbar and enter AOL Keyword: **Travel** and click the **Go** button to display the AOL **Travel** channel.

2. Click **Adventure** under the **Interests & Activities** category on the **Travel** channel to display the **Adventure & Outdoors** Web site.

3. Select a destination or activities from the drop-down selection boxes and click the **Go** button.

30 Traveling with disabilities

If you're one of the 43 million Americans with disabilities, you've probably found traveling to be less than a positive experience. Before your next trip, learn about available resources and what your rights are as a traveler from AOL's Seniors Interests & Activities Web site. It provides information about the importance of understanding symbols and signage and how they promote accessible travel for all, and it also offers government and non-government accessibility resources. Here's how to find this helpful site:

1. Click the **Keyword** button located on the AOL toolbar and enter AOL Keyword: **Senior Travel** and click the **Go** button to display the **Seniors Interests & Activities** Web site.

2. Click **Traveling with Disabilities** to display resources for accessible travel and disabled travelers' rights.

31 Finding senior travel discount opportunities

Seniors can save on travel expenses as long as they know where to look. The Senior Travel Special Interests Web site lists hot deals, and offers discounts from AARP and others on airline tickets, hotels, car rentals, train and bus tickets, amusement park tickets, and much more. Visit the Senior Travel Special Interests Web site to find great savings on your next vacation or trip. Here's how:

1. Click the **Keyword** button located on the AOL toolbar and enter AOL Keyword: **Senior Travel** and click the **Go** button to display the **Seniors Interests & Activities** Web site.

2. Click **Saving Money** to display information and links to valuable travel coupons, deals, discounts, and newsletters.

3. Click the link that you'd like to see more information on.

32 Searching for a little romance

Would you like to add a little romance to your life, access a searchable personals database, or get online dating advice that will win you big points in the game of love? You can with Love@AOL. Love@AOL is the single most popular romance site online. It lists hundreds of thousands of personals and thousands of success stories from couples that fell in love after using Love@AOL. It offers a variety of services and features including love tips and advice, chat rooms and message boards, e-mail goodies including love letter generators and an InstaRose to send to that special someone, and the ability to access the largest personals database with pictures online anywhere, as well as the ability to create your very own personal. Here's how you can take advantage of this exciting and fun AOL service:

1. Click the **Keyword** button located on the AOL toolbar and enter AOL Keyword: **Love** and click the **Go** button to display the **Love@AOL** channel.

2. In the **Search for Singles** area of the **Love@AOL** channel, check the box corresponding to what gender you are: **Woman** or **Man**, then check the box corresponding to whether you're looking for a **Woman** or **Man**. Then enter an age range that you're looking for, and then enter your zip code, shown in Figure 11-7.

3. Click the **Search** button to begin your search.

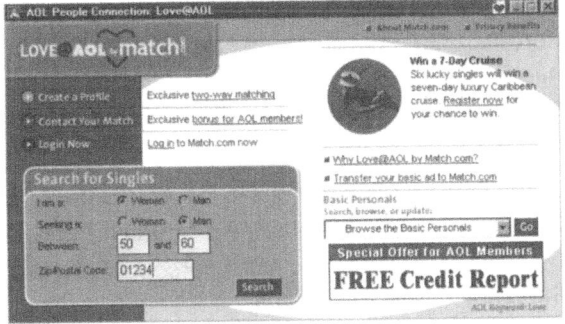

Figure 11-7. Finding romance is a snap on the Love@AOL channel.

33 Accessing the latest arts news

The Arts News channel provides access to the latest news in the world of arts. From the week's top box office winners to weekly book reviews, you'll stay current with all the latest news. You'll also find other exciting news in the areas of movies, music, TV, celebrities, and more. Visit the Arts News channel for all your entertainment news. Here's how:

1. Click the **Keyword** button located on the AOL toolbar and enter AOL Keyword: **Arts News** and click the **Go** button to display AOL's **Arts News** channel.

2. Double-click the folder of interest under the **Arts News** category or click one of the many links under the **More on Arts** category.

34 Finding local art and cultural events

Finding local entertainment for the city you live or any other city is as simple as pointing-and-clicking your mouse. The AOL Entertainment Local Guide

Web site provides schedules and listings of local events happening in and around your city such as musicals, plays, theater, movies, museums, and other art and cultural events. Visit the Entertainment Local Guide Web site to find cultural events in and around your city. Here's how:

3. Click the **Keyword** button located on the AOL toolbar and enter AOL Keyword: **Books** and click the **Go** button to display the **Books & Art** channel.

4. Click **Cultural events near you.** On the **Books & Art** channel to display the **Local Guide** for the city you live in.

35 Accessing sporting and gambling sites

If you love the action of playing Slots, Roulette, Blackjack, Poker, Bingo, or the Lottery, you'll love the free games offered on AOL's Free Casino & Lottery Web site. You'll find great games with real gambling action, and best of all it's free. Visit the Free Casino & Lottery Web site for all the excitement of Las Vegas and Atlantic City brought right to your computer screen. Here's how:

Click the **Keyword** button located on the AOL toolbar and enter AOL Keyword: **Casino** and click the **Go** button to display the **Free Casino & Lottery** Web site, shown in Figure 11-8.

Figure 11-8. Sporting, casino, and lottery games are free on the Casino & Lottery Web site.

36 Getting cooking insights and recipes

If cooking is your passion, then AOL's Food & Recipes channel is just what the doctor ordered. You'll find mouth-watering and scrumptious recipes for your favorite foods, information about cook books and wine, a food index, and you can print weekly savings coupons, view member recipes, receive a free newsletter, and much more. This is one terrific site that will satisfy the gourmet in anyone. Visit the Food & Recipes channel for cooking help, advice, or anything that tastes nice. You'll be glad you did. Here's how:

Click the **Keyword** button located on the AOL toolbar and enter AOL Keyword: **Food** or **Recipes** or **Cooking** and click the **Go** button to display the **Food & Recipes** channel.

37 Accessing gardening sites

If you have a little green thumb in you, then you'll love AOL's Gardening channel. You'll be able to find information on your favorite plants, solve problems with your lawn or plantings, learn gardening basics, get gardening tips, buy tools and supplies online, find a landscaper in your area, access helpful Q&A forums and chat rooms, subscribe to a free weekly newsletter, and more. This site will help with all your gardening questions and then some. Visit the Gardening channel and learn all the best techniques for making your lawn and garden healthy and beautiful year around. Become green-minded—you won't regret it. Here's how:

Click the **Keyword** button located on the AOL toolbar and enter AOL Keyword: **Gardening** and click the **Go** button to display AOL's **Gardening** channel.

Retirement & Estate Planning

38 Ensuring your financial security

Do you want to ensure financial security during your retirement years, for your children, and grandchildren? If you're like most people, you're aware of the pitfalls of not being prepared, but you may not know where to start. AOL's Personal Finance channel provides a wealth of knowledge to help you have enough money leading up to and during your retirement years. It's wise to consult a qualified financial planner or investment counselor for the specific plans that are right for you and your family, but you can find a lot of great resources here. Get business news, stock prices, mutual fund topics, retirement planning information, savings & planning strategies, banking & loan advice, real estate basics, financial tools, access to helpful Q&A forums, chat rooms, financial games, a free newsletter, and more. Visit the Personal Finance channel today for you and your family's well being. Here's how:

Click the **Keyword** button located on the AOL toolbar and enter AOL Keyword: **Finance** and click the **Go** button to display AOL's **Personal Finance** channel, shown in Figure 11-9.

< or >

Click the **Personal Finance** channel button located on the left side of your screen to display AOL's **Personal Finance** channel.

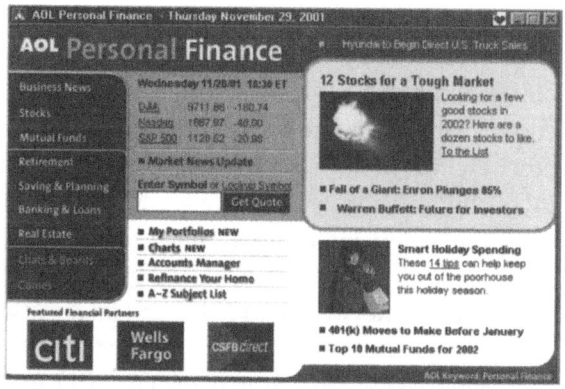

Figure 11-9. Getting a basic understanding of personal finance on the Personal Finance channel

39 Accessing online investing message boards

Would you like to share ideas, information, and opinions with others about investment strategies, stocks, and market fundamentals? AOL's Personal Finance Message Boards Web site lets you do just that. Though it's a good idea to consult a financial planner for investment information for your needs, you'll find a host of resources here including: a company stock board directory, investing boards, planning boards, ask an expert, and more. Visit the Personal Finance Message Boards Web site to communicate with a vibrant and thriving online community of investment-minded people. Here's how:

Click the **Keyword** button located on the AOL toolbar and enter AOL Keyword: **Investing** and click the **Go** button to display AOL's **Personal Finance Message Boards** Web site.

40 Accessing retirement and financial planning resources

Are you planning on retiring soon? Are your retirement savings and investments going to meet your retirement goals and needs? AOL's Personal Finance Retirement Planning Web site provides information that will help you answer these and related questions for peace of mind and financial security when you retire. Though you should plan to consult a qualified financial planner or investment counselor for specific plans right for you and your family, this site provides retirement resources galore. It covers such topics as 401(k)s, IRAs, self-employed retirement plans, long term care planning, a variety of retirement calculators, Q&A forums, chat rooms, financial games, a free retirement newsletter, and more. Here's how to get there:

Click the **Keyword** button located on the AOL toolbar and enter AOL Keyword: **Retirement** and click the **Go** button to display AOL's **Personal Finance Retirement** Web site.

41 Estate planning–Lifestages Estate channel

Are your loved ones adequately provided for in your will? Do you understand the difference between an estate plan versus a will? These and many other questions are answered on AOL's Personal Finance Estate Planning, Wills & Trust Web site. Don't leave your survivors in financial chaos—give yourself and your loved ones the peace of mind they deserve with a well thought out estate plan. Of course, you should plan to consult a

qualified financial planner, investment counselor, or lawyer for specific plans that are right for you and your family. This site provides comprehensive estate planning resources covering such topics as wills, trusts, money tips, retirement calculators, message boards, chat rooms, a free money newsletter, and more. Here's how to access this site:

Click the **Keyword** button located on the AOL toolbar and enter AOL Keyword: **Estate** and click the **Go** button to display AOL's **Personal Finance Estate Planning, Wills & Trust** Web site.

CHAPTER 12

Family Matters

AOL OFFERS A VARIETY of tools, services and advice that will help busy families get everything done and have fun, too. Planning a vacation with the kids? Check out Family Events, Outings and Vacations. You'll find travel tips for all ages and plenty of good ideas for the younger set. Share your pictures across the miles. Is home schooling an option? Chat with other parents on this very topic. From dealing with aging parents to coping with loss, share your ideas, feelings and suggestions with other AOL members. And best of all, this information is easily accessible to the entire family without leaving the comforts of home.

In this chapter you'll learn how to:

- Find information on outings and vacations that are fun for the whole family

- Use resources to help you handle family issues and relationships

- Locate family living and parenting resources

- Access family services resources

Family Events, Outings, and Vacations

1 Finding family adventures

AOL's Family Adventure Web site opens a world of fun and excitement for the whole family to enjoy. It provides ideas on cool things you and your family can do in your local community including theme parks, kid-friendly events, zoos, parks, aquariums, museums, movies, and much more. You can also use it to find adventures in major cities around the United States. Here's how it's accessed:

1. Click the **Keyword** button located on the AOL toolbar and enter AOL Keyword: **Family Adventure**. Click the **Go** button to display AOL's **Family Adventure** Web site.

2. Click the city hyperlink that you'd like to find family adventure for.

2 Dining out with kids

Does your busy schedule prevent your family from sharing quality time at dinner or other meals? AOL's Family Dinner channel provides family- and time-friendly ideas on preparing sit-down meals that give your family the opportunity to discuss events that occurred during the day. According to recent statistics, a family that dines together fosters a bond of togetherness while staying connected to daily events, issues, and other important family matters. The Family Dinner channel offers tips on proper etiquette, easy table talk, great timesaving recipes, and more. Here's how it's accessed:

Click the **Keyword** button located on the AOL toolbar and enter AOL Keyword: **Family Dinner**. Click the **Go** button to display AOL's **The Dinner Table** channel.

3 Grilling tips the whole family will enjoy

The Grilling channel is your single-source to wonderful and tasty grilling tips and ideas that family and friends are sure to enjoy. You'll learn great recipes for high-flavor sauces and rubs, how to arrange coal, test grill temperature, light and clean a gas grill, grill tasty hamburgers and brats, and much more. Visit the Grilling channel for all your grilling needs. Here's how:

Click the **Keyword** button located on the AOL toolbar and enter AOL Keyword: **Grilling**. Click the **Go** button to display AOL's **Grilling** channel.

4 Searching for family entertainment

AOL's Family Entertainment channel is your resource for finding family-oriented television shows and movies, toys and books, travel and activities, and much more. You'll also discover what other parents are doing for family entertainment, find great children's book by age, view a gallery of toys by age, learn about the 10 worst toys for kids, and get family travel ideas. Make AOL's Family Entertainment channel your online destination for family entertainment ideas and tips. Here's how:

Click the **Keyword** button located on the AOL toolbar and enter AOL Keyword: **Family Entertainment**. Click the **Go** button to display the **Family Entertainment** channel.

5 Entertaining craft ideas

AOL's Crafts channel provides cool crafts and projects that'll be fun for the whole family. You'll find great ideas for under $10, simple projects that can be done to enhance the appearance of your living space, and how to utilize interior room planners to visualize what your room will look like before you rearrange your furniture. Shop for housewares and appliances, share ideas to make jewelry, get quilting ideas, capture your memories with scrapbook ideas, find needlepoint and sewing supplies, search for carpentry projects, and more. Here's how to get to the Crafts channel:

Click the **Keyword** button located on the AOL toolbar and enter AOL Keyword: **Crafts**. Click the **Go** button to display AOL's **Crafts** channel.

6 Planning a family vacation

The Family Vacation Web site lets you find and book a family vacation to anywhere in the world. It provides vacation tips and tools, a vacation finder, hot deals, vacation discounts, travel guides, photo galleries, and more. You'll find vacation packages, including details about air, cruise, bus, tours, hotels, and meals, by specifying a travel destination, month of travel, price per person, and length of stay. Here's how to visit:

Click the **Keyword** button located on the AOL toolbar and enter AOL Keyword: **Family Vacation**. Click the **Go** button to display AOL's **Family Travel** Web site, shown in Figure 12-1.

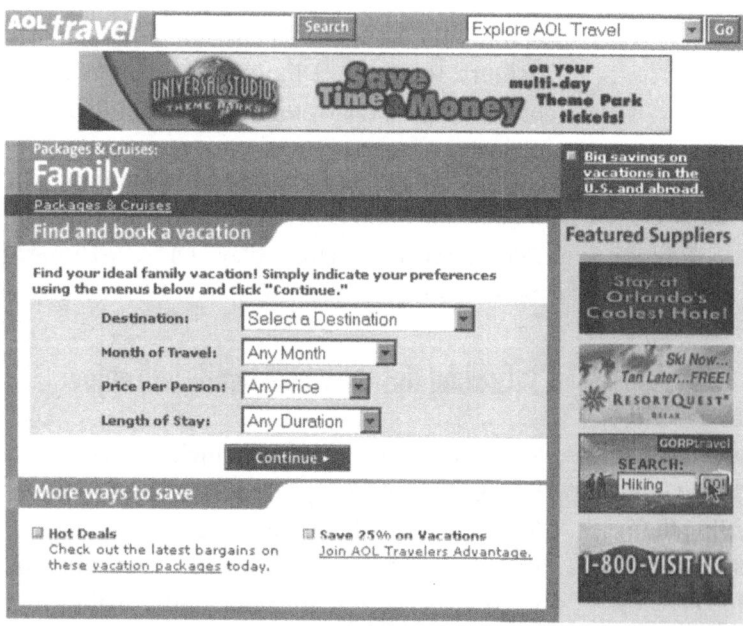

Figure 12-1. Finding and booking a family vacation on AOL's Family Vacation Web site

7 Traveling by car with the kids

Traveling by car with the kids can be a trying experience. AOL's Parents' Survival Kit: Travel channel provides travel games and other goodies that are sure to be a hit on those trips away from home. You'll find travel games, classic car games, questions and memory games, travel snack bags, and gear, among other things. Visit the Car Travel folder for problem-free traveling for your whole family. Here's how:

1. Click the **Keyword** button located on the AOL toolbar and enter AOL Keyword: **Family Entertainment**. Click the **Go** button to display the **Family Entertainment** channel.

2. Click the **Travel/Activities** tab on the **Family Entertainment** channel.

3. Click the **Car Travel** folder from the drop-down selection box titled **More Travel & Activities**, and click the **Go** button to display the **Parents' Survival Kit: Travel** channel.

8 Traveling with toddlers

Before you travel with a young toddler, first visit BabyCenter's Traveling With a Baby Web site. You'll find seven secrets to successful travel with a young child to make your travel experience an enjoyable and memorable one. Make BabyCenter's Traveling With a Baby Web site your online destination for parent-tested ideas and suggestions. Here's how to find it:

1. Click the **Keyword** button located on the AOL toolbar and enter AOL Keyword: **Family Entertainment**. Click the **Go** button to display the **Family Entertainment** channel.

2. Click the **Travel/Activities** tab on the **Family Entertainment** window.

3. Click the **Traveling with tots** folder from the **More Travel & Activities** drop-down selection box, and click the **Go** button to display **Baby-Center Traveling With a Baby** Web site.

9 Keeping toddlers safe on trips

BabyCenter's Traveling Safely with Toddlers Web site provides health and safety tips to keep your small child safe while traveling. You'll learn useful and helpful tips to make sure your toddler is an active participant in your travel adventures—all from leading experts. Here's how it's accessed:

1. Click the **Keyword** button located on the AOL toolbar and enter AOL Keyword: **Family Entertainment**. Click the **Go** button to display the **Family Entertainment** channel.

2. Click the **Travel/Activities** tab on the **Family Entertainment** window.

3. Click the **Keeping tots safe on trips** folder from the **More Travel & Activities** drop-down selection box, and click the **Go** button to display **BabyCenter's Traveling With a 3-Year-Old** Web site.

10 Traveling games for kids

Traveling with kids should be a fun and enjoyable experience for everyone. Moms Online provides terrific ideas on the type of games kids can play when traveling. From simple conversation to jokes, question and answer games to snacks and radio stations, you'll find some great ideas for families on the go. Here's how it's accessed:

1. Click the **Keyword** button located on the AOL toolbar and enter AOL Keyword: **Family Entertainment**. Click the **Go** button to display the **Family Entertainment** channel.

2. Click the **Travel/Activities** tab on the **Family Entertainment** window.

3. Click the **Traveling games for kids** folder from the **More Travel & Activities** drop-down selection box, and click the **Go** button to display **Travel Games for Kids—Moms Online** channel.

11 Singing and storytelling for kids while traveling

Moms Online provides a series of great tips and suggestions for helping families on the go. The Songs and Stories for Travel channel provide suggested songs and stories for toddlers and school-age children. You'll also learn other valuable techniques for keeping children active while on those road-trips. Here's how:

1. Click the **Keyword** button located on the AOL toolbar and enter AOL Keyword: **Family Entertainment**. Click the **Go** button to display the **Family Entertainment** channel.

2. Click the **Travel/Activities** tab on the **Family Entertainment** window.

3. Click the **Songs and Stories for Travel** folder from the **More Travel & Activities** drop-down selection box, and click the **Go** button to display Songs and **Stories for Travel—Moms Online** channel.

12 Flying with kids

Flying with kids is a challenge at anytime. iVillage's Trip Tips: Flying With Kids provides wonderful suggestions on making your flight a more pleasurable experience. The parents of Parent Soup and ParentsPlace.com offer these tips. Here's how you'll be able to find these valuable suggestions:

1. Click the **Keyword** button located on the AOL toolbar and enter AOL Keyword: **Family Entertainment** and click the **Go** button. The **Family Entertainment** channel appears.

2. Click the **Travel/Activities** tab on the **Family Entertainment** window.

3. Click the **Flying with kids** folder from the **More Travel & Activities** drop-down selection box, and click the **Go** button to display the **iVillage Family Travel** Web site.

4. Click **10 tips for flying** under **Stress-Free Family Travel** to display **Trip Tips: Flying with Kids.**

13 Having fun at amusement parks

If you're looking for that ultimate thrill ride, then AOL's Amusement Parks channel is for you. It provides a search function to help you find theme parks located anywhere in the United States, along with thrill rides, roller coasters, family resources, lodging facilities, and much more. Visit the Family Amusements and Theme Parks channels for fun and excitement for the whole family to enjoy. Here's how:

Click the **Keyword** button located on the AOL toolbar and enter AOL Keyword: **Family Amusement**. Click the **Go** button to display the **Parents' Survival Kit: Amusement Parks** channel, shown in Figure 12-2.

< or >

Click the **Keyword** button located on the AOL toolbar and enter AOL Keyword: **Theme Parks**. Click the **Go** button to display AOL's **Theme Parks** Web site.

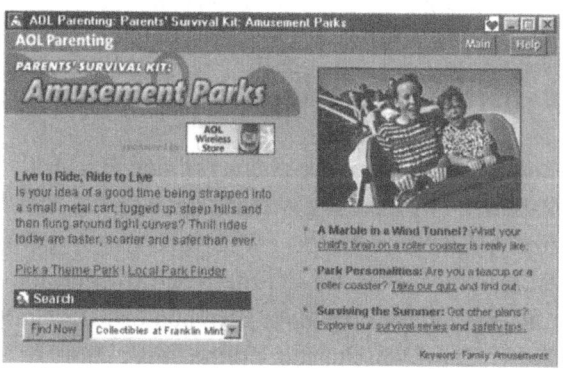

Figure 12-2. Finding family fun on the Family Amusements channel

14 Beaching it with the kids

Does your family enjoy the beach? AOL's Family Beach channel is your all-in-one beach survival kit for parents and kids everywhere. It provides tips and suggestions for happy beaching, building sand castles, creating beach crafts, learning to surf, and more. Make the Family Beach channel your online destination for all your beach needs. Here's how:

Click the **Keyword** button located on the AOL toolbar and enter AOL Keyword: **Family Beach**. Click the **Go** button to display the **Parents' Survival Kit: Beach** channel.

15 Camping with the kids

Would you like your kids to experience nature first hand? AOL's Family Camping channel is your family's doorway to the wild side. You'll learn where the best camps sites are, cooking safety techniques, how to animal proof your campsite, how to teach a child through singing, storytelling, and stargazing. Visit the Family Camping channel and find hiking and walking trails in your area or anywhere in the United States. Here's how:

Click the **Keyword** button located on the AOL toolbar and enter AOL Keyword: **Family Camping**. Click the **Go** button to display the **Parents' Survival Kit: Camping** channel.

16 Planning a safari to your local zoo

AOL's Zoo finder lets you find safaris and zoos close to your home or in another city. You'll understand animal habitat communities and species, encounter animals in real-life settings, locate and visit public land refuges, view photo galleries of animals from around the world, and much more. Visit AOL's Zoos channel for regional wildlife guides, vacation packages, and other great fun for the whole family. Here's how:

Click the **Keyword** button located on the AOL toolbar and enter AOL Keyword: **Zoos**. Click the **Go** button to display AOL's **Safaris and Zoos** Web site.

Family Issues and Relations

17 Deciding whether to work from home or not

AOL's Working Moms and Work from Home channels provide the resources busy moms can use to find balance in their hectic lives. You'll find career topics and a variety of techniques to learn how to take charge of your life: use timesaving tips to make your day more productive, decide whether a career outside the home is right for you, get suggestions on telecommuting, explore daycare options, and even schedule carpools online. There

are also chats, message boards, and much more. Here's how these valuable resources are accessed.

Click the **Keyword** button located on the AOL toolbar and enter AOL Keyword: **Working Moms**. Click the **Go** button to display AOL's **Working Moms** channel, shown in Figure 12-3.

< and >

Click the **Keyword** button located on the AOL toolbar and enter AOL Keyword: **Work from Home**. Click the **Go** button to display AOL's Work from Home channel.

Figure 12-3. Taking charge of your busy schedule on AOL's Working Moms channel

18 Finding reliable daycare for your children

Are you looking for quality daycare for your little one? Find out what the experts think at AOL's Child Care channel. This great site is a must for working parents who need to work but also want the very best care for their children. It provides a built-in search to help you find reliable daycare options in your neighborhood, including nannies, and what legal requirements exist for nanny employers. AOL's Child Care channel is a savior when it comes to daycare issues and solutions. Here's how you can find it:

Click the **Keyword** button located on the AOL toolbar and enter AOL Keyword: **Child Care**. Click the **Go** button to display AOL's **Child Care** channel, shown in Figure 12-4.

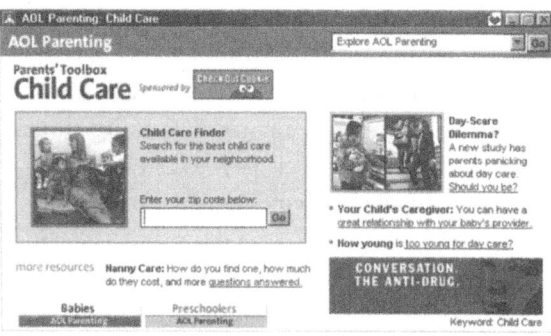

Figure 12-4. Finding neighborhood daycare for your child on AOL's Child Care channel

19 Saving for your family's security

Are you worried about your family's financial security? Do you have escalating credit card debt? AOL's Family Finance channel can help by providing important financial information to families everywhere. You'll learn techniques for building a better financial future, how to curtail out-of-control spending, manage debt, protect your loved ones if the unthinkable should happen, start and fund a 401(k), and stretch your dollars. An online library of finance topics and expense calculators make the Family Finance channel your online destination to ensure a secure tomorrow for you and your family. Here's how to access it:

Click the **Keyword** button located on the AOL toolbar and enter AOL Keyword: **Family Finance**. Click the **Go** button to display AOL's **Family Finance** channel.

20 Understanding finance and money issues

AOL's Personal Finance channel is your all-in-one online financial resource and advisor. You'll find business and financial news, money management techniques, stock reports and charts, mutual fund investing, tax planning guides, free money tips newsletter, real estate tips, refinancing tools, banking and loan resources, chats, message boards, and much more. Make AOL's Personal Finance channel your financial center for fast, accurate, and timely information on finance and money issues. Here's how:

Click the **Keyword** button located on the AOL toolbar and enter AOL Keyword: **Finance**. Click the **Go** button to display AOL's **Personal Finance** channel.

21 Avoiding debt

Would you like to get better control over your spending behavior and find out the effect of compounding your investment savings? AOL's Personal Finance How Much Am I Spending? Web site lets you enter actual versus desired monthly expenditures to see how much money is being spent and where specific cutbacks could increase your personal savings and investment opportunities. You'll learn what effect additional savings off monthly expenses can have when invested and compounded over a 10 year period. Visit the Family Finance channel to learn how investment earnings can make a difference in ensuring a more secure future for you and your family. Here's how:

1. Click the **Keyword** button located on the AOL toolbar and enter AOL Keyword: **Family Finance**. Click the **Go** button to display AOL's **Family Finance** channel.

2. Click **Spend Too Much?** to display the **How Much Am I Spending?** Web site, shown in Figure 12-5.

How Much Am I Spending?

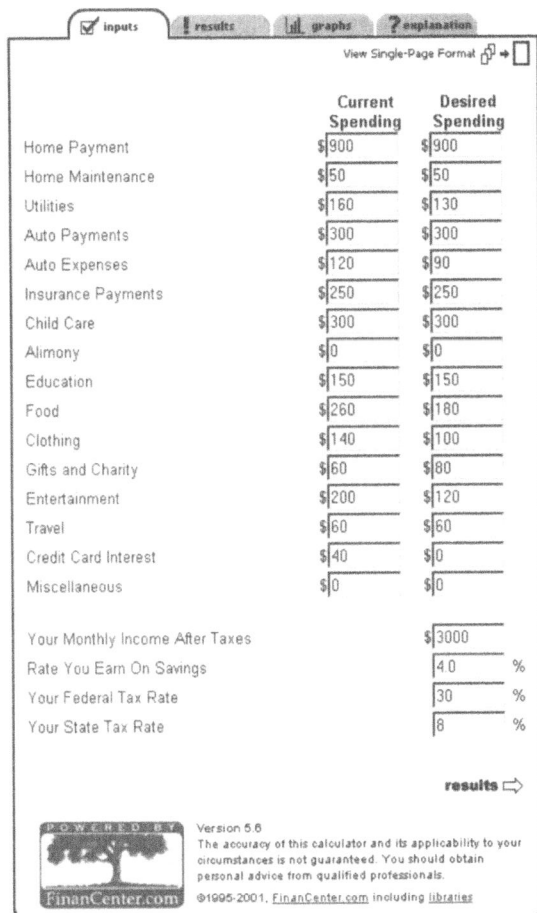

Figure 12-5. Learning compound investing techniques on the Personal Finance Web site

22 Disciplining children

If you're looking for a little advice on how to discipline your kids, AOL's Discipline channel provides tips on what to do when your little one acts up. Find out what your discipline style is, get advice from parents and experts alike, and check out the message boards. Find out how AOL's Discipline channel can help you turn unruly kids back into good kids. Here's how:

Click the **Keyword** button located on the AOL toolbar and enter AOL Keyword: **Discipline**. Click the **Go** button to display AOL's **Discipline** channel.

23 Understanding sibling rivalry

AOL's Sibling Rivalry channel offers a variety of resources to better understand the basis for sibling rivalries. You'll learn the effect of birth order and how it influences sibling personalities, reasons for tensions and problems among siblings, advice on building stronger relationships between siblings, tips, quizzes, and much more. Whether you're a parent or the oldest, middle, youngest, or only child, you won't want to miss AOL's Sibling Rivalry channel for valuable information on why siblings are so important. Here's how it's accessed:

Click the **Keyword** button located on the AOL toolbar and enter AOL Keyword: **Sibling Rivalry**. Click the **Go** button to display AOL's **Sibling Rivalry** channel.

24 Preparing your kids for divorce

Preparing your kids for a divorce is no easy matter. As you would expect, a divorce often brings about many changes not only for the parents, but for the children, too. Not only does divorce mean that there is a loss of the presence of a parent, children often experience an even greater problem. They grieve the loss of a family atmosphere they have come to depend on. It's a very emotional and trying time for children, often resulting in increased stress levels and other problems. AOL's Kids & Divorce channel offers wonderful resources to help parents better understand the difficulties their children are going through and the issues brought on by divorce. As a parent, you have a responsibility to help your kids through this difficult process and to make sure they are equipped to cope with the many changes they will be confronted with. Make AOL's Kids & Divorce channel one of your resources during a divorce crisis. Here's how:

Click the **Keyword** button located on the AOL toolbar and enter AOL Keyword: **Kids & Divorce**. Click the **Go** button to display AOL's **Kids and Divorce** channel.

25 Bonding with stepchildren

The bonding process for parents and stepchildren isn't always easy. AOL's Stepfamilies channel can help parents and children deal with the lifestyle changes stepfamilies often experience by providing advice on building a happy and healthy stepfamily. Learn how to resolve difficult parenting issues through increased communication and realistic expectations, help your children and your spouse's children cope with the lifestyle changes, and build respect for each other's feelings. Visit AOL's Stepfamilies channel for resources that can help you bond with stepchildren. Here's how:

Click the **Keyword** button located on the AOL toolbar and enter AOL Keyword: **Stepfamilies**. Click the **Go** button to display AOL's **Stepfamilies** channel.

26 Coping with elderly parents

People in the United States and other developed nations are living longer and healthier lives, which means many children have to learn to cope with their aging parents. Increased longevity frequently results in unforeseen physical and mental deterioration. Being able to cope with elderly parents as they become less able to care for themselves brings about challenges that, until confronted, are rarely understood. AOL's Caregiving channel provides comprehensive resources to help you better understand the dynamics of the day-to-day support issues as well as the social and emotional needs of your aging parents. You'll also learn how to handle your own issues as caregiver with online search tools, archives of advice and tips from leading experts, chats, message boards, and more. Visit AOL's Caregiving channel for the information you'll need to better cope with the issues confronting families with elderly parents. Here's how:

1. Click the **Keyword** button located on the AOL toolbar and enter AOL Keyword: **Caregiver**. Click the **Go** button to display AOL's **Caregiving** channel, shown in Figure 12-6.

2. Double-click the folder of interest from the list of topics displayed in the selection window.

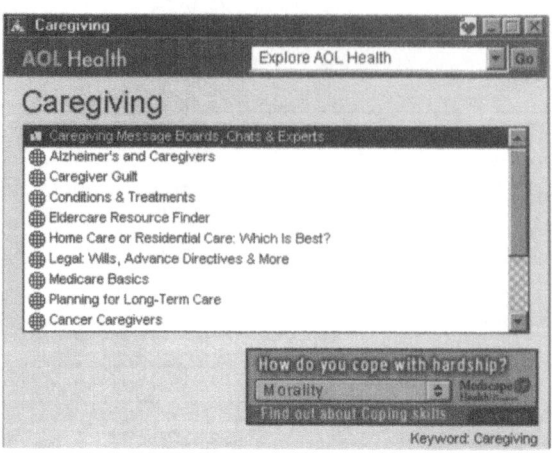

Figure 12-6. Finding resources to cope with aging parents on AOL's Caregiving channel

27 Seeking help with elder care

If you're seeking help with elder care, Learning Network's Elder Care Resources Web site is for you. You'll find wonderful articles, and tools to help you find the proper care for your loved ones. This site offers a free newsletter, articles covering the basics of finding the right care to long term care insurance, including how to identify elder abuse and stop it, planning your health care decisions in advance, and much more. Get the help you need in finding the best care for your loved ones. Here's how:

1. Click the **Keyword** button located on the AOL toolbar and enter AOL Keyword: **Family Issues**. Click the **Go** button to display AOL's **Family Issues** channel.

2. Select the **Elder Care** folder in the Info A-Z drop-down selection box and click the **Go** button to display the **Learning Network's Elder Care Resources** Web site.

28 Coping with loss

Coping with loss, personal grief, or other tragic situations can be difficult for families, and especially children, to handle. Often it's important to find adult and child support groups and centers so that everyone involved can cope with the loss. AOL's Coping With Loss channel provides numerous resources for being able to handle emotional issues in times of crisis. You'll find articles and other resources on emotional and grief management, handling fear, understanding death, dealing with sadness, finding hope in faith, maintaining your health, support chats, message boards, and much more. Here's how to access this channel:

Click the **Keyword** button located on the AOL toolbar and enter AOL Keyword: **Coping With Loss**. Click the **Go** button to display AOL's **Coping With Loss** channel.

29 Sharing your sympathy with others

For families experiencing loss, grief, or sadness, receiving a sympathy greeting can be a heart-warming and welcome gesture of caring and kindness. American Greetings.com is your online source of electronic cards. You'll find several types of sympathy cards that you can customize and send including cards expressing loss of a loved one, loss of a pet, and Spanish language greetings. Show your concern and share your sympathy with others by sending an American Greetings.com's sympathy card:

1. Click the **Keyword** button located on the AOL toolbar and enter AOL Keyword: **Coping with Loss**. Click the **Go** button to display AOL's **Coping With Loss** channel.

2. Click **Send Cards** under **Share Your Sympathy** section to display **American Greetings.com Sympathy Cards** Web site, shown in Figure 12-7.

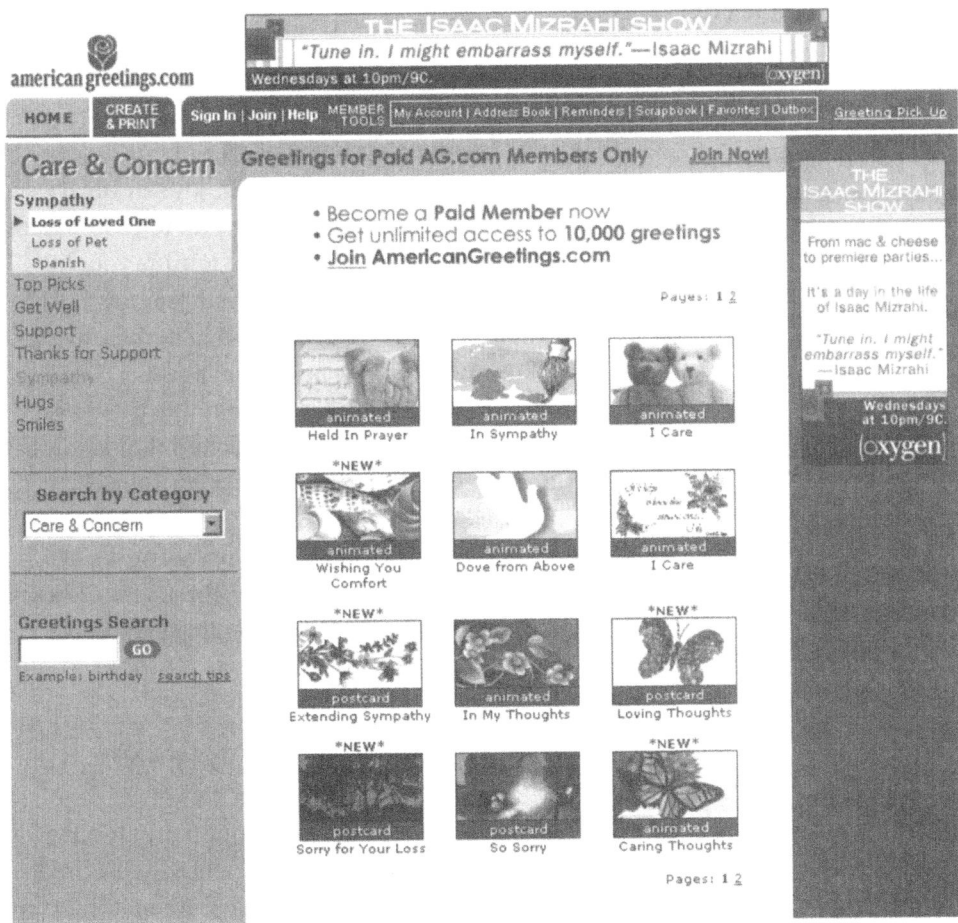

Figure 12-7. Sharing your sympathy with others on American Greetings.com's Web site

30 Communicating with people who share your spirituality

Connect with people who share your same spiritual beliefs. AOL's Spirituality Web site provides thought-provoking articles, tips, and expert advice on all religious communities and denominations. You'll also be able to request a free newsletter to be sent to your e-mail address. Here's how:

Click the **Keyword** button located on the AOL toolbar and enter AOL Keyword: **Spirituality**. Click the **Go** button to display AOL's **Lifestyles Community- Spirituality** Web site.

Family Living and Parenting

31 Parenting tips

AOL's Parenting channel provides wonderful information for parents everywhere. You'll find insightful parenting advice, parenting tips by age, work and family issues, entertainment, news, single parent topics, health warnings, parenting with a disability, and an assortment of tools such as coupons, a newsletter, chats, and message boards. Here's how to visit AOL's Parenting channel:

Click the **Keyword** button located on the AOL toolbar and enter AOL Keyword: **Parenting**. Click the **Go** button to display AOL's **Parenting** channel.

32 Accessing the Parents Hotline for expert advice

AOL provides a 24/7-advice hotline for parents. AOL's Parents Hotline channel provides a community of leading experts—parents who help answer the questions and issues important to parents everywhere. From baby to teen issues, parenting tips to safety alerts, child health to family issues, you'll find electronic postings on a variety of topics. Access AOL's Parents hotline channel to get answers to your questions from other parents. Here's how:

1. Click the **Keyword** button located on the AOL toolbar and enter AOL Keyword: **Parents Hotline**. Click the **Go** button to display AOL's **Parenting Hotline** channel.

2. Click **Enter Help Area** to list, read, and find posts and answers by parents everywhere.

33 Understanding baby's early years

The early years of a baby's life are often referred to as the bonding years between baby and parent. This is the time when you and your baby build a healthy and loving relationship that will endure throughout your lives. AOL's Parenting Babies channel offers a variety of resources including month-by-month baby development guidelines, immunization schedules, baby feeding and nutrition advice, breastfeeding guidelines, baby safety tips, and sleep problem tips.. Visit AOL's Parenting Babies channel and develop a better understanding of your baby's early years. Here's how:

Click the **Keyword** button located on the AOL toolbar and enter AOL Keyword: **Baby** or **Babies**. Click the **Go** button to display AOL's **Parenting Babies** channel.

34 Understanding the preschooler years

AOL's Preschoolers channel provides resources galore for how to experience the joys and deal with the challenges of a preschool child. You'll find great articles, tips, and guidelines to nurture your little one's developmental needs. From learning how to handle bed-wetting issues to what the best toys are to buy, and managing health and learning disability issues to finding out various learning resources. AOL's Preschooler channel is your online resource for children in their preschool years. Here's how it's accessed:

Click the **Keyword** button located on the AOL toolbar and enter AOL Keyword: **Preschool**. Click the **Go** button to display AOL's **Parenting Preschoolers** channel.

35 Understanding the grade school years

Does your child possess a unique natural ability for mathematics, music, art, or science? AOL's Grade Schoolers channel provides a wealth of resources that can help you identify your child's innate abilities while nurturing hidden talents. You'll find an assortment of self-help tools including techniques for improving a child's grades, a quiz to identify and nurture a child's inner abilities, an online homework helper, discipline issues and techniques, science fair project ideas, chats, and message boards. AOL's Grade Schoolers channel is an online resource that you and your child will benefit from using. Here's how:

Click the **Keyword** button located on the AOL toolbar and enter AOL Keyword: **Grade School**. Click the **Go** button to display AOL's **Parenting Grade Schoolers** channel.

36 Understanding the teen years

As your child enters the teen years, a series of new challenges and issues can arise. The pressures facing today's kids are immense. From issues such as peer pressure to fashion trends, from relationship and behavioral problems to various forms of depression, a teen's world is a pressure-cooker of contrasts and contradictions. AOL's Parenting Teens channel provides valuable resources for parents of today's teens. You'll find articles, tips, and guidelines for preteen, teen, and late teen issues and concerns. Visit AOL's Parenting Teens channel for insightful tips and techniques on being a supportive and responsible parent to your. Here's how:

Click the **Keyword** button located on the AOL toolbar and enter AOL Keyword: **Parenting Teens**. Click the **Go** button to display AOL's **Parenting Teens** channel.

37 Accessing a variety of parenting tools

If you're looking for an all-in-one resource of valuable parenting tools then look no further. AOL's Parents' Toolbox channel provides basic parenting tools such as a baby namer, a baby registry, childcare resources, a homework helper, local activity guides, and parents' hotline, to list just a few. It also provides tools for want-to-be parents such as fertility advice recommendations, ovulation detection kits, and conception advice. For soon-to-be parents, an assortment of tools can be found including a baby budget calculator, trimester checklists, tips for choosing a pediatrician, pregnancy calendar, and personalized birth plan. Infant and toddler care tips are available, including an immunization

guide, a sleep deprivation checklist, and medicine chest checklist. Parents of preschoolers also have an assortment of essential tools including a kindergarten readiness checklist, social and emotional development guidelines, and vaccination guidelines. Plus, you can request a free newsletter to keep you informed of new and revised parenting tools, as well as other useful guidelines. Make AOL's Parents' Toolbox your online destination for all your parenting needs. Here's how:

Click the **Keyword** button located on the AOL toolbar and enter AOL Keyword: **Parents Toolbox**. Click the **Go** button to display AOL's **Parents' Toolbox** channel, shown in Figure 12-8.

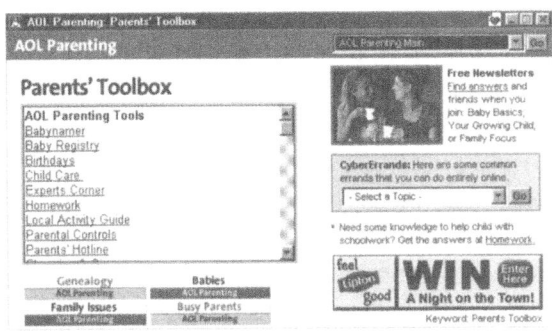

Figure 12-8. AOL's Parents' Toolbox channel is a parent's best online resource for information.

38 Finding romance after baby

Has the romance gone out of your bedroom after baby? Do you find little or no time for each other now that your baby has arrived? Has your libido done the disappearing act due to hormonal loss during pregnancy? AOL's Sex After Baby channel provides wonderful information on how you as parents can light that fire again and find a little romance. You'll discover how you can make time for each other, and once again experience the joys that come from romance with your partner. AOL's Sex After Baby channel is a must resource for parents wanting to find and put a little romance back into their lives. Here's how:

Click the **Keyword** button located on the AOL toolbar and enter AOL Keyword: **Sex After Baby**. Click the **Go** button to display AOL's **Is There Sex After Baby?** channel.

39 Learning to be a good dad

As a dad, you want to be a major positive influence in your child's life. Recent studies show that more dads are learning not only to be dads, but also to be good dads. However, learning to be a good dad isn't always easy. AOL's Dad channel can help by letting you get involved in all aspects of your child's life. You'll find insightful information on the challenges facing dads everywhere, as well as tips, advice, and guidelines that dads can follow. Learn to become a great father figure to your child. Here's how:

Click the **Keyword** button located on the AOL toolbar and enter AOL Keyword: **Dad**. Click the **Go** button to display AOL's **Parenting Dads** channel.

40 Being Mr. Mom

Recent statistics show that more and more moms are returning to work after baby is born than ever before. This means that more dads are staying home to care for baby, clean the house, and perform other duties once performed by mom. Parents often decide on this type of arrangement because the wife makes more money, they want to have their child cared for by a parent, or for a host of other reasons. AOL's Mr. Mom channel offers tips, advice, and guidelines for dads who have hung up their suits and work boots in favor of diapers and caring for their child. You'll find an assortment of must-read articles and other help areas including the challenges and issues faced by Mr. Mom, online support groups, chats, message boards, and much more. Here's how it's accessed:

Click the **Keyword** button located on the AOL toolbar and enter AOL Keyword: **Mr. Mom**. Click the **Go** button to display AOL's **Parenting Mr. Mom** channel.

41 Teaching your kids to love sports

Are your kids active in sports? Are you a fan or a fanatic when it comes to your kids' sporting events? Would you like to see your kids act less like couch potatoes and be more active in sports? AOL's Kids & Sports channel gives you the information you need as a parent to become your child's biggest fan. You'll find wonderful resources to help you coordinate your responsibilities as a working parent with your kid's sporting activities, find the right sport(s) for your child to participate in, find the right coach to work with your child, and much more. If your child is active in sports, you must visit AOL's Kids & Sports channel. Here's how:

Click the **Keyword** button located on the AOL toolbar and enter AOL Keyword: **Kids and Sports**. Click the **Go** button to display AOL's **Parenting Kids and Sports** channel.

42 Homeschooling tips

Is your child being taught in a homeschooling type of program? Have you decided to homeschool your children? Do you want to identify existing support groups that can provide a pre-packaged curriculum? Homeschooling is legal in all 50 states in the United States, although each state has its own unique requirements. AOL's Homeschooling Web site provides valuable information and other resources to help you develop a top-notch homeschooling curriculum. You'll find homeschooling curricula, teacher's aides and supplies, resource books, workbooks, arts and crafts ideas, support groups, chats, message boards, and more. Make AOL's Homeschooling Web site the one destination for your home schooling needs. Here's how:

Click the **Keyword** button located on the AOL toolbar and enter AOL Keyword: **Homeschooling**. Click the **Go** button to display AOL's Parenting **Homeschooling** Web site.

43 Setting Internet parental controls for your children

You can control what type of access is available for a particular screen name through parental controls. AOL's Parental Control channel lets you assign a safety net for members to prevent unauthorized contact by other members while online. This feature controls member access while using Instant Message, chat rooms, newsgroups, message boards, and other online communication mediums. AOL lets you set parental controls for the following age categories:

• Kids Only (ages 12 and under)

- Young Teens (ages 13–15)

- Mature Teens (ages 16–17)

- General Access (ages 18 and older)

Here's how you can set parental controls for any screen name:

1. Verify that you're currently signed on as the primary or "Master" screen name.

2. Select **Parental Controls** from the **Settings** menu on the AOL toolbar or click the **Keyword** button located on the AOL toolbar and enter AOL Keyword: **Parental Controls**. Click the **Go** button to display AOL's **Parental Controls** channel.

3. Select the screen name you want to assign parental control settings for from the **Edit controls for:** list.

4. Click **Chat control** under the **Custom Controls** heading in the **Parental Controls** window.

5. Click the check box corresponding to the option you want to allow or restrict chat options, and click the **Save** button.

44 Online safety tips

A safe online environment is something every family member should have and enjoy. Protect your family from online viruses, hoaxes, and scams. Here are a few safety tips your children should remember each time they get online:

- Tell your parents about any bad or threatening language you see.

- Never give your AOL password to anyone, ever.

- Never tell anyone your name, address, telephone number, or school name without your parents' permission.

- Never respond to anyone who makes you feel bad, uncomfortable, or unsafe. Instead, contact keyword: **Tell AOL**. Remember that people aren't always who they say they are.

- Get your parents' permission before telling someone you'll meet them in person.

- Never accept e-mails, file attachments, pictures, or Web site addresses from someone you don't know.

- Don't degrade, harass, or discriminate against other people.

- Don't swear or use vulgar language.

AOL's Neighborhood Watch channel provides important information to help you and your family have an enjoyable online experience. Here's how you'll be able to control your kids' online safety, manage junk mail, avoid viruses and Trojan horse programs, and much more:

1. Click the **Keyword** button located on the AOL toolbar and enter AOL Keyword: **Security** or **Safety** or **Neighborhood**. Click the **Go** button to display AOL's Neighborhood **Watch** channel, shown in Figure 12-9.

2. Click the **Online Safety Tips** link to display AOL's **Online Safety Tips** channel.

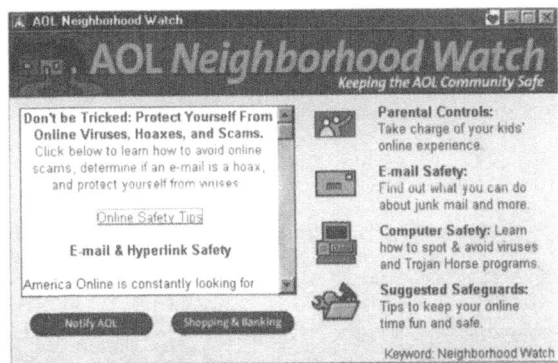

Figure 12-9. Ensuring online safety and enjoyment with AOL's Neighborhood Watch channel

45 Understanding past generations

Are you looking for long-lost relatives? Do you want to research your surname on the Internet? AOL's Genealogy and Roots channels provide online resources to help you search for your ancestors. You'll find the most common surnames, be able to access census data and government resources, records by state, chats, message boards, genealogy books, and much more. Discover who your ancestors were and where your roots began on AOL's Genealogy and Roots channels. Here's how:

Click the **Keyword** button located on the AOL toolbar and enter AOL Keyword: **Genealogy**. Click the **Go** button to display AOL's **Parenting Genealogy channel**.

< and >

Click the **Keyword** button located on the AOL toolbar and enter AOL Keyword: **Roots**. Click the **Go** button to display the **Golden Gate Genealogy Forum** channel.

46 Considering adoption

Are you one of the millions of couples who want a child but are unable to conceive? There are many resources that can help including infertility treatments, drugs, or in vitro. But if you've already tried these methods or prefer not to experiment with these approaches, you may want to consider growing your family through adoption. AOL's Thinking About Adoption? channel provides valuable resources to help you decide what approach is best for you. You'll find articles, state-by-state summaries of adoption laws, advice centers, agency resources to help locate the child of your dreams, support centers, databases of photographs, chats, message boards, books, and much

more. Growing your family through adoption is a wonderful way to express your love. Here's how:

Click the **Keyword** button located on the AOL toolbar and enter AOL Keyword: **Adoption**. Click the **Go** button to display AOL's **Parenting Thinking About Adoption?** channel.

Resources for Families— Family Services

47 Accessing Sesame Workshop

You and your child will love the wonderful stories, coloring pages, letter and number games, and other special activities on K.O. Jr's Sesame Street and Sesame Workshop Web site. You'll find parent and kids resources including games, stories, art, music, mail, Elmo's World, TV information, and much more. Here's how to access a Web site that will be sure to give your child hours of fun and be a great learning tool:

Click the **Keyword** button located on the AOL toolbar and enter AOL Keyword: **Sesame Street**. Click the **Go** button to display **K.O. Jr. Sesame Street** Web site, shown in Figure 12-10.

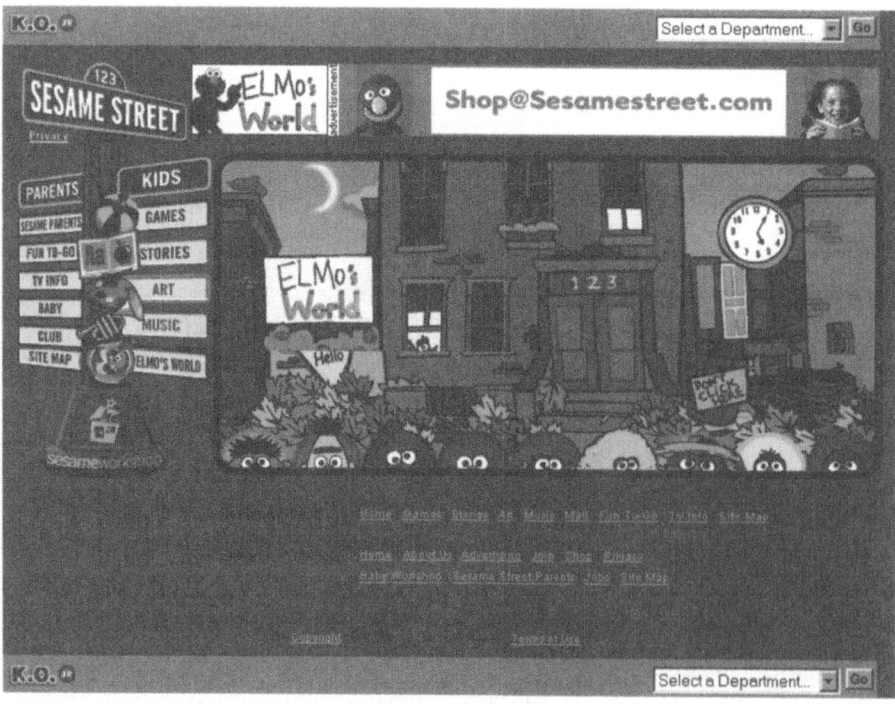

Figure 12-10. Exploring stories, games, art, and other fun things on the Sesame Street Web site

48 Reading as a family—the family newsstand

Do you enjoy browsing popular magazines while you relax? Would you like your very own newsstand delivered right in your home or office? AOL's Families Newsstand channel lets you browse magazines anytime you like. You'll find publications for women, men, and children including Better Homes and Gardens, Consumer Reports, Cosmopolitan, Country Living, Family PC, Good Housekeeping, Home Magazine Online, Home Office Computing, Home PC, House Beautiful, Marie Claire, Metropolitan Home, Parenting, Redbook, Seventeen Online, Teen People, Travel & Leisure Magazine, and many more. Access AOL's Families Newsstand channel and never have to leave home again for your favorite magazines. They're yours anytime, 24 hours a day, 7 days a week. Here's where you'll find them:

Click the **Keyword** button located on the AOL toolbar and enter AOL Keyword: **Families Newsstand**. Click the **Go** button to display AOL's **Parenting Newsstand** channel.

49 Learning to read

Do you want your children to develop strong reading skills? Has your child developed pre-reading skills such as storytelling? Do you know what signs to look for to determine if your child has a reading problem? AOL's Learning to Read channel provides valuable resources to help your child develop good reading skills. You'll find articles, parent tips, and expert advice on reading diagnostic tools, resources for parents, phonics resources, software, chats, message boards, and much more. Develop your child's reading skills on AOL's Learning to Read channel. Here's how:

Click the **Keyword** button located on the AOL toolbar and enter AOL Keyword: **Learning to Read**. Click the **Go** button to display AOL's **Learning to Read** channel.

50 Becoming a great storyteller

Storytelling is a marvelous way for parents to communicate to a child. It's also a way for young children to cross the boundaries of reality to the world of make believe. Stories help a child view a problem in an optimistic way and then teach the child how it can be solved. This serves a useful purpose that will help them throughout their lives. AOL's Storytelling channel provides advice on how parents can tell stories that teach children valuable lessons, encourage kids to seek and develop creative thoughts and ideas, build an interest in cultural themes, pass family history from generation to generation, and much more. Access AOL's Storytelling channel and you'll learn to become a great storyteller for your child. Here's how:

Click the **Keyword** button located on the AOL toolbar and enter AOL Keyword: **Storytelling**. Click the **Go** button to display AOL's **Parenting Storytelling** channel.

51 Getting started with a family scrapbook

Preserve a piece of your family's history for future generations. Get your children, loved ones, and friends involved in creating lasting memories that will endure for a lifetime. AOL's Family Scrapbook channel shows how to organize childhood memories, how to make baby scrapbook pages, how kids can make their own scrapbooks, how to restore and preserve photographs, how to add a family tree to your scrapbook, and much more. See how you can preserve precious memories of your children, loved ones, and friends on AOL's Family Scrapbook channel. Here's how:

Click the **Keyword** button located on the AOL toolbar and enter AOL Keyword: **Family Scrapbook**. Click the **Go** button to display AOL's **Parenting Family Scrapbook** channel.

52 Learning for the whole family

AOL's Learning Network Web site is an all-in-one resource for parents, families, teachers, and kids of all ages. You'll find articles, tips and expert advice for parents, teachers, and kids, homework help by grade, an idea exchange, gift ideas, recipes, lesson planning resources, teacher tools, free software, professional development resources, e-mail newsletters, chats, message boards, and much more. Make AOL's Learning Network your choice for stimulating ideas, chat, and a variety of resources anytime and anyplace. Here's how:

Click the **Keyword** button located on the AOL toolbar and enter AOL Keyword: **Learning Network**. Click the **Go** button to display AOL's **Research & Learn Learning Network** Web site.

53 Volunteering in your local PTA

Are you interested in improving the education, health, and safety of children in your local community? Parent-Teacher Associations (PTAs) consist of volunteers who work closely with home and school to provide students with every possible advantage in intellectual and physical education. Working with public and private schools at the elementary, junior high, and high school levels, each PTA develops programs to suit the needs of its school and community. AOL provides online resources to help interested parents and teachers better understand what Parent-Teacher Organizations are all about. Here's how you'll be able to find this useful information:

1. Click the **Keyword** button located on the AOL toolbar and enter AOL Keyword: **Education** or **Homework**. Click the **Go** button to display AOL's **Homework Help** channel.

2. Enter **PTA** in the **Encyclopedia Search** field and click the **Search** button to display the **World Book Encyclopedia's Parent-Teacher Organizations** Web site.

3. Click the article that interests you from the search results displayed. For example, clicking **Parent-teacher organizations** displays information about PTAs as volunteer groups.

54 Planning a party or other event

Are you planning a party or other event anytime soon? Whether you're throwing a birthday or dinner party, anniversary celebration, backyard BBQ, beach party, or celebrating any other event, AOL's Invitations Web site makes party planning as easy as 1-2-3. All you do is create a graphical AOL invitation, come up with a list of e-mail addresses, and AOL Invitations does the rest. Once this is

done, your guests open your invitation containing a link to the AOL Invitation site describing your event. Each guest then sends an RSVP indicating their decision of Yes, No, or Maybe along with an optional comment. Here's how it's accessed:

1. Click the **Keyword** button located on the AOL toolbar and enter AOL Keyword: **Party Planner**. Click the **Go** button to display AOL's **Invitations** Web site.

2. Select the appropriate event under the categories **Celebration** or **Parties**, shown in Figure 12-11.

Another popular way AOL users can plan a party is to access AOL's Holiday Party channel. You'll find exciting ideas, tips, and expert advice on delicious snack recipes, how to send invitations, party tips, self-help party guides, where to buy party supplies, and much more. Visit AOL's Holiday Party channel the next time you plan that special party. Here's how:

Click the **Keyword** button located on the AOL toolbar and enter AOL Keyword: **Holiday Party**. Click the **Go** button to display AOL's **Holiday Party** channel.

Figure 12-11. Sending invitations for a party or event is simple on AOL's Invitations Web site.

55 Accessing You've Got Pictures

Would you like to share pictures of loved ones and friends with others online? AOL's You've Got Pictures channel provides advice, tips, and links to photo processing services to help you share your pictures with anyone else. You'll be able to request a free starter kit containing sample pictures of your film, upload pictures, receive photo quality prints, visit the photo gallery, create holiday photo scrapbooks, and much more. Access AOL's You've Got Pictures channel for all your photo needs. Here's how:

Click the **Keyword** button located on the AOL toolbar and enter AOL Keyword: **Pictures**. Click the **Go** button to display AOL's **You've Got Pictures** channel, shown in Figure 12-12.

Figure 12-12. Creating holiday photo scrapbooks on AOL's You've Got Pictures channel

56 Listening to Internet Radio

You can listen to music and talk radio on the Internet if you're using the Windows 95/98/2000/ME/XP operating system, have a sound card and speakers connected to your computer, a 28.8Kbps or faster modem, AOL version 5.0 or higher, RealPlayer G2 or higher, and a stable connection to the Internet. The Radio@AOL channel provides more than 75-programmed AOL stations for your listening pleasure including classical, country, jazz, inspirational, Latin, lite sounds, news, sports, talk, pop, rock, rap, hip-hop, soundtracks, and more. You'll also be able to listen to exclusive performances and live interviews by popular artists. Visit the Radio@AOL channel anytime for your 24/7 listening pleasure. Here's how:

Click the **Keyword** button located on the AOL toolbar and enter AOL Keyword: **Radio**. Click the **Go** button to display the **Radio@AOL** channel.

Information Superhighway

Part Three

Advanced Topics

CHAPTER 13

Privacy and Security

ENSURING COMPUTER PRIVACY from unwanted exposures and outside forces due to security violations, terms of service violations, viruses, and Trojan horse programs isn't an option—it's a must. AOL offers a variety of methods to control privacy preferences via communication mediums such as e-mail and chat, as well as account controls like passwords, marketing, and newsgroups. AOL also offers expert advice on maintaining a computer's health and well being by safeguarding against viruses and Trojan horse programs, which appear to perform a valid function but are designed to steal private information from your computer. These types of problems and issues not only raise frustration levels, they hinder productivity, and in the worst cases, may cause you lost or damaged data. Whether you're a seasoned AOL expert or new to AOL, you'll find AOL services and features to help with privacy and security issues and their resolutions.

In this chapter, you'll learn how to:

- Handle e-mail issues and solutions

- Set and modify parental controls for a safe and secure online experience

- Set Instant Messenger and newsgroup controls

- Shop and bank safely and securely from your own home

E-mail Issues and Solutions

1 Ensuring e-mail privacy

Ensuring and maintaining e-mail privacy is crucial, and AOL members have a couple methods to ensure their privacy. The easiest method is to send messages using a process referred to as a blind courtesy copy (BCC). This protects the privacy of the address you specify in a blind copy. It also speeds up the process of opening an e-mail message—since fewer addresses are displayed. To specify a blind courtesy copy for an e-mail address, simply surround each e-mail address in parentheses, e.g., (KPLConsultant). To specify a blind courtesy copy for a group of e-mail addresses, separate each address with a comma and then add parentheses around the entire set of addresses, e.g., (KPLConsultant, MacFamily).

> *You can use the Address Book window to send blind copies too—just click the Blind Copy button.*

The second method of ensuring e-mail privacy is to block advertisements from businesses, offers from adult-oriented sites, chain letters, and countless other types of unwelcome and unsolicited junk mail. Never again will you be forced to take time away from your busy schedule to delete mail you have no interest in and never asked for. AOL makes it easy to eliminate unsolicited junk mail, known as spam, while giving you greater control over your e-mail situation. Here's how:

1. Click the **Settings** menu button on the AOL toolbar, and select **Parental Controls**.

2. Click **Set Parental Controls** from the AOL **Parental Controls** window.

3. In the **Edit controls for:** field, select the **screen name** you want to block junk mail for.

4. Click the **E-mail control** button on the **Parental Controls** window.

5. Choose the settings you prefer from the **AOL Mail Controls window** and click the **Next** button, shown in Figure 13-1.

6. Click the **Yes** button corresponding to the prompt, **Are you sure you want to block all e-mail?**

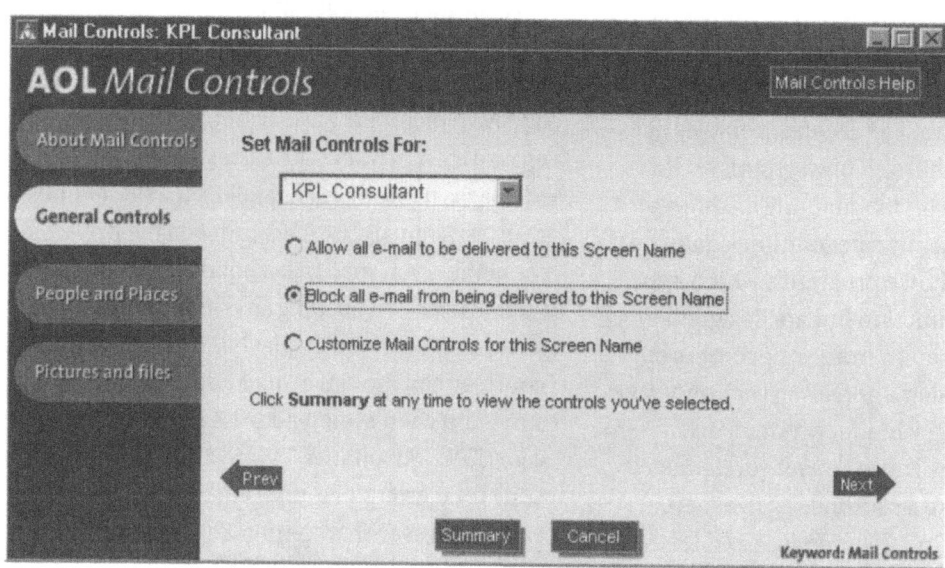

Figure 13-1. Blocking all e-mail on AOL's Mail Controls channel

2 Recognizing unsolicited bulk e-mail or junk mail

Unsolicited e-mail, commonly referred to as junk mail, is a problem for every Internet user. It's almost always invasive, annoying, and all too often offensive in nature. AOL members should be on the lookout for this troubling form of unsolicited mail. You may want to set up who you can receive mail, pictures, and files from by using mail controls for any and all of your screen names (discussed in Chapter 2 in the Junk E-mail section). In the absence of mail controls, you can resort to a less than scientific method of identifying junk mail.

Although no perfect technique exists for identifying junk mail, here are a few ways that I've used over the years. So before you click, keep these tips in mind:

1. **Inspect who sent you the e-mail.** Is it someone you know? If not, then it probably can be classified as unsolicited, and taken a step further, treated as junk mail.

   🖊 *It is common practice for junk mail senders to use invalid mail addresses in the "from" and "reply-to" fields so that if you try to contact them using these addresses the message usually gets sent back to you as being Undeliverable.*

2. **Inspect the subject line carefully.** Frequently, junk mailers use alluring words such as "Free," "Hot," or "Sex," in the subject line to entice you to open the mail and any attachments. Other times a catch phrase is used to attract your curiosity such as "Don't Miss This Opportunity," "Work from Home Part-time," "You've Been Approved," "Want To Be Your Own Boss," and "Make More Money." Another favorite trick is to infer some level of familiarity with you or someone you know such as "Great Meeting You Last Week," "Here Are the Slides You Requested," or "Your Wife Asked For ..." The general rule of thumb is that if you don't recognize who the sender is and the subject line implies something too good to be true, it can probably be treated as junk mail. You should avoid opening any message when you're unable to interpret what the subject line is saying.

3. **Be skeptical of official sounding addresses.** Junk mailers will go to any means to get you to open their message—including using addresses with official sounding names such as TechSupp7, Admin33, or Dept321.

4. **If in doubt, never open an attachment or picture**, and never click on a hyperlink in the mail. These actions can lead to unwanted viruses.

3 Reporting junk mail to America Online

Naturally you can delete any and all junk mail you receive. But you can step up your campaign a notch and do something about the nuisance created by junk e-mailers. Here's how: When you receive any junk mail that violates AOL's Terms of Service, forward the junk mail through e-mailing to screen name TOSEmail1. If the junk mail contains an attached file, forward it to screen name TOSFILES. For all other types of junk mail, forward it to screen name TOSSPAM. AOL will review and take the necessary and appropriate action against the junk e-mailer.

4 Understanding e-mail scams and schemes

E-mail scams occur all the time. In an attempt to access your AOL billing and password information, thieves may try to get you to download files that break into you computer, ask you to click hyperlinks that automatically download computer viruses, or ask you to enter your screen name and password on official-looking Web sites. These types of scams frequently result in damage to your computer system or the transmission of crucial information such as passwords and other account information. With this type of information, a scammer can then access your account in your name, read your e-mail, send e-mail under your screen name, make online purchases, and cause havoc everywhere they go. You should never enter your AOL screen name and password into an unknown Web site, and never click on hyperlinks sent to you by strangers in e-mails.

5 Keeping your identity anonymous

Every AOL account can have a maximum of seven screen names (or e-mail addresses) assigned. A screen name is your unique alias to the online world, and is the way others find you in cyberspace. It's recommended to keep your identity anonymous. By doing this, you maintain a level of privacy and security from undesirable Internet users. AOL provides separate passwords, mailboxes, filing cabinets, and favorite places for each screen name. The screen name you specify is yours to use each time you sign on to AOL. It's considered your primary master screen name, and once assigned can never be deleted or changed.

6 Understanding viruses and Trojan horses

Computer viruses and Trojan Horse programs have been known to destroy or erase computer files stored on hard drives, open up your AOL account to theft or vandalism, or contain attachments consisting of objectionable content. To minimize the possibility of infiltrating your computer with a virus or Trojan horse program, install an anti-virus software program to scan files you download, and never download a file from a stranger. Also, avoid electronic greeting card scams where someone sends you what appears to be a greeting card, but in actuality contains a Trojan horse program. Not only can these types of programs compromise your computer system, they can access your account and billing information without you knowing it.

7 Virus protection tips

Viruses can make your computer run slower, delete or damage files on your hard drive, prevent you from accessing the Internet, and get you bumped off the Internet more frequently. They result in heightened frustration levels, lower productivity, and the worst situation of all, lost or damaged files. Downloading a file attached to your e-mail can spreads viruses. The best advice for preventing the spread of viruses is to follow these simple tips:

- Keep your anti-virus software up-to-date. McAffee and Norton offer the latest updates and can be downloaded for a small fee.

- Never download files sent in e-mails from strangers.

- Never click hyperlinks sent in e-mails from strangers.

8 Protecting yourself from Trojan horses

Trojan horse programs are basically programs that appear to perform a valid function, but destructive forces hidden within the code itself cause damage to your computer. They are often designed to access your AOL account, password, and billing information. Guarding against Trojan horse programs is

relatively easy, but you'll need to follow a few simple tips:

- Install anti-virus software on your system.

- Apply recent anti-virus updates as they become available. Inoculating your computer with the latest anti-virus updates often prevents the spread of Trojan horse programs.

- Never download files attached to your e-mail from strangers.

9 Understanding what you can do if you've been infected with a virus

If you suspect your computer has been infected with a virus, or you feel your standard anti-virus software has either failed to detect the virus or isn't able to eliminate it, you'll need to follow these simple steps to remove the virus:

1. Identify the virus, if possible, by going to AOL's **Anti-Virus Computer Community**. Enter AOL Keyword: **Anti Virus Community**, shown in Figure 13-2.

2. Click either **PC: Anti-Virus Downloads** or **Mac: Anti-Virus Downloads** under the **Features** heading depending on the type of computer you're using.

3. Select the subject from the listed items in the **Anti-Virus & Security** window, and click the **Read Description** button to view the purpose of each program or update.

4. Download the program or update by clicking the **Download Now** button.

5. Navigate to the desired directory and click the **Save** button.

6. Run the downloaded program or anti-virus update to remove the virus.

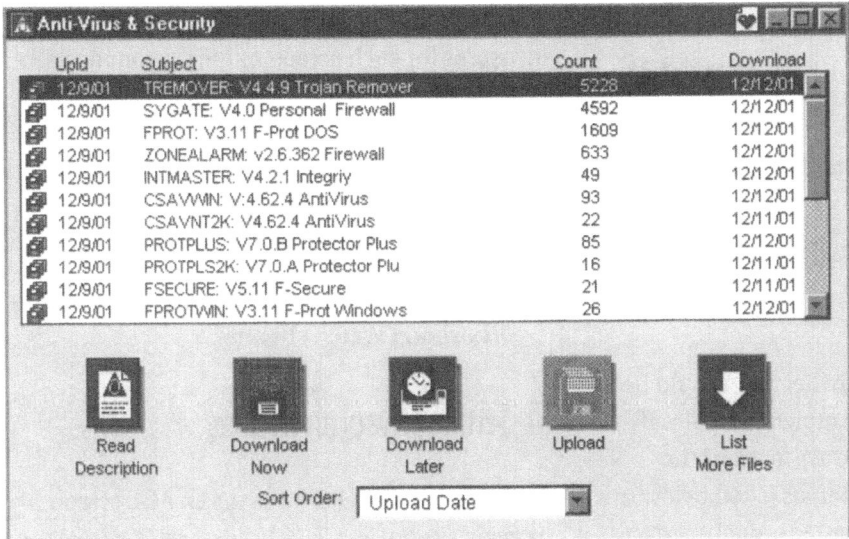

Figure 13-2. Downloading anti-virus programs and files to your computer

10 Accessing anti-virus message boards

AOL's Anti-Virus message boards provide an electronic community of helpful discussion on virus-protection issues, programs, and updates. You'll find like-minded individuals asking for help in understanding virus- and Trojan horse-related problems and issues, program and anti-virus updates, removal tools, and much more. Here's how to get the help you need:

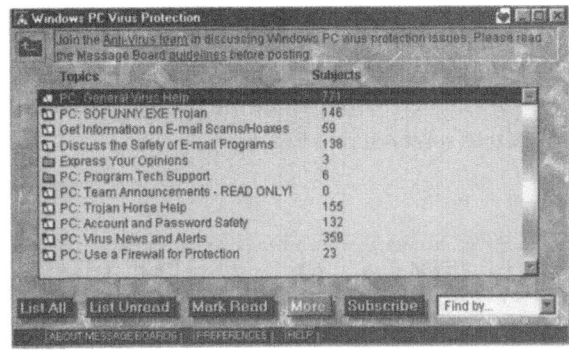

Figure 13-3. Getting answers to anti-virus protection questions via electronic message boards

1. Click the Keyword button on the AOL toolbar and enter AOL Keyword: **Virus**.

2. Click the **Go** button to display AOL's **Anti-Virus Center** channel.

3. Click **Anti-Virus Message Boards** to display the **Anti-Virus Center**. Double-click the topic that interests you from the items listed.

4. Double-click the folder of interest from the items listed, shown in Figure 13-3.

11 Using anonymous remailers

An anonymous remailer is basically a computer service that provides anonymity to e-mail. What this means is that anonymous remailers protect

the identity or privacy of the person sending an e-mail message as well as the person receiving the e-mail message. This level of privacy represents an important service for people who wish to express opinions about something while remaining anonymous. An increasing number of people are abusing e-mail by spamming and flaming (sending insulting e-mail), making the concern for privacy more important. Consequently, anonymous remailers let you maintain anonymity while you continue to go about your business. Although AOL doesn't offer anonymous remailer services, there are countless free as well as for-a-fee organizations. Here's how you can find them:

1. Click the Keyword button on the AOL toolbar and enter AOL Keyword: **Remailers**.

2. Click the **Go** button to display AOL's search results on remailers.

3. Click the remailer of interest from the list.

12 Contacting AOL Security with e-mail security violations

Violations of the AOL Terms of Service should be reported in e-mail or in a file attached to e-mail. When reporting violators, always forward the violating mail to the screen names listed below. AOL can't accept copied and pasted e-mail messages. Please include any background information on the problem. This helps AOL security get to the root of the problem more quickly so they can put a stop to the security violation.

For e-mail-only violations, forward the e-mail to screen name TOSEMail1. For e-mail with files attached, forward the mail to screen name TOSFiles. For unsolicited, commercial e-mail, forward the e-mail to screen name TOSspam.

Parental Control Issues and Solutions

13 Watching the neighborhood— AOL Neighborhood watch

AOL's Neighborhood Watch channel provides articles, tips, and expert advice on privacy and security issues. It's like having an online security police force working for you anytime you're on the Internet, reading or sending e-mail, chatting, or shopping. You'll find an assortment of valuable information to ensure everyone in your household has an enjoyable online experience. From tailoring parental controls to handling junk mail, from identifying and removing viruses to handy online

security tips, you'll have everything you need to implement the appropriate privacy and security measures for each screen name on your account. Here's how:

1. Click the Keyword button on the AOL toolbar and enter AOL Keyword: **Security** or **Neighborhood Watch** or **Safety**.

2. Click the **Go** button to display AOL's **Neighborhood Watch** channel.

14 Setting privacy preferences

Setting privacy preferences for an AOL screen name is as easy as 1-2-3. Privacy settings let you control what, if any, screen names can contact you. You'll be able to let all screen names contact you, only the people in your buddy list, only selected screen names that are specified, or block screen names. You can also allow or block other screen names from seeing your screen name in their buddy list. Here's how you can tailor the level of privacy for each screen name.

1. Verify that you're currently signed on as the primary or master screen name.

2. Select **Preferences** from the **Settings** menu on the AOL toolbar.

3. Click **Privacy** under the **Accounts Control** heading on the **Preferences** channel.

4. Click the **Privacy** tab heading on the **Buddy List Preferences** window.

5. Click the check box corresponding to the desired privacy preference option you want, and click the **Apply** button, shown in Figure 13-4.

6. Click the **Save** button to set the desired privacy preferences for the selected screen name.

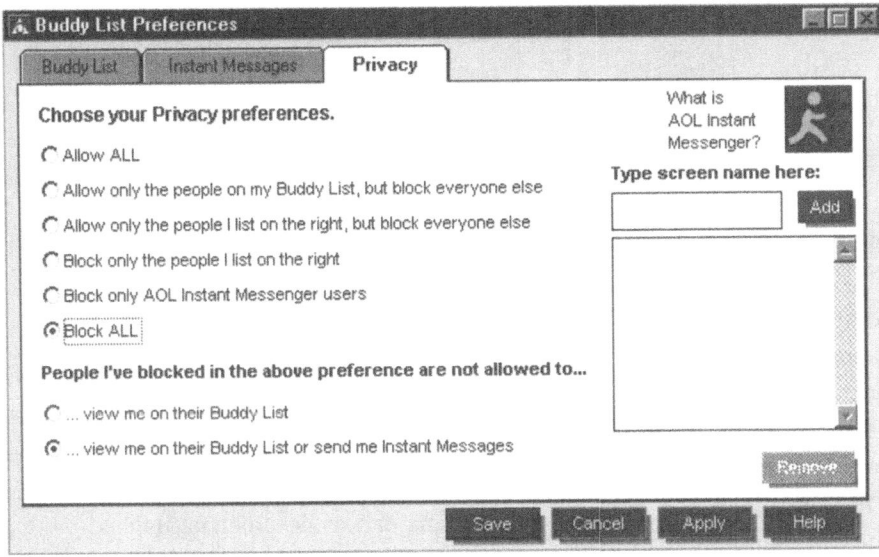

Figure 13-4. Blocking all screen names on AOL's Buddy List Preferences Privacy tab

15 Understanding parental controls

Parental controls let you decide which type of mail access is to be available for a particular screen name. By selecting a parental control, a safety net for each screen name is created to prevent unauthorized contact by other members while online. This feature controls member access while using e-mail, Instant Message, chat rooms, newsgroups, message boards, and other online communication features.

16 Setting parental control levels

To limit the amount and type of mail and other content one is able to receive online, AOL lets you set parental controls for specific age categories. Although normally set at the time a screen name is created, changes can be made at any time as an account management function. The following age categories are available for each screen name:

- Kids Only (ages 12 and under)

- Young Teens (ages 13–15)

- Mature Teens (ages 16–17)

- General Access (ages 18 and older)

17 Changing parental controls for children

As children grow, parents will need a way to make parental control changes to their children's screen name. In order to set or modify a parental control setting for children, the person doing this task will need to be signed on as a master screen name. AOL lets you change the parental control age setting to one of the following: Kids Only (12 and under), Young Teen (13–15), Mature Teen (16-17), or General Access (18+). Here's how it's done:

1. Verify that you're currently signed on as the primary or master screen name.

2. Select **Screen Names** from the **Settings** menu on the AOL toolbar.

3. Click **Edit Parental Controls Settings** under the **Parental Controls** heading on AOL's **Screen Names** channel.

4. Select the screen name you want to assign parental control settings for from the **Edit controls for:** list.

5. Click an age category from the list displayed at the bottom of the **Edit Parental Controls Settings** window.

6. Click the **Accept New Category** button on the **Alert! Parental Controls Category Change** window.

7. Click the **OK** button in the **Your changes to Category Setting have been saved** dialog box.

18 Restricting access to premium services

Would you like to restrict the access to premium service content providers? Premium service providers generally charge a special fee for their content such as games and, when accessed, automatically charge an hourly or one-time access fee on the credit card you use for AOL billing. AOL lets you block the ability to access premium services easily by following these simple steps:

1. Verify that you're currently signed on as the master screen name.

2. Select **Screen Names** from the **Settings** menu on the AOL toolbar.

3. Click **Edit Parental Controls Settings** under the **Parental Controls** heading on AOL's **Screen Names** channel.

4. Select the screen name you want to block premium services for from the **Edit controls for:** list.

5. Click **Premium Services** from the **Custom Controls** on the **Edit Parental Controls Settings** window.

6. Click the **Block Premium Services** checkbox, and click the **Save** button.

7. Click the **OK** button in the **Your changes to Premium Services Controls have been saved** dialog box.

19 Kids' safety tips

As a parent, you'll want to do everything you can to let your kid have a safe and enjoyable online experience. AOL, through the Neighborhood Watch channel, offers kid-friendly online safety tips that parents should share with their kids. Here's how you and your child can access these useful tips:

1. Click the Keyword button on the AOL toolbar and enter AOL Keyword: **Kid Safety.**

2. Click the **Go** button to display AOL's **Neighborhood Watch** channel.

3. Click **Kids' Online Safety Tips** to display **Kids' Safety Tips.**

20 Setting the online timer for your children

For kids-only screen names, AOL lets you limit how long your child can be online.

1. Verify that you're currently signed on as the primary or master screen name.

2. Select **Screen Names** from the **Settings** menu on the AOL toolbar.

3. Click **Edit Parental Controls Settings** under the **Parental Controls** heading on AOL's **Screen Names** channel.

4. Select the child's screen name for whom you want to restrict online time from the **Edit controls for:** list.

5. Click **Online Timer** from the **Custom Controls** on the **Edit Parental Controls Settings** window.

6. To set or modify online timer settings, review the existing settings and click the **Next** button on the **Custom Control Settings: Online Timer** window.

7. Click the level of flexibility you want from the available radio boxes (**Same Limit Daily, Weekday/Weekend Limits, Custom Daily Limit,** or **Unlimited**) on Step 1 of 4, and click the **Next** button.

8. Select the number of hours you will allow your child to be online each day from the available options (**# of Hours, Starting Time,** and **Ending Time**) on Step 2 of 4, and click the **Next** button.

9. Select the time zone where your child resides and whether AOL should adjust for daylight savings time on Step 3 of 4, and click the **Next** button.

10. Confirm the online timer settings you established for your child's online enjoyment, and click the **Save** button if it's correct on Step 4 of 4, shown in Figure 13-5.

11. Click the **OK** button in the **Your changes to Online Timer Controls have been saved** dialog box.

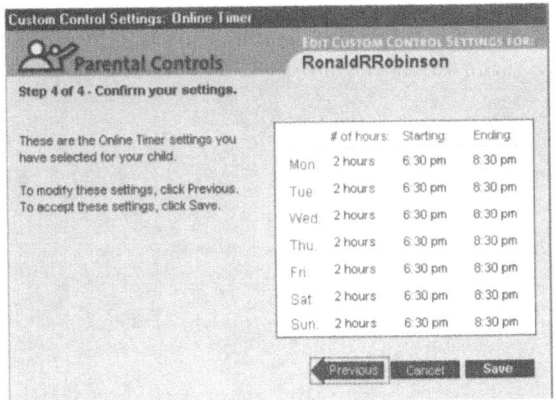

Figure 13-5. Confirming online timer settings

21 Turning off product and service offers to kids

According to recent studies, advertisers are spending over $2 billion to target kids with the latest products and services. The reason is pure economics: These same studies show the average consumer will spend over $100,000 on goods and services during his or her lifetime. You may feel that your kids don't need to be bombarded with invasive product and service offers levied by marketers in pursuit of your kid's mind and money. If so, you can turn off those annoying product and service offers and provide your children a fun, marketing-free, online experience. It's easy to turn off marketing offers from various mediums including the U.S. Mail from non-AOL organizations, U.S. Mail from AOL, telephone, e-mail, and pop-up windows. Here's how:

1. Verify that you're currently signed on as the primary or master screen name.

2. Select **Preferences** from the **Settings** menu on the AOL toolbar.

3. Click **Marketing** under the **Accounts Control** heading on the **Preferences** channel.

4. Click a preference button on the **Marketing Preferences** window, and click the **Continue** button to display the specific preference window you'd like to turn off promotional ads for.

5. Click the check box corresponding to **No, I do not want to receive special AOL members-only _____ offers.** and click the **OK** button.

6. Click the **OK** button corresponding to **Your Preference has been sent** dialog box.

7. Repeat steps 5-6 for each type of marketing medium.

Instant Messenger and Newsgroup Issues and Solutions

22 Understanding parental controls and Instant Messenger

You can control what type of Instant Messenger access is available for a screen name through parental controls. The selected parental control assigns a safety net for members to prevent unauthorized contact by other members while online. This feature determines who can access a screen name while using Instant Message, chat rooms, newsgroups, message boards, and other online communication mediums.

23 Blocking Instant Messenger notes for privacy

You can make sure you don't get bombarded with Instant Messenger notes during an online session by turning this feature off. You can also use this parental control to determine who can access a given screen name using Instant Message, chat rooms, newsgroups, message boards, and other online communication mediums. Here's how:

1. Verify that you're currently signed on as the master screen name.

2. Select **Screen Names** from the **Settings** menu on the AOL toolbar.

3. Click **Edit Parental Controls Settings** under the **Parental Controls** heading on AOL's **Screen Names** channel.

4. Select the screen name you want to block Instant Messenger notes for from the **Edit controls for:** list.

5. Click **IM control** from the **Custom Controls** on the **Edit Parental Controls Settings** window.

6. Click the **Block Instant Messenger notes** checkbox to restrict all notes from other members, and click the **Save** button.

7. Click the **OK** button in the **Your changes to Instant Message Controls have been saved** dialog box.

24 Notifying AOL with Instant Messenger violations

When you are messaging with your friends, there is little concern over security, as when you're opening attachments or visiting Web sites. Viruses don't transmit via AOL Instant Messaging. This is a major advantage of Instant Messenger over other AOL communication methods.

Still, if you receive a request from someone you don't know for chat on Instant Message and you become suspicious, you can click on the button to Notify AOL and your message window will close, and the AOL security team will be notified to look into the situation.

🖊 AOL correspondence is always sent in a blue envelope on your screen. That way you know it's official.

There are a number of discussion groups on virus prevention and countermeasures to check out, if you're interested in these areas. You can start with the AOL area called AOL Computer Center, AOL Keyword: Anti-Virus. Fellow AOL user volunteers run the anti-virus boards on AOL. If interested, you

can become a volunteer and help other AOL members in this important area.

If you witness inappropriate behavior on AOL, you should report it. Here's how:

1. Click the Keyword button on the AOL toolbar and enter AOL Keyword: **Notify** or **Notify AOL**.

2. Click the **Go** button to display AOL's **Notify AOL** channel, shown in Figure 13-6.

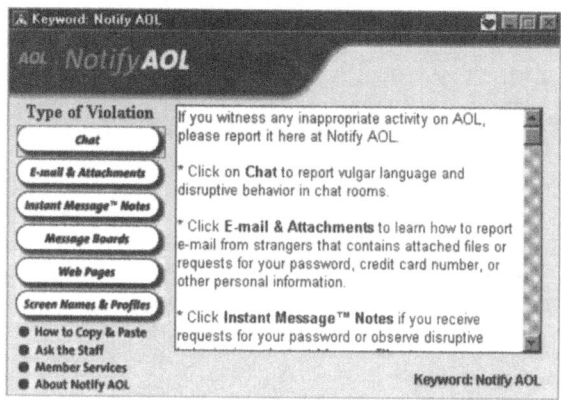

Figure 13-6. Notifying AOL about inappropriate online behavior

25 Blocking buddy list displays for added privacy

Your Buddy List can display useful information about who on your list is signed on, screen names that recently signed on or signed off, and how many screen names in each group are signed on. But if you wish to block AOL members on your buddy list from seeing when you've signed on or signed off, follow these simple steps:

1. Sign on with the screen name you want to block buddy list displays for.

2. Select **Preferences** from the **Settings** menu on the AOL toolbar.

3. Click **Privacy** under the **Account Controls** heading on AOL's **Preferences** channel.

4. Click the **Privacy** tab on the **Buddy List Preferences** window.

5. Click the **Block All** checkbox under the **Choose your Privacy** preferences heading and click the **... view me on their Buddy List or send me Instant Messages** checkbox under **People I've blocked in the above preferences are not allowed to ...** heading, and click the **Apply** button, shown in Figure 13-7.

6. Click the **Save** button on the **Buddy List Preferences** window.

26 Blocking others from knowing when your computer is in "idle" mode

Your Buddy List can show others when your computer is sitting "idle" or not being used. AOL determines that your computer is idle when there hasn't been any interaction with your mouse or keyboard for a number of minutes. To prevent other AOL members from seeing if your computer is in an idle state, you may block this information from appearing by following these simple steps.

1. Sign on with the screen name you want to block buddy list displays for.

2. Select **Preferences** from the **Settings** menu on the AOL toolbar.

3. Click **Privacy** under the **Account Controls** heading on AOL's **Preferences** channel.

4. Click the **Buddy List** tab on the **Buddy List Preferences** window.

5. Remove the check in the **Allow other members to see that I am idle** checkbox under the **Choose your Buddy List** preferences heading, and click the **Apply** button.

6. Click the **Save** button on the **Buddy List Preferences** window.

27 Turning chat room preferences off for added privacy

You can set and save special chat preferences that enable you to get the most from your online chat experience. You can choose to have AOL notify you when members arrive or leave a chat room, enable chat room sounds, alphabetize the member list in a chat room, even double-space incoming messages for enhanced readability. It's easy to let AOL know whether you want these features on or off. By

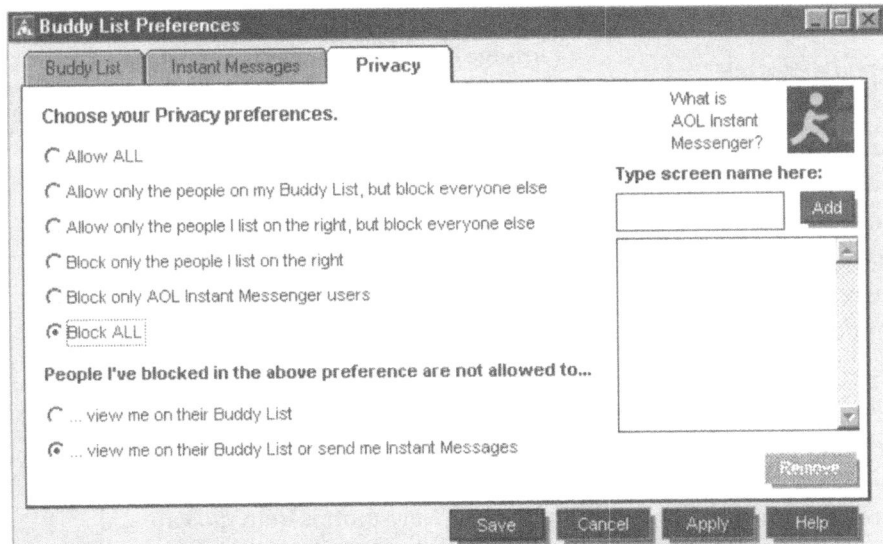

Figure 13-7. Blocking Buddy List displays for added privacy during an online session

turning them off, you provide yourself additional privacy. Here's how:

1. Sign on with the screen name for which you want to block buddy list displays.

2. Select **Preferences** from the **Settings** menu on the AOL toolbar.

3. Click **Chat** under the **Communications** section in the **Preferences** window.

4. Select the specific chat preferences you want turned off by removing the check mark in each check box, and click the **Save** button, shown in Figure 13-8.

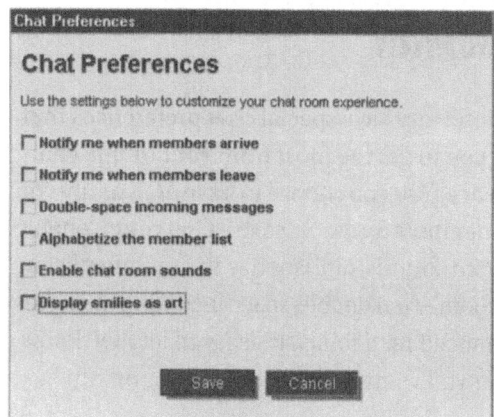

Figure 13-8. Turning all chat room preferences off for added privacy during an online session

28 Setting newsgroup parental controls

Unlike message boards, newsgroups are open to anyone on the Internet and consequently aren't subject to AOL's terms of service guidelines. Because postings could contain objectionable content such as vulgar language, sexual comments, or files of an unsuitable nature, you may find it necessary to limit your child's access to newsgroups. AOL lets you control how much or how little you'll interact with newsgroup content. Here's how:

1. Click **Parental Controls** from the **Settings** menu on the AOL toolbar.

2. Click **Set Parental Controls** from the AOL **Parental Controls** window.

3. Select the screen name you want to set parental controls for from the **Edit controls for:** list.

4. Click **Newsgroups** from the **Parental Controls** window.

5. Click the appropriate check box to control what your child can or can't do in newsgroups from the **Custom Control Settings: Newsgroups** window. For example, to block access to all newsgroups, click the **Block all newsgroups** check box.

6. Click the **Save** button to save new settings.

7. Click the **OK** button in the **Your changes to Newsgroup Controls have been saved** dialog box.

29 Creating a spam-free environment for your kids

Is your child receiving unsolicited messages from newsgroups? Messages like these are known as spam. Spamming is the process of sending the same message to multiple newsgroups. Not only is this unacceptable netiquette, it has the potential of hurting the integrity of the newsgroups where the message is posted. Here's why: If everyone posted a message to every newsgroup, it would make finding messages related to that newsgroup virtually impossible. So only post a message to a single newsgroup. Create a spam-free online environment for your children and turn off those annoying messages. Here's how:

1. Click **Parental Controls** from the **Settings** menu on the AOL toolbar.

2. Click **Set Parental Controls** from the AOL **Parental Controls** window.

3. Select the screen name you want to set parental controls for from the **Edit controls for:** list.

4. Click **Newsgroups** from the **Parental Controls** window.

5. Click the **Block all newsgroups** from the **Custom Control Settings: Newsgroups** window.

6. Click the **Save** button to save new settings.

7. Click the **OK** button in the **Your changes to Newsgroup Controls have been saved** dialog box.

Shopping & Banking Issues and Solutions

30 Shopping safely online

AOL protects you against transaction fraud when using credit cards by ensuring that all Certified Merchants provide a safe and secure shopping community. AOL's secure Web browser is used during shopping trips to the online shopping communities. It automatically scrambles any information that you provide AOL's Certified Merchants including name, credit card number, expiration date, and other critical information. Consequently, should a transmission be intercepted by an unknown party, the information would be indiscernible and useless. To provide the highest level of security, you should verify what browser software is being used by AOL. Entering AOL Keyword: **Browser** can check this for you.

31 Accessing AOL's shopping guarantee

AOL's shopping guarantee is the best in the industry. It guarantees shoppers everywhere secure transactions and privacy protection. Plus, Shop@AOL offers the highest quality customer service anywhere giving shoppers the ability to contact AOL by toll-free telephone, via e-mail, or live chat, 24 hours a day, 7 days a week. If you're unhappy with the product you purchased or the service you received, access AOL's customer service to see how the problem can be resolved or the product returned for a full refund including shipping and handling charges. Here's how:

1. Click the **Keyword** button on the AOL toolbar and enter AOL Keyword: **Shop Help** or **Shopping Help**.

2. Click the **Go** button to display AOL's **Shopping Help** channel.

3. Click the **Our promise to you** hyperlink on AOL's **Shopping Help** channel to display AOL's **Guarantee** Web site.

32 Contacting AOL about a shopping problem

Do you need assistance getting a problem resolved? AOL's Shopping Help team can help with shopping-related problems, such as not being able to find what you're looking for, not getting the assistance you need from a vendor, or anything else regarding an online purchase. Contacting AOL is easy, and most importantly representatives can be reached 24 hours a day, 7 days a week. Here's how:

1. Click the Keyword button on the AOL toolbar and enter AOL Keyword: **Shop Help** or **Shopping Help**.

2. Click the **Go** button to display AOL's **Shopping Help** channel.

3. Click the **Contact Shopping Help** hyperlink to display the three convenient ways to contact AOL's shopping representatives.

33 Setting marketing preferences

AOL makes it easy to block the marketing of product and service offerings to specific screen names. Not only can you choose not to receive these offerings from AOL by e-mail, phone, snail mail, or pop-up screens, you can choose to block your name and address from third party mailing lists. Here's how:

1. Sign on with the screen name you want to block product and service offers for.

2. Select **Preferences** from the **Settings** menu on the AOL toolbar to display AOL's **Preferences** channel.

3. Click **Marketing** to display AOL's **Marketing Preferences** window, shown in Figure 13-9.

4. Click the marketing medium you'd like to change from the marketing preferences list, and follow the on-screen instructions.

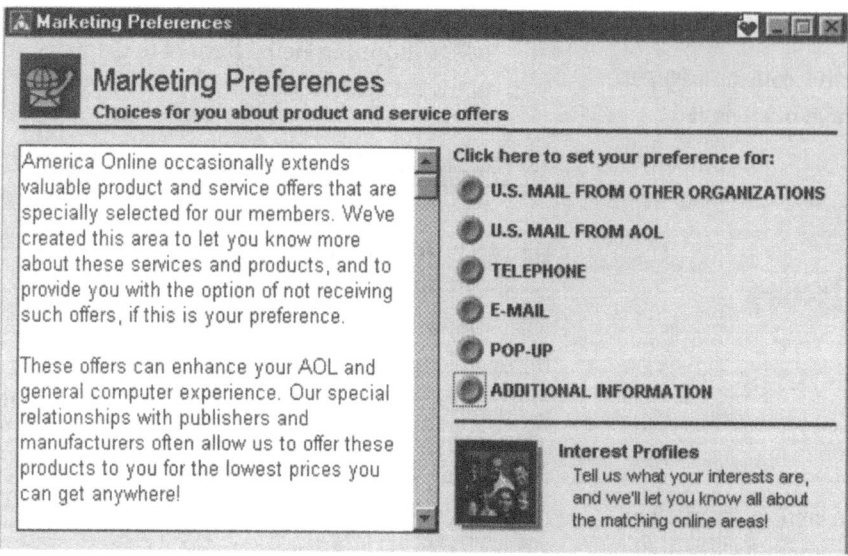

Figure 13-9. Controlling product and service offerings with AOL's Marketing Preferences

34 Banking from the comfort of your own home

Would you like to save time by doing all your banking online? Many banks offer online services that let you pay your bills, see balance alerts, and view account statements. These services are designed to save you time and, in many cases, postage as well. The best part of all is that you can access them 24 hours a day, 7 days a week. Visit one of AOL's featured banking providers for further details. Here's how:

1. Click the Keyword button on the AOL toolbar and enter AOL Keyword: **Bank**.

2. Click the **Go** button to display AOL's **Banking** channel, shown in Figure 13-10.

3. Click the bank you'd like to transact business with from the **Featured Banking Providers** list on AOL's **Banking** channel.

4. Follow the on-screen instructions.

Figure 13-10. Banking from the comfort of your own home with AOL's Banking channel

CHAPTER 14

AOL Customizations

HAVE YOU EVER WANTED to turn off the sounds AOL makes, add or remove content on My AOL, store your password so you don't have to enter it each time you go online, or control when and how files are downloaded? AOL provides numerous preferences that, when customized, control the way online services and features behave. From AOL interface customizations to tailoring My AOL with just the content you're interested in, you'll find a wealth of handy tips to personalize your online experience. You'll find everything you need to change the way AOL looks, behaves, sounds, and operates, just by changing a few options.

In this chapter, you'll learn how to :

- 📖 Customize the AOL interface
- 📖 Tailor My AOL with content that's set to your specific needs
- 📖 Customize mail and download processes
- 📖 Set Internet properties for a faster, safer, and more efficient Internet experience
- 📖 Customize commonly performed tasks using Automatic AOL
- 📖 Tailor chat communication using cool features and tips

AOL Interface Customizations

1 Setting Auto Start options

Would you like to schedule AOL to automatically get your mail before arriving at the office? AOL lets you program what tasks to perform as well as when

to perform them. This automatic feature is handy when sending and retrieving mail during off hours or before you arrive at your office each morning. You can even have it automatically get unread newsgroup postings, send postings, and download files using the built-in scheduler. Automatic AOL can eliminate all that wasted time opening and downloading mail and attachments on demand, and instead perform these time-consuming steps in the wee hours. You'll have your mail waiting for you so you can read it each morning when you arrive at the office, and sent each evening after you've left the office. Here's how it's done:

1. Select **Preferences** from the **Settings** menu on the AOL toolbar.

2. Click **Auto AOL** under the **Communications** section in the **Preferences** window.

3. Select the tasks you want **Automatic AOL** to perform, such as **Send mail**, **Get unread mail**, **Download files**, **Send postings**, or **Get unread postings**, from the **Automatic AOL** window.

4. Click the **Select Names** button.

5. Click the screen name you want **Automatic AOL** to run by checking the appropriate check box, and enter the password to use during the sign on process.

6. Click the **OK** button.

2 Setting automatic AOL preferences

You can set AOL to automatically send mail, get unread mail, download and save files attached to mail, send and receive postings, and download files marked to be downloaded later. Taking advantage of this feature enables you to maximize your time to the fullest by scheduling time-consuming tasks when you're away from the office, after hours, while on vacation, or while you sleep. After the tasks are completed, everything is waiting for you in your personal filing cabinet. Just sign on and go about your usual business. Here's how:

1. Select **Preferences** from the **Settings** menu on the AOL toolbar.

2. Click **Auto AOL** under the **Communications** section in the **Preferences** window.

3. Select the tasks you want **Automatic AOL** to perform from the **Automatic AOL** window.

4. Click the **Schedule Automatic AOL** icon.

5. In the **Schedule Automatic AOL** window, specify the days you want it turned on, click **Enable Scheduler**, the starting time, and how often (e.g., every hour, every 2 hours, every 4 hours, every 8 hours, every day).

6. Click the **OK** button.

3 Customizing parental control settings

Parental controls let you decide the type of access that is to be available for a particular screen name. By selecting a parental control, a safety net for each screen name is created to prevent unauthorized contact by other members while online. This feature controls member access while using e-mail, Instant Message, chat rooms, newsgroups, message boards, and other online communication features.

To limit the amount and type of mail and other content one is able to receive online, AOL lets you set parental controls for specific age categories. Although normally set at the time a screen name is created, AOL lets you make changes at any time. AOL lets you customize a maximum of seven screen name settings per account for the following age categories:

- Kids Only (ages 12 and under)

- Young Teens (ages 13–15)

- Mature Teens (ages 16–17)

- General Access (ages 18 and older)

Here's how it's done:

1. Verify that you're currently signed on as the primary or master screen name.

2. Select **Screen Names** from the **Settings** menu on the AOL toolbar.

3. Click **Edit Parental Controls Settings** under the **Parental Controls** heading on AOL's **Screen Names** channel.

4. Select the screen name you want to assign parental control settings for from the **Edit controls for:** list.

5. Click an age category from the list displayed at the bottom of the **Edit Parental Controls Settings** window.

6. Click the **Accept New Category** button on the **Alert! Parental Controls Category Change** window.

7. Click the **OK** button in the Your changes to **Category Setting have been saved** dialog box.

4 Changing and saving your password

AOL lets you change and save your password to manage how your account is accessed. Changing your password lets you protect your AOL account from intruders. A password should be easy to remember, but not so easy that others can guess what it is. It must be at least six characters in length and should be a combination of letters and numbers. You should change your password anytime you feel your account has been compromised in any way.

Saving your password is a handy feature that prevents you or another person from typing additional keystrokes. Although this feature makes signing on easier, it can be misused if put in the wrong hands. When your password is saved, anyone with access to your computer (e.g., family members, perhaps even your kids' friends) can sign on to AOL with your account. For this reason, you may want to weigh the pros and cons of using this AOL feature. Here's how it's done:

1. Verify that you're currently signed on to the screen name you want to change the password for.

2. Select **Passwords** from the **Settings** menu on the AOL toolbar to display AOL's **Screen Names** channel.

3. Click **Change Your Password** under the **Password Options** heading on AOL's **Screen Names** channel.

4. Click the **Change Password** button on the **Password** window.

5. Enter your current password and then enter your new password 2 times for verification.

6. Click the **Change Password** button.

5 Removing a stored password

You may find that a stored password makes it too easy for others to gain access to your account. If that's the case, you can remove a stored password at any time. Here's how:

1. Verify that you're currently signed on to the screen name for which you want to remove a stored password.

2. Select **Passwords** from the **Settings** menu on the AOL toolbar to display AOL's **Screen Names** channel.

3. Click **Store Your Password** under the **Password Options** heading on AOL's **Screen Names** channel.

4. Remove the check mark corresponding to the **Sign-On** check box in the **Password Preferences** window.

If you have the Filing Cabinet check box checked, you'll still need to enter a valid password for the screen name.

5. Click the **OK** button to complete the process.

6 Customizing the Welcome screen

Your Welcome screen is the first screen you see when you sign on to the AOL network. For this reason you may want to customize the way it looks. The area of the Welcome screen that can be customized is located on the right side—and is aptly named My Places. My Places lets you customize your Welcome screen with links to the areas you consider most important to your online experience. You'll also be able to display local city information by clicking Zip Code and entering your zip. Follow these steps to customize My Places:

1. Click the **More** button located on the bottom right side of your **Welcome** screen.

2. Click any one of the buttons on the drop-down selection list to customize your **Welcome** screen.

My Places offers up to 12 customizable buttons for your use.

3. Click the **Change My Places** button from the **My Places** drop-down selection list, shown in Figure 14-1.

4. When you're done, click the **Save My Changes** button located at the bottom of the **Change My Places** window.

7 Customizing the way your Web browser behaves

Your AOL Web browser is your interface to everything the Internet has to offer. AOL lets you customize the way your browser behaves by selecting various Internet options. You'll be able to control which Web page is used as your home page, where temporary Internet pages are stored, how long Web pages are stored in your history folder, how security is handled, what type of content can be viewed, whether Web graphics will be compressed, and whether the AOL Shopping Assistant will appear while shopping online. Here's how:

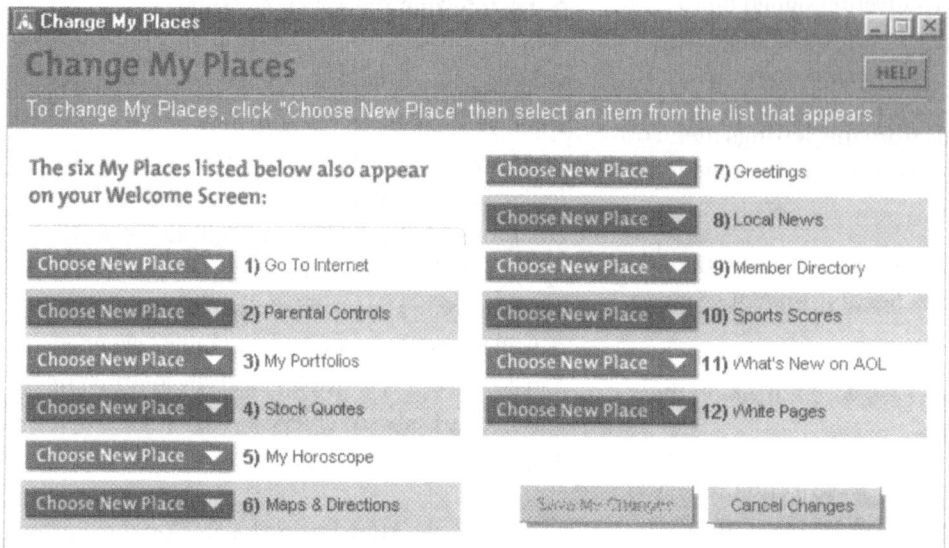

Figure 14-1. Customizing My Places on your Welcome screen

1. Select **Preferences** from the **Settings** menu on the AOL toolbar.

2. Click **Internet Properties (WWW)** under the **Organization** heading on AOL's **Preferences** window.

3. Select your preferences from the following **Internet Options** tabs: **General**, **Security**, **Content**, **Web Graphics**, and **Shopping Assistant**.

4. Click the **Apply** button.

5. Click the **Save** button.

8 Changing local telephone access numbers

It's essential to be able to change a local telephone access number to take advantage of a more reliable connection or when you are traveling. Changing a local telephone number is easy—just follow these steps:

1. Sign off AOL.

2. From the **Sign On** screen, select **Setup**.

3. Click **Add a new AOL access phone number** on the AOL **Setup** window.

4. Enter the area code you are looking numbers for in the **Area Code** field (e.g., 619).

5. Select a country from the list of countries provided, and click the **Next** button.

6. Select the desired location in the **Location Name** field from the **Select AOL Access Phone Numbers** window, and click the **OK** button.

7. Select one or more access numbers from this list, and when done click the **Next** button.

8. Select any special circumstances applicable to the selected phone number(s) on the **Access Numbers You've Selected** window, and click the **Next** button.

9. Click the **Finish** button on the **Confirm Current Locations** window.

9 Setting toolbar preferences and customizations

The AOL toolbar provides a colorful array of task or menu buttons located at the top of your AOL screen. The toolbar is organized into five colored groups: Mail (blue), People (green), AOL Services (violet), Settings (aqua), and Favorites (purple). AOL lets you customize the way your toolbar looks by displaying icons and text, or just text by itself. It also lets you place the toolbar at the top or bottom of your screen. Here's how:

1. Select **Preferences** from the **Settings** menu on the AOL toolbar.

2. Click **Toolbar & Sound** under the **Organization** heading on AOL's **Preferences** window.

3. Select the preferences you want from the Toolbar & Sound Preferences window.

4. Click the **Save** button.

10 Customizing font, text, and graphics preferences

Controlling how your e-mail, chat, and Instant Message text looks is simple. You'll be able to select the style of font, font size, text color, and graphics preferences to suit your particular interests. Once they're set, you'll have them for all your text-based communication tools. Here's how you can do this:

1. Select **Preferences** from the **Settings** menu on the AOL toolbar.

2. Click **Font, Text & Graphics** under the **Communications** heading on AOL's **Preferences** window.

3. Select font, text size, text color, and graphics preferences from the **Font, Text, & Graphics Preferences** window, shown in Figure 14-2.

4. Click the **Save** button.

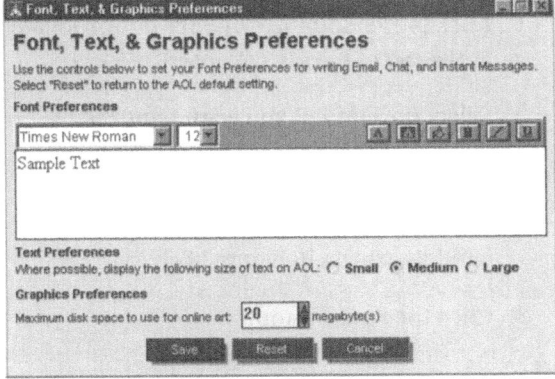

Figure 14-2. Customizing e-mail, chat, and IM text with Font, Text, & Graphics Preferences

11 Setting font and text preferences for the sight impaired

If you're colorblind or need bigger fonts than the default settings, you can customize the text and font preferences easily. AOL lets you control the font and text preferences for writing e-mail, chat, and Instant Messages. You'll be able to select the type and color font to use in all your correspondence, as well as the size of your displayed text. Here's how:

1. Select **Preferences** from the **Settings** menu on the AOL toolbar.

2. Click **Font, Text, & Graphics** under the Communications heading on AOL's **Preferences** window.

3. Select your font preference such as Times New Roman or Arial Black, your color preference such as black or blue, and your text preference from small, medium, or large.

4. Click the **Save** button.

12 Setting sound preferences

AOL lets you set sound preferences such as the Welcome greeting, Instant Message chimes, and chat room sounds. Here's how:

1. Select **Preferences** from the **Settings** menu on the AOL toolbar.

2. Click **Toolbar & Sound** under the **Organization** heading on AOL's **Preferences** window.

3. Select **Enable AOL sounds such as the Welcome greeting and Instant Message chimes** from the **Toolbar & Sound Preferences** window.

4. Click the **Save** button.

< or >

1. Select **Preferences** from the **Settings** menu on the AOL toolbar.

2. Click **Chat Preferences** under the **Communications** heading on AOL's **Preferences** window.

3. Select **Enable chat room sounds** from the **Chat Preferences** window.

4. Click the **Save** button.

13 Turning off modem sounds

AOL lets you turn off those annoying modem sounds by following a few simple instructions:

1. Click **Setup** on the AOL Sign On screen.

2. Click **Expert Setup**.

3. Click the **Devices** tab and select your modem in the selection list.

4. Click **Edit** and select the volume in the **Speaker Volume** field from the **Expert Edit Modem** screen.

5. Click the **OK** button.

6. Click the **Close** button.

My AOL Customizations

14 Customizing My AOL

You can customize My AOL to display only the information that interests you. Get the latest news from around the world, discover great travel bargains, look at your portfolio of stocks and bonds, view your calendar of scheduled appointments and events, find out what the weather is in sunny Miami, or get a few laughs with today's comics. Here's how:

1. Click the **Personalize My Page** button located at the top of the My AOL page or click the **Add Content to Left Side** or **Add Content to Right Side** drop-down selection boxes located at the bottom of the page.

2. Select the content you want added or removed by clicking the desired box.

3. Click the **Save** button.

4. **My AOL** will display the content you selected.

15 Adding content to My AOL

My AOL can be customized with as little, or as much, information as desired. You decide on what content you want, and then using your mouse, point-and-click to add one or more windows of content. Frequently, content is added by clicking the Personalize My Page button located at the top of the My AOL page. See the previous tip on how it's done. Content can also be added to My AOL using the Add Content to Left Side or Add Content to Right Side drop-down selection boxes located at the bottom of the screen. Here's how:

1. After clicking either the left or right **Add Content** menu, click the window(s) you'd like to add, and click the **Add** button.

2. Additional windows will be added to the left or right window your **My AOL** page.

16 Removing content from My AOL

If you decide you don't want a particular content window anymore, AOL makes it easy to remove it. Here's how:

1. Click the **Personalize My Page** button located at the top of the **My AOL** page.

2. Select the content you want removed by clicking the box (clears the check mark) corresponding to the type of content you want removed in the **Personalize My AOL** window, shown in Figure 14-3.

3. Click the **Save** button.

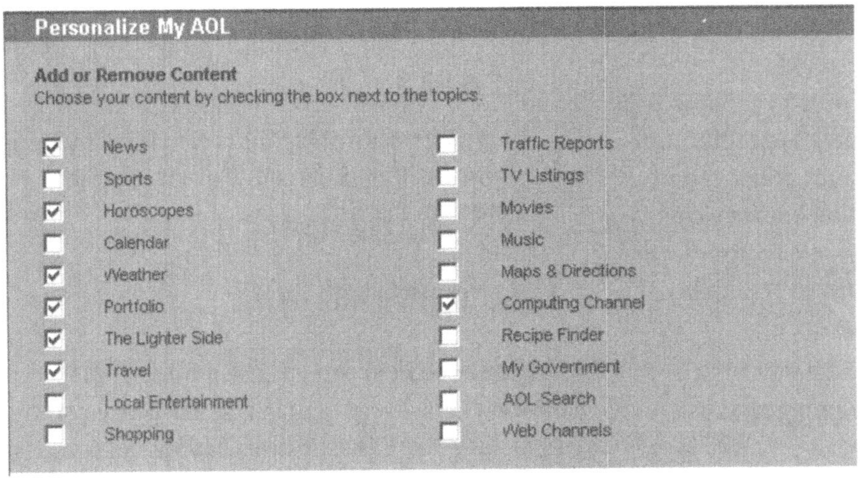

Figure 14-3. Removing content on My AOL

17 Personalizing content on My AOL

You can personalize the content of your My AOL by clicking the **Personalize My Page** button located at the top of the My AOL page (see Tip #13) or by clicking the **Personalize** button located at the top of any window. If you decide to personalize a window's content, you'll have three options displayed when the Personalize button is clicked: Customize, Remove, and Help. The Customize option lets you add or remove content based on your interests. The Remove option physically removes the window and all its content. The Help option displays instructions on how to customize a window's content. Here's how to do it:

1. Click the **Personalize** button located at the top of any content window on your **My AOL** page.

2. Select the content you want added or removed by clicking the box (check mark indicates add) corresponding to the type of content you want added or removed in a specific window.

3. Click the **Save** button.

18 Moving content windows around on My AOL

If more than one AOL window is open at the same time on your My AOL, you can arrange one or more windows by dragging the window from its original location and dropping it to another location. Here's how it's done:

1. Using your mouse, point to the gray textured portion of the title bar and click the title bar.

2. Hold the mouse button down while you drag the window to a new desired location (the entire window will be outlined in red).

3. A **Reposition Here** message will display in the area where the window will be moved.

19 Setting My AOL's data refresh rates

The contents of each window on My AOL automatically change with updated information. AOL lets you set the how often you would like them to be updated on My AOL. You'll be able to instruct AOL how frequently to retrieve the latest news, stock quote updates, sports scores, traffic reports, and much more. Once the refresh rate is set, your Web browser will automatically refresh the contents of each My AOL window. Here's how:

1. Click the **Personalize My Page** button located at the top of **My AOL** Web page.

2. Select how often you want AOL to refresh **My AOL** window contents (for example, Never, Every 20 minutes, Every 40 minutes, or Every 60 minutes).

3. Click the **Save** button.

20 Refreshing My AOL anytime

The contents of each window on My AOL can be refreshed with updated information anytime. AOL lets you refresh My AOL anytime to get the latest news, stock quotes, sports scores, traffic reports, and more by clicking the **Reload** button located just below the AOL toolbar. Your Web browser will automatically refresh the contents of each My AOL window. That's all there is to it.

21 Setting My AOL's connection speed

AOL let's you control how many graphics are displayed on My AOL based on your connection speed. If you connect to AOL with a slower speed modem, you may want to select the option corresponding to Low (fewer graphics) for the Connection Speed to prevent long delays with displaying graphic-intense content. Generally, faster modems are better equipped to handle graphic-intense Web content. Here's how you can set this option:

1. Click the **Personalize My Page** button located at the top of **My AOL** Web page.

2. Select the connection speed that corresponds with the speed of your modem.

3. Click the **Save** button.

22 Adding your calendar and scheduler to My AOL

Would you like to have your personal calendar and scheduler displayed on My AOL? AOL lets you add your calendar with just a few clicks of your mouse. You'll have your personalized planner and event service wherever you're at. Its 24/7/365 accessibility makes it a great tool for viewing current and future appointments while you're at the office, home or away. Here's how easy it is to add your calendar to **My AOL**.

1. Click the **Personalize My Page** button located at the top of **My AOL** or click the **Add Content to Left Side** or **Add Content to Right Side** drop-down selection boxes located at the bottom of the page.

2. Select **Calendar** from the drop-down selection box.

3. Click the **Save** button.

4. **My AOL** will display your calendar containing appointments and other events for the current month.

23 Getting help with My AOL

Do you need help personalizing your My AOL window? The My AOL Help window is your 24/7 help desk. You'll find answers to your questions here too. Here's how it's accessed:

1. Click the **My AOL Help** button located at the top of **My AOL**.

2. Click the help topic that interests you from **My AOL Help** window.

AOL Mail and Download Customizations

24 Controlling how mail is read

AOL's e-mail feature gives you the ability to receive mail from practically anyone in the world. It's a marvelous tool that has seen dramatic increases in usage over the years, but with this increase has come a host of problems and issues. AOL recognizes this, so they provide several user-selected options to help you manage your mail after it's been read. From automatically saving e-mail to a folder on a hard drive to notifying you before opening e-mail containing pictures, AOL allows you to control how your mail is read.

25 Specifying the number of days to keep mail after it's been read

After e-mail has been read, it's automatically saved to your Old Mail box. Mail in your Old Mail box will remain there for 3–7 days. To increase or decrease the number of days old mail remains in your online mailbox, follow these steps:

1. Click **Preferences** on the **Settings** menu on the AOL toolbar.

2. Select **Mail** under the **Communications** heading on the **Preferences** window.

3. Change the number of days in the **Keep my old mail online __ days after I read it** by clicking the increase/decrease button associated with the number of days.

4. Click the **Save** button.

26 Requesting a reminder when e-mail contains pictures

To be reminded of e-mail containing pictures, you can have AOL automatically display a confirmation window. This way, you won't accidentally open an e-mail that could contain a virus without having a confirmation window display first. This is especially useful if you decide to read e-mail from people you don't know. To have AOL notify you of e-mail containing pictures, follow these steps:

1. Click **Preferences** from the **Settings** menu on the AOL toolbar.

2. Select **Mail** under the **Communications** heading on the **Preferences** window.

3. Click the **Notify me before opening mail containing pictures** box.

   🖉 *This may be the default setting—so don't accidentally "unset" this option.*

4. Click the **Save** button.

27 Making e-mail easier to read with white mail headers

To enable easier reading of e-mail, AOL displays the Subject, Date, From, and To information on a white background rather than a gray background. Here's how:

1. Click **Preferences** from the **Settings** menu on the AOL toolbar.

2. Select **Mail** under the **Communications** heading on the **Preferences** window.

3. Click the **Use white mail headers** box.

4. Click the **Save** button.

28 Displaying next e-mail when current one is deleted

To save a few mouse clicks, you can have the next message in your message list automatically open when you delete the current message. Otherwise, if this feature is not turned on, the message list will reappear. To turn this feature on, follow these steps:

1. Click **Preferences** from the **Settings** menu on the AOL toolbar.

2. Select **Mail** under the **Communications** heading on the **Preferences** window.

3. Click the **Display next message when current message is deleted** box.

4. Click the **Save** button.

29 Reading e-mail offline

You don't have to be online to read your e-mail messages. Sometimes it's handy to postpone reading e-mail that you downloaded from your online mailbox until a later time. Here's how:

1. Click **Filing Cabinet** from the **File** menu located at the top of your screen.

2. Click the **Mail** tab on the **Filing Cabinet** window, and double-click the desired e-mail message of choice in the **Incoming/Saved Mail** folder.

3. The e-mail message appears so you can read it.

30 Saving e-mail to a folder on a hard drive after it's been read

After you've read an e-mail message, you have the choice of leaving it in your online mailbox, deleting it, or saving it to a folder of your choice. Saving it to a folder is easy as long as you follow these steps:

1. From your online mailbox, click the folder where you want the e-mail to go, either the **New Mail**, **Old Mail**, or **Sent Mail** tab.

2. Select the e-mail message you want to save by clicking it once.

3. Click the **Save to Filing Cabinet** menu, and select the location where you want mail saved (e.g., Incoming/Saved Mail).

Generally, you'll want your messages saved automatically. Here's how:

1. Click **Preferences** from the **Settings** menu on the AOL toolbar.

2. Click **Filing Cabinet** under the **Organization** heading of the **Preferences** window.

3. To save all incoming messages, select the **Retain all mail I read in my Filing Cabinet** check box.

31 Reading e-mail sent to another screen name on your account

If you have multiple screen names associated with your AOL account, you can read e-mail messages sent to another screen name without signing off. Not only does this save time—it's a handy way to access the other screen names on your account too. Here's how:

1. Click **Switch Screen Names** from the **Sign Off** menu located at the top of your screen.

2. In the **Switch Screen Names** window, double-click the screen name you want to switch to.

3. Sign on to your screen name as usual.

32 Requesting a return receipt on sent e-mail

AOL provides several user-selected features to help you manage how your mail is sent. From spell-checking mail before it's sent to providing helpful reminders when mail is waiting to be sent, AOL lets you control how mail is sent. Sometimes it's handy to know when someone else has opened his or her e-mail. Here's how:

1. Click the **Write Mail** button on the AOL toolbar.

2. Address and compose your e-mail message as usual.

3. Click the **Request "Return Receipt" from AOL members** check box.

4. Click the **Send Now** button.

33 Customizing spell preferences

If your spelling is less than perfect, why not have AOL perform a spell check on your e-mail message before you send it. You can tell AOL what to look for by selecting one or more of the following preferences: capitalization of sentences and proper nouns, doubled words, "a" vs. "an," compound words, punctuation, and even add words to a personal dictionary from the Spelling preferences window. Here's how:

1. Click **Preferences** from the **Settings** menu on the AOL toolbar.

2. Select **Spelling** under the **Communications** heading on the **Preferences** window.

3. For advanced spell preferences, click the **Advanced** button and select desired features.

4. Click the **OK** button.

34 Resizing pictures in e-mail

When writing mail and inserting a picture, you can have AOL automatically display a selection window to help resize the image. To turn this feature on, follow these steps:

1. Click **Preferences** from the **Settings** menu on the AOL toolbar.

2. Select **Mail** under the **Communications** heading on the **Preferences** window.

3. Click the **Present resizing options when inserting pictures in e-mail** box.

4. Click the **Save** button.

35 Controlling download preferences

If you download files from others or the Internet, you'll want to set specific preferences to better control the download process. You can set AOL download preferences to notify you before downloading questionable files, automatically display images after downloading, confirm when files are added to the download list, delete zip files after they are decompressed, tell you when to decompress zip files, and suggest where to store downloaded files. Here's how you can customize the behavior of the AOL download process:

1. Click **Preferences** from the **Settings** menu on the AOL toolbar.

2. Select **Download** under the **Organization** heading of the **Preferences** window.

3. Select the one or more options from the available choices by clicking the appropriate check boxes on the **Download Preferences** window.

4. Click the **Save** button.

36 Specifying when to decompress Zip files

More often than not, files that have been uploaded for sending via the Internet are automatically grouped together and compressed in order to save time during download. You'll be able to tell when your download is in compressed format because the file name will end in .ZIP for PC files and .SIT for Macintosh files. AOL is able to automatically decompress downloaded files at the time they are downloaded. Here's how:

1. Click **Preferences** from the **Settings** menu on the AOL toolbar.

2. Click **Download** under the **Organization** heading on the **Preferences** window.

3. In the **Download Preferences** window, the available options for decompressing zip files are displayed:

   • When I download them

   • When I sign off

   • Do not decompress

4. **Select** the option which best meets your needs for decompressing downloaded files and click the **Save** button.

AOL Internet Properties Customizations

37 Changing the Web page to use as your home page

Do you have a favorite Web page that you'd like to always display as your home page? AOL lets you specify this Web page in your AOL Internet Properties. Here's how:

1. Click **Preferences** from the **Settings** menu on the AOL toolbar.

2. Select **Internet Properties (WWW)** from the **Organization** heading on the **Preferences** window.

3. Enter the Web page address or URL of your choice in the **Home page Address** field. For example, http://www.software-intelligence.com/ displays the Software Intelligence Corporation home page.

4. Click the **Apply** button.

5. Click the **OK** button.

38 Setting parental controls

AOL lets you set parental controls for each screen name on an account. Parental controls set up a safety net for each screen name to prevent unauthorized contact by other members while online including while using e-mail, Instant Message, chat rooms, newsgroups, message boards, and other online communication features.

Setting parental controls limits the amount and type of online communication and content you'll receive online. Although normally set at the time a screen name is created, changes can be made at any time for specific age groups as an account management function. The following age group settings are available for each screen name:

- Kids Only (ages 12 and under)

- Young Teens (ages 13–15)

- Mature Teens (ages 16–17)

- General Access (ages 18 and older)

To modify parental control settings, you'll need to be signed on as a master screen name. AOL lets you change the parental control age setting to one of the following: Kids Only (12 and under), Young Teen (13–15), Mature Teen (16–17), or General Access (18+). Here's how:

1. Select **Screen Names** from the **Settings** menu on the AOL toolbar.

2. Click **Edit Parental Controls Settings** under the **Parental Controls** heading on AOL's **Screen Names** channel.

3. Select the screen name you want to assign parental control settings for from the **Edit controls for:** list.

4. Click an age category from the list displayed at the bottom of the **Edit Parental Controls Settings** window.

5. Click the **Accept New Category** button on the **Alert! Parental Controls Category Change** window.

6. Click the **OK** button in the **Your changes to Category Setting have been saved** dialog box.

39 Setting how often your Web browser checks for newer versions of stored pages

Would you like to reduce the time it takes to view Web pages? You can by storing frequently viewed pages in a special folder on your hard drive. By storing them on your hard drive, you decrease the time it takes to display a Web page because the page isn't downloaded from the Internet each time it's accessed. It's stored in the special folder you designate for quick and easy access by your Web browser. You can also set how often your browser checks for newer versions of stored pages. This AOL setting lets you control whether newer versions of the page will be downloaded. You'll be able to select from the following settings: every visit to the page, each time Internet Explorer is started, automatically, or never. Here's how it's done:

1. Click **Preferences** from the **Settings** menu on the AOL toolbar.

2. Select **Internet Properties (WWW)** from the **Organization** heading on the **Preferences** window.

3. Click the **General** tab on the Internet **Options** window.

4. Click the **Settings** button under the **Temporary Internet Files** heading on the AOL **Internet Properties** window.

5. Select the setting that best meets your needs under the **Check for newer versions of stored pages** heading.

6. Click the OK button on the **Settings** window.

7. Click the **OK** button on the **AOL Internet Properties** window.

40 Setting the number of days to keep Web pages in your history folder

AOL lets you control how many days URL addresses or links to pages you've recently visited are stored in the History folder. These links give your browser easier and quicker access to recently viewed pages. Here's how you can control how long links are kept:

1. Click **Preferences** from the **Settings** menu on the AOL toolbar.

2. Select **Internet Properties (WWW)** from the **Organization** heading on the **Preferences** window.

3. Click the **General** tab on the **Internet Options** window.

4. Select the numeric value by clicking the up or down arrows for the **Days to keep pages in history** field on the **Internet Options** window.

5. Click the **Apply** button.

6. Click the **OK** button.

41 Changing the space requirements for temporary Internet file folders

AOL lets you control how much space to use to store temporary Internet files. Web page addresses are stored in the Temporary Internet Files folder on your hard drive to permit quicker access to frequently accessed Web pages. If you find that the space setting is insufficient, you may need to change the space allocation. Here's how:

1. Click **Preferences** from the **Settings** menu on the AOL toolbar.

2. Select **Internet Properties (WWW)** from the **Organization** heading on the **Preferences** window.

3. Click the **General** tab on the **Internet Options** window.

4. Click the **Settings** button under the **Temporary Internet Files** heading on the **AOL Internet Properties** window.

5. Select the amount of disk space to use by clicking the up or down arrows for the **Amount of disk space to use** field on the **Settings** window.

6. Click the **OK** button on the **Settings** window.

7. Click the **OK** button on the AOL **Internet Properties** window.

42 Displaying Web graphics more quickly using compression

The Web is a graphics-oriented environment. To receive and display Web pages faster, AOL lets you control whether graphic images are compressed. By compressing Web graphics, you'll receive the images quicker, although your browser may appear a little slower. AOL lets you choose from the following options: always compress graphics, never compress graphics, or compress graphics when not using a broadband (high-speed) connection. Here's how it's done:

1. Click **Preferences** from the **Settings** menu on the AOL toolbar.

2. Select **Internet Properties (WWW)** from the **Organization** heading on the **Preferences** window.

3. Click the **Web Graphics** tab on the **Internet Options** window.

4. Select the compression option from the choices displayed in the **Do you want Web graphics to be compressed?** on the AOL **Internet Properties** window.

5. Click the **Apply** button on the **AOL Internet Properties** window.

43 Requesting the availability of AOL's Shopping Assistant while you shop online

AOL's Shopping Assistant provides valuable information while you shop online. It's easy to turn on. Here's how:

1. Click **Preferences** from the **Settings** menu on the AOL toolbar.

2. Select **Internet Properties (WWW)** from the **Organization** heading on the **Preferences** window.

3. Click the **Shopping Assistant** tab on the **Internet Options** window.

4. Select the check box corresponding to **View the Shopping Assistant** option.

5. Click the **Apply** button on the **AOL Internet Properties** window.

Automatic AOL Customizations

44 Sending mail with Automatic AOL

Would you like to have AOL automatically send your outgoing mail at the end of each day? Any mail that you've identified as wanting to send later by clicking the Send Later button on the Write Mail window is set-aside in the "Mail Waiting to be Sent" folder. Automatic AOL can be instructed to send your outgoing mail any time and as many times as necessary during the day. You can have it perform this task on demand or schedule it for different times of the day. Here's how:

1. Click **Preferences** from the **Settings** menu on the AOL toolbar.

2. Select **Auto AOL** under the **Communications** heading on the **Preferences** window.

3. Click the **Send mail from the "Mail Waiting to be Sent" folder** box.

4. Click the **Select Names** button on the **Automatic AOL** window and select one or more screen names and enter the passwords so **Automatic AOL** can sign on the account.

5. Click either the **Schedule Automatic AOL** button or the **Run Automatic AOL Now** button to instruct AOL when to send outgoing mail.

45 Getting unread mail with Automatic AOL

Would you like to have your unread mail automatically picked up for you each day? Automatic AOL can be instructed to get your unread mail and place it in the Incoming Mail folder. You can have it

perform this time-consuming task on demand or schedule it for different times of the day. Here's how:

1. Click **Preferences** from the **Settings** menu on the AOL toolbar.

2. Select **Auto AOL** under the **Communications** heading on the **Preferences** window.

3. Click the **Get unread mail and put it in "Incoming Mail" folder** box.

4. Click the **Select Names** button on the **Automatic AOL** window and select one or more screen names and enter the passwords so **Automatic AOL** can sign on the account.

5. Click either the **Schedule Automatic AOL** button or the **Run Automatic AOL Now** button to instruct AOL when to get unread mail.

46 Scheduling when and how often Automatic AOL is to run

You can schedule Automatic AOL when to run. Taking advantage of this feature enables you to maximize your time to the fullest by doing time-consuming tasks such as downloading files when you're away from the office, before you arrive at the office, after hours, while on vacation, or while you sleep. It's a great feature that can save you time by letting you do other more important things. Here's how:

1. Click **Preferences** from the **Settings** menu on the AOL toolbar.

2. Select **Auto AOL** under the **Communications** heading on the **Preferences** window.

3. Select the tasks you want **Automatic AOL** to perform from the **Automatic AOL** window.

4. Click the **Select Names** button on the **Automatic AOL** window and select one or more screen names and enter the passwords so **Automatic AOL** can sign on the account.

5. Click the **Schedule Automatic AOL** button to instruct AOL when to run.

6. Specify one or more days you want **Automatic AOL** to run.

7. Click the **Enable Scheduler** box, the starting time, and how often (e.g., every hour, every 2 hours, every 4 hours, every 8 hours, every day) on the **Schedule Automatic AOL** window.

8. Click the **OK** button.

47 Specifying what screen names will run with Automatic AOL

In order for Automatic AOL to perform the tasks you want, you'll need to specify one or more screen names it should automatically sign on to. This will require you to select the screen names you want Automatic AOL to use as well as the passwords for each. It's worth noting that once Automatic AOL is set up with your screen names and passwords, your account could be compromised by anyone with physical access to your computer. So use the utmost care in safeguarding your computer at all times. Here's how you'll specify the screen names and passwords to use with Automatic AOL:

1. Click **Preferences** from the **Settings** menu on the AOL toolbar.

2. Select **Auto AOL** under the **Communications** heading on the **Preferences** window.

3. Select the tasks you want **Automatic AOL** to perform from the **Automatic AOL** window.

4. Click the **Select Names** button on the **Automatic AOL** window and select one or more screen names and enter the passwords so **Automatic AOL** can sign on the account.

5. Click the **OK** button on the **Select Screen Names** window.

48 Making Automatic AOL run immediately

You can make Automatic AOL run on demand anytime you like. Just follow these simple instructions:

1. Click **Preferences** from the **Settings** menu on the AOL toolbar.

2. Select **Auto AOL** under the **Communications** heading on the **Preferences** window.

3. Select the tasks you want **Automatic AOL** to perform from the **Automatic AOL** window.

4. Click the **Select Names** button on the **Automatic AOL** window and select one or more screen names and enter the passwords so **Automatic AOL** can sign on the account.

5. Click the **OK** button.

6. Click the **Run Automatic AOL Now** button on the **Automatic AOL** window.

7. Click the **Begin** button on the **Run Automatic AOL Now** window.

< or >

If you've already set up the tasks you want performed as well as selected the screen names and passwords, you can perform the following steps to run Automatic AOL now. Here's how:

1. Click **Automatic AOL** from the **Mail** menu on the AOL toolbar.

2. Click the **Run Automatic AOL Now** button on the **Automatic AOL** window.

3. Click the **Begin** button.

49 Getting help using Automatic AOL

If you find yourself needing help using Automatic AOL, you'll find a handy self-contained help facility built right into AOL. Just follow these simple instructions to access help:

1. Click the **Help** button located on the **Automatic AOL** window.

2. Click the **Using Automatic AOL** button under **Select a Topic**.

3. Select a folder of interest and click the **View** button for information on the help topic.

50 Specifying where files are to be downloaded with the Download Manager

Any downloaded file saved during an Automatic AOL session is stored in the directory specified by the Download Manager. The default location in Windows AOL Version 7.0 is C:\America Online 7.0\download. The default location in Windows AOL Version 6.0 is: C:\America Online 6.0\download. You'll need to specify an alternate directory location if you don't want the default location. Here's how:

1. Click **Preferences** from the **Settings** menu on the AOL toolbar.

2. Select **Auto AOL** under the **Communications** heading on the **Preferences** window.

3. Select the tasks you want **Automatic AOL** to perform from the **Automatic AOL** window.

4. Click the **Select Names** button on the **Automatic AOL** window and select one or more screen names and enter the passwords so **Automatic AOL** can sign on the account.

5. Click the **OK** button.

6. Select **Download** under the **Organization** heading on the **Preferences** window.

7. Click the **Browse** button to change the directory location for storing downloaded files by navigating to the desired directory in the **Put files I download in the following directory** field.

8. Click the **Save** button.

9. Click the **Run Automatic AOL Now** button on the **Automatic AOL** window.

10. Click **Automatic AOL** from the **Mail** menu on the AOL toolbar.

11. Click the **Run Automatic AOL Now** button on the **Automatic AOL** window.

12. Click the **Begin** button.

Chat Customizations

51 Customizing chat preferences

AOL lets you set special chat preferences that enable you to get the most from your online chat experience. You can choose options that will have AOL notify you when members arrive or leave a chat room, enable chat room sounds, alphabetize the member list in a chat room, even double-space incoming messages for enhanced readability. It's easy to let AOL know whether you want these features on or off. Here's how:

1. Select **Preferences** from the **Settings** menu on the AOL toolbar.

2. Click **Chat** under the **Communications** heading on the **Preferences** window.

3. Select the desired chat preferences by clicking the corresponding check boxes, and then click the **Save** button.

52 Requesting notification when AOL members come and go

AOL lets you play sounds when a buddy in your Buddy List signs on or signs off. When sound settings are turned on, AOL defaults to a squeaky door opening when a buddy signs on and a door slamming closed when a buddy signs off. Otherwise no sound is played. This notification feature is easy to use and can be set at anytime by following a few simple steps. Here's how:

1. If your Buddy List isn't open, select **Buddy List** from the **People** menu on the AOL toolbar.

2. Click the **Setup** button on the **Buddy List** window.

3. Click the **Preferences** button on the **Buddy List Setup** window.

4. Click the **Buddy List** tab on the **Buddy List Preferences** window.

5. Click the **Play sound when buddies sign-on** and **Play sound when buddies sign-off** checkboxes on the **Buddy List Preferences** window.

6. Click the **Apply** button on the **Buddy List Preferences** window.

7. Click the **Save** button.

53 Double-spacing incoming messages

AOL lets you avoid the normal clutter associated with incoming messages by having the Instant Message window automatically double-space incoming message text. This makes your buddy's incoming message text not only more readable, but can help reduce eye fatigue. Here's how:

1. Select **Preferences** from the **Settings** menu on the AOL toolbar.

2. Click **Chat** from the **Communications** heading on the **Preferences** window.

3. Click the **Double-space incoming messages** checkbox on the **Chat Preferences** window.

4. Click the **Save** button.

54 Blocking hyperlinks in chat rooms

AOL lets users of Version 4.0 or higher block the blue underlined text links, commonly referred to as hyperlinks from appearing in chats. This prevents links to external sites from appearing in a chat window. You'll also prevent children from being redirected to an external site or Web page by clicking a link. Here's how it's done:

1. Verify that you're currently signed on as the primary or master screen name.

2. Select **Parental Controls** from the **Settings** menu on the AOL toolbar.

3. Click **Set Parental Controls** in the **AOL Parental Controls** window.

4. Click **Chat control** under the **Custom Controls** heading in the **Parental Controls** window.

5. Select the check box, **Block viewing and using hyperlinks in rooms** in the **Custom Control Settings: Chat** window, and then click the **Save** button.

6. Click the **OK** button in the **Your changes to Chat Controls have been saved** dialog box.

55 Displaying smiles as art

AOL lets you display emoticons or smileys in your chat correspondence when using Instant Messenger. Emoticons can be displayed as art or text-based notes to express feelings of emotion. Here's how to insert art-based emoticons:

1. Select **Buddy List** from the **People** menu on the AOL toolbar.

2. Click the **Setup** button on the **Buddy List** window.

3. Click the **Preferences** button on the **Buddy List Setup** window.

4. Click the **IM** tab on the **Buddy List Preferences** window.

5. Click the **Display smiles as art** checkbox on the **Buddy List Preferences** window.

6. Click the **Apply** button.

7. Click the **Save** button.

56 Enabling chat room sounds

Before you can play and hear chat room sounds, you'll need to verify that your computer has the necessary sound capabilities. If your computer has sound, then you can play the desired sound to others in the chat room.

Only members in the chat room with the same .WAV filename as yours will be able to hear the sound. Here's how chat room sounds are enabled.

1. Select **Preferences** from the **Settings** menu on the AOL toolbar.

2. Click **Chat** from the **Communications** heading on the **Preferences** window.

3. Click the **Enable chat room sounds** checkbox on the **Chat Preferences** window.

4. Click the **Save** button.

5. In a chat room, type {S filename} followed by your message. **Filename** refers to the .WAV file stored in your America Online folder.

57 Using alternate Buddy List sounds

The default sounds you hear when a buddy signs on or signs off AOL can be changed to alternate sounds. This is part of the AOL customization process and requires you to download the Buddy Sound Installer from the AOL Sound Library. The Buddy Sound Installer is only available under the PC operating system. Once downloaded, you'll be able to select various .WAV (Windows Audio Format) files for the BuddyIn and BuddyOut sound events. You can select a specific sound to play as a buddy signs on and another sound when your buddy signs off. Here's how:

1. If your **Buddy List** isn't open, select **Buddy List** from the **People** menu on the AOL toolbar.

2. Click the **Setup** button on the **Buddy List** window.

3. Click the **Preferences** button on the **Buddy List Setup** window.

4. Click the **Buddy List** tab on the **Buddy List Preferences** window.

5. Click the **Go to Sound Library** button on the **Buddy List Preferences** window.

6. Click the **Buddy List Sound Library** button on the **Buddy List Sounds** window.

7. Select the sound you want to download from the **Buddy List Sounds** selection window and click the **Download Now** button.

8. Save the selected .WAV sound file in the desired location using the **Download Manager** window. The default download location on your hard drive for AOL Version 6.0 is `C:\America Online V6.0\download` and AOL Version 7.0 is `C:\America Online V7.0\download`.

9. Click **Sounds** from your **Windows Control Panel** and point the **BuddyIn** and **BuddyOut** sound events to the desired .WAV files.

Privacy, Marketing, and Association Customizations

58 Setting Buddy List privacy controls

AOL lets you set Buddy List privacy preferences for any of your account's screen names. Privacy settings let you control what, if any, screen names can contact you. You'll be able to let all screen names contact you, only the people in your Buddy List, only selected screen names that are specified, or block screen names. You can also allow or block other screen names from seeing your screen name in their Buddy List. Here's how you can limit who contacts you except those people listed in your Buddy List:

1. Select **Preferences** from the **Settings** menu on the AOL toolbar.

2. Click **Privacy** under the **Accounts Control** heading on the **Preferences** channel.

3. Click the **Privacy** tab heading on the **Buddy List Preferences** window.

4. Select the checkbox corresponding to **Allow only the people on my Buddy List, but block everyone else** and click the **Apply** button.

5. Click the **Save** button to set the desired privacy preferences for the selected screen name.

59 Setting Instant Message preferences

AOL lets you set Instant Message preferences for any of your account's screen names. You'll be able to choose your privacy preferences, display timestamps on Instant Message notes, display smiles as art, display icons from AOL members, and use you Address Book to auto-suggest screen names. Here's how:

Setting IM Privacy

1. Select **Preferences** from the **Settings** menu on the AOL toolbar.

2. Click **Privacy** under the **Accounts Control** heading on the **Preferences** channel.

3. Click the **Privacy** tab heading on the **Buddy List Preferences** window.

4. Select the level of privacy you desire from the list of choices, and click the **Apply** button.

5. Click the **Save** button.

Setting IM Preferences

1. Select **Preferences** from the **Settings** menu on the AOL toolbar.

2. Click **Privacy** under the **Accounts Control** heading on the **Preferences** channel.

3. Click the **Instant Messages** tab heading on the **Buddy List Preferences** window.

4. Select the IM preferences you desire from the list of choices, and click the **Apply** button.

5. Click the **Save** button.

60 Specifying marketing preferences

AOL makes it easy to block the marketing of products and services to designated screen names. Not only can you choose not to receive these offerings by e-mail, phone, snail mail, or pop-up screens, you can choose to block your name and address from any third-party marketing mailing lists. Here's how:

1. Sign on with the screen name you want to block product and service offers for.

2. Select **Preferences** from the **Settings** menu on the AOL toolbar to display AOL's **Preferences** channel.

3. Click **Marketing** to display AOL's **Marketing Preferences** window.

4. Click the marketing medium you'd like to change from the marketing preferences list, and follow the on-screen instructions.

CHAPTER 15

Create Your Own Web Page

BEFORE EMBARKING ON the creation of your own Web page, you should ask yourself why you want one in the first place. Once you can answer this question, you'll have a better idea about what it should contain. Analyzing the purpose of your page and your reasons for wanting a Web page will help you provide something of value while leaving a lasting impression on your intended audience. A Web page should be fresh and exciting, providing a reason for your audience to revisit your page often. As one of the most dynamic mediums in the world, the Internet is always changing. To better cope with these changes, you'll need to be aware of your target audience and the available resources on AOL.

In this chapter you'll learn how to:

- Create your own Web page

- Access AOL's Web publishing software and tools

- Customize your Web page with HTML and JavaScript

- Download and add clip art graphics to your Web page

- Find shareware Web publishing tools

Web Page Basics

1 My own Web page—why and how?

The rise of the World Wide Web, or Web for short, over the last decade has been phenomenal. In the early 1990s when graphical browsers were first introduced, home pages were simple one-pagers in newsletter-style format about some topic with a few snapshots of the owner's favorite pets, or cars. Now, Web browsers have developed the capability to handle multimedia effects such as video, audio, frames, and Java applets, everyone from personal users to large corporate behemoths is taking full advantage of the Web as an efficient means of self-expression. Larger business-oriented Web sites come complete with product and service promotions, customer feedback, electronic commerce, banner advertising, chat and discussion group capabilities, and everything in between.

So why create a Web page? The Web is a well-established medium for an ever-growing audience in addition to being an avenue for self-expression. Many AOL members and Internet users from around the world have created Web pages for a list of reasons. Let's take a look at some of the reasons that others have expressed as to why they created a Web page:

- To share information about a topic of interest such as recipes, cars, trading card collections, political beliefs, and countless other topics.

- To display pictures of family members and friends.

- To share favorite vacation memories.

- To promote artistic talent.

- To display a resume.

- To sell products or services.

- To promote a business.

- To have fun.

So, how do you create a Web page, you ask. The answer to this question isn't an easy one. Since Web pages can run the gamut from simple one-page text and graphic presentations to highly complex 24/7 online business centers, this question usually leads to a myriad of other questions that need to be answered. The type of Web page you create is entirely up to you. But, before creating your first Web page, you should carefully evaluate and answer the following questions:

- How do you want your Web page to look and work?

- What purpose will your Web page have?

- Who is your target audience?

- Will you be using Web editing software?

- Do you know HTML and JavaScript?

- Where are you going to publish your finished Web page?

- How will you publish your finished Web page?

2 Deciding what a Web page should contain

Before creating a Web page, you should know what content you want to put on your page. Making sure your page has a worthwhile purpose involves a considerable degree of planning. This is critical because you'll want to provide something of value that leaves an impression on your intended audience. You'll also want to keep your Web page fresh and exciting, providing a reason for your audience to revisit your page often. To achieve this, you'll need to be aware of some important information about your target audience. By answering the following questions, you'll be in a better position to address specific content matters:

- What are the age ranges of your target audience?

- What are the educational backgrounds of your target audience?

- Are there specific gender groups you're writing content for?

- What are the ethnic backgrounds of your target audience?

- What nationalities will visit your Web page?

- What income level will your target audience be in?

- Does your target audience have any special language requirements or is one language adequate?

- What is the marital status of your target audience?

- What are the social attitudes of your target audience?

- What is the technical proficiency of your target audience?

- Are you planning to target specific professions?

3 Understanding what is needed to build a Web page

You don't have to be a computer engineer or software developer to build a Web page anymore. Now anyone can do it. AOL's Build Your Web Page channel provides everything you need from start to finish so you can get a great-looking Web page up and running in the shortest amount of time possible. You'll find comprehensive online resources to help you every step of the way. You'll learn everything necessary to create a Web page including: how to use Web publishing tools; write basic HTML and JavaScript code; create Web content; set up a Web store that earns you money; and build return traffic. AOL's Build Your Web Page channel is great starting point for anyone who wants to build a Web page, but doesn't know where to start. Here's how it's accessed:

1. Click the **Keyword** button located on the AOL toolbar and enter AOL Keyword: **Web Page**.

2. Click the **Go** button to display AOL's **Build Your Web Page** channel.

4 Taking advantage of Web Publishing Tutorials Web page

Get all the online help you need to build a great-looking Web page. AOL's Web Publishing Tutorials channel provides free self-paced tutorials that will teach you everything you need to know about HTML basics, making text stand out, hyperlinks, graphics, sound, tables, counters, forms, guest books, frames, and an assortment of other skills.

1. Click the **Keyword** button located on the AOL toolbar and enter AOL Keyword: **Web Tut** or **Web Tutorial**.

2. Click the **Go** button to display AOL's **Web Publishing Tutorials** channel, shown in Figure 15-1.

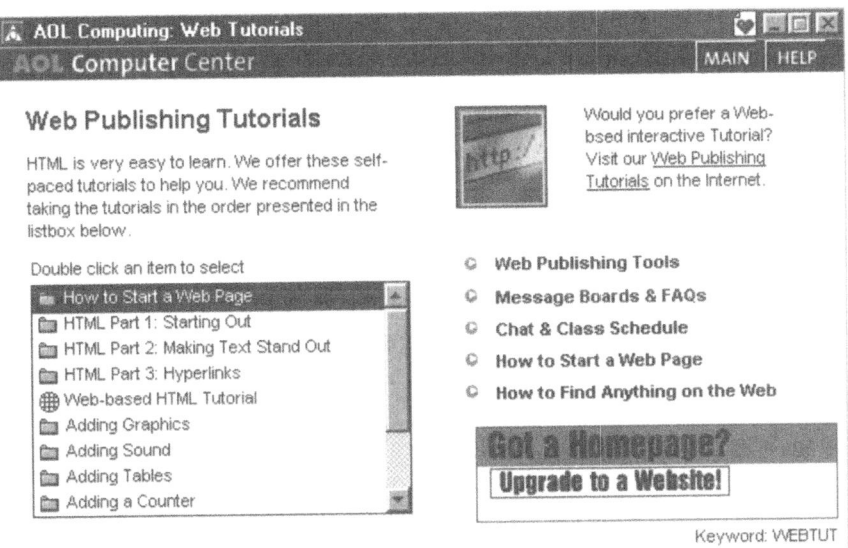

Figure 15-1. Creating a Web page is a snap with AOL's Web Publishing Tutorials channel

5 Building a Web page is free!

Building a Web page doesn't have to cost a lot of money. In fact, it doesn't have to cost anything at all. AOL lets you choose and build a Web page of your dreams or helps you improve the one you have. You'll be able to select a template from over 90 different choices, or, for the more adventurous, drag and drop images and text to create a cool Web page. Here's how:

1. Click the **Keyword** button located on the AOL toolbar and enter AOL Keyword: **Authoring Tools** or **Publishing Tools**.

2. Click the **Go** button to display AOL's **Publishing Tools** channel, shown in Figure 15-2.

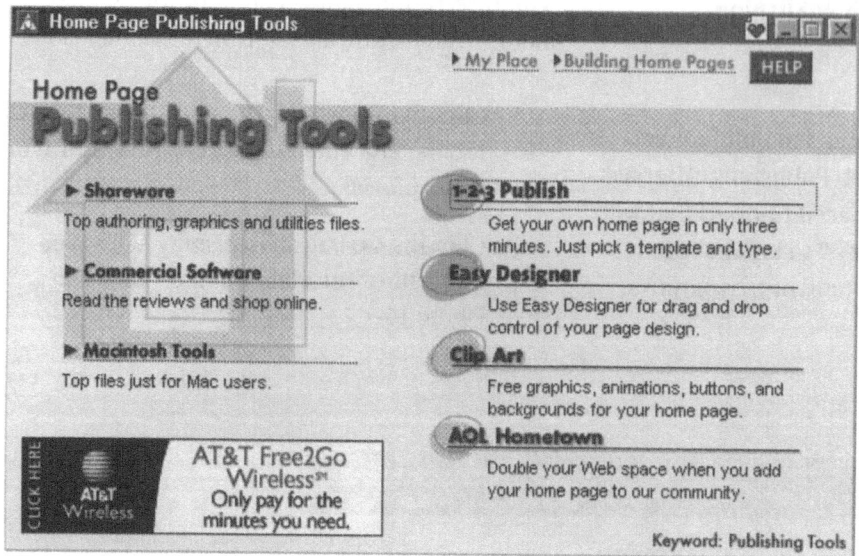

Figure 15-2. Accessing the free Web building tools is easy with AOL's Publishing Tools channel

6 Getting help—it's just a click away

AOL has a variety of resources for aspiring Web page builders to choose from including computer communities such as chat rooms, message boards, Web classes, FAQs, and tutorials; image download centers, upload centers, publishing tools; and much more. You'll be amazed at the number of Help channels and Web sites that are available for your use anytime you need them. Table 15-1 shows a list of popular AOL Help channels and Web sites.

Table 15-1. Web Publishing Resources

CHANNEL/WEB SITE	AOL KEYWORD
Authoring Tools/Publishing Tools	Publishing Tools
Build Your Web Page	Web Page
Computer Center	Computer Center
Computer Community	Web Community
Easy Designer	Easy Designer
PC Upload Center	Upload Center
Web Art & Artists Center	Web Art
Web Publishing Tutorials	Web Tutorial

Web Design & Templates for Beginners

7 Choosing AOL Web site building tools

If you've never designed or built a Web page before, you should visit AOL's Computer Center Build Your Web Page channel. Here you'll find quick and easy tools to design and build a Web page from simple to complex. Using 1-2-3 Publish you'll be able to have a simple Web page up and running in minutes, or you can use Easy Designer to design and build more advanced pages.

AOL's 1-2-3 Publish Web site provides over 90 existing templates of popular Web page designs for you to choose from. You'll find an assortment of Web page designs and themes that cover horoscopes, vacations, music, holidays, memorials, hobbies, sports, cities, auctions, and much more. Here's how you can select one of these popular 1-2-3 Publish templates:

1. Click the **Keyword** button located on the AOL toolbar and enter AOL Keyword: **1-2-3 Publish**.

2. Click the **Go** button to display AOL's **1-2-3 Publish** Web site.

3. Select the desired template from the list and follow the on-screen instructions to begin designing a great looking Web page.

8 Building a simple Web page with 1-2-3 Publish

Building a simple Web page with 1-2-3 Publish is not only fast but easy. You'll be asked to decide on a background color, a picture for the top of your Web page, a title, a divider style to use between major sections of your page, your message, which links to include, whether to display promotional banners, and whether AOL Instant Messenger Remote will be available. Here's how it's done:

1. Click the **Keyword** button located on the AOL toolbar and enter AOL Keyword: **1-2-3 Publish**.

2. Click the **Go** button to display AOL's **1-2-3 Publish** Web site.

3. Select the desired template from the list and follow the on-screen instructions to begin designing a great looking Web page.

4. Enter the message you want displayed and select the options from the list of choices, shown in Figure 15-3.

9 Previewing your 1-2-3 Publish Web page

Once your message has been added in the fill-in-the-blank fields and the desired options selected, you'll be able to preview your Web page. Here's how:

1. Click the **Preview My Page** button. Your Web page will appear with the text you entered and the options you selected, shown in Figure 15-4.

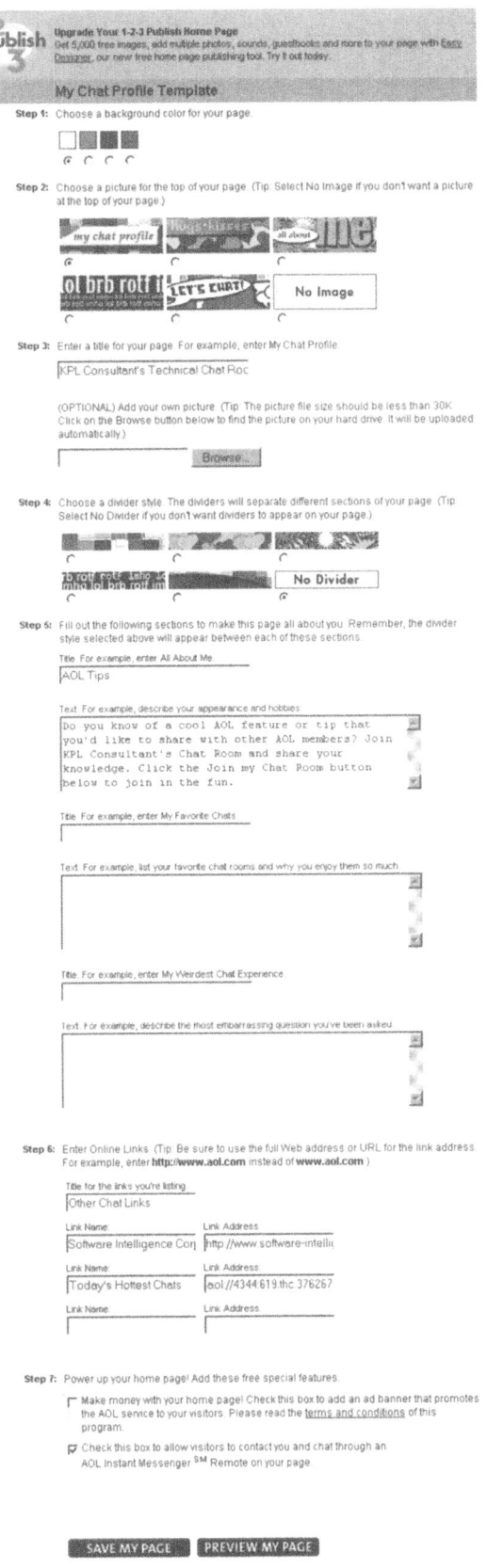

Figure 15-3. Building a Web page with 1-2-3 Publish is as easy as 1-2-3

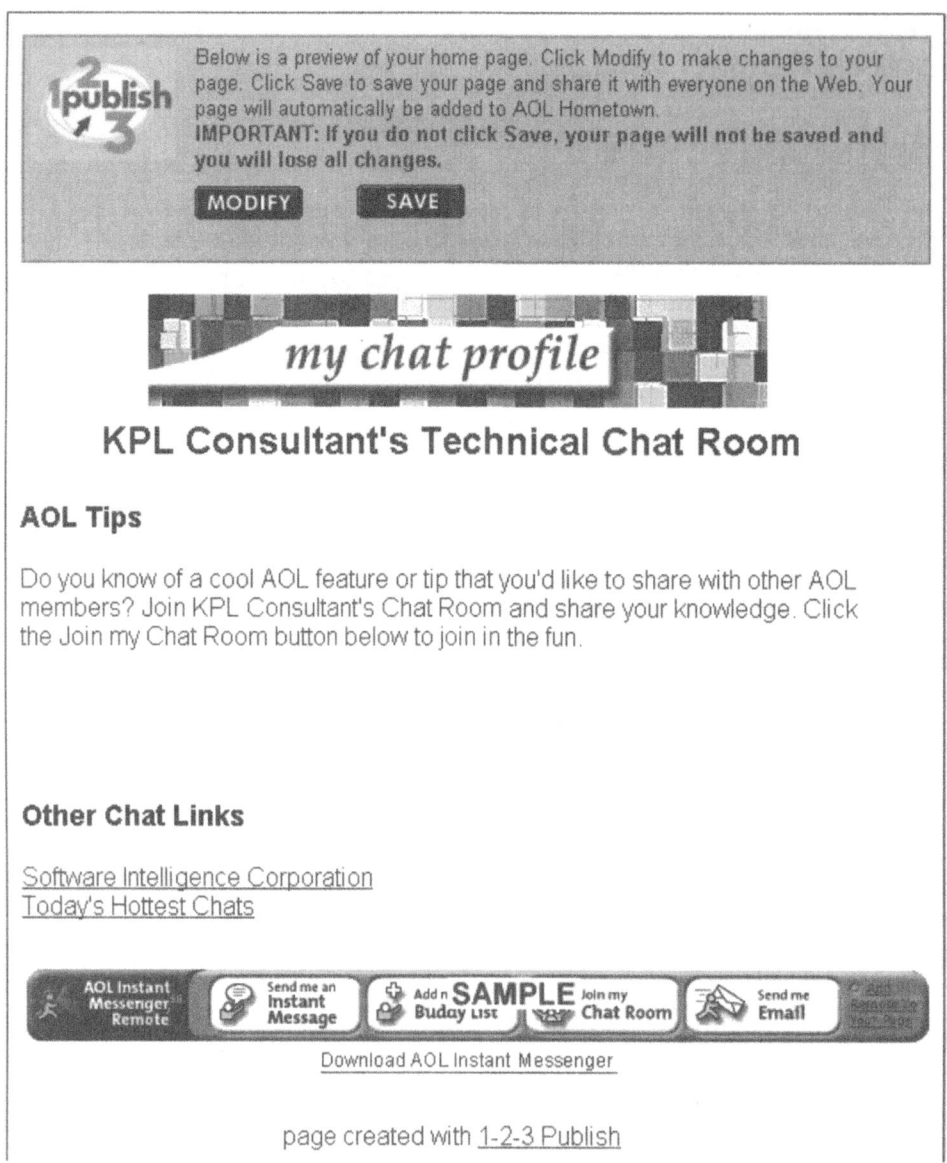

Figure 15-4. Previewing your 1-2-3 Publish Web page lets you see how your page will look.

10 Publishing your 1-2-3 Publish Web page

Once you've got your 1-2-3 Publish Web page just the way you like, you'll want to publish it. The good part is that publishing it is easy and will automatically add your page to AOL Hometown so everyone on the Web can see it. Here's how:

1. Click the **Save** button located at the top of the **Preview** window.

2. When the **Congratulations** screen appears, you'll know you have successfully created your Web page, shown in Figure 15-5.

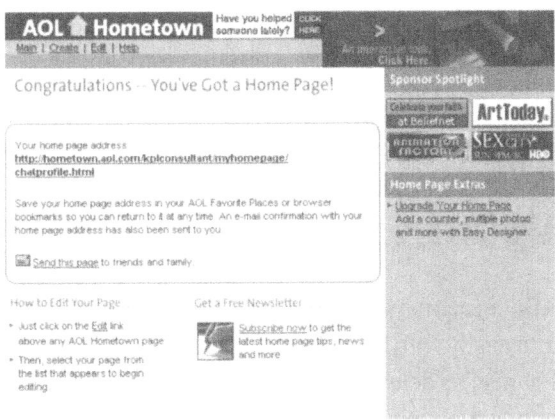

Figure 15-5. The Congratulations screen appears when your Web page has been published

II Making changes to your 1-2-3 Publish Web page

Is your Web page in need of updating? Do you need to remove content and/or links that aren't relevant anymore? Would you like to add some cool new features to make your visitors online experience a more enjoyable one? Well, you're in luck. As one of the most dynamic mediums in the world, the Internet and its content are always changing. No matter what the circumstances, changes are inevitable. Because of this, you'll want and need to make changes to your Web page as frequently as necessary to prevent visitors from shying away from your page.

From fixing broken or out-of-date links, removing content that isn't relevant anymore, or adding new and exciting features for your online visitors to enjoy, AOL lets you make changes to your Web page with easy-to-use Web tools. To speed up the task of making changes to your Web page while making the job less of a chore, you'll want to use a good HTML editor, and other publishing tools. Using the right tools can make all the difference in the world. For more information on Web publishing tools for the PC and Macintosh, see earlier tips in this section. Here's how you can make changes to your Web page as often as you like:

1. Click the **Keyword** button located on the AOL toolbar and enter AOL Keyword: **1-2-3 Publish**.

2. Click the **Go** button to display AOL's **1-2-3 Publish** Website.

3. Select the template you used to design your Web page from the list and follow the on-screen instructions to begin the customization process with AOL's **Easy Designer**.

4. Click the **Click to get started!** button on the **Easy Designer** Web site.

5. Make the necessary changes to your Web page using the **Easy Designer** menu tools and/or editing HTML code.

6. Click the **Save** button located on the **Easy Designer** toolbar to save your Web page.

7. Click the **OK** button on the **Your page has been saved. The page address is ...** dialog box.

8. Close the **Easy Designer** customization window.

9. Close all open windows and test the Web page by entering your Web address (URL).

I2 Opening an existing 1-2-3 Publish page

AOL lets you open an existing 1-2-3 Publish Web page quickly and easily. You'll be able to add, change, or delete content anytime, and as often as you like. Here's how:

1. Click the **Keyword** button located on the AOL toolbar and enter AOL Keyword: **1-2-3 Publish**.

2. Click the **Go** button to display AOL's **1-2-3 Publish** Web site.

3. Select the template you used to create your **1-2-3 publish** Web page.

4. Click the **Modify** button located at the top of your Web page.

5. Click the **Check this box to allow visitors to contact you and chat through an AOL Instant Messenger(SM) Remote on your page** checkbox.

6. Click the **Preview My Page** button to see how your Web page looks.

7. Click the **Save My Page** button to save your page.

13 Adding a chat room to your 1-2-3 Publish page

Would you like other online users to be able to contact you or join in chat room conversations through your Web page? AOL lets you add a chat room to your 1-2-3 Publish Web page for easy communication with your online visitors at anytime. Here's how:

1. Click the **Keyword** button located on the AOL toolbar and enter AOL Keyword: **1-2-3 Publish**.

2. Click the **Go** button to display AOL's **1-2-3 Publish** Web site.

3. Select the template you used to create your **1-2-3 Publish** Web page.

4. Click the **Modify** button located at the top of your Web page.

5. Click the checkbox corresponding to **Check this box to allow visitors to contact you and chat through an AOL Instant Messenger(SM) Remote on your page.**

6. Click the **Preview My Page** button to see how your Web page looks.

7. Click the **Save My Page** button to save your Web page.

Web Page Building for More Advanced Users

14 Building a Web page with Easy Designer

If you're eager to build a Web site that has a few more features, and is a little more tailored to what you want, Easy Designer provides more advanced tools than 1-2-3 Publish, but it's still quite easy to use. Here's how to get started with Easy Designer:

1. Click the **Keyword** button located on the AOL toolbar and enter AOL Keyword: **Easy Designer**.

2. Click the **Go** button to display AOL's **Easy Designer** Web site.

3. Click **Create a New Page** to display the **Easy Designer is Ready!** page.

4. Select the desired template from the list, or select a blank page to start from scratch, and follow the on-screen instructions to begin designing a great looking Web page.

15 Opening an existing Web page with Easy Designer

AOL lets you open an existing Web page quickly and easily with Easy Designer. You'll be able to add, change, or delete content anytime, and as often as you like. Here's how:

1. Click the **Keyword** button located on the AOL toolbar and enter AOL Keyword: **Easy Designer**.

2. Click the **Go** button to display AOL's **Easy Designer** Web site.

3. Click **Open an Existing Page** to display the **Easy Designer is Ready!** page.

4. Click **Click to get started!** on the **Easy Designer is Ready!** page to display the **Easy Designer— Open Existing Page.**

5. Click the desired Web page to open from the list and click the **Open** button, shown in Figure 15-6.

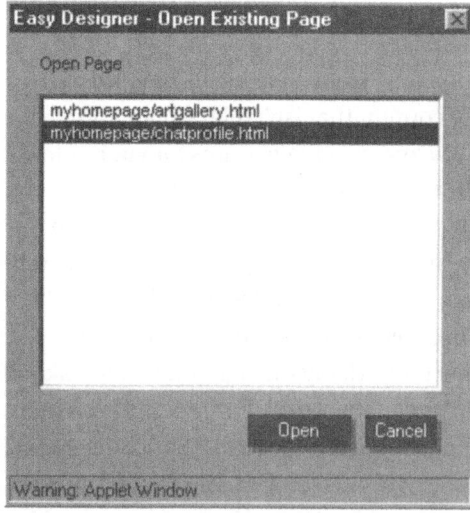

Figure 15-6. Opening an existing Web page is easy with AOL's Easy Designer.

16 Making changes to your Web page with Easy Designer

As with 1-2-3 Publish, Easy Designer gives you Web page tools to let you change the way your page looks and behaves. In fact, it gives you an incredible number of tools to make the job a breeze. From fixing broken or out-of-date links, removing content that isn't relevant anymore, or adding new and exciting features for your online visitors to enjoy, AOL lets you make changes to your Web page with easy-to-use Web tools. To speed up the task of making changes to your Web page while making the job less of a chore, you'll want to use a good HTML editor, and other publishing tools. Using the right tools can make all the difference in the world. For more information on Web publishing tools for the PC and Macintosh, see earlier tips in this section. Here's how you can use Easy Designer to make changes to your Web page as often as you like:

1. Click the **Keyword** button located on the AOL toolbar and enter AOL Keyword: **Easy Designer**.

2. Click the **Go** button to display AOL's Easy Designer Web site.

3. Select the template you used to design your Web page from the list and follow the on screen instructions to begin the customization process with AOL's Easy Designer.

4. Click the **Click to get started!** button on the **Easy Designer** Web site.

5. Make the necessary changes to your Web page using the **Easy Designer** menu tools and/or editing HTML code.

6. Click the **Save** button located on the **Easy Designer** toolbar to save your Web page.

7. Click the **OK** button on the **Your page has been saved. The page address is ...** dialog box.

8. Close the **Easy Designer** customization window.

9. Close all open windows and test the Web page by entering your Web address (URL).

17 Adding text to your Web page with Easy Designer

Adding text to your Web page is easy with AOL's Easy Designer. It lets you add text anywhere you want quickly and easily. Here's how:

1. Click the **Keyword** button located on the AOL toolbar and enter AOL Keyword: **Easy Designer**.

2. Click the **Go** button to display AOL's **Easy Designer** Web site.

3. Select the template you used to design your Web page from the list and follow the on-screen instructions to begin the customization process with AOL's Easy Designer.

4. Click the **Click to get started!** button on the **Easy Designer** Web site.

5. Click the **Add Text** button located on the **Easy Designer** toolbar.

6. Add the text you want added to your Web page in the **Easy Designer—Text Editor** window, and when done, click the **OK** button, shown in Figure 15-7.

7. Move the text box you just added to the desired place on your Web page by dragging it, if necessary.

8. Click the **Save** button located on the **Easy Designer** toolbar to save your Web page.

9. Click the **OK** button on the **Your page has been saved. The page address is ...**" dialog box.

10. Close the **Easy Designer** customization window.

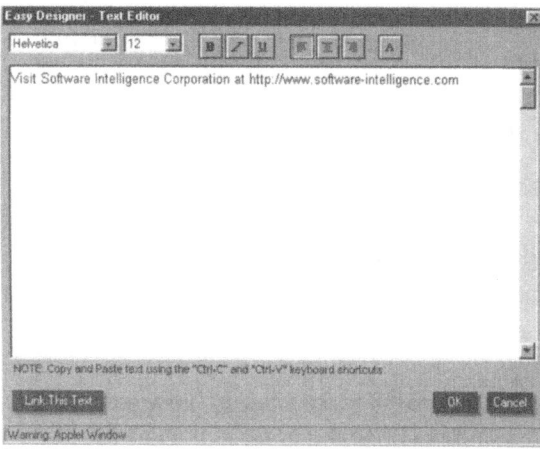

Figure 15-7. Adding text to your Web page is quick and easy

18 Adding graphics and art to your page with Easy Designer

AOL makes it easy for the more advanced Web page builder to add graphics and art. With AOL's Easy Designer, you'll be able to choose from a gallery of graphic images that are sure to improve the way your Web page looks. Easy Designer's image gallery includes these categories: Animals and Nature, Buildings and Homes, Bullets and Buttons, Business and Careers, Entertainment and The Arts, Holidays and Seasons, People and Cultures, Science and Technology, Sports and Recreation, and Travel and Transportation. If you want to choose from more varied sources, there are many clip art sites available. Here's how you can spice up your Web page by adding graphics and art using Easy Designer:

1. Click the **Keyword** button located on the AOL toolbar and enter AOL Keyword: **Authoring Tools** or **Publishing Tools**.

2. Click the **Go** button to display AOL's **Publishing Tools** channel.

3. Click **Easy Designer** on AOL's **Publishing Tools** channel to display AOL's **Easy Designer** Web site, shown in Figure 15-8.

4. Click **Open an Existing Page** on AOL's **Easy Designer** Web site to display the **Easy Designer** tool.

5. Click the **Click to get started!** button to display the **Easy Designer—Open an Existing Page** window.

6. Select the page you want opened and click the **Open** button to display your Web page in the **Easy Designer** window, shown in Figure 15-9.

7. Select an area of your Web page where you want a graphics image inserted, shown in Figure 15-10.

8. Click the **Add Image** button located on the **Easy Designer** toolbar.

9. Double-click a **category** from the **Easy Designer—Picture Gallery** to select it, and double-click a gallery name to enter it.

10. Click the **right and left arrows** to display the gallery of images in a category.

11. Select the desired graphic image from the **Easy Designer—Picture Gallery**.

12. Click the **Resize picture to fit object size** button and click the **OK** button, shown in Figure 15-11.

13. Select the graphic image and stretch or shrink the image on your Web page, shown in Figure 15-12.

14. Click the **Save** button located on the **Easy Designer** toolbar, select the file name to save your page, and click the **Save** button on the **Easy Designer—Save Your Page** window, shown in Figure 15-13.

15. Click the **Yes** button on the **A page with this file name already exists. Do you want to replace it with the page you are saving?** dialog box.

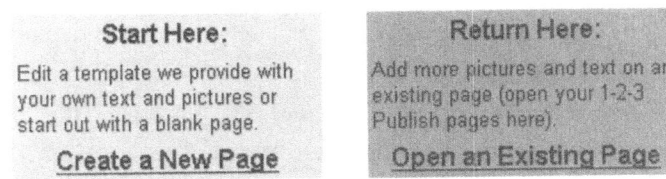

You are about to start Easy Designer, an easy to use home page publishing tool, to create your own home page for AOL Hometown.

Start Here:

Edit a template we provide with your own text and pictures or start out with a blank page.

Create a New Page

Return Here:

Add more pictures and text on an existing page (open your 1-2-3 Publish pages here).

Open an Existing Page

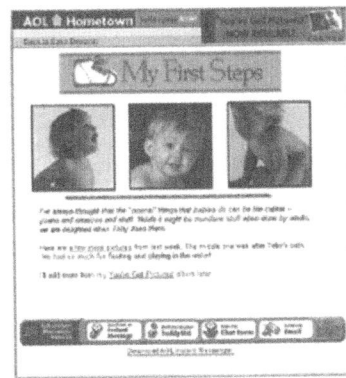

Easy Designer Highlights:

• Drag and Drop images and text to move them around a page.

• Add multiple pictures and resize them right on the page.

• Get access to a gallery of thousands of pieces of clip art.

• BONUS for advanced users: You can add your own html to produce sounds and banners and guest-books.

Figure 15-8. Modifying an existing Web page is easy with AOL's Easy Designer.

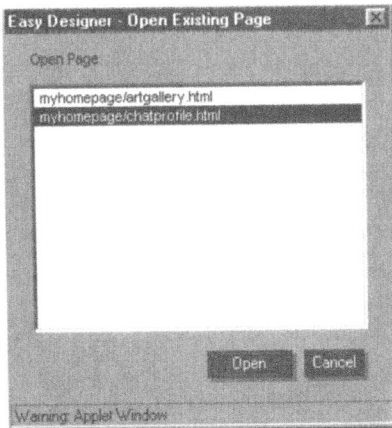

Figure 15-9. Selecting and opening a Web page in the Open Existing Page window

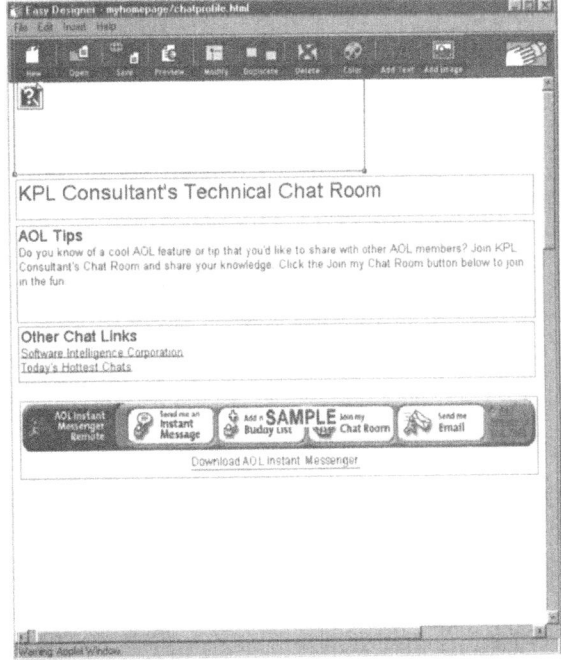

Figure 15-10. Modifying a Web page in the Easy Designer customization window

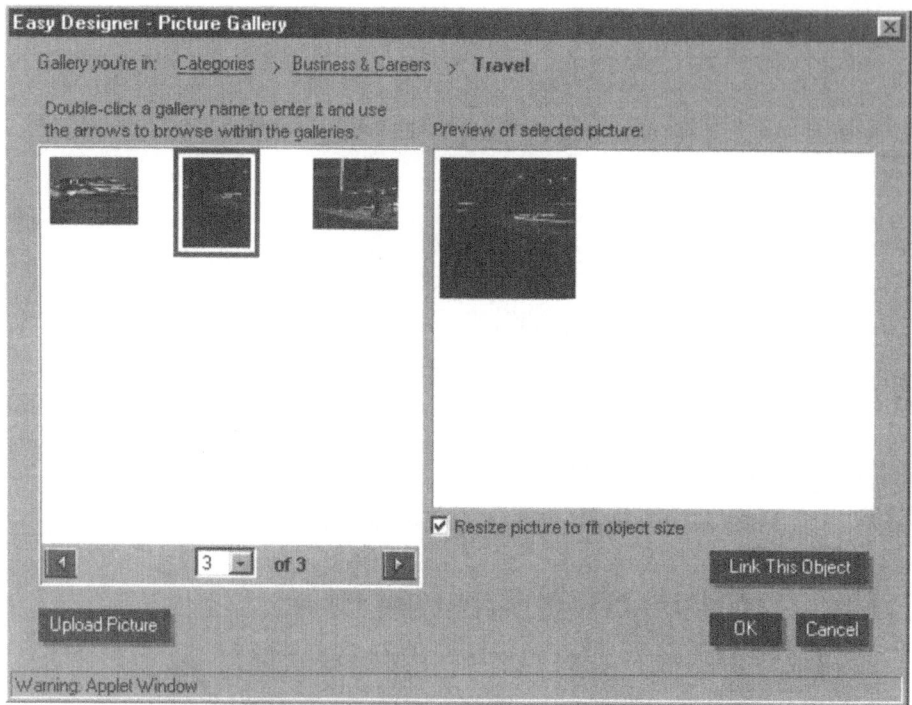

Figure 15-11. Selecting a graphic image from Easy Designer's Picture Gallery window

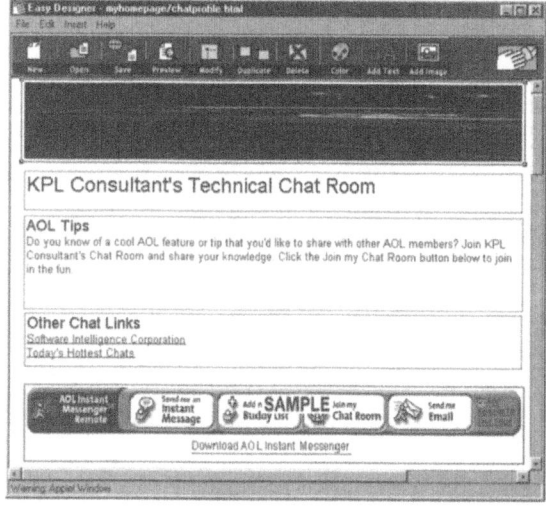

Figure 15-12. Sizing the image to fit on your Web page

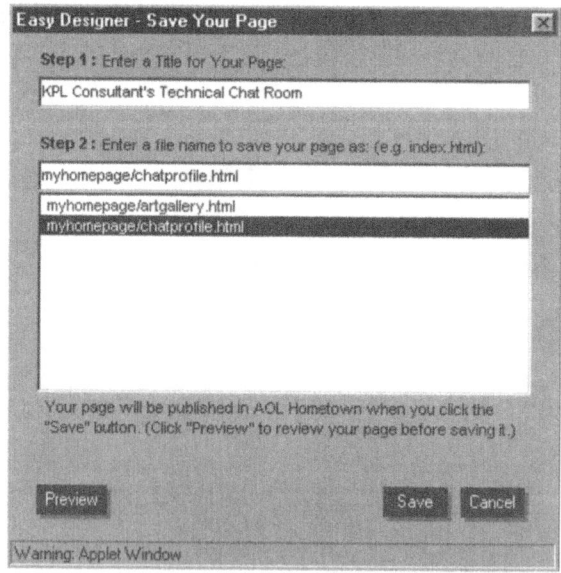

Figure 15-13. Previewing and saving your Web page changes

19 Adding hyperlinks to your page with Easy Designer

AOL lets you add hyperlinks, which allow users to move from one Web page to another in just one mouse click. Hyperlinks are displayed in color, usually in blue underline text, and your mouse pointer changes to a pointing finger as the mouse is moved over a link. With AOL's Easy Designer, you'll be able to add hyperlinks to text or graphics, whatever objects you choose. Here's how it's done:

1. Click the **Keyword** button located on the AOL toolbar and enter AOL Keyword: **Authoring Tools** or **Publishing Tools**.

2. Click the **Go** button to display AOL's **Publishing Tools** channel.

3. Click **Easy Designer** on AOL's **Publishing Tools** channel to display AOL's **Easy Designer** Web site.

4. Click **Open an Existing Page** on AOL's **Easy Designer** Web site to display the **Easy Designer** tool.

5. Click **Click to get started!** button to display the **Easy Designer—Open an Existing Page** window.

6. Select the page you want opened and click the **Open** button on the **Easy Designer— Open an Existing Page** window to display your Web page in the **Easy Designer** window.

7. Right-click the desired object (e.g., graphic image) on your Web page and select **Modify** from the drop-down selection list that appears.

8. Click the **Link This Object** button on the **Easy Designer—Picture Gallery** window.

9. Enter the Web Address (URL) you want to link to on the **Easy Designer—Link To** window and click the **OK** button, shown in Figure 15-14.

10. Click the **OK** button on the **Easy Designer— Picture Gallery** window to complete the hyperlink process.

11. Click the **Save** button located on the **Easy Designer** toolbar to save your Web page.

12. Click the **OK** button on the **Your page has been saved. The page address is ...** dialog box.

13. Close the **Easy Designer** customization window.

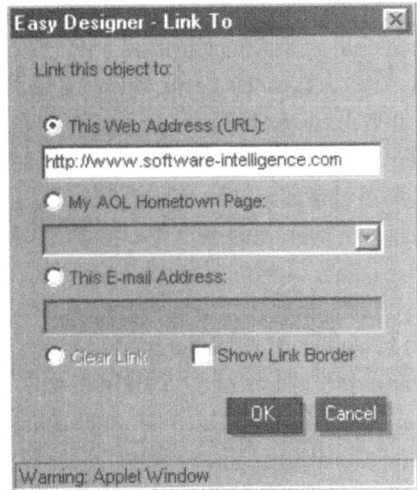

Figure 15-14. Adding a hyperlink to a Web page object with AOL's Easy Designer Web site

20 Checking hyperlinks to see if they work

The Internet is a dynamic medium with content always changing. Hyperlinks let you transfer your user from one place on a Web page to another place. Consequently, you should check hyperlinks periodically to make sure they are not broken or out-of-date. This will prevent visitors from becoming frustrated with your Web content, or worse yet, shying away from your page altogether.

21 Avoiding the risks associated with hyperlinks

AOL lets users of Version 4.0 or higher block the blue underlined text links, commonly referred to as hyperlinks from appearing in e-mails, chats, Instant Message notes, and message boards. This prevents children or others from clicking on a link and being redirected to a Web page that is inappropriate or has undesirable content. To avoid the risks associated with hyperlinks on a Web page, always move your mouse over the link and hold it there for a second before you click. This will display the address of the link at the bottom of your screen. You can then decide whether or not to click the mouse and visit that site or not.

22 Changing your background color with Easy Designer

Do you want to change the background color of your Web page? AOL's **Easy Designer** makes it easy to change your Web page's background color anytime, and as often as you'd like. But before you do, use care when choosing a background color. Make sure that your Web page will not be difficult for sight-impaired or colorblind visitors to read. Colorblindness is the inability to distinguish between certain shades of color. Certain background and hyperlink colors can be difficult to read when combined together. So in choosing your Web page colors, be aware that certain shades of red and green may be indistinguishable to some visitors, while others may experience this problem with certain shades of blue and yellow. You'll want to provide all your visitors with the greatest and most satisfying online experience possible. So choose your colors wisely. Here's how you'll be able to change your background color:

1. Click the **Keyword** button located on the AOL toolbar and enter AOL Keyword: **Easy Designer**.

2. Click the **Go** button to display AOL's **Easy Designer** Web site.

3. Select the template you used to design your Web page from the list and follow the on-screen instructions to begin the customization process with AOL's **Easy Designer**.

4. Click **Click to get started!** button on the Easy Designer Web site.

5. Click the **Customize** button on the **Easy Designer—Select a Color Style** window.

6. Click the **Color** button under the **Background** heading to see a list of color choices, shown in Figure 15-15.

7. Select the background color you want from the **Color Selector** window and click the **OK** button.

8. Click the **OK** button on the **Easy Designer— Customize Colors** window.

9. Click the **OK** button on the **Easy Designer— Select a Color Style** window.

10. Click the **Save** button located on the **Easy Designer** toolbar to save your Web page.

11. Click the **OK** button on the **Your page has been saved. The page address is ...** dialog box.

12. Close the **Easy Designer** customization window.

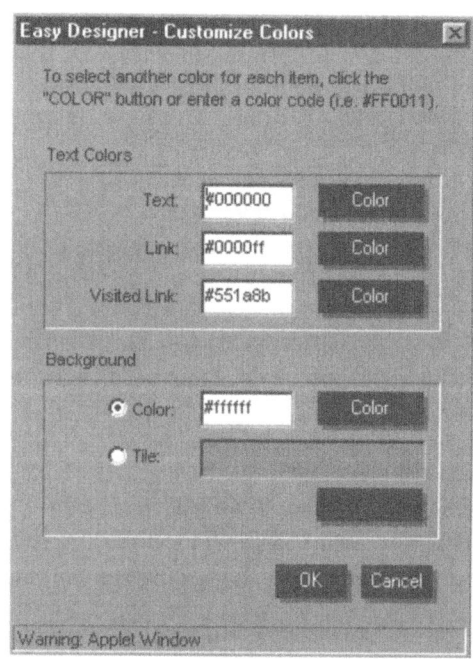

Figure 15-15. Changing your Web page's background color is easy.

23 Linking text to a URL with Easy Designer

AOL's **Easy Designer** let's you link text to a Web Address (URL) to create a point-and-click capability. You'll be able to create a custom Web page quickly and easily. Here's how:

1. Click the **Keyword** button located on the AOL toolbar and enter AOL Keyword: **Easy Designer**.

2. Click the **Go** button to display AOL's **Easy Designer** Web site.

3. Select the template you used to design your Web page from the list and follow the on-screen instructions to begin the customization process with AOL's **Easy Designer.**

4. Click the **Click to get started!** button on the **Easy Designer** Web site.

5. Right-click the text box where your text is located and select **Modify** from the drop-down selection list to display the **Easy Designer—Text Editor** window.

6. **Highlight the text** you want to link to a URL, and click the **Link This Text** button, shown in Figure 15-16.

7. Enter the Web address in the **This Web Address (URL):** field on the **Easy Designer—Link To** window, and click the **OK** button, shown in Figure 15-17.

8. Click the **OK** button on the **Easy Designer—Text Editor** window.

9. Click the **Save** button located on the **Easy Designer** toolbar to save your Web page.

10. Click the **OK** button on the **Your page has been saved. The page address is ...** dialog box.

11. Close the **Easy Designer** customization window.

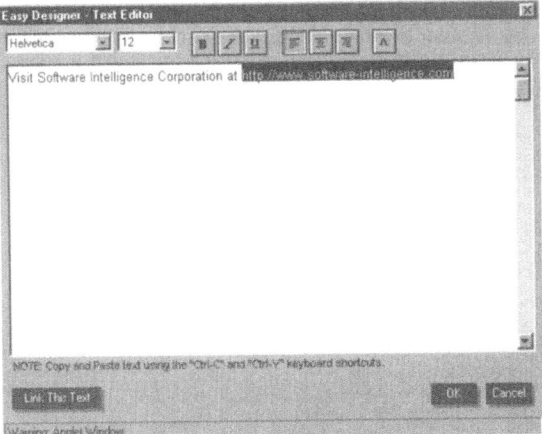

Figure 15-16. Selecting text to link to a Web address (URL)

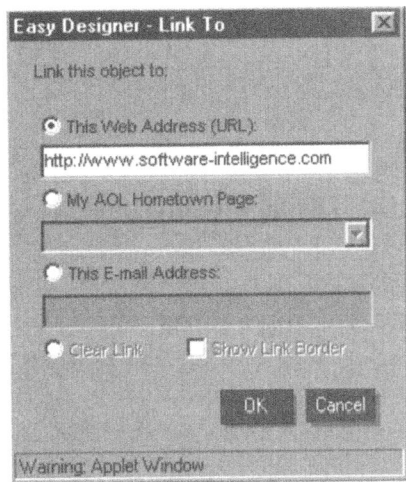

Figure 15-17. Entering a Web address corresponding to the selected text

24 Adding a counter with Easy Designer

Adding a counter to your Web page is a great way to see how many visitors have visited your page. You'll be able to add this valuable tool to your Web page easily and quickly with AOL's Easy Designer. It lets you add text anywhere you want quickly and easily. Here's how:

1. Click the **Keyword** button located on the AOL toolbar and enter AOL Keyword: **Easy Designer**.

2. Click the **Go** button to display AOL's **Easy Designer** Web site.

3. Select the template you used to design your Web page from the list and follow the on-screen instructions to begin the customization process with AOL's Easy Designer.

4. Click the **Click to get started!** button on the **Easy Designer** Web site.

5. Select **Counter** from the **Insert** drop-down menu at the top of the **Easy Designer** window.

6. Move the counter to the desired location on your Web page by dragging it, and resize, if necessary.

7. Click the **Save** button located on the **Easy Designer** toolbar to save your Web page.

8. Click the **OK** button on the **Your page has been saved. The page address is ...** dialog box.

9. Close the **Easy Designer** customization window.

25 Adding music or sound with Easy Designer

Adding music or sound to your Web page creates a unique experience for visitors. Treat visitors with music or sound that augments the theme of your page. AOL lets you access an assortment of music and sound files directly from the Web and then add them to your Web page and to your FTPSPACE. Here's how:

Downloading Music and Sound Files

1. Click the **Keyword** button located on the AOL toolbar and enter AOL Keyword: **Music and Sound**.

2. Click the **Go** button to display AOL's **Music & Sound** Website.

3. Click **Music & Sound Libraries** under the **Related Links** heading to display AOL's **Music & Sound Libraries**, shown in Figure 15-18.

4. Double-click the library or folder of interest to open it.

5. Double-click a category and then double-click a library to display the MIDI and .WAV files in a selection window.

6. Select the file you want to download from the list and click the **Download Now** button to save the file to your computer's hard drive. Using the **Download Manager**, navigate to the desired folder on your computer's hard drive.

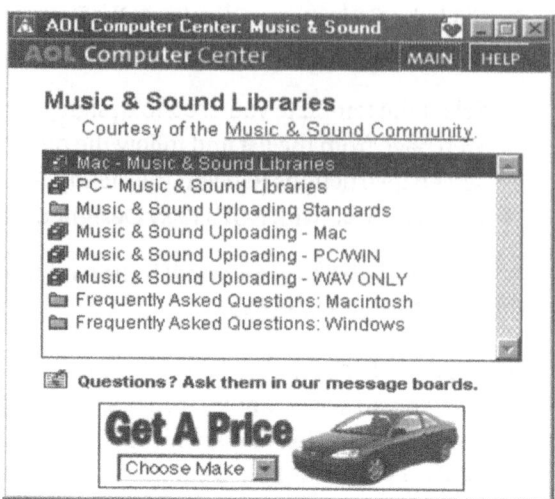

Figure 15-18. Accessing PC and Mac music and sound libraries is easy with AOL

Adding Background Music or Sound to Your Web Page

Adding background music or sound to your Web page requires that you add a single line of HTML code and upload the music or sound file to AOL Keyword: **FTPSPACE** as a binary file. Here's how it's done:

1. Click the **Keyword** button located on the AOL toolbar and enter AOL Keyword: **Easy Designer**.

2. Click the **Go** button to display AOL's **Easy Designer** Web site.

3. Select the template you used to design your Web page from the list and follow the on-screen instructions to begin the customization process with AOL's **Easy Designer**.

4. Click the **Click to get started!** button on the **Easy Designer** Web site.

5. Select **Advanced HTML** from the **Insert** drop-down menu at the top of the **Easy Designer** window.

6. Enter the following HTML tag: **<embed src="sound-file-name.midi">** where sound-file-name is the name of the music or sound file you want to use in the **Easy Designer—Advanced HTML Source Code Editor**, shown in Figure 15-19.

7. Click the **OK** button.

8. Move the music or sound object to the desired location on your Web page by dragging it, preventing the object from becoming overlapped with another object.

9. Click the **Save** button located on the **Easy Designer** toolbar to save your Web page.

10. Click the **OK** button on the **Your page has been saved. The page address is ...** dialog box.

11. Close the **Easy Designer** customization window.

12. Click the **Keyword** button located on the AOL toolbar and enter AOL Keyword: **FTPSPACE**. Click the **Go** button to display AOL's **My FTP Space** channel.

13. Click **See My FTP Space** to upload the music or sound file to your personal Web space.

14. Double-click the **MyHomePage** folder to display the files in your Web page space.

15. Click the **Upload** button.

16. Enter the name of the music or sound file in the **Remote Filename** field, click the **Binary** radio button, and click the **Continue** button, shown in Figure 15-20.

17. Click the **Select File** button on the **Upload File** window and navigate to the location of the music or sound file on your computer's hard drive, and select the file to be uploaded, shown in Figure 15-21.

18. Click the **Send** button on the **Upload File** window. You'll see the **File Transfer** window appear as it uploads the file.

19. Click the **OK** button on the **File transfer complete** dialog box.

20. Close all open windows and test the Web page by entering your Web address (URL).

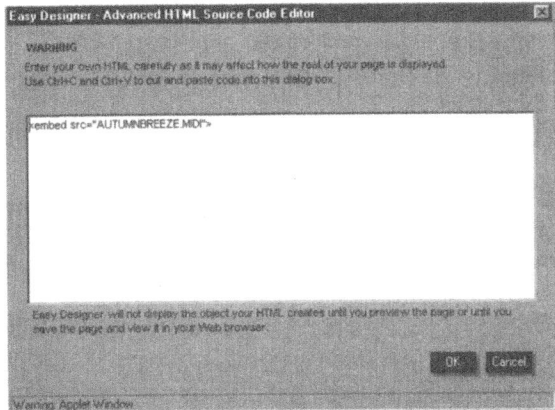

Figure 15-19. Adding background music or sound to your Web page can be done by anyone

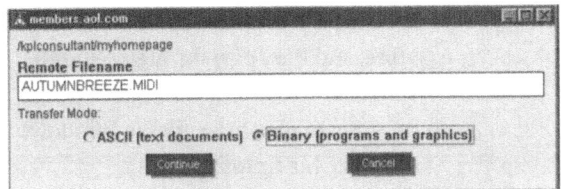

Figure 15-20. Uploading the music or sound file to your FTPSPACE in binary format

Figure 15-21. Selecting the music or sound file to upload to your FTPSPACE on AOL

26 Understanding sound file types and extensions

Understanding sound file types and extensions is helpful in making your Web page the best it can be. Although a variety of sound and music file types exist, you'll want to know which file types offer the best sound and access speed, especially when selecting files to be downloaded or when creating your own. This will make your Web page shine while giving your visitors the greatest online experience possible.

.AVI	Represents an audio visual file, used for Windows video files. AOL's Windows software will display these files.
.MID (.MIDI)	Represents a Musical Instrument Digital Interface file. MIDI files are songs for most sound cards and MIDI boards. AOL's software will play these files.
.MOD	Represents a music module that includes the instruments as well as the score, and they play through a sound card, not MIDI. You will need a special program to play these files in Windows or on the Macintosh.
.SIT	Represents a StuffIt file. These are Macintosh compressed files that can be extracted by Windows users with programs such as UnSit and UnStuff. Some of the files with this extension will not run on Windows, even after extraction. AOL's Macintosh software will open these files.
.SND	Represents a sound file for Macintosh System 7 sounds that can be played on Windows using converters such as SOX. AOL's Macintosh software will run these files.
.WAV	Represents a Windows sound file. Mac users can find utilities in the Software Center at Keyword: Software to convert them to sound files that the Macintosh can play. AOL's Windows software will play these files.

27 Adding animation with Easy Designer

Adding animation to your Web page can create visual impact like nothing else. AOL lets you add images that blink, move, twirl, scroll, and much more. You can even treat your visitors with a movie that they can download and view on their own computer. Here's how you can create a stimulating environment for anyone visiting your page.

Downloading Animated GIF Files

1. Click the **Keyword** button located on the AOL toolbar and enter AOL Keyword: **Animated GIFS** or **AGIF**.

2. Click the **Go** button to display AOL's **Animated GIF Resources** channel, shown in Figure 15-22.

3. Double-click the library or folder of interest to open it.

4. Select the animated GIF file you want to download from the list and click the **Download Now** button to save the file to your computer's hard drive. Using the **Download Manager**, navigate to the desired folder on your computer's hard drive.

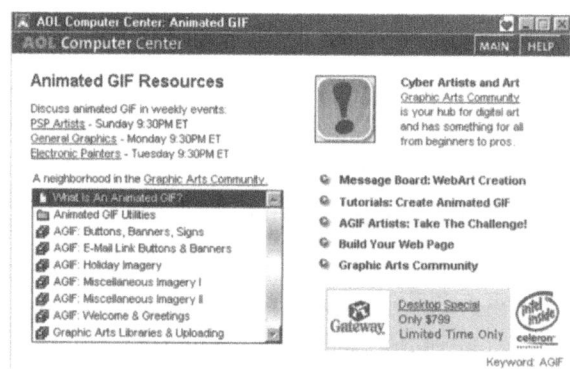

Figure 15-22. Downloading an animated GIF file from an assortment of categories is easy.

Adding Animated GIF Files to Your Web Page

Adding an animated GIF file to your Web page requires that you add a single line of HTML code to your page and uploading the GIF file to AOL Keyword: **FTPSPACE** as a binary file. Here's how it's done:

1. Click the **Keyword** button located on the AOL toolbar and enter AOL Keyword: **Easy Designer**.

2. Click the **Go** button to display AOL's **Easy Designer** Web site.

3. Select the template you used to design your Web page from the list and follow the on-screen instructions to begin the customization process with AOL's **Easy Designer**.

4. Click the **Click to get started!** button on the **Easy Designer** Website.

5. Select **Advanced HTML** from the **Insert** drop-down menu at the top of the **Easy Designer** window.

6. Enter the following HTML tag: **<img src="animated-file-name.gif">** where animated-file-name is the name of the GIF you want to use in the **Easy Designer—Advanced HTML Source Code Editor**, shown in Figure 15-23.

7. Click the **OK** button.

8. Move the animated GIF object to the desired location on your Web page by dragging it, preventing the object from becoming over-lapped with another object.

9. Click the **Save** button located on the **Easy Designer** toolbar to save your Web page.

10. Click the **OK** button on the **Your page has been saved. The page address is …** dialog box.

11. Close the **Easy Designer** customization window.

12. Click the **Keyword** button located on the AOL toolbar and enter AOL Keyword: **FTPSPACE**. Click the **Go** button to display AOL's **My FTP Space** channel.

13. Click **See My FTP Space** to upload the animated GIF file to your personal Web space.

14. Double-click the **MyHomePage** folder to display the files in your Web page space.

15. Click the **Upload** button.

16. Enter the name of the animated GIF file in the **Remote Filename** field, click the **Binary** radio button, and click the **Continue** button.

17. Click the **Select File** button on the **Upload File** window and navigate to the location of the animated GIF file on your computer's hard drive, and select the file to be uploaded.

18. Click the **Send** button on the **Upload File** window. You'll see the **File Transfer** window appear as it uploads the file.

19. Click the **OK** button on the **File transfer complete** dialog box.

20. Close all open windows and test the Web page by entering your Web address (URL).

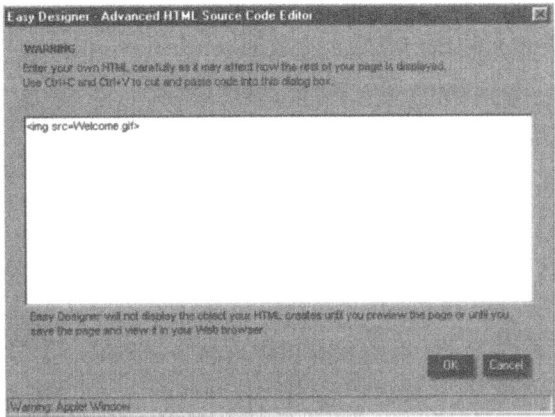

Figure 15-23. Adding the HTML tag for an animated GIF can be done quickly and easily.

Clip Art Graphics

28 Understanding graphic file types and extensions

Understanding graphic file types and extensions is helpful in making your Web page the best it can be. Although a variety of graphic file types exist, you'll want to know which file types offer the best resolution and access speed, especially when selecting files to be downloaded or when creating your own. This will make your Web page shine while giving your visitors the greatest online experience possible. Table 15-3 provides a brief description of each graphic file type.

TABLE 15-3. GRAPHIC FILE TYPES

ART	Represents a compressed graphics file using AOL's Johnson-Grace system. These files can be viewed using your AOL software.
.AVI	Represents an audio visual file, used for Windows video files. AOL's Windows software will display these files.
.BMP	Represents a Windows bitmap graphics file. AOL's software can display these files.
.EPS	Represents an Encapsulated Postscript File. These are images designed for vector, or line-based, drawing programs such as Adobe Illustrator. AOL's software cannot display these files.
.GIF	Represents Graphics Interchange Format type of graphic images that are very common in online services and the Internet. GIF includes file compression as part of its definition, so no additional file compression software is needed. AOL's software can display these.
.JPG or .JPEG	Represents Joint Photographers Expert Group type of graphics format designed to take up as little space as possible while retaining as much quality as possible. JPG files are smaller than GIF files, but take longer to display. AOL's software will display these files.
.PCX	Represents older graphics files, commonly used for clip art.
.PCT or .PICT	Represents the original Macintosh graphics format. AOL's Macintosh software will display these files.
.SCR	Represents a Windows screen saver file. These will not work unless placed in your C:\Windows directory.

TABLE 15-3. GRAPHIC FILE TYPES (CONTINUED)

.SIT	Represents a StuffIt file. These are Macintosh compressed files that can be extracted by Windows users with programs such as UnSit and UnStuff. Some of the files with this extension will not run on Windows, even after extraction. AOL's Macintosh software will open these files.
.TIF	Represents a Tagged Image Format or bitmapped graphic image. These are popular among desktop publishers. AOL's software will not display these files.
.TTF	Represents a True Type Font and are scalable fonts commonly used in Windows. You will need to run the Windows Control Panel to install them.

29 Adding clip art to your Web page

Finding and downloading clip art to add to your Web page is easy with AOL's Web Art & Artists Center. Not only is it easy but it's also free. You'll find GIF and JPEG backgrounds and images, banners and text images, bars and bullets, buttons and icons, online classes, graphics arts communities, chats, message boards, and much more so you can spice up your Web page. Here's how:

1. Click the **Keyword** button located on the AOL toolbar and enter AOL Keyword: **Authoring Tools** or **Publishing Tools**.

2. Click the **Go** button to display AOL's **Publishing Tools** channel.

3. Click **Clip Art** on AOL's Publishing Tools channel to display AOL's **Web Art & Artists Center** channel, shown in Figure 15-24.

   <or>

1. Click the **Keyword** button located on the AOL toolbar and enter AOL Keyword: **Web Art**.

2. Click the **Go** button to display AOL's **Web Art & Artists Center** channel.

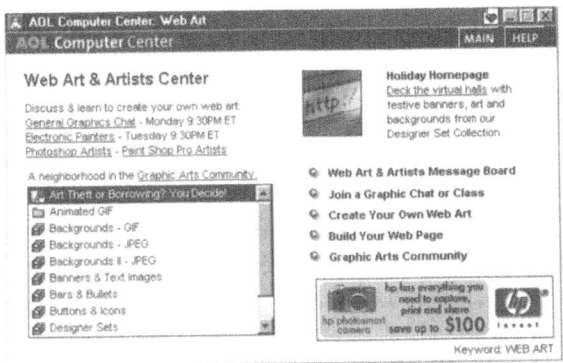

Figure 15-24. There's a wealth of good clip art on AOL's Web Art & Artists Center channel.

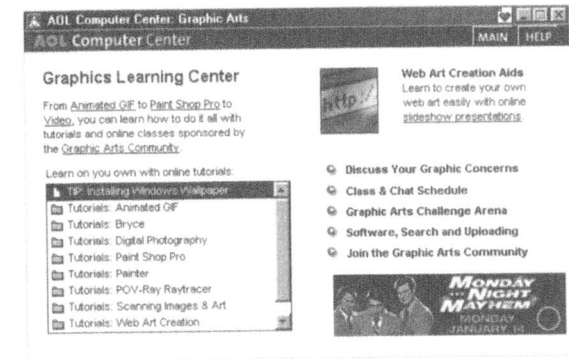

Figure 15-25. AOL's Graphics Learning Center

30 Creating your own Web art

Would you like to create your own Web art? AOL provides an online graphics learning center with slideshow presentations, online tutorials, chats, and message boards, to show you how to create great-looking Web art. You'll learn how to create animated GIFs, use 3D rendering software from Corel, brighten and dim images, invert and rotate pictures, use Paint Shop Pro, scan images and art, create Web textures, convert GIF to JPEG and JPEG to GIF, and much more. Here's how:

1. Click the **Keyword** button located on the AOL toolbar and enter AOL Keyword: **Web Art**.

2. Click the **Go** button to display AOL's **Web Art & Artists Center** channel.

3. Click **Create Your Own Web Art** to display AOL's **Graphics Learning Center** channel, shown in Figure 15-25.

4. Click **Slideshow presentations** under the **Web Art Creation Aids** heading to display the assortment of **Web Art Creation Slideshows**, shown in Figure 15-26.

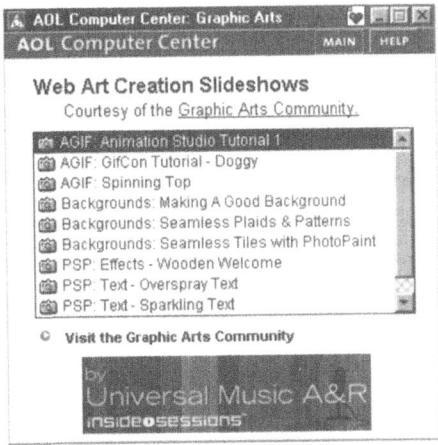

Figure 15-26. Learning how to create Web art with online slideshows

31 Downloading background art

You'll find a broad assortment of GIF and JPEG background art to choose from on AOL's Web Art & Artists Center channel: rainbows, colorful borders, waving flags, grids, textures, bubbles, smoke patterns, shooting stars, planets, and much more. AOL's downloadable backgrounds are freely distributed, but only for use on an AOL member's personal Web site. Here's how to download the art to your PC's hard drive:

1. Click the **Keyword** button located on the AOL toolbar and enter AOL Keyword: **Web Art**.

2. Click the **Go** button to display AOL's **Web Art & Artists Center** channel.

3. Double-click the desired GIF or JPEG background art folder from the selection list.

4. Select the background art file of interest and click the **Read Description** button for a detailed description of the file including information on the author, uploaded by, date written, image size, resolution, and copyright information. When done, close the **Read Description** information. Click the **List More Files** button to see additional background art files.

5. Select the desired file and click the **Download Now** or **Download Later** button to navigate to the desired directory and/or folder on your PC's hard drive. AOL's **Download Manager** window will handle the download process.

32 Downloading banners and text images

Would you like to include banners on your site? You'll find numerous GIF and 24-bit banner and text images on AOL's Web Art & Artists Center channel in the shape of banners. Choose from welcome banners, holiday-oriented and Christian banners, Web art greetings, under construction signs, and much more. Take note: AOL's downloadable banners and text images are freely distributed for use on a member's personal Web site only. Here's how to download the banners to your PC's hard drive:

1. Click the **Keyword** button located on the AOL toolbar and enter AOL Keyword: **Web Art**.

2. Click the **Go** button to display AOL's **Web Art & Artists Center** channel.

3. Double-click the **Banner & Text Images** folder from the selection list on AOL's **Web Art & Artists Center** channel.

4. Select the **Banner & Text** image file of interest and click the **Read Description** button for a detailed description of the file including information on the author, uploaded by, date written, image size, resolution, and copyright

information. When done, close the **Read Description** information. Click the **List More Files** button to see additional background art files.

5. Select the desired file and click the **Download Now** or **Download Later** button to navigate to the desired directory and/or folder on your PC's hard drive. AOL's **Download Manager** window will handle the download process.

33 Downloading animated art

Animated art can really liven up a Web page. Choose from a variety of GIF animated art images on AOL's Web Art & Artists Center channel including: animated buttons, banners, signs, e-mail link buttons and banners, holiday imagery, and welcome art. AOL's downloadable animated art is freely distributed for use on a member's personal Web site only. Here's how to access those files:

1. Click the **Keyword** button located on the AOL toolbar and enter AOL Keyword: **Web Art**.

2. Click the **Go** button to display AOL's **Web Art & Artists Center** channel.

3. Double-click the **Animated GIF** folder from the selection list on AOL's **Web Art & Artists Center** channel to display AOL's **Animated GIF Resources** channel.

4. Double-click the animated GIF folder of interest on the **Animated GIF Resources** channel.

5. Select the desired file and click the **Read Description** button for a detailed description of the file including information on the author, uploaded by, date written, image size, resolution, and copyright information. When done, close the **Read Description** information. Click the **List More Files** button to see additional background art files.

6. Select the desired file and click the **Download Now** or **Download Later** button to navigate to the desired directory and/or folder on your PC's hard drive. AOL's **Download Manager** window will handle the download process.

<or>

1. Click the **Keyword** button located on the AOL toolbar and enter AOL Keyword: **AGIF.**

2. Click the **Go** button to display AOL's **Animated GIF Resources** channel.

3. Double-click the animated GIF folder of interest on the **Animated GIF Resources** channel.

4. Select the desired file and click the **Read Description** button for a detailed description of the file including information on the author, uploaded by, date written, image size, resolution, and copyright information. When done, close the **Read Description** information. Click the **List More Files** button to see additional background art files.

5. Select the desired file and click the **Download Now** or **Download Later** button to navigate to the desired directory and/or folder on your PC's hard drive. AOL's **Download Manager** window will handle the download process.

34 Using care when borrowing someone else's work

With all the wonderful and valuable resources on the Web and in libraries, the temptation to borrow someone else's work is huge. It can't be overemphasized, to take someone else's work IS stealing and is called plagiarism.

The Author(s) of an original work of computer art is protected under U.S. Copyright laws. Using or borrowing someone else's work without their express permission is against the law. Only the author or, if the work was created as a work for hire, the employer may lay claim to ownership of computer art. Using computer art and other works without the express permission of the rightful owner threatens the livelihood of artists and other specialists. As a personal property right, copyright is subject to the numerous state laws and regulations that govern ownership. It's recommended that anyone needing specific advice about copyright law should consult an attorney. To request further information, you can contact the United States Copyright Office:

Copyright Office
LM 455
Library of Congress
Washington, D.C. 20559-6000
Web site Address:
`http://lcweb.loc.gov/copyright/`

35 Accessing graphic arts communities

Would you like to communicate with computer artists and other like-minded individuals? AOL's Computer Community—Graphics Arts Web site covers a variety of graphic arts topics including 3D Rendering, Digital Photography, Web Art, Animation and Video, Electronic Paint, and Computing, as well as chat, message boards, home pages, related links, computing communities, and much more. Here's how you can access the stimulating graphics arts communities:

1. Click the **Keyword** button located on the AOL toolbar and enter AOL Keyword: **Web Art.**

2. Click the **Go** button to display AOL's **Web Art & Artists Center** channel.

3. Click **Graphic Arts Community** to display AOL's **Computer Community—Graphics Arts** Web site, shown in Figure 15-27.

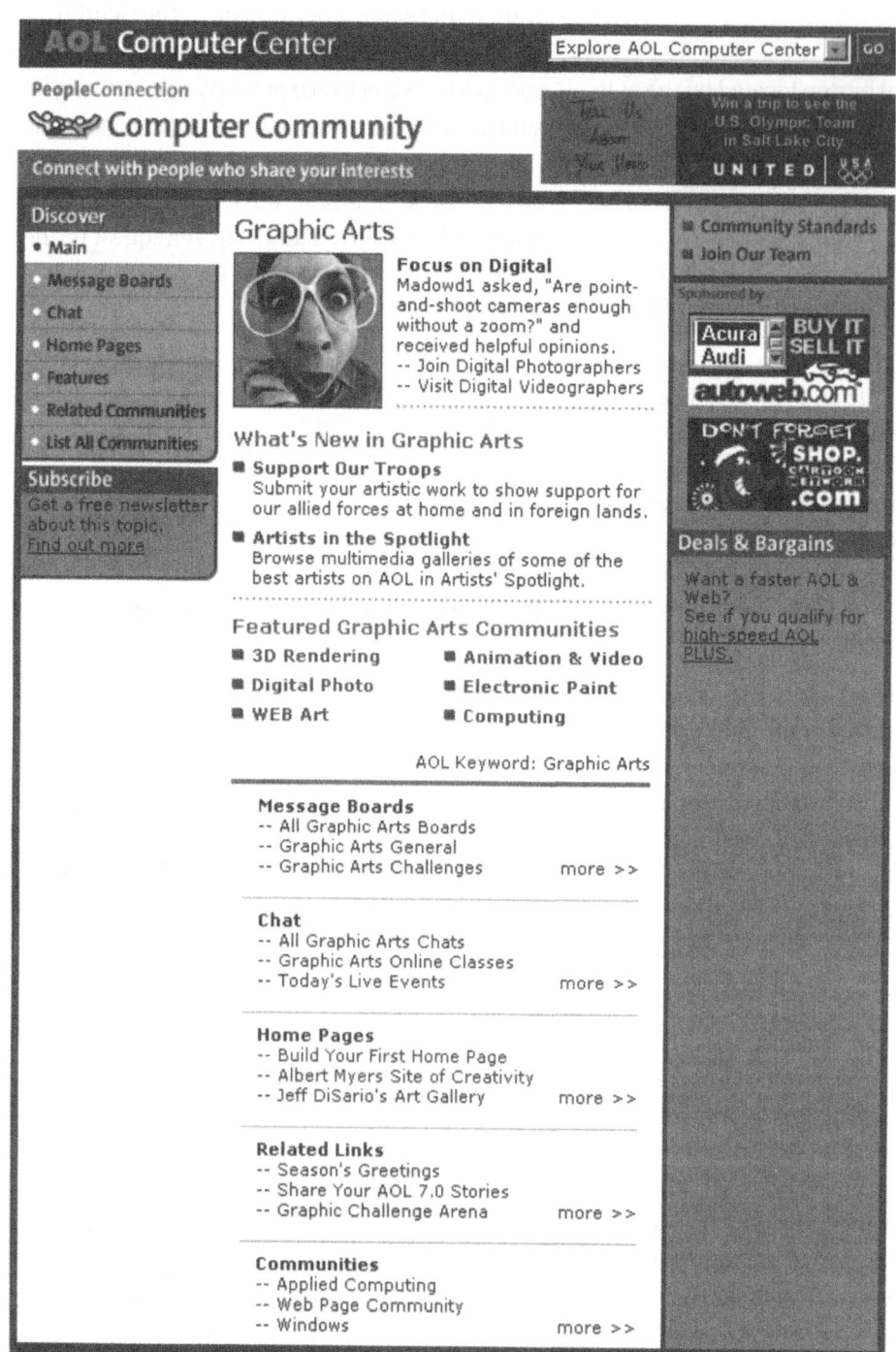

Figure 15-27. Accessing the exciting world of graphics arts on AOL's Graphics Art Web site

Shareware Web Tools and Web Publishing

36 Deciding on PC publishing tools

AOL provides an assortment of PC shareware publishing tools for you to test-drive and use for your own Web publishing needs. Most are inexpensive full-featured publishing tools that will let you create wonderful looking Web pages. You'll find HTML and Web authoring programs, Web graphic programs, and Web and HTML utilities. Here's how you can access these PC publishing tools:

1. Click the **Keyword** button located on the AOL toolbar and enter AOL Keyword: **Authoring Tools** or **Publishing Tools**.

2. Click the **Go** button to display AOL's **Publishing Tools** channel.

3. Click **Shareware** on AOL's **Publishing Tools** channel to display AOL's **Tools We Recommend** window.

HTML & Web Authoring Programs

CoffeeCup Express V5.0 is a free HTML editor that allows novices to create professional-looking pages. Files can be uploaded to your Web site with a right-click of your mouse.

Under Construction 98 is a Web editor that provides features for both the beginner and advanced Web author.

HOMESITE: V4.5 Web Page Maker is an HTML design tool for professional Web developers.

ARACHNOPHILIA: V4.0 HTML Editor is a Web project organizer. Arachnophilia helps you get started if you are a beginner, and it will help you organize larger projects as you acquire more experience.

Web Graphic Programs

PSP: Paint Shop Pro Win 3.x PaintShop Pro is a graphic editing tool that helps prepare graphics for your Web pages. It lets you convert graphics between formats, resize graphics and create special effects.

It is developed by JASC and provides features similar to the more costly commercial graphics software.

ULEAD: V5.0 PhotoImpact Trial Version is an easy-to-use graphic editing tool designed to work with graphics, animations, buttons and text effects for the web. It comes with a 30-day trial and requires Windows 95, 98, or NT 4.x or later.

GIFWEB: V3.1 Transparent Gifs GifWeb makes it easy to put transparent graphics on your web page. It's used when you want to design Web buttons or icons that let the foreground show but want the Web page background to show through.

GIFCON: V1Q Animated Gifs GifCon is a popular Web graphic animator. GifCon lets you add animation to your Web page by building animated gifs and then adds them to your Web page as if they were standard graphics. It's available in a 32-bit version for Windows 95/98, and a 32-bit professional version.

LIVEIMAGE: V1.29 Imagemap Editor AOL supports "client side" ImageMaps that were uploaded and reside on your Web space in My FTP Space along with your page and graphics. LiveImage for Windows 95/98 creates an image map file, but does require some experience with HTML and Graphics before using the product.

Web & HTML Utilities

WS-FTP: V5.8 FTP LE Client WS_FTP permits batch uploading, point and click delete and rename, and more. A 16-bit version is also available for use with Windows 3.x. Please note that the 32-bit client requires both Win95/98+ and a 32-bit version of the AOL software. WS_FTP LE is free to non-commercial users.

COLOR: V2.0 Color Picker Mix, browse, and pick the exact color you want for your Web page background, links, and more. Color Picker returns the RGB values so you can paste them into your Web page.

CACHEK: V1.40 Cache Killer Pro Delete cache and history files for Netscape, MSIE, and AOL browsers easily and quickly. Eliminating your computer's cache of older Web page versions allows you to see the newly published version.

37 Macintosh publishing tools

AOL provides an assortment of Macintosh shareware publishing tools for you to test-drive and use for your own Web publishing needs. Most are inexpensive full-featured publishing tools that will let you create wonderful looking Web pages. Here's how you can access these Macintosh publishing tools:

1. Click the **Keyword** button located on the AOL toolbar and enter AOL Keyword: **Authoring Tools** or **Publishing Tools**.

2. Click the **Go** button to display AOL's **Publishing Tools** channel.

3. Click **Macintosh Tools** on AOL's **Publishing Tools** channel to display AOL's **Recommended Tools** window.

Mac Publishing Tools

AOLpress for MacOS 7.x or 8.0 is a do-it-yourself Web publishing software package that includes a WYSIWYG (What You See Is What You Get) editor that allows you to create a page without having HTML knowledge. AOLpress is a free tool, and is available for a limited time. Note, this version of AOLPress is not currently compatible with MacOS 8.5 or later.

PageSpinner is an HTML Editor for MacOS. It's designed for beginners and advanced Web developers and supports HTML 3.2 plus additional Netscape extensions. The editor gives you quick access to often-used formatting tools and supports interactive help with AppleGuide and an HTML Assistant to help you compose dynamic Web pages.

Wallaby is a small, easy-to-use HTML Editor for the Macintosh. It is designed for both the experienced Web designer and the beginner. It combines a simple-to-use user interface and is packed with lots of features. It includes drag-and-drop text editing and JavaScript samples.

HTML Editor offers simple text editing of files smaller than 32k. The editor lets you insert HTML tags via button clicks and menu selections. Includes an undo command, find-and-replace, and an HTML checker.

BBEdit Lite V4.6 is a powerful text manipulation and development tool that makes it easy to create and edit HTML documents. The "lite" version is fully functional and freely distributed. A demo of BBEdit 5.1.1 is available to let you test-drive it before purchasing the professional version.

Cinnamon WebMaster Suite (CWMS) V1.4 is a very compact, simple, yet feature-packed HTML text editor. If you're looking for something with a little more convenience than Mac SimpleText but not as cumbersome as a full-fledged Web authoring program, this one may be for you.

Texplore is a fast text editor that has a macro system with a set of HTML macros for Web page editing. Texplore also lets you use auto-scrolling capabilities to make reading text documents on your screen easier.

TextureMill is a Web publishing tool that allows the creation of seamless textures for Web pages, multimedia, 3D rendering, and desktop patterns. Select up to 20 unique patterns, change the way your page looks with different surface treatments, colorize any image with a multicolor selector, preview the image as a background in a Web page, then save the image in PICT or GIF file format.

ColorSieve is a utility that will display the color information for any pixel on the screen. It supports displaying color information in RGB, HSL, HSV, and CMY.

RTF to HTML is a tool to convert RTF documents (from Microsoft Word, WordPerfect, etc.) into HTML documents for the Web. It's also available for the Macintosh.

Fetch is an easy-to-use Macintosh FTP client. It allows point-and-click, drag-and-drop file transfers to and from any machine with a FTP server, over a TCP/IP network. Fetch is used to publish your web pages to AOL's FTPSpace.

38 Uploading a template script file to your Web space

Once your Web page is written, tested, and validated, you'll need to upload it to your AOL Web space. AOL provides a fast and easy way to upload a script file, and best of all, it's available for any AOL member to use free of charge. Here's how:

1. Click the **Keyword** button located on the AOL toolbar and enter AOL Keyword: **FTPSPACE.**

2. Click the **Go** button to display AOL's **My FTP Space** channel.

3. Click **See My FTP Space** to upload the script file to your personal Web space.

4. Double-click the **MyHomePage** folder to display the files in your Web page space.

5. Click the **Upload** button.

6. Enter the name of the script file in the **Remote Filename** field, click the **ASCII** radio button, and click the **Continue** button.

7. Click the **Select File** button on the **Upload File** window and navigate to the location of the script file on your computer's hard drive, and select the file to be uploaded.

8. Click the **Send** button on the **Upload File** window. You'll see the **File Transfer** window appear as it uploads the file.

9. Click the **OK** button on the **File transfer complete** dialog box.

10. Close all open windows and test the Web page by entering your Web address (URL).

CHAPTER 16

Problem Solving and Errors

THIS CHAPTER PRESENTS problem solving and error resolution tips to help make your AOL experience a happier one. Many of the error messages you may encounter while using AOL are explained with one or more appropriate solutions. Instead of the all-too-pervasive mumbo-jumbo tech talk that's often associated with resolving an error message—you'll get explanations and solutions presented in plain English. This not only will reduce your frustration levels, but also will give you the help you need to resolve those nagging and often confusing error messages quickly.

In this troubleshooting chapter, errors are classified and diagnosed in these categories:

- ☐ Detecting and dealing with errors
- ☐ Connecting problems
- ☐ Explaining e-mail issues
- ☐ Troubleshooting Instant Messenger, telnet, mailing lists, and FTP
- ☐ Diagnosing Web problems
- ☐ Problems that can be avoided by performing preventative maintenance

Detecting and Dealing with Errors

1 Decoding error messages

An error message is an on-screen warning telling you that something is about to go wrong or already has gone wrong. Although error messages are something not always accepted with open arms,

they do play a vital and important role in providing information related to mistakes and situations that could compromise an otherwise successful computing experience. Error messages exist to alert you to a problem and explain how you can use AOL more effectively.

Some typical reasons for error messages are:

- no dial tone
- a lost connection
- the printer is out of paper
- a paper jam
- an unsuccessful attempt to reach a Web site
- a Web site not responding
- a full online mailbox
- an application that has stopped responding
- data corruption

2 Analyzing an error message

Error messages don't have to be confusing or difficult to understand. And they definitely don't have to be difficult to correct. But all too often they are viewed with fear, frustration, and a sense of anger. This is too bad, because an error message is really meant to provide information that will correct a wrong turn.

Essentially error messages describe a problem that either has already occurred or a problem that is about to occur. That's all they do—nothing more. So the next time you receive an error message, don't get angry, use it as an opportunity to understand

333

the problem. The best way to do this is to recognize its most important parts. This not only will help you identify the source of the problem more quickly, but allow you to apply the best solution to correct the problem. So here are the most important parts of an error message:

- **Message title bar**—the heading at the top of the message box. It often identifies the application that caused the problem.

- **Message Body**—describes the error and its cause. This is the most important part of an error.

- **Message buttons**—permits you to decide how to react to an error message by either closing the error window or viewing more detailed information, as you see in Figure 16-1.

- **Message details**—contains the technical mumbo-jumbo associated with an error, such as page faults and registers, as you see in Figure 16-2.

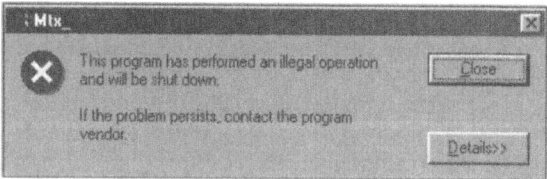

Figure 16-1. Displaying an Error Message's explanation

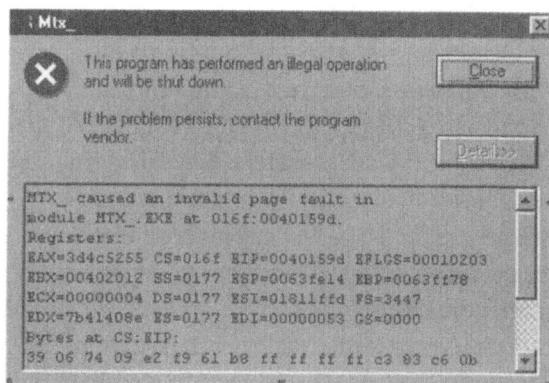

Figure 16-2. Viewing the details of an Error Message

3 Understanding error types

Being able to recognize the differences between the various types of errors will help you resolve them and make your online experience a better one. Here's a description of a few common errors:

- **Fatal exception error**—This type of error generally is caused when AOL or your operating system attempts to access a nonexistent program component or executes an invalid instruction. The result of such an action causes the system to lock up or crash without notice. The best solution for fixing this problem is to reboot or shut your system down.

- **General Protection Faults (GPFs)**—This type of error is the result of a conflict between an application such as AOL and your operating system. This is caused by an application that tries to access a location in memory that isn't allocated to it. The best way to fix a GPF problem is to reboot your computer. You can also try to shut down the application using the **CTRL-ALT-DELETE** keys on a PC.

- **Invalid page fault**—This type of error is a result of a program that tries to access data in memory that is corrupt, already in use by another application, or doesn't exist. This error may not affect the entire system. The best way to fix the problem is to restart the affected application, again using **CTRL-ALT-DELETE** and then clicking the **Task Manager** button.

- **Windows protection error**—This type of error is a result of your operating system having a problem communicating with system hardware or virtual device drivers. Errors of this type are a bit tricky and often require a Windows reinstall.

- **Runtime error**—This type of error is often the result of an application running out of memory. This error rarely affects the entire system. The best way to fix the problem is to restart the affected application.

Connecting Problems

4 Connecting using local numbers

Accessing AOL has never been easier. Because of AOL's vast selection of telephone access numbers you should be able to connect with one or more of the local access numbers near you. And even if there is no local number near you, you'll still be able to access the AOL network anywhere in the United States (including Puerto Rico and the U.S. Virgin Islands) using the toll free telephone number 1-800-716-0023. This access number connects at speeds up to 28.8 Kbps and costs may vary, so it's recommended that you visit AOL's Billing Center at AOL Keyword: **Billing** for further details.

5 Diagnosing modem problems

If you think you're experiencing modem problems, you can attempt to troubleshoot the problem before contacting the modem manufacturer. Here are a few suggestions that may be worth trying:

1. Verify that the phone cord coming from your wall jack is connected to your computer's modem marked with the words **Jack**, **Line**, or **To Wall**.

2. Check to make sure no phones are off the hook.

3. Exit any other software application that may be using the modem (for example, fax software).

6 Detecting a dial tone

Problem:

If you receive the error message, "Modem cannot detect a dial tone," this could mean that your phone line, phone cord, or modem are not working.

Solution:

Here are a few suggestions for determining whether the problem is in your phone line, phone cord, or in your modem:

1. Verify that the phone cord coming from your wall jack is connected to your computer's modem marked with the words **Jack**, **Line**, or **To Wall**.

2. If the phone cord is plugged in, then test whether the phone line works by unplugging the line going to the modem and connecting it to a working phone. Listen for a dial tone. If there's no dial tone, then the problem is probably with your phone line. Contact your telephone company.

3. If you hear a dial tone when performing Step 2, then the problem is probably with your computer's modem. Contact your modem manufacturer or computer warranty provider for assistance.

7 Losing your AOL connection

Problem:

When you receive the error message "Your connection to the AOL service has been lost," it could mean any number of things including:

- your modem may have problems with the access number you dialed

- you may be experiencing excessive noise on your phone line

- your computer system may be low on system resources

- an incoming call may have disrupted your connection

- you may have modem-related problems

Solution:

Here are a few suggestions that you can try to resolve problems related to lost connections:

1. Choose a different AOL access number by clicking the **Access Numbers** button on the **Sign On** screen. Your modem may be having problems with the number you're currently using.

2. Try reducing line noise by connecting your modem directly into the wall jack with a single cord. Avoid using splitters, and don't plug in copy machines, fax machines, answering machines, fans, stereos, or other devices with the modem connection.

3. Check and replace phone cords that are frayed, cut, or damaged.

4. When you're low on system resources, close any unnecessary programs that may interfere with AOL's use of the modem.

5. Disable call waiting to prevent an incoming call from disrupting your connection.

6. Verify that no other phone is off the hook or in use by another person. You won't be able to use the phone line for other purposes while accessing the AOL network.

7. Try re-detecting your modem by clicking **Setup** on the **Sign On** screen and then clicking **Add Modem** on the AOL **Setup** screen.

8 Dealing with "No carrier signal"

Problem:

When you receive the error message "No carrier signal," this means that your AOL connection has been disrupted. The possible reasons for this are:

- an incoming call broke your connection (e.g., call waiting)

- the connection was broken when another extension on the phone line picked up

- there may be noise on your phone line

- you're attempting to connect at an incorrect modem speed

Solution:

Here are few suggestions that should help resolve problems related to no carrier signal.

1. Choose a different AOL access number by clicking the **Access Numbers** button on the **Sign On** screen. Your modem may be having problems with the number you're currently using.

2. Disable call waiting to prevent an incoming call from disrupting your connection.

3. Verify that no other phone is off the hook or in use by another person. You won't be able to use the phone line for other purposes while accessing the AOL network.

4. Try reducing line noise by connecting your modem directly into the wall jack with a single cord. Avoid using splitters, and don't plug in copy machines, fax machines, answering machines, fans, stereos, or other devices with the modem connection.

5. Check and replace phone cords that are frayed, cut, or damaged.

9 Coping when the host fails to respond

Problem:

When you receive the error message "Host has failed to respond," it could mean that there's a problem with a modem at the access number site. Usually, the access number you're dialing is temporarily out of service.

Solution:

Here a few suggestions for dealing with a host that fails to respond within one or two minutes:

1. Try the access number again in a few minutes—you may have experienced a temporary problem with the access number.

2. Choose a different AOL access number (if possible) by clicking the **Access Numbers** button on the **Sign On** screen.

3. Write down the access number you're having problems with and click **Report a Problem** at AOL Keyword: **Access** (if you're able to get online).

10 Diagnosing HTTP 500 internal server errors

Problem:

When you receive the error message "HTTP 500 internal server error," it means that you were unable to view the requested Web page because of an error with your browser software, which is most likely (AOL, Netscape Navigator or Microsoft Internet Explorer).

Solution:

To resolve this problem, you'll need to perform the following steps:

1. Sign off and close America Online.

2. Click **Start** on the Windows taskbar, and point to **Programs**.

3. Point to America Online and click **AOL System Information**.

4. Click the **Utilities** tab in the AOL **System Information** window.

5. Click **Clear Browser Cache**.

6. Click **Uninstall AOL Adapter** and then click the **Close** button.

7. Restart your computer when prompted.

8. Try accessing the site again.

11 Dealing with modem hang ups at Step 4

Problem:

When your modem locks up or hangs up at Step 4: "Requesting Network Attention," it means that you identified the wrong network for the access number that was selected in your setup.

Solution:

You'll need to follow these steps to correct problems related to your modem locking up or hanging up at Step 4:

1. Sign off AOL.

2. Click **Setup** on the **AOL Sign On screen**. The **Connection Setup Wizard** should automatically appear.

3. Click **Add a new AOL access phone number**, and click the **Next** button. The **Search for AOL Access Numbers** screen should appear.

4. Type in the three-digit telephone area code for your location, and click the **Next** button.

5. Click the access number with the correct speed for your modem, and click the **Add** button.

6. Select and/or adjust dialing options (e.g., call waiting or outside line) if needed in the popup screen, and click the **OK** button when ready.

7. To add additional access numbers, repeat steps 5 and 6 as many times as necessary.

8. When complete, click the **Done** button.

12 Disconnecting modems—electromagnetic interference

Problem:

If your modem disconnects it could be due to electromagnetic interference. What this means is that residential-grade phone line is not always shielded from the signals produced by digital electronic equipment such as computers, CD players, TVs, radios, fax and copier machines, as well as appliances such as microwave ovens, fans, lights with dimmer switches that use fluorescent bulbs, and other appliances.

Solution:

To minimize the effect of electromagnetic interference, especially in older homes and establishments that may have older wiring, keep these suggestions in mind:

- Avoid placing your computer's modem near major electronic equipment.

- Avoid passing phone lines too close to electronic equipment.

- Since not all phone line wiring is equipped to handle today's electronic gadgets, you may need to contact your telephone company for assistance.

13 Diagnosing the problem when the modem won't initialize

Problem:

When a modem doesn't initialize, communication settings required for the successful connection with America Online will not occur. Consequently, you'll be unable to access AOL or any other online service.

Solution:

To resolve problems related to an external modem not initializing, try these steps:

1. Turn the modem off.

2. Make sure the modem's power cord is plugged in securely and that the modem cable is securely attached to the modem and computer.

3. Turn the modem on again to reset it. Verify the modem's lights are on.

4. Verify that the modem isn't in use by another software application (e.g., fax software). Exit any application that is currently using the modem and restart your computer to free the modem and allow it to initialize.

🖊 *To resolve a problem related to an internal modem not initializing, simply verify that the modem isn't in use by another software application (e.g., fax software). Exit any application that is currently using the modem and restart your computer to free the modem and allow it to initialize.*

14 Troubleshooting tips for the modem

Here are a few modem troubleshooting tips to keep in mind:

1. Verify that the modem's power cord is securely plugged in.

2. Verify that the phone cord coming from your wall jack is connected to your computer's modem marked with the words **Jack, Line,** or **To Wall.**

3. Try reducing line noise by connecting your modem directly into the wall jack with a single cord. Avoid using splitters, and don't plug in copy machines, fax machines, answering machines, fans, stereos, or other devices with the modem connection.

4. Check and replace phone cords that are frayed, cut, or damaged.

5. Disable call waiting to prevent an incoming call from disrupting your connection.

6. Verify that no other phone is off the hook or in use by another person. You won't be able to use the phone line for other purposes while accessing the AOL network.

7. Exit any other software application that may be using the modem (e.g., fax software).

Explaining E-mail Issues

15 Fixing long e-mail truncation and large attachments

Problem:

AOL users with a Rockwell Protocol Interface (RPI) modem or a modem that utilizes the RPI technology may have problems sending long e-mail messages and messages containing large attachments. This type of modem apparently uses software as part of its operation and you will need to obtain and install a special modem driver to make it function properly with America Online.

Solution:

To fix the problem associated with RPI modems, you'll first need to determine which type you have and then install the WinRPI driver, and create a custom modem profile for use with America Online. For more information, type AOL Keyword: **RPI.**

16 Compressing or decompressing file problems

Problem:

If you experience problems related to the compression or decompression of files, it could mean that the compressed file is damaged or you're lacking sufficient hard drive space to store the file.

Solution:

Here are a couple of suggestions to help resolve this type of problem:

- You may need to contact the person who sent you the file to inform them that the file may be damaged. If this is the case, you'll want them to try resending the file again.

- Try deleting files that aren't needed anymore to reclaim hard drive space. If this isn't possible, store seldom used files to secondary storage (e.g., a Zip drive) so you can reclaim this space. Another option may be to purchase and add another hard drive.

17 Dealing with an overflowing mailbox

Problem:

When your online mailbox becomes full, any e-mail messages you receive will be automatically returned to the sender without being stored in your mailbox. This will prevent you from receiving e-mail communication from others.

Solution:

The best way to prevent your online mailbox from becoming full is to clean it out regularly by deleting and filing messages that have been read or are no longer needed.

18 Dealing with disappearing e-mail

Problem:

When you're unable to find e-mail that was in your mailbox earlier but is no longer available, the problem may be that the e-mail has expired.

Solution:

AOL retains e-mail that has been read for a period of 3-7 days. After that time it's automatically deleted to make room for new e-mail. Also, if you don't read your new e-mail for a period of 27 days, it will be deleted automatically. In these cases, there is nothing that can be done to retrieve the e-mail.

19 Coping when e-mail delivery is slow

Problem:

AOL processes more online mail than any other single service in the world. Generally, mail delivery from AOL member to member is within a few seconds, and mail delivery to Internet users (non-AOL members) is rarely delayed more than 15 minutes, unless factors occur which are outside the control of AOL.

Solution:

When Internet e-mail services are too slow, keep these considerations in mind:

- Mail sent to Internet addresses must be processed by the AOL Internet Mail Gateway. Occasionally the Internet Mail Gateway may be unavailable resulting in a delay in transmitting mail.

- Internet sites can experience unexpected delays, disruptions, and other technical problems outside the control of AOL. When this is the case, AOL attempts to make contact with them until a connection is made so mail can be transmitted.

- Some sites have limited bandwidth (the rate at which a communication system can transmit data) preventing mail from being transmitted, especially during peak periods.

- Poor Internet communications can prevent proper server connections resulting in mail being rejected.

- Some Internet sites may not be able to transmit mail on the first time resulting in delays due to the retransmission of mail over several hours.

- If you are sending a very important e-mail and want to be sure it gets through to the intended address, consider using the e-mail confirmation and receipt features mentioned in Tips 2-57, 2-58, 2-59, 2-60.

20 Receiving the "Internet e-mail cannot be sent at this time" message

Problem:

When you receive the message "Internet e-mail cannot be sent at this time," it means that the AOL Internet Mail Gateway is unavailable. This can occur during peak demand periods for e-mail services.

Solution:

The best suggestion for handling peak demand for e-mail services is to wait for a short period of time and try sending your e-mail again. Generally these conditions occur infrequently and are usually short in duration.

21 Temporarily unable to list or access e-mail during down times

Problem:

During times when AOL is performing routine maintenance or applying upgrades to the mail system, your e-mail may be unavailable. These conditions may prevent you from being able to send or receive e-mail.

Solution:

Since the AOL network operates on a 24/7 basis, the best advice during these normally brief periods is to wait a little while and try accessing e-mail at a later time.

22 Checking unrecognized or unknown E-mail addresses

Problem:

The error message "E-mail address unrecognized" means that the screen name or Internet address to which you're trying to send an e-mail message to is

not valid. Another problem that will prevent you from sending an e-mail message occurs when you receive an error message that says, "This is not a known member." This means that the AOL network is unable to find the member by the screen name you've asked for.

Solution:

Try the following suggestions when an e-mail address is unrecognized or unknown:

1. Verify that you entered their screen name or Internet address correctly, making sure there are no spelling, punctuation, or capitalization errors. If there are errors with the address, correct them and send your message again.

2. Search for the AOL member using the AOL People Directory.

> *If this person is not an AOL member, then you will not be able to use People Directory.*

23 Receiving e-mail from mailer_daemon

Problem:

What is the menacing sounding mailer_daemon? When you receive e-mail from mailer_daemon, it typically means that there was a problem sending a mail message to an Internet address. Common reasons for this error are: an invalid or unknown user name, an unknown host or site domain name, the receiving site is currently unavailable, or a critical error occurred at the receiving site.

Solution:

Here are a few suggestions for handling e-mail received from mailer_daemon:

1. Verify that you entered the correct Internet address making sure there are no spelling, punctuation, or capitalization errors.

2. Check the address for extraneous quotation marks or unbalanced parentheses.

3. Verify that you spelled the site domain name correctly making sure there are no spelling, punctuation, or capitalization errors.

4. Try sending your e-mail again later—by then the receiving site may have resolved any technical difficulties they were having.

5. Contact the site or host domain to get further assistance.

Troubleshooting Instant Messenger, Mailing Lists, Telnet, and FTP

24 Dealing with an invalid screen name message in IM

Problem:

When you're using AOL Instant Messenger and you receive the error message "The screen name or password you entered is not valid," it means that you may have typed your screen name and/or password incorrectly and you should re-enter the correct information. Another possible reason may be that you never registered for the Instant Messenger service in the first place.

Solution:

Here are a couple of suggestions that you might try when the screen name or password you enter isn't valid:

1. Verify that you entered your screen name and/or password correctly. If not, try again.

2. If the error continues to appear, you may not have registered for the AOL Instant Messenger service. To sign up if you're an AOL member, access the Registration form for AOL members at: http://register.oscar.aol.com/reuse, or if you're not an AOL member, sign up at http://register.oscar.aol.com/create.

25 Receiving too many mailing list messages

Problem:

With the huge popularity of mailing lists, the possibility of receiving hundreds, maybe even thousands, of messages each day is very real. If you find that you're receiving too many mailing list messages, you'll have to act fast before it gets out of control.

Solution:

To limit the number of messages you receive from mailing lists, check to see if the mailing list offers a digest version of posted messages from a given period into a single message.

26 Understanding why mailing list messages stop coming

Problem:

When your mailing list messages stop coming, you may be experiencing the result of an overstuffed online mailbox. This condition often causes mailing list messages to stop altogether because the mailing list will automatically unsubscribe after a certain number of e-mail bounces.

Solution:

The best way to prevent the stoppage of mailing list messages is to clean out your online mailbox frequently by deleting or filing messages that have been read or are no longer needed.

27 Determining when your online mailbox is full

Problem:

When your online mailbox becomes full, any e-mail messages you receive will be returned automatically to the sender without being stored in your mailbox.

Solution:

The best way to prevent your online mailbox from becoming full is to clean it out frequently deleting or filing messages that have been read or are no longer needed.

28 Suspending mailing list messages

Problem:

The suspension of mailing list messages can occur automatically when your online mailbox becomes full. Since messages don't have anywhere to go they bounce back to the sender and the mailing list will often suspend further messages from being sent to your mailbox.

There are times when you may want to suspend mailing list messages yourself, such as when you're on vacation or away for a period of time. Using this service prevents your online mailbox from filling up while you're away and means you don't have to leave the list permanently.

Solution:

The best way to find out more information about suspending mailing services is to contact the list owner for details. Usually by accessing the list, directions will be provided on how to suspend service.

29 Dealing with subscribing or unsubscribing difficulties

Problem:

If you can't subscribe to or unsubscribe from a mailing list, it may be because you aren't sending mail to the correct subscription address. An address misspelling may be the cause.

Solution:

To correct this problem, verify that you have the correct address for subscribing or unsubscribing. Also, make sure there are no spelling, punctuation, or capitalization errors in the address itself. Sometimes, it may take a couple of days for a subscribe or unsubscribe request to take effect.

30 Connecting to telnet:domain.edu

Problem:

Currently, the AOL browser doesn't support connections using telnet, which gives you the ability to log in to another site or computer. To connect and access another computer using telnet, you'll need to download telnet software from the Software Center at AOL keyword: **Software**. If you do download it and then receive the error message "Can't connect to telnet:domain.edu," this means that your computer is having a problem connecting and logging onto another computer.

Solution:

Here are a few things to keep in mind when using Telnet software to access other computers:

- After downloading the telnet software from the Software Center, but before you use it, read the instructions very carefully. You'll want to read and understand how to use the various commands for connecting to computers, setting up your display, disconnecting from computers, and other essential commands.

- Telnet is a text-only interface—so it will not have the same appearance as Windows-based applications.

- Telnet access can frequently be slow due to excessive server demands.

- Almost every site that you'll connect to using telnet will require an account to be established. Some will be free, but others such as universities may prevent access unless you are affiliated in some way with the university. Still others will limit your capabilities and access privileges.

31 Timing out of a telnet connection

Problem:

If your telnet connection gives you the boot or times out before you're finished, this means that the remote computer system may have placed certain time limits or restrictions on your account. Often accounts are assigned certain default settings that control your access time. Time limits are also frequently enforced during peak load periods to control the length of time you've been on as well as the amount of time you've been idle between command requests.

Solution:

If this presents a problem with you using the remote computer system effectively, then you'll need to talk to the system administrator to see if you can arrange to have any time limits removed or have time increased for your account.

32 Coping with FTP/Word errors

Problem:

The error message "FTP: Unknown remote PC error #255," means that you've attempted to upload a Microsoft Word document using File Transfer Protocol (FTP) while it's still open in the Microsoft application.

Solution:

To correct this problem, you'll need to close the open Word document and try uploading it again using FTP. You don't have to exit from the Microsoft Word application itself, just close the individual document.

33 Troubleshooting FTP upload errors

Problem:

When you encounter errors while uploading a file to your FTP space, this may mean that you either have the file opened in another application or the file is not named correctly.

Solution:

Here are a couple of suggestions to allow the successful uploading of a file to your FTP space.

1. Verify that the file is not open in another software application (e.g., MS Word). If it is, you'll need to close the file before it can be uploaded.

2. Verify that the file name doesn't contain spaces or special characters.

34 Session interrupted during upgrade download

Problem:

When this problem occurs, it interrupts the download process causing downloaded AOL upgrade software to be cancelled prematurely.

Solution:

To recover from a session interruption during a software download process, just return to the software upgrade area and start the download

process again. The download process will automatically determine where the download was interrupted and resume where it left off.

35 Connecting to FTP sites

Problem:

When you receive the error message "Unable to connect to FTP site," it means that your Web browser isn't able to access the FTP site you want. This is usually a result of an address being typed incorrectly, the FTP site being moved or closed down, the FTP server malfunctioning, or the FTP server not permitting anonymous logins.

Solution:

Here are a few suggestions that you might try when you're unable to connect to an FTP site:

1. Verify that you entered the correct FTP site address making sure there are no spelling, punctuation, or capitalization errors.

2. Wait and try accessing the site at another time; it may not be busy later and any server problems may have been fixed.

3. Check to see if you are able to connect to other FTP sites. If you can't, then the problem may be with your Internet connection. Under these conditions, it's best to restart the FTP application or to restart AOL.

36 Dealing with "Permission denied"

Problem:

The error message "Permission denied" appears when you attempt to read, write, modify, create, or delete directories or files during FTP operations. This error is a result of not having the permissions necessary to perform these types of activities in non-public areas of an FTP site.

Solution:

The only way to resolve this problem is to contact the representative for the FTP site and obtain the required permissions to perform the operation.

37 Getting an I/O error message

Problem:

The error message "FTP: I/O error message," may occur when a file upload or download operation is interrupted and then the same upload or download is attempted again.

Solution:

This should resolve I/O error messages during an interrupted FTP process:

1. Sign off and exit America Online.

2. Restart AOL and sign back on.

3. Initiate the upload or download without any interruptions.

38 Learning more about My FTP Space

Here's some interesting information on how AOL assigns disk space for My FTP Space. AOL automatically sets aside free disk space on the "members.aol.com" Web server for storing Web pages and downloadable files. Each AOL screen name is given a maximum of 2 megabytes of storage space giving each account (with seven screen names allotted to it) a maximum of 14 megabytes of space. One screen name can't be given more than another—each screen names is given the same 2 megabytes.

Diagnosing Web Problems

39 Clearing your browser cache

Problem:

AOL's browser software stores Web pages including graphic images and text on your hard drive in an area known as the cache. It saves the images and text from each Web page you visit. Occasionally the cache fills your hard drive causing performance to slow down and your hard drive to run out of space. The reason the AOL browser uses caching is to prevent large slow-to-download images from having

to be downloaded from the Web page each time you visit that page. Instead, the Web page's images and text are stored on your hard drive enabling information to be displayed much more quickly.

Solution:

To clear the contents of your browser's cache, follow these instructions:

1. Click **Preferences** from the **Settings** menu on the AOL toolbar.

2. Click **Internet Properties (WWW)** in the **Organization** section of the **Preferences** window.

3. Click **Delete Files** in the **Temporary Internet Files** section.

4. Click the **OK** button.

40 Difficulty accessing a previously visited Web pages

Problem:

When you're unable to access a Web page you visited earlier, this can mean one of a number of things. The server that stores the page may be experiencing difficulty; the page may have been moved or deleted; your Internet connection may be down; or the Web address you entered may not be correct.

Solution:

Here are a few suggestions that you might try when you're unable to access previously visited Web pages:

1. Verify that you entered the correct Web site address making sure there are no spelling, punctuation, or capitalization errors.

2. Wait and try accessing the site at another time, perhaps after any server problems have been fixed.

3. Click the **Reload** button to attempt accessing the Web site again.

4. Check to see if there is a forwarding address or wait a few seconds to see if you'll automatically be directed to the new page.

5. See if you are able to connect to other Web sites. If you aren't able to visit other sites, then the problem may be with your Internet connection. Under these conditions, it's best to restart AOL.

41 Trouble connecting to a Web site

Problem:

The "Unable to connect to a Web site" error message is produced when your Web browser is unable to get to a desired Web site. The reasons for this: you may have mistyped the Web address; the Web site may no longer exist; the Web site could have been moved; the Web server could be temporarily down; or the network could be experiencing technical problems.

Solution:

Here are a few suggestions to try when you're unable to connect to a Web site:

1. Verify that you entered the correct Web site address making sure there are no spelling, punctuation, or capitalization errors.

2. Wait and try accessing the site at another time, perhaps after any server problems have been fixed or during off-hours.

3. See if you are able to connect to other Web sites. If you aren't able to visit other sites, then the problem may be with your Internet connection. Under these conditions, it's best to restart AOL.

42 Determining why you got a blank Web page

Problem:

When a blank Web page appears, this can mean that the Web page has no content, the site has a large number of graphic images, or the server is busy with other users attempting to access the same site at the same time.

Solution:

Here are a few suggestions that you might try when a blank Web page appears:

1. Verify that you entered the correct Web site address making sure there are no spelling, punctuation, or capitalization errors.

2. Check whether the AOL logo is spinning or look at the bottom of your Web browser window to see the status of the page. If the AOL logo is spinning or the status indicates that the browser is still trying to connect, you may want to wait a little longer. Otherwise, you can click the **Stop** button and click the **Reload** button to attempt accessing the Web site again.

3. Attempt accessing the Web site at a later time when it may not be so busy.

43 Dealing with too much network traffic

Problem:

The error message "Too much network traffic" means that too many people are already connected to the Web site you are trying to access.

Solution:

Here are a few suggestions that you might try when you're stuck in a network traffic jam:

1. Click the **Reload** button to attempt to access the site again or simply wait until a later time to access the site.

2. Your disk cache could be full, slowing your browser's performance. Clear or empty your Web browser's disk cache.

3. Check to see if you are able to connect to other Web sites. If you aren't, then the problem may be with your Internet connection. Under these conditions, it's best to restart AOL.

44 Checking why a requested URL was not found

Problem:

When you receive the error message "The requested URL was not found," it means that the Web site you requested by entering the Universal Resource Locator (URL) or Web address can't be found.

Solution:

Here are a few suggestions that you might try when the requested URL is not found:

1. Click the **Reload** button to attempt to access the site again or simply wait until later to access the site.

2. Clear or empty your Web browser's disk cache, which may have become full. Web browsers place data that is frequently read or accessed (e.g., Web site pages) in disk cache, and when the cache fills up, this can affect your browser' performance.

3. Check to see if you are able to connect to other Web sites. If you can't, then the problem may be with your Internet connection. Under these conditions, it's best to restart AOL.

45 Getting the L2TP Connection error message

Problem:

The error message "Do you want to close the connection to L2TP?" refers to users of Encompass, Inc.'s Internet Registration software being automatically started when you run Windows software (or boot your computer). Encompass Internet registration software is often preinstalled on computers and runs in the background. When present on your machine, it's automatically activated when Windows is started. This often produces this error message.

Solution:

If you've got Encompass' Internet registration software running, you'll want to follow these steps to prevent the automatic startup of Encompass' Internet Registration software:

1. Click **Run** on the Windows **Start** menu.

2. Type **MSCONFIG** in the **Open dialog** box, and click the **OK** button.

3. Select the **Startup** tab on the **System Configuration Startup** window.

4. Clear the check box for **Encompass_ENCMONTR**, and click the **OK** button.

5. Verify no other programs are running, and click the **Yes** button to restart your computer.

46 Getting the 401–Authorization Required message

Problem:

The error message "401—Authorization Required," means that you're trying to view a page that has limited or controlled access. Sometimes the authors of a Web page may only want certain people to have access to it and a password may be required.

Solution:

Here are a few suggestions that you might try when you receive the 401—Authorization Required message:

1. Verify that you entered the correct Web site address. Then verify that you entered the correct password (if you indeed have one) noting any special capitalization of letters and words.

2. If you continue to get the error message and you don't think you should, contact the Web site's representative or person maintaining the site with an e-mail message and explain the problem.

47 Decoding the 403–Forbidden message

Problem:

The "403—Forbidden" error message is generated by a server when a Web site file, or the site itself, is not properly configured or installed correctly.

Solution:

Here are a few suggestions that you might try when you receive the 403—Forbidden error message:

1. Verify that you entered the correct Web site address making sure of spelling and capitalization.

2. This error message can also be generated when a Web site is down for maintenance, or too many people are trying to access the server at once. If this is the case, it may be best to click the **Reload** button or to try accessing the site at another time.

3. If the problem still occurs after you've followed the first two steps, send an e-mail message to the site's Webmaster with the error message you're getting.

The Webmaster's address is usually located at the bottom of the Web page.

48 Determining why you got a 404-Not Found message

Problem:

The "404—Not Found" error message is almost always a result of a Web page that was renamed or moved.

Solution:

Here are a few suggestions that you might try when you receive the 404—Not Found error message:

1. Verify that you entered the correct Web site address making sure of spelling and capitalization.

2. This error message may be generated when a Web site has been renamed, shut down, or moved to another location. If you still can't access the site after poking around, you may have to accept that the person may no longer have a site with that name.

49 Coping with Server-related Error messages

Problem:

When you receive any of the following error messages, "500—Server Error," "502—Connection Failed," or "Web site not responding," it means that the server is experiencing some sort of mechanical problems or has not being configured properly.

Solution:

Here are a couple of suggestions that you might try when you receive either of these server messages:

1. Verify that you entered the correct Web site address making sure there are no spelling, punctuation, or capitalization errors.

2. Wait and try accessing the site at another time, possibly after any server problems have been fixed.

50 Understanding the 501-Not Implemented message

Problem:

The "501—Not Implemented" error message is almost always related to a problem in the HyperText Markup Language (HTML) code.

Solution:

Contact the site's Webmaster and describe the problem you're having

The Webmaster's address is usually located at the bottom of the site.

51 Dealing with Can't Parse HTTP messages

Problem:

The "Can't Parse HTTP" error message means that your Web browser isn't able to figure out the address you typed. When your Web browser doesn't understand a Web address, it has no choice but to issue this error message.

Solution:

Here are a few suggestions that you might try when you're unable to parse HTTP:

1. Verify that you entered the correct Web site address making sure there are no spelling, punctuation, or capitalization errors.

2. Click the **Reload** button to attempt to access the site again or you could simply wait until a later time to access the site.

3. You might also try clearing or emptying your Web browser's disk cache, which may be full, affecting your browser's performance.

4. Finally, check to see if you are able to connect to other Web sites. If you aren't, then the problem may be with your Internet connection. Under these conditions, it's best to restart AOL.

52 Getting MSIE connection to the server not established

Problem:

If you're using Microsoft Internet Explorer to surf the Web and you receive the error message "Internet Explorer cannot open Internet site http://_____, a connection to the server could not be established." This usually means that your Internet connection has probably been lost.

Solution:

To resolve this problem you'll need to exit AOL and any other open applications and then shut down your PC by clicking **Start** and **Shut Down**. Wait at least ten or more seconds before starting up your computer again.

Miscellaneous Errors

53 Understanding No helper application defined

Problem Explanation:

The error message "No helper application defined," shown in Figure 16-3, means that your Web browser has accessed a file that it doesn't know how to process or find. Helper applications are stand-alone programs that process certain files that AOL isn't equipped to handle. A few examples of helper applications include programs that play special sound formats, encode and compress files, decode and decompress file archives, or play animated movies.

Solution:

To resolve this problem you'll need to access the AOL **Preferences** or **Options** windows to add the necessary programs, helpers, or viewers to be able to handle these file types. For example, to use the AOL **Media Player** to hear supported file types, you'll need to select the appropriate option.

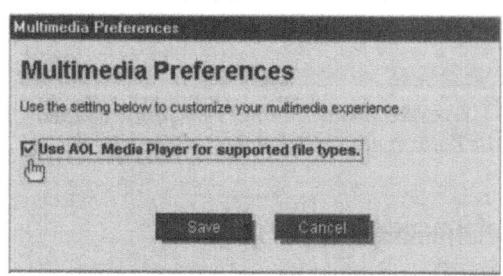

Figure 16-3. Displaying the Multimedia Preferences window

CHAPTER 17

Miscellaneous Tips

THIS CHAPTER PRESENTS a potpourri of tips covering many exciting new services that can definitely have an impact on your online experience. Take advantage of the latest version features offered by AOL; improve accessibility with screen readers and keyboard alternatives; send and receive e-mail and Instant Message notes even when you don't have AOL software; disable call waiting and modem sounds; and access AOL services using high-speed connections such as DSL, satellite, and cable. Tips like these and many more are presented to make the online experience a total and comprehensive one.

In this chapter, you'll learn how to:

- 📖 Upgrade to new AOL versions

- 📖 Determine what the system requirements are for Windows versions

- 📖 Troubleshoot installation and upgrade problems

- 📖 Improve accessibility with AOL Version 7.0

- 📖 Enable and disable connection features

- 📖 Upgrade your modem

- 📖 Access e-mail and Instant Messages using wireless and AOLTV services

- 📖 AOL Versions, Upgrades and System Requirements

1 Finding what's new in AOL Version 7.0

Would you like to learn what new features are available with AOL Version 7.0? You can find out all

the great new features, content, and more by visiting AOL's Upgrade Center. You'll even be able to watch an online movie describing what's new in Version 7.0. And when you're ready, AOL lets you download the Version 7.0 upgrade right to your computer or you can request the latest 7.0 CD to be mailed to you. It's your choice. Here's how you can find out what's new in AOL Version 7.0:

1. Click the **Keyword** button located on the AOL toolbar and enter AOL Keyword: **Upgrade**.

2. Click the **Go** button to display AOL's **Upgrade Center**.

2 Finding out what version of AOL you're using

Do you know what version of AOL you're currently running? With several versions available, you'll want to determine what version you're running so you can upgrade to the latest and greatest. Finding out is easy. Here's how:

Select **About America Online** from the **Help** drop-down menu located at the top of your screen to display the **About AOL** window, shown in Figure 17-1.

3 Assessing AOL 7.0 System Requirements under Windows

The minimum system requirements for your computer to run AOL 7.0 adequately depends on the version of Windows you're running under. Here are the recommended system requirements that America Online suggests members should have before upgrading to 7.0:

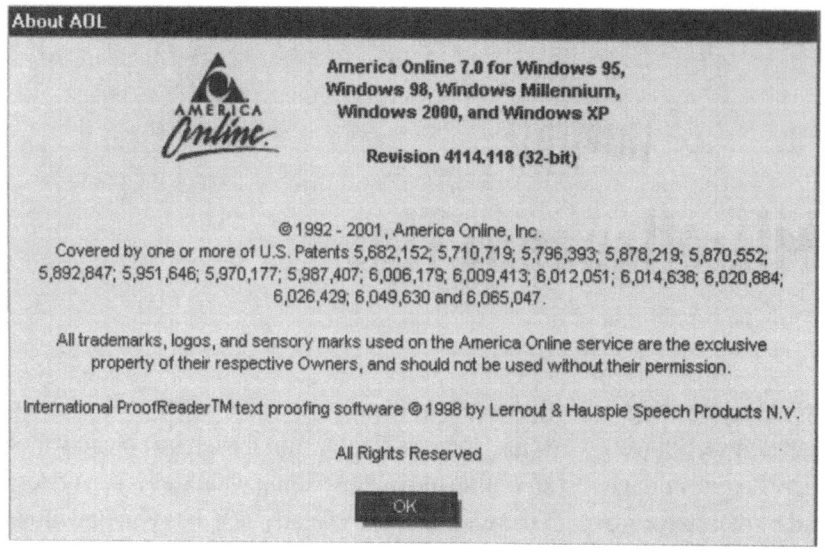

Figure 17-1. Displaying the version of AOL you're running in the About AOL window

Minimum System Requirements for Windows 95/98/ME

- Pentium-class processor (166Mhz or better)

- 32 MB (megabytes) of RAM minimum

- Hard drive free space required for install:

  - 161 MB for Windows 95**

  - 147 MB for Windows 98/ME**

  - VGA, SVGA or better display

  - 640x480, 256 colors or better screen (optimized for 800x600)

  - 28.8 Kbps or faster modem or other means of Internet connection

  - Internet Explorer 5.0 or higher

  - Up to 233 MB of free hard disk space if Internet Explorer version 5.5 is installed.

Minimum System Requirements for Windows 2000

- Remote Access Services (RAS) Installed

- Pentium-class processor (166Mhz or better)

- 64 MB (megabytes) of RAM

- 118 MB Hard drive free space required for install**

- VGA, SVGA or better display

- 640x480, 256 colors or better screen (optimized for 800x600)

- 28.8 Kbps or faster modem or other means of an Internet connection

- Internet Explorer 5.0 or higher

- Requires 177 MB of free hard disk space if Internet Explorer version 5.5 is installed.

Minimum System Requirements for Windows XP

- Pentium-class processor (166Mhz or better)

- 64 MB (megabytes) of RAM

- 118 MB Hard drive free space required for install

- VGA, SVGA or better display

- 640x480, 256 colors or better screen (optimized for 800x600)

- 28.8 Kbps or faster modem or other means of an Internet connection

- Internet Explorer 6.0 or higher (packaged with the operating system)

4 Obtaining the latest AOL software

Getting the latest AOL software is easy and it's free. AOL gives you three ways to get Version 7.0: by download, on CD through the mail, or on CD at one of the many stores near you. If you decide to download Version 7.0, hourly billing plan members won't get charged for the connect time. Here's how:

Downloading to Your PC

1. Click the **Keyword** button located on the AOL toolbar and enter AOL Keyword: **Upgrade**.

2. Click the **Go** button to display AOL's Upgrade Center.

3. Click the **Start UPGRADE Now!** button.

4. Follow the on-screen instructions to download the AOL Version 7.0 application.

Through the Mail

1. Click the **Keyword** button located on the AOL toolbar and enter AOL Keyword: **Upgrade**.

2. Click the **Go** button to display AOL's **Upgrade Center.**

3. Click the **Get AOL 7.0 on a CD** button.

4. Click Order your **AOL 7.0 CD Here.**

5. Enter your name, address, and phone number information in the AOL 7.0 **Software Orders** window, and click the **Order** button. Your CD will arrive in the mail.

Getting a Copy at a Store Near You

You'll find Version 7.0 at popular stores in your area. Look for a store in the following list, shown in Table 17-1.

Table 17-1. Finding AOL Version 7.0 at Your Favorite Store

7-Eleven	Eckerd Drugs	Safeway
A&P Food Market	Food Lion	Savemart
B. Dalton Bookseller	Fry's Electronics	Sears
Barnes & Noble	Gateway	Smiths Food & Drug
Bashes	Giant Eagle	Spencer Gifts
Bergen Brunswig Drug	Giant Food	Target
Big Y Foods	Grand Union	United News Stands Inc.
BiLo Foods & Riverside	Homeland Stores	Vons
Blockbuster	Independent Pharmacy Co-Op	Wawa
Brooks/Maxi Drug	Kash n' Karry	Wal-Mart
Circle K	Kinko's	Weis Markets
Circuit City	Kroger	Western Supermarkets
Comp USA	Marsh Supermarkets	Wherehouse Music
Cumberland Farms	May's Drug Stores	Wilson Farms
CVS/pharmacy	Office Depot	Winn-Dixie
Drug Emporium	Pick n' Save	Xtra Mart
Eagle Food Centers	Ralph's	

5 Quitting other programs before installing Version 7.0

As with any program installation, it's recommended that you close out of any and all programs and applications, including shareware, freeware, and screen saver programs, before attempting to install or upgrade AOL Version 7.0. This should enable a clean install without problems.

6 Installing AOL

Installing AOL is automatic and easy. If you downloaded Version 7.0 from the AOL Upgrade Center, AOL will sign you off at the completion of the download and the software installation will begin. If you received a copy of the software on CD in the mail, just insert the CD in your drive and it should automatically start. Follow the on-screen instructions to install Version 7.0 on your computer. That's all there is to it.

7 Copying your address book and filing cabinet to Version 7.0

You can choose to have the AOL installation process automatically copy your address book and filing cabinet to Version 7.0. That way you'll have these handy tools available for your use when you launch AOL. Not only that, but you'll also save time. Just click **Current Member** at the beginning of the installation process. When the **Current** members screen appears, click **Upgrading to a new version of AOL on this computer**. The contents of your address book and filing cabinet will automatically copy to Version 7.0.

8 Troubleshooting installation/upgrade problems

Are you having problems installing or upgrading to Version 7.0? Occasionally, a problem can occur during the installation or upgrade process. Before pulling your hair out, let's look at a few things that could lead to problems during the installation/upgrade or operation of Version 7.0:

Download Gets Interrupted

If you're downloading Version 7.0 and the download process gets interrupted for any reason, just return to AOL Keyword: **Upgrade** and click the **Upgrade to AOL 7.0 Now!** button. The download process will resume right where it left off prior to the interruption. This not only saves time, but also makes the upgrade process automatic and trouble-free.

Can't Upgrade to Version 7.0

If AOL displays the message, "Can't upgrade to Version 7.0," your computer may not be adequately equipped with the minimum system requirements. To verify that you meet the minimum system requirements for the machine and operating system you're running, refer back to Tip #3 in this chapter.

AOL's Not the Default Web Browser

Under Microsoft Windows, a single Web browser is set for accessing Web pages, e-mail, newsgroups and the like. During the Version 7.0 installation/upgrade process, AOL lets you set the default Web browser. If you chose another software product as your default browser, you can reset this by selecting AOL as your default by following these instructions:

1. Select **Preferences** from the **Settings** menu on the AOL toolbar.

2. Click **Association** under the **Account Controls** heading on the **Preferences** window.

3. Click the **OK** button on the **Association Preferences** window to select AOL as your default Web browser for pages, e-mail, and newsgroups.

9 Keeping earlier versions of AOL software

Would you like to keep and use earlier versions of AOL and install/upgrade to Version 7.0 on your machine? AOL lets you install/upgrade Version 7.0 in a separate directory so earlier versions of AOL are not affected. This lets you use the earlier versions anytime you want. The only thing you have to have is adequate disk space to accommodate the different versions.

10 Upgrading MS Internet Explorer during the installation process

AOL Version 7.0 uses MS Internet Explorer (MSIE) 5.0 or later as its Web browser. If AOL finds an earlier version of IE on your machine during the installation process, it will automatically upgrade your IE browser software to Version 5.5. This assures you of the greatest online experience available.

11 Getting the latest version of MS Internet Explorer anytime

As new versions of MS Internet Explorer (MSIE) become available, you'll be able to upgrade anytime. It's easy and best of all it's free. The Browser Upgrade window will display whether you're using the latest version of MSIE and, if not, will let you upgrade your browser software. Here's how:

1. Click the **Keyword** button located on the AOL toolbar and enter AOL Keyword: **Browser**.

2. Click the **Go** button to display AOL's **Browser Upgrade** channel.

3. If you're not using the latest version of MSIE, AOL will let you upgrade by clicking the **Upgrade** button in the **Browser Upgrade** window.

4. Follow the on-screen instructions to download the latest version of IE.

12 Removing earlier versions of AOL from my computer

Since AOL automatically creates a new directory when you upgrade to Version 7.0 from an earlier version of AOL, you'll have two versions of AOL on your computer. To remove the earlier version of AOL from your computer, you'll want to remove the application using the Add/Remove Programs in the Control Panel. Here's how:

1. Click the **Start** button on the Windows desktop and select **Control Panel** from the **Settings** drop-down selection list.

2. Click **Add/Remove Programs** from the **Control Panel**.

3. Select the version of AOL you want removed and click the **Add/Remove** button.

AOL Accessibility Tips

13 Improving accessibility with AOL Version 7.0

AOL Version 7.0 offers greater accessibility to members with disabilities than ever before. With improved features in the areas of sign-on, e-mail, buddy list, Instant Message, chat, parental controls, and usability tools on the AOL toolbar, members have many new improvements in Version 7.0. You'll find assisted technologies such as screen readers, screen magnifiers, keyboard or mouse alternatives, voice recognition, wireless technology, and speech deployment to make AOL accessible to everyone. Here's how you can find more about the many accessibility features in Version 7.0:

1. Click the **Keyword** button located on the AOL toolbar and enter AOL Keyword: **Accessibility**.

2. Click the **Go** button to display AOL's **Accessibility Help** screen.

14 Accessing local AOL and international access numbers

Getting local AOL and international access numbers is essential for a successful online experience. The good news is that it's never been easier. By going to AOL's Connecting to AOL channel, you'll find new access phone numbers available in your area, learn how to change an existing access number, use AOL's dependable 1-800 access number while traveling, report a connectivity problem, find international access phone numbers, and much more. Here's how:

1. Click the **Keyword** button located on the AOL toolbar and enter AOL Keyword: **Access**.

2. Click the **Go** button to display AOL's **Connecting to AOL** channel.

15 Accessing surcharged access numbers

If you want to avoid having to pay additional charges beyond your AOL subscription fee, don't dial access numbers outside your calling area, or use AOL's 1-800 access number. Access charges for using AOL's 1-800 access number are billed in addition to your subscription fee and will appear on your AOL billing statement, however using access numbers outside your local calling area will not be billed to your AOL statement. Instead, your telephone provider will bill these charges on your monthly statement as long distance charges. To monitor any and all accrued charges for your current or previous month's online activities, you can access your account charges anytime. Here's how:

1. Click the **Keyword** button located on the AOL toolbar and enter AOL Keyword: **Billing**.

2. Click the **Go** button to display AOL's **Billing Center** channel.

16 Determining international access costs

The costs for accessing AOL from international locations are charged in addition to your regular AOL fees and are based on the country access number you use and connection time. To obtain a listing of the costs for international access, go to AOL's Web site: `http://intlaccess.web.aol.com/`. Here's how:

1. Click the **Keyword** button located on the AOL toolbar and enter AOL Keyword: **Access**.

2. Click the **Go** button to display AOL's **Connecting to AOL** channel.

3. Click the **International Access** button.

4. Double-click the **International Access Costs** folder.

5. Click **International Access Numbers** to view the applicable hourly surcharges for each country access number, URL: `http://intlaccess.web.aol.com/`.

6. Click the **Full List of International Access Numbers** button to display AOL's **International Access** search results.

17 Using AOL and Globalnet— for the foreign traveler

AOL Globalnet Plus lets you access AOL from anywhere in the world. Currently only AOL members using AOL Version 5.0 under Windows 95 and Windows 98 can use the AOL Globalnet Plus software. Members connecting to AOL with Globalnet Plus will be billed an hourly surcharge in addition to your normal monthly billing. Members are recommended to check the surcharge fees before connecting. Here's how:

1. Click the **Keyword** button located on the AOL toolbar and enter AOL Keyword: **Access**.

2. Click the **Go** button to display the **Connecting to AOL** channel.

3. Click the **International Access** button.

4. Double-click the **AOL Globalnet Plus International Access numbers** folder.

5. Click **International Access Numbers** to view the applicable hourly surcharges for each country access number.

18 Contacting international technical support

You can ask a technical question and usually get a reply back within 24 hours. All you need to do is type in your question with as much detail as possible and send it. An AOL representative will contact you via e-mail. Here's how it works:

1. Click the **Keyword** button located on the AOL toolbar and enter AOL Keyword: **Access**.

2. Click the **Go** button to display the **Connecting to AOL** channel.

3. Click the **International Access** button.

4. Double-click the **Ask a technical Question** folder.

5. Enter your question in as much detail as you can in the **Ask a Technical Question** window and click the **Send Report** button.

19 Accessing AOL e-mail without AOL software

AOL members can access their AOL e-mail even without AOL software. AOL NetMail is a free service that lets you send and receive AOL e-mail anytime and from anywhere. You just have to register for AOL NetMail and the rest is easy. Here's how:

1. Enter the URL http://www.aol.com/aolmail/ to display AOL Mail on the Web. First-time users must register to use the software.

2. Follow the on-screen instructions to begin using AOL **NetMail**.

20 Sending an access number request to AOL

If you can't find an international access number in a country and city, then send your request to AOL. Here's how:

1. Click the **Keyword** button located on the AOL toolbar and enter AOL Keyword: **Access**.

2. Click the **Go** button to display the **Connecting to AOL** channel.

3. Click the **International Access** button.

4. Double-click the **Access Number Request** folder.

5. Enter the country and city where you'd like to have an **International Access Number** in the **Access Number Request** window and click the **Send Report** button, shown in Figure 17-2.

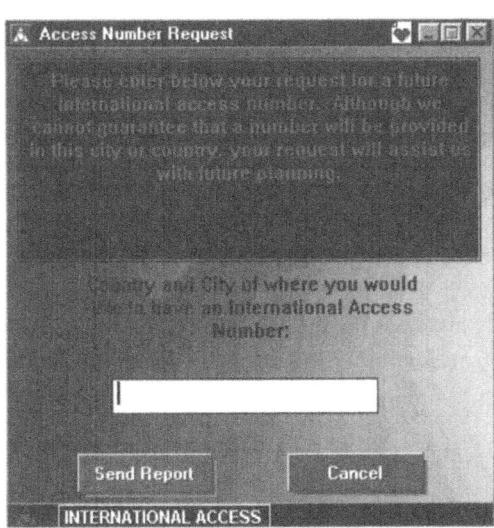

Figure 17-2. Sending an access number request to AOL

AOL Connection Options

21 Changing modem sound settings

Tired of hearing those loud and annoying sounds your modem makes? AOL lets you change your modem sound settings by following a few simple instructions. Here's how:

1. Click **Setup** on the AOL **Sign On** screen.

2. Click **Expert Setup**.

3. Click the **Devices** tab and select your modem in the selection list.

4. Click **Edit** and select the volume in the **Speaker Volume** field from the **Expert Edit Modem** screen.

5. Click the **OK** button.

6. Click the **Close** button.

22 Disabling call waiting

Do you have call waiting? Are you tired of losing your connection each time you receive an incoming call? Then why not disable the call-waiting feature while you're online and make your experience a more enjoyable one. Here's how:

1. Sign off America Online.

2. Click **Setup** on the AOL **Sign On** screen.

3. Click **Expert Setup**.

4. Select the phone number you want to have call waiting disabled for.

5. Click **Edit** and select the volume in the **Speaker Volume** field from the **Expert Edit Modem** screen.

6. Click the check box labeled, **Dial *70, to disable call waiting**.

7. Click the **OK** button.

8. Click the **Close** button.

23 Identifying a modem manufacturer

Before you can update or upgrade your computer's modem, you first need to identify your modem manufacturer. Here's how:

1. Sign off America Online.

2. Click **Setup** on the **AOL Sign On** screen.

3. Click **Expert Setup.**

4. Click the **Devices (modems, etc)** tab on the **Connection Setup** window. Your modem should be displayed next to an icon resembling a telephone.

5. Click the **OK** button.

6. Click the **Close** button.

24 Upgrading a modem's firmware

Occasionally a modem manufacturer may make software updates available so you can upgrade your modem's built-in software. Software that's built into your modem is referred to as firmware. Your modem manufacturer may provide these software upgrades on their Web site or they may be available through AOL's Connecting to AOL channel. Once the upgrade is downloaded and installed, the update is automatically made part of the modem. Not only is upgrading cheaper than buying a new modem, it may provide greater speed, quality, and reliability for a better online experience. Check with your modem manufacturer's Web site to see if updates are available for your modem.

When upgrading a modem's firmware, you'll need to know who the modem manufacturer is and the model number of your modem. Use extreme care and follow on-screen instructions. Applying the incorrect firmware to your modem can render your modem inoperable. In the event you're unable to successfully download the firmware upgrade, you may be able to request that the modem manufacturer send the firmware upgrade on a disk. Here's how you can access information on your modem's firmware:

1. Click the **Keyword** button located on the AOL toolbar and enter AOL Keyword: **Stay Connected.**

2. Click the **Go** button to display AOL's **Connecting to AOL** channel.

3. Click the **Modem Manufacturers** under **Click on a Subject** heading.

4. Double-click your modem's manufacturer to access information.

25 Upgrading a modem's hardware and driver

When the only way to upgrade a modem is to replace or fix the modem's hardware, you'll need to either send it back to the manufacturer or take it into a reputable service establishment. Either way, your modem manufacturer's Web site should provide details related to modem hardware upgrades.

Upgrading a modem's driver involves updating the software that controls the way the modem works with your computer's hardware and software. As you start your computer, the modem's driver is initialized. Your modem manufacturer's Web site should provide details related to modem hardware upgrades. Check with your modem manufacturer's Web site to see if updates are available for your modem's driver.

Here's how you can upgrade your modem's hardware and driver:

1. Click the **Keyword** button located on the AOL toolbar and enter AOL Keyword: **Stay Connected.**

2. Click the **Go** button to display the **Connecting to AOL** channel.

3. Click the **Modem Manufacturers** under **Click on a Subject** heading.

26 Understanding AOL and cable modems

Would you like to surf the Web up to 50 times faster or have an instant connection? AOL's high-speed cable modem access lets you connect without the need for a second telephone line. A cable modem provides access to the Internet and other AOL services over coaxial or fiber-optic television cables rather than telephone lines. Using a cable modem as your Internet connection, you'll be able to experience the Web like never before and be able to download files and Web pages much faster. From listening to music to watching movie previews, to getting the news, you'll access everything offered on the Internet at lightning speeds. Learn more about AOL and cable modems. Here's how:

1. Click the **Keyword** button located on the AOL toolbar and enter AOL Keyword: **Cable**.

2. Click the **Go** button to display AOL's **High Speed Cable** channel.

27 Finding out if AOL's cable modem service is available in your neighborhood

Finding out if AOL's cable modem service is available in your neighborhood is easy. Here's how:

1. Click the **Keyword** button located on the AOL toolbar and enter AOL Keyword: **Cable**.

2. Click the **Go** button to display AOL's **High Speed Cable** channel.

3. Click the **Is it available in my neighborhood?** under the **Click on a Topic** heading.

4. Scroll through the list of cities to see if AOL's cable modem service is available.

28 Assessing AOL cable modem system requirements

America Online suggests the following minimum system requirements for running a cable modem on your computer. These requirements are direct from the America Online Web site:

- Pentium-class processor (200Mhz or better)

- Windows 95, 98, 2000, XP, or ME

- CD-ROM drive

- 32 MB (megabytes) of RAM minimum

- 32 MB Hard drive free space

- VGA graphics adaptor (Video card)

- VGA monitor

- USB port or free PCI card slot

29 Understanding what AOL Plus DSL is

Like the high-speed cable modem, AOL's high-speed Digital Subscriber Line (DSL) access lets you connect to the Internet without the need for a second telephone line, download files and access Web pages faster, and much more. Unlike a cable modem, DSL technology uses existing copper lines by splitting the line between voice and data. Using DSL as your Internet connection brings you a Web experience like never before. AOL provides a wealth of support and help with everything you'll need to get DSL up and running with your computer. Here's how to find out more:

1. Click the **Keyword** button located on the AOL toolbar and enter AOL Keyword: **DSL Help**.

2. Click the **Go** button to display the **High Speed AOL Resource Center** channel.

30 Assessing AOL Plus™ DSL system requirements

America Online suggests the following minimum system requirements for running AOL Plus DSL with your computer. These requirements are direct from the America Online Web site:

- Pentium-class processor (200Mhz or better)

- Windows 95 or 98

- AOL Version 4.0 or higher

- CD-ROM drive

- 32 MB (megabytes) of RAM minimum

- 32 MB Hard drive free space

- VGA graphics adaptor (Video card)

- VGA monitor

- USB port or free PCI card slot

31 Connecting to AOL with your current DSL service

Even if you already have a DSL service, you can still connect to AOL with your current DSL carrier. You'll have all the advantages offered by a high-speed Internet connection combined with the powerful features of the AOL network. Here's how:

1. Connect to your DSL service provider network as usual.

2. Start America Online.

3. Click the **Setup** button on the AOL **Sign On** screen.

4. Click **Create a location for use with new access phone numbers or an ISP**, and click the **Next** button on the **AOL Setup** screen.

5. Enter the location in the **Name:** field on the **Add Location** window.

6. Click **Add a custom connection**, and click the **Next** button to create the new location.

7. Click the **Sign On** button to connect to the America Online network using the connection provided by your DSL Internet Service Provider.

32 Understanding AOL Plus DirecPC satellite system

Satellite technology lets you download files and access Web pages faster, work with your existing screen name, view music and videos, news headlines, and much more. AOL's high-speed satellite access also lets you connect without the need for a second telephone line. Unlike a cable modem or DSL, you'll get a free satellite dish installation so you can surf the Web with lightning speed. You'll also find a wealth of support and help with everything you need to get satellite up and running with your computer. Here's how to find out more about this exciting way to connect to the Internet and the many AOL services:

1. Click the **Keyword** button located on the AOL toolbar and enter AOL Keyword: **Satellite**.

2. Click the **Go** button to display the AOL **High Speed Satellite** channel.

3. Double-click the folder you'd like to open.

33 Assessing AOL's high speed satellite system requirements

America Online suggests the following minimum system requirements for running AOL high-speed satellite with your computer. These requirements are direct from the America Online Web site:

- Pentium-class processor (200Mhz or better)

- Windows 98 or ME

- AOL Version 4.0 or higher

- CD-ROM drive

- 32 MB (megabytes) of RAM minimum

- 80 MB (180 MB when Internet Explorer 5.01 is installed) hard drive free space

- VGA or SVGA graphics adaptor (Video card)

- High-resolution monitor

- USB port hardwired to motherboard

- Unobstructed southwestern view (for North America)

AOL Wireless, Mobile Communications, and AOL TV

34 Using an Internet-enabled phone

Would you like to be able to access your e-mail, instant messages, news, and other worthwhile information on your phone? AOL's AOLbyPhone offers ease and convenience in one affordable package for AOL members everywhere. You'll be able to send and receive e-mail, chat with Instant

Messages, get news and weather reports, access stock updates, and more—anytime and anywhere you like. For a small monthly fee, you can use AOLbyPhone on any phone to access your AOL Anywhere features. Here's how you can find out more about this handy service:

1. Click the **Keyword** button located on the AOL toolbar and enter AOL Keyword: **AOLByPhone.**

2. Click the **Go** button to display the **AOLbyPhone** channel.

35 Accessing AOL with the Mobile Communicator

AOL's Mobile Communicator two-way messaging device provides ease and convenience for AOL members to access their e-mail and Instant Messages. You'll be able to chat virtually anywhere with friends, family, and business associates without tying up a phone line. Because of its wireless technology, e-mail and Instant Messages can be sent and received using the built-in, and easy to use keypad. Here's how you can access AOL's Mobile Communicator Web site for further information:

1. Click the **Keyword** button located on the AOL toolbar and enter AOL Keyword: **My AOL MC.**

2. Click the **Go** button to display the AOL's **Mobile Communicator** channel.

3. Click the buttons located on the left of the Web site to display **Mobile Communicator** content, shown in Figure 17-3.

Figure 17-3. Communicating with friends and family is easy with AOL's Mobile Communicator

36 Accessing AOL on a PDA

Access AOL on your Personal Digital Assistant (PDA) anytime and anywhere is a snap. AOL makes it easy and convenient to reach AOL Anywhere with a Palm OS, Windows CE, or Pocket PC PDA. Here's how:

1. Click the **Keyword** button located on the AOL toolbar and enter AOL Keyword: **Wireless.**

2. Click the **Go** button to display the AOL's **Wireless Web** site.

3. Click **PDAs** under the **More Resources** heading to display AOL's **PDAs** Web site, shown in Figure 17-4.

4. Click the **Find Out More!** button for more information on how AOL works with your PDA.

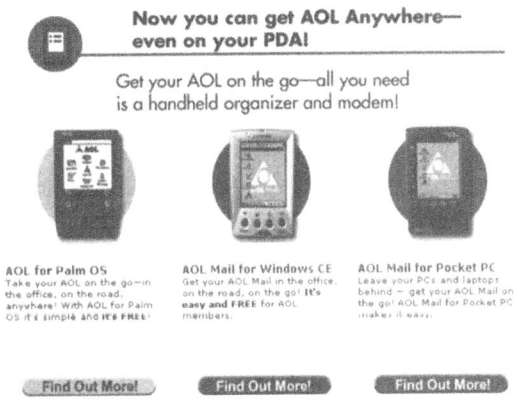

Figure 17-4. Accessing AOL on the go with your favorite PDA

37 Sending and receiving e-mail and Instant Messages without a PC

Sending and receiving e-mail and Instant Messages without a PC has never been easier. AOLbyPhone lets you listen and reply to your e-mail messages anytime and anywhere. Whether you're at the office, in your car, at the airport, or anywhere else, you'll be able to communicate by e-mail or Instant Message anytime and anyplace.

You'll also be able to receive additional services such as news updates, stock quotes, restaurant guides, movie listings, and much more. Here's how you can find out more about this exciting service from AOL:

1. Click the **Keyword** button located on the AOL toolbar and enter AOL Keyword: **AOLbyPhone.**

2. Click the **Go** button to display the **AOLby-Phone** channel.

3. Click the **Try It Free! Click Here** button.

38 Accessing AOL TV™

Would you like to chat, send and receive Instant Messages, e-mail, and surf the Internet on your TV? AOL offers an exciting service that lets AOL members access AOL services on their television sets for a small monthly fee. You'll have access to e-mail with up to seven screen names, thousands of chat rooms, built-in parental controls, message boards, newsgroups, shopping, 24/7 technical support, and much more. The best part is that AOL TV works with your existing phone line and television. There's no special wiring or phone service you have to use. Here's how you can order this exciting service from AOL:

1. Click the **Keyword** button located on the AOL toolbar and enter AOL Keyword: **AOLTV.**

2. Click the **Go** button to display the **AOL TV** channel, shown in figure 17-5.

3. Enter your name and address and click the **Order Now!** button.

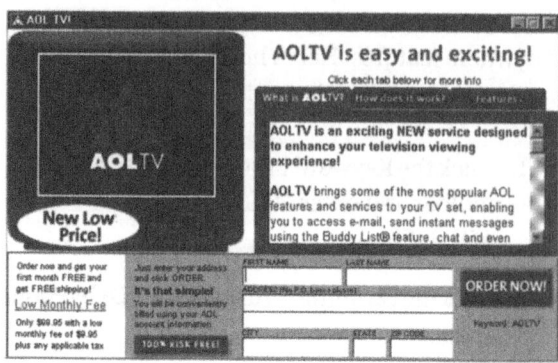

Figure 17-5. Enhancing your television viewing experience with AOLTV

39 Assessing AOL TV™ system requirements

America Online provides everything you need to use AOL TV. Follow the instructions to connect AOL TV to your TV and phone line for an exciting online experience. In your AOL TV package you'll receive the following items:

- AOL TV set top box

- 56K modem

- Coaxial/RCA cables

- Phone cord

- Phone splitter

- Installation guide

- User manual

- Video

Index

Symbols and Numbers

A

Q

R

S

Apress Titles

ISBN	PRICE	AUTHOR	TITLE
1-893115-73-9	$34.95	Abbott	Voice Enabling Web Applications: VoiceXML and Beyond
1-893115-01-1	$39.95	Appleman	Dan Appleman's Win32 API Puzzle Book and Tutorial for Visual Basic Programmers
1-893115-23-2	$29.95	Appleman	How Computer Programming Works
1-893115-97-6	$39.95	Appleman	Moving to VB. NET: Strategies, Concepts, and Code
1-59059-023-6	$39.95	Baker	Adobe Acrobat 5: The Professional User's Guide
1-893115-09-7	$29.95	Baum	Dave Baum's Definitive Guide to LEGO MINDSTORMS
1-893115-84-4	$29.95	Baum, Gasperi, Hempel, and Villa	Extreme MINDSTORMS: An Advanced Guide to LEGO MINDSTORMS
1-893115-82-8	$59.95	Ben-Gan/Moreau	Advanced Transact-SQL for SQL Server 2000
1-893115-91-7	$39.95	Birmingham/Perry	Software Development on a Leash
1-893115-48-8	$29.95	Bischof	The .NET Languages: A Quick Translation Guide
1-893115-67-4	$49.95	Borge	Managing Enterprise Systems with the Windows Script Host
1-893115-28-3	$44.95	Challa/Laksberg	Essential Guide to Managed Extensions for C++
1-893115-39-9	$44.95	Chand	A Programmer's Guide to ADO.NET in C#
1-893115-44-5	$29.95	Cook	Robot Building for Beginners
1-893115-99-2	$39.95	Cornell/Morrison	Programming VB .NET: A Guide for Experienced Programmers
1-893115-72-0	$39.95	Curtin	Developing Trust: Online Privacy and Security
1-59059-008-2	$29.95	Duncan	The Career Programmer: Guerilla Tactics for an Imperfect World
1-893115-71-2	$39.95	Ferguson	Mobile .NET
1-893115-90-9	$49.95	Finsel	The Handbook for Reluctant Database Administrators
1-59059-024-4	$49.95	Fraser	Real World ASP.NET: Building a Content Management System
1-893115-42-9	$44.95	Foo/Lee	XML Programming Using the Microsoft XML Parser
1-893115-55-0	$34.95	Frenz	Visual Basic and Visual Basic .NET for Scientists and Engineers
1-893115-85-2	$34.95	Gilmore	A Programmer's Introduction to PHP 4.0
1-893115-36-4	$34.95	Goodwill	Apache Jakarta-Tomcat
1-893115-17-8	$59.95	Gross	A Programmer's Introduction to Windows DNA
1-893115-62-3	$39.95	Gunnerson	A Programmer's Introduction to C#, Second Edition
1-59059-009-0	$39.95	Harris/Macdonald	Moving to ASP.NET: Web Development with VB .NET
1-893115-30-5	$49.95	Harkins/Reid	SQL: Access to SQL Server
1-893115-10-0	$34.95	Holub	Taming Java Threads
1-893115-04-6	$34.95	Hyman/Vaddadi	Mike and Phani's Essential C++ Techniques
1-893115-96-8	$59.95	Jorelid	J2EE FrontEnd Technologies: A Programmer's Guide to Servlets, JavaServer Pages, and Enterprise JavaBeans
1-893115-49-6	$39.95	Kilburn	Palm Programming in Basic
1-893115-50-X	$34.95	Knudsen	Wireless Java: Developing with Java 2, Micro Edition
1-893115-79-8	$49.95	Kofler	Definitive Guide to Excel VBA
1-893115-57-7	$39.95	Kofler	MySQL
1-893115-87-9	$39.95	Kurata	Doing Web Development: Client-Side Techniques
1-893115-75-5	$44.95	Kurniawan	Internet Programming with VB
1-893115-38-0	$24.95	Lafler	Power AOL: A Survival Guide
1-893115-46-1	$36.95	Lathrop	Linux in Small Business: A Practical User's Guide
1-893115-19-4	$49.95	Macdonald	Serious ADO: Universal Data Access with Visual Basic
1-893115-06-2	$39.95	Marquis/Smith	A Visual Basic 6.0 Programmer's Toolkit
1-893115-22-4	$27.95	McCarter	David McCarter's VB Tips and Techniques
1-893115-76-3	$49.95	Morrison	C++ For VB Programmers
1-893115-80-1	$39.95	Newmarch	A Programmer's Guide to Jini Technology
1-893115-58-5	$49.95	Oellermann	Architecting Web Services
1-893115-81-X	$39.95	Pike	SQL Server: Common Problems, Tested Solutions
1-59059-017-1	$34.95	Rainwater	Herding Cats: A Primer for Programmers Who Lead Programmers
1-59059-025-2	$49.95	Rammer	Advanced .NET Remoting
1-893115-20-8	$34.95	Rischpater	Wireless Web Development
1-893115-93-3	$34.95	Rischpater	Wireless Web Development with PHP and WAP
1-893115-89-5	$59.95	Shemitz	Kylix: The Professional Developer's Guide and Reference
1-893115-40-2	$39.95	Sill	The qmail Handbook
1-893115-24-0	$49.95	Sinclair	From Access to SQL Server
1-893115-94-1	$29.95	Spolsky	User Interface Design for Programmers

ISBN	PRICE	AUTHOR	TITLE
1-893115-53-4	$44.95	Sweeney	Visual Basic for Testers
1-59059-002-3	$44.95	Symmonds	Internationalization and Localization Using Microsoft .NET
1-893115-29-1	$44.95	Thomsen	Database Programming with Visual Basic .NET
1-59059-010-4	$54.95	Thomsen	Database Programming with C#
1-893115-65-8	$39.95	Tiffany	Pocket PC Database Development with eMbedded Visual Basic
1-893115-59-3	$59.95	Troelsen	C# and the .NET Platform
1-893115-26-7	$59.95	Troelsen	Visual Basic .NET and the .NET Platform
1-59059-011-2	$39.95	Troelsen	COM and .NET Interoperability
1-893115-54-2	$49.95	Trueblood/Lovett	Data Mining and Statistical Analysis Using SQL
1-893115-16-X	$49.95	Vaughn	ADO Examples and Best Practices
1-893115-68-2	$49.95	Vaughn	ADO.NET and ADO Examples and Best Practices for VB Programmers, Second Edition
1-59059-012-0	$49.95	Vaughn/Blackburn	ADO.NET Examples and Best Practices for C# Programmers
1-893115-83-6	$44.95	Wells	Code Centric: T-SQL Programming with Stored Procedures and Triggers
1-893115-95-X	$49.95	Welschenbach	Cryptography in C and C++
1-893115-05-4	$39.95	Williamson	Writing Cross-Browser Dynamic HTML
1-893115-78-X	$49.95	Zukowski	Definitive Guide to Swing for Java 2, Second Edition
1-893115-92-5	$49.95	Zukowski	Java Collections
1-893115-98-4	$54.95	Zukowski	Learn Java with JBuilder 6

Available at bookstores nationwide or from Springer Verlag New York, Inc. at 1-800-777-4643; fax 1-212-533-3503. Contact us for more information at sales@apress.com.

Apress Titles Publishing SOON!

ISBN	AUTHOR	TITLE
1-59059-022-8	Alapati	Expert Oracle 9i Database Administration
1-59059-015-5	Clark	An Introduction to Object Oriented Programming with Visual Basic .NET
1-59059-000-7	Cornell	Programming C#
1-59059-014-7	Drol	Object-Oriented Flash MX
1-59059-033-3	Fraser	Managed C++ and .NET Development
1-59059-038-4	Gibbons	Java Development to .NET Development
1-59059-030-9	Habibi/Camerlengo/ Patterson	Java 1.4 and the Sun Certified Developer Exam
1-59059-006-6	Hetland	Practical Python
1-59059-003-1	Nakhimovsky/Meyers	XML Programming: Web Applications and Web Services with JSP and ASP
1-59059-001-5	McMahon	Serious ASP.NET
1-59059-021-X	Moore	Karl Moore's Visual Basic .NET: The Tutorials
1-893115-27-5	Morrill	Tuning and Customizing a Linux System
1-59059-020-1	Patzer	JSP Examples and Best Practices
1-59059-028-7	Rischpater	Wireless Web Development, 2nd Edition
1-59059-026-0	Smith	Writing Add-Ins for .NET
1-893115-43-7	Stephenson	Standard VB: An Enterprise Developer's Reference for VB 6 and VB .NET
1-59059-032-5	Thomsen	Database Programming with Visual Basic .NET, 2nd Edition
1-59059-007-4	Thomsen	Building Web Services with VB .NET
1-59059-027-9	Torkelson/Petersen/ Torkelson	Programming the Web with Visual Basic .NET
1-59059-004-X	Valiaveedu	SQL Server 2000 and Business Intelligence in an XML/.NET World

Available at bookstores nationwide or from Springer Verlag New York, Inc. at 1-800-777-4643; fax 1-212-533-3503. Contact us for more information at sales@apress.com.

a!™
apress™

books for professionals by professionals™

About Apress

Apress, located in Berkeley, CA, is a fast-growing, innovative publishing company devoted to meeting the needs of existing and potential programming professionals. Simply put, the "A" in Apress stands for *"The Author's Press™"* and its books have *"The Expert's Voice™"*. Apress' unique approach to publishing grew out of conversations between its founders Gary Cornell and Dan Appleman, authors of numerous best-selling, highly regarded books for programming professionals. In 1998 they set out to create a publishing company that emphasized quality above all else. Gary and Dan's vision has resulted in the publication of over 50 titles by leading software professionals, all of which have *The Expert's Voice™*.

Do You Have What It Takes to Write for Apress?

Apress is rapidly expanding its publishing program. If you can write and refuse to compromise on the quality of your work, if you believe in doing more than rehashing existing documentation, and if you're looking for opportunities and rewards that go far beyond those offered by traditional publishing houses, we want to hear from you!

Consider these innovations that we offer all of our authors:

- **Top royalties with *no* hidden switch statements**
  Authors typically only receive half of their normal royalty rate on foreign sales. In contrast, Apress' royalty rate remains the same for both foreign and domestic sales.

- **A mechanism for authors to obtain equity in Apress**
  Unlike the software industry, where stock options are essential to motivate and retain software professionals, the publishing industry has adhered to an outdated compensation model based on royalties alone. In the spirit of most software companies, Apress reserves a significant portion of its equity for authors.

- **Serious treatment of the technical review process**
  Each Apress book has a technical reviewing team whose remuneration depends in part on the success of the book since they too receive royalties.

Moreover, through a partnership with Springer-Verlag, New York, Inc., one of the world's major publishing houses, Apress has significant venture capital behind it. Thus, we have the resources to produce the highest quality books *and* market them aggressively.

If you fit the model of the Apress author who can write a book that gives the "professional what he or she needs to know™," then please contact one of our Editorial Directors, Gary Cornell (gary_cornell@apress.com), Dan Appleman (dan_appleman@apress.com), Peter Blackburn (peter_blackburn@apress.com), Jason Gilmore (jason_gilmore@apress.com), Karen Watterson (karen_watterson@apress.com), or John Zukowski (john_zukowski@apress.com) for more information.